Serving Herself

Althea Gibson, enigmatic and relaxed, in November 1958 as she began to embark on new pursuits after amateur tennis. "I don't want to be put on a pedestal," she wrote. "I just want to be reasonably successful and live a normal life with all the conveniences to make it so. I think I've already got the main thing I've always wanted, which is to be somebody, to have identity. I'm Althea Gibson, the tennis champion. I hope it makes me happy."

Portrait by Carl Van Vechten. Everett/Shutterstock.

Serving Herself

The Life and Times of Althea Gibson

ASHLEY BROWN

OXFORD

UNIVERSITY PRESS

OXFORD

UNIVERSITY PRESS

Oxford University Press is a department of the University of Oxford. It furthers
the University's objective of excellence in research, scholarship, and education
by publishing worldwide. Oxford is a registered trade mark of Oxford University
Press in the UK and certain other countries.

Published in the United States of America by Oxford University Press
198 Madison Avenue, New York, NY 10016, United States of America.

© Oxford University Press 2023

Library of Congress Cataloging-in-Publication Data
Names: Brown, Ashley, author.
Title: Serving herself : the life and times of Althea Gibson / Ashley Brown.
Description: New York, NY : Oxford University Press, 2023. |
Includes bibliographical references and index.
Identifiers: LCCN 2022040682 (print) | LCCN 2022040683 (ebook) |
ISBN 9780197551752 (hardback) | ISBN 9780197551769 (updf) |
ISBN 9780197551776 (epub) | ISBN 9780197551783
Subjects: LCSH: Gibson, Althea, 1927-2003. | African American tennis
players—Biography. | Women tennis players—United States—Biography. |
Tennis—United States—History—20th century.
Classification: LCC GV994.G53 B76 2023 (print) | LCC GV994.G53 (ebook) |
DDC 796.342092 [B]—dc23/eng/20220901
LC record available at https://lccn.loc.gov/2022040682
LC ebook record available at https://lccn.loc.gov/2022040683

DOI: 10.1093/oso/9780197551752.001.0001

1 3 5 7 9 8 6 4 2
Printed by Sheridan Books, Inc., United States of America

For Ruby

Contents

Acknowledgments

THE CLICHÉ IS true: it isn't how you start that's important, it's how you finish. *Serving Herself: The Life and Times of Althea Gibson* began as my doctoral dissertation and represents more than a decade of research and writing. In that time, many people and institutions contributed to the completion of this book. I offer my heartfelt thanks to them here.

I could not have asked for a better editor for my first book than Susan Ferber. Susan saw the strengths and possibilities of this biography at the right time and consistently gave me the time, space, support, and trust that I needed. She is everything—scout, coach, analyst, cheerleader, teammate, talent manager, problem solver, and visionary. She is also a very fine person. Susan has been a dream to work with, and publishing with Oxford University Press has been a dream come true. Assembling the final product would not have happened without the careful diligence of copy editor Sue Warga, indexer Colleen Dunham, proofreader Bob Land, and production editor Amy Whitmer.

The University of Wisconsin–Madison has been my ideal professional home since 2017. The History Department is an all-star team. Whether an assistant, associate, or full professor, every member of the faculty has contributed to my growth here. My Madison story begins with the dedicated members of the search committee that brought me to campus in February 2017: Sue Lederer, Tony Michels, Karl Shoemaker, and co-chairs Susan Lee Johnson and David McDonald, both of whom became my mentors. Susan (now of the University of Nevada–Las Vegas) opens doors and creatively paves paths. David is an astute reader and a terrific conversationalist, especially about the world and history of golf. In subsequent years, other colleagues stepped forward to further support my work. Brenda Gayle Plummer is a trailblazer whose encouragement has meant a great deal to me. Lee Palmer Wandel is a keen listener whose clear-sightedness has positively impacted my approach to pedagogy. Leonora Neville stands out as an advocate and a creative leader. As I entered the final stages of this project, Mary Louise Roberts became my mentor and friend. Lou's attention to detail, wit, wisdom, and commitment to excellence have enhanced my work.

Allan H. (Bud) Selig plays an important role in my work. In 2010, Commissioner Selig, a UW-Madison alumnus, made a major gift to the History Department to create the Allan H. Selig Chair in the History of Sport and Society, the position that I have held since January 2020. The chair, a rarity at an American university, enables me to do what I love: encourage my students to think about the people, places, productions, institutions, and reach of American sports in new and expansive ways. My students teach me, and they apply their knowledge and skills to innovate their chosen fields. I draw much energy and inspiration from their examples. Teaching the course Biography in U.S. Sport History in the fall of 2021 was especially helpful as I completed the final chapters of the manuscript. The Selig Faculty Fellowship in Sport History, awarded during the 2017–2018 academic year, gave me the time and resources required to write, among other things, "'Uncomplimentary Things': Tennis Player Althea Gibson, Sexism, Homophobia, and Anti-Queerness in the Black Media," which the *Journal of African American History* published in 2021. The research support of the Selig Chair has been invaluable to bringing *Serving Herself* to fruition and thus familiarizing historians, students, and others with Althea Gibson's preeminent place in the history of sports. Commissioner Selig's generosity and leadership are signal reminders of the need for and vast impact of philanthropy in higher education.

Institutional support has been essential to *Serving Herself*. George Washington University backed my studies and research through its Presidential Merit Fellowship, the Jeffrey C. Kasch/GWU Horton-Vlach Fund for American Studies Research Fellowship, and multiple American Studies Academic Excellence Awards for Summer Research. The North American Society for Sport History's 2015 Graduate Student Essay Prize, which led to the publication of my first article, "Swinging for the State Department: American Women Tennis Players in Diplomatic Goodwill Tours, 1941–1959," in the *Journal of Sport History*, helped establish my reputation as a scholar. Giving the graduate student keynote address at the 2015 NASSH conference in Miami was an experience that I will savor for the rest of my career. The opportunity gave me a view of what the future might bring. The Alumnae Association of Mount Holyoke College's 1905 Fellowship funded an important research trip to Tallahassee, Florida, in 2017. An associateship at the Five College Women's Studies Research Center, led by Banu Subramanium, was a pivotal launchpad for my transition from graduate school to the professoriate. That same year, Lucas Wilson, Preston Smith, Lynda J. Morgan, and the Africana Studies Department at Mount Holyoke gave me a bridge that added to my appreciation for my alma mater. In 2017–2018, a postdoctoral fellowship at Emory University's James Weldon Johnson Institute for the Study of Race and Difference, led by Andra Gillespie, became an essential landmark on my professional journey. The University of Wisconsin–Madison has buttressed my endeavors through the Selig Chair, support from the Office of the Vice Chancellor for Research and Graduate Education, and, in 2020–2021, an invaluable Nellie McKay Research Fellowship. Accessing resources at UW-Madison would not have been possible without the diligent efforts and knowledge of Todd Anderson, Sophie Olson, and Jana Valeo. Leslie Abadie, Scott Burkhardt, Mike Burmeister, Lisa Normand, John Persike, and Jenny Schumacher make everything better. The support of the organizations and people named here supplied much-needed time to work, access to the many sources required to write this book, and additional authorial motivation.

Along these lines, I extend my thanks to the many colleagues who have shared encouraging words, insights, and, in some cases, invitations to share my work with their campus communities. Leaders in this respect are the late Craig Lanier Allen, Amy Bass, Madeleine Blais, Andy Bruno, Aram Goudsouzian, Pamela Grundy, Eric Allen Hall, Felipe Hinojosa, Tera W. Hunter, Jane Kamensky, Rita Liberti, Mary G. McDonald, Michele Mitchell, Elizabeth Odders-White, Martin Polley, Randy Roberts, Jaime Schultz, Johnny Smith, Susan Ware, Brandon Winford, Darius Young, and Oxford University Press's anonymous reviewers. The author of groundbreaking works, Susan K. Cahn is a major reason this book exists. I have been influenced by Susan's scholarship, encouraged and enriched by her interest in my research, and strengthened by her reminder that we must care for ourselves as people rather than exclusively as producers of scholarship.

My first intellectual homes were in Massachusetts and Washington, D.C. When I was an undergraduate at Mount Holyoke College, David Sanford, Preston Smith, Paul Staiti, and Elizabeth Young sparked my dream of becoming a professor. At George Washington University, Kip Kosek, Erin Chapman, Suleiman Osman, Melani McAlister, Jennifer Nash, and Tom Guglielmo helped make that dream come true. During a chance meeting at GW's Gelman Library in 2014, the late Jim Miller said the right thing at the right time.

Sources are the lifeblood of scholarship. I appreciate the efforts of the staff at each of the institutions whose archives I accessed. I give special praise to Meredith Miller Richards, Nicole Markham, Ymelda Rivera Laxton, Troy Gowen, and Doug Stark of the International Tennis Hall of Fame and Museum; Rebecca Baugnon and Gerald Parnell at the University of North Carolina–Wilmington; Gloria Woody at Florida Agricultural and Mechanical University's Coleman Library; E. Murrell Dawson of the Meek-Eaton Black Archives Research Center and Museum; Beatrice Hunt and the archives of the West Side Tennis Club; Toni Wiley and Sportsmen's Tennis and Enrichment Center; and the employees of the Library of Congress and the National Archives and Records Administration in College Park, Maryland. This project would have suffered immeasurably without the consistent support of Carolyn Eaton, the youngest daughter of Dr. Hubert A. and Celeste Eaton. Not only did Carolyn grant me permission to access her father's papers in 2013, but she also offered terrific and timely advice that Althea Gibson would have liked: "Just do you." Like her parents, Carolyn is a champion of integrity and African American history. The Eaton family has my respect and my gratitude. Michelle Curry, executor of the Gibson estate, is an important figure in sharing Gibson's legacy. Don Felder, Gibson's second cousin, came through in a big way by sharing original sources to which I had sought access for years. Don and Michelle's joint efforts in many forums are teaching people across the country and around the world about Gibson.

—·—

In any life and career, time, interests, geography, and fate intervene in such a way that we get to know some colleagues better than others. The COVID-19 pandemic brought welcome opportunities to forge new bonds and strengthen old ones. I could fill a book with memories of Jennifer Ratner-Rosenhagen's many gestures of goodwill before and during the pandemic. Jennifer is a friend, muse, guide, and sounding board with a generous spirit. My experience of this unprecedented time in history would have been very different without the kindnesses of Jennifer and her family, especially Ulrich, Miriam, and Mabel. Nan Enstad has been equally munificent. Time with Nan allowed me to laugh and relax. Nan and her partner, Finn, embody living and working with honesty. Emily Callaci, my running buddy in the pre-Prefontaine sense of the word, is a model of benevolence and persistence. Sharing in the childhoods of Emily's sons, Theo and Otis, has delighted me beyond words. .

The past dozen years brought opportunities to reflect on the meaning of friendship. Friends are there for you with positivity and generosity when things go well, not just when things go wrong. Friends enhance the afterglow of your victories, great and small, and the things that give you joy. Lila Webb's frankness, wit, confidence, and laughter have enriched my life for more than twenty years. Her children, Rowan and Juna, have grown up alongside this book. Catherine Connor's optimism is contagious. Cathy and my grandfather have convinced me that cheerfulness is essential to becoming a nonagenarian. Sally Sheaffer Lehman's company and her belief in me have never wavered. Discussions with Doc Pye led me to make the leap to graduate school. Doc was the first to believe in this project. My journey would have been much more difficult without her. Whenever I shared good news about some breakthrough or honor, Doc always said, "I am happy for you, and I am not surprised." Mickey Goldmill has been a consistent source of fun, clarity, challenge, patience, and strength. Wherever I have been, Mickey has been there, too. Wherever I go, she will be there, too.

My family is ever-present in my life. I thank my grandfather Willie James for telling me when I was four years old that I should go to college. My brother, Dudley, influenced my early interest in sports. My aunt and uncle, Michelle and Craig, showed me that tennis and golf are magical games. I thank my parents, Richard and Iva, for accepting my wish to pursue my dreams wherever they lead me. More than anyone else, Mom and Dad remind me of the importance of being ambitious and true to myself, maintaining discipline and focus, persevering, having faith, and deriving pleasure from work.

Ruby, my dear niece and daughter of Dudley and Rochelle, my very kind sister-in-law, is the pride and joy of our family. I sincerely hope Ruby and her generation will read works of history and learn—by thinking deeply about the successes, shortcomings, failures, and unrealized ambitions of our predecessors—how to make lives of happiness, purpose, productivity, and fulfillment. May they also find the ingredients for making a compassionate country and a peaceful world.

Serving Herself

Introduction

ALTHEA GIBSON SHOULD have been on top of the world in the summer of 1957. Instead, she found herself at odds with it yet again. In July, Gibson won the women's singles title at Wimbledon, six years after becoming its first Black American competitor. Queen Elizabeth II presented her with the victor's plate, marking the first time a Black person, male or female, had claimed the top prize in tennis. Gibson was the belle of the Wimbledon Ball that night, dancing the traditional first dance with Lew Hoad, the men's singles champion from Australia. Blond and White, Hoad guided her around the dance floor. Some attendees watched in admiration; others stared with displeasure.[1]

Days later, Gibson was back in her hometown, New York, riding up Broadway in an open convertible and waving at the thousands of people who lined the streets during the ticker-tape parade held in her honor. The mayor gave her the key to the city, and a series of speakers lavished her with praise during a banquet at the Waldorf-Astoria Hotel. Gibson was a "wonderful ambassador and saleswoman for America," said one, a reference to the dozens of tournaments she had won around the world. She "came up the hard way and now stands at the top of her class," remarked another.[2]

The mood changed in Chicago, where Gibson went to compete in the U.S. Clay Court Championship the following week. Because she was Black, none of the hotels in River Forest, the leafy suburb that hosted the tournament, would give her a room, forcing her to find lodging miles away. Intent on maintaining her form through the end of the season, she prioritized practice and rest over media obligations before the tournament began. Reports emerged that Gibson gave "brush-offs" to the mostly male press corps, refusing requests for interviews and photographs. Some journalists got close enough to ask Gibson questions. With the civil rights movement under way, they wanted to talk about race. Did she think that her accomplishments in tennis "helped" other African Americans? Did she "cherish" being compared with Jackie Robinson, who ten years earlier had become the first Black man to play in baseball's major leagues in the twentieth century?[3] "No, I don't consider myself to be a representative of my people. I am thinking of me and nobody else," she reportedly answered.[4] "I'm trying to help myself."[5] Gibson won the tournament decisively, but her image was tarnished as writers called her "arrogant," "non-cooperative," and "as ungracious as a stubborn jackass."[6]

Apologies and appeals for understanding were not Gibson's style; doubling down and going on the offensive were. Speaking outside Pittsburgh in early August, she gave her version of what had happened in Chicago: "They said I was hostile and wouldn't cooperate. I say I wasn't given a fair opportunity to be helpful." She had no plans to be helpful going forward. "Frankly, I'm tired of being pushed around by people who don't seem to have any concern for my feelings," she told the press pool, living up to the derisive labels—"Jackie Robinson without charm" and "Ted Williams without his skills"—that some sportswriters had given her.[7] "I'm ready to start speaking out and saying what I think is right. I might lose some friends, but there are those who will understand my viewpoint. . . . [F]rom now on I'm going to do what I think is right and not worry about what some people who don't mean anything to me say. Then when I get mad, I'm going out on the tennis court and [will] take it out on whoever's across the net."[8]

Gibson soon made good on her promises. The subject of *Time*'s cover story for the last week of August, she spoke candidly about her fraught relationship with the notion that she carried a special duty to be a racial representative or spokesperson as the only African American in elite amateur tennis. "I tried to feel responsibilities to Negroes, but that was a burden on my shoulders," she admitted. "If I did this or that, would they like it? Perhaps it contributed to my troubles in tennis. Now I'm playing tennis to please me, not them."[9]

Two weeks later in September, Gibson won the United States National Lawn Tennis Championship at Forest Hills (now the U.S. Open), where she had been the first Black player allowed to enter in 1950. Vice President Richard Nixon presented her with the trophy. When asked which victory that summer was more meaningful, she replied, "Winning Wimbledon was wonderful, and it meant a lot to me. But there is nothing quite like winning the championship of your own country. That's what counts the most with anybody."[10]

The victory meant that Gibson had achieved another historic racial first. She would accomplish still more. She successfully defended both her

Wimbledon and U.S. Nationals titles in 1958, giving her, with her capture of the French Championship in 1956, a career total of five Grand Slam singles titles, joining her six others in doubles and mixed doubles. In 1963, she was the first African American to compete on the Ladies Professional Golf Association (LPGA) Tour. In 1971, she was the first African American inducted into the International Tennis Hall of Fame. Between 1975 and 1977, she was the athletic commissioner for the state of New Jersey, the first woman and the first African American to hold that position. Every opportunity, every setback, every accolade, and every criticism that Gibson received was linked to her identity as an African American woman who dared to defy social norms and expectations of what tennis players, golfers, race leaders and pioneers, and even Black women said and did and how they looked. She persevered in the face of it all as her audacity and achievements challenged the progressiveness of the communities and institutions that she entered and occupied.

Serving Herself explores the history of sports integration by taking readers on a journey with Althea Gibson, the preeminent African American female athlete of the mid-twentieth century, through her rise, falls, triumphs, and repeated comebacks. No apologist, Gibson fought valiantly for control over her life, career, image, and future at a time when women were expected to be passive. A restless and insatiable competitor, she was determined to win, and she put in the work and made the sacrifices to do it. A fiery competitor with little regard for social graces, she cared more about winning games and matches than winning friends and fans. Gibson was a world champion who was all too human. In a world that placed limits on opportunities for someone of her race and her gender, she gambled, taking risks and making hard choices that paid off. Yet she also paid a high price for her decisions. She traveled the streets and the world as a woman alone. She enjoyed the perks of being an "exceptional" African American. With her talents and ambitions, she circulated among the social elite, galaxies away from her humble origins, and moved in the same orbits as some of the most acclaimed people of her era in sports, politics, and entertainment. She lived with surveillance, exploitation, being made into a spectacle, and constant criticism all because the world had never seen a woman like her. The result is a very different story about sports integration and its outcomes than the familiar narrative, one that instead is intended to reflect on what we ask of our cultural heroes and "pioneers," whether they owe us anything at all, and what our responsibilities to them are.

Unlike most histories of sports integration, this is not a saga of men.[11] Rather, it is the story of a complex, unorthodox, courageous, and vulnerable woman who navigated uncharted territory in the face of an unjust society to create a blueprint and path for herself and to become the first Black female superstar in sports. Gibson had to be her own model, revisiting techniques that she devised as the lone African American in elite amateur tennis to make it as the lone Black woman in professional golf. Those strategies included calculated silences and dissembling, approaches adopted by many other Black women who sought to make room for themselves in hostile places where their worth was doubted.[12] At the same time, she was remarkably candid about her joys, frustrations, and troubles, in hundreds of interviews and two autobiographies. Gibson's existence requires that we recalibrate the tendency for the phrase "Black athlete" to refer exclusively to men. She reveals the underappreciated role of women in sports integration, seeing beyond traditional roles they held as wives, mothers, and status symbols.[13] For Gibson, women were fellow athletes and allies who supported her cause as well as antagonists who stood in her way. Her interactions with men were just as mixed. Most of her mentors and role models were men she could depend on for advice and charity, especially as she made her way in tennis. Yet she also encountered paternalism from those who tried to make decisions for her. The battles of Gibson and her athletic peers beg women's history to move sports away from its margins and to its center, where so many singers, dancers, actresses, writers, and other performers and cultural figures have been welcomed in recent years.[14]

Class and place are essential to this story. It follows Gibson in the high-toned and ultra-White settings of tennis and golf, sports with cultures, connotations, and expectations for comportment that differed dramatically from those in the worlds of baseball, football, basketball, boxing, and track and field where Black athletes traditionally found success and where most other books have trailed them, especially on American soil with American protagonists. Gibson's life is indeed an American story: she pursued her dreams and sought to support herself with ingenuity and determination across the United States. It is also a global one, set in the Caribbean, Europe, Southeast Asia, the Middle East, Canada, Mexico, Australia, and Latin America—all places where it was often easier for her to find respect as a Black American. Yet no matter where Gibson competed, and whether it was in amateur or professional tennis or in golf, attention was always paid to whether her clothes and hair sufficiently upheld the gender and class norms of her sports and represented Black people well, aesthetic concerns and pressures not foisted upon male athletes.

Gender and sexuality are essential to this biographical history of sports integration. Masculinity, marriage, and assumed heterosexuality have long been glossed over as important factors in the stardom of Black sportsmen.[15] The scrutiny, inquisitions, and innuendoes that Gibson endured for being unmarried for most of her career in sports force us to confront the impact of sexism, heterosexism, and homophobia on sports integration. Indeed, she was subjected to sexism and racism. Her life upends the dominant story that when African Americans, whether as individuals or on teams, crossed the color line in sports, the entire race won. Gibson faced higher expectations and harsher standards, ambivalence, and even outright animosity within African American communities as she reached racially unprecedented heights in tennis ahead of Black men. That she was a woman who crossed the color line had lasting, negative implications on her life until the end. This makes for a darker, more unsettling story about sports integration than has previously been told.[16]

———

America and the world began remembering and rediscovering Gibson even before her death in 2003 at the age of seventy-six. The news in the mid-1990s that she was in poor health and had fallen on hard times, subsisting on Medicare and Social Security, led to a flurry of articles, editorials, and fundraisers. In 2001, General Mills placed a picture of Gibson on its iconic Wheaties cereal box. The year 2004 brought the publication of two biographies by journalists and a close friend. In 2012, Branch Brook Park in Newark, New Jersey, the state that she called home for the last four decades of her life, honored her with a statue near the tennis complex that carries her name. In 2013, the United States Postal Service commemorated Gibson's career with a stamp bearing her image in its Black Heritage series. Two years later, filmmaker Rex Miller released a documentary, *Althea*, that has been screened around the world and featured as part of the long-running PBS series *American Masters*. CBS Sports has released its own documentary, *Arthur and Althea*, a dual portrait of Gibson and Arthur Ashe, the first African American man to win the U.S. Open (1968), the Australian Open (1970), and Wimbledon (1975). Biopics are in development, too. In 2022, Gibson's first autobiography, *I Always Wanted to Be Somebody* (1958), was reissued, and the block of West 143rd Street on which she lived during the 1930s and the 1940s was renamed for her.[17]

Opening day of the 2019 U.S. Open brought a particularly grand commemoration of the trailblazer's enduring significance. The United States

Tennis Association (USTA) unveiled a statue of Gibson on the grounds of its Billie Jean King National Tennis Center in Flushing, New York. For years, the USTA had recognized Gibson primarily in brief memorials. In September 2004, star players King, John McEnroe, and Zina Garrison, journalist and commentator Bud Collins, and former New York mayor David Dinkins paid tribute to her in a program before the start of the quarterfinals match between Jennifer Capriati and Serena Williams, who, like her older sister Venus, had been inspired as a child when she learned that tennis had a Black champion in the 1950s. Future salutes at the U.S. Open coincided with the major anniversaries of Gibson's victories there. Gibson was featured in or the central subject of several works of children's and young adult literature during her lifetime, and still more have told sunnier versions of her story in recent years. A letter-writing campaign by a group of children contributed to the USTA's decision to establish the permanent memorial. The statue was a priority for Katrina Adams, the association's first Black female president and its CEO from 2015 to 2018. As a child, Adams met Gibson during a tennis clinic in Chicago in the 1970s. Adams came to view their chance encounter as a mandate: "Whatever I was going to do in my life and career as a player, it had to somehow involve the continuation of Althea's work breaking down barriers for women and people of color."[18]

Made of granite and bronze, weighing more than eighteen tons, and scaled at three and a half times life size, the "monument," as its sculptor, Eric Goulder, refers to it, stands in front of Arthur Ashe Stadium, named in 1997.[19] Goulder chose to present Gibson from the shoulders up, rising from a cube and looking as she did in August 1950, when, at the age of twenty-three, she made her historic debut at the U.S. Nationals. While Gibson's right shoulder remains in the cube, her left shoulder is uncovered. Alluding to Gibson's impact on sports, Goulder explained during the unveiling ceremony, "Her shoulder is exposed because that's the shoulder that everybody since has stood on."[20]

Gibson was indeed a foundational figure in sports. Serena Williams has said that Gibson "paved the way for all women of color in sport."[21] Certainly, the Williams sisters, Garrison, Lori McNeil, Chanda Rubin, Sloane Stephens, Cori "Coco" Gauff, and every other woman of African descent in tennis are part of her legacy. So are Renee Powell, LaRee Sugg, Shasta Averyhardt, Sadena Parks, Cheyenne Woods, Ginger Howard, and Mariah Stackhouse, the small group of Black women who have played on the LPGA Tour.[22] Characterized by a powerful serve and all-around speed, her style of play influenced subsequent generations of champions in women's tennis, including

Christine Truman, Darlene Hard, Maria Bueno, and Billie Jean King. Gibson, moreover, toured as a professional tennis player and tried her hand at being a promoter in the game more than a decade before the founding in 1970 of the Virginia Slims Circuit, the forerunner of the current-day Women's Tennis Association (WTA). Gibson's rise was integral to Arthur Ashe's career. They shared a mentor, Dr. Robert Walter Johnson, who applied the techniques that he had crafted while preparing Gibson for elite amateur tennis to guiding Ashe, who was nearly sixteen years younger than Gibson and won the U.S. Open and Wimbledon eleven and eighteen years, respectively, after she did. Always more popular with the press and the public, Ashe was able to capitalize financially on his abilities and celebrity in ways that Gibson never could.

Time, like gender, was not on Gibson's side. She competed before the 1970s, a crucial decade in sports. When she turned to professional tennis at age thirty-two in 1959, open tennis did not exist. Professional tennis players were barred from competing against amateurs at the Grand Slams—the national championships of Australia, France, England, and the United States—or anywhere else. Gibson and other professionals played on barnstorming tours. Though these engagements could be exciting, filled with enthusiastic crowds often made up of people who had never before attended a tennis match, they lacked the prestige, luxury, and order associated with the private club hosts on the amateur circuit.

The arrival of open tennis in 1968 allowed professionals to get paid as they vied for august titles and product endorsements, and it sparked the "tennis boom" that followed, bringing more fans and recreational players, tournaments, media interest, and money into the game. In 1972, the growth of tennis was helped further by the passage of Title IX, the federal requirement that institutions that receive government funding provide equal resources to men and women in education, including in athletic programs. More women and girls took up sports, and many turned to tennis. Like golf, the elite origins of tennis led to its acceptance as a "ladylike" sport, making it possible as early as the late nineteenth century for an amateur tennis circuit and, beginning in 1949, the Ladies Professional Golf Association to exist.[23] Not only did the open era and the tennis boom come too late for Gibson, they also rendered the history of tennis and women in sports prior to 1968 and Title IX irrelevant and insignificant, as many publications, media producers, and members of the public focused on the "modern era."

Undoubtedly, Gibson's detachment from the civil rights struggle during the prime of her tennis and golf careers has contributed to her relegation to the sidelines of history. Of course, many (one might even say most) star athletes did not and do not participate in social justice initiatives at all, let alone in significant and sustained ways, and yet still become the subjects of multiple and meaningful biographies, films, and commemorations. Increasingly, though, proof of activism, political engagement, and actively pushing against social restrictions have become essential to claiming that an athlete, especially those who are African American and female, "transcended sport." Suggesting gravitas and a charitable spirit that is at once humanizing and heroic, demonstrations of social consciousness readily give biographers and others deeper and more complex ways of interpreting athletes' lives and their social and cultural importance. It is why Curt Flood, Muhammad Ali, Arthur Ashe, and Bill Russell have come to join Jackie Robinson, Joe Louis, and Jesse Owens in the pantheon of Black athletes, and why Billie Jean King has become the leading living legend of women's sports. The political identities of Flood, Ali, Ashe, Russell, and King were cast during their respective playing careers, when, in addition to winning important titles, they stepped forward to deliberately speak and act in ways intended to challenge the conventions of the organizations that ran their sports and to create a more just and equitable society.[24]

"Journalism is the first draft of history" is more than a cliché. The media play an important role in how cultural figures, including athletes, are remembered. In Gibson's case, journalists wrote that she was "an American Negro of stature" and repeatedly noted that she was "the first of her race" to reach the heights that she did in tennis and golf.[25] Journalists also took note when she made controversial statements about race, like the ones she uttered in Chicago and for a *Time* interview in 1957, and in London in 1956, where she told a correspondent for the *New York Times*, "I am just another tennis player, not a Negro tennis player. Of course, I am a Negro— everybody knows that—but you don't say someone is a white tennis player, do you?"[26] They paid attention, too, when, writing in her 1958 autobiography, she declared, "I am not a racially conscious person. I don't want to be. I see myself as just an individual. I can't help or change my color in any way, so why should I make a big deal out of it?"[27] Today, such comments suggest that Gibson was ahead of her time, but to many influential figures in the African American press of the mid-twentieth century, she sounded as if she was not proud to be Black. Others were troubled that she did not take an active role in trying to get more Black tennis players, especially men, into elite tennis tournaments.

By 1965, Gibson was called "an aloof representative of the colored race."[28] The tag reflected the distance between Gibson and ideas about Black women's responsibilities to their communities, giving historians further reasons to overlook her. The oversight is ironic because between the mid- and late 1950s she had been one of the most famous women in the world, living a life of glamour, fame, and international travel that is seldom associated with Black women of the era. She appeared on the covers of major Black magazines, including *Ebony* and *Jet*, as well as mainstream publications *Sports Illustrated*, *Sport*, and *World Tennis*, in addition to *Time*, and she was the subject of major stories in *Life*, *Saturday Evening Post*, and *Look*, too. Gibson was also, to use the phrase coined by sociologist Patricia Hill Collins, an "outsider within." Like the Black domestic workers for whom Collins originally created the term, Gibson lived and worked near people, Black and White, who were well-off and whom she enriched by helping them reach their goals, but she was not always treated as their equal.[29] Still, altruism and sacrifice have become the dominant narratives in histories of African American women, influenced by the generations of Black women who found meaning in the powerful intraracial mandate that they prioritize their families, kin, social networks, and other African Americans through voluntarism or careers in education, social justice organizations, and the law, in order to combat white supremacy.[30] It was a call that Gibson did not heed as she gave all of herself to all that she did and put her personal interests first, hence the title of this book. As she explained in 1971, "I wasn't fighting any case. I was [on the tennis court] trying to do a good job for myself and if it was worthy enough to be good enough for my people, beautiful."[31]

Several elements combined to shape Gibson's reluctance to become a vocal advocate for change in tennis, golf, and society. She believed in self-reliance in the face of adversity, a conviction formed on the streets of Harlem and within her working-class family of former sharecroppers who moved to New York as part of the Great Migration. Moreover, the middle- and upper-class African Americans who introduced Gibson to tennis and prepared her to become their test subject to integrate the U.S. Nationals and the elite amateur tennis circuit emphasized respectability politics and individual success as the methods to improve conditions and open doors.

Gibson, furthermore, could ill afford the selflessness and the duties traditionally expected of racial representatives. Speaking up for social causes and seeking to change their organizations from the inside have always carried risks for athletes, especially people of color and women. Gibson was especially vulnerable. She had no money of her own, nor did she have a contract or teammates to back her up. Elite amateur tennis was run by wealthy White men whom even White players feared for ruling over the game with more arbitrariness than fairness. Crossing the United States Lawn Tennis Association (USLTA) could reduce any player's opportunities to compete and could even end their careers, as indeed happened to some. Players learned to wait until their amateur careers were over to express their criticisms.

From her first "White" amateur tennis tournament in 1949 to her last in 1959, Gibson was the only African American with a consistent presence in the sport and, like other Black athletes of the era, she knew what that meant. "I was always aware of my behavior on the court," she wrote in 1988. "I [knew] that if I had made [any] gesture or argued one call they would have tried to boot me out of the game."[32] Of course, that did not stop Gibson from occasionally and dramatically arguing with linespersons, who often gave her questionable rulings. At the U.S. Nationals in 1953, for example, she acted out with such vehemence in response to what she thought were unfair penalties that her opponent, Maureen Connolly, the teen prodigy and the first woman to win the single-season Grand Slam, asked her to "either play or default."[33] Three years later, Gibson was so overcome with frustration after being called for twenty-one foot faults during a match in Australia that she launched a tennis ball into the stands, nearly striking Australian prime minister Robert Gordon Menzies.[34]

The women's tennis scene of the 1950s further impacted Gibson's decision-making about where she should devote her time, energy, and thoughts. Dominated by a cadre of Americans—Doris Hart, Margaret Osborne duPont, Louise Brough, Shirley Fry, and Connolly—the sport was a minefield of competition. In the United States and abroad, Gibson faced players who had more tournament experience and had been matched up against better opponents than she had in her years in the American Tennis Association (ATA), the governing body for Black tennis. Her opponents also had more experience playing on grass. Producing fast and unpredictable bounces, grass separated the good players from the great ones and was the surface of choice at the most prestigious events, including Wimbledon and the U.S. Nationals. As a mentor observed, Gibson had to "put untold hours" into her game to become the number one tennis player in the world, and she did.[35] An eight-month international tour in 1955–1956, sponsored in part by the State Department, gave Gibson, a student of tennis, the necessary preparation to win her major titles. Maintaining a mutually beneficial relationship with the State Department, which she did until 1959, further influenced her reluctance to say or do anything that might make her appear to occupy any space other than the center or even just right of center where race was concerned.[36]

Later, when she turned to golf in her mid-thirties, Gibson again found herself a racial outsider playing a game of catch-up in yet another environment controlled by White leaders and players, leaving her to feel once more that she needed to concentrate on her new sport and nothing else. On the LPGA Tour, she competed against not only her aging body but also women in their teens and twenties who had been playing golf for much longer than she had and under conditions that were superior to those on the public courses where she initially honed her game. Gibson played against several women, including Mickey Wright, Kathy Whitworth, and Marlene Bauer Hagge, whose skills and victory totals would earn them induction into the World Golf Hall of Fame. Determined to succeed, she dove into her new craft, taking lessons from multiple instructors, spending hours at the driving range and on the putting green, and reading every book she could find about the mental and physical aspects of golf. She ignored those who were surprised, dumbfounded, or offended by the sight of a Black woman playing golf.

Money factored into Gibson's calculations about whether, when, and how to discuss racial inequality as she played her new game. She believed that her race and her gender made corporations, famously conservative and concerned about offending White consumers, wary of offering her endorsement deals, an issue that most Black athletes of the period faced. Clubs and businesses that the LPGA partnered with were unwelcoming, too, refusing to allow her to enter their tournaments. Gibson had no money from playing amateur tennis, no family wealth to tap into, and, for most of her time on the tour, no spouse to pay her way. In golf as in tennis, Gibson lacked the financial freedom and the career circumstances to be a champion for civil rights.

Highly competitive by nature—the kind of person who hated to lose as much as she loved to win—and passionate about sports and learning, Gibson organized her tennis and golf careers around the principle that athletes "must be willing to sacrifice all but the very essential activities of ordinary day to day living and give undivided attention to the development of [their] mental attitudes and physical skills" if they were going to be the best. "There is," she believed, "a great deal more involved in this than the average observer might think."[37] Gibson brought a similarly zealous determination to realizing her dream of being a vocalist, culminating in the production of an album, *Althea Gibson Sings*, in 1958; to her foray into acting, including a role in *The Horse Soldiers* (1959), a Civil War epic directed by Academy Award–winner John Ford and starring John Wayne; and to her professional tennis tours between

1959 and 1960, which made her into an opening and halftime act for the Harlem Globetrotters.

Although Gibson was never at the forefront of activism, she found ways—sometimes earnest, sometimes convoluted, and always influenced by the restrictions of the temporal moment and her specific cultural milieu—to show her solidarity with social justice initiatives. In her first autobiography, she wrote about her support for school integration. She also appeared at fundraisers for the National Association for the Advancement of Colored People (NAACP) and scholarships for Black college students. Gibson demanded that her part in *The Horse Soldiers* be rewritten to remove its more stereotypical dimensions. On her professional tennis tour, she spoke out against segregated seating in Virginia. Gibson admired Dr. Martin Luther King Jr. and the aims of the March on Washington in 1963 and emphatically applied its rhetoric about ending employment discrimination to the racial prejudice that stymied her golf career. She found a personal cause in speaking to audiences of children, teenagers, and parents about the importance of staying in school; most of her listeners were Black. Gibson changed further in the 1970s. She led tennis clinics for inner-city children to diversify the sport and broaden the horizons of boys and girls whose backgrounds were similar to her own. She used speaking engagements and media interviews to support women's rights, Title IX, and the expansion of competitive opportunities and increases in prize money for women in professional sports. She frustrated many in the WTA for not supporting a program designed to add more tennis players of color. "I've never been militant. I don't believe in fights. Talent wins out," she told reporter Grace Lichtenstein in 1973. Gibson added, "I sincerely feel as the only Negro player, I have an image to maintain to young ladies. I don't mean to be blowing any horns, but whom do they have to look up to?"[38] She coached Leslie Allen and Zina Garrison, two of the leading Black women in tennis in the 1980s.

To be sure, self-interest guided Gibson's involvement in each of these matters. In most cases, she either was paid for participation or stood to gain from the changes that she discussed. Nevertheless, her stances, like her deviance from gender norms, reflect her contradictions and challenge claims made by other scholars that she was merely "an accommodationist," was "stoic," and simply "rolled with the punches" when it came to social issues.[39]

Taken together, the titles of Gibson's two autobiographies, *I Always Wanted to Be Somebody* and *So Much to Live For* (1968), tell us how she saw herself and how she wanted to be seen—as a leader. "So Much to Live For" was the title of a song that was written for her and which she sang to audiences, including on *The Ed Sullivan Show* in 1958. The title captures her spirit as a Renaissance woman and her belief that living without restrictions was the key to happiness.

I Always Wanted to Be Somebody was even more personal and political. The title alluded to "I Am Somebody," a poem of history and race pride popularized in the 1940s by Reverend William Holmes Borders, a civil rights activist in Atlanta who had a radio program. In the poem, Borders named African Americans who had accomplished important feats and were seen as leading and inspiring other African Americans and the country through their actions and examples. Langston Hughes, Frederick Douglass, Sojourner Truth, and W. E. B. Du Bois were among the figures Borders identified. So were Jesse Owens and Joe Louis.[40] For years, "I Am Somebody" was reprinted in Black newspapers and dramatized in Black churches, the lines and names changed to reflect more recent figures. As a youth in Atlanta, Martin Luther King Jr. tuned in regularly to Borders's program. In the 1960s, King spoke of the concepts of "somebodiness" and "nobodiness" in his own speeches and writings, including his famous "Letter from a Birmingham Jail."[41] By titling her first book *I Always Wanted to Be Somebody*, Gibson was announcing to the world that she had long aspired to be respected and to emulate the "somebodies" of African American history, and that she believed that her many firsts in tennis made her a social leader. King agreed. In his last book, *Where Do We Go from Here?* (1968), King described Gibson as one of several Black celebrities, including athletes Joe Louis, Muhammad Ali, Jackie Robinson, Bill Russell, Jesse Owens, and Arthur Ashe, who "remind [African Americans] that, in spite of our lack of full freedom, we can make a contribution here and now."[42]

———

Listening to Gibson, then in her mid-fifties, recount the highs and lows of her careers, an interviewer in the early 1980s concluded that her "life was a mosaic."[43] It was an apt description of Gibson. The pieces are, to be sure, varied and fascinating, and they show a woman who challenged the attitudes—and sometimes tried the patience—of the communities and institutions she passed through on the way to grandly realizing her dreams and, more mundanely, to merely trying to survive.

The mosaic is a colorful and deep portrait of a maverick and iconoclast. As a girl and teen, Gibson was "the wildest tomboy you ever saw," playing sports with boys and grown men when she was not fighting them, with her father's encouragement, on the streets of Harlem.[44] A working-class and

less-than-genteel figure, she learned tennis in Sugar Hill, Harlem's best neighborhood, and was looked upon by members of its Black elite with a blend
of curiosity, concern, and offense as she took to their tennis courts wearing
blue jeans, the uniform of rebels. With her bid to play in the U.S. Nationals
and other "White" tennis tournaments, she forced the USLTA to publicly
confront its attitudes and policies toward African Americans. Later, her
ambitions in golf pushed the LPGA to do the same. Whether it was finishing
high school, winning her Grand Slam tennis titles, joining the LPGA Tour, or
marrying, Gibson always seemed to reach milestones years after what society
considered "normal."[45] She flouted norms concerning dress, too. In her early
twenties, Gibson "wore slacks and a t-shirt every chance I got." She admitted
that well into her teens, "a sweater and skirt combination was as far as I was
willing to go in the direction of looking feminine."[46] Gibson's stardom made
her a sensation in the African American, White, and international media, but
in each case, coverage revealed that journalists often lacked the sensitivity and
the acumen to write with fairness and respect about her life and the fierce devotion with which she played tennis and golf, because of her race, her gender,
and her tenacity. "People thought I was ruthless, which I was," she once said
practically. "I didn't give a darn who was on the other side of the net. I'd
knock you down if you got in the way."[47] Gibson was often the only African
American in the circles in which she traveled. Other times, she was the only
woman. Together, the pieces merge to portray a social misfit whose broad
gender nonconformity was so at odds with her settings and times that it is
fitting to call her expansively queer.

    In describing Gibson as queer, my purpose is not to add to conjectures
about her sexuality.[48] While conducting research for this book, I did not un-
cover sources that revealed that Gibson had intimate female partners. Rather,
"queer" is fitting as a concept for understanding the degree to which she was
a social misfit. Since the 1990s, theorists have reclaimed the word "queer,"
expanding its meaning beyond homosexual, its primary and "derogatory"
connotation, during the mid-twentieth century.[49] The term "queer" is not
"defined solely by the gender of [an individual's] sexual partners," explains
Lisa Duggan, but is instead "unified only by a shared dissent from the dominant organization of sex and gender."[50] The latter definition applies to
Gibson. She was frequently the subject of efforts to make her more feminine
during her teen years and young adulthood as she came under the influence
of the African American middle and upper classes and as she moved closer
to crossing the color line that surrounded tennis, where adherence to gender
norms was a major aspect of the culture. In addition, homophobic innuendo

and rumors circulated about her in the African American media along with other gender-based expressions of ambivalence and derision.

Neither the gender-based corrections nor the homophobic gossip that Gibson endured was coincidental. Rising since the 1930s, the lesbian athlete stereotype was firmly in place when her tennis career began in earnest in the 1940s. It was utilized broadly to stigmatize women in sports as trespassing in a field that was dominated by and which many assumed should be reserved exclusively for men. African American reformers and their followers, including in the Black media, had long viewed gender conformity and abiding by heterosexual norms as central strategies to achieve full citizenship. Black women were enjoined that marrying, having children, tending to their homes, and serving their husbands as "helpmates," rather than partnering with them as equals, was a vital way to advance beyond the wide gulf of segregation. The civil rights movement pushed this credo into overdrive.[51]

Domesticity and compliance, however, were not Gibson's modus operandi. An unmarried female athlete from a working-class background, she prioritized her career over marriage and sometimes dressed and expressed herself in ways that society deemed masculine. In the sociopolitical climate of the Cold War, when gays and lesbians were labeled as national security threats in the face of Communism, the Black media, like the rest of America, viewed those traits as signs of lesbianism.[52]

Gibson would make some concessions over the years. She was "a tactical renegade with regard to gender, choosing to defy or adhere to protocols, depending upon whichever approach would help her get her way."[53] She became more mindful of her public appearance, wearing dresses, skirts, and makeup, and became especially attentive to her hair. She played coy with the media about her relationships with men as often as she shut down questions. As a public relations representative for the Ward Baking Company, she participated in public engagements purported to suit the tastes of female consumers. It was all part of a performance well known to sportswomen of the era no matter their race. Society expected female athletes to repeatedly prove their femininity and heterosexuality because they were athletes. Male athletes, meanwhile, were given a pass. Since sport was a traditional proving ground for masculinity, sportsmen's masculinity and heterosexuality were never in doubt.[54]

Yet Gibson remained committed to her independence, no matter what people thought of her, making her more radical for her times than she has been given credit for being. "I'm not going to throw away whatever chance I have of doing something with the success I've been able to achieve," she wrote in 1958. "I'm not about to throw away everything for love. I can do without a man if I have to. I've done it for fifteen years and I guess I can do it for a while longer."[55] And she did, bucking trends and social pressure. When Gibson did marry for the first time, she was nearly forty years old, and she largely continued to live as she had before: putting her career first. Self-focused, she never became a parent and seems never to have wanted to be one.

"Homophobia is a powerful political weapon of sexism," writes sports and sexuality scholar Pat Griffin. "When a woman is called a lesbian, she knows she is out of bounds."[56] The homophobic disparagement that Gibson endured—"uncomplimentary things," she understatedly called the remarks—served a purpose beyond condemning her sexuality, even as she did not identify as a lesbian. It was a way for her African American critics to assert that she did not fit their image of the ideal Black woman even though she was the face of Black tennis.[57]

———

There have been other biographies of Althea Gibson.[58] Bruce Schoenfeld's *The Match* and Frances Clayton Gray and Yanick Rice Lamb's *Born to Win* were both published in 2004. A well-crafted story, *The Match* is a dual biography of Gibson and Angela Buxton, the friend and doubles partner with whom she won her first Wimbledon title in 1956. Useful in its interviews with people who knew Gibson at different times in her life, *Born to Win* is the "authorized biography" and, as such, neglects to take seriously its subject's shortcomings and her complexities. Neither book is invested in a sustained exploration of the ways in which Gibson negotiated the challenges as well as the opportunities wrought by race and gender throughout her life and in her career pursuits. The Gibson of *The Match* and *Born to Win*, moreover, is decidedly static and inaccurately stoic. Swift in their treatments of her life after she left amateur tennis, neither book allows readers to see how Gibson's ideas about and approaches to social matters as well as her sense of herself as an athlete, a performer, and, to use one of her oft-used phrases, someone who could "make a contribution" evolved as her circumstances and the times changed.

The result of more than a decade of research, *Serving Herself* sets and examines Gibson's singular life within the context of the major historical developments of the twentieth century, utilizing newly discovered and available sources. These materials include interviews and personal correspondence, records, and recordings from university, government, presidential, family, and museum archives as well as several hundred articles, including interviews, from newspapers and magazines published around the world.

Uncovering Gibson's presence in the African American media has been essential to recouping her symbolism and varied meanings to a community that often embraced her with ambivalence as much as enthusiasm but which she still considered her own, especially the working class. The result is a narrative history that chronicles Gibson's domestic and global exploits as a seminal cultural figure who crossed the color line as few others did and that provides accounts of those who knew her as a person, an athlete, a symbol, a colleague, and a friend. Most of all, these sources allow Gibson's one-of-a-kind voice and thoughts to be front and center, enhancing the perspectives that she left behind in her autobiographies and supporting this book as a "biography of an age"—of two ages in fact: the era and aftermath of sports integration and the years before Title IX and widespread opportunities for women in sports.[59]

The advanced state of women's sports makes this the ideal time for a substantial, full-scale biography of Gibson. Led by tennis, women's sports have achieved unprecedented popularity. There are more star sportswomen as well as competitive and lucrative opportunities for them than ever before. Yet the disparity between the number of studies of sportswomen's lives and those of their male counterparts demonstrates that many stories of sports history, women's history, and African American history have yet to be told. Furthermore, gender inequities in sports remain, making it even more important to illuminate the narrow path that sportswomen from previous generations trod and their perseverance in creating space for themselves just the same. Because they were women, Gibson and her peers in tennis and golf faced scrutiny of their bodies, facial expressions, attire, and life choices, especially when (not whether) they would marry; low expectations for excellence; intense sexualization from the sports press; reduced opportunities to explore and thrive in sports; suppositions that they were odd; assumptions that they were inferior athletes; and the pervasive notion that they should not take their careers seriously. Because she was a Black woman, Gibson also encountered doubts in the media about her work ethic, her intelligence, and her legitimacy as a champion. Some fans admired her, but spectators also subjected her to hostility. Linespersons made calling her for foot faults a form of entertainment. Examining these conditions and addressing how Gibson and her colleagues met them sheds light on the similar injustices sportswomen continue to face.

The ongoing attention paid to the activist and political engagements of African American athletes makes this examination of Gibson's life and career even more timely. Athletes of African descent face pressure to make statements and take stands in favor of social justice and just as much pressure not to get involved. No matter what choice they make, they incur risks.

This book offers Gibson as an addition to the list of athletes, including Jack Johnson, Roy Campanella, Willie Mays, O. J. Simpson, Michael Jordan, and Tiger Woods, who were criticized for their reluctance to discuss racial issues and support African American causes during their playing careers.[60] Only by exploring their personal backgrounds, the times in which they lived, their sports' cultures, their financial obligations, the survival strategies they adopted, and their personal ambitions can we understand rather than judge their decisions. Athletes support all kinds of movements and initiatives during and after their careers. Some are race-specific; others are not. What is more, athletes grow and change over their lives, leading some to find in retirement that they have the time, interest, resources, and freedom to take up issues and find new outlets. Gibson's life encourages us to think about athletes' lives as long games that play out in many different arenas.

Serving Herself aspires to place Althea Gibson, as both hero and antihero, where she belonged and longed to be: in the pantheon of Black athletes and thus in the assembly of consequential American athletes. In her achievements, her legacy, her symbolism, her departures from expectations for women, and the sheer drama of her life and all that it tells us about the opportunities and impossibilities of sports in the twentieth century, she was as important and as impactful as any of the leading Black sportsmen who captured the public's imagination long ago. "If I see something and it appeals to me, I do it," she once told an interviewer.[61] It was a defiant, elastic, and freewheeling approach to life, gender, and race that brought her to historic heights and devastating lows. It also gave Gibson a story that is as compelling as that of any other American sports star who ever lived.

I

Coming Up the Hard Way

Sometimes, in a tough neighborhood, where there is no way for a kid to prove himself except by playing games and fighting, you've got to establish a record for being able to look out for yourself before they will leave you alone. If they think you're an easy mark, they will all look to build up their own reputations by beating up on you. I learned always to get in the first punch.

—ALTHEA GIBSON, 1958

FOUR DAYS AFTER her historic victory at Wimbledon in July 1957, Althea Gibson sat at the head table between her parents during a luncheon held in her honor at New York City's famed Waldorf-Astoria Hotel. Wearing a dress of red and blue silk with a corsage pinned to her lapel, she listened as local officials sang her praises. Gibson was "an American girl," "a real lady," and "a wonderful ambassador . . . [and] saleswoman" for the country, they said.[1] Speaker after speaker reached for superlatives and generalities to pay tribute to Gibson for rising improbably from "the sidewalks of New York," in the words of Mayor Robert F. Wagner, to winning the most prestigious tennis tournament in the world. The commissioner of the department of commerce and public events cut closest to the truth with six words: "She came up the hard way."[2]

Gibson did not begin her life as the ladylike figure feted by the mayor. Instead, she had been in her own estimation "the wildest tomboy you ever saw."[3] As an adult, Gibson candidly described the hardships of her youth and the hardness of her own ways in her autobiography *I Always Wanted to Be Somebody*, and people who knew her in those days concurred. Eschewing the "politics of respectability" in her public accounts of her early life, she diverged sharply from the entrenched script of gentility and femininity that society expected women, especially race-conscious Black women, to follow in living, and in telling the stories of, their lives.[4] That Gibson not only defied gender norms in her youth but looked back in adulthood with neither shame nor apology for fighting, committing acts of daring and disobedience, displaying tactics of self-reliance and self-defense, and experiencing physical and emotional pain—long before she ever picked up a tennis racket—during a tough upbringing in Harlem all marked her as decidedly nonconformist.

Gibson believed that her father, Daniel Gibson, was let down when she was born in the family's cabin on August 25, 1927, for a simple yet significant reason: she was not a boy. The day was his nineteenth birthday, too, and a male child would have been a munificent gift. A son, according to the thinking of the times, could grow up to carry out the kinds of hard chores that needed to be done on the farm in Silver, South Carolina, the "three-store town" where Daniel, short, muscularly stocky, and round-faced, sharecropped cotton and corn with his father-in-law.[5] A boy could be a buddy, too, someone to play sports and games with. Whatever his perceptions of the different meanings of having a daughter as his firstborn instead of a son, Daniel, creative if unorthodox in his thinking, devised a solution: he would parent Althea in the way that he thought was appropriate for a male child.[6]

Daniel started early. He began with his daughter's name. Annie, his eighteen-year-old wife, was enchanted by the name Althea; that was the name of the woman her brother Charley was dating at the time. Meaning "healer" or "wholesome," it was another name for the hibiscus plant. It also just happened to look like the word "athlete." To Annie and Charley, the name was "pretty-sounding."[7] Daniel might have agreed, but he sometimes called his new daughter by the masculinized derivative "Al."[8] Later, Daniel claimed that he and the toddler Althea "used to shoot marbles in the dirt road with acorns for marbles" in Silver and that she would win. The story, which Gibson later recognized as hyperbole, captures Daniel's devotion, including in his imagination, to bringing her up in ways that ran against social expectations for a very small child, as well as his interest in teaching his daughter to be competitive, a trait that society forbade for girls lest they seek to challenge and surpass men.[9]

By marrying Annie Bell Washington, Daniel had chosen a rural-born wife who had experience breaching standards of gender for women. Born in South Carolina on November 14, 1908, she was the last of ten children born to Charles Canty Washington, alternately a farmer, store owner, and preacher, and his wife, Mary Emma. Annie played baseball as a girl. After her marriage to Daniel on April 4, 1927, she devoted herself to working on the farm. Annie, full-figured and as tall as Daniel, found ways to make the hard and dirty work fun. Gibson recalled Annie telling her about riding not only horses but also pigs and cows. Decades later, Annie longed to rough-ride atop the animals again and believed she could do so without any trouble. To Gibson, Annie was a "strong woman" who was proud that she had been "no delicate flower" in her own youth.[10] Annie was plain-spoken, too, describing her newborn first child as a "big fat one" for weighing eight pounds at birth.[11]

Sharecropping was dirty in its own way, replete with exploitative ravages for southern Black tenant farmers. White landowners were notorious for cheating Black farmers out of earnings that they were rightfully owed for a year's harvest. Claiming that they themselves were owed money, the landowners kept tenants in severe debt. Sources vary on Daniel and Annie's exact position in farming. Gibson wrote that they "lived in a cabin on a cotton farm" where they "had five acres of land" that they tended with one of her uncles, possibly Charley.[12] Listed on Gibson's birth certificate as doing "public work," Daniel told an interviewer later that he worked on a farm owned by Annie's father and added that the couple owned "thirty acres" (possibly inherited in later years) that they "rented . . . out" in the 1950s.[13]

Whether owners or renters, little or nothing could buffer Daniel and Annie against the capriciousness of the weather and the vicissitudes of the stock market. They endured three straight years of ruined crops. Daniel estimated that they produced only a bale and a half of cotton in the final year, to make seventy-five dollars, not nearly enough money to support their family, which had grown to four with the birth of daughter Mildred in June 1929. The onset of the Great Depression in the fall of 1929 made matters worse in Silver, a small town whose economy depended on agriculture. Recalling the intense pressure, Daniel admitted decades later, "I had to get out of there."[14]

South Carolina, including Clarendon County, gave Black residents no shortage of reasons to want to leave. Silver was located a few miles from Fort Sumter, the site of the first battle of the Civil War. More than eighty years after the Confederacy lost, and stoked by the "separate but equal" doctrine of *Plessy v. Ferguson* (1896), division still governed daily life. Blacks were denied the right to vote through poll taxes, literacy tests, and threats on their lives. Elected positions, from the governorship to the state legislature to judgeships and local public offices, were held exclusively by Whites. Segregation was just as entrenched socially. Blacks and Whites lived in separate neighborhoods and attended different churches.[15]

Long after the Gibsons left, school segregation became Clarendon County's claim to fame and infamy. For decades, Black children attended public schools with facilities that were in no way equal to those afforded their White counterparts and, later, buses were not provided for them, either. Fed up, Black residents, including twenty parents, challenged the situation by filing lawsuits, first about the buses and later about the unconstitutionality of segregation itself. The NAACP joined one of those suits, *Briggs v. Elliott*; this suit plus four others from Washington, D.C., Virginia, Delaware, and Kansas that each took aim at school segregation were consolidated as *Brown v. Board of Education* (1954), the landmark case in which the Supreme Court struck down "separate but equal" in public school. Before the ruling, some of the men and women from Clarendon County who brought their suit saw their homes and places of worship burned to the ground by defenders of white supremacy, lost their jobs, and were forced to leave the state.[16]

Clarendon County in the late 1920s was a long way from watershed judicial decrees, and closer to a low point in legal history that made the county stand out for all the wrong reasons. In 1944, an all-White jury would deliberate for ten minutes after a day-long trial in which the prosecution presented specious evidence. The jury found George Stinney Jr., a fourteen-year-old Black boy who lived in the small town of Alcolu, guilty of the double homicide of Mary Emma Thames, seven, and Betty June Binnicker, eleven. Both girls were White. Stinney seems never to have been interrogated with either his parents or an attorney present, nor was he given the opportunity to appeal the conviction. Stinney was sent to the electric chair on the same day that the trial ended, making him the youngest person executed for a crime in the twentieth-century United States.[17]

The presence of the kind of anti-Black conditions that made Stinney's conviction and execution possible and that kept school segregation alive in Clarendon County were among the cruel facts of life that led more than one million Black southerners to decide to head for the North, Midwest, and West between World War I and the end of the 1920s in the first stage of the movement known as the Great Migration.[18] Several members of Daniel and Annie's families had already fled South Carolina. Reminiscent of Gibson's pattern in adulthood of downplaying and even disavowing the ways that racism negatively impacted her sports careers, Daniel, in interviews, did not attribute the family's departure from Silver to racial prejudice. He insisted that money, or the lack thereof, drove them out. Yet money, specifically the ability to earn it, was always mixed up with race. He also gave little voice to Annie's thoughts about leaving, describing the decision as his own, verbally establishing his position as the patriarch of the Gibson household. Sources vary on precisely when the family left, but by 1931, the year that Daniel Jr., whom they called Danny and Bubba, was born in August, the Gibsons were living in New York City.[19]

Althea went first. Sally Washington, Annie's sister, already lived in New York. She came back to South Carolina for the funeral of their sister Blanche. When Sally returned to New York, she took Althea with her. Daniel promised Sally that he would move there in two months. Annie would follow. Bundled in Sally's arms and separated from her parents, Althea made the first of her many migrations.[20]

———

Daniel had looked out for the fortunes of his family by leaving the South, and he soon learned that he would have to be on his guard in the North, too. Family lore had it that Daniel chatted with a porter, probably another Black man, on the train to New York. Brimming with bluster and pride and wearing by his own admission "a cheap blue suit," Daniel talked of life in South Carolina and his joy at going up north, putting his status as a southern greenhorn on full display.[21] Porters were sophisticated men well versed in both serving and sizing up travelers. Innocently, Daniel asked for directions to Harlem from Pennsylvania Station. The porter volunteered to show Daniel the way for five dollars and said that the trip would take an hour. After a twenty-minute subway ride that cost a nickel, the porter took him to Harlem's famed 125th Street and left, taking Daniel's five dollars with him. There was a dark lesson in the experience. Other people, including Blacks from whom Daniel might have anticipated respect and solidarity, could act in self-interested, exploitative ways in his new town.[22]

Harlem was a hard landing spot for migrants like Daniel. By the 1930s, the celebrated Black mecca was home to more than two hundred thousand people with African roots that stretched from the American South to the Caribbean and Puerto Rico. It was not, however, the glittering place romanticized in the poetry, prose, and songs of the cultural renaissance of a few years earlier. There was a housing crunch. It was difficult to find a home in Harlem in the best of times. Landlords, taking advantage of the cachet of the city, high demand, and low supply, charged high rents for often small and ramshackle spaces. The Great Depression heightened the problem. Migrants kept moving in, but new buildings were not going up. Jobs were scarce, too. The majority of Harlem businesses were owned by Whites who did not hire Blacks or at best doled out only service jobs. Subject to "last hired, first fired" syndrome nationwide,

Blacks were also vulnerable to termination as businesses sacrificed employees in bids to survive. Most Blacks in Harlem, as in the rest of the country, worked service jobs and were paid less than Whites, who seldom welcomed Blacks into their labor unions. Poverty persisted among Black Harlemites, leading many families and individuals to turn to charitable organizations for sustenance. That merchants charged exorbitant prices for basic groceries hardly helped. Blacks protested with some success in the 1930s, most famously the "Don't Buy Where You Can't Work" initiative and the efforts of women associated with the Communist Party to see rent and meat prices reduced. Yet frustration over continued unfairness born from racism remained, eventually fueling uprisings in Harlem, first in 1935 and again in 1943.[23]

Daniel boasted that he found a job in a garage as a handyman quickly, and he was proud of the "big money" that he earned—ten dollars every week, a vast improvement over what he had made farming in Silver. The high rents and the housing shortage, though, slowed his momentum. Like many migrants, Daniel and Annie moved in with a relative. They turned again to Sally Washington.[24]

Gibson remembered very little about living with Washington and seemed to know even less about her decades later, but her aunt proved an important and influential early role model of an independent woman. Throughout her autobiography, Gibson wrote of her desire to "be somebody." Each reference described living on her own without being financially dependent and with the respect of others. Washington as Gibson remembered her had all of that.[25] Harlem was famous for its hustlers, big and small, who skirted the law to survive. Washington appears to have been one of them. Despite the restrictions on alcohol wrought by Prohibition until 1933, she sold whisky and, according to Gibson, "made good money" doing it. "Men," Gibson remembered, "were always coming to the house" to buy the stuff. More than once the whisky sickened her. She remembered guzzling it late at night while thirsty, confusing it with a container of water. Men, uncles as well as Washington's friends and buyers, plied the young Gibson with whisky during daytime trips out of the house, too, leaving Daniel to force her to vomit by putting his fingers down her tiny throat. Despite the dangers of Washington's business and her way of operating the household, Gibson was impressed by her aunt, or what she had been told about her: "There was always lots of food to eat in her house, the rent was always paid on time, and Aunt Sally wore nice clothes every day in the week. She did all right for herself." Washington seems to have done so without a male partner, at least not one who was consistently present in the apartment; in Gibson's account, Washington was unmarried and had no children. Self-sufficient with either the bootleg whisky alone or another way of making money, she kept up the apartment on her own.[26]

Taking care of themselves without the support of others remained beyond the grasp of Daniel and Annie, and in 1934 or 1935 they sent Althea to Philadelphia, another popular destination for Black migrants from the South. She lived there with another aunt, Daisy Kelly, Annie's sister. The Gibson family was growing: Ann, the third daughter and fourth child, was born in February 1935. Having Althea live with Kelly eased some of the financial pressure, but it meant breaking up the family for extended periods. Gibson lived with Daisy "off and on for a couple of years."[27]

Kelly provided Gibson with another model of independent Black womanhood. Though later accounts state that Kelly was married to a Pullman porter, a prestigious service job among Blacks that offered entrée to the middle class, Gibson remembered her aunt as a woman who was on her own.[28] She also remembered Kelly as frequently inattentive. In one story, Kelly forbade Gibson from joining her and a cousin, Pearl, on an outing. Secretly, and dangerously, Gibson defied her aunt. "When the car pulled up at the house they were going to, and Aunt Daisy and Pearl got out, I was standing on the sidewalk," she recalled. "I had made the whole trip standing on the running board and holding on to the door handle, with my head scrooched down underneath the window so nobody could see me."[29]

Then there was the Sunday morning when Gibson jumped into a bucket of automobile grease, ruining the white frock, stockings, and bow in which Kelly had dressed her. Kelly let Gibson roam the streets of the neighborhood, and one time Gibson caused a stir when she came home chased by two boys who appeared ready to attack her; over what, neither she nor Kelly could remember more than twenty years later. It was clear, though, that Gibson was neither defenseless nor afraid. She repeatedly swung a tree branch at the boys, leaving Kelly scared that they would be the ones to get hurt, not Gibson. Looking back, Gibson savored the story as emblematic of her strength and tenacity. "I could always take care of myself pretty well, that's a fact," she wrote.[30]

Despite the impossibility of verifying these anecdotes from Gibson's stays in Philadelphia, their cartoonish qualities, and their likenesses to caricatures of Black children as impossible to hurt, the reminiscences—or their spirit— have worth. They made Gibson feel good in her thirties, providing important insight into what she valued. The Philadelphia stories reveal that Gibson took pride in these portrayals because they showed her challenging expectations that females be passive, polite, compliant, and pretty as early as her childhood.[31]

Gibson was back in Harlem for good sometime between 1938 and 1939, but her return was not seamless. Sources, including Gibson's first memoir, suggest that she was eleven years old before the family had a home of their own for everyone. Until then the family appears to have shifted from one apartment to another between 115th and 130th Streets. Before the decade's end, they had found permanence at last with their move into the five rooms of an apartment on the third floor of 135 West 143rd Street, between Seventh and Lenox Avenues, a six-story walk-up that was built in 1920. Gibson said later that though her family was "poor," her parents made sure they "never went hungry."[32] Still, their household was under tremendous stress. With the birth of Lillian in August 1940, the family had grown to seven people, with five children ranging from infant to adolescent. Daniel's wages at the garage were the only source of income. Gibson's birth certificate listed Annie's occupation as "domestic," but Gibson seems never to have stated that her mother worked in anyone's household except theirs. Annie appears not to have worked in New York, a rarity among Black women of the working class and the working poor. Gibson had lived in three different households during her first twelve years. Readjusting to her parents and the change from being able to explore the streets during the daytime to attending school were difficult and catalyzed her independent streak. "I didn't like people telling me what to do," she explained, a reaction that led her to "real trouble."[33]

Gibson's problems manifested in her approach to school. New York City had so many public schools that the buildings were known not by names but by numbers. Overcrowded in deteriorating classrooms in buildings that could not be expanded or repaired amid the Depression, the students might as well have been mere numbers, too. The Great Migration made the population of Harlem's schools almost entirely Black. Most of the teachers, though, remained White. Gibson was enrolled at P.S. 90 for her elementary years and the all-girls I.S. 136 (Harriet Beecher Stowe Junior High School) after that.[34] She frequently skipped class, a habit begun, and punished, when she was very young. "Teachers used to try to change me; sometimes they would even spank me right in the classroom," she remembered. Gibson, though, was defiant more than daunted. "It didn't make any difference, I'd play hooky again the next day."[35] She hung out with friends who also skipped school, sometimes going to the movies at the Apollo Theater on 125th Street. Daniel, not nearly so flippant about truancy, beat Gibson, one of many "terrible whippings" that he meted out to her.[36]

"Daddy would whip me . . . and I'm not talking about spankings," Gibson wrote. "He would whip me good, with a strap on my bare skin, and there was nothing funny about it."[37] "He would slap the hell out of you," Daniel Jr. said as a man in his seventies when asked about his father's strikes, which were delivered, he said, either by hand or "from an ironing cord."[38] Several times Gibson went to a local police station and told them the truth: "I was afraid to go home because my father was going to beat me up." She kept going to the station, even though her first use of it as a harbor from the storm of Daniel was a debacle. North and south, east and west, African Americans were wary of police forces; law enforcement, in their eyes, prioritized, served, and protected the interests of Whites. Annie was no different. She refused to come to the station to retrieve Gibson after receiving a call from an officer. Another officer went to the family's apartment and confronted her, asking, "Don't you want your daughter?" Gibson came home, but she received a rude welcome: "I got it good that night."[39] Another time, in 1939 or 1940, Daniel gave Gibson a "sore bottom for a week" after he found out that she and a friend, Charles, had rented a bike at a shop in Harlem and then sold it to an unwitting man on the street. Like Annie, Daniel "didn't want to have any trouble with the police," so he rectified the matter on his own.[40] Daniel tracked down the buyer, told him about the children's misdeeds, refunded the money, and brought the bike back to the shop owner.[41]

Writing in *I Always Wanted to Be Somebody*, Gibson connected the beatings from Daniel with disciplining tactics in response to her disobedience (truancy, staying away from home, and petty theft), not with abuse. She described his actions as taking place only after she moved in with the family for good—and acted out—but not before. She discussed the whippings with notable forbearance. "Poor Daddy must have wished there was some way he could whip me hard enough to make me behave like the other kids in the family," she wrote, explaining that her siblings were "good in school" and "never got into any trouble at all."[42] Gibson emphatically defended her father's actions, as if anticipating that readers would look askance at him. Daniel was "teach[ing] me right from wrong," she wrote, and was not "harder on me than he ought to have been."[43]

Gibson also blamed herself for her father's vicious acts. "If he had whipped me every day of my life from the time I was seven years old," a potential clue that Daniel had beaten her from an earlier age, "I would have deserved it. I gave him a whole lot of trouble," she said, adding that "somebody had to knock a little sense into me, and it wasn't easy." In Gibson's view, her father was a paradox. "Even though when he got mad he got very mad," she wrote, "he was actually a patient man."[44] Daniel Jr. saw their father in a similar light: "But when he got mad get out of his way! When he talked, you listened—and he didn't repeat himself."[45]

Gibson remembered Annie sympathetically, noting that her mother "walk[ed] the streets of Harlem until two or three o'clock in the morning" searching for her in vain. Annie stood between Daniel and Gibson or another child, "sometimes catching errant swings," during the disciplining battles.[46] Still, Gibson said that she was frequently "yell[ed] at" when home; by which parent is unclear, leaving the possibility that Annie, too, may have spoken harshly to her at times.[47] Gibson was still defending her parents as a woman in her sixties. Interviewed in the late 1980s for a photography book about notable Black women, she said, "My parents were doing their best to raise me, but I just didn't let 'em."[48]

Gibson's interpretation of the dynamics of Daniel's abusive tendencies was multilayered. The self-blaming rhetoric she used is sometimes adopted by the abused and reflected the limited discourse and understanding of domestic violence in this era, a dialogue that would not begin to widen until the 1960s.[49] Corporal punishment was widely accepted in the 1930s and the 1940s. Gibson's description of the beatings as necessary held racial significance, too. African American communities have long held a comparatively permissive view of spanking and physical discipline compared to White communities. Such tactics were considered important for controlling the behavior of Black children, who are more apt to come under the surveillance of authorities—like the police—in childhood and as adults, to be thought of as older and bigger than they really are, and to be punished more harshly than their White peers for infractions imagined and real, even minor ones. Beatings are not beatings at all, the rationale has gone, but forms of protection and education imparted in the present to keep Black children out of trouble in the future.[50]

Abuse, discipline, and self-protection collided when Daniel began giving Gibson boxing lessons when she was twelve or thirteen. According to her brother, whom Daniel also taught to fight, the lessons took place on the roof of the family's apartment building.[51] "Put up your dukes," their father would say. If Gibson did not do it fast enough, Daniel would start without her. "I had to get ready to defend myself or I would take an even worse beating," she said.[52] Gibson's recollections of the hour-long sessions indicate that coercion and fear were part of the tutorials. Father and daughter agreed in the 1950s that thoughts of survival fueled the lessons, too.

Money was one consideration. Daniel was searching for ways to provide for his five children and saw a potential source of revenue in Gibson. "I had to think of the kids' future," he said in 1957. A fight fan, Daniel had read about "lady boxers" in newspapers and the "big money" they made.[53] He believed that Gibson had what it took to win as a prizefighter. "The minute I saw this natural left hook that Al had, I started teaching her how to mix it up with a right cross. It was a beautiful combination from the beginning. . . . I knew right away that Al would make a world's champion."[54]

Women had indeed boxed in the United States since the early nineteenth century, generally on the quiet and typically in the form of impromptu brawls, as the boxing canvas and the surrounding grandstand were considered improper places for so-called ladies. As prizefighting rose in popularity and acceptance for men in the 1870s, women's participation grew, too. They were paid and given prizes in fights organized by promoters. Female boxers, though, were typically relegated to vaudeville and burlesque theater settings, giving their participation in pugilism an air of entertainment and spectacle rather than that of legitimate sport and competition, which were reserved for male boxers.[55] The public and the press were more comfortable with women as spectators at boxing matches in the 1920s and the 1930s, when promoters came to like the presence of women, especially celebrities and the wives of famous men, in the stands, believing their attendance conferred respectability and cultural sophistication to their perpetually controversial sport. However, women who boxed then, as in the nineteenth century, were ridiculed as "amazons," a term used to deride them for breaching codes of ladylikeness and veering into behaviors and activities considered appropriate only for men. Boxing was re-legalized in New York in 1920, although the New York Athletic Commission routinely denied women's applications for prizefighting licenses, despite there being no formal ban.[56]

Daniel's interest in putting Althea in the boxing ring may have been inspired by two famous African American female boxers in the late 1920s and early 1930s. Emma Maitland and Aurelia Wheeldin fought in a boxing skit as part of a theatrical revue performed in New York City and Europe, where they were "a sensation," according to the *New York Amsterdam News*, the local Black newspaper.[57] Maitland and Wheeldin were "putting over some serious looking swings and uppercuts" that "knocked [spectators] off their seats" in 1926.[58] By 1927, they were promising to challenge Jeanne La Mar, a White woman who was petitioning New York for a license to fight. If La Mar was given a license, Maitland and Wheeldin said, they, too, would pursue a state permit.[59] A license appears never to have come through for any of the women, but Maitland and Wheeldin kept up their act, performing "three rounds of socko (and no fooling)" onstage in the early 1930s, including on Long Island, where they were accompanied by singers and dancers, and for five months in cities in the West.[60] They may have earned as much as $500 per performance.[61] The *Amsterdam News* was not put off by the idea of "girl boxers." "Although their act is one of the most strenuous young ladies ever voluntarily engaged in," according to a reporter, "it has not taken away any of their good looks or one iota of that personal charm which has made them a favorite everywhere."[62] Similarly, Daniel seemed unconcerned that fighting might compromise Gibson's femininity.

New York's refusal to license female fighters ended Gibson's career in prizefighting before it began, but Daniel found another use for the boxing lessons: self-defense. She was spending more time away from home and on the streets while dodging him and playing hooky from school. Gibson was tempting fate. Harlem was a lot of things. To her it was "a mean place to grow up in; there's always somebody to gall you no matter how much you want to mind your own business," she wrote. "If Daddy hadn't shown me how to look out for myself, I would have got into a lot of fights that I would have lost, and I would have been beaten up a lot of times."[63] Fighting was required in Harlem "for a kid to prove himself," she said. "You've got to establish a record for being able to look out for yourself before they will leave you alone. If they think you're an easy mark, they will all look to build up their own reputations by beating up on you. I learned always to get in the first punch."[64] In Gibson's view, Daniel saw the state of the neighborhood and reacted by looking out for his family, especially his unusual oldest daughter.

The gangs were especially concerning. The Sabres wore skullcaps of red trimmed in black. The Hornets donned yellow jackets that advertised their gang's name, stitched in green letters, on their backs. The Rainbows, a Puerto Rican gang, claimed wine as their hue. These and other gangs robbed, attacked, beat up passersby, and guarded their turfs. In the 1950s, it was said that Gibson herself was in a "gang," though their degree of organization is unclear, and she seems never to have confirmed the association.[65] Undoubtedly, though, she was a girl on the streets night and day as men and boys sought to prove their masculinity, making her vulnerable to physical attacks and assaults.

Gibson indeed got into a fight with a gang member, the leader of the Sabres, when he tried to rob her uncle Charlie, whom she called Junie. Junie was drunk and defenseless in the hallway of his apartment building when the Sabre made his move. He gave up the robbery attempt after Gibson called him out, but he did not go quietly. The Sabre threw a "sharpened screw driver" at Gibson, and that was it—she chased him out of the building. "We fought all over the block," she remembered. Attacking Gibson with "his fists and his elbows and his knees and even his teeth," she said, the Sabre "didn't even think of me as a girl, I can assure you." Years later, Gibson took pleasure in the knowledge that people on 144th Street "still talk[ed] about" the fight and how she had held her own. Roger Wilkins, who became an assistant attorney general in the administration of Lyndon Johnson and the head of the Ford Foundation, also grew up in Harlem in the 1940s and remembered the Sabres as the toughest of tough customers. They "had dudes as old as twenty, and all had knives and could stomp and even kill. They were said to be the baddest motherfuckers in the [Harlem Valley]."[66] Gibson's fight with the Sabre raised her street credibility. "Those Sabres respected me from then on. None of them ever tried to use me for a dartboard again."[67]

Gibson got into other fights, too. There was the time she calmly turned around and gave "a black eye" to a man six feet tall who tried to "play the dozens" on either Danny, the entire family, or just Annie as she and her brother walked down the street. Danny remembered, "We never had no trouble out of that bully again."[68] Gibson did not spare Junie, either. She whisked in, a "little lady Robin Hood in the flesh," to punch him after she saw him slap his wife, Mabel.[69] She got into fights with girls on the street and at school. Gibson remembered challenging one bully to a fight after school after the girl had tugged her pigtails one time too many. Gibson matched the expletive-filled taunts of the other girl word for word and applied Daniel's lessons. "I tried to get myself into position, so I'd have enough leverage to get off a good punch," she explained. Then she caught the bully by surprise. "I brought my right hand all the way up from the floor and smashed her right in the face with all my might. I hit her so hard she just fell like a lump. Honest to God, she was out cold." Gibson and the bully had been surrounded by watching schoolmates, including Althea's "gang," who, thrilled by the spectacle, egged them on. "Everybody backed away from me and just stared at me, and I turned around like I was Joe Louis and walked on home."[70]

The connection with the grown man who was the heavyweight champion of the world between 1937 and 1949 captured Gibson's pride in the ice that she imagined was running through her veins. The deadpan look that Louis wore on his face, win or lose, and the steady way that he walked away from opponents after he downed them were intended to minimize the reactions of Whites who might have interpreted a smile, arms raised above his head, or a dip in his step as gloating. Either way, Louis's unreadable expression made him a portrait of coolness and stoicism.[71] The comparison also conveyed Gibson's awareness that she wanted to be associated with and possess the power, physical and otherwise, that she observed as wielded by men.

Daniel, the major male figure in Gibson's life, encouraged her way of thinking. He refused to let her allow kids in the neighborhood and at school to bully her without retribution. Gibson recalled that she once came home and told Daniel that a girl in the neighborhood had punched her "right in the breadbasket" without provocation. "If you don't go back out there and find her and whip her," he said, "I'll whip the behind off you when you come home." Gibson complied.[72] In her first autobiography, she recounted one story after another about fighting. Each account showed both her awareness that her behavior was not standard girlhood biographical fare and her pride in her ability to defend herself. "I know it sounds indelicate, coming from a girl, but I could fight, too. Daddy taught me the moves," she confessed without apology.[73]

But pain is the other side of pride, and though Gibson remembered always standing her ground in her early battles, there is reason to believe that she was hurting, too. "I was tough, I wasn't afraid of anybody, not even [Daniel]," she said, a statement contradicted by her efforts to avoid her home. Gibson claimed not to have cried when Daniel struck and whipped her. Her sister Mildred agreed, saying, "She just stood there and took it."[74] To Gibson, holding back tears was proof that she had "the right temperament" for a fighter.[75] Yet her refusal to cry also suggested that, though only an adolescent, she had absorbed the trope of the strong Black woman who is uncomplaining in the face of unrelenting pain and trauma.[76]

Fighting, and Daniel's encouragement of it, was but one way in which Althea was queer for a girl. In the early twentieth century, teaching girls the norms of femininity was considered a responsibility for parents, especially mothers. Adolescence was a period when girls were supposed to give up being tomboys and begin to adopt the feminine modes of dress and genteel behavior that would prepare them for heterosexual womanhood. Among African Americans—the elite, the middle class, and aspirants to those groups— imparting such lessons was seen as a necessity to challenge white supremacist stereotypes of Black girls and women as aggressive, masculine, and hypersexual, and, as a result, not deserving of respect or rights.[77]

Yet neither Annie nor Daniel seems to have forced Gibson to present and carry herself femininely. In her autobiography, she makes no mention of her mother either teaching or forcing her to don dresses, wear makeup, or style her hair. Daniel, meanwhile, was undisturbed by either Gibson's attire or her attitude. "If I had gone to school once in a while like I was supposed to," she said, "Daddy wouldn't have minded my being a tomboy at all."[78]

By age twelve, Gibson was lean and stood near or at her full adult height, which she reported as 5′10½″.[79] She preferred to wear shorts and pants and claimed not to have owned a "real dress" since she was a "little girl."[80] People who encountered Gibson in the early 1940s recalled that she routinely wore pants, specifically "dungarees," as denim slacks were called. Pants were a sartorial expression of her personal preferences and the family's poverty.[81] Some in the neighborhood called her "Tomboy,"[82] and a girl who initiated a fight with her on the street picked her out precisely because she thought Gibson was deliberately carrying herself as if she were "tough" or "bad."[83] Their fight was effectively a competition to see who was tougher. Gibson had no camouflage for gender nonconformity, and it would seem that she did not want it.

Harlem was a permissive place for queerness. Its performance stages in the 1920s were famous for it. Gladys Bentley, a Trinidadian and African American, danced and sang the blues while wearing men's clothes, including a white tuxedo, as her costume. Bentley and other female blues performers sang openly about homosexuality and gender nonconformity. Same-sex-loving women flocked to Harlem, where they lived with partners and among women with whom they formed a subcultural community. Like gay men in the neighborhood, lesbians socialized and danced not just at house parties but at bars and cabarets, though Black newspapers derided the women as immoral, improper, and prone to violence. Through the 1940s, Harlem was the site of drag balls, including the famous Hamilton Lodge Ball, an annual affair in which men and women, mostly working-class, showed off their sartorial flair as thousands of people watched.[84] Born in Harlem, James Baldwin was Gibson's contemporary and spent his childhood and adolescence on the same streets where she walked and played. While the adolescent Baldwin agonized as he sought to square his effeminacy and attraction to men with his life as a young Pentecostal minister, he nevertheless recognized the latitude the neighborhood offered. "All of the American categories of male and female, straight or not, black or white, were shattered, thank heaven, very early in my life," Baldwin reflected.[85] Gibson similarly experienced and exercised an elasticity in standard conceptions of gender. Although she was not persecuted during her youth on the streets of Harlem by people who took offense at either her queer appearance or her hardened demeanor, that was about to change.

2

A Queer Cosmopolitan

*You only had to see her hit one ball to forget the blue jeans
she first wore to the [tennis] court.*

—COSMOPOLITAN TENNIS CLUB MEMBER

GIBSON HAD BEEN drawn to sports for years. Annie saw the attraction
early on. "She was always running and playing with a ball of some kind, almost as soon as she learned to walk."[1] In Harlem, she would "shoot marbles
on the manholes."[2]

Gibson's urge to compete was so great so early in her life that she came to
believe she possessed "a God-given talent for being able to do things with a
ball."[3] "She was around 12 or 13 when she really started playing games much,"
her sister Mildred said.[4] Mildred remembered that Gibson "didn't want to
stay in the house any longer than she had to. She wanted to get out there and
play."[5] Gibson's objective was to "play, play, play" and have "fun, fun, fun."[6]
"Any kind of ball" would do, she said. "My mother would tell me to go down
to the store for a loaf of bread in the morning, and I would get into a ball
game, and that would be the last I thought of the loaf of bread. I would play
until it got dark and then I would be afraid to go home because I knew I'd be
punished."[7]

The Harlem sports streetscape enticed Gibson. New York City, aided by
philanthropy, the zeal of Progressive-era reformers, New Deal dollars, and an
ambitious city planner and parks commissioner named Robert Moses, added
dozens of public recreational facilities in Harlem, including playgrounds and
sporting areas. Along with the surrounding neighborhood, West 143rd Street
abounded with opportunities for Gibson to compete. It was a play street,
closed to traffic in the afternoons, on weekends, and for hours during summer
days by the Police Athletic League (PAL). In the late 1930s, PAL remained
guided by the ambitions that led to its founding in 1914: to give children like
Gibson in densely populated neighborhoods across Manhattan, Brooklyn,

the Bronx, and Queens safe spaces to learn and play games, develop cordial relations with the police, and choose alternatives to gangs and crime.[8] She did not think about the racial backgrounds of the children that she met: "I played with any kid on the block. It didn't matter whether he was white, brown, black, or yellow."[9]

The perception that sports were a "male preserve, an all-male domain in which men not only played games together but also demonstrated and affirmed their manhood," had persisted since the nineteenth century and remained intact in the 1930s and the 1940s.[10] The sporting ground was effectively a training ground for boys, where they were introduced to and developed the "physical size, strength, power, mental toughness, [and] competitiveness" that society deemed requisite for men to be masculine and that were simultaneously judged as incongruous to femininity.[11] The games that Gibson played, the passion with which she played them, and the fact that her teammates and opponents were often boys added to her queerness as a girl and teenager. Through PAL and her own explorations, she bowled and played baseball, football, stickball, volleyball, shuffleboard, badminton, ping-pong, and basketball, the last of these her absolute favorite. She roamed south to Central Park to play softball. Ted Poston, the only Black reporter for the *New York Post*, later described her as having been "the only female member and pitcher on the city-wide softball championship team" as a youngster.[12] Most of the sports and games that Gibson played and preferred were of the rough-and-tumble team variety considered acceptable only for boys and men. Neither Daniel nor Annie stopped her. Looking back on her childhood, Gibson commented in 1983 that her father's insistence that she never lose a fight made her into a fierce competitor. Winning shifted from being a "desire" to being a "necessity." She was also keenly confident in her abilities, feeling "a step ahead of the other kids, boy or girl, from early childhood."[13]

PAL led Gibson to tennis. Invented in 1898 by Frank Peer Beal, a fourteen-year-old boy in Albion, Michigan, paddle tennis was an inexpensive derivative of lawn tennis that could be played on virtually any flat surface and took up less space than a traditional tennis court. It became a uniquely New York game in 1921 when Beal, then a chaplain, persuaded James V. Mulholland, the director of recreation for the Manhattan Department of Parks, to allow several courts to be drawn in the center of Washington Square. Soon, PAL began to outfit play streets with paddle tennis courts and equipment. Within two decades, the game had spread to the parks and playgrounds of nearly five hundred cities across the United States. By the late 1930s, paddle tennis had reached Gibson's block in Harlem.[14]

One summer morning, she and a close girl friend saw two small wooden rackets and a white rubber ball lying on the street in front of Gibson's building. Intrigued by their discovery, the two girls began to play. "It got to us," Gibson told an interviewer in 1979. "So, we would anticipate every summer morning to be the first on the paddle tennis court, practicing it, hitting balls, enjoying it. And, as a matter of fact, it got to a point where we owned the paddle tennis court. Nobody could get on the court but us." Imaginations afire, Gibson and her friend led day-long tournaments that they called "Losers Weepers." Players competed against each other in singles. The winner of one match then faced the winner of another, and so on. Gibson kept winning, ensuring that she was hardly a loser or a weeper. She savored the memory of playing paddle tennis "all day." When she ventured to the new paddle tennis courts at nearby Colonial Park she faced off against and defeated girls as well as boys. "The fellows in the block were more fun to compete with than the girls," she told Poston. "They made it worth while."[15] Mildred proudly recalled her sister's paddle tennis record: "Not even the boys could beat her."[16]

Gibson soon came to the attention of PAL staffer Osborne "Buddy" Walker. The well-to-do of Harlem knew him as an orchestra leader who conducted the music they danced to at invitation-only balls, cocktail soirees, club dances, and fashion shows. Youngsters, especially those among the disadvantaged, saw him as a community leader. Tall, lean, and ever ready with a broad smile, Walker worked for the *Amsterdam News* Boys Club in the 1930s, organizing sports gatherings, coaching its basketball team, and mentoring its musicians. To support his family, he also turned to PAL and became an instructor. When he met Gibson, she was playing paddle tennis in a way that set her apart from the other kids. "Her aggressive strokes and swift movement caught my attention immediately," Walker said. He later took credit for encouraging her to enter New York City's paddle tennis tournament.[17]

Mystery surrounds precisely when Gibson won medals in paddle tennis tournaments organized by PAL and the Department of Parks, but she undoubtedly demonstrated her queerness at an event in which her skills were recognized. The first photo plate in *I Always Wanted to Be Somebody* shows Gibson wearing what looked like a man's suit, minus the necktie, at a paddle tennis awards ceremony. The jacket, baggy on her lean frame, was dark and buttoned to just below her suprasternal notch. A handkerchief thrust out of a pocket on the left breast. Her shirt had a floral or paisley print and a collar of exaggerated length that fell over the lapels of the jacket. The reactions of the other guests and the dignitaries, including Frank Beal himself, are unknown, but her appearance was remarkable. She was already as tall as the three men with whom she posed for photographs and who all wore suits of their own. Gibson, in a moment of glory and public recognition, had chosen to present herself as boyish, a look augmented by her hair, which she wore swept up and back, away from her face. The caption states that the picture was taken in 1939, but Gibson looks older than twelve and the *New York Times* does not list her among the girls who placed first or second in the PAL paddle tennis tournament that year. In some sense, the year does not matter. What does matter is that she included the photograph in her book twenty years later, demonstrating her lack of shame for her early gender nonconformity.[18]

Walker looked beyond Gibson's appearance to see her potential. In the summer of 1941, he invited his friends to come to 143rd Street to match their racquet-wielding skills against hers. All were beaten. Walker soon decided that Gibson was ready for a more advanced game. "One day I realized she probably could make a good tennis player," he told the press after she won her first Wimbledon singles title. Walker spent ten dollars of his own money on two secondhand tennis rackets. He gave them to Gibson and took her to Morris Park, where she hit balls back and forth against a wall used for handball. Soon Walker enlisted the help of more friends, asking them to hit balls with her at the new Harlem River Tennis Courts at 153rd Street and Seventh Avenue, built with money donated by industrialist and philanthropist John D. Rockefeller Jr. Gibson more than held her own, despite being new to maneuvering a bigger racket as well as to playing on a bigger court and in front of so many people—her first gallery. She played for more than an hour. People from surrounding courts and elsewhere stopped what they were doing to watch. Walker relished the day: "It was wonderful to see this 12-year-old kid hypnotize so many people with her speed and power strokes the very first time she had ever been on a tennis court."[19]

Walker had an idea of what Gibson might become through tennis. He did not speak of Wimbledon and Forest Hills or of race and changing the image of an American sport. He did, however, have class on his mind. Walker pitched tennis as not just a game but as a game-changer in Gibson's life. Early on, she remembered, "he started telling me all about how much I would like the game and how it would be a good thing for me to become interested in because I would meet a better class of people."[20] That introduction had already begun. Walker invited Gibson to his apartment at the Harlem River Houses and introduced her to his young daughter, Fern, and wife, Waltrine "Trini" Hawkins. Trini was considered one of the most "fashion-minded" women in Harlem, and Fern's christening, like her parents' wedding at the grandiose St. James Presbyterian Church on St. Nicholas Avenue, was reported in the

Amsterdam News.[21] Gibson would have seen that the Harlem River Houses, a brand-new triumph in public housing, had steam heat, private bathrooms, and reams of sunlight, along with courtyards and outdoor spaces where children could play safely. The buildings were "an oasis in the desert" of Harlem tenements like the one where her family lived.[22]

Walker and Trini agreed that, through tennis, Gibson could "have a chance to make something out of myself."[23] She liked what she heard. Years later, she would boast of Walker's support for her: "I suppose in his own mind he must have seen raw talent."[24]

———

Gibson's background—southern and working poor—made her a decidedly unlikely tennis player. The ancient Greeks were the first to play the game, followed by European royalty in the Middle Ages. The French and the Italians played "the palm game," wearing a corded glove to slap around a ball made of leather and stuffed with hair. The French came to call it "tenez." In England, Germany, and Austria between the sixteenth and eighteenth centuries, rackets replaced gloves, but the association of the game with the royal and the well-off remained intact.[25]

Not much changed in the early 1870s when Major Walter Clopton Wingfield of Wales invented lawn tennis. The British leisure class adopted the game and played it at their homes and throughout the empire. In April 1874, a White American socialite, Mary Ewing Outerbridge, discovered lawn tennis in Bermuda, then a British outpost. Outerbridge sailed back to America with a tennis kit, which she brought to the Cricket and Baseball Club in Staten Island, her hometown. Soon members of similar clubs across the Middle Atlantic and the Northeast were playing lawn tennis. In 1881, White Americans founded the governing body of the sport, the United States National Lawn Tennis Association in New York City ("National" was dropped in 1920), and hosted the first annual National Lawn Tennis Championships. By the end of the century, tennis had taken hold among the White American elite, first on the East Coast and then spreading west. For the next several decades, these influencers and tastemakers built tennis courts at their homes, on the grounds of their country clubs and resorts, and on the campuses of their selective schools and colleges. Expectations of Victorian deportment governed the culture and play of tennis no matter the location of the club or court. Players were to wear white (pants and later shorts for men, dresses and skirts for women), maintain a cool and indifferent demeanor, keep their voices down, be polite, and, whether victorious or vanquished, shake hands with their opponents at the end.[26]

African Americans were playing tennis by the 1880s, with the first known Black southerners taking to the courts by the 1890s at Tuskegee Institute in Alabama. Shut out of the USLTA, Blacks made their own tennis world, though it too was associated with the social elite. The first Black interstate tennis tournaments took place by 1899 and became a tradition over subsequent decades. Black tennis enthusiasts in Washington, D.C., and Baltimore, Maryland, founded the American Tennis Association in November 1916 to popularize the sport and raise the level of play among Black people. African Americans sometimes competed in local tournaments held on public tennis courts outside the South. The ATA was different and special. It gave African Americans a regular circuit on which to compete and the chance to vie for an annual national title, an honor denied to them by the USLTA.[27]

Historically Black colleges and universities (HBCUs) further developed tennis among the race, adding tennis courts to their campuses at the encouragement of ATA leaders. The facilities were vital to spreading the game among African Americans. Segregationist attitudes about recreation and approaches to urban planning restricted their access to tennis. HBCUs became the sites of most ATA tournaments, including the highly anticipated Nationals. Players and attendees entertained themselves on campuses at pool parties, dances, and other social affairs that led some to see the ATA as a playground for "'the mink coat, Cadillac' set."[28] By 1939, the ATA supervised twenty-one sanctioned tournaments nationwide and boasted a hundred and fifty clubs, including chapters in the Bahamas and Bermuda. The faithful among the twenty-five thousand members of the ATA played in interclub tournaments as well as championships staged around the country in the four months of the late spring and summer. Clubs had rivalries, and the stars of the ATA found their photographs and tournament results published in Black newspapers. Yet, like so much else in segregated America, they were mostly ignored by the White press. Players looked forward each year to packing their cars and traveling from tournament to tournament to compete and commune with other Black tennis enthusiasts. *Time* magazine praised the ATA as a standout among Black sports associations, including the famed Negro League of baseball, writing that in "no [other] sport are [African Americans] more firmly organized than at tennis."[29]

New York State was a hub of Black tennis, with one of the highest numbers of ATA chapters in the country. Like the ATA's other chapters, clubs in its New York Tennis Association carried grandiose names. The Nassau and St. Thomas groups tipped off the Caribbean origins of club founders. The Atlas and Hermes tennis clubs took their monikers from mythology. Brooklyn Merit, Ideal, Progressive, Rhythmic, and Utopian were no less ambitiously named. In the summer of 1941, Gibson was given a place on the membership roster of the most rarefied chapter—the Cosmopolitan Tennis Club, the jewel that glittered brightest in the ATA's crown.[30]

At 443 Convent Avenue near 149th Street in Harlem, the Cosmopolitan was a mere six blocks north of Gibson's street, but it might as well have been in another world. Begun as the Colonial Tennis Club, the Cosmopolitan was among the oldest tennis clubs for Blacks in New York.[31] The club had four clay courts, locker rooms for men and women, showers, lavatories, the only veranda in Harlem, and, the *Amsterdam News* marveled, "a beautiful pavilion for guests, with radio and other appointments for their comfort."[32] Black journalist Roi Ottley described the Cosmopolitan as having a "resort atmosphere," making it an oasis in Harlem.[33] The White *New York Herald Tribune* acknowledged that the Cosmopolitan was "the leading Negro tennis club of the country."[34]

Following the ATA's goal of bringing more juniors into tennis, the Cosmopolitan kept up a youth membership drive. One of the people who had watched Gibson hit shots on the tennis courts at Morris Park arranged for her to come to the Cosmopolitan to play a few games with Fred Johnson, the club's teaching professional. A coterie of members eyed the proceedings. Impressed, the group pooled their funds to pay for Gibson's membership and regular lessons with Johnson.[35]

Cosmopolitan Club members fit the high-toned character of its neighborhood, Sugar Hill, where "blacks who had made it," according to local lore, "live[d] the sweet life."[36] Some of the most eminent African Americans in the country had chosen to live "on the Hill," as it was called, moving into its elegant brownstones and vaunted apartment buildings. Roy Wilkins, Thurgood Marshall, Walter White, and W. E. B. Du Bois, luminaries of the NAACP, lived on the Hill. So did artists, writers, musicians, and performers, including Aaron and Alta Douglas, George Schuyler, Count Basie, and Paul and Eslanda Robeson.[37]

Gibson was keenly aware of the status of the Cosmopolitan. She called it "the ritzy tennis club in Harlem" where "all the Sugar Hill society people belonged."[38] She knew that Cosmopolitan members had the disposable income to afford tennis, with its expensive rackets, white clothes, shoes, and balls that required frequent replacement, along with club memberships and lessons.[39]

On the evening Gibson was awarded the club membership, Fred Johnson learned just how much her circumstances differed from those of the other Cosmopolitan members. Johnson, a short, dark-skinned, small-framed man in his early fifties, walked to 135 West 143rd Street and climbed the three flights of stairs to pay a visit to the Gibson family. Daniel was not home; he worked the night shift at the garage. Annie let Johnson into the cramped apartment. Johnson told Annie about the club membership and asked for her permission to give tennis lessons to Gibson. Annie responded with a question of her own: "How much money is there in it?" It was an indication of the financial straits of the family of seven. Johnson replied, "None now, but probably some later." Annie's question affirmed Johnson's decision to combine the five dollars given to him by one club member and another ten dollars of his own money to buy a new tennis racket for Gibson.[40]

Gibson, in a moment of self-aggrandizement, boasted to an interviewer in 1979 that the members of the Cosmopolitan "took me as one of theirs," but the situation was more complicated and less flattering than that.[41] She was a spectacle in the ordered and elegant confines of the Cosmopolitan. Thirteen going on fourteen when she arrived, she stood out as a long, straight figure clad in jeans. After Gibson won Wimbledon, club members who knew her in those early days still remembered her as "the skinny little tomboy you couldn't tell from a boy or girl."[42] Gibson breached tennis etiquette not only in her attire but also in her manners. "When balls came onto her court from the other courts," said one member, "she would simply bat them out of the way in any direction instead of politely knocking them back to the players who wanted them, as is done in tennis." Such gestures revealed Gibson's background in sports: "She had played in the street all her life and she didn't know any better."[43] While abhorring Gibson's mien, members could not dismiss her abilities. One conceded, "You only had to see her hit one ball to forget the blue jeans she first wore to the court."[44] Nevertheless, they felt that something had to be done about the way she looked and behaved.

Fred Johnson was the man to do it. He was a consummate student of the protocols that governed the game and expected the same from Gibson. Johnson dressed neatly in white at the club and lived by the dictum of the era that tennis coaches model good behavior for their students. Having lost his left arm in an accident as a teenager, he was nicknamed "One-Arm Johnson" in press reports of his matches.[45] Despite his disability, Johnson astounded onlookers and undoubtedly opponents with his serve. He had at least two techniques. In one, he "placed one tennis ball beneath the upper part of his left arm," all that remained after the accident, and "would hold the other ball in his right hand, with his racket, and toss it up. As he released the ball, he swung the racquet back and around, striking the ball as the racquet came up and around."[46] In the other, Johnson would "put a ball on the face of his racquet, toss it up with the racquet and serve."[47] Johnson won three ATA senior men's national singles championships between 1934 and 1938 and shared the men's doubles championship of the Bahamas as part of the association's first international delegation in 1936. Johnson knew that he would have to meet Gibson where she was. "A good instructor," Johnson believed, "must learn how to get over to his pupil."[48]

Johnson taught Gibson the fundamentals, tennis grips, footwork, and the area in which he was most renowned as a player, strategy. "She was very apt, but not the studious type," Johnson later said. He found that the best way to teach her was through demonstrations: "She would stand behind me and imitate me."[49] Getting Gibson to address her social comportment proved more difficult. "He also tried to help me improve my personal ways. He didn't like my arrogant attitude and he tried to show me why I should change," Gibson admitted. "I don't think he got too far in that department; my mind was set pretty strong.... I wasn't exactly ready to be a fine lady."[50]

Johnson had a female ally in his project of getting Gibson to conform to the standards of the Cosmopolitan and of tennis. One of the most admired women at the club, socialite Rhoda Worrell Smith was a native of Barbados who had emigrated to the United States as a young woman in 1912 and took up tennis sometime around 1920. By 1930, Smith ranked in or around the top ten of the ATA women's circuit. When she met Gibson, Smith was transitioning from playing competitively to becoming a more active volunteer for the Cosmopolitan. She was building a reputation as a supporter of younger players, especially girls.[51]

Smith, who claimed to be "the first woman [Gibson] ever played with," was nonplussed by her mentee's differences. She had watched her during her tryout with Johnson. To Gibson's irritation, Smith used their time together to teach her to have better manners on the tennis court. Gibson "resented it," Smith noticed. "I was always trying to improve her ways. I had to keep saying, 'Don't do this,' and 'Don't do that.'" Smith chided Gibson, saying she should gently tap errant tennis balls to players on other tennis courts rather than belt them back. Smith also bought clothes for her: "She only had dungarees and that wouldn't do."[52] When she learned one winter that Gibson did not have a warm coat, Smith took her downtown and bought one for her, along with new underwear.[53]

Johnson and Smith's campaign to change Gibson was rooted in the standards of region, class, and gender that guided the outlooks of most middle- and upper-class African Americans on racial representation in the early twentieth century. Black northerners had judged since the start of the Great Migration that southern migrants needed to be reformed and schooled in the ways of life beyond the Mason-Dixon Line, lest the newcomers affirm racist stereotypes. African Americans observed the tendency of Whites to look upon Blacks as a mass. White supremacists, they argued, considered the actions, primarily and particularly the perceived lapses, of one Black person as indicative of the character and habits of the entire race and then pointed to the supposed errors as evidence of black inferiority and as justification for segregation. African Americans who founded and led institutions like the ATA, the Cosmopolitan, and HBCUs responded by advocating strict protocols of self-presentation that they believed were in the best interest of their maligned race. The "politics of respectability," as historian Evelyn Brooks Higginbotham put it, was a survival strategy deployed and mandated by middle- and upper-class African Americans to combat Whites' negative notions of the race that undermined Black progress, instill pride in individual Blacks, and demonstrate pride in being Black.[54]

Gender was integral to respectability politics for generations of the Black elite and to Black strivers. The dominant White culture stereotyped all African Americans as hypersexual and made further distinctions between the sexes. Black men were cast as weak, inept, and unmanly in comparison to White men. Black women were characterized as aggressive, dominant, and unfeminine in contrast to White women. African American social leaders prescribed gender conformity as essential to challenging such ideas and used all manner of cultural products at their disposal to call for men and women, boys and girls to adhere to traditional ideas about masculinity and femininity in yet another effort to improve the image of and chances for African Americans, individually and as a race. Leaders and followers branded Blacks who transgressed norms of gender, sexuality, and upward mobility as harmful to the race and believed that personal choices reflected on their entire race.[55]

Gibson discovered that the Cosmopolitan and the ATA used tennis as a vehicle for teaching and expressing respectability. "The Cosmopolitan members were the highest class of Harlem people and they had rigid ideas about what was socially acceptable behavior," she wrote. "They were undoubtedly more strict than white people of similar position for the obvious reason that they felt they had to be doubly careful in order to overcome the prejudiced attitude that all Negroes lived eight to a room in dirty houses and drank gin all day and settled all their arguments with knives."[56] Her chosen description—crowded households, alcoholism, and sudden yet routine violence—overlapped with her own life. That the Cosmopolitan had White members added to the attention that Black club members paid to etiquette and social correctness.

While the middle- and upper-class Blacks who belonged to the Cosmopolitan and other chapters undoubtedly would have enforced propriety on their own, the ATA established in its literature the expectations that members be socially and politically productive rather than exclusively recreational. ATA leaders used the pages of the program booklet for the Nationals in 1941, the year that Gibson joined the Cosmopolitan, not only to inform attendees of the events scheduled at tournament host Tuskegee Institute but also to reflect on the association's principles on its twenty-fifth anniversary. The goodwill and understanding that ATA members facilitated through camaraderie and fellowship at tournaments and elsewhere "made a substantial contribution to the Democracy in which we live," wrote ATA president Dr. D. Ivison Hoage. Consequently, he explained, ATA members deserved "respect and recognition from other groups who no longer classify us as an isolated class but as individuals whose lives form an integral part in the progress of the nation."[57] Juniors were not exempt from the constructive and even political dimensions of tennis for the ATA. "The program of the ATA goes far beyond the development of the game of tennis as a sport, it is interested in the physical and cultural development of the life of every young person," administrators reported in 1941. "It reaches wherever possible into the home, the school, the college, and the every day community activity."[58]

The ATA and the Cosmopolitan shared and promoted the popular idea that tennis could mature players, positively shape their character, and, consequently, enhance the country. Edwin Bancroft Henderson, who headed the physical education programs in the Washington, D.C., public schools of the era and admired the ATA, noted, "Tennis has a carry-over value of more worth to participants than any of the other games." ATA tournaments were "wholesome," according to Henderson, and tennis itself was a "splendid game" with innumerable "possibilities and advantages."[59] The ideas of Henderson, the ATA, and the Cosmopolitan aligned with mainstream White conceptions of tennis as didactic. The game could be "utilized to effect habits that make toward moral, emotional, mental, and physical health," wrote the author of *Tennis for Women*, a guidebook published for tennis teachers in 1926. Tennis was ideal for "establishing standard habits and attitudes of behavior," including gender.[60]

Rhoda Smith typified the kind of women that the ATA, the Black press, and indeed middle- and upper-class Black America celebrated for being good at tennis and for behaving according to the ideals of femininity, the standards that Smith and Johnson sought to cultivate in Gibson. Smith and other women in the ATA were known, and praised, for showing that women could be both athletic and feminine. Known as a fashion plate, Smith traveled to ATA tournaments with, in the memory of one acquaintance, a "bottomless trunk" filled with splendid clothes.[61] The *Amsterdam News* reported on her many social activities, published photographs of her wearing evening attire at the ATA Nationals, and sometimes described what she wore to events.[62]

The ATA and the Black press likewise celebrated other women in the association. Elise "Elsie" Conick won several ATA tournaments and was respected for her comportment. In 1929, Arthur Francis, an ATA member who refereed matches and chronicled the events of the association in the *Amsterdam News*, wrote approvingly of Conick as "brilliant and charming" and a "credit to Negro tennis in America" who possessed a "very pleasing disposition" and a "lovable, competitive spirit." Conick was quick to express her gratitude to others and neither boasted of her victories nor complained about her losses.[63] Hers was the kind of bearing that was associated with Henderson's concept of "ladylike sportsmanship"—generosity to all and equanimous reactions no matter the outcome of a match.[64] Conick was adulated for her looks, too. In October 1918, she appeared without her tennis racket on the cover of *The Crusader*, a magazine targeted at middle- and upper-class African Americans. In 1938, she was featured holding her tennis racket in an advertisement for Ramsdell's Rita-Sav, a product that promised to clear blemishes from the skin of Black women. Flora Lomax, winner of four ATA women's national championships between 1938 and 1942, was Smith and Conick's successor in attaining ideals of femininity among Black women. Black sportswriters hailed Lomax as "comely," "winsome," a "classy little athlete," "graceful," and "dainty."[65] The most emphatic reaction to Lomax's appearance and personality appeared in the *Amsterdam News* in 1940, when a reporter opined that Lomax, short and petite with impeccably coiffed hair, was "a glamour girl queen," a "lissome dark-brownskinned lass," and "one of the most fetching sights on the court in those little white outfits she wears—and which always seem spotlessly clean, no matter how tough a match she's had."[66]

Gibson, meanwhile, was not a devotee of either standardization or femininity and bristled at attempts to make her such. Thirty years later, she credited Johnson with "start[ing] me on my way to become the champion that I became," but as an adolescent, she did not immediately see the constructiveness of his teachings.[67] "I was willing to do what [Fred Johnson] said about tennis," she remembered, "but I figured what I did away from the courts was none of his business." She felt similarly about Rhoda Smith, whose efforts, well-meaning by the standards of the Black elite, the Cosmopolitan, and the ATA, amounted to "always pickin'" on her.[68]

Survival, self-reliance, and self-defense were the watchwords in Gibson's family, not mutual aid, group representation, and respectability. As for femininity, she had little interest in or use for mainstream conceptions of the proper way for women and girls to either look or behave. Above all, Gibson had not grown up thinking of any of the sports that she played as opportunities to demonstrate either femininity or racial equality. Her mantra was simple: "Win at any cost."[69] Everything else could take care of itself.

In August 1942, the ATA held its annual New York State Open at the Cosmopolitan. A year had passed since Gibson joined the club. Fred Johnson, believing that she was ready to compete, entered her. It was Gibson's first tennis tournament, and she won.[70]

The victory held personal significance to Gibson for two reasons tied to race and gender. In their sporadic coverage of ATA tournaments, White newspapers like the *New York Times* noted that the events were "Negro."[71] The New York State Open, though, was just that—open to anyone regardless of race who submitted an entry form and paid the registration fee. Nina Irwin, Gibson's opponent in the final round of the week-long event, was White and her bona fides in tennis were strong. Irwin, another of Fred Johnson's students, played doubles with her mother, Natasha, an amateur tennis player who won the New York City Parks Department Tennis Championships that year. Nina herself had won the girls' open tennis tournament at the Great Neck Country Club on Long Island in July.[72] In adulthood, Gibson would rarely ascribe racial significance to her athletic achievements. Yet, when looking back on her first win, she acknowledged the pride that she took in beating "a white girl." "I can't deny that that made the victory all the sweeter to me," she wrote in *I Always Wanted to Be Somebody*. "It proved to my own satisfaction that I was not only as good as she was, I was better."[73] Gibson knew the socially constructed racial hierarchy and felt that she had disproved it. Significantly, she also held that first win in the same light that she would see the many others that made up her career—as attained by and belonging to her and her alone, not to the entire Black race.

Intraracial dynamics of class made Gibson's win personally meaningful, too. She felt that Cosmopolitan members were cold toward her, and she suspected that many of them, trading in schadenfreude rather than hewing to racial solidarity, wanted Irwin to win. "They thought I was too cocky and they figured it would do me good to get beat," she remembered. Gibson's self-confidence showed in her reaction to the victory. "I was a little surprised about winning, but not much," she said. After years of playing sports and games, she was "accustomed to winning." Society frowned upon such self-assurance in women, who were not supposed to take pleasure in their own success, and tennis players were always to be phlegmatic. Yet for Gibson, such mettle was an essential part of her makeup. She had no intention of changing.

Gibson carried such chutzpah to her next tournament. With her expenses paid by members of the Cosmopolitan, she traveled to Lincoln University, the prestigious men's HBCU in Pennsylvania, to compete in the ATA Nationals. She reached the semifinals, and before the match she displayed a confidence more redolent of a prizefighter than of the equanimity and politesse associated with tennis players. "Who's this Nana Davis?" Gibson asked smugly as she took to the court.[74] A native of Elizabeth, New Jersey, Davis came from a family of winning tennis players, and her older sisters had won the New York State Open in 1940 and 1941. Davis, who was considerably shorter than Gibson, noticed her opponent's nerve but was neither distracted nor intimidated, even when Gibson made it clear that she was gunning for her. "Let me at her," Gibson wailed before the match.[75] Davis deemed her "a very crude creature," promptly beat her, and went on to win the tournament title. Gibson did not accept the loss graciously. She did not shake Davis's hand at the net after the match, and when she heard a young man laugh at her, Davis recalled, Gibson "headed right for the grandstand," determined to "throw him out."[76]

That Gibson brought her street background to the match showed that her life was still much closer to the culture of the blacktop than it was to that of the tennis club. She was fourteen going on fifteen and leading a double life. The year 1942 was emblematic. Althea had won her first ATA tournament and made her first trip out of town as a tennis player. She also dropped out of high school.

The decision was years in the making, beginning in junior high school. "I didn't like school and I didn't like anybody telling me what to do," Gibson said.[77] Classrooms, with their rules and walls, were confining, but she felt freedom on Harlem's streets, where she "played hooky" more and more. Sports were her favorite diversion, but she also loved going to the movies. Gibson would spend hours at the Apollo Theater watching one production after another. Friday was her favorite day to go. There was "a big stage show" and she and her best friend, Alma Irving, would settle into their seats and take it all in. Gibson would see anything that starred Bette Davis, her favorite actress. Gibson was becoming fascinated with performing. She loved jazz and bought sheet music to learn the lyrics of songs. On the rare occasions when she was at her family's apartment, she sometimes stood in front of a mirror and sang, imagining herself as the girl singer backed by a band.[78]

Gibson felt alienated in school. "It wasn't that I really cared which school I went to, or played hooky from," she said wryly. "It was just that a lot of my girl friends were going to one of the downtown high schools, and I wanted to stay with them."[79] She was enrolled at the Yorkville Trade School, while her friends were likely sent to Wadleigh, an all-girls high school on West 114th Street where the student population, while increasingly Black after the Great Migration and with the surge of new migrants during World War II, was mixed in race and class. Wadleigh had an orchestra, choirs, and theater groups, extracurricular activities that matched Gibson's interests in music and the movies.[80] In comparison, Yorkville was a perceived disappointment. Educating students in vocations rather than in the humanities or sciences was then a judgment on their potential, based in a spurious dichotomy between mental acumen and manual labor. Gibson described the decision as being made by school administrators. They were undoubtedly aware of her chronic truancy and may also have taken account of her tomboyish ways. Her parents might have approved. Daniel continued to work at the garage, and Annie had the idea that Gibson could become a seamstress; she could make dresses even if she did not want to wear them.[81]

Gibson tried to make the best of Yorkville. She went to class with some regularity during her first year. The sewing classes interested her, just as Annie hoped, and she "got to be pretty good" at making things. Gibson also found stimulus in the sewing machines themselves. Once, when her machine stopped working properly, she took it apart and did the repair. "The teacher was amazed," she remembered.[82] "I always had a desire to see what made them go. I guess it was one of my 'tomboy' tendencies to be mechanical-minded." After the first year, though, Gibson's attendance at Yorkville waned until she did not go at all.[83]

Soon Gibson left home, too. The apartment had continued to be a fraught place. Sports, including tennis, had become a refuge for her. "I didn't know nothin' about tennis, and that's all she was interested in," Daniel said years later.[84] That tennis and the Cosmopolitan were foreign to her father may have added to their appeal. That she was good at the game and was earning rewards and positive attention through it undoubtedly did. Even though she felt like an outsider at the Cosmopolitan, the club and its courts became part of Gibson's collection of hideouts, joining restaurants, movie theaters, the rooms of friends, and, when all else failed, the subway. "I would just ride the subway all night. I would ride from one end of the line to the other, from Van Cortlandt Park to New Lots Avenue, back and forth like a zombie. At least it was a place to sit down."[85]

Once Gibson stayed away from the family apartment "for a couple of nights." Daniel, enraged, was waiting when she came back. "He didn't waste any time going for the strap," she said. "When I finally sashayed in, he just walked up to me and punched me right in the face and knocked me sprawling down the hall." Gibson, resilient in her memory, did not stay down for long. She rose and punched her father in the jaw. The fight went on for some time. It is not clear whether Annie, Mildred, Daniel Jr., Ann, or Lillian saw what was going on, but the fight was serious. "We weren't fooling around, either," Gibson said.[86] It was the one fight that she never claimed to have won.

Gibson sought refuge with the Society for the Prevention of Cruelty to Children (SPCC). She had learned about the organization from a friend who had been mistreated by her own parents. Incorporated in 1875, the New York SPCC called itself the first agency in the world to seek to protect children. Gibson approached the arched entrance of the six-story SPCC building at Fifth Avenue and East 105th Street one night when she had "stayed out so late that I didn't dare go home." A woman greeted her at the door and listened as Gibson asked to be allowed to stay. "I'm scared to go home," she confessed. "My father will whip me something awful."[87] Gibson stayed for one night. Then Daniel, notified by SPCC officials, came for her the next morning, brought her home, and beat her again. Gibson returned to the shelter the next week and stayed, even after Daniel came back and tried to bring her home once more. She preferred the shelter to her family's apartment. "At home I'd had to work a lot harder, the food was nowhere near as good, and somebody was always yelling at me or, worse, hitting me."[88]

Even so, the SPCC dormitory could be a mean place, too. After getting into a fight with another ward, Gibson remembered, she was placed in solitary confinement. She spent a night in a small, barren room in the basement with only a mattress on the floor and was given a skimpy meal. The night in the cell shook Gibson. "I behaved myself after that experience; I didn't want to go back there again. It was too nice up in the dorm."[89]

Gibson eventually grew "tired" of living at the shelter, finding it "a little too restricted" in comparison to her life on the streets of the city, and chose to be returned to her parents. Going back home was a risk. She remained afraid of what her father might do to her. Indeed, the reconciliation did not last long. She started avoiding home and skipping school once more. Soon the Welfare Department got involved. Labeled a "wayward child," Gibson was given a room in the private residence of a family she left unnamed, and she was required to report weekly to the agency and get a job. She received an allowance check during periods when she was unemployed. The arrangement was to end when she turned eighteen.[90]

Gibson's move to a private family home around the age of fifteen was an important turning point in her adolescence. If she had refused, she wrote, she would have been sent away to a place the SPCC referred to benignly as "the girls' correction school" in Hudson.[91] Yet everything about the New York State Training School for Girls was caustic. Built in 1887 as the House of Refuge for Women, it changed its mission in 1904 to supervise female adolescents between the ages of twelve and sixteen. Most are thought to have been truants or runaways from difficult and impoverished family circumstances like Gibson's. Segregation was a clear and present danger at Hudson, where a racial caste system was prescribed for the incarcerated in at least its first three decades. Black girls, including jazz artist Ella Fitzgerald, who spent more than a year there, could not join the choir and were subjected to the most derelict of living conditions in the crowded, euphemistically named "cottages," where they were beaten by male staff. Black girls were made to do the harshest work, including the laundry of the other charges, while the White wards could participate in more forms of education and recreation. Segregation was officially ended at the training school in 1936, but Jim Crow ideas have a way of lingering. Had Gibson been sent to the training school at Hudson, her talent and passion for tennis might, at worst, have been lost; at best she might have emerged more troubled than when she entered.[92]

It was good that Gibson enjoyed working because she would have many jobs between 1943 and 1946. Working gave her the "feeling of being independent, like I was somebody." Gibson could buy the things that she wanted and make her own choices, something that was missing from her life at home and at school. She preferred "doing what I wanted to do instead of being what you might call dictated to. It was very important to me to be on my own." Gibson was a counter attendant at a Chock full o' Nuts restaurant on

Chambers Street and a processor in a chicken plant on Long Island, tasked with removing the innards from the birds. She was an elevator operator at the low-budget Dixie Hotel in midtown Manhattan and a packer in a button factory. She put her dexterity and curiosity to use in at least one job in a machine shop. Her favorite job was as the mail sorter and distributor for the New York School of Social Work, where, she said, she had her own office: "I liked the job because it was the first one I'd had that gave me some stature, that made me feel like I was somebody." The job gave Gibson a sense of responsibility, but she lost that position for being irresponsible. One Friday, she skipped work to join a group of friends for a Sarah Vaughan concert at the Paramount Theatre. When she came back to work on Monday, her boss fired her. She had lasted six months, a personal record.[93]

The other jobs proved fleeting because, as much as Gibson enjoyed the rewards of work, she craved playing sports even more. "I didn't keep any [job] long," she told Sam Lacy, the sports editor for the *Baltimore Afro-American*, in 1956. "I'd either quit or get fired. You can't keep work, you know, when you have your mind on playing tennis."[94] Yet, with the Cosmopolitan closed in wintertime, tennis was not her only sport.

Gibson was one of the thousands of young women across the country who were taken by the sensation of indoor basketball. In the 1930s, the Northeast and the Mid-Atlantic were hotbeds for the game in African American communities. Named for its newspaper sponsor, the Philadelphia Tribunes was among the best teams in the country, winning eleven straight National Colored Basketball championships between 1932 and 1942 under the leadership of Ora Washington, who was also a leading player in the ATA. Gibson was in the throes of establishing herself as a dominant two-sport athlete. She was a member of the Mysterious Girls A.C. (Athletic Club), Harlem's famed basketball team, between 1943 and 1945. Her entry into the state ward system may have brought her to the attention of the team's founder, coach, and manager. Marsden "Scoop" Burnell worked for the Harlem Welfare Association. Burnell started the team in 1939 with members of the Harlem YWCA and quickly made it into a squad revered for its rotation of talented players. The Mysterious Girls were soon regarded as the best women's basketball team in the New York area and on the East Coast, earning the title of world champions after multiple seasons of dominant runs. The team reportedly won two hundred games and lost only seven between the 1939–1940 and 1942–1943 seasons. The *Amsterdam News* actively followed the Mysterious Girls, which played industrial teams—Black and White—and was no less successful during the years when Gibson belonged.[95]

Gibson earned acclaim through basketball. Some of her first media notices appeared in the *Amsterdam News* and were about her play on the hardwood, not the tennis court, though reporters often misspelled her name—first and last. She was among the highest scorers on the team, making her one of its two "fleet forwards," according to reporter Dan Burley. Her contributions guided the Mysterious Girls to at least seventeen straight wins in the 1943–1944 season and the title of "World Girls Basketball champions." The squad had an unbroken string of at least twenty-seven wins in 1944–1945.[96] One observer called Gibson the "fastest player on the team" and a "speedy shot under the basket" who was good for "ten to 12 points a game." The Mysterious Girls were lauded for their "machine"-like "teamwork" and for playing "aggressively" and "defensively."[97] Gibson was briefly the face of their brilliance. In October 1943, she appeared beside Burnell in an advertisement for Bond bread. It may have been the first time her photograph appeared in the press. The caption described Burnell as "coach of the famous Harlem Mysterious Five, championship girl basketball team," and quoted him praising the bread as "just right for my young athletes." Gibson, the only team member in the ad, wore her basketball uniform, a dark T-shirt and belted bottoms, and smiled at Burnell as he pointed approvingly to the packaged loaf. The suggestion that Gibson strengthened herself on bread fortified with protein was ironic, since her diet at the time consisted of street food.[98]

Gibson did not hold back on the basketball court. The Mysterious Girls played boys' and men's teams, too. Joe Bostic, a sportswriter for the *Amsterdam News*, met Gibson when she was a young basketball player. Burnell had invited Bostic and other men to work out against the team in the gymnasium at Harlem's Mother African Methodist Episcopal Zion Church on West 137th Street. Gibson left an indelible impression on Bostic. Her "winning attitude" and "competitive" spirit shone then, he said. "That quintet, led by the Gibson girl, ran us 'til we were ragged." The Mysterious Girls held a twelve-point advantage after a half hour, when the men decided to end the game. Gibson, Bostic concluded, was "a wow of an athlete" and "a terror in skirts," a description that conveyed the supposed monstrosity of athletic excellence by women and girls.[99]

Basketball was on the borders of respectability in the 1940s. White physical educators had spent the previous two decades opposing basketball as too exhausting and rough for women and criticized male coaches and the businesses that backed teams and leagues as poor influences on players' character, leading to a reduction in the number of girls' teams at predominantly White institutions. African American physical educators and social leaders, always mindful of the image of the women of their own race, paid attention and in many instances followed suit. Several HBCUs in the 1940s revised their tolerance for basketball for female students on the basis that it perpetuated stereotypes of Black women and girls as unrefined. Gibson, the Mysterious Girls, and women's industrial teams were outside the control of school administrators. Even so, playing basketball vigorously and not by "girls' rules" marked them as bucking the status quo. The experience was not entirely radical. There were White teams that refused to play the all-Black Mysterious Girls.[100]

The Mysterious Girls A.C. gave Gibson a group of Black female friends who, in their passion for and success in sports, provided her with a queer community that she did not have at the Cosmopolitan. Some of the girls she met through the club became her "boon coons," a racially dubious term that she picked up in Harlem that meant "block buddies, good friends."[101] Bea Jenkins captained the softball team, which Gibson also played on, was a guard on the basketball team, and was one of Gibson's partners on the bowling team. When Gibson was "around 16," Bea beat her at paddle tennis, a defeat that Gibson claimed was the only one she ever had in the game.[102] Alma Irving, Gibson's best friend, was a fellow forward on the basketball team. They spent hours shooting baskets on courts in public parks during the day. At night, they went to the gym at P.S. 136 for more, "challen[ging] anybody, boy or girl, man or woman" to play against them in half-court games. Gibson and Alma "played hard" and, after their games, went out for meals at "a cheap restaurant," savoring their hours away from home.[103] Gibson and Gloria Nightingale, a forward and captain of the Mysterious Girls who was also a local track star, bowled together after basketball games, too. Gibson earned attention in the local press as "a graceful, cool bowler," if an inconsistent one.[104]

Gloria and the late-night visits to bowling alleys brought Gibson to the attention of Sugar Ray Robinson, widely regarded as the greatest welterweight boxer in history. Gloria knew Robinson's wife, the singer, dancer, and model Edna Mae Robinson. Gibson and Gloria spotted him one night at a bowling alley in the Bronx. Gibson admired Robinson for his boxing skills, but she did not melt into a puddle of fandom at the sight of him. Instead, she threw down the gauntlet. "So you're Sugar Ray Robinson?" she bellowed. "Well, I can beat you bowling right now!"[105] Robinson may have been impressed by Gibson's brashness, as she later said, but he was worried about her. Robinson was a champion athlete and a successful businessman. He was also a southern migrant from a poor background, a night owl, and a man with a soft spot for kids, hosting hundreds of them for picnics and the opportunity to watch him work out at his training camp at Greenwood Lake, New York, and donating money to PAL. Gibson "really endeared herself to him and he became concerned about her being in the bowling alley at any hour that he'd show up," Edna Mae explained years later. Robinson was particularly concerned that Gibson was not in school.[106]

The Robinsons looked after Gibson. She sometimes slept at their apartment on St. Nicholas Avenue in Harlem or at their home in Riverdale, New York. She accompanied them to Greenwood Lake and appointed herself Edna Mae's "Girl Friday" when he entered the army in 1943. Gibson was enamored with the way that the couple lived, surrounded by "nice things" and equipped with "fancy cars," which Robinson allowed her to drive even though she did not have a driver's license. Robinson even paid $125 for a used tenor saxophone that Gibson coveted in a pawn shop. Gibson described the instrument as a gift given in kindness and as encouragement that she take her interest in music seriously. Buddy Walker gave her lessons. Edna Mae, though, remembered the saxophone as a soft bribe by Robinson and as an example of cunning by Gibson, who had admitted to Ray that she had trouble in school. Ray "worried her so much about continuing her education that [Gibson] told him she'd be willing to go back if he bought her a saxophone."[107]

Edna Mae's beauty, background, and interests coaxed Gibson to compare herself to other girls and to think about how she measured up against ideals of womanhood. Edna Mae, twelve years older than Gibson , had been born to a prominent family in Miami. Her father was an Episcopal minister. She spurned her family's ambitions that she become a teacher or a social worker, professions deemed worthwhile and respectable for well-heeled and educated Black women, and left Hunter College to pursue a career as a dancer. She toured with Duke Ellington's and Cab Calloway's bands and became a star attraction at Harlem's Cotton Club, where she danced on an oversized drum before Whites, the only patrons allowed. Gibson continued to sing and dance after her marriage to Robinson in 1938 and modeled, too. Gibson let her guard down with Edna Mae to reveal her dissatisfaction with her own life, including her appearance. "She was unhappy," Edna Mae recalled. Gibson "had a gaunt build and she felt that she was the least good-looking girl she knew. She had insecurity and went into herself. She used to talk wild." Edna Mae tried to lift her spirits by telling her that she could "be somebody."[108] Gibson looked to sports, not powder and paint, to do it.

Gibson continued to excel at tennis, and her vigorous style of play further distinguished her from the girls that she knew through the Mysterious Girls and in the ATA. She successfully defended her title in the New York

State Open in August 1943. The ATA Nationals were not played that year due to the war, so she had to wait two years to have a second chance at the girls' national title. In August 1944, she beat her rival Nana Davis decisively in the final round, 6–1, 6–3, and rose to the number one ranking among the association's girls nationwide. She was the only girl in the Mysterious Girls A.C. to hold a national tennis title.[109] Gibson's resolute type of play brought her the wins as well as a reputation in the Black press. She did not play "patty-cake" tennis, a term dropped by critics to decry the game as lacking action compared to other sports and, in particular, to ridicule men as supposedly playing in the style of women.[110] Gibson played with zest. Sam Lacy, the sports editor for the *Baltimore Afro-American*, traveled to the Cosmopolitan, the host site of the 1944 Nationals, and was impressed by her game. Lacy called her "hard-driving Althea Gibson" who "outplayed" Davis with "superior baseline play."[111] Gibson enjoyed the best of two worlds: she played tennis, which was socially acceptable for women and girls, and succeeded by competing in the powerful way that was considered the hallmark of the men's game.

Gibson would later write that she adjusted her behavior at the Cosmopolitan to meet the social expectations of tennis, but that did not mean that she altered her style of play to suit gender norms. "The polite manners of the game, that seemed so silly to me at first, gradually began to appeal to me. So did the pretty white clothes," she wrote. Yet Gibson adapted to tennis culture by blending her street sports background with her new genteel setting. "I began to understand that you could walk out on the court like a lady, all dressed up in immaculate white, [and] be polite to everybody, and still play like a tiger and beat the liver and lights out of the ball." Gibson also imagined herself as akin to a certain kind of male athlete. "I remember thinking to myself that [taking to the tennis court and playing] was kind of like a matador going into the bull ring, beautifully dressed, bowing in all directions, following the fancy rules to the letter, and all the time having nothing in mind except sticking that sword into the bull's guts and killing him as dead as hell."[112] Inspired by the movies, that idea conveyed Gibson's hybrid approach to gender as she expansively combined the rigid customs of tennis with her unique imagination, strong shots, and intense desire to win.

Alice Marble bestowed Gibson with a vision of a woman playing the bold brand of tennis that she preferred and admired. Marble had become the greatest female tennis player in the world by breaking with gender norms. Sportswriters during and after Marble's career noted that she took "a man's approach to the game," from her "American twist serve to the leaping volleys and jump overheads" as well as her "fierce competitive spirit and coolness under pressure."[113] Standing 5'7", she wore shorts during her matches to increase her mobility, allowing her to run freely to the net. Marble won the singles title at the United States National Lawn Tennis Championships at Forest Hills four times between 1936 and 1940 and captured Wimbledon in 1939. She spent the war years playing exhibition tennis matches with Mary Hardwick, the leading player among British women. Marble and Hardwick played before military personnel and civilian audiences to boost morale and grow the game of tennis. On August 19, 1944, the pair played three exhibition matches—singles versus each other and doubles and mixed doubles while partnered with Black players—during the ATA Nationals at the Cosmopolitan.[114]

Marble's play mesmerized Gibson. Marble's "effectiveness of strike, and the power that she had, impressed me terrifically," Gibson wrote. "It was the aggressiveness behind her game that I liked. Watching her smack that effortless serve, and then follow it into the net and put the ball away with an overhead as good as any man's, I saw possibilities in the game of tennis that I had never seen before." Impressionable at nearly seventeen, Gibson decided that she wanted to play just like Marble, who, in the space of an afternoon, had become "the only woman tennis player I'd ever seen that I felt exactly that way about." Gibson, in three years of playing tennis, had "always had eyes for the good men players."[115] Marble's performances at the Cosmopolitan were a revelation for her.

Gibson moved on from the exhibition matches, but she could not shake what she saw. She successfully defended her ATA national girls' title in August 1945. It was her last tournament as a junior. Sometime after Marble and Hardwick's visit to the Cosmopolitan, Gibson went to Forest Hills as a spectator for the first time. If the Cosmopolitan was another world for her, the West Side Tennis Club was a whole other galaxy. The annual host site of the U.S. Nationals, the club had courts made of lush green grass, cloth awnings of pink and white, and a cottage-style clubhouse. One color, however, was noticeably absent from the club grounds. Like the people whose names were listed on the membership roster, none of the players in the tournament bracket were Black. Gibson was undaunted. From her seat in a grandstand high above a freshly mown court at one of the most revered and exclusive—and Whitest—shrines in all of sports, she made a promise to herself: "One of these days, I'm going to be down there."[116]

3

The Making of a Strong Black (Woman) Contender in the South

I believe you are the key to unlock the door.

—DR. ROBERT W. JOHNSON, 1946

AFTER TURNING EIGHTEEN in August 1945, Gibson was no longer a ward of New York City. She missed the allowance check but little else. "I was able to run my own life at last," she remembered. The transition from ward to adulthood was one of Gibson's earliest realizations that money was no guarantor of freedom. She rented a room in the apartment where Gloria Nightingale, a friend from the Mysterious Girls, lived with her grandmother and took a job as a waitress, possibly at a Chock full o' Nuts restaurant.[1]

Gibson was not living according to the norms of adolescence. "When other girls were putting on lipstick," Mildred said wryly in 1957, "she was playing stickball."[2] Gibson and Gloria were passing some of their days and many of their nights enjoying the amusements of New York. Gibson was not dating boys in preparation for marriage and starting a family. Nor was she going to school to lay the groundwork for college and a career, symbols of productivity. She instead devoted her time to supporting and satisfying herself, especially through sports, and Gloria was her sidekick. "Gloria was like me," Gibson wrote. "All she cared about was playing games and having a good time." Together, the two played basketball and bowled late at night and did not arrive at home "until three or four in the morning." Even after becoming famous and winning the most coveted titles in tennis, Gibson looked back wistfully and without shame on her untraditional adolescence with Gloria and their friends Bea Jenkins and Alma Irving. "I still consider those years as the liveliest of my whole life," she wrote. "We were really living. No responsibilities, no worries, just balling all the time."[3]

Gibson remained a queer presence at the Cosmopolitan and in the ATA as she brought her dominant style of playing tennis from the junior division into her first bids for titles in women's tennis. She donned pants and shorts and wore her hair combed "straight back."[4] Reporters assessed her unorthodox appearance as "colorful" and her tenacious game as making her "the fighting young threat from New York."[5] In July 1946, Gibson defeated Lillian Van Buren to win the Eastern Sectional Tennis Championships in Scotch Plains, New Jersey, at Shady Rest Country Club, the premier resort for African Americans. It was a stunning victory and "the biggest upset" of the tournament, wrote the *Baltimore Afro-American*.[6] Van Buren, who had teamed with Mary Hardwick in the mixed-race women's doubles portion of the exhibition series at the Cosmopolitan in 1944, was the second-ranked woman in the ATA. Van Buren, the Cleveland *Call and Post* said, was "unable to match [Gibson's] steady play."[7] Gibson followed her victory by winning the New York State Open weeks later, beating Nana Davis in the final round.[8]

Gibson traveled next to Wilberforce University, in Ohio, for the ATA Nationals, where she played in the title match for the women's championship on August 24. She split the first two sets of the final match, 6–4, 7–9, with Roumania Peters, a thirty-two-year-old physical education teacher from Tuskegee Institute who had won the title in 1944. With her sister Margaret, Peters belonged to one of the most dominant doubles teams in ATA history, having won the doubles title seven times since 1938.[9] Gibson was on her way to winning the third set, the match, and the tournament when Peters made what one reporter called "a come-back" but what Gibson came to recognize as a deployment of gamesmanship.[10] Peters "began dropping around the court as though she was half dead," Gibson remembered. "She looked for all the world as though she was so exhausted she couldn't stand up." Admittedly "overconfident" that she would beat the seemingly sick Peters handily, Gibson eased up.[11] It was a mistake. Peters came charging back with quick volleys and hard drives that sent Gibson crisscrossing the court. Peters won the set 6–3 and the match.[12] Frank A. "Fay" Young, the lead sportswriter for the *Chicago Defender*, understood what had happened: "Miss Peters was content to take advantage of her wide tournament experience and allow the spunky easterner to defeat herself."[13]

The outcome of the match hurt Gibson, as all her tournament losses did throughout her life. She was disappointed in herself for, she thought, giving the match away: "I probably wouldn't have minded [the defeat] much at all if I hadn't felt so strongly that I had let Roumania 'psych' me out of the match."[14] Gibson learned never to let up until the chair umpire called "game, set, match," but the lesson came at the cost of the most prestigious prize that she could win in Black tennis.

The reaction of some of the spectators added extra sting for Gibson, reinforcing her perception that she was merely tolerated as a means to a desired end for some ATA people. The loss at Wilberforce gave her a primer in fair-weather friendship—or sponsorship, as it were. Gibson had concluded that she was being "groomed to win" the ATA national women's singles championship; her honorary membership at the Cosmopolitan was part of the deal.[15] The dramatic loss at Wilberforce suddenly cast the investment, and tolerance for her eccentricities, in doubt, and some folks did not hesitate to tell her as much. "Some of the A.T.A. people who had come out from New York were pretty disappointed in me," she remembered. She suspected that the critics who approached her with unkind words "thought they hadn't got their money's worth out of me because I had lost."[16] Instead of offering reassurance, "the people I had expected sympathy or a kind word from told me they thought I should have won."[17] Years later, the biting words of someone she chose not to name came back to her. "One of them [said] something to the effect that they were through with me, that they didn't think much of my attitude."[18] The comments gave bitter and ironic credence to Gibson's belief, fomented after her first tournament victory, that "not many people . . . find fault with a winner."[19] Gibson had lost, and the fault-finding was intense. She sat alone in the grandstand, "a pretty dejected kid" in what felt like "life's darkest moment."[20]

———

Dr. Hubert A. Eaton Sr. and Dr. Robert Walter Johnson had watched the match from their seats in the grandstand. Gibson "should have won the title easily," Dr. Johnson conceded.[21] Nevertheless, neither man was put off by her loss. Dr. Eaton thought that Gibson "moved well on the court, with good concentration," while Dr. Johnson observed that she "had agility, power, everything. Everything, that is, but consistency and accuracy."[22] They saw that Gibson had been plainly bewildered by her opponent's game of possum during the match and that she was dispirited by the naysayers afterward. "Her New York sponsors gave her the devil. They said they were through with her," Dr. Johnson remembered.[23] "I wish we could do something to help that girl," he said.[24] Dr. Eaton agreed. Both doctors had more than Gibson on their minds.

The color of the American professional sports landscape was becoming a little less monochrome. Before World War II, Black journalists had connected the playing fields of sports and the battlefields of combat. "Colored Americans will be conscripted for duty in our Army. If war comes there can be no doubt of his loyalty and courage. But," wrote noted Black illustrator Ollie Harrington in the *New York Amsterdam News* in August 1940, "in professional athletics the same men who are expected to defend democracy are barred because of color."[25] Six years later, the battle cry of the Black press that World War II should yield a "Double Victory"—one over fascism abroad and another over Jim Crow at home—appeared to be taking root in the highest rungs of American sports.[26] The Los Angeles Rams had signed Kenny Washington and Woody Strode to contracts in the spring of 1946. On August 23, the day before Gibson's match with Roumania Peters, Washington and Strode had played in their first game, an exhibition at Soldier Field, in Chicago, making them the first Black men to compete on a National Football League (NFL) team in twelve years. Jackie Robinson, Washington and Strode's teammate on the football team at the University of California, Los Angeles, had spent the season playing baseball for the Montreal Royals. Robinson's success as the first Black man in organized baseball since the nineteenth century raised the hopes of some and the fears of others that he would be promoted from the triple-A farm team to its owner, the Brooklyn Dodgers of the major leagues.[27]

Dr. Eaton and Dr. Johnson saw in Gibson the opportunity to join their love for tennis with their devotion to racial uplift. "Knowing that the Jim Crow signs on the tennis courts of the world had to come down sooner or later and that a strong black contender should be waiting in the wings," Dr. Eaton wrote in his autobiography, "Dr. Johnson and I began to plan Gibson's future."[28] Unaware that Gibson had dropped out of junior high school, they started from the proposition that she could earn a college scholarship, most likely at Tuskegee, and that they could coach and sponsor her. Spotting Gibson seated alone in the grandstand, they approached her and pitched their plan as an opportunity for her to "make something of herself," eventually get a college education, and "be a tennis champion" if she put in the effort.[29] Their accounts differ, though, on when Gibson learned that the doctors operated with thoughts of preparing her for the possibility of competing at Forest Hills. In 1951, *American Lawn Tennis* published an open letter that purported to have been penned by Gibson but was most likely composed by the doctors. The letter says that Dr. Johnson asked her, "How would you like to play at Forest Hills?" and told her that he believed that she was "the key to unlock the door" that kept Blacks out of the national championship.[30] It made for a nice story, but it may not have been accurate. Dr. Eaton did not describe in interviews he gave in 1957 or in his autobiography that either he or Dr. Johnson expressly mentioned Forest Hills in that first meeting at Wilberforce. Dr. Johnson, however, told Ted Poston of the *New York Post* that he "asked [Gibson] if she would like to really work hard at tennis and someday compete at Forest Hills."[31] Gibson herself said in her autobiography that, while she "often wondered if, even then, at that early stage of the game, they were thinking in terms of me someday playing at Forest Hills or Wimbledon," neither man broached the subject of integration then. Gibson knew nothing about the possibility, she wrote, until three years later.[32]

This much is clear: though Gibson claimed to have enjoyed her life on the streets, by 1946 she wanted something different. She was skeptical of the generous offer at first, especially after the way her New York patrons had treated her that afternoon. Nevertheless, she was interested. Gibson told Dr. Eaton and Dr. Johnson that she was "just drifting" in New York.[33] Yet she was also reluctant to leave. Still, getting Gibson to practice and play tennis was not a hard sell and the idea of going to college especially appealed to her. Upon hearing the name Tuskegee, her mood brightened, but she admitted that there was a hitch: "That would be great, except I never even been to high school."[34] It was pure Gibson.

The doctors approached Gibson later that afternoon with an amended plan. They decided that she could divide her time between their respective homes. Dr. Eaton would host Gibson during the school year in Wilmington, North Carolina, where she would live with his family and enroll in high school. Dr. Johnson's house in Lynchburg, Virginia, would be her base during summers, when she would train with him and, together, they would travel to ATA tournaments across the country. The heads of thriving medical practices in their communities, Dr. Johnson and Dr. Eaton agreed to pay Gibson's personal and tennis expenses for the length of the arrangement and give her intensive lessons and virtually unlimited opportunities to play on the tennis court that each man had in his backyard. With their sponsorship, Gibson would have the resources of time and money to develop her tennis game as few other African Americans had ever had. Tentatively, Gibson said yes.[35]

Gibson remained unsure until the Robinsons pointed her toward her future. When she returned to New York, she went to see Sugar Ray. He had long thought that Gibson needed to be in school. "You'll never amount to anything just bangin' around from one job to another like you been doin'," he told her. "No matter what you want to do, tennis or music or what, you'll be better at it if you get some education."[36] Edna Mae agreed, and Gibson made up her mind to move to Wilmington.

But first she had to go to 143rd Street one last time. Gibson had turned nineteen on August 25, the day after the ATA Nationals. Even so, Dr. Eaton told her to get her mother's permission before she moved into his house in early September. Gibson complied, though what she told Annie is unknown; she did not record what happened during this, their last meeting for at least two and a half years. Daniel seems not to have entered Gibson's thoughts or the decision process. Annie wrote and mailed a brief missive to Dr. Eaton: "God bless you for your help with my child."[37]

The integration of elite amateur tennis was not unlike Annie's letter—a project based in faith. Dr. Eaton and Dr. Johnson had to believe that Gibson could adjust to living a regulated life with them in the South and that her game and her resolve could hold up under the scrutiny, change, and pressure that were to come. Gibson had to trust that Dr. Eaton and Dr. Johnson would do right by her. And all three had to hope that the USLTA and the White men and women who controlled tennis would cooperate—or could be made to cooperate—and allow Gibson to enter matches and, eventually, Forest Hills.

Gibson found two cardboard suitcases and prepared for her next migration.

———

Dr. Eaton, Dr. Johnson, and Gibson, whether she knew it or not, had united to challenge the racial restrictions that surrounded elite amateur tennis. They were also embarking on a multifaceted battle with gender. The idea that sports integration was a project exclusively for Black men was as entrenched as the notion that sport itself was a male domain, and it existed in the ATA, too.

Gibson's selection for the integrationist project was proof of her potential: the ATA had a record of prioritizing men and boys in its integration efforts. In 1930, association leaders stood behind Gerald L. Norman and Reginald Weir when the USLTA denied them the opportunity to compete in the National Junior Indoor Tennis Tournament. Both Norman and Weir regularly competed with and against White boys; Norman, son of an ATA founder who was also executive secretary, was the captain of the Flushing High School tennis team. Weir, the association's national junior champion of 1928, was a member of the tennis team at City College and was later selected as its captain. When the Cosmopolitan hosted elite White players for exhibition matches, men were guaranteed opportunities to play. Donald Budge, who in 1938 became the first player to win the Grand Slam (national singles championships in Australia, France, Wimbledon, and the United States) in a single season, came to the club as a professional in 1940. He defeated Jimmie

McDaniel, the reigning ATA men's national champion, and then teamed with McDaniel in a doubles match against two other ATA men, Weir and Richard Cohen. USLTA amateurs Bill Talbert and Francisco "Pancho" Segura, a native of Ecuador, visited in 1945 and played singles and doubles, too. None of these three elite players, though, played mixed doubles with ATA women.[38]

Alice Marble's and Mary Hardwick's involvement with the ATA in 1944, when they teamed with Frances Gittens and Lillian Van Buren, respectively, in doubles led to opportunities for its women to participate in integrated exhibition matches. In 1946, Lula Ballard, the 1936 ATA national women's singles champion, and McDaniel defeated Hardwick and her husband, Charles Hare, a former Davis Cup player for England, in a mixed doubles exhibition at Wilberforce during the Nationals. That same week, Hardwick and Flora Lomax, a past ATA national champion, met in a singles match. Lomax lost soundly, 6–1. It was a one-set exhibition. Lomax had been given only half the chance that McDaniel had received six years earlier against Budge.[39]

The *New York Herald Tribune*'s Al Laney once observed a gendered division at the Cosmopolitan. The ATA looked upon Laney as friendly to their cause and invited him to the club in 1941 to evaluate its strengths and weaknesses for the purpose of making their players more competitive. Laney pulled no punches. "Be particularly concerned over the fact that the game has not made the same progress among Negro girls and women that it has among the men," he told the ATA. Laney conjectured that the "reason" for the chasm boiled down to the possibility that "no one has bothered much about the girls until one of them began to get good." He recommended a solution. "Let the younger girls be encouraged to play more and let the best men players in the clubs give some time to them. It will pay dividends."[40] Five years later, Gibson had become too good for anyone to ignore, in part because she patterned her game on the methods used by the men of the ATA.

Interracial matches, whether between men or women, happened on ATA turf because the USLTA was the holdout on integration. "The U.S.L.T.A. has never paid much attention to the Negro tennis association, although it maintains an officially friendly attitude," Laney wrote in 1944.[41] The USLTA perpetuated the logic of white supremacy, which held that for a White athlete to compete with or against a Black athlete was to sully the value and dignity of the White game and the White athlete. Fear buttressed sports segregation, too. A victory by a Black player or team undermined white supremacist claims of black inferiority. The sturm und drang that preceded Jack Johnson's bout against Jim Jeffries for the world heavyweight boxing title in 1910 and the race riots and bitter editorials that followed Johnson's decisive victory had made those fears plain for all to see.[42] In comparison, tennis had a reputation as a genteel sport, but its governing body had taken a hard line for decades against its players trading shots with African Americans.

Budge's, Marble's, and Hardwick's interactive visits to the Cosmopolitan validated Laney's assertion that professionals, free of the restrictions imposed by the USLTA, were not "squeamish" about playing with or against African Americans and had even "done a lot to help the Negroes' game by playing with them and showing them what the best game is like."[43] Yet Budge, Marble, and Hardwick are not known to have either voiced or acted in opposition to segregation in tennis during their amateur careers. "Politically comatose and socially hyperactive" is the way historian Larry Engelmann describes the generation of amateurs who played tennis before World War II. "Not a single white player" in the USLTA "raised a voice of dissent or protest. They accepted the segregation as normal and required and even as good."[44]

Integration had to be a two-way street to succeed, but halfway through 1946, the USLTA remained stalled.

———

Gibson was changing before she had even arrived in Wilmington. Eager to make a good impression on the Eatons, she wore a skirt, albeit "a tired old" one that she had chosen "because I figured it wouldn't matter if it got beat up on the train ride."[45] Anxiety and vulnerability replaced the braggadocio and self-confidence that she had clung to in New York. Between naps and snacks, questions entered Gibson's mind. "Would the movie houses refuse to let me in because I was colored?" she wondered. "Would I have to get off the sidewalk if a white person came along?" Thoughts of race, segregation, and violence had plagued her since she first talked with Dr. Eaton and Dr. Johnson about their plan. To her, the South was "this strange country where, according to what I'd heard, terrible things were done to Negroes just because they were Negroes, and nobody was ever punished for them."[46]

Recent history bore out Gibson's fears. Outside Monroe, Georgia, on July 25, a White mob pulled two married Black couples from a car and dragged them to the Moore's Ford Bridge before beating and shooting them to death. Tens of people, possibly more, were believed to have known the identities of the killers, but no one—not even African Americans, fearful of reprisals—would come forward. No one was prosecuted for the crime, either. The *New York Amsterdam News* covered the mass lynching on its front page. Rallies were held in Harlem, including at Mother AME Zion Church on 137th Street and Seventh Avenue, where Gibson played basketball in the basement gymnasium.[47]

Gibson's mind shifted from gratitude to uncertainty and back again. "I thought about how lucky I was to be asked to live in a good home with people like the Eatons." She also worried about losing this new, good thing that had suddenly come her way. "I hoped I would do everything right, so they wouldn't be sorry they had started the whole thing. I made up my mind that I would adjust myself to whatever came along."[48] Gibson had two dreams in life: freedom and tennis. On the train, she decided to relinquish one in exchange for the other and hoped that someday she could have both.

Gibson's anxiety abated when she reached Wilmington and saw the way the Eaton family lived. A "big car" and a uniformed chauffeur awaited her at the station. Gibson relaxed as she sank into the plush backseat. "Ain't this a blip," she thought. Marveling at the doctor's "nice things," she "felt pretty good" and imagined that the experience that awaited her "shouldn't be too hard to take."[49] The chauffeur drove her to 1406 Orange Street, the two-story bungalow where Dr. Eaton and his wife, Celeste, lived with their son, Hubert Jr., three, and daughter, Faustine, known in the family as Tina, nearly seven months old.[50] In the kitchen, Mrs. Eaton, twenty-six, greeted Gibson with a hug and a kiss—"as though I were her favorite niece"—introduced her to the children and their beloved caregiver, and invited her to make herself at home by making lunch for herself and unpacking her things in her room upstairs.[51] Standing before her new foster mother, Gibson was self-conscious that she "looked every bit as uncomfortable as I felt" in her skirt and top, rumpled from the hours on the train. Mrs. Eaton's gestures, though, put her at ease. Making her way through the house, Gibson marveled at its orderliness and was awed by each room, which came together to form "a home of luxury."[52] "It was a far cry from what I'd been used to," she said later. "Everything was as clean and as fresh as it could be."[53]

Mrs. Eaton embodied her class of New Negro women and was a model of the brand of Black womanhood that integration-minded African Americans advocated. She was attractive, with clear, light bronze skin and straight hair. *Jet* magazine, which covered the couple's extensive social life in the 1950s, called her "the North Carolina beauty" who could "pass any studio's screen test."[54] Well educated, she had attended Palmer Memorial Institute, a private day and boarding school for Black girls and boys, in Sedalia, North Carolina, that prioritized college preparation.[55] At Talladega College, in Alabama, Mrs. Eaton pledged Alpha Kappa Alpha (AKA), joining the oldest Black sorority in the country and formally entering the ranks of African American women

who were committed to racial uplift through civic engagement and respectability. After marrying in December 1938 and graduating from Talladega in the
spring, she joined her husband in Ann Arbor, Michigan. He studied for his
medical degree at the university and she pursued a master's degree in physical
education. In Wilmington, she founded its chapters of The Links, Inc., a community service organization for Black women, and Jack and Jill, which gave
Black children further education and chances to socialize.[56]

Mrs. Eaton was the quintessential wifely helpmate to her husband, who
praised her for supporting "my efforts to bring about social change."[57] However,
he made a self-admitted "serious blunder" by forgetting at Wilberforce the
wisdom of discussing Gibson's move into their house as a foster child and
his plan to coach and mentor her with Dr. Johnson.[58] Once it was clear that
Gibson intended to come, Dr. Eaton explained, apologized, and gave his wife
the final word on Gibson's future. Mrs. Eaton acceded to the plan on two
conditions: Gibson was to comport herself as if she were a "member of our
family," and she would not be the source of "any trouble." The Eatons agreed
that if Gibson did not comply, they would send her back to New York.[59]

———

Trouble was the last thing that any Black man, woman, or child wanted anywhere in America in 1946, let alone in Wilmington. In that coastal city in
November 1898, white supremacists, feeling aggrieved by the presence of
African Americans in positions of authority in local as well as state government and law enforcement, carried out a riot that they had been planning
for up to a year. Sixty African Americans were killed. In the aftermath, nearly
120,000 African Americans were purged from Wilmington's voter registration rolls. Black people, the majority population before the riot, fled "Port
City" in droves. Within two years, Wilmington was majority white. Dr. Eaton
observed that the toll of the riot was still being felt a half century later. The violence had "frightened the colored community into pitiful docility," he wrote,
while White residents accepted segregation and encouraged subjugation.[60]

As a newcomer, Dr. Eaton was uniquely positioned to judge race relations in Wilmington. His wife's father, Dr. Foster Flavorial Burnett, had
practiced medicine there for decades and co-founded a Black medical facility,
Community Hospital, and its nursing school in 1920, the year after she was
born. Dr. Eaton, whose father was also a doctor, moved to Wilmington after
graduating from the medical school at Michigan in 1942 and completing his
residency the following year in Winston-Salem, where his family had lived
since 1928. When Dr. Eaton arrived in the summer of 1943 to join his aging

father-in-law's practice, he was twenty-six years old and brought the total number of Black doctors in Wilmington to six, available to serve the city's more than thirteen thousand African American residents. None of the Black doctors had medical privileges at James Walker Memorial Hospital, the public facility that had neither Black nurses nor doctors and that maintained only twenty-five beds for Black patients in a ward that was unattached to the main building. "There were no black policemen, firemen, city councilmen, county commissioners, or board of education members," he recalled.[61] Wilmington's schools, movie theaters, restaurants, recreational spaces, and libraries were segregated, too. Later, Dr. Eaton discovered that the local courthouse kept two different Bibles, one labeled "Colored," the other "White," for administering oaths. When the Eatons bought their house on Orange Street in 1945, they did so "through a dummy intermediary owner" rather than directly from the real estate agent because White families who lived nearby would have opposed the sale of the home to African Americans.[62]

The Eaton family's tennis court was among the few integrated spaces in Wilmington. A champion tennis player in his own right, Eaton had won the North Carolina State Inter-Scholastic Tennis Tournament in 1932. Impressed by Hubert's abilities, Dr. Charles W. Furlong invited the young man to spend the summer at his home in Smithfield, North Carolina, to receive coaching. He accepted and won the ATA boys' junior singles title in 1933. The victory earned Eaton a tennis scholarship to Johnson C. Smith University, the men's HBCU in Charlotte, where he pledged Omega Psi Phi and was steeped in a rhetoric of service and uplift as principles of Black masculinity.[63] Dr. Eaton's observations of the senselessness of Jim Crow while growing up in North Carolina and his experiences with integration at the University of Michigan affirmed his belief that segregation was wrong. He saw to it that the tennis court, built in the backyard shortly after he and his wife moved into the house, "was color-integrated from the start."[64] Soon after the court was in place, Dr. Eaton hosted Fred Perry, the first man to win the career Grand Slam in tennis, for an afternoon of exhibition matches and invited the public to watch—regardless of race. The event was part of Dr. Eaton's vision that his tennis court would be a progressive space in Wilmington.[65]

Gibson was part of that vision. Their arrangement was akin to Dr. Furlong's mentorship and coaching years earlier. Gibson and Dr. Eaton played and practiced together on the tennis court nearly every afternoon until winter came. He tried to build upon the work that she had done on her fundamentals and strategy with Fred Johnson at the Cosmopolitan and sought to enhance her powers of "concentration," which had impressed him at Wilberforce.[66]

Gibson met the many Black tennis players who came to the Eatons' home because it was the only place in town where they could play. She also met White players who played cordially with and against the African Americans and bemoaned the segregation in Wilmington. Gibson "agreed" with their complaints. The mixed-race membership of the Cosmopolitan, Marble and Hardwick's exhibition matches, her own victory over Nina Irwin in the New York State Open, and the basketball games in which the Mysterious Girls had faced off against White teams had shown her the peaceful and indeed edifying possibilities of interracial competition. Still, she remained silent on the matter in Wilmington. "I kept my mouth shut about it because I knew it would only embarrass Dr. Eaton if I started popping off in his home town."[67]

Gibson was learning that being measured and methodical was the Eatons' way of carrying themselves, and she modeled herself accordingly. This was not her natural tendency. Rather than being phlegmatic in either victory or defeat or after she mastered techniques during lessons, Gibson allowed the results of her practice and playing sessions to govern her mood and interactions with the family. "On the days she won she was all smiles; on the days she lost her face went blank and she seemed depressed, saying little all afternoon and barely managing 'good night' when she went upstairs to bed," Dr. Eaton wrote.[68] Gibson's actions may have stemmed from self-induced pressure to win. She wanted to show Dr. Eaton that she was worthy of the opportunity that he and his wife were giving her, a sentiment that in later years she wrote about and discussed. He gave her primers on modulating her behavior and attitude to fit tennis etiquette and made a point of coaching her not only in tennis but also in life. Dr. Eaton was pleased that Gibson "listened respectfully" as he spoke. "I took her aside on the tennis court after practicing and emphasized the importance of self-discipline off the court as well as on the court," he said. "I reminded her that it was as important to build character as to build her tennis game."[69]

The Eatons decided that Gibson's appearance needed attention, too. Dr. Eaton distinctly remembered being put off by the way that she looked when he encountered her for the first time, at the Cosmopolitan in August 1945 during the ATA Nationals: "She was such a tomboy in those days that I didn't know whether she was a boy or girl with her hair straight back and wearing slacks. So I didn't pay much attention to her then."[70] Mrs. Eaton stepped in to give Gibson lessons in femininity, picking up the work started by Rhoda Smith in New York. Gibson had arrived in Wilmington with only two skirts and no dresses. "I'd never owned a real dress since I'd been a little girl; a sweater and skirt combination was as far as I was willing to go in the direction of looking feminine," Gibson wrote later.[71] Mrs. Eaton bought dresses for Gibson, arranged for her to have her hair "curled" at a salon, and taught her to apply lipstick.[72]

Together, the Eatons were applying the gendered politics of respectability to prepare Gibson for her life with them and for her multifaceted future as a Black sportswoman integrationist. Gibson and the integration of tennis represented among Dr. Eaton's first forays into social activism combined with respectability politics—the belief that each Black person's outward form and composure communicated the pride, esteem, and modernity of the individual as well as his or her community and the entire Black race. He believed that "Negro parents" and "Negroes who have been successful in their various fields" were responsible for "constantly advis[ing] and encourage[ing] our youth" to prepare them for the lives and careers that would be available after segregation.[73] Gibson had brushed off Fred Johnson's and Rhoda Smith's insistence on respectability, but living in the South and with the Eatons made it difficult for her simply to go her own way not just in her looks but also in her personality, which some considered abrasive.

Furthermore, there were interracial implications for the Eatons' expectations. Along with Dr. Johnson, their goal was to get Gibson into White tennis tournaments, culminating in Forest Hills. She had to prepare to overcome the intertwined barriers of race and class that kept African Americans out of the sport and the fashionable private clubs where tournaments were staged. The presence of a Black person in the tournament bracket at the U.S. Nationals, the oldest and most prestigious tennis tournament in the country, and at its annual host site, the all-white West Side Tennis Club, challenged "the commonplace," as noted by one historian, "that elite spaces must be white spaces and that no matter how respectable and well-mannered, black people did not belong."[74] The Cleveland *Call and Post* had identified the connected racism and classism that undergirded the segregation of USLTA tournaments as early as 1939 and speculated that efforts to integrate elite amateur tennis would be more difficult than those to erase the color line in professional baseball: "It will be harder because the clan that rules the U.S.L.T.A. is a snobbish one. A great deal of emphasis is placed on the way you use your fork, the sort of color combinations you sport on the tennis courts and the way your tie hangs. Of course in all these things our net stars could shape up well but unfortunately, our white friends don't believe it."[75] The Eatons knew that Gibson, aesthetically and behaviorally, would have to demonstrate that she, a Black woman, could meet the social standards that gave tennis dual status among the privileged as an elite game and as an acceptable and even ideal sport for the White women who played it.

The expectations were overwhelming for Gibson, and she struggled to adapt. "I wasn't used to living according to somebody else's plan," she later admitted. "I'd been on my own for so long that I chafed under the discipline."[76] Life in the Eaton household revolved around looking out for each other, mutual respect, and maintaining order. Living with the family, Gibson faced a stark fact about her nature: "It just wasn't in me to be that good all the time."[77] Some mistakes were minor. In the beginning, she did not help with household chores such as doing the dishes. She did not follow basic table etiquette, either. Dr. Eaton noticed that she had been "underfed" in New York.[78] Gibson's voracious appetite and her habit of eating street food in Harlem had spoiled her table manners. The Eatons and their small, impressionable children took their meals in the dining room, while she ate in the kitchen until her manners improved.[79]

Gibson committed other infractions that posed risks to the family's social standing and even their safety as well as her own. A month after she moved to Wilmington, Dr. Eaton received a telephone call from a friend who had spotted her visiting the poolroom on a corner downtown. He summoned Gibson home. "Althea," he explained, "here in the South girls do not go to poolrooms." "Puzzled" and "mystified," she digested the news.[80]

Another time, Gibson borrowed a car without either the owner's permission or a driver's license. Dr. Eaton's mother, Estelle, left her car at the Orange Street house when she, the doctor, and Mrs. Eaton went to an event together in another car. Gibson took Mother Eaton's car and picked up a young man from school. Together, they cruised and parked for make-out sessions. Gibson brought the car back home, confident that no one had seen her. But Wilmington was full of eyes, as she learned yet again. Someone saw her and told on her. Dr. Eaton prided himself on his composure, first learned, he said, as a Black boy in the South and then embodied as a Black man who chose to live there. This slip-up, though, infuriated him. "He was so angry he just walked away from me," Gibson wrote. "I guess I came pretty close to being sent away from there that very day. Dr. Eaton had no intention of letting me mess up things for his family."[81] And mess things up she might have, if, uninsured and unlicensed, she had been in an accident or gotten pulled over by a police officer who was guaranteed to be White. On darkened back roads, she was also vulnerable to any carnal-minded ne'er-do-well, White or Black, who might have come her way.[82]

Then there was the time Gibson severely tested the mercy and trust of Dr. and Mrs. Eaton while babysitting their children. One night, the couple left her to look after Hubert Jr. and Tina. The boy locked himself and his sister in a downstairs bathroom during a game of hide-and-seek. Telling the story in the 1980s, Dr. Eaton wrote that Gibson went to sleep in her bedroom upstairs. But when Hubert Jr. was in his sixties, he recalled that Gibson may have left the house with the children trapped in the bathroom.[83] Either way, Mrs. Eaton was livid to arrive home to find the two small children unattended. She gave her husband an ultimatum: "Either [Althea] goes or I go." Dr. Eaton confronted Gibson the next day and told her that he was going to send her back to New York. She "pleaded" with him to let her stay with the family and tearfully apologized to Mrs. Eaton. Faced with the tears and her husband's reminder that in New York Gibson was unlikely to "realize her full potential in school or tennis," Mrs. Eaton agreed to let her stay.[84]

Over time, Gibson and the Eatons adjusted to each other. She came to see the benefits of compromise. "Gradually, living in Dr. Eaton's house as one of the family, I learned to obey rules and get along with people." The Eatons gave Gibson "the first real family life I had ever known," and she was reluctant to lose it.[85] She called Dr. and Mrs. Eaton, who were only eleven and eight years her senior, "Dad" and "Mom," respectively, and acted as a "big sister" to Hubert and Tina.[86] The Eatons came to understand that the living situation was not easy for Gibson, who "had to be careful to remain in our good graces." Region made her adjustment even more difficult. "Many customs of the South were different and strange to this Yankee girl from Harlem," he mused. Together, they resolved to make "as comfortable a situation as possible for her." "I had taken Althea out of Harlem, but I was having difficulty taking the Harlem out of Althea," Dr. Eaton realized.[87] He learned to "head off trouble when I saw it coming." He continued to give his advice about meeting the demands of life during their time together on the tennis court, and she, in turn, continued to listen.[88]

Jim Crow, however, would not adjust to Gibson, and she found it difficult to adjust herself to it as she faced its daily, dispiriting grind. She might have felt differently had she grown up in the South. Being from the North, though, made her an outsider to the color codes that organized everyday life in Wilmington. Gibson knew that being a "city kid" in "a small town" would be tough, but the thought of the segregationist laws worried her even more. She rationalized that "up north, the law may not exactly be on your side, but at least it isn't always against you just because of the color of your skin."[89]

"Disgusted" and "ashamed," Gibson rode amid the "White" and "Colored" signs on the city buses that took her downtown. She resented the dictate that Black customers who bought hot dogs at the five-and-ten-cent store eat outside rather than while seated at the counter. She learned that while Black did not match White in Wilmington, green and Black suited the White store owners just fine. "They didn't mind taking your dime, no matter how black you were," she said.[90] In Harlem, Gibson had loved choosing a seat in the Apollo's balcony to watch the "flickers," as she called movies. In Wilmington, though, her joy at sitting high above the crowd was dulled because Jim Crow laws demanded that she sit there. She had no other choice. Gibson experienced the insidiousness of segregation in recreation as did most African Americans—as an accumulation of indignities and flagrant restrictions that limited not only her access to recreation but her pleasure in taking leisure.[91]

Gibson navigated Jim Crow in Wilmington and maintained her sense of dignity by observing the law but not respecting it. Basic acts became political acts of defiance for her. She sat as close to the front of the bus "as I thought I could possibly get away with," continued to go to the movies, and went to the five-and-dime, but she did so with the knowledge that she had made a promise to herself—living under southern apartheid would not be her permanent way of life. "I managed to conform to whatever the program was wherever I went. But I hated every minute of it," she remembered. "I made up my mind once and for all that I was never going to live any place in the South, at least not as long as those laws were in existence."[92] Wilmington and the South, like the Cosmopolitan and the Eaton household, were yet more places where Gibson learned to outwardly accept and conform enough to get by while inwardly she believed that she was in control of rather than controlled by the situation. Adjusting thus became a means of achieving her desired end of getting what she wanted. Gibson was devising a strategy for negotiating the demands for her future.

Negotiating gender at Williston Industrial, the Black high school in Wilmington, proved just as difficult for Gibson as maneuvering race—if not more so. The principal allowed her to enroll in the tenth grade rather than begin in the ninth. The freshman class was more appropriate for Gibson given her academic record in New York, but enrolling as a sophomore lessened the age and size difference between herself and her peers.[93] Yet no matter the grade level, she did not—and could not—fit the gender norms of the high school, and her female classmates let her know it.

They teased Gibson for her voice, low and resonant. Soon after starting at Williston, she joined its choir, "figuring that that was one place where I ought to be able to fit in easily." The year before, she had placed second in the Harlem Amateur Hour competition at the Apollo, where she sang Cole Porter's "Night and Day."[94] Though praised at the Apollo, her voice was a problem at Williston. Finding her voice too low for her to stand with the girls in the alto section, the choral teacher placed her among the all-male tenors. Moving her balanced the choir but distressed her because the other girls laughed at her position among the boys. Feeling defeated and humiliated, she quit.[95]

Gibson's penchants for sports and pants really set the tongues of the local mean girls wagging. "'Look at her throwin' that ball just like a man,'" they said upon seeing her playing football, baseball, and basketball with Williston's boys. Years later, she remembered the pain she felt when she heard the jeers and saw the hostile stares of the schoolgirls as she frolicked in her pants and T-shirts: "They looked at me like I was a freak."[96] Her female classmates were subjecting her to the harsh critiques of mannishness increasingly leveled against female athletes, especially given the postwar era's increased policing of gender norms for men and women.[97] Excelling in sports and wearing pants, Gibson offended the thinking of her classmates, who, in her recollection, had plainly bought into their race and region's ideas about what women and girls were supposed to do and the way they should look.

Cast yet again in the role of outsider, Gibson ached with feelings of anger and being misunderstood: "I felt as though they ought to see that I didn't do the things they did because I didn't know how to, and that I showed off on the football field because throwing passes better than the varsity quarterback was a way for me to express myself, to show that there was something I was good at."[98] Years later, Wilmington would honor Gibson with a star on the walkway of its Cotton Exchange. Nearly a dozen women from the Class of 1949, some of whom might have been her tormentors, gathered to pay tribute to her memory in the fall of 2003. The women, some of whom wore pants, stood before a picture taken of Gibson wearing makeup, coiffed hair, a tennis skirt, and a smile—precisely the way her female classmates thought she should have looked way back then.[99]

Gibson was frustrated in her first year of high school, but she refused to give up her nonconformist qualities. She joined Williston's girls' basketball team and played forward, as she had with the Mysterious Girls. Her basketball skills made her a star at school. She was Williston's leading scorer, despite being guarded by two and sometimes three members of the opposing team, and led the Tigers to an undefeated season.[100]

Gibson also found a new outlet for her love for music. Unpacking the tenor saxophone that Sugar Ray had bought her, she joined a small jazz ensemble as well as the high school band. She wore her band uniform proudly, donning the military-style hat and brass-buttoned blazer—albeit with a dreaded skirt. Still, the blazer, the band, and the saxophone, an instrument traditionally associated with male musicians, showed her further flouting gender norms and enjoying every minute of it.[101]

———

The summer of 1947 was the first of many that Gibson spent with Dr. Johnson in Lynchburg, Virginia. He lived at 1422 Pierce Street, a corner lot with a two-story house shingled in brown and white that was larger than the others on the street. The basement held a bar, lounge area, and ping-pong table. Four bedrooms accommodated the many guests that Dr. Johnson invited, first to a tennis retreat for adults and in later years to a full-fledged tennis camp for younger players. Outside there were gardens and fruit trees. Dr. Johnson kept his Buick, which impressed Gibson with its size and grandeur, in the garage. Connected to that was a tool shed that housed an ever-increasing array of devices advertised as capable of improving even the most woeful of tennis games. The backyard tennis court was raised well above the sidewalk for added privacy and minimal distractions. The amenities of the Pierce Street property gave the doctor some buffer from the racist restrictions in Lynchburg.[102]

Altogether, the property reflected Dr. Johnson's status among the Black elite. Born in Roper, North Carolina, in 1899, he had played football at both Shaw and Virginia Union Universities, finally graduating in 1924 from Pennsylvania's Lincoln University with a degree and the nickname "Whirlwind" because of the way his long hair fluttered around his helmetless head as he ran for touchdowns as a record-setting star running back. After earning his medical degree from Meharry Medical College in Nashville, Dr. Johnson took up tennis while completing his residency at Prairie View University in Texas. Having played casually at Shaw and Virginia Union, he became more serious about the game. It helped him stay fit and challenged him in a way football and baseball had not.[103]

Dr. Johnson made sure that his tennis court was an integrated space. He welcomed all who wanted to either play or watch a match. Starting in 1943, he held an annual round-robin men's doubles tournament. White players entered for the first time in 1944. Bobby Riggs would play an exhibition match on the tennis court in 1953, more than a decade after winning Wimbledon and Forest Hills. Still, Dr. Johnson could not overcome the laws, customs, and fears in Lynchburg. The seating for the exhibition was segregated. Whites sat in chairs placed inside the court; African Americans sat on benches behind and above them, further separated by a barbed wire fence.[104]

Dr. Johnson's training of Gibson aligned with her lessons with the Eatons, right down to the efforts to mitigate her queerness. She described that first summer as "the most intensive tennis drill of my life."[105] Day in and day out for weeks, Gibson faced off against machine and man. Dr. Johnson brought his Tom Stow Stroke Developer from the tool shed and had her hit ball after ball that came rushing at her across the court and over the net. Dr. Johnson, his son, Bobby, and their friend William "Babe" Jones of Baltimore were her sparring partners. The sessions were exhausting, but Gibson undoubtedly enjoyed the rigor and had her practicing preferences affirmed in Dr. Johnson's backyard. "I usually practice with men," she said in 1957. "They give me the type of practice I need. I admire the aggressiveness of the male player."[106]

That, however, was where Dr. Johnson's support for Gibson's interest in doing anything with—and certainly like—men ended. She roomed on the third floor of the house, separated from male guests on the lower floors by a full flight of loudly creaky stairs. Dr. Johnson did not allow her to attend the many parties he held in the basement lounge, where alcohol flowed freely. Nor did Gibson's wardrobe escape his surveilling gaze. Dr. Johnson did not permit her to wear pants. "We used to hide her slacks to keep her from wearing them," he told the *New York Post Daily Magazine* without self-consciousness but instead with laughter. "Had it been left to her she wouldn't have worn anything else."[107]

Such was the doctrinaire and single-minded approach that Dr. Johnson took to preparing Gibson, and later other young Black tennis aspirants, for playing across the color line. She turned out to be Dr. Johnson's premier protégé in the program that grew into the ATA's Junior Development Team. Three years after meeting her, he decided to invest his resources into developing the games of younger tennis players. In the 1950s, he invited girls and boys to the house every summer to teach them to play tennis. Rather than pay room and board, the youngsters did chores in and around the house and agreed to follow his orders. The groups of campers were multiracial but most were Black, and Dr. Johnson insisted that they carry themselves in ways that would give members of the White tennis establishment and the players who hailed from it few reasons to find fault with their presence either on the court or in the high-toned social settings that surrounded the game. "I want you to be accepted without being a center of attraction," he told them. "I want you to be able to take care of yourself in any situation where habits or manners are important, so that you don't stand out." Poise included "no raquet throwing, no hollering, [and] no indication of discontent with officials' calls" on the tennis court, even when it appeared that decisions were erroneous and made to the other player's advantage. Dr. Johnson expected his players to pay close attention to table etiquette and social graces. Men, for example, were to stand when a woman entered the room, a form of decorum that presupposed that women would act as "ladies." The "new world," as he called elite amateur tennis, demanded this behavior if the players were to enter and find acceptance at best.[108]

Gibson obeyed the conformist rules of Dr. Johnson, who, like the Eatons, could potentially disinvite her and take back his sponsorship, but her individuality still shone through. Dr. Johnson was pleased that she was a "hard worker who did everything we told her to do," but he saw that some of her traits could not be stamped out, no matter how much time she spent with him. Gibson was occasionally "stubborn" and could "get wheels in her head on the court," though he did not explain what he meant by the latter characterization.[109]

The stubbornness, self-centeredness, and disinterest in concealing her disregard for others could surface during the most routine parts of daily life. Once, Dr. Johnson's neighbor Mrs. Case invited Gibson and the other tennis players home for dinner. Mrs. Case served chicken to her guests in the dining room. She saved the breast for her husband, who was away, and stepped into the kitchen. Violating expectations of ladylikeness, Gibson voiced her displeasure. Why should she be left to pick from the bone-in legs, wings, and thighs of the bird when the breast, thick and succulent, was, she thought, the best part? The other players called out Gibson for her audacity and rudeness. Hearing Gibson's complaint, the ruckus from the others, or both, Mrs. Case returned from the kitchen and invited her to eat the chicken breast.[110] Years later Gibson would say of segregation, "There's a big difference between what you do because you want to and what you do because you're made to do it."[111] She got what she wanted that evening at the Case house, and she was unashamed of the behavior that helped her get it.

—·—

In June 1947, Gibson set off for the ATA circuit, facing her first tests on the journey to integrate amateur tennis. With Dr. Johnson in the driver's seat, she piled into the Buick with Bobby, Babe Jones, and their friends Biddie Woods and Carl Williams.[112] These critical first excursions to desegregate elite amateur tennis were bound by segregation, making traveling while Black from one tournament to the next part of Gibson's test.

The group rose early on travel days. Early morning departures meant more daylight and fewer motorists, including any hostile White drivers who might have been looking to start trouble. The Johnsons, Gibson, and the rest stayed in Black-owned hotels, too; there were no guarantees that any other hotel, motel, or inn, even those in the North, would take Black travelers. Gibson distinctly remembered suffering through long, hot hours in the sedan and at least one sweltering night in a hotel without air-conditioning in Kansas City, Missouri, a situation not uncommon for Black travelers, as Black-owned inns had a reputation for not improving their facilities, either because of a lack of revenue or as a way to hold on to their money; as unpleasant as it was, segregation gave owners a form of monopoly.[113]

The tennis matches themselves marked another test for Gibson, and she excelled. She dominated the ATA women's division that summer. Dr. Johnson entered her in tournaments in Virginia, North Carolina, Connecticut, Washington, D.C., Pennsylvania, Missouri, Indiana, New Jersey, and Alabama. Skipping the New York State Open, where she was the defending champion, freed Gibson for the Kansas City Open and the Mid-Western Open in Indiana. She faced Flora Lomax, Elizabeth Stanfield, and Lillian Van Buren, the best ATA women in the middle of the country. She defeated each one. The win over Stanfield in the Mid-Western was monumental. Stanfield, who was favored to win, had experience playing against White players. She won the Detroit Open in 1945 and, days before losing to Gibson, had captured the women's singles title in the Indianapolis City Parks Tournament, where most of the entrants were White. Stanfield was as athletic as Gibson was, too. She was considered a "crack bowler" and was the first Black woman to earn a varsity letter in sports at Butler University.[114] All told, Gibson won the women's singles title in every one of the nine tournaments she played that summer, without dropping a single set. Together, she and Dr. Johnson won eight mixed doubles tournaments, too.[115] The doctors' investment appeared to have been a wise one.

The tennis season culminated in the ATA Nationals at Tuskegee Institute, where the association was forced to contend with Jim Crow. Mary Hardwick, the well-respected British professional, and her husband, Charles Hare, attended as guests. The night before the finals, Black society columnist and ATA member Betty Granger noticed that "officialdom of the ATA flipped" when they realized that laws in Alabama forbade Hardwick and Hare from sharing a table with them in the cafeteria. Granger and ATA leaders surreptitiously brought Hardwick and Hare to the home of a Black couple nearby, where everyone ate together anxiously. The next day, Hardwick and Hare met

Gibson and George Stewart, a native of Panama and a rising star in the ATA, in an exhibition match. Granger was stunned to see two deputies from the sheriff's office watching the match "with guns in their laps."[116]

That would not be the only unnerving experience Gibson would have during her tennis travels in the Deep South. The next year, she was in the car with Babe Jones and a group of players after the ATA Nationals in Orangeburg, South Carolina. Late at night after the finals, Jones realized his car was dangerously low on gas. He found a station, but it was closed and the owner was asleep. After Jones honked the car horn, the owner, a White man, came out with a rifle. "You niggers better go," he warned. The owner eventually let Jones fill up the tank, but he did not let go of the gun.[117]

Tuskegee proved the site of Gibson's greatest victory in the summer of 1947. She faced Roumania Peters in the title match, giving reporters who had hyped the possibility that the pair would meet again precisely what they—and the tournament committee, which had placed them on opposite sides of the draw—wanted. The *Chicago Defender* anticipated a "bitter battle" and reminded readers of the women's history: that Gibson "went to the finals at Wilberforce University last year only to be disposed of by the stout-hearted, confident Miss Roumania Peters."[118] In the end Peters looked more tuckered out than stout-hearted. She gave the first set everything she had but still lost 7–5. Then Gibson charged ahead in the second and never looked back, winning 6–0 and taking the ATA's women's national title. Gibson defeated her rival decisively on Peters's home turf, her alma mater, and her workplace. It was sweet and cold payback.[119]

After the match, Gibson met Hardwick in a single-set exhibition. The event was freighted with meaning. Major League Baseball, as everyone knew, was experimenting with integration. Jackie Robinson had been playing for the Dodgers since April, and Larry Doby had joined the Cleveland Indians in July.[120] The match with Hardwick was Gibson's first time challenging herself against a White tennis player from the elite ranks. She was the ATA woman with the greatest likelihood of giving Hardwick stiff competition.

Gibson was confident on the heels of her win against Peters earlier in the day. She wore long shorts and a V-neck sweater of the type that Dr. Johnson, Dr. Eaton, and other men in the ATA preferred, but, nodding to feminine norms, her hair appeared glossy and upswept in curls. She racked up a lead of four games to zero. Then, suddenly, two games shy of the biggest victory of her career, the unexpected happened. Hardwick mounted an improbable comeback, winning the next six consecutive games and the match. Afterward, Hardwick beamed with joy, but Gibson was sullen and strained to smile. The outcome-dependent mood that Dr. Eaton had noticed and worried about was back.[121]

After losing the match, Gibson lost her temper. Laura V. Junior, a Philadelphia schoolteacher and respected elder of the ATA who served as the chairwoman of the association's rating committee, approached Gibson to advise her on the errors that led to the loss. Breaking with the lessons of Dr. Eaton and Dr. Johnson, Gibson turned on Junior. Harshly, she told Junior that she did not need anyone to give her a point-by-point account of the match that she had just played. Junior fired back: "I only thought I was helping you, young lady. I took the point score down to point out your faults, believing you would correct them, but all I get is a bawling out. You don't want to be told—and I shall never tell you anything in the future."[122] Spectators stopped and stared.

Among them was Frank A. "Fay" Young, the lead sportswriter for the *Chicago Defender*. He wrote about the tense exchange in his next column and sided with Junior. Young lumped Gibson with "most youngsters" for whom "gratitude" was "something they never learned at home," all but calling her common. Young judged Gibson severely on gender grounds, too, deciding that "as a young woman, Miss Gibson has much to learn." He acknowledged that she had the sponsorship of Dr. Eaton and Dr. Johnson, but that, he said, was not enough because "all the money these two men can muster will not make her a lovable and worthwhile champion if Miss Gibson doesn't start right now to learn that role."[123] Young valued propriety in racial representation. He wrote in 1946 that the ATA Nationals "draws the best we have in tennis" and insisted that "the following which follows it is a credit to any group."[124] Gibson's reaction to Junior ran afoul of the composure associated with tennis players and which Young, like the ATA, expected of its members.

Young's column about Gibson not only marked her earliest experience with bad publicity but showed that her tennis career was making her a noted female figure in the national Black press. As such, Gibson was subject to examination for her interrelated performances of gender and class, and thus of racial representation. Together, they formed yet another test—precisely as her mentors knew that they would.

Young's assessment was anomalous, as Gibson overwhelmingly received praise in the national Black press during and after her first undefeated season and intrigued the reporters who saw her. Observers recognized her dedication and her work ethic, noting that she had "greatly improved" since her loss to Peters in the 1946 season and was a "determined contender."[125] That improvement included "a marvelous repertoire of strokes," including "a beautiful overhead smash," the shot that Alice Marble used to such impressive effect when Gibson saw her play at the Cosmopolitan.[126] Gibson's figure became an object of fascination, with reporters appraising her body as "wiry," "tall and lanky," "willowy," and "slim."[127] The consensus was clear: she had "a beautiful physique."[128] That Gibson played a power game did not escape notice, either. Descriptions of her opponents as "victims" surfaced, alongside more general yet still suggestive notes that she possessed a "hard-driving attack" and was a "dire threat" in tournaments. The rhetoric underscored her queerness in the women's tennis of the ATA, highlighting that her strong abilities were considered unorthodox and, even while recognized as effective, out of place for a woman.[129]

Gibson's success furthered expectations that she would become a legendary ATA player. When she won the ATA national girls' junior title in 1945, Sam Lacy declared that she "[gave] promise of following in the footsteps of Ora Washington, regarded [as] the all-time peer of colored feminine racqueteers."[130] Gibson's second consecutive undefeated season in 1948 resurrected the comparisons. The Associated Negro Press (ANP) humorously noted after she won the ATA's prestigious Eastern Championship at Shady Rest Country Club for the second time that she "threatens to become another Ora Washington by holding the title until senility takes its toll."[131] The other women in the association began to lose hope that they could beat Gibson. Said one ATA competitor, "She was feared."[132]

The comparisons with Washington highlighted the changes that Gibson had made since joining the Eatons and Dr. Johnson as well as the postwar preferences of the Black press and the Black public. As she prepared to defend her ATA national women's title at South Carolina State College in Orangeburg, the *Pittsburgh Courier* lavished her with praise and appeared to pillory Washington. The newspaper, one of the most widely circulated among African Americans during and after the war, predicted that Gibson would win more ATA Nationals than Washington's record-setting eight. The *Courier* credited her with having a femininity that Washington, tall, lean, and muscular, lacked. "Unlike the muscled knobby-legged women athletes who formerly typified excellence in athletics," the *Courier* snidely noted, "Miss Gibson is a slender type and the owner of the cursive lines." Feminine with a dominant tennis game, Gibson, according to the *Courier*, was "the representation of the graceful, gazelle-like racqueteer which American Tennis Association enthusiasts hoped for, but vainly, for many years."[133] With those comments, the *Courier* stressed that Washington did not fit the image that the image-conscious, uplift-minded ATA sought to project.

The *Courier* did not only employ words to laud Gibson. The illustration "Three-Star Performer," drawn by noted Black sportswriter and artist Ric Roberts, celebrated Gibson as she defied gender norms across athletic settings. Roberts drew her behind a pool table, where she was "a 'shark'" and "too much for the average male." He showed her wearing shorts as she dribbled a basketball, described as her "top favorite" sport. Roberts rendered Gibson in a T-shirt and shorts with a determined look on her face as she played tennis. The last image captured her in the ladylike mode that was becoming de rigueur for sportswomen across America. Gibson, wearing a windblown dress and high-heeled shoes, was depicted carrying an armload of trophies to represent her success on the tennis court that season, but the awards could just as easily have been granted as approval for her changed appearance, her youth, and her mien.[134] Roberts's and the *Courier*'s respective messages were clear: Gibson was a commendable female athlete because she was outstanding in sports and because she presented herself away from competition as a womanly figure, just the way that the Black sports press and the public preferred sportswomen to be.

The year 1949 brought the national Black press new reasons to be proud of and pleased by Gibson as she traveled to New York to compete in her first tournaments across the color line. In March, she entered the Eastern Indoor Tennis Championships, where she lost in the semifinals to Betty Rosenquest, the fifteenth-ranked player in the country. Seven hundred people came to the 15th Regiment Armory in Harlem to see the match. Gibson lost 8–6, 6–0, but she left an impression. "Hers will be a game to remember in tennis as the Southern girl is young and definitely has a big-time game," noted *American Lawn Tennis*. "She can scramble to retrieve a shot, she can attack, she picks her openings well and she is at ease in the forecourt."[135] While Gibson was in New York, the USLTA invited her to compete in its National Indoor Championships at the conclusion of the Eastern.[136] With these two historic tournament admissions, her quest to compete at Forest Hills had entered a new phase.

Dr. Reginald Weir, Gibson's mixed doubles partner in the National Indoors, had paved the way for her the previous spring. Weir, a dentist, had been competing in White tennis tournaments in the New York area since at least the middle 1940s. His membership and captaincy on the City College of New York tennis team had given him contacts across the color line, and practicality as much as politics influenced his decision to enter "White" events.

The schedules and travel associated with ATA tournaments were becoming a poor match for his appointments with patients.[137] In March 1948, the tournament committee for the National Indoor accepted Weir's application, making him the first African American to enter the competition.[138]

Neither the USLTA nor Weir agreed with the assertions in the media, Black and White, that the news was groundbreaking. Reporters likened Weir's entry to Jackie Robinson's debut in Major League Baseball. The USLTA, however, made no promises that Weir would compete at Forest Hills, "our real championship," according to executive secretary Edwin S. Baker. Baker explained the admission as both exceptional and run-of-the-mill. "Dr. Weir has been a good player for a number of years, he is a gentleman and he is well liked by all the other players. He is not a member of a U.S.L.T.A. club, but his non-membership has been waived."[139] For his part, Weir played down the precedent, assuring the tournament committee that he "would probably withdraw if [news of his acceptance] caused any commotion."[140] Facing Bill Talbert, runner-up at Forest Hills in 1944 and 1945, Weir lost in the second round 6–1, 6–1 and was not invited to play at Forest Hills in August.[141]

Gibson, twenty-one, was a racial trailblazer and an anomaly at the Eastern and the National Indoors. The Black press reported that a record nine African American men were entered in the Eastern Indoors, and Weir was the only Black man in the National. Gibson, however, was believed to be the first Black woman to enter either event.[142] In both tournaments, she lasted until the quarterfinals, when she lost to Californians. Nancy Chaffee, winner of the USLTA national girls' title in 1947, beat her in the Eastern, while Gussie Moran prevailed over her in the National.[143] To Gibson, the sheer fact that she had been given the chance to compete in the National, a USLTA-run tournament, mitigated her usual disappointment over losing. "I was glad I had lasted until the round of eight. I had been there, I had been invited to play with the white girls in one of the important tournaments, and I felt good about it." She felt that her fellow players in the women's draw in both the Eastern and the National Indoors showed no malice or rudeness. "I was made to feel right at home by the other girls," who she said were "genuinely friendly. It was as though they realized how much strain I was under, and they wanted to do whatever they could to help." Gibson remembered Moran, the eventual winner, as being particularly kind. Moran was not "going through any diplomatic motions," Gibson decided. She was simply "that kind of girl." The acceptance gave Gibson "a lot of hope for the future, and a lot of confidence."[144] Indeed, Moran publicly supported Gibson, whose game she thought showed tremendous promise, and the integration of their sport. "Why shouldn't a

Negro play tennis?" Moran asked a reporter several months later. "I think a few more like [Gibson] would stir up the smugness of this stuffy game."[145]

Integration was so new that the press treated it as a novelty. Robinson's entry in baseball was likened to an "experiment," capturing the uncertainty that integration would take hold in baseball as well as the spectacular quality of those first meetings between one Black man and dozens more who were White—not counting the tens of thousands who sat in the stands.[146] Critics of integration in sports nursed the concern that violent altercations would erupt when Blacks and Whites encountered each other in close spaces like grandstands. New York was not free of the idea. In a few years, Walter O'Malley, president and co-owner of the Brooklyn Dodgers, the very team that initiated integration in baseball, would agonize that a race riot might explode at Ebbets Field, among the smallest of the sport's cathedrals.[147]

Nothing so eventful happened at either the 369th Regiment Armory or the Seventh Regiment Armory, where Gibson's tennis tournaments were played, but the Black press still saw the lack of drama as newsworthy. Reporters probed the way in which the White players and spectators received her at both the Eastern and the National Indoors. Dick Edwards of the *Pittsburgh Courier* wrote that she was "warmly received by the large gallery."[148] Cal Jacox, writing for the *Norfolk Journal and Guide*, found inspiration and affirmation in the integrated matches of Gibson and Weir: "For those who maintain that integration in sports can be accomplished without the incidents that diehard conformists predict will happen the successful participation in the tournament by Miss Gibson and Dr. Weir should serve as an example for those who still refuse to give the colored athlete a chance."[149] The Black press used Gibson and Weir's experiences in the National Indoors as a barometer of society's readiness for integrated tennis and judged the conditions as favorable.

Gibson's play added hope, too. American racial logic and history decreed that she and Weir were representing African Americans in the tournaments. There was no way around that. All they could do was their individual best. In the eyes of many, Gibson and Weir "more than held their own."[150] Jacox pointed to the fact that each lost to the eventual winners, Moran and Richard "Pancho" Gonzales, winner of the men's singles title at Forest Hills in 1948, as proof of their strength and evidence that African Americans could be proud of them.[151] The National Negro Press Association (NNPA) graded both as having made a "good showing." Borrowing from the *New York Times* without attribution, the NNPA spotlighted elements of Gibson's game, specifically that she "drove vigorously" and "got in spectacular winners with her backhand and at the net."[152]

The same American racial logic and history that had made Gibson and
Weir representatives of their race had also made sports, including a USLTA-
run national tennis tournament, into a political event. Gibson and Weir had
participated in a display of "democracy in tennis," even if society itself lacked as
much.[153] Some White media reportage of Gibson's play underscored the gap.
American Lawn Tennis called Gibson "the unseeded North Carolina invader"
and headlined its article about her "Negress Stars in Eastern," using a common
and offensive term for Black women rife with animalistic connotations.[154]

The measure of Gibson's rising stature among African Americans would
not be fully known until the end of the year, when the *Norfolk Journal and
Guide* placed her on its annual list of Black women who had achieved notable
racial firsts or acted in a way that the newspaper considered as having brought
pride to African Americans. Honorees included Mary McLeod Bethune,
educator and presidential advisor; Dr. Dorothy Ferebee, healthcare activist;
and social reformer Mary Church Terrell. Gibson was the only sportswoman
listed.[155] Queerness and all, she had been labeled as a race woman.

———

Gibson returned after the matches to Wilmington and her senior year at
Williston. She was on the verge of graduating tenth in her class and in three
years, achieving the goal that she had set for herself when she came to town.
She had captained the girls' basketball team since her junior year and was its
lead scorer, averaging twenty-two points each game and propelling the squad
to three consecutive undefeated seasons. She still played her saxophone in the
marching band, too.[156]

In late April, Gibson received another opportunity indicative of her
stardom. Florida Agricultural and Mechanical College (FAMC) invited her
to its campus in Tallahassee to participate in an exhibition series during its
first Florida High School Tennis Tournament. The trip doubled as a scouting
and recruitment visit. William H. Wiggins, FAMC's director of physical
education, and Walter M. Austin, its tennis coach, watched Gibson execute
shots and glide around the tennis court. She was in fine form. The *Baltimore
Afro-American* called her visit "one of the highlights of the tournament."[157]
Wiggins and Austin agreed. In May, Dr. Eaton received solicitous letters from
both men laying out the terms of an athletic scholarship that would cover her
room, board, laundry, and funding for travel to tournaments, and give her a
part-time campus job for spending money.[158]

Gibson's scholarship was generous as well as almost unheard of. Before
the passage of Title IX of the Education Amendments of 1972, few colleges

and universities provided athletic scholarships for women. Officially, FAMC had none for female athletes and said as much to those who inquired.[159] The institution, however, made an exception for Gibson. Her athleticism and rapidly growing recognition in tennis were too good for Wiggins, Austin, and FAMC president William Gray to pass up. Her queerness was being rewarded yet again.

As Gibson began to look ahead to living in Tallahassee, she could reflect on the ways that her life in Wilmington with the Eatons had changed since her arrival three years earlier. She and the family had reached a place of comfort with each other. The couple gave her, she said later, "love, encouragement, and a great deal more," including the will to persevere in high school when either the classes, the attitudes of the other schoolgirls, or both felt too hard and sparked in her thoughts of quitting yet again.[160] To Gibson, the parental care and concern that Dr. Eaton had shown her, even with the initial impositions, were deeply meaningful. As she would later tell *Sports Illustrated*, he was "the guy who took such good care of me."[161] The Eatons, in turn, derived pleasure from having Gibson with them. She became fond of Hubert Jr. and Tina, who developed sisterly feelings toward her.[162]

Gibson's gender non-conformity amused and edified Dr. Eaton. Her leadership on the basketball team amazed him. Making a joke out of the "girls' rules" that the team played by, she set scoring records at Williston. Dr. Eaton also delighted in watching her outplay men who challenged her on the tennis court. All the while, Gibson's passion for winning never abated. Dr. Eaton came to see that her desire "to win every set and match" and her habit of "play[ing] every day as if she were in the finals of a tournament" were not sins of either gender or sportsmanship but an asset. "I realized that her behavior was a mark of all champions." Gibson taught Dr. Eaton that "[a] true champion never wants to lose. Losing is not acceptable; winning is all that counts."[163]

Gibson compromised in her life with the Eatons and in Wilmington, too. She wore her pants and T-shirts "every chance I got" and still played sports with the boys of Williston, but she also wore the dresses, lipstick and makeup, and styled hair that Dr. and Mrs. Eaton hoped to cultivate as habitual for her.[164]

The compromise and persistence of Gibson and the Eatons culminated in one event—Williston's junior-senior prom. She did not want to go, but Mrs. Eaton, an inveterate socialite, persuaded her to attend as a show of unity with the Class of 1949. Mrs. Eaton and a family friend, Elizabeth Holmes, directed Gibson's makeover. They made an appointment for her at the salon, applied her makeup, and stood watch as she dressed in "a long pink evening gown." They even found a young man, Joe Davis, to escort her to the dance. When Dr. Eaton came home, he hardly recognized her. Gibson was no longer the raggedly dressed young woman who had come to Orange Street nearly three years before or the tomboyish-looking one he had encountered at the Cosmopolitan the year before that. He was overcome with pride at the sight of her. "Her appearance overwhelmed me," he admitted forty years later. "I have never told Althea how close she came to flooring me. At that moment I somehow felt rewarded for all my efforts in her behalf."[165] Gibson had passed another test on her way to Forest Hills.

4

From Florida A&M to Forest Hills

Have courage—remember that you're just like all the
rest of us.

—ALICE MARBLE, 1950

IN JUNE 1949, Gibson moved to Tallahassee to begin her first year at
Florida A&M. Forgoing her usual trip to Lynchburg and her travels with
Dr. Johnson, she spent the summer doing course work, playing in collegiate tournaments with her new teammates, and traveling to ATA events
with the tennis team. Gibson impressed from the start. She had "very few
weaknesses and . . . felt right at home on the court with any male member
of the squad," remembered Henry Singletary, a teammate who acted as her
sparring partner in the fall. Paul Buie, another teammate, agreed. She clearly
had "championship ability." Gibson again won every singles tournament
that she entered, including sectionals in Pennsylvania, New Jersey, New
York, and North Carolina. In August, she won the women's singles title at
the ATA Nationals at Wilberforce. It was her third straight victory in the
Black championship.[1]

During tournament week at Wilberforce, Gibson spent time with
Dr. Eaton. He and others were convinced that she was not only the most
dominant woman playing in the ATA but also competitive enough to be
put forward as the Black candidate to integrate the USLTA's National
Championships. "Althea, how would you like to play at Forest Hills?" he
asked nonchalantly. She responded in her distinctive way as the Harlem-bred
skeptic, answering his question by posing a question of her own: "Who you
kidding?" Overlooking her lapse in syntax, Dr. Eaton let Gibson know that
the possibility loomed. "It could happen. People are working on it," he said.
"I'm ready," she replied. "I'm ready any time they are."[2]

In the meantime, Gibson could only face the high hurdles in her path for the coming year. She would need help to get over them. And she got it, often from unexpected and surprising sources.

—•—

Gibson was glad to have the scholarship at FAMC and to "feel a little bit independent again" after living with the rules of the Eatons and Dr. Johnson. Yet taking the award represented a compromise.[3] In Wilmington, she had resolved "once and for all that I was never going to live any place in the South, at least not as long as those laws were in existence."[4] Yet by coming to Tallahassee, she had moved further south and more deeply under segregation.

Jim Crow ran Tallahassee, Florida's capital city. African Americans composed more than 30 percent of the population of the city, but they were not full citizens. They were barred from White-owned hotels and restaurants, as well as public libraries, parks, swimming pools, golf courses, and tennis courts. Only two hospitals, the one on campus and Laura Bell Campbell Hospital and Clinic, treated Black patients, just as only one movie theater allowed Black patrons. White bus drivers, the only kind the city hired, firmly maintained segregation in the seats of the buses, too.[5]

FAMC itself represented the ways in which segregation limited Gibson's options. The Southeast was ideal for tennis in terms of climate as well as traveling to tournaments. The region was also home to many HBCUs, the only institutions that Gibson seems to have contacted about scholarships. No predominantly White colleges anywhere recruited her and certainly none in Florida, where Black-White segregation was ironclad in education, public and private, and would remain so until the 1960s.[6] In Tallahassee and at FAMC, which had the official name of Florida State College for Negroes, Gibson had to compromise—follow the plans of others or at least appear to—on the way to achieving her personal goal of getting a college degree and the independent life she craved. Her course of study was her first compromise. "I wanted to take music as a minor subject in college," she wrote in her autobiography, "but my faculty advisers talked me out of it. They said that being an athlete and a musician wouldn't mix."[7]

Founded in 1887 as the State Normal College for Colored Students, FAMC had decades of experience steering pupils through the daily social dilemmas and rejections posed by segregation. FAMC's answer—to make a Black world of its own—was not unlike that offered by other HBCUs. The campus location reinforced the solution. In the 1890s, the physical plant was relocated to a new campus, literally on the other side of the tracks, atop a steep

hill a little less than a mile away from the Tallahassee train station.[8] Students'
fondness for the campus was laced with memories of the lackluster qualities
of some of the facilities and equipment at Florida's only public HBCU. The
gymnasium "rocked and reeled during basketball games" and its lights went
out "whenever it rained." The movie projector was faulty, too, "breaking
down at least twice" during screenings.[9] These were the quirks of Gibson's
new, state-supported home, whose funding depended in part upon decisions
made by White politicians in the state legislature and the governor's mansion
of the Jim Crow state.

Gibson remembered the FAMC campus as the wellspring of student life.
Dorm rooms were for sleeping, studying, and listening to the radio, while the
gymnasium occasionally hosted dances. She soon found her favorite spots.
Despite the projector's problems, she still went to the auditorium to see first-
run movies, where she was not hassled into sitting according to segregationist
dictates. The canteen served fast food, featured a jukebox, and had a pool
table that she used openly and unselfconsciously, unlike in Wilmington.[10]
Still, Gibson knew that a whole segregated world existed in Tallahassee beyond the hillside, and administrators tried to keep students away from it to
lessen the potential for trouble.[11]

Respectability enforced by the FAMC administration mediated what
students did, where they went, and how they looked when they went there.
When Gibson arrived on campus, she landed in another bastion of Black-
enforced propriety. FAMC, like all HBCUs, was an elite institution that
saw itself as preparing future generations of race leaders and felt obligated to
challenge mainstream White suppositions of black inferiority in ways large
and small.

The requirement that students attend nondenominational church services three times a week—twice on Sunday, for one formal and one informal
service, and once at midweek for a prayer session—was an example of the
inculcation of respectability at FAMC that still puzzled Gibson years after
she graduated. The dress requirements for women, which she considered "ridiculous," irritated her as much as the mandatory church attendance.[12] The
official college bulletin instructed students on the "proper clothing and other
personal items" for the school year. Women received detailed instructions on
the garments they were to own. As a FAMC woman, Gibson was required to
have "1 Tailored navy blue coat suit, 2 Plain tailored white blouses with long
sleeves, 1 Pair black low heel shoes, [and] 1 Black or Navy Blue full length
coat." The college also expected women to have "woolen and silk street dresses"
that were appropriate for church and social gatherings, including dinners and

parties, and to "bring one hat, matching pocketbook, and gloves of a neutral color" as accessories for their "Sunday wardrobe" and their church attire.[13]

FAMC also advised female students on hair care. The Women's Beauty Shoppe was open from 7:00 A.M. until 7:00 P.M. Monday through Friday, and FAMC's women were strongly encouraged to use it. "All boarding women students," the bulletin explained, "are expected to take advantage of these services," which came at "average prices." Women could also avail themselves of allocated spaces in dormitories where they could groom their hair on their own.[14] The salon spaces represented convenience as well as administrators' expectations that Black female students would discipline their bodies at not inconsiderable costs of time and money.

It did not take long for Gibson to become stressed by FAMC and its standards. She did her part by following the dress code—she wore skirts and dresses to class and saved her shorts for tennis and basketball. The college made early missteps with Gibson. Her scholarship freed her of the $175 fee required of out-of-state students, but early in her first semester she was nonetheless billed for it. Making matters worse, the wages from her job as an assistant in the P.E. department were directed erroneously toward her scholarship. Strapped for cash, she could not buy the things that she needed, including her textbooks, school supplies, and the white blouses that she was required to wear to chapel. President Gray could not help her, having been forced to resign earlier in the year amid speculation that he had committed financial misdeeds. Suddenly alone, Gibson had to be her own negotiator.[15]

On top of the transition to college, the mix-ups and lack of money were too much too soon. Gibson wanted to be independent, but after three years with the Eatons she had come to enjoy the solace and structure of family life. She now faced a series of adjustments—a new town and professors, more challenging coursework, being four to five years older than her peers once again, and coming home not to a house brimming with activity but to a single dorm room. She wanted to know what was happening with Hubert Jr. and Tina, and even to hug them. Homesick and wearied by the confusion over her scholarship, she wrote to Dr. Eaton in a state of distress and asking for help. "Everything has changed," she said. "If I had known that it was going to be like this, I would not have come."[16]

Gibson found support on campus from Alonzo "Jake" Gaither, FAMC's famed football coach and the newly appointed director of physical education. Football enthusiasts, Black and White, knew him to be a leader on the gridiron, but his players also respected him as avuncular and even as a father figure. Gibson was another beneficiary of his warm, familial, and sensible treatment. Gaither allowed her to charge some of her books to his account and told her to pay him back only when she could. She was relieved, though she did not like the feeling of being indebted to anyone.[17]

The administrative and financial turmoil revealed that Gibson, outwardly and deliberately stoic to people she did not know, felt a keen sense of vulnerability and could be easily addled by the unexpected. To be sure, her tenacity and abilities drove her success, but the generosity of others—the Cosmopolitan members, the ATA, the Eatons and Dr. Johnson, and Coach Gaither and FAMC—can hardly be dismissed or forgotten. Bounties were not guaranteed to last, and the grace and favor of others could be lost at a moment's notice.

The instability passed by the end of the semester: Gibson received her paychecks, and the fee was handled appropriately. Personally, things changed for her, too. She kept a resolution that she had made to Dr. Eaton to "stick it out and try to make the best of things" at FAMC rather than give up in the face of the challenges.[18] She joined the Freshman Women Council and was elected to the Women's Senate. Gibson met her scholarship's terms, too, following the rules laid out for all students and maintaining a passing grade in each of her classes. In the fall, she pledged a sorority, choosing Alpha Kappa Alpha, just like Mrs. Eaton. Gibson earned A's in English 101, Introduction to P.E., and Health and P.E., and B's in geology and math. She earned her lowest grade, a less than stellar C, in History 101.[19]

For Gibson, 1950 was more than the start of a new year or even a new decade. It began with a brief stay at the FAMC hospital to get treatment for the flu. Then two events, four weeks, and a singular goal made the year extraordinary.[20] At the end of it all, she would be launched as a celebrity, a subject of controversy, and a race heroine.

In February, Gibson returned to New York to compete in the USLTA's two major indoor tennis tournaments again. Earlier that month, Clifford Blackman, a longtime member of the ATA and the Cosmopolitan, mailed her an entry form for the Eastern Indoors, scheduled for February 22 to March 6 at the Kingsbridge Armory in the Bronx. Eleven days later, she was to enter the week-long National Indoors at the Seventh Regiment Armory on Manhattan's Upper East Side.[21] The invitations bolstered Dr. Eaton's confidence that ATA leaders were making progress in their efforts to get a Black player into Forest Hills and that figures in the USLTA were open to the idea.

Even the Black press was reporting on the possibility that Forest Hills would integrate soon.[22]

Gibson quickly tested the theories. Carved on a mantelpiece at Kingsbridge was the Latin phrase *paratus et fidelis*, meaning "ready and faithful."[23] Gibson showed that she was both at the Eastern Indoors. On March 4, she won the women's singles title, beating Millicent Hirsch Lang, a resident of Forest Hills.[24]

Exuding calm and confidence, Gibson next went to the National Indoors. Seeded second, she nearly blanked her opponent, 6–0, 6–1, to reach the quarterfinals and steadied herself in the semifinals when her back was against the wall to win over Midge Buck, a veteran player, 6–2, 4–6, 7–5. Two days later, on March 25, Gibson met Nancy Chaffee in the final. Chaffee was out to prove, if only to herself, that she was more than the fun-loving, dark-haired pin-up that the sports media portrayed her as. Runner-up to Gussie Moran in the National Indoors the previous year, she overwhelmed Gibson, winning 6–0, 6–2.[25]

During the match, Gibson might have been preoccupied with thoughts of its potential stakes. That week, Bertram Baker, the executive secretary of the ATA, and Arthur Francis, its assistant executive secretary, along with future president Dr. Sylvester B. Smith of Pennsylvania, met two USLTA representatives, Dr. Ellsworth Davenport, treasurer and referee, and Alrick Man Jr., chairman of the tournament committee, in New York for a secret meeting. Gibson's victory at the Eastern outpaced the expectations of the ATA. "We wanted to be sure that we could offer a player who would be worthy of competing in the national championships," Francis later said. "We preferred to wait a year or two more, if we had to, before asking for an entry to be sent to a Negro player."[26] Gibson's success, including her march through the early rounds at the National Indoors, caused the group to revise their gradualist approach and plan. "We were," he admitted to the *New York Post Daily Magazine* years later, "sure by 1950 that we had a proper candidate in Miss Gibson."[27] At the spring meeting, the two groups of men discussed the possibility of Gibson entering Forest Hills in August. Davenport and Man, along with others within the USLTA but not present for the meeting, supported the idea. A Black player would play at Forest Hills "sooner or later," they told Francis, Baker, and Smith, but the decision did not rest with Davenport and Man alone. Thirty-six people belonged to the national tournament committee and "a majority . . . would have to give their approval," an outcome that was not guaranteed.[28]

Faced with the press after the match with Chaffee, Gibson spoke maturely and cautiously. Asked to assess her play, she judged that she "didn't do so badly" and did not blame a balky ankle for her loss. Instead, she was gracious and praised the other women in the field, all of whom were White, calling them "very, very nice" and "good sports." Gibson added, "After all, if you can't be a good sport in sports, you can't be a good sport in anything," a lesson learned from Dr. Eaton.[29] Asked about Forest Hills, Gibson was measured. She allowed that she had never played on grass courts as pristine as those at the West Side Tennis Club and mentioned that she was willing to give them a chance if she received an invitation. She did not, however, use the post-round interviews to ask to be invited to play in the tournament, nor did she suggest that she had qualified.[30]

Others, however, imagined that Gibson's name would be printed in the program. Al Laney, the ATA's old friend at the *New York Herald Tribune*, had covered tennis for decades and knew skillful play, the kind that was worthy of an invitation to Forest Hills, when he saw it. Laney was forthright that the Gibson-Chaffee final at the National Indoors was hardly riveting. "This was not a good match," he said, and pulled no punches, writing that Gibson, who had "done so well earlier [in the tournament], did badly when the big chance came." Nevertheless, Laney concluded that she had proven that she could be competitive in the most important tennis tournament in America. "Miss Gibson did not win the title, but she definitely won the right to have her entry accepted for the championships at Forest Hills next September."[31]

Even *Life* magazine weighed in. The preeminent American pictorial devoted a half-page to Gibson.[32] Photographer Gordon Parks snapped several pictures of her during her practice sessions in New York. Unlike her appearance during a match, she looked tomboyish again, wearing a T-shirt and tab-front shorts. Juxtaposed on the page with a photo of actress and dancer Ginger Rogers in an evening gown and pearls, *Life* published a shot of Gibson, mouth agape and eyes focused on the ball, preparing to unleash her power into an overhead smash above a provocative caption: "Her performance in the Indoors posed a question for tennis moguls: would she be the first Negro to play in the outdoor championships at Forest Hills next August?" *Life* called the half-page feature "New Tennis Threat," underscoring that Gibson differed from the image of the sport.[33]

The Black press did not require persuasion that Gibson was ready. The idea that she might play at Forest Hills had floated in the Black media since she reached the quarterfinals at the National Indoors in 1949.[34] Her second-place finish turned conjectures into celebrations. The *Pittsburgh Courier* and the *Baltimore Afro-American* ran headlines—"Althea Gibson Earns Chance to Play in National Tennis Tourney" and "Althea Gibson Earns Bid to U.S. Tennis Nationals," respectively—that touted her entry as a lock. For good measure, the *Afro-American* clarified that Gibson was "in position to be invited" and pointed out the historic nature of the invitation. Playing at Forest Hills was "something no colored person has yet done."[35]

That history was not lost on Florida A&M. Interim president H. Manning Efferson was in the gallery during the title match at the Eastern Indoors and congratulated Gibson on her victory when she won. When she returned to Tallahassee, Efferson met her at the train station, and FAMC's marching band played the alma mater as she disembarked. The sight of a "big sign" on campus that said "Welcome Home, Althea" moved her. "For a freshman," the celebrations were "a real big thing," she remembered. "I was overwhelmed, and very happy."[36] Gibson's happiness came from the unprecedented nature of the display. "It was my first touch of fame and it was wonderful."[37] She recognized, though, that the gestures were about more than her personal success. The chorus of FAMC's "The College Song" declared that students "fight and win whate'er the battle be." In the eyes of the college community, Gibson had fought and won a battle over white supremacy, even though she did not agree with the perception. "Obviously, they all felt that what I had done was important not just to me but to all Negroes."[38]

Gibson was more interested in what the tournament results meant for herself. Before she had been allowed to enter the Eastern and the National Indoors, it "rankled" and "ate at" her that she could not "play against the white girls."[39] She wanted to play against them because she was a fierce competitor who sought to challenge herself against the best players in the world so that she might become the best herself, not to prove something about the Negro people.

Dr. Eaton saw both sides. In early April, he wrote to Gibson to express his pride in her success. He also sought to keep her focused and grounded. She had acquitted herself well in the two tournaments, and he was convinced that she had "what it takes to become one of the greatest women tennis players of all time, white or colored." Doing so, he said, required her own "sacrifice" and "hard work," as "there is much room for improvement" in her game as well as "still greater fields to conquer." Only practice would allow her to become the world-beater that he believed she could be. The situation was bigger than Gibson: "You need to constantly remember that the eyes of the tennis world are on you and what you do this summer can make or break the immediate future of negro tennis."[40] The message once again was respectability and bearing a responsibility to the race.

Gibson received yet another reminder that her success on the tennis court gave her the stature, weight, and responsibilities of a race heroine. On April 5, Dr. George W. Gore gave his first speech as the new president of FAMC to the students, faculty, and staff. Gore organized his address around a rhetorical question: "What should Florida A. and M. College stand for?" He called Gibson a representative of the "quality" for which the college should strive and wrapped her into his necessarily wishful and survivalist theory of achieving greatness despite Jim Crow. Gibson's "name is a byword in America because she stands for quality," he told the audience. "Whenever you excel people respect you regardless of race, color, or creed."[41] The statement spoke volumes about the perseverance and outlook of Gore, a Columbia Ph.D. who, despite being appointed the president of a public university, would not be allowed to join members of the all-white Florida State Board of Control for meals or use the same restroom facilities they did when the committee convened for official meetings.[42]

Gibson, surely gratified by yet another public sign of esteem, faced different questions. Did the USLTA respect her or, barring that, the quality of her tennis game? If so, was it enough to get her into Forest Hills? Perhaps unintentionally, she revealed her caution and uncertainty to the public. Chestine Everett, a FAMC journalism teacher, interviewed her shortly after she returned from New York for a piece that would be published in Black newspapers nationwide. Everett asked Gibson to name the thing that most "impressed" her about playing in the Eastern and the National Indoors. "Everyone was extremely nice. I felt no aversion by others to my color," she responded, as if she anticipated that the question of the way that Whites treated her was on everyone's mind. Gibson allowed that "it is not pessimistic to feel that [such emotions] perhaps will come as I go on—and I hope up." She continued, "I hope that I shall be able to go to Forest Hills. The possibility of my race would seem to pose a question."[43] The answer reflected Gibson's candor and her balancing act.

———

When the semester ended in late May, Gibson went back to Wilmington. She decided to take advantage of Dr. Eaton's offer to practice and play with her. Nathaniel Jackson, his friend and doubles partner, was available to help, too. Together, Gibson and Dr. Eaton planned that she would limit her play in Black tennis during the season. He believed that playing as many tournaments as she had during the previous summers would erode her game. Besides, spending hours in a car on the road and in shoddy hotels to play nearly a dozen events was fatiguing and pointless. Gibson was without a doubt the best player among women in the ATA. She was not going to lose a set, or even a game in most cases, let alone a match. Her energy and stamina were resources best marshaled for the task of preparing for Forest Hills.[44]

Those preparations tentatively included one significant White tournament. Before Gibson left Tallahassee, she had received an entry form for the National Clay Court Championships in Chicago, to be held at the River Forest Club in July. The sender was Charles Hare, a former star of the British Davis Cup team, an executive with Wilson Sporting Goods, the husband of Mary Hardwick, and a postwar transplant to Chicago. After speaking with officials at River Forest, Hare gleaned correctly that Gibson's entry into the Clay Courts stood a good chance of being accepted.[45]

The River Forest invitation was a good omen, but the acquisition of an invitation to Forest Hills remained uncertain. As Gibson focused on her workouts in Wilmington, the ATA triumvirate of Baker, Francis, and Smith met again with the USLTA representatives. Since the first meeting in April, Davenport and Man had been in touch with other USLTA officials. Instead of carrying the good news that the entire national tournament committee had voted in favor of admitting Gibson to Forest Hills, Davenport and Man presented concerns raised by some of their colleagues.

Together, the topics raised pointed to suppositions that Gibson differed from USLTA players. One involved her merit as a tennis player. Some thought, Smith recalled, that "she had not compiled any praiseworthy record of achievement" in USLTA tournaments. The ATA delegation retorted that the argument was ridiculous, as it ignored the prejudice of the USLTA-member clubs that approved players for tournaments. "We, of course, wanted to know how she could ever be expected to compile this suitable record in U.S.L.T.A. competition if her entries in such tournaments were to be repeatedly rejected by the tournament officials." Another concern struck Smith as particularly trifling: "The subject of her use of the locker room facilities was even raised in spite of the minor aspect of this facet of her competition." The matter was inconsequential to the ATA men but real all the same: Negro League teams that played in White-owned baseball stadiums were not guaranteed use of the locker rooms. Smith, Baker, and Francis found themselves confronting White America's centuries-long association of African Americans with disease and contamination, the kind of fear that kept water fountains, swimming pools, and restrooms segregated by law in the South and by custom in the North and elsewhere.[46]

Moving past the concern about the locker room, the men reached a compromise about Gibson's immediate future. Davenport and Man produced a sheet of paper. It held a short list of the names and addresses of clubs that were to hold tournaments in the coming weeks. They recommended that the ATA write to the tournament committees to request entry forms for Gibson. Tournaments were invitationals. Each club carried the authority to choose players based on its own criteria. Davenport and Man cautioned that southern tennis clubs might not be the only ones to reject them. Francis knew that the events were being presented as qualifiers. His background in sports journalism, dating back to tennis articles he wrote for the *New York Amsterdam News* in the 1920s, stoked another idea about the value of the appearances. Playing in the tournaments "would permit her to show what she could do against first-class players as well as build up her reputation."[47]

The list brought a new dimension to the campaign to get Gibson into Forest Hills. Dr. Eaton and Francis believed that the application of "pressure" would get her there.[48] Her play was one form of pressure. Gibson did her part by playing and practicing nearly every day on the Eaton family's tennis court. Words and, as Francis put it, "reputation" were another. In mid-June, he typed letters to Robert Clark, chairman of the tournament committee at Cherry Valley Club on Long Island, host of the New York Women's Championships, and to the Maplewood Country Club in Maplewood, New Jersey, where the New Jersey State Championships were to be played in July. Francis's letters did not mention that Gibson was a Negro, nor did he characterize the ATA as a Negro organization. Instead, they praised her as a player and person whom the clubs would welcome on their sophisticated grounds. He reminded the recipients of Gibson's recent achievements at the Eastern Indoors and the National Indoors and informed them of her victories in major ATA-sanctioned tournaments—the New York State, Pennsylvania State, and Eastern Sectional championships—and her status as the ATA's national women's singles champion. Gibson, Francis concluded, was "a very fine player," the holder of "a very fine tennis temperament" and a "very fine tennis disposition," and "a credit to the game of tennis."[49]

Davenport and Man's warning to the ATA delegation about the boundlessness of prejudice proved accurate, as neither club reciprocated the respect that Francis had shown them. Maplewood's treatment of Francis was emblematic. Before sending the letter, he had twice called a club official to request an entry form. Each time, the official said that he would mail the paperwork. Francis, however, never received it.[50] In the end, Gibson played in neither tournament. Maplewood Country Club eventually issued a denial, claiming that there was "not enough information" about her record. She interpreted that to mean that she "hasn't played in enough recognized tournaments to qualify."[51] The response was part of the circuitous rejection loop: USLTA clubs were unwilling to give her the chance to play in their tournaments, where she could prove herself.

At the end of June 1950, Gibson boarded a train bound for New York. The tournament committee at River Forest had accepted her entry form. With its clay courts, the Cosmopolitan was the best place for her to practice.[52]

———

If Gibson felt any smug contempt for the way that some people at the Cosmopolitan had once treated her, given the way her life was turning out, she kept it to herself. Eyes trained on the future, she devoted her time to practicing and playing tennis, not to pettiness or the past. A gesture initiated by Rhoda Smith helped. The club gave Gibson a special suitcase for her tennis togs. It was a far cry from the pair of cardboard suitcases held together by worn leather belts that she had carried to Wilmington. Touched, she deemed the suitcase "beautiful" and appreciated that members were "kind enough" to give her something that she could use in her travels.[53] She was living well— indeed its own revenge—and everyone at the club knew it. That was enough.

People at the Cosmopolitan stepped forward to help Gibson. She played with some of the best members to get ready for the National Clay Court Championships and received financial support, too. Baker and Francis set up a fund for contributions to cover her tournament travels and quickly raised $125 at a meeting of the New York Tennis Association. Baker "advanced" $100 from the ATA to the fund, too. Gibson trusted his and Francis's stewardship, assessing that the pair "seem to have things well in hand."[54] That trust was important. Knowing that others were overseeing the finances freed her to focus on her tennis. Together, the Cosmopolitan and the ATA were rallying behind her to push her over the color line.

Sarah Palfrey came to the Cosmopolitan to practice with Gibson to try to pull her across that line.[55] In Palfrey, she had one of the most respected and skillful players in women's tennis on her side. Born to a prominent family outside of Boston in 1912, Palfrey learned tennis from Hazel Hotchkiss Wightman, winner of four U.S. National singles titles between 1909 and 1919 and founder of the Wightman Cup, the prestigious annual event that matched the four best women in American tennis against their British counterparts for two days of competition. Palfrey played on ten Wightman Cup teams and won fifteen titles at Forest Hills, including the women's singles championship in 1941 and 1945.[56] Palfrey's ideas about tennis were in sync with those of the ATA. In her first book, *Winning Tennis and How to Play It* (1946), she called the game "an all-American sport" that should be accessible for all, "rich and poor," and praised the men's Davis Cup for having "shown that people of many races and temperaments can enjoy the game at its best."[57]

Palfrey had reasons to question the decision-making of the USLTA. In April 1947, the association banned her and suspended Pauline Betz, four-time winner of the U.S. Nationals and 1946 champion of Wimbledon, without warning. The ban was precipitated by administrators' discovery that Palfrey's husband, Elwood Cooke, had written letters to several country clubs to gauge their interest in hosting the two women on a professional tour. Both Palfrey and Betz were still amateurs, though the former had not played a competitive match since winning Forest Hills in 1945. The suspension, sudden and immediate, overlapped with Wimbledon and Forest Hills, rendering both women ineligible to compete. It also struck some in the tennis community as unfair. Leading male amateurs Jack Kramer and Donald Budge had spoken openly about their intentions to play professionally even as they still competed as amateurs, but they were not suspended for it. A writer for *American Lawn Tennis* observed in 1947 that Palfrey and Betz "had some well thought out criticism to make" against the USLTA.[58]

Shoring up Gibson's game and making her competitive was one way that Palfrey could push the association to be more just. Palfrey had first met her the previous year, when, as Gibson remembered, they "batted balls back and forth on Manhattan's East Side at the start of my big-time tournament career."[59] Palfrey canceled a trip to Europe and told Francis that she was "able to play with Gibson as long as they both were in New York."[60] Palfrey worked with her for several days and grew increasingly pleased by her pupil's progress and the versatility of her game. Gibson's strokes, Palfrey decided, were "well adapted for grass," the playing surface at Forest Hills. Still, she saw areas for improvement. Gibson needed "a good follow-up volley" to match her serve and her "ground strokes were erratic," but Palfrey, mindful of time, decided that "with the tournament season almost at hand there was no sense in her trying to change them at this stage."[61]

While practicing with Palfrey, Gibson received an unexpected endorsement. In "A Vital Issue," an opinion essay published in *American Lawn Tennis*, Alice Marble wrote that Gibson should be allowed to compete at Forest

Hills. Marble knew Palfrey well, since they had won the women's doubles title together four times at the U.S. Nationals and twice more at Wimbledon. Marble, though, did not link Palfrey's support for Gibson to her decision. Instead, she described making the choice entirely on her own.

Marble had been in the gallery for the final round of the National Indoors in March. She noted that Gibson "performed beautifully" in the match, possessed "lovely strokes," and "exhibited a bold, exciting game that will doubtlessly improve against first-class competition." After the tournament, Marble embarked on a speaking tour where she encountered people who asked whether Gibson would be allowed to compete at Forest Hills at the end of the summer. Marble decided to pose questions of her own to a member of the USLTA tournament committee. Gibson's play in the spring was unremarkable because she faced subpar competition, he explained. Furthermore, she needed to prove herself by playing in "major Eastern tournaments," all of which were invitationals. No invitation meant no chance to prove herself. Marble revealed the strategy in "A Vital Issue" and unreservedly attributed the antics of the USLTA to racial prejudice. The national tournament committee and its clubs, said Marble, "were not judg[ing]" Gibson "by the yardstick of ability but by the fact that her pigmentation is somewhat different." She added that the tactics amounted to "injustice perpetuated by our policymakers." To Marble, Gibson was "a fellow human being to whom equal privilege ought to be extended."[62]

American Lawn Tennis backed Marble. A brief preamble to the essay stated that the magazine "wholeheartedly support[ed]" her sentiments and opinions. The same issue featured a glowing profile of Gibson. Written by journalist Howard Cohn, "The Gibson Girl" introduced her to the White American tennis community as a prodigy of the sport and a hardworking college student from a humble background who, as "the greatest Negro woman tennis player in history," was ready to test her developing skills against the best in the game.[63] Photos accompanying the article presented Gibson as a dynamic yet conventional coed—delivering her overhead smash, studying in her dorm room at FAMC, smiling while standing side by side with Nancy Chaffee, playing table tennis, and tooting her sax. In all but the tennis scenes, she wore either a dress or a skirt. The ATA shone as businesslike and moderate. Cohn made clear that the association "had no desire to create a 'stir,' and try to bludgeon tournament committees into accepting [Gibson's] entry."[64] Without naming Maplewood Country Club, Cohn reported that at least one club had reneged on its promise to send an entry form to the ATA. Bertram Baker was thrilled by the publication. He had cooperated with Cohn on the story, submitting to "several conferences" and listening as the author read a draft to him over the telephone. "Both the editors of this magazine and Miss Marble," he wrote Dr. Eaton, "have gone all out in championing our cause in a most courageous and fearless manner."[65]

Bravery turned out to be contagious, at least for some. Marble was among the most respected sportswomen in the country, and *American Lawn Tennis* was the flagship magazine of the sport. After the essay and the article appeared, other outlets released endorsements of their own. On July 5, the *New York Herald Tribune* published "Justice at Forest Hills." Calling Gibson "a New Yorker of demonstrated ability," the editors declared that "to any fair-minded outsider, Miss Gibson has shown that she has the stuff" to play at Forest Hills. Rather than using "unofficial restrictions" to keep Gibson out, the USLTA should "let the girl show what she can do." The matter was one of "human fairness" and would reveal "the full spirit of justice."[66] *Life* agreed. Two weeks later, the magazine took up her cause in "Justice and the Courts (Tennis)." The brief piece acknowledged that her game was still a work in progress. The editors, though, did not hold back in accusing the USLTA of behaving unfairly. "Miss Gibson is certainly a better player than many who are ordinarily invited to participate in the nationals, and it is about time that the U.S. tennis fathers, who have been drawing a *de facto* color line at Forest Hills all these years, got over their ancient prejudices."[67]

———

On July 12, Gibson departed New York for the National Clay Courts. She traveled alone by train to Chicago and slept on the lower berth of a private Pullman car. The ATA network was vast, and members beyond New York were eager to help break the seal that contained elite amateur tennis. Richard Hudlin, a teacher at Sumner High School in St. Louis, Missouri, was among them. In 1928, Hudlin had been elected the captain of the tennis team at the University of Chicago, making him the first Black varsity captain of any sport in the Big Ten. Baker and Francis were pleased when Hudlin volunteered that he and his wife, Jane, would be willing to come to Chicago to "act as chaperone[s]" for Gibson.[68] She was approaching twenty-three, but she also represented the future of African Americans in tennis, which was too precious not to be supervised by the Black elite.

That representation made Gibson into a social threat that needed to be contained, including by her benefactors. Clubs like River Forest were places where people mingled and socialized on equal and intimate terms, leading to friendships and even romances and marriages. Mitigating interracial sexual

contact was a major raison d'être for segregation. Gibson's presence at the social events that accompanied the tournament risked offending the sensibilities
of Whites who valued the racial homogeneity of their country club and the
tournament. Aware of this, Dr. Johnson telegrammed advice to Gibson after
she arrived in Chicago: "I would not attend any of their social functions. Go
home and rest. One of the reasons they don't want you to play at Forest Hills
is because of the social functions. Pass these up to get to Forest Hills."[69]

Once at the tournament, Gibson discovered that Dr. Johnson was right
about her outsider status. River Forest had approved her entry, but it also
took steps to contain the spread of the Black game. Gibson was not allowed
to bring a partner for doubles, either women's or mixed, ensuring that she was
the only Black player in the bracket. Instead, tournament officials decided to
pair her with players upon her arrival at the club. Deprived of a Black com-
rade and thrown into competition with a partner whom she had not yet even
met, let alone gelled with, Gibson felt "handicapped" by the setup.[70] On top
of that, the *Chicago Daily Tribune* ran a story on the eve of the tournament
about the impressive array of men and women from around the country and
the world who were in town to compete for the title, and in it the paper literally segregated her. Under the heading "Negro Girl Entered," reporter Robert
Cromie described her as "working to look good enough in the River Forest
competition so that she will be invited to Forest Hills, where no Negro has
ever played."[71] Following mainstream standards of the period, the *Tribune*
referred to Gibson's race in every story in which it mentioned her for the
remainder of the tournament. The isolation in the tournament and the publicity left her without camouflage.

Gibson's sudden celebrity also meant that she had to deal with intrusions
from the press. One night as she ate dinner at the private residence where
she was staying, famed Black sportswriter Wendell Smith dropped in, apparently unannounced. Smith had a special interest in integration. Years before
organized baseball dropped the color barrier, he had criticized the segregation of the sport in his columns and articles for the *Pittsburgh Courier*, and
in the 1940s he arranged tryouts for Black players but to no avail. In 1945,
Smith recommended Jackie Robinson to Branch Rickey as the best Black
candidate for Major League Baseball. Rickey signed Robinson and also hired
Smith as Robinson's companion and confidant. Smith spent the next two
seasons chronicling Robinson's career. When Smith interviewed Gibson, he
was working for the *Chicago American*, a White daily newspaper.[72] Still, his
column, "Sports Beat," was published in the *Courier*. Despite Smith's background, Gibson did not rush to finish her dinner to meet him.

When she appeared, Gibson was faced with a man who treated her differently than he did Robinson or any other male athlete. Smith was so pleased by the sight of her that he made note of her appearance to share with his readers. He was taken with Gibson's attire, the "summer smock" that was "short and sleeveless and dangled from her trim body in a casual sort of way." Indeed, he was fascinated by her body. Gibson was tall (she gave her height as 5′10½," though Smith put her at an inch shorter) and a "well proportioned 130 pounds" with "marvelously efficient arms" of a "smooth bronze color" that were only "slightly muscular," while her legs were "like two columns of polished mahogany." Altogether, she struck Smith as "a handsome woman with an abundance of personal charm," so much so that he asked her whether she was dating anyone.[73]

Gibson's answer, straightforward with youthfully quixotic notes, made it clear that her career was her priority, not a relationship. "I haven't had time to think of boys or marriage," she told Smith, though she might have been fibbing, as she briefly dated William Burrough, a fellow student, in Tallahassee. "All my time has been devoted to tennis. I eat and sleep the game and when I go to bed I dream of playing at Forest Hills. The game of tennis absorbs my very life." Smith was impressed by her dedication, but he was also smarmy about it. "Any game that can make a girl as attractive as Althea ignore the birds and bees and starry nights . . . must be associated with some kind of racket!" he remarked, adding, "In her case 'love' is nothing more than tennis parlance and belongs up on the scoreboard."[74] Smith's objectification was surely sexist, but it also had a purpose.

The lesbian athlete stereotype was alive and well. In the two years since the *Courier* compared Ora Washington and Gibson, the widespread perception that gender nonconformity was a sign of homosexuality had not abated.[75] Smith, by presenting Gibson as feminine, attractive, and physically appealing, was signaling that she was heterosexual, an acceptable female athlete, and, in the language of the era, a normal woman.

Gibson's time in the National Clay Court tournament was short but effective. She received favorable press in the *Tribune* when she told a reporter that she aspired to become a "policewoman" and "straighten out some of New York's juvenile delinquents."[76] Unseeded, she lasted until the quarterfinals, where she lost to Doris Hart, 6–2, 6–3.[77] There was no shame in the defeat. Hart, twenty-five, was seeded first for good reason. Except for Forest Hills, she had won every women's singles major, including that year's French International, which also was played on clay. Gibson solidified her place in the American national championship by convincingly defeating

Mela Ramirez, the women's national champion of Mexico, 6–3, 6–1, in the first round. The *Chicago Daily Tribune* described the result as one of the two "major upsets" of opening day and found it doubly surprising given that the event marked Gibson's "first major outdoor tourney."[78] She was heading back east earlier than she wanted. Nevertheless, she had played well enough to still be a viable candidate for Forest Hills.

Others agreed. After Chicago, Harold LeBair, chairman of the USLTA's umpires' association, told Bertram Baker, the ATA executive secretary, that if Gibson submitted an entry form for the U.S. Nationals, it would be accepted. Gibson filled out the form as soon as she received it. The decision to accept her at Forest Hills amounted to a more progressive version of the gentlemen's agreement that had kept Blacks out of the tournament; it, too, was not announced in the press.[79]

Gibson resumed her practice sessions with Sarah Palfrey after returning to New York. Her next tournament was the Eastern Grass Court Championships in East Orange, New Jersey. Palfrey liked the ways in which Gibson's game was developing, but she felt that their preparations lacked the crucial experience of playing on high-quality grass. Palfrey called Ralph Gatcomb, president of the West Side Tennis Club, and asked whether she could bring Gibson there for a practice session. He could have refused; Palfrey was not a member of the club. Gatcomb, however, said yes without hesitation, Palfrey recalled, a further sign that the conflict over Gibson's admission was over. Two days later, on July 30, she and Palfrey boarded the subway in midtown Manhattan. Within twenty minutes they were in Forest Hills.[80]

The West Side Tennis Club was like nothing that Gibson had ever seen. Although she had been a spectator, there was a world of difference between sitting in a grandstand staring down into the court below and walking on the grounds dressed in her tennis whites with her own equipment, preparing to play. The club was more than a place; it was a shrine. "America's answer to Wimbledon," some called it. At its heart was a massive clubhouse designed in 1913 in the style of an English cottage. Flat, green, and pristine, twenty grass courts stretched across the club's twelve acres.[81] The tournament was not to begin for another four weeks, but Gibson likely broke history the moment she walked onto the court that she and Palfrey had been assigned and took her first practice strokes. The West Side Tennis Club had no Black members, a common exclusion at the time that underscored its claims to exclusivity.[82]

After changing in the ladies' dressing room, Gibson and Palfrey practiced for nearly two hours in blazing heat. Being on the courts was "a big help,"

Gibson realized. "[Getting] the feel of the place" would make it seem less strange once the tournament began.[83] She had also come to trust and admire Palfrey. "She's one of the finest tennis players I've ever had the pleasure of hitting against," Gibson wrote. "She knows everything about tennis strokes and strategy that's worth knowing."[84] Palfrey's confidence that Gibson could be a good grass court player was reinforced, even though this was her pupil's "first taste of playing on a real 'lawn' tennis court." Gibson's dominant style of play—"big serve, good volley and smash"—was a strength on the turf. So, too, was her physical presence, Palfrey thought. "Her natural timing and big, catlike strides were useful for the faster pace of a grass court." Dressed in her shorts and a johnny-collar shirt, Gibson moved with no inhibitions. Her height, an asset otherwise, posed one notable liability: she struggled to bend for low retrievals. Palfrey was not worried by it and judged the session an "impressive workout."[85]

It looked as if much of what made Gibson stand out would give her a real chance at succeeding at Forest Hills.

———

And yet there was still time for Gibson's idiosyncrasies to do her in.

The day after Gibson visited the West Side Tennis Club, she was in South Orange for the Eastern Grass Court Championships. She recognized the tournament as "major-league."[86] Only Forest Hills bested it in prestige. The setting was impressive, too. As with Chicago, Gibson's presence was treated as a spectacle. Reporters noted repeatedly, including in their headlines, that she was "a Negro." "Principal interest centered" on her match, said the Associated Press (AP), because it was the first time that a Black player had ever played in a USLTA grass court championship. Another precedent was set, too: her match marked the first time in tournament history that all of the lines callers and the umpire were women.[87]

On day one, Gibson took down Virginia Rice Johnson, an established player from New Haven, Connecticut, 6–1, 6–3. *New York Times* tennis reporter Allison Danzig lauded Gibson's performance. Danzig thought she played "with poise," "made an excellent showing," and had a "forehand and backhand" that were "soundly wrought." He also saw the gender-defying elements of her game: "She follows her fast service to the net as do few women, and no other player of her sex hits an overhead more emphatically." Danzig believed that Gibson "has the equipment to be a very good tennis player." She just needed more "experience" playing against "the best players in match competition."[88]

Gibson got such an experience the next day in the second round. She faced Helen Pastall Perez of Encino, California, ranked fifth in the nation. Playing on a court made soggy by rain, Perez broke Gibson's game. The quick net action that had served her so well only the day before was gone, Danzig wrote, as her volleys "often went astray." Gibson's overhead smash, among the strongest weapons in her arsenal and one of which she was inordinately proud, all but disappeared. Danzig counted that seven of those were offline, too.[89] In the end, she lost, 6–1, 6–1. The score looked like one of her ATA routs, only this time she was the one who was routed. The reporter who covered the match for the AP took a cheap shot at her and at African Americans, writing that "[a] major disappointment turned up in Althea Gibson, first Negro player ever to compete in a grass court title tourney."[90]

Undoubtedly, disappointment did characterize Gibson's feelings and, according to some, her conduct after the match. The poor reaction to losing that Dr. Eaton had observed reappeared, along with the disregard for tennis etiquette that Rhoda Smith had addressed years earlier. Gibson did not shake Perez's hand after the match, according to an ATA member who was there. She also refused to sign autographs for children. Saying that she was "thirsty," Gibson walked away. She stood off to the side of the court and stared daggers at Perez. People nearby claimed to have heard her muttering to herself, "I could have beaten her. I could have won that match."[91] Addressing reporters, a hurt Gibson said that she still had hopes of playing at Forest Hills and getting more exposure to grass.[92] Otherwise, Gibson could only wait.

The next three weeks illuminated the duality of Gibson's life. As she waited for the USLTA to announce her admission into Forest Hills, the White national championship, she prepared to compete in the ATA Nationals, the Black event. Back at the Cosmopolitan, she beat a White opponent, Isabel Troccole, the women's City Parks champion, to win the New York State Open. Since it was her third straight victory in the tournament, she was given the trophy permanently instead of having to return it after a while so that it could be presented to the next year's winner. Then Gibson headed for Ohio, where she beat Jane Hudlin, 6–3, 6–0, to win the ATA's Midwestern Open in Columbus, another tournament that she had won before.[93] Each victory, dominant and decisive, proved that she needed a more challenging circuit on which to play.

—*—

When Gibson arrived at Wilberforce for the ATA Nationals, she was all business. Her attitude was present long before she easily won the title for the fourth straight year, defeating Nana Davis yet again. A reporter for the *Afro-American* approached Gibson shortly after she arrived on campus on the morning of Monday, August 21, the first day of tournament week, and asked her for a statement about her future. Conflicting reports were circulating in the media. The *Pittsburgh Courier* reported that an unnamed USLTA official confirmed after the Eastern Grass Court tournament that her entry form to Forest Hills would be accepted. Meanwhile, the *New York Times* wrote that while the association confirmed that it had received her paperwork, no one could say for sure what was going to happen.[94] Gibson told the reporter that she had not heard from the USLTA. Pressed for more details, including remarks about what it was like to play in the National Clay Court and the Eastern Grass Court championships, she said that she had "no comment" to make and cited fatigue: "I have just finished a long overnight drive. I'd rather not talk about the possibility of my playing at Forest Hills."[95]

Gibson's matter-of-fact response, which struck the reporter as "terse" and "non-committal," surely indicated her caution amid the uncertainty surrounding Forest Hills as well as the likelihood that she did not want to be in Ohio.[96] Being there was an obligation. She needed the sponsorship of the ATA, its influence and its leadership in negotiations, to get her into White tournaments and the ATA Nationals so that she could continue to be recognized as the Black national champion. The ATA circuit, though, was of little use for her as a competitive vehicle. Playing at Wilberforce would help her stay in shape, but neither its hard courts nor the players entered were going to make her sharper for Forest Hills.

On the afternoon of August 21, the tournament committee released the names of the fifty-two women selected to compete at Forest Hills. Gibson's name was among them. Addressing a band of reporters in New York, Lawrence A. Baker, the USLTA president, said nothing about Marble's essay or Palfrey's coaching. He omitted any reference to the past prejudice of his association or the precedent that Gibson's entry set. Instead, Baker explained the decision in a fashion as straight and as simple as a baseline: "Miss Gibson was accepted on her ability."[97]

Reflecting in 1957 on Baker's remarks, Gibson conveyed an understated reaction. Acceptance based upon ability, she said, "was all I had ever asked."[98] She was, however, more effusive as she spoke with a reporter after the decision became public: "From the day I began playing tennis, I've looked forward to getting in the Nationals. Getting an invitation to play in this event is about the biggest honor I've ever experienced on the court." Smiling, Gibson explained what Forest Hills meant to her and to every other American tennis player.

"You simply can't go any higher," she said. "Unless you win it, of course."
The statement was an acknowledgment, albeit unintentional, that the ATA
Nationals, the very tournament in which she was entered, was not the best.[99]

Gibson admitted that she was unsure how her game would fare at Forest
Hills. She promised that she would "be in there giving my best every minute
of the way."[100] Never, it seems, did she volunteer to make those efforts as a self-
appointed ambassador of Negroes.

———

Unlike either the USLTA or Gibson, the press, Black and White, did not hesitate to acknowledge the racial precedent and even found themselves grappling
with gender as part of the social milestone. To be sure, tennis was considered
a White sport, but sport itself remained a male bastion and proving ground.
Black men were the recognized and expected leaders in its integration. In covering Gibson's admission to Forest Hills, the press on both sides of the color
line confronted gender in sports integration while at the same time inadvertently revealing the factors that made it difficult for Black women to gain a
foothold in almost any realm considered exclusively male.

Shock that the first Black player at Forest Hills would be a woman
emanated from the front-page headlines of the two major White newspapers
in New York. "Title Tennis Admits First Negro, a Girl," blared the *Times* on its
front page. The comma was a tool of emphasis that made the two words that
came after it akin to a punch line.[101] The *Herald Tribune* was less blatant, but
even so, "New York Negro Girl Will Enter National Tennis Championship"
underscored that Gibson was an anomaly.[102] Both articles noted that she was
twenty-two years old and would play in the women's rather than the junior division, but they referred to her as a girl all the same, displaying the casual and
normalized infantilization to which women were routinely subjected.

Black newspapers took all manner of pride in Gibson's entry into Forest
Hills, politicizing it in a multitude of ways. The *Baltimore Afro-American's*
possessive embrace of her as "our top woman tennis champion" captured
the general feeling in Black America.[103] Other sentiments were strong, too.
Her achievement was to many a major advancement of class. Writing for the
Amsterdam News, Moneta Sleet spoke for many when he observed that the
"racial barriers" that had "been broken down in football, baseball, basketball,
and many other sports" were "beginning to crumble in one of the most staid
and aristocratic of competitive games—tennis."[104] A third common theme was
that Gibson's debut in the national tennis championship was a hopeful sign of
equal opportunity for Americans regardless of race. "It took a woman—and

more power to her—to erase the color line at historic Forest Hills, N.Y., the tennis capital of the world," wrote the editors of the *Norfolk Journal and Guide*. With Gibson's hard work rewarded, "tennis," they declared, "now joins the parade of democracy in sports."[105] Hovering over the editorial was the long-standing hope that democracy, once achieved in sports, would spread to every other aspect of American life.

Amid the pride and praise, the patriarchal bent of the Black press was still evident. The industry operated on the principle that a rising tide for Black men lifted the boats of all Black people. In other words, Black women were not thought to be in need of a wave of their own.[106] Plenty of articles described Gibson neutrally as "the first of her race" to play at Forest Hills, but some writers and news outlets felt the need to put a fine point on her accomplishment by marking it as distinctly female. Gibson was slated to be, said the *Pittsburgh Courier*, "the first Negro to participate in the National Women's Singles championship at exclusive Forest Hills," not just the entire tournament.[107] Even Sam Lacy, an unabashed Gibson fan at that time, pointed out in a celebratory profile in the *Baltimore Afro-American* that her debut would mark "the first time in history that a colored girl has been given a shot for a world championship in tennis."[108] The editors of the *Philadelphia Tribune* openly stated that the meaning of her admission to Forest Hills was limited. Thanks to Gibson, wrote the editors, "the door will be open from now on to other qualified women players of color."[109] The implication was clear: Gibson's success and historic first were of no use or meaning to Black men and boys.

———

Forest Hills was a home game for Gibson. Sure, neither she nor anyone who looked like her had ever played in the tournament before. Still, it was in New York—Queens, to be exact. And so on Monday, August 28, 1950, opening day of the seventy-fifth U.S. National Lawn Tennis Championships, she rose and took her first stretch of the morning in Harlem.

Staying with her own family was not an option—at least not a good one. Being one of seven people in five rooms had been challenging when she had to live there, especially with Daniel's volatility. Gibson needed to be in a serene setting to be at her best, so Rhoda Smith's brownstone at 415 West 154th Street was her base during the tournament.[110]

That extraordinary, long-anticipated day began ordinarily. Gibson had always been lean, but the months of practice, play, and stress had left her even thinner. Smith rose early and prepared a hearty breakfast of bacon, eggs, toast, and milk. She and Gibson had been together since Friday night, when they left Wilberforce together by train and came back to New York. As Smith cooked in the kitchen, Gibson gathered her belongings. Flannel was the tech fabric of the day, so into her "small kit bag" went "a pair of tailored white flannel shorts and a flannel shirt" (a collared shirt rather than a crewneck T-shirt), followed by a flurry of still more white—socks, tennis shoes, and a "knitted sweater" made for her by an ATA member.[111] Just three years earlier, Gibson had proudly sported cable-knit, V-neck sweaters like the top-tier male players in the ATA wore. Now she donned a loose cardigan that was socially acceptable for a young woman. The sweater told the story of Gibson's gender transformation as she, and Black tennis, moved across the color line.

The subway added to the mundaneness of the morning. Palfrey had been on to something by taking Gibson to Queens via the train for their practice session at the end of July. Gibson and Smith traveled there just that way, too. Emerging from the station at 71st Street and Continental, they walked three blocks to the main entrance of the West Side Tennis Club. Although Gibson's travel time to the club was "short," the journey there "had taken me a long time."[112]

The spell of ordinariness was broken once Gibson and Smith entered the club. The clubhouse was not a sanctuary for her as it was for the other players. Not because Gibson was not allowed to enter the space or use the ladies' dressing room—she was. The problem was that members of the press were there, too. "There were reporters and photographers all around, clamoring for interviews and pictures," she remembered. Smith managed the melee as best she could. Gibson recalled, "The whole thing awed me. All this attention, all these people wanting to talk to me and get me to say things, patting me on the back and telling me that they knew I could do it—it was hard for a girl who had never been through the mill before."[113]

The tournament committee had assigned Gibson to Court 14, dismissed by sportswriters as "a field court" and a practice patch "far out in the 'country.'"[114] Court 14 seated only three hundred people, far fewer than the actual number who craved a glimpse of the first Black player at Forest Hills. By one estimate, as many as a hundred and fifty of the five thousand people on the club's grounds were African Americans, easily a tournament record. A few minutes before 1:00 P.M., the start time for Gibson's match against Barbara Knapp of Birmingham, England, spectators left the stadium where the popular Jaroslav Drobny of Czechoslovakia was still playing, and descended on Court 14, searching for the few available seats. Those left standing pressed against the barbed wire fence. Photographers and cameramen added to the circus. Officials, in an unheard-of decision, allowed them to take pictures on the tennis court during the first two games. The lights and noise of flash bulbs disrupted the ambience as Gibson sought to take control early and establish her rhythm. Buddy Walker, who had given Gibson her first tennis rackets, was dismayed. She "was being treated badly," he thought, from the out-of-the-way side court to the surrounding frenzy. Just as the USLTA had not prepared for the scene, officials did not intervene once it was clear that there was a problem. Gibson played above the madness, but she thought about it, wondering why "officials didn't give me a little more protection."[115] Her status as an outsider undercut her usual assertiveness. Knapp was her official opponent on the court, but Gibson had dozens of unofficial adversaries on the periphery.

Not wanting to "make any complaints," Gibson continued to play, and in doing so further inequities were revealed. Knapp was surely daunted by the frenetic atmosphere, but her skills—and Gibson's dominance—inadvertently underscored the ludicrousness of the USLTA's opposition to Gibson in the preceding months. Knapp was powerless as Gibson moved quickly across the court, jumping from the service line to the net and unleashing her overhead smash at every opportunity. Laney thought Knapp was "not really a first-class player" and yet she had had no known trouble securing an invitation. She also had "much more tournament experience than" Gibson.[116] Winning 6–2, 6–2, Gibson gave Knapp a tournament experience she was unlikely to forget.[117] Gibson learned something, too. With every camera pop, flash of light, and body crushed against the fence, her status as a spectacle was undeniable and only grew, leaving her with the responsibility of dealing with distractions unknown to White players.

An emotional reunion awaited outside the court. Standing in her proper tennis outfit with her hair freshly straightened and neatly curled, Gibson faced her benefactors while looking like the kind of middle-class young lady they believed she could be. Buddy Walker and Fred Johnson, from the Cosmopolitan, were there. Francis and Baker brought the greetings of the ATA, while Edna Mae Robinson represented herself and Sugar Ray. Dr. Johnson was there, and so was Dr. Eaton, who had brought his movie camera. Neither man was given to either expansive gestures or displays of emotion, but Dr. Eaton showed signs that he might give in to his feelings. Living together as a foster family, they had seen each other a thousand times, but never on such a momentous day. Dr. Eaton could only look into Gibson's eyes and shake her hand to convey his pride in her accomplishment, and when he did, both looked as if they would cry.[118]

Alice Marble was there, too. Separating herself from the crowd of reporters, photographers, well-wishers, and gawkers, Marble introduced herself to Gibson. Trailed by the throng, veteran and newcomer exchanged congratulations and gratitude, and chatted amiably. Before they parted, Marble offered Gibson words of encouragement: "Have courage—remember that you're just like all the rest of us."[119]

———

Gibson spent the rest of the day trying to recover a sense of calm. She returned to the clubhouse, where she showered, dressed, and, with Baker, met with reporters. The ordeal, combined with the drama of the match, had left her "too excited to eat" lunch, even as USLTA officials, concerned about appearances as much as comfort, made sure she knew that she was "welcome" to have a meal there. All through the press session, Gibson dissembled. "I tried hard to be calm and poker-faced with the reporters," she wrote in her memoir, "but I was pretty emotional deep down inside."[120]

The questions that might have hit Gibson hardest were about her family. They were at such a remove from her public image that a reporter wrote in the spring that she was an orphan.[121] Neither Daniel nor Annie had come to any of her matches, whether for the ATA or the USLTA, including the events that she played in New York, New Jersey, and Connecticut. At the most important event in her career, Sam Lacy asked about her people. Gibson said nothing about Daniel. Instead, she explained that Annie "didn't want to watch [because her] nerves wouldn't let her."[122] Forest Hills was an hour away from Harlem by subway, but not a single member of her family was in the stands.

Gibson was leading a double life, at least as far as tennis and her family were concerned. Daniel and Annie, southern, boisterous, and humbly educated, were not part of her public life then and would not be for a long time. Gibson's tennis kin were the people she knew through the ATA, people like Baker, who stayed planted by her side during the question-and-answer session—all the better for representing Black tennis as respectable and getting it across the color line. Baker, in fact, had a ready answer for questions about the Gibsons: "They were a respectable but very poor family with no financial resources. But they were very respectable in every way."[123]

Gibson stayed at the club after the interviews—or, as she put it, "after the reporters had finished with me," suggesting a budding wariness of the press. She watched a few matches. Then, with thoughts of an early dinner and a few extra hours of sleep on her mind, she headed back to Harlem with Rhoda Smith, whom the *Amsterdam News* called her "mother-chaperone."[124]

———

Unlike Barbara Knapp, Louise Brough was no pushover. An Oklahoman who lived in Beverly Hills, California, Brough, twenty-seven, had won Forest Hills in 1947. She was also the reigning Wimbledon champion, having won it in July for the third year in a row. Al Laney expected Brough to beat Gibson in Forest Hills's second round. He had thought it ever since the draw was released. Cynically, Sam Lacy even wondered whether the draw was on the up-and-up. When Reginald Weir had debuted in the National Indoors two years earlier, Lacy recalled, he, too, had faced a little-known, easy opponent in the first round, only to meet—and get demolished by—a powerhouse, Bill Talbert, in the second. Lacy had no evidence, and tournament draws were supposed to be made at random with names literally drawn from a hat, but he openly wondered whether the USLTA deliberately matched Gibson against Brough to get her out of Forest Hills as soon as possible while still giving the public a feel-good story.[125]

Gibson nearly complied. The match began at 3:30 in the afternoon in the stadium court, but she played as if it were 3:30 in the morning. Visibly nervous, she lost the first set badly, 1–6, and was down 2–3 in the next. Shots that had come easily to her only the day before slid by her racket, landed in the net, or sailed offline. For all the world, it looked as if she was going to lose in straight sets.[126]

Suddenly, though, Gibson found her form. She won the second set 6–3. That was a victory of its own. Gone, it seemed, was a habit that Dr. Eaton had observed in the past—giving up after falling behind. When it mattered most, she charged back.[127]

While Gibson and Brough played, strange things were happening—things that were not supposed to happen during a tennis match, that surely had never happened in a Grand Slam, and that only happened because Gibson was a Black woman playing the match. Two thousand people could fit in the grandstand at the stadium court, but, just like the day before, the crowd exceeded the space's capacity as more and more people crammed their way inside. There was standing room only. Laney noticed that there were very few Blacks in the stadium and those who were there "were by no means the most vociferous in their cheering." Listening to the murmured conversations around him, Laney sensed a shift in the mostly White crowd. At the end of Gibson's woeful first set, people were hoping that she would not be "humiliated" out of the tournament. Then, when she mounted her comeback, she seemed to win over the gallery. There was, however, one clear exception. Her competence, composure, success, and mere presence were too much for a nameless, nondescript White man sitting in the gallery. Breaking etiquette, he made his displeasure known, demanding of Brough, "Knock her out of there! Knock her out of there!" Seated beside Dr. Johnson, Dr. Eaton heard the jeering White man. He also saw that Gibson drew perverse inspiration from the verbal attack. She was down 1–4 in the third set when the heckler cried out, but she soon caught fire. Relying on her serve, rushing to the net, and smashing one overhead after another, Gibson won the next three games in a row, tying the set. A counter-heckler, a young woman, yelled in favor of Gibson, "Give it to her now!"[128]

Brough refused to give in, but so did Gibson. Her decision-making was impeccable. Brough had been bothered by a shoulder injury all year, and just the day before a newcomer, Laura Lou Jahn, had pushed her to the limit in the second set before falling 11–9. The struggle led Laney to report in that morning's paper that Brough "now shows definite signs of declining."[129] Gibson read the papers and had a keen eye. Steadily wearing Brough down, she hit a torrent of smashes and lobs. Laney watched in amazement. The tennis match looked increasingly like pugilism, and Brough was decidedly on the ropes. He began to think that he was watching the best woman tennis player in the world and certainly the best to play at Forest Hills in many a year. He was talking about Gibson, not Brough.[130]

Gibson led 7–6 in the third set—one game away from defeating the reigning Wimbledon champion and advancing to the third round at Forest Hills—when the unimaginable happened. As she and Brough changed sides, a gust of wind rushed into the stadium. The sky turned black, interrupted only by a flash of lightning. A great, thunderous bang shot through the air. Rain began to descend in sheets. The spectators scurried for cover. It was almost biblical, and so the chair umpire hastily called the match. Like everyone else, Gibson and Brough sought shelter. The scene had gone from almost historic to certainly chaotic, a circumstance heightened by what came next. The top of the grandstand was adorned with American eagles carved out of concrete.[131] A bolt of lightning struck one of the eagles, splitting it and sending it plummeting to the ground, where it shattered. For a moment, it seemed that the match and the outcome—the Black underdog on the cusp of victory—had broken America.

Back at Rhoda Smith's apartment in Harlem, Gibson passed a rough night, thinking that only four points stood between her and victory. Smith gave her dubious encouragement: "Even if you lose tomorrow, honey, it won't make a particle of difference. You did yourself proud already." Years later, Gibson considered Smith's words well-meaning but wrong. She needed to hear more affirmations about what she had done well during the match and how she could repeat that approach to win the next day. Sleep did not come until 2:30. The match was to resume at noon. Gibson forced herself not to think about race, that she was "a Negro"—the only Negro—in the tournament. "I just didn't think about it," she replied to a reporter later.[132] Not thinking about race, she thought, was the way to win.

Wednesday, match day, was a debacle. Gibson lost the calmness, order, and routine that had characterized the previous days and even the weeks and months that came before. She read the morning newspapers' accounts of the match, ratcheting up her anxiety by seeing what the sportswriters thought. The accounts made her "a nervous wreck."[133] The daily newspapers in New York were White and each one described her repeatedly as a "Negro," making it impossible for her to escape race. Seeing Palfrey at the club, she asked for a practice session. Her walk to the match was delayed when a man and a woman, both Black, created a fracas. Misguided by a sense of racial loyalty, they stepped in front of Gibson to try to keep away the onslaught of photographers and reporters.[134] The disruption made her late. Tired and agitated, with her concentration broken, she was finished before she started.

Brough, meanwhile, was ready. Blending caution with attack, serving powerfully, attacking the net, and hitting forehand winners, she again looked like the Wimbledon champion that she was. Brough won the opening game, tying the match 7-all. Gibson helped. Out of sorts, she stopped playing in the freewheeling way that had brought her to the brink of victory. Tense, she double-faulted while on serve. When her shots were not bounding out, they were speeding into the net. In the end, Brough won the set 7–9. The whole thing was over in eleven minutes.[135]

5

Dis/Integration

I have no explanation of Althea's conduct nor do I know
what stress she may have been under.

—MAUREEN CONNOLLY, 1957

IN THE HOURS and days after Gibson lost to Louise Brough, she carried regrets and wondered what might have been. She was convinced that she would have won "if the rains hadn't come," a thought that was on the minds of many sportswriters and tennis fans, too.[1] Brough agreed, telling reporters, "The rain was probably the only thing that saved me" and that she was "lucky to win."[2] The statement was gracious and apt. Between the obligatory interviews with the press and the subway ride back to Harlem that afternoon, Gibson had a long time to think about what happened and why. "My court strategy was all wrong," she decided. Instead of keeping her mind in the present, she had been preoccupied with thoughts of "those last four points," the ones that would have led to victory. Caution, too, played a major role in the defeat. "I should have gone on the offensive" on Wednesday, she said. That approach, not "play[ing] it careful," had brought her within a game of winning on Tuesday.[3]

Gibson had lost the match, but she maintained her ability to look ahead with perspective and resilience. "I'll be back again next year," she told the *Courier*. To make it back, she had to be honest about her weaknesses. They were not insignificant, she conceded. To beat Brough, "a darned good player," required more experience playing on grass and learning the strokes suited for the surface, becoming "more confident [in] my game," and developing a better backhand.[4]

Gibson got to work right away. Still the visual learner that Fred Johnson had recognized nine years earlier, she returned to the West Side Tennis Club in the days after her loss to Brough to study the games of other players. Instead of copying their exact moves, she began to think about ways to make the actions her own. The observational tutorials ended on September 2, when she and Torsten Johansson of Sweden lost in the mixed doubles quarterfinals, 6–3, 6–1, to Patricia Canning Todd and John Bromwich. Racial representation still did not motivate Gibson, though she appreciated the interest that others— no matter their color—had taken in her brief time in the tournament: "I just hope I justified the confidence all the folks across the country had in me." Gibson left Forest Hills disappointed but grateful. "It was a privilege to play here with the world's greatest tennis players," she said. The chance to "watch top-seeded men and women whose names I read about in the papers all the time" had given her "quite an education."[5]

Weeks later, Gibson was back in Tallahassee to resume her formal educa- tion. An appendectomy, the *Tallahassee Democrat* reported, delayed her re- turn. When she arrived at the train station on September 26, she received the surprise of "a very nice reception." President Gore, the marching band, and the FAMC student body were there to greet her, duplicating the celebration that had followed her return from the National Indoors in March. Gibson found the display "very inspiring." It was the campus community's way of again expressing its view that she was representing Black America through her tennis, even as she herself did not agree.[6]

FAMC was not the only Black institution that felt that way about Gibson. The drama at Forest Hills amplified her status as a national race heroine. As she settled into her sophomore year, Black newspapers published outpourings of celebration of her. Hosannas were not limited to the sports section, where coverage of Gibson sometimes took up as much as half a page. News, society, and editorial pages hailed her, too. Writers praised her as "courageous" for "carrying the burden of race on her shoulders."[7] She did so with aplomb, many said. Gibson's poise as a player buttressed arguments that she had broken the class barrier that interlaced with racial stereotypes to keep African Americans out of Forest Hills. Sam Lacy wrote that she "pioneer[ed] for her race in the stodgy atmosphere that belongs to the prim West Side Tennis Club."[8] The editors of the *Chicago Defender* agreed, crediting Gibson with "[striking] a blow for democracy . . . that is still echoing in the snooty precincts of country clubs and exclusive sports associations throughout the land."[9]

Gibson spent the fall semester of her sophomore year basking in her celeb- rity. She was a regular attendee at FAMC football games. Under Jake Gaither's leadership, the squad was in the midst of an impressive fifteen-year run of 121 wins against a mere 20 losses, with thirteen conference championships and four national titles. Football games were major social events where alumni and friends of the opposing colleges networked, socialized, and jockeyed for bragging rights. Gibson's growing fame made her a desired attendee whom others wanted to meet. Virtually anyone who knew anything about her knew that she was enrolled at FAMC. Most of the profiles and articles in the press mentioned it. That fall, two college presidents made special efforts to get Gibson to games. The president of Southern University in Shreveport, Louisiana, requested her presence at his school's meet with the Rattlers in Tallahassee, and President Gore gave her permission to travel to Miami to see the Rattlers compete in the most important game of the year, the Orange Blossom Classic. Gibson, an athlete and sports fan who liked being the center of attention, found the football atmosphere "thrilling."[10]

The fall brought more distinctions that showed just how esteemed Gibson had become in Black America. The November issue of *Ebony*, the country's premier Black news source, published a glowing profile on her. *Ebony* was only five years old, but with color photography, coverage of the public and private lives of Black entertainers, politicians, athletes, and artists, and an emphasis on social progress rather than problems, it had quickly distinguished itself in the Black media industry. The "*Ebony* philosophy," according to its publisher, John H. Johnson, was to focus on "men and women who were building the campfires of tomorrow" for Black America.[11] "Althea Gibson: Tomboyish Coed Startles Tennis World" presented her as a tennis player who belonged in the Black campfire circle. The six-page spread contended that Gibson was wholly accepted in elite amateur tennis regardless of being Black. She was the only Black person featured in any of the pictures, and only Whites, including Mary Hardwick and Sarah Palfrey, who penned a short essay about their practice session at Forest Hills in July, were quoted. "She makes friends readily and has had no trouble with spectators or players while competing in tournaments at exclusive clubs," one picture caption stated, plainly ignoring the White heckler who had disquieted her match with Brough and the entire saga that preceded the tournament. Just as importantly, *Ebony* had no qualms with Gibson's presentation of gender; her youth, emphasized with each reference to her as a "young lady," made her queerness acceptable, and she was said to exude "charm and cooperation," making her a "great favorite with gallery, officials and other players." If anyone missed the magazine's acceptance of her queerness in the title, the clues were clear in the profile, where the uncredited reporter said that Gibson "is proving that Negro women today deserve a place in the sports spotlight right alongside Jackie Robinson and Joe Louis," and its accompanying images, where action shots showed her competing in shorts. She was, moreover, quoted as saying, "At school I play against men and boys all the time. My timing is off against the soft returns of some of these women."[12]

Gibson returned to New York in November to receive the annual Sports Achievement Award given by the Harlem YMCA. This was a major honor personally and socially for someone who so recently had been a kid at the Y, playing basketball and passing the time.[13] Banquet attendees were well-heeled members of the "Century Club," those who had raised $100 or more during fund drives for the Y throughout the year. Jackie Robinson, who reportedly raised $9,000 and donated his weekly salary as an ambassador back to the organization, presented her with the award. Alice Marble was a guest speaker, and Edith Sampson, the first Black delegate to the United Nations, to whom Gibson had been compared as a symbol of democracy at work, was the keynote speaker. That Gibson was "thrilled" about the award was clear to anyone who saw her at the banquet on November 29.[14] She wore a dark skirted suit with shoulder pads worthy of Joan Crawford and had a giant corsage pinned to her jacket. Gibson smiled broadly as she posed for pictures with Robinson, Marble, and Sampson. No longer roaming the streets of Harlem wearing denim trousers with her hair slicked back, Gibson looked like the sophisticated college sophomore and young lady that so many people wanted their Black sportswoman integrationist and race heroine to be.[15]

———

The fall of 1950 brought another unexpected development: Gibson cut back on her practice time. FAMC, she decided, did not give her "the best conditions possible" to work on her game.[16] An airplane hangar had served as the college gymnasium since 1948, and even after its refurbishment in 1952 it would still lack showers. She needed more experience playing on grass courts, which FAMC lacked; the college's tennis courts were made of clay. Even with these deficiencies, FAMC, along with South Carolina State and Tuskegee, was one of the "strongholds" of tennis for African Americans.[17]

Gibson was not the only person to question FAMC's fitness as her tennis training base. In October, the *Amsterdam News* criticized her enrollment there. Gibson, who came back to New York to spend Christmas 1950 with her family, including her brother, who was on leave from the army, may have seen the piece. Sportswriter Joe Bostic, who had been wowed by her basketball skills years earlier, thought she should leave FAMC and be "put . . . in a school where she'd rub elbows with and probably engage top flight tennis talent." Gibson "need[ed] that contact to develop her marvelous potentialities, assuming she intends to become a serious challenger for the national tennis crown." Bostic believed that Gibson "could win it too, all things being equal."[18]

But all things were not equal. The state of Florida was a breeding ground for tennis talent—and a hotbed of segregation. Its predominantly White public and private colleges, including Rollins College and the University of Miami, claimed stars such as Dorothy Bundy, Pauline Betz, Jack Kramer, and Doris Hart as alumni. These institutions, like most of the others in the South, would also fail to admit Black students—including athletes and certainly not with scholarship offers—until the 1960s. She was advancing in tennis across the color line, but Jim Crow determined where she could get an education.[19]

Gibson was anxious, struggling, searching, and questioning what to do with her life and tennis career. No single decision more fully summed up how adrift she was than her decision to join the Episcopal Church, where she sought spiritual solace for her internal conflicts. It was a turn away from the Baptist faith of her mother. Gibson's conversion was rooted in a desire to develop a deeper understanding of herself beyond that of athlete. "I also have other attributes that I wish to explore and perfect with God's help," she told Dr. Eaton.[20] She did not name what those traits were, but it was clear that she was looking for a satisfaction in life that was impossible to find in tennis, school, and her celebrity status. She soon developed the habit of praying before the start of her tennis matches.[21]

Gibson resolved that playing in more tournaments in 1951 was the solution to her problem. The events would give her more experience against top-tier players, opportunities to examine their games, and access to the best facilities. Tournament officials were pleased to have her participation. Surely some were well-meaning, but money, too, could not have been far from their minds. The spectacle of the much-talked-about Negro tennis sensation sold tickets. By January, Gibson had been accepted into three tournaments for the first three months of the year.[22] Competitive, impatient, and craving independence, she may or may not have realized that the time away from campus would come at great risk and cost.

Gibson started her campaign in February in Montego Bay, Jamaica, for the Caribbean Championship and was a sensation on the island even before the tournament, her first international one, began. The majority-Black islanders longed to see her. Locals crowded into the bleachers that surrounded the grass courts of the Fairfield Country Club to watch her win, 6–2, 6–3, in an exhibition match against the Jamaican champion, Ivy Cover Ramsey. If it was not the first match played abroad between two Black tennis players, as the Jamaican and American press reported, it was rare and called to mind the trip to Nassau, Bahamas, that Fred Johnson, Rhoda Smith, and other members of the ATA had made in 1936. Local newspapers plastered Gibson's picture and headlines about her across their front pages. Denizens honored her with cocktail parties, dances, and invitations to area nightclubs, trailed her for autographs, and set attendance records on title day, when she beat Betty Rosenquest 5–7, 6–4, 6–4. The victory was a sure sign of progress, as Rosenquest had defeated her just two years earlier in the Eastern Indoors.[23]

Two days after the Caribbean Championship ended, Gibson flew to New York. She was supposed to be there for business, but she found time for pleasure. She teamed with Bill Talbert in a one-set mixed doubles exhibition against Nancy Chaffee and Don McNeil as part of a benefit program for the American National Theater and Academy (ANTA). Jackie Robinson, the surprise guest for the three thousand spectators, showed off his tennis skills against some of the biggest names in the game, including Sarah Palfrey. Dozens of other popular sports and entertainment figures participated in the star-studded affair. Model Jinx Falkenberg, comedian Milton Berle, television producer Ralph Edwards, and gossip columnist Igor Cassini, better known as Cholly Knickerbocker, wowed the crowd. Alice Marble was on hand, too.[24] Gibson was in the thick of the celebrity culture, which she loved.

Teddy Tinling, the preeminent designer of women's fashions in tennis, was among those Gibson met. Tinling was famous—some would say infamous—for designing the lace-trimmed panties and shortened skirt that Gussie Moran had worn at Wimbledon in 1949. The design was seen as so beyond the pale that Tinling lost his position as the tournament's master of ceremonies and was barred from Wimbledon for more than thirty years. Watching Gibson in New York, Tinling decided that he wanted to add her to his gallery. The complexity of her physicality fascinated him. In racially insensitive language, Tinling wrote of her body and movements in 1963: "Althea had a rangy, primitive grace with liquid yet angular movements . . . although masculine in face and figure, her feminine mannerisms and fluid style added an extra dimension to her appearance." He was struck by Gibson's hairstyle at the National Indoors. She wore "a sophisticated, up-swept hair-do, which added greatly to her presence." Introduced by a friend, Tinling excitedly told Gibson of his interest in designing for her. Gibson's response appalled him: "Don't you mind that I'm coloured?" Tinling was offended. He assumed that she was accusing him of being prejudiced. In time, he came to understand her question as "a pathetic commentary on her unhappy experiences." Gibson's question was also an astute observation of the fashion industries, whether American or European, haute couture or mass-produced: Black models, even mannequins, were a rarity because Madison Avenue did not imagine that White consumers wanted to emulate anyone who was Black. Getting over his shock, Tinling reassured Gibson: "You won't find us so sensitive in Britain." Though that proved naive, Tinling surmised that she appreciated his response, and they stayed in touch.[25]

Gibson won her first match in the National Indoors at the Seventh Regiment Armory without dropping a set, but she could not keep up the momentum. She needed two hours to defeat Midge Buck, whom she had beaten the year before. Four times, Buck had her within a point of defeat in the third set. Relying on her lob and overhead smash, Gibson dug out the match 7–5, 3–6, 8–6, but, as Allison Danzig reported, it was "a harrowing experience."[26] Things were no better the next day. Hoping to see an exciting match and siding with Gibson, the sizeable gallery was disappointed when she lost in the quarterfinals 6–1, 6–3 to Nancy Chaffee, who went on to win the tournament for the second straight year. The matches with Buck and Chaffee revealed a pattern in Gibson's troubles—a lack of confidence, unforced errors often brought on by hitting the ball hard but into the net, and losing games after she had mounted a lead.[27]

None of this was what tennis experts in the mainstream media expected. Their anticipation was premature, but journalists had thought that Gibson would be better six months after her near defeat of Brough. "It was believed that Miss Gibson, with another year's experience, would offer stiffer competition," *American Lawn Tennis* reported after she lost to Chaffee.[28] Al Laney still contended that she was "a most promising player" and had "made progress." Her serve, volleys, and firm ground strokes were among the best in the women's game. Still, Laney was forthright in his criticism. Gibson, a half-year removed from defeating a Wimbledon champion, "still retains her worst faults."[29]

The Good Neighbor Tournament, Gibson's last event of the spring semester, gave her a shot at redemption. It was a new tournament, first organized in 1949 with a title that alluded to the Roosevelt administration's policy toward Latin America. Staged at Miami Beach, the Good Neighbor was a domestic stop on the so-called Sunshine Circuit, a series of tournaments played between Florida, South America, and the Caribbean in the late winter and early spring that were low-key, cushy starts to the new tennis season. Instead of beginning their year playing indoors in one of New York's massive armories, players could compete comfortably for a week in a major resort center.[30]

Before traveling to Miami, Gibson participated in a match on the FAMC campus orchestrated to inspire African Americans. She joined

Edward Whitsey, a fellow member of the tennis team, in an exhibition for All-American News. The company produced newsreels focused on African Americans and billed its footage as showing "our people's contributions to America and freedom." Photographer J. R. Zimmerman filmed Gibson and Whitsey in action, and took pictures of her with Jake Gaither, tennis coach Walter Austin, and Pete Griffin, the track coach. The footage was to be distributed to Black film audiences across the country, allowing them to see Gibson, the rare and rising Black tennis star who was, the media hailed, making gains across the color line.[31]

The exclusivity of Miami Beach made Gibson's entry in the Good Neighbor a landmark moment for her chroniclers in the African American press. She was the first Black player to enter a tennis tournament organized by Whites in the South, Black newspapers reported excitedly. Black journalists were just as interested in the integrationist aspect of Gibson's accommodations. Days before she arrived, the *Courier* announced that she "will be a guest at a most fashionable Miami Beach hotel."[32] Tournament organizers had arranged for her to stay at the Admiral, a four-story white stucco hotel that billed itself as "thoroughly modern" and "located in the heart of Miami Beach."[33] Despite assertions that it was in the South but not of it—"hardly more than a geographical associate" of the region, according to noted White sportswriter Furman Bisher—Miami Beach was a bulwark of Jim Crow.[34] Leisure on Miami Beach was off-limits to Blacks, who could not reside as guests in the hotels and were required to carry work permits to justify their presence. The restriction even applied to crossover entertainers such as Ella Fitzgerald, Harry Belafonte, Louis Armstrong, Sammy Davis Jr., and Nat "King" Cole. With the Admiral, Miami Beach, and the Good Neighbor, Gibson's tennis skills and fame had given her entrée to yet another set of exclusive and glamorous places where no other African American had gone before.[35]

Paving the way proved a trying experience. The travails started with the Admiral. Gibson spent her first night in one of its hundred rooms. The next day, she discreetly asked to be moved to the Mary Elizabeth, the Black-owned and -operated hotel in mainland Miami that was popular with Black entertainers. "I was lonesome at the Admiral, all by myself," Gibson explained in her autobiography. "I'm an authority on what it feels like to be the only Negro in all-white surroundings, and I can assure you that it can be very lonely." She "appreciated the gesture" of being accommodated at the Admiral and "what it meant" in terms of racial progress and hospitality, but it was not enough to make her stay.[36]

Gibson was just as isolated once the tournament at Flamingo Park began. She was the only Black player among the 120 people entered. Covering the tournament for the *Afro-American*, Sam Lacy saw only progress, from the Black spectators who came to the tennis courts and sat amiably with Whites to Gibson's interactions with the other players and tournament staff: "The players laughed with Althea, admired her hair-do, enthused over her strokes, and even asked for advice."[37] Gibson's experience, though, did not fit Lacy's halcyon narrative of racial unity in sports integration. "It was quite an experience," she later wrote of playing in the Good Neighbor. "I felt as though I were on display, being studied through a microscope, every minute."[38] The attention to her hair and the requests for advice might have been microaggressions directed at the lone Black player. Under the circumstances, the Mary Elizabeth was a retreat. By staying there, Gibson put a physical and, at least partially, psychological barrier between herself and the other players. Dissembling, she posed for photographs with them and kept her feelings about the hostilities to herself.[39]

Gibson did not socialize with the other players. The tournament director, Eddie Herr, had seen to that. He beamed with pleasure on the night in early March when he announced to members of the tennis committee over dinner that she had accepted the invitation to enter the tournament. A native of Atlantic City who owned a successful dry-cleaning business in Miami, Herr was a tennis enthusiast with integrationist leanings and a streak of realism. He told no one, certainly not the press, when a woman from Palm Beach saw the draw and, upon realizing that she would have to face Gibson, withdrew. Herr kept the matter so quiet that Gibson herself knew nothing about it until 1958. (When a young White reporter learned of the story in that year and told Gibson, she simply smiled and offered no comment.) Herr also secured the help of a key member of Miami's Black community, Dr. I. P. Davis, a well-connected dentist, who was chosen to lead a reception committee specifically created for Gibson's visit. Players and others partied nightly at hotels in Miami Beach. On at least one night a local socialite, Roy S. Evans, entertained them on his yacht in Biscayne Bay. Gibson, sequestered on the mainland, seems not to have participated in any of this. Davis took her to City Hall, where she, *Pittsburgh Courier* writer Billy Rowe, and Sugar Ray Robinson, who was in the city for his fight at Miami Stadium with Holley Mims, met the mayor, William Wolfarth. Any socializing she did was with the African Americans to whom Davis and his fellow committee members introduced Gibson, Sugar Ray, and a female friend of the Eatons, Leonora, who met her in the city. At the end of the tournament, the Negro Jaycees and the Negro Junior Chamber of Commerce, respectively, honored Gibson as the outstanding athlete of 1950 and the outstanding woman athlete of the year. Black Miami went all out for Gibson, showing her what her crossing of the color line at Forest Hills and in their city meant to them.[40]

Not all of Gibson's interactions with Whites, some of whom may or may not have had antics on their mind, could be limited and managed. She experienced either a terrible faux pas on the part of tournament staff or a deliberate attempt at sabotage soon after she reached Miami Beach. She arrived four days before the tournament began and brought her tennis rackets to the pro shop for restringing. The staffers took six days to do the job, leaving Gibson to practice and play the first two days with rackets borrowed from fellow competitor Gladys Heldman. Lacy told the story as a shining example of sharing, one in which Gibson was "shown every courtesy to be found in the code of sports and sportsmanship" and Heldman was "a new-found friend," but the staffers' lollygagging could have thwarted her.[41]

Instead, she won. After Montego Bay, Gibson still had the upper hand on Rosenquest, whom she beat 6–4, 6–2 before a crowd of a thousand. Lacy later reported that segregated seating was not enforced and that spectators ignored the color line, but the "colored section" sign was still up, and the *Miami Daily News* announced in its own section devoted specifically to "news about the Miami Negro community" that 350 seats were "allocated each day for those that wish to see Miss Gibson in action," an apparent euphemism for the "colored section" at Flamingo Park.[42] Calm and unrelenting, Gibson played above seats and signs and segregation. She placed her serve exactly where she wanted it to go, and her groundstrokes were so deep that Rosenquest was held back at the baseline, unable to mount a charge at the net. Rosenquest was gracious about her latest loss to Gibson, telling Lacy, "Of course there's never anything pleasant in being defeated but I can think of no one to whom I'd rather lose than Althea. She has rare skill and an uncanny ability to make the most of your mistakes. And she's a fine person as well. There's no disgrace in being beaten by a real artist."[43] After the singles final, Gibson teamed with Tony Vincent, a player from Coral Gables, to win the mixed doubles title, 6–2, 6–1, over Elaine Lewicki, a junior at Rollins College, and Orlando Garrido of Cuba. She came close to a clean sweep of the Good Neighbor's titles, but she and Suzanne Herr, daughter of the tournament director, lost to Rosenquest and Rhonda Hopkins in the women's doubles final. Gibson's record was even more impressive because she played all three finals on the same day.[44]

Before the Good Neighbor ended, Gibson had a chance meeting with someone who suggested they could give her game the boost she so desperately wanted. E. John "Slim" Harbett was among the most renowned teachers in tennis. He taught Doris Hart and Dick Savitt, both of whom finished their careers as champions of Wimbledon and Forest Hills, as well as popular winners Gardnar Mulloy and Gussie Moran. Nothing was certain, but Gibson excitedly wrote to Dr. Eaton to tell him that "if plans and finance comes through I will go to Miami and take pro. lessons under" Harbett.[45]

Gibson left Miami with more than her second victory in three months and shiny new trophies. She headed back to Tallahassee with a bold and risky idea.

Gibson was contemplating dropping out of college. Likely influenced by someone she encountered during the winter and early spring, she had a vague notion of leaving FAMC and moving to France, the romanticized mecca for Black expatriates. She thought that she could play tennis there.[46]

FAMC was a fertile place for Gibson in some ways. Her athleticism and growing celebrity as a Black sportswoman playing across the color line continued to make her popular on campus. The FAMC chapter of Omega Psi Phi fraternity awarded her its annual achievement plaque that year, and she sat in the highest seat on the sports float, "Fitness Through Athletics," at the homecoming parade. She earned varsity letters in three sports—tennis, basketball, and golf.[47] Yet none of this changed her feeling that FAMC could not give her what she increasingly wanted: independence, including money.

Money was the carrot that was just out of reach for Gibson. She was twenty-four, living in a college dorm, and managing the modest stipend that FAMC gave her for working in the P.E. department. Tennis brought her into close contact with moneyed people, but she was not one of them and could not be if she remained an amateur.

The rules of amateurism barred all players from playing for pay. Amateur athletes played for honor and the love of the game. Profits were for professionals. If Gibson were paid to play and were caught, she risked losing her amateur status and, with it, the ability to play on the tennis circuit, including the four coveted majors. The USLTA allowed players to receive a daily expense allowance during tournaments and coverage for their travel. Clubs also gave additional money for "incidentals," with those amounts often inflated and serving as under-the-table payments to players whom officials believed would attract more spectators. Bobby Riggs admitted after turning professional that during his own amateur career he made as much as $250 per tournament under the table, on top of all expenses paid, and he said that he made even more after he won at Wimbledon and Forest Hills in 1939.

Officials opposed the system publicly but did little or nothing to stop it be-hind the scenes. The payments were a widely known practice, leading critics to lambast amateurism as "shamateurism."[48]

Sexism undergirded the system. Perceived to be more exciting to watch than women and thus driving the momentum of ticket sales, men received most, if not all, of the under-the-table payments. The notion that men were "breadwinners" for their families and needed money more than women was pervasive, too. Jack Kramer received payments years before he won Wimbledon and Forest Hills in 1947. That same year, Ellsworth Davenport, a Forest Hills referee and a member of several USLTA committees, confronted Kramer about a "rumor" that he was "taking money under the table." Kramer admitted that the rumor was a fact. "I explained that I was a man of twenty-six, that I had a wife and a baby, that I had no family money behind me, no money in the bank. I told him that I took what I could, merely to be able to play the game." Davenport did not flinch. Instead, he told Kramer "that if he were in my shoes, he would do exactly what I was doing."[49]

Race made Gibson attractive to tennis organizers. Hundreds, and at Forest Hills thousands, of people came to her matches, curious to see the Black tennis phenomenon. Everyone—the tennis associations, clubs, even area businesses—profited. Everyone, that is, except Gibson.

Meanwhile, promoters wooed, and distracted, her. Jake Gaither saw the results up close as sports producers of questionable legitimacy and integrity reached out to Gibson with offers. "I remember many afternoons when she would come into my office and argue about quitting school," Gaither told *Ebony* in 1960. Frustrated that Gaither would not hear of it, "she'd wind up running out into the hall and slamming the door." Soon enough, Gibson would return, contrite and worried that "Pop," as she called the coach, might be "mad with" her. He never was. Echoing Edna Mae Robinson's sentiments from when Gibson was a teen in Harlem, Gaither empathized with her new plight in Tallahassee. He concluded that "she needed understanding."[50] Promoters were not the only people who saw dollar signs when they looked at Gibson. *Pittsburgh Courier* sportswriter Wendell Smith had, too. Smith titled their interview in Chicago in 1950 "Thar's Gold in Them Thar Forest Hills" and explained to readers, "The Nationals are the world series of tennis. The player who finally comes through on top can turn professional and get rich. There's a pot of gold at the end of the Forest Hills rainbow and anyone with enough coordination to bounce a tennis ball knows it."[51]

Gender limited the likelihood that Gibson would have a long and lucra-tive career in professional tennis. Since the 1920s, few American and English women—Mary K. Browne, Ermyntrude Harvey, Phoebe Holcroft Watson, Ethel Burkhardt, Jane Sharp, Alice Marble, Mary Hardwick, Sarah Palfrey, Pauline Betz, and Gussie Moran—had toured as professionals, and their success had been short-lived, curtailed by attitudes that both amateur tennis and the men's game were "the real thing" as well as by a paucity of women to play.[52]

Being a woman, moreover, made Gibson more likely to be severely penalized by the USLTA if she were caught doing anything close to skirting the rules. Female players could not switch from amateur to professional and back again; while some men had been permitted to do so, women seemingly could not, as Palfrey and Moran discovered during the 1950s. Patricia Canning Todd, winner of the 1947 French International Tournament, perceived that the major domos of the USLTA were petty and inconsistent in meting out punishments. In an interview published in *Sport* magazine in April 1951, Todd accused the association of assigning rankings based on favoritism and controlling opportunities for international travel. Few players spoke up about such offenses, she said, because they feared further retribution and damage to their careers. Bill Tilden, widely regarded as the greatest male tennis player in history, charged that the USLTA's "manner of enforcing the amateur rule" was unfair: "It seems as if personal likes or dislikes, rather than policy, determine how the rule is interpreted."[53] Being a Black woman further increased the likelihood of scrutiny and censure. The association was run by wealthy White men, and as the events of the previous summer had shown, plenty of people did not want Gibson anywhere near their tournaments.

Gibson was six hundred miles away from Wilmington, and yet the eyes of the city still watched her as closely as they did when she lived there. Dr. Eaton learned about her thoughts of quitting college when a contact, Mr. Rogers, likely the principal at Williston High, visited him at home and told him about it. Rogers had heard about her desire from none other than George Gore, FAMC's president. A rumor of Gibson's plan had reached the Eatons once before, but Rogers's utterance of it added veracity and urgency. Dr. Eaton also knew from Dr. Johnson that Gibson was "already anticipating a pro offer," even though she had only played on the amateur circuit for two years.[54] Dr. Johnson was opposed to Gibson leaving school, too. "I do not believe she is the type who can stay out of school at irregular intervals and still have enough desire to finish after being exposed to too much luxurious tournament tennis."[55]

Dr. Eaton warned Gibson not to be careless in her talk or her actions. Otherwise, she risked losing her amateur status and inflaming bad feelings with her peers. He suspected that "your success so far has caused undoubtedly some resent[ment] among White women players." Dr. Eaton advised that she "consult with the USLTA" if she found herself "in doubt about anything." The USLTA was, he thought, "going all out helping you up the ladder of Tennis Fame."[56]

Race influenced Dr. Eaton's advice, too. He understood Gibson's desire to be paid for her skills. "It is a natural instinct for an individual to want to make some money and become to a certain degree financially independent," he wrote. Yet he also expected her to put those individual interests aside for the supposed good of the group: "You should forgo any personal ambitions that you may have because of what you can do for the Negro Tennis players who are to follow you in years to come. It is true that it may mean a certain amount of personal sacrifice on your part in the next few years." Her benefactors, he emphasized, would be "disappointed" if she did "anything to impede your progress as our top amateur tennis player." Gibson could "commercialize on your success" after graduating from college and "develop[ing] your game to a higher peak."[57]

Gibson pulled back from the brink, but not before news of her thoughts of dropping out of college reached the Black papers in April 1951. Sourced by unidentified "friends" of Gibson, the Associated Negro Press reported that she thought coursework interfered with her ability to practice, play, and improve her game. By May, the story had changed. Gibson released a statement that denied the reports. "I do not plan to withdraw from Florida A&M college," the statement said. "My relation here is most pleasant. The academic requirements of me are the same as for other students. I want it that way."[58]

Gibson's statement stopped the story cold, but several hard truths remained. Being a Black woman on the White tennis circuit gave Gibson social capital but not money or independence. And no one asked White tennis players to make personal sacrifices in their careers for the supposed good of their race. Nevertheless, she was getting ahead of herself, allowing expectations and desires to outpace likelihoods, reality, and common sense. "I sincerely hope," Dr. Eaton exhorted, "that your crown of success does not grow too heavy for you to wear."[59] He also worried for her future. "I would admonish you . . . to be very skeptical in going against the advice and decisions of those whom you must know are personally interested in you and your welfare."[60] It was advice that Gibson needed.

———

As Gibson pondered her future at FAMC, she looked ahead to traveling abroad. The All England Club had invited her to compete at Wimbledon, the oldest and, to many, the most prestigious tennis tournament in the world. Mary Hardwick, who had made the dramatic come-from-behind win against Gibson at Tuskegee four years earlier, had envisioned Gibson playing in the namesake tournament of her hometown, Wimbledon Village, even before Forest Hills accepted her, and less than a year later, the historic development happened: Gibson was slated to become only the third known Black player to play at Wimbledon, following B. M. Clark of Jamaica in 1924 and David Samaii of South Africa in 1949, and the first Black American entrant in its history.[61]

The Black press saluted the news of Gibson's Wimbledon invitation. Her entry in the tournament was yet another symbol of racial progress in sports and in society. The class implications thrilled Sam Lacy. Gibson, a product of "Harlem's crowded tenement district," was playing a sport favored by "heiresses-to-be" and "blue-bloods," he wrote, astonished that the king and queen of England might even see her play.[62] Lacy boldly posited that Gibson's debut at Wimbledon would be "one of the greatest advances our race has made in the history of athletics," outshining the achievements of Jackie Robinson, Joe Louis, and Jesse Owens as "the top accomplishment of any tan athlete in history." Robinson, Louis, and Owens had made their names in sports associated with the working classes, but Gibson played a sport that was neither "highly commercial" nor "for the crowd from the other side of the tracks."[63]

Others remarked upon the transnational significance of Gibson's debut at Wimbledon. "In a sense," said the *Pittsburgh Courier*, "Wimbledon will be providing a world-setting where Miss Gibson's presence will be indicating to players and spectators from all over the world that the American Negro is coming on fast, that he has arrived." The editors saw no conflict in applying male pronouns to the entire race, underscoring the socially accepted invisibility of Black women. "Her presence and play will bring credit and prestige to the American Negro people."[64] Gibson's invitation to Wimbledon meant that a Black American had leapt over one of the highest social barriers not only in sports but in the world to enter a bastion where sophistication mattered.

Yet not every Black sportswriter was pleased that Gibson was set to break the color barrier at yet another tournament. Marion E. Jackson, the sports editor for the *Atlanta Daily World*, was puzzled by her singular status in elite amateur tennis. "Miss Althea Gibson's rise to eminence in the tennis world presents us with a first-rate enigma," he wrote after her historic entry and triumph at the Good Neighbor Tournament. "It is why there is no Negro male counterpart for her success on the national amateur tennis scene."[65] With Wimbledon in sight for Gibson, Jackson revived his tune. He accused the

ATA of giving Black male tennis players "the sheer brush-off" as the association prioritized Gibson, he said, rather than fighting for its men. Jackson demanded that the ATA "move . . . for the full inclusion of all Negro sexes in USLTA [competition] . . . at once."[66]

———

The Wimbledon milestone quickly became a source of strain revealing once again that Gibson's racial singularity made her vulnerable to exploitation. FAMC administrators, while proud of her latest honor, were left to balance her stardom—and the latest unprecedented opportunity that came her way—with her membership in the student body, and had to withstand pressure from outside, influential forces whose commitment to her long-term well-being was unclear. Without the knowledge of either Dr. Eaton or Dr. Johnson, Bertram Baker, the executive secretary of the ATA, wrote to Jake Gaither to outline a plan through which Gibson would end the spring semester early so that she could train for up to three weeks with Jean Hoxie, a noted tennis instructor based in Hamtramck, Michigan, a suburb of Detroit. Hollis Dann of the USLTA recommended that Gibson work with Hoxie to get ready for Wimbledon. Baker thought Gibson could then travel to Europe and spend the entire summer playing tournaments there in preparation for the 1952 season.[67]

Baker was also on the lookout for money. Tennis was not cheap, and traveling to Europe to play tennis was even more expensive. Slazenger, a British sporting goods firm, stepped up as a sponsor. A company representative arranged for a custom-made set of rackets to be waiting for Gibson when she arrived in London and recommended the tournaments that she should play to best prepare for Wimbledon, "her main target," and to "get the most publicity."[68] Baker sought still more funds from FAMC. He asked Gaither how much money the college could contribute to finance the plan for Gibson to spend more time abroad and for details on how much of the semester she would be allowed to miss. Baker argued that "the school and its Athletic program" would benefit from his plan because of the publicity, while "the Race in General" would gain, too.[69]

Gaither was unmoved. Writing on behalf of President Gore, he was unequivocal that FAMC could not "justifiably spend funds . . . on anyone for reasons which are personal rather than institutional." The college had already made compromises for Gibson. FAMC covered portions of her travel expenses. Gore and Gaither, moreover, consented to allow her—at her suggestion after the National Indoors in March, when she, Baker, Arthur Francis,

Hoxie, and Dann discussed the proposal—to withdraw after the spring semester and not return until the fall of 1953. This would enable her to train
with Hoxie and spend at least a year in Europe playing tournaments without
academic penalty or the loss of her scholarship. Gaither and Gore disliked
that they were left out of the meeting in New York. Gaither told Baker that
he "realize[d] the contribution that Miss Gibson has made for the school
and to our people, in general, as a result of her accomplishments in tennis."[70]
Nevertheless, FAMC refused to commit to funding Baker's plan.

Gaither shared Dr. Eaton's and Dr. Johnson's belief that Gibson needed to
remain in college until she graduated. The coach and the doctors were in ac-
cord: Gibson was contributing to the greater good of the race, but sacrificing
her education and career prospects after tennis by turning her into a full-time
commodity for the race was not an option. In the end, Gibson's professors
and Gore granted her permission to take her exams two weeks early with the
senior class so that she could head to Michigan and spend ten days training
there before flying to England. Baker received credit for the move. The
Amsterdam News described itself as learning through "an exclusive interview" with Baker that he had "arranged" the "intensive course" for her after
"work[ing] in harmony" with Eaton and Johnson.[71]

———

Gibson arrived in Michigan in mid-May and received treatment that
demonstrated her growing fame and the special care that race-conscious
African Americans felt she deserved. William Matney, a reporter for the
Michigan Chronicle, Detroit's Black newspaper, picked her up at the airport.
Matney brought her to the Hotel Gotham, hailed by *Ebony* as the "undis-
puted holder of the title of best Negro hotel in America." The management
did not assign Gibson just any room. She was given the suite used by Joe
Louis, her childhood hero, at Louis's request.[72]

Gibson found her brush with Louis more meaningful than her ten days
with Jean Hoxie. Hoxie, the longtime tennis coach at Hamtramck High
School and the city tennis director, had aspirants come from across the
country to train with her. In 1947 alone, Hoxie's students won thirty-seven
titles nationwide. She was internationally known, too, traveling to Mexico,
South America, and Europe to observe as well as give tennis clinics. Hoxie's
methods, though, were not well suited to Gibson's tastes—she missed the rep-
artee, badinage, and encouragement that came with playing and practicing
with others, particularly Dr. Eaton and Dr. Johnson and their male friends—
or her preference for visual learning.[73]

The Hoxie program was decidedly different. Gibson had sparring sessions with a male opponent, but just as often she faced her toughest opponent—a concrete wall sixty feet long and nearly twenty feet high. Hoxie and her husband, Jerry, made their students face "The Wall" at Veterans Memorial Park, a public facility in Hamtramck that included six to eight tennis courts built under the Works Progress Administration in the 1930s. Students had to stand between forty and fifty feet away as they targeted their shots, forced to hit with enough ferocity to make the ball come back to them again and again, no easy feat against a surface that was the equivalent of the side of a fortress. Fred Kovaleski, the first of Hoxie's students to win national titles, remembered that she "had the temperament of a volcano."[74] She shouted the strokes that she wanted players to hit in between bellows of ominous encouragement: "The first 10,000 shots are the hardest."[75] Gibson had her own thoughts about the usefulness of the Hoxies' program. "I don't know how much I improved my tennis while I was in Detroit," she admitted seven years later.[76]

Gaither and Dr. Johnson concluded that when Hoxie saw Black, she also saw gold, putting lucre ahead of interracial goodwill. "Miss Jean Hoxie's interest in Althea was mercenary and not a purely amateurish desire to help the girl," Gaither told Dr. Johnson.[77] Gaither sent Hoxie a copy of the letter in which he informed Baker that FAMC would not provide financial support for Gibson's time in Hamtramck or in Europe. Hoxie spoke with Gaither and, according to Dr. Johnson, she "insulted" the athletic director, the college president, and the college itself because the men remained adamant that Gibson stay in school, a decision that disappointed Hoxie. Hoxie also courted donors in Detroit. The leadership of the Central Motor City Tennis Club, a Black organization, contacted her about a reception for Gibson upon her arrival in the city. The president of the club told Baker, "Mrs. Hoxie said a reception would be fine, but Althea was in need of financial assistance." Hoxie appears to have attempted to use Baker's rhetoric that Gibson needed to quit school and focus on tennis full-time for "the Race in general" for her own benefit.[78] Hoxie made sure that she was paid for her work, promptly sending the ATA a bill for $325. Hoxie also received free publicity, as the Associated Negro Press and the *New York Times*, informed by Betty Granger, a member of the ATA's board of directors, reported that she had coached Gibson.[79]

Other well-wishers acted with more strategy and taste. The Detroit Duffers Golf Association, a Black group, offered to raise $500. Eventually, according to Gibson, she received $770 through a benefit for her trip to Wimbledon. Their generosity led her to conclude that "the people in Detroit have been very good to me."[80]

The Wimbledon invitation revealed the degree to which African Americans were eager and willing to give money to support Gibson as a young Black woman with ambitions and skills that placed her in all-White realms. Intentions sometimes exceeded means, too. In April, two Detroit ministers offered to provide funding for her lessons with Hoxie in a classic example of mutual aid. They "balked," however, upon learning the cost, according to the Cleveland *Call and Post*.[81] Joe Bostic of the *Amsterdam News* made supporting Gibson's career a sign of race pride and loyalty. Bostic devoted space in several editions of his column, "The Scorecard," to over-the-top and impolitic fundraising appeals. "ALTHEA NEEDS MONEY TO CONTINUE HER GALLANT ONE-WOMAN FIGHT! So why in the hell don't YOU send her some?" he wrote in one. In his view, whenever Gibson stepped onto the court at an all-white tournament, she was "going into the lion's den singlehanded to fight a battle for all of us . . . Every Negro who has failed to make a contribution to this girl's fight ought to be made to stand in the corner for a week to think it over." Bostic argued that Gibson waged her battle to enter and to win the White tennis tournaments for the entire Black race: "What Althea is doing isn't so much a personal triumph as it is a door for YOUR kids when they come along. Shame! Shame! Shame!"[82] It's unclear how much money Bostic raised, but one thing was undeniable: all kinds of people looked upon race-based heroics and pioneering as worthy of charity and as potentially profitable.

Joe Louis, Detroit's favorite son, joined Black America's fervor for Gibson. His generosity went beyond the suite at the Gotham. Louis, according to the *Call and Post*, was part of a committee that pledged to raise $3,000 for Gibson's trip to Wimbledon. "Every sports minded person who has read of Althea's tennis playing and feels pride in what she has done, should be more than willing to contribute to this campaign," he said.[83]

Louis came to the Gotham one morning in May to treat Gibson to breakfast. She was awestruck as the boxer lavished attention on her. Instead of regaling her with stories about his past glories, he "talked to me about how I was doing," she remembered. Louis also committed one of his characteristic acts of kindness. Apparently acting apart from any committee, he told Gibson that "he would have a round-trip airplane ticket to London left for me at Idlewild Airport in New York." She veritably swooned at the news. "What a guy," Gibson recalled.

But the guy was also a cautionary tale.[84] Louis's gesture typified his pattern of being generous to a fault. A race man and humanitarian, Louis gave away hundreds of thousands of dollars to charities, social causes, and individuals during and after his career. He was also bilked by the people he trusted to manage his money. On top of all that, he lived the high life. Louis sat before Gibson in the elegant Gotham in the early throes of a financial downward spiral that would last the rest of his life. Even as he comped her suite, picked up the breakfast tab, and paid for her air travel, Louis stood in deep trouble with the Internal Revenue Service, owing more in back taxes than he could possibly pay.[85]

Gibson wanted for nothing when she left Detroit for New York on May 30. She spent the day and the night with her family in Harlem. At Idlewild the next day, she cashed in the ticket that the Duffers Association had paid for and gave the money to Bertram Baker for safekeeping for the future. She chose to fly to London on Louis's ticket and kept "leftover cash" from the Duffers' fundraiser to cover her other European travel expenses. Just before she got on a Pan-American Clipper, she told reporters that she was optimistic about her odds at Wimbledon. At 4:00 P.M., Gibson boarded the plane, hair coiffed, face buffed, and lips painted. She clutched her shoulder bag filled with cash.[86]

Gibson was hardly anonymous when she arrived in London. Newspapers across the United Kingdom had reported on Alice Marble's effort to get her into Forest Hills in 1950 and on her subsequent performance there. Nine months later, Fred Perry, the English tennis hero admired and once hosted by Dr. Eaton, was hyping Gibson as a player to watch during the 1951 tennis season. She struck Perry as "perhaps [the] most interesting" of the "newcomers" for several reasons, chief among them her victories in Jamaica and Miami as well as the mettle that she showed against Brough. Yet her race—and the rewards that others could reap from it—made her notable to Perry, too. Gibson, "the first coloured woman to compete" at Forest Hills, was "certainly a drawer of crowds, and therefore good for the gate."[87] With that, Perry affirmed that she would be a spectacle and a commodity on both sides of the Atlantic.

The English had never seen anyone like Gibson on a tennis court. England was the birthplace of lawn tennis; the three tournaments there that she entered in advance of Wimbledon had been played for decades, and Americans had entered and excelled in them for nearly as long. But she was literally marked as different. Local newspapers said nothing about the race of Doris Hart, Betty Rosenquest, Margaret duPont, or any of the other Americans who competed in the tournaments, but Gibson was singled out at nearly every turn as the "coloured American champion," "coloured girl," "American coloured lawn tennis player," "coloured American tennis girl," or simply a "negress," usually accompanied by "American" or "New York."[88]

British journalists searched for controversy, too. Some papers reported that individuals and the ATA (misnamed as the "American Lawn Tennis Association . . . consisting of coloured folk") rather than the USLTA funded her trip abroad, a sure sign to the British press that she was unwelcome in elite American tennis.[89] Russell D. Kingman, chairman of the USLTA's International Play Committee, spoke about Gibson's struggle with the association the previous summer. "Some people had hard feelings when Miss Gibson was accepted for the U.S. championships at Forest Hills," Kingman said. "But," he added, "I guess that those who didn't like it just had to lump it. There's a federal law making it illegal to discriminate against coloured people." Kingman suggested that the troubles were in the past, but he still contributed to the racial noise that the press piped around Gibson.[90] Stories that her chances to play the best American women were "limited" popped up, too.[91] Each report was another way that racial prejudice, including fascination with it, followed her abroad.

Gibson responded by blending caution with openness in her interactions with the press. Shortly after arriving in London, she submitted to an interview with Denzil Batchelor, a well-known journalist who specialized in sports, for *Picture Post*, the English equivalent of *Life*. *Picture Post* was not above ginning up racial controversy around Gibson or underscoring that she was an anomaly on the English tennis scene. The magazine titled its profile "The Different Gibson Girl" and opened with a preamble that raised the specter of verboten intimate interracial contact on the hallowed grounds of Wimbledon. She was "the first Negress to compete" in the tournament, *Picture Post* noted. "If she wins—and there will be other years besides this—it is the normal custom at the [Lawn Tennis Association Ball] for her to have the first dance with the champion: who may well be a white American from the South."[92] Gibson sidestepped such matters. She told Batchelor that race had never hampered her career. She was being necessarily careful in her speech. The American press and government scrutinized the words and actions of African Americans who traveled abroad, and Paul Robeson, Josephine Baker, W. E. B. Du Bois, and others who had spoken the truth about American racism and Jim Crow had been penalized.[93] One wrong word, Gibson surely knew, and she risked losing not only her travel privileges but also her playing privileges with the USLTA.

Gibson was candid in other ways. She confidently told Batchelor that her goal was to win Forest Hills and Wimbledon by 1955 or 1956, predicted that Wimbledon 1951 would not be won by duPont, Brough, or Hart, and admitted her love for the movies, especially ones with Bette Davis or Kirk Douglas. Batchelor was charmed by Gibson's personal insight but skeptical of her remarks about race. "I am bringing up all my reserves of faith in the hope of believing" that race had never impeded her rise, he wrote. Batchelor also saw through her feigned nonchalance after losses and revealed a dimension of Dr. Eaton and Dr. Johnson's lessons: "She hates to lose; but to do honor to her race, she has trained herself to be more impersonal about it than anyone else in the tournament."[94] Batchelor was not taken in by her dissembling.

Gibson played through the scrutiny, earning praise for her bold game and singular tactics. Jim Dear watched her play a practice match, her first time on English soil, at London's Queen's Club, where he was the teaching professional. Dear believed that she would "make a few people sit up and take notice," and not because of her color: "She has a fine service and a better backhand than most of the world's best women players."[95] Gibson felt comfortable enough in England to drop her studied on-court stoicism once tournament play began. In the second round of the Northern Lawn Tennis Tournament in Manchester, her first event, she complimented Norma Potts, her opponent, on several of her shots and laughed aloud when one of them bounced across the tape of the net before falling onto her own side, giving Potts the point. The laughter was, said the *London Daily Mirror*, indicative of her "irrepressible tom-boy sense of humor."[96]

Gibson did not win any tournaments in the run-up to Wimbledon, but she earned confidence and developed a reputation for being a contender. Plagued by double faults, she lost to Doris Hart 6–1, 6–4 in the semifinals at Manchester, but observers saw enough of her in the early rounds to declare that she had potential. "Miss Gibson possesses a stylish, all-around game and a fast spin service of the highest class," wrote the *Belfast Telegraph*. "She has a powerful forehand drive, which she follows to the net. Crisp volleys are her specialties."[97] Gibson's body and physicality fascinated observers, too. A tennis scribe for the *Daily Mirror* thought that she used her height and wingspan to "great advantage" before her loss in the semifinals of the Kent Lawn Tennis Tournament to Betty Rosenquest, making herself "almost impassable at the net" and taking down "anything overhead . . . with great force and certainty." She won her quarterfinal match easily after taking the first ten games in a row.[98] Gibson lost to Shirley Fry in the semifinals at the London Lawn Tennis Championships at the Queen's Club, the final event before Wimbledon, but she received plaudits for her tenacity in the second set, where she "offered stubborn resistance" before bowing 6–1, 6–4.[99]

Gibson was growing even as, and because, she lost. She was gaining at last consistent and concentrated exposure to grass, and she was enjoying it. "The grass courts here are very fast and beautiful. They are well kept," she reported to Dr. Eaton.[100] In England, she again was exposed to the top-notch conditions that the best White players had known for years. She also made a course out of her time at the tournament sites. Seated as a spectator in the stands, Gibson studied the methods of other players and humbled herself enough to take seriously Batchelor's criticisms that her backhand, her net game, and even the groundstrokes that she was so proud of needed work.[101]

Gibson was not all business while abroad, though. The social exposure made for "a wonderful time," she said. "The people [of England] were very good to me," she would remember.[102] She was the only Black person in most of the places she traveled to, but somehow she did not have the same uncomfortable feeling of being on display that she had experienced in Miami. Three times a week, she ate steaks flown to her from America by her Detroit supporters. (Begun during the war, rationing remained in effect in England.) She went to the movies at the end of most days. She went sightseeing in London, visiting the Festival of Britain, the House of Parliament, and the National History Museum.[103]

———

Gibson saw at Wimbledon the height of what she had been missing behind the color line. Stepping onto the hallowed grounds of the All England Lawn Tennis Club, she joined competitors from twenty-five countries, the most internationally diverse field in tennis, who represented the best players in their nations. It was revered as the most smoothly run tournament, too. The conditions of the fifteen courts—firm, fast, and smooth—were the best that Gibson and every other entrant would ever know, even better than those at Forest Hills. The grandstands and stadium held the most knowledgeable and devoted spectators of the game. According to lore, Wimbledon's patrons maintained the highest respect for decorum and good play as a matter of national duty.[104] The tournament was as much a symbol of Great Britain as the royalty who watched the matches during the fortnight of play at Wimbledon.

Even the dressing rooms inspired awe. Unseeded, Gibson was assigned to the lower dressing room, one of the two for women at the club. The upper dressing room was the haunt of Wimbledon champions, seeded players, and club members. There, a board held the gold-lettered names of past champions and the dates of their victories. Whether assigned the upper or the lower room, players were well cared for. Hairpins, makeup, and cologne were at their disposal. Tight muscles could be worked out by a masseuse who was on standby. The mistress of the dressing room, Mrs. Ward, was ready to launder a player's apparel at a moment's notice. Remembered one player, "Nothing in the United States approaches [Wimbledon's] impeccable service."[105]

Gibson did not take public transportation to the All England Lawn Tennis Club. Private cars picked up Wimbledon's players and delivered them to the club for their matches, then returned later to drop them back at their accommodations. Officials gave her a first-round bye, leaving an additional day to practice and rest, and scheduled her debut on June 26 on the famed Centre Court, "the holiest of holies" according to one writer, where the legends of the game—including Alice Marble and Donald Budge—had played and won.[106]

The morning of her first match, Gibson was sick with anxiety until she settled herself down. She recounted the experience in 1987: "I said to myself, 'Althea, all you have to do is watch the ball. Don't look around at everyone and laud the fact you're the first black to do this or that or you'll forget about why you're here. Just concentrate on looking at the ball.'"[107] She was confused about the location of her match. The twelve-sided stadium for Centre Court held seventeen thousand people. This was just the first match of a Wimbledon rookie, she thought. Another thought crossed her mind: the tournament committee had put her on the grandest stage in tennis to "show me off or to see me get beaten."[108]

Playing against Pat Ward, the local favorite, Gibson showed herself off. Wearing a nylon outfit designed by Teddy Tinling, she played before her biggest audience and did not disappoint. Gibson won the first set 6–0. A surge of satisfaction came over her. "I looked around as if to say, 'How do you people like that?'" The feeling was short-lived. It also broke her concentration, giving Ward an opening. Ward won the second set 2–6.[109] Gibson then scrambled to take the third set 6–4, winning in dim light, a feature of being the last match on a cloudy day that had begun with rain and cool temperatures that lingered. The impressive win met with applause from the spectators, who had hoped the weather and light would hold out.[110]

The next day brought a complete reversal of Gibson's fortunes. The vicissitudes of English weather revealed themselves in the third round. The heat was as much her foe as Beverly Baker of Santa Monica. Baker's pedigree included winning the U.S. junior championship title of 1948 and the Pacific Southwest Tennis Championship in 1947, when she was only seventeen. Baker impressed reporters as much because of her looks and her body as because of her ambidextrous play; she hit a left-handed forehand as her backhand. "The glamorous Miss Baker from California is all lissom grace as she makes a crisp return on the way to her 6–1, 6–3 victory over the coloured girl, Althea Gibson," wrote the *Daily Mirror* beneath a picture of Baker stretching to make a shot in her short shorts and sleeveless top. "It's just a spot more proof that glamour and tennis ability can go hand in hand."[111] The British press saw no such glamour in Gibson. Instead, reporters agreed that she possessed talent but suffered from "a lack of experience" and a persistent case of "nerves."[112] The following day, Doris Hart and Frank Sedgman beat Gibson and Narendra Nath of India in the third round of mixed doubles.[113]

In the passage between the court and the dressing rooms was a wooden sign inscribed with lines from Rudyard Kipling's famous poem "If" that every player saw: "If you can meet with triumph and disaster and treat these two imposters just the same."[114] Getting bounced from Wimbledon so soon in her first try was not exactly a disaster for Gibson, but it was disappointing. She could only take solace in her thoughts before the tournament had begun. "It's tough over here," she had told a band of reporters. "You've got to be good to win. The competition is getting better all the time. You can't be good all the time. I always try to do my best."[115]

A surprise visit with old friends helped Gibson recover. Sugar Ray Robinson was spending the summer in Europe on tour. On July 4, Gibson greeted Edna Mae and Ray with hugs and kisses as they arrived at London's Victoria Station. As the English gawked, Gibson dove right into the Robinsons' garish style. Ray and Edna Mae stepped into a bright pink Cadillac, reported to be eighteen feet long, as their entourage—Ray's sister, two secretaries, his manager, two trainers, his barber, sparring partners, and a French interpreter—organized themselves into two other Cadillacs, two Rolls-Royces, and a bus with room for twenty. All told, there were eighty-two pieces of luggage supporting the pack. Reporters wondered over Edna Mae, "coffee-coloured" and "chic," in her "tight-fitting" sailor-style "costume."[116]

The visit with Ray and Edna Mae, first at Piccadilly and then at Windsor, rejuvenated Gibson. She won three titles in the next month. In Germany, she won the Dortmund International. She returned to England for the Essex Lawn Tennis Tournament in Frinton-on-Sea, winning the singles and, with Australian Don Candy, the mixed doubles title.[117]

The tournaments were not Wimbledon, but they brought Gibson her favorite things—wins. Each added to her newfound love for Europe, especially England. She would have bottled the feeling if she could have.

By the third week of July, Gibson was back in New York. She deplaned at Idlewild in a smart dark skirted suit with a corsage pinned to the left lapel. She also wore a smile that told the story of the glories of Europe. Yet behind the lipstick she was frustrated by her immediate future.[118]

Gibson's schedule was packed with ATA commitments. Days after her return, she went to Philadelphia to play in two exhibition matches, women's singles and mixed doubles, at the Pennsylvania Open, where she reconnected with Dr. Johnson. Then, on August 8, she was the guest of honor at a three-hour reception organized by the ATA Guild and *Our World*, a short-lived magazine that rivaled *Ebony*. *Our World* made her the subject of a pictorial, "Queen of the Courts," in its September issue. Held in the Peacock Lounge at the Waldorf-Astoria Hotel, the reception raised funds and publicity. Attendees paid $25 or more to be listed in the program as sponsors. New York mayor Vincent Impelliteri and William H. Hastie, the first African American to be selected for the United States Circuit Court of Appeals and the honorary president of the ATA for 1952, attended. Horace Mann Bond, president of Pennsylvania's Lincoln University, and diplomat Ralph Bunche, winner of the Nobel Peace Prize in 1950, sent congratulatory notes. Others queued up to shake hands with Gibson, who was presented with gifts and awards from the ATA, *Our World*, and F. & M. Schaefer Brewing Company. Wearing heels, a light-colored skirted suit, and a pearl choker, she towered over Daniel, Annie, and Mildred, who, dressed in their finest, attended the celebration, too. Gibson talked excitedly to anyone who would listen about how well she had been treated abroad, particularly by the spectators and townspeople in Dortmund.[119]

Yet all had not been pleasant in Europe. Gibson clashed with Teddy Tinling over what outfits were best for her. Since meeting her in New York, Tinling had disliked her preference for "plain, tailored clothes." He "persuaded her to tolerate a skirt instead of shorts." Tinling wrote proudly in his first book that he "combined both our interests" by designing for her a special divided skirt that "was widely copied." The two, however, remained at odds over how she should wear her hair. After days of play, Gibson's hair had lost some of its luster and her natural curls and waves had begun to show. To his later regret, Tinling—White, male, and bald—commented upon its change. Gibson's hair "looked much less effective," he thought, and he said as much. Gibson did not politely or patiently accept his input. "You don't seem to realize that you have no de-frizzing irons over here," she said. Gibson cut down the 6'7" Tinling, succinctly pointing out his privilege and his obtuseness. Tinling, to his credit, accepted the rebuke: "I blamed myself for not having been more observant."[120]

For all the excitement of the reception, Gibson wanted no part of the third ATA event, the Nationals, scheduled at Wilberforce in August. Her feelings were another sign of her desire to take control of her career rather than accept the duties attendant to race loyalty. She had lost in the quarterfinals of the Eastern Grass Court Championships in South Orange, New Jersey, to Maureen Connolly, the latest promising protégé of Eleanor "Teach" Tennant, an instructor based at the Beverly Hills Tennis Club who had coached Alice Marble, Bobby Riggs, and Pauline Betz to the winner's circle at Wimbledon and Forest Hills. The match was close, 6–4, 6–4, and Gibson had hung tough against Connolly's volleys, leaving some, including Al Laney, to believe that she could someday best Connolly. Gibson wrote to Dr. Eaton to say that she preferred to spend several days practicing with Dr. Johnson in Lynchburg before returning to New York to practice with Sarah Palfrey on grass before the start of Forest Hills at the end of the month.[121]

Though Gibson's request pushed Dr. Eaton's patience to the limit, he intervened once more. For the second straight year, organizers of the ATA Nationals accelerated the women's singles and mixed doubles matches to enable Gibson to finish on Friday so that she could travel back to New York for Forest Hills. While in New York to attend the reception at the Waldorf, he had the chance to say some version of words that he drafted but seems never to have typed and mailed to Gibson in response to her plan: "It is past time for you to start thinking for yourself and stop having other people weave you into their patterns and schemes." Just who Dr. Eaton had in mind with the reference to "other people" is unclear. The line of schemers forming around Gibson grew annually. It is certain that he felt she needed a firm reminder: "You have made much progress in a few years. Don't forget those who . . . helped you."[122]

In the end, Gibson played the ATA Nationals and, after dropping only one game in the final against Kansas City's Mary Etta Fine, won for the fifth consecutive year. Fissures over her career were forming within the association. Some agreed that she should have skipped the tournament to play on grass to prepare for Forest Hills. Dr. Johnson seemed to be among them. He and Gibson lost in the mixed doubles semifinals, 8–6, 4–7, 7–5, to Nana Davis and her fiancé, Quentin Vaughn. Gibson's game was out of sorts. In the last game of the last set, she double-faulted her serve, handing the match to Davis and Vaughn. "She made errors today that she has never made before,"

Dr. Johnson said, before explaining, "She has been playing too much tennis under this rush schedule."[123]

Others were not sympathetic. Some ATA members believed that Gibson owed a debt to the association that could only be paid by playing in its tournaments. "She never would have gone to Forest Hills, Wimbledon, or any other place without the ATA," an attendee told the *Afro-American*. The paper also reported that an unnamed ATA leader "threatened to keep Althea out" of Forest Hills if she skipped the Nationals. Gibson set out to quell the chatter that displeased her: "I don't know what all the talk's about—I'm here to play tennis at Wilberforce." However, she gave a sharp response when asked for comment on a report that Bertram Baker said that his office "outlined" her "tennis program." This went to the heart of Gibson's desire for independence, including in her career, and her blunt response betrayed her frustration that she had no control at all: "Nobody told me anything about running my tennis program. It's the first I've heard of it."[124]

But it was not. Gibson had already received a strong reminder that she was not a free agent within the ATA. Over the summer, Dr. Johnson was contacted by a Mr. Craig who represented the Detroit Duffers, the group that had raised money for Gibson before she flew to England. Craig shared "information" about "the amount of funds received in Detroit." Exactly what Dr. Johnson learned was not recorded in the minutes of the meeting held by the ATA subcommittee that strategized about Gibson's career. What is clear is that the group decided they needed to establish parameters. They passed two motions. The first decreed that any player who represented the ATA was "under the direct supervision and control of the ATA through the Executive Secretary." The second stated that "when any player represents the ATA in any tennis activity, all matters related to such activity, as interviews, newspapers, letters for publication, magazines, radio, television, et cetera, and any opportunities for advertisements and fund-raising campaigns, must be cleared through the office of the Executive Secretary."[125]

Dramatically, after the motions carried, Dr. Johnson left the room. When he returned, Gibson was with him. The ATA president led "an interrogation" of her. Bertram Baker, the executive secretary, read the "new regulations" aloud and asked for her "reactions." According to the meeting minutes, she "reacted favorably." If she hoped to continue her tennis career under the auspices of the ATA, she had no other choice.[126]

That Gibson played in two national tennis championships in the United States—one Black, the other White—spoke to the way that Jim Crow bifurcated America and gave her two identities in sports, one as an integrationist and another as a subject of segregation. At Forest Hills, she lasted until the third round, where she met Maureen Connolly again and lost 6–2, 6–4. She was just one of Connolly's casualties on her path to win the women's singles title the following week.[127]

Gibson and Connolly had much in common. Both came from families of modest means. Connolly's first teacher, like Gibson's, had a disability: Wilbur Folsom, who taught her on the public University Playground courts in San Diego, had an artificial leg. Connolly had also been a sports-loving tomboy as a child and preferred playing and practicing with boys and men. She also took a fanatical approach to tennis and had to learn to control her temper. Gibson imagined herself as a matador in the ring, while Connolly envisioned herself as a "hunter" and a "warrior" on the tennis court, her "secret jungle."[128] The press, Black and White, called Connolly and Gibson tennis queens but, in that way, they were not on the same level. With her Forest Hills trophy in hand and her sights firmly set on Wimbledon for 1952, Connolly could back up the title of queen. Revered for her baseline and net games, she had just bagged her first Grand Slam at age sixteen. Before that, she had won the U.S. Junior Nationals girls' title twice in a row. When Gibson was sixteen, she was still competing in the junior girls' division of the ATA on clay and cement. If she was really going to become a tennis queen and reach her full potential, she could not keep playing and beating Mary Etta Fine in the ATA Nationals. She needed to meet—and defeat—the Maureen Connollys of American tennis, and on grass.[129]

—◦—

When Gibson returned to Tallahassee in September 1951 for her junior year, she faced the sobering news that FAMC had placed her on academic probation for the semester. Leaving college would have skirted the outcome. Instead, she faced the consequences of prioritizing her career over her classes, two of which she had dropped in the spring.[130]

Gibson's predicament resulted in President Gore playing an active role in her academic life. Gore, acting in loco parentis, assumed the power to refuse her permission to travel to tournaments. He exercised that authority in September, when organizers of the Pan-American Tennis Tournament requested her presence in Mexico at the end of the month. The group lobbied Gore to permit her to play, arguing without evidence that her participation "certainly would not affect [her] matriculation and classes" and that her presence as a Black tennis player was important "from the symbolic angle," contributing to the "lofty cause" of showing "international and racial amity."[131] These were the "promoters and bounders" that Jake Gaither looked upon with contempt and the questionable "well-wishers and fortune hunters [that] always manage to surround her to give her 'a helping hand,'" a group that Mary Hardwick observed, too.[132] Gore denied Gibson permission to enter the Pan-American on the grounds that she had already been "granted too many leaves of absence."[133] She completed the coursework required to restore her academic standing by the end of the semester. It was, she said, "the devil to go through," and she wished never to put herself so far behind in her studies ever again.[134]

Gibson committed to graduating from college with her bachelor's degree in P.E., but she remained discontented. Her relationship with the basketball coach Julia Lewis was fraught. Older than the other players, Gibson disobeyed curfew when the team traveled, and she smoked. Lewis's efforts to discipline her failed. "Coach Lewis could hardly manage her, because she always had an answer back," one teammate recalled. Another noticed that she had few friends among the female students "because the women didn't really understand what she was all about."[135] There was no women's tennis team at FAMC. Two other women were on the college's single tennis team during Gibson's first year; men were the majority. The yearbook for 1951 suggested she had become the only woman by then and an important member of the team because of her ATA achievements and her entries in USLTA tournaments. In the yearbook, she was pictured with Coach Austin as one of "Famcee's Net Stars." With her shorts, T-shirt, and short hair brushed back with a lone curl falling over her forehead, she struck a tomboyish pose.[136] In later years, Gibson boasted that the tennis team "won our conference championships every year I was on the team," but how much playing time she received is unclear. It does not appear that she competed against men from other colleges.[137] The situation contributed to her belief that FAMC lacked all manner of resources to advance her tennis ambitions. "If I expect to become a good tennis player, I will need to be in a different environment," she told Dr. Eaton. At FAMC, "there is not enough interest in my tennis here from the standpoint of practice and development." She believed that she was "losing a great [deal] by staying in school." Her conclusion was clear: "My tennis is suffering."[138]

The trip to Europe had intensified Gibson's dissatisfaction. She had returned to America with a widened view of tennis and of the world but also the impression that everything overseas was better than what she had at home. She brought back helpful lessons learned by watching other players but also criticism, including of her coaching. "I picked up as much from observation over there as I did in all my years of assorted coaching," she told Sam

Lacy during an interview at the end of the summer. Abroad she learned "how important it is to develop a completely all-around game." Gibson had come to realize that her serve and overhead, the strongest weapons in her arsenal, were not enough. "Now I know I not only need a good backhand . . . I need one that offers a variety of strokes, so that I can alter my game to suit surface and wind conditions." Her chief takeaway from seeing and being beaten by the best players in the world was simple: "In top tennis circles, if you can't come up with a variation from every stroke, you're lost."[139] Lacy, who had heaped masses of praise on Gibson amid her debut at Forest Hills and celebrated her play at Wimbledon in 1951, was unconvinced. He decided that "experimentation"—his term for her decision to observe and study the methods of the game's best players—"has played havoc with [her] tennis."[140] The *Los Angeles Sentinel* agreed, or at least parroted Lacy's opinion with a brief article of its own: "Althea Gibson's Experimentation Hurts Game."[141] The problem was that she had limited access to the people and places at the top.

Like Dr. Eaton and Dr. Johnson, Gaither was steadfast in his refusal to support Gibson's interest in quitting or the intimation that her professors asked too much of her. Gaither followed the paternalistic methods of his generation of Black coaches, regarding a college degree as armor with which to meet Jim Crow. He had ready responses for anyone who believed that sports took precedence over studies: "Athletes are admitted to the university just as other students are admitted. They are required to maintain the same academic standards as other students, no special favors are asked and none are granted." FAMC was "no winter resort."[142]

The gendered construction of FAMC's physical education program further stymied Gibson. Like most colleges and universities, FAMC offered two decidedly different sets of P.E. curricula, one for men and another for women. Both male and female students were expected to perform calisthenics and gymnastics, but after that their programs diverged. The program for male P.E. students "emphasize[d] strenuous distance running, balance and agility activities," according to Lua Stewart Bartley, FAMC's longtime P.E. instructor for women. Meanwhile, FAMC women learned the less physically demanding activities of "body mechanics, rhythms, [and] tumbling." Some P.E. classes were single-sex, such as P.E. 300–400, in which men and women were separately exposed to archery, golf, basketball, swimming, tennis, volleyball, shuffleboard, softball, and horseshoes. However, differences were woven into the curricula, too. The men could do touch football, speedball, basketball, badminton, table tennis, boxing, wrestling, weightlifting, gymnastics, and track and field. Women instead participated in dance (square, modern, folk, and tap) and darts, which were not offered to the men.[143]

Such divisions underscored that Gibson's gender-defying abilities, background, and vision exceeded the FAMC landscape. She knew that being a woman did not make one too fragile for strenuous exercise. She could have undertaken the course offerings for men and excelled. The gendered limitations of the P.E. program contributed to her feeling of being "mentally unsatisfied" at FAMC.[144] Gibson was an athletic star in the P.E. department, but she was, in her own way, among the women there who felt that it had, in the words of one female staff member, "major problems" and needed the "sympathy and help" of Gaither, who was the department head.[145] By early 1952, the department was considering making a dramatic change that spoke volumes about the way FAMC viewed women. In January, the staff raised the possibility of discontinuing the women's varsity basketball team, a move that would pave the way for FAMC to join the retrograde trend that had taken hold at educational institutions nationwide.[146]

Gibson toughed out her last three semesters at FAMC, focusing on her studies more than tennis practice. She "had to [train] night and day in order to get in shape" for the four tournaments that she played in the spring of 1952 to keep up her rankings—eleventh in the USLTA and second in the Eastern Lawn Tennis Association.[147] The *Tallahassee Democrat* reported in early February that Gibson was "working out daily in the Famcee gym" with Edward Whitsey from the tennis team for as much as six hours.[148] The cramming yielded mixed results. Between February and March, she made it only as far as the semifinals of the National Indoors, the Caribbean Lawn Tennis Championships in Montego Bay, and the Good Neighbor, where members of the majority-White crowd reportedly booed her for calling Florida her "second home."[149] At the St. Andrew International Tennis Tournament, she lost in the finals to Betty Rosenquest, who had married since their last meeting. It was another measure of the ways in which the lives of her peers and rivals were moving on as she remained in school.[150]

While Gibson's status as the premier Black tennis player in the world earned her no latitude in academics at FAMC, her fame was still rewarded with special treatment elsewhere. In July, she made her first trip to Bermuda to compete in the first International Lawn Tennis Tournament of the Somers Isles Lawn Tennis Association. She won the singles and mixed doubles titles. She also beat one of Bermuda's best male players, Alex Romeo, in an exhibition match, 6–2, 6–3. Bermuda continued her streak of being welcomed warmly in the arms of the Black diaspora. Gibson had such a good time that she extended her stay in Hamilton from one week to two and a half. "Everyone is treating me as if I were a queen," she mused.[151] She shopped, accepted invitations to cruises, went sightseeing, swam, fished in the sea, cycled, and attended beach parties, some at midnight. She sang, too. Gibson did a guest spot on local radio and, wearing a thin-strapped evening gown, joined the band at the Leopard Club, a popular nightclub.[152]

Gibson sailed back to New York on a luxury liner, the *Queen of Bermuda*. In August, Grossinger's, the famed Jewish vacation spot in the Catskills, hosted her for exhibition matches and demonstrations with Anita Kanter, club pro Eli Epstein, and Epstein's assistant, Nat Jesser. The Grossinger family welcomed many athletes and their families, including Jackie Robinson's, to enjoy their facility, which included tennis, golf, trails, a swimming pool, and horseback riding. Gibson's stay at the resort was another sign of the doors that being the Black tennis phenomenon allowed her to walk through.[153]

———

Gibson committed to graduating from FAMC in four years. Doing so meant putting her tennis career on hold. She played in no tennis tournaments and practiced only on Sundays during her senior year.[154]

Previous springs had seen Gibson living and traveling in luxury in New York, the Caribbean, and Miami, but in 1953 she made a more practical trip to a less glamorous place. In May, she went to Jefferson City, Missouri, to interview for a job as a P.E. teacher and the men's tennis coach at Lincoln University, an HBCU. *The Clarion*, Lincoln's student newspaper, reported the news on its front page, touting Gibson as a "nationally famous tennis star" who "broke precedent" at Forest Hills and Wimbledon and other English tournaments. The university made her an honored guest at its annual sports banquet, held during her campus visit.[155] Lincoln was not simply interviewing Gibson; it was recruiting her. She left Jefferson City without a contract but with the tentative expectation that she would accept the position.

Gibson graduated from FAMC on Monday, June 1. Dr. and Mrs. Eaton attended the Memorial Day weekend activities and the ceremony. None of Gibson's relatives were there, a matter, Dr. Eaton thought, of their material poverty. Dr. Eaton, only a few years her senior, commented, "We were as proud of Althea when she walked down the aisle in her black cap and gown as if she were our own daughter."[156] Gibson indeed looked upon Dr. Eaton as a father figure. Later, when asked to name the people most responsible for her achievements, she named him along with Dr. Johnson, Fred Johnson, and

Buddy Walker as well as three men from FAMC, Jake Gaither, tennis coach Woody Austin, and William Gray, the former president. She did not mention Daniel, her real father.[157]

Gibson was proud, relieved, and ready to launch herself back into tennis and an independent life. She dove back into the game, but the outcome was not what she wanted. Maureen Connolly stood in her way, becoming her nemesis, just as she was to every other woman in amateur tennis. Connolly successfully defended her Wimbledon and Forest Hills titles in 1952. In 1953, she won the Australian, French, and Wimbledon championships, too.

Connolly was indisputably the number one player in the world, but some still thought that Gibson could beat her. She could "match [Connolly's] speed and drive," according to the Associated Press.[158] They had last met in May 1952 in an exhibition match played for the Chicago Tennis Patrons. Gibson lost in three sets, 6–1, 4–6, 6–1, but her serve and her volleys were more effective than Connolly's. In July, Gibson tried to capitalize on them. At the National Clay Court Championships in Chicago, her first tournament since graduating from FAMC, she faced Connolly in the title match. Connolly won again, and the result left a bitter aftertaste. Gibson was not at her freshest, worn down by the two hours and thirty-five minutes it had taken her to win her semifinal match against Anita Kanter the day before.[159]

Next came the Pennsylvania State Tennis Tournament at the famed Merion Cricket Club in Haverford. Standing on the other side of the net in the semifinal was Louise Brough. The gallery buzzed with anticipation, recalling the second round at Forest Hills three years earlier. Brough had only become more vulnerable since then, contending with injuries to her wrist, arm, shoulder, and elbow. The crowd rallied behind Gibson after she came back from being down 1–4 in the first set. Brough, however, held on to win 7–5 and then took charge for the second set, 6–1. The desired showdown never materialized. Gibson had wilted and showed that her game had the same deficits under pressure that it had had two and a half years earlier. "Miss Gibson lost her control and rhythm, and, both at the net and off her ground strokes, she made costly errors with little provocation," wrote Allison Danzig.[160] She endured a second setback after the match. Eager to practice, she asked Merion officials for permission to remain and work out on their immaculate grass courts. They said no.[161]

–—–

Since the summer of 1951, when she needed housing while competing in the Eastern Grass Court Championships in East Orange, Gibson lived in

Montclair, New Jersey, whenever she needed to be in the New York metropolitan area. Her hosts were Miriam and Robert Darben. Rosemary, their
daughter, was Gibson's closest friend and one of the better ATA players in the
New York area. Rosemary also played in amateur tournaments in New Jersey.
In addition to tennis, the two women shared interests in golf, basketball,
bowling, card games, and listening to albums. Whenever Gibson came to stay,
she and Rosemary shared a room. Over time, Gibson's trophies, scrapbooks,
travel souvenirs, and so much else gave her a fixed presence there. William
Darben, Rosemary's brother, soon developed an interest in her. They went on
dates whenever she was in town. He "had taken a shine to me" and they "saw
a lot of each other," she wrote.[162]

By the standards of the day, Will was a respectable catch. The Darbens
had much in common with the Gibsons, but there were clear differences, too.
Like Daniel and Annie Gibson, Robert and Miriam Darben were natives
of South Carolina. Robert was born sometime around 1877 in Edgefield,
the hometown of Strom Thurmond, among the most famous of segregationist senators blocking progress and the conferral of Black civil rights in
the 1950s and 1960s. Born in Aiken in 1888, Miriam had studied at Black
schools in Denmark, South Carolina, first at Bettis Academy and later at
Voorhees Industrial School. Robert and Miriam were "old settlers" among
Black migrants. They were living in the Northeast just after the turn of the
twentieth century and married at Saranac Lake, New York, in 1909. Church-
going Baptists, the couple soon moved to Montclair, New Jersey, where they
raised their six children, three daughters and three sons, on Robert's wages
as a chauffeur and eventually bought a home.[163] Since his discharge from the
navy, their son Will, twenty-eight, had worked as an administrative assistant
at the Bendix Corporation and had ambitions for promotion. Away from the
plant, he was a devoted son. A casual tennis player, Will was lean and tall, fitting Gibson's physical preference in a husband.[164]

Yet when Will proposed to Gibson in 1953, she said no. She "thought
seriously about him," she wrote later, just not as seriously as he thought of
her. "There wasn't any spark between us," she concluded. The way that Will
proposed did not help. He did not ask her to marry him or present an engagement ring. He simply said "he thought it would be a good idea for us to get
married." Gibson saw that he made the proposal "in dead earnest," but she was
unmoved. "I couldn't help but think, isn't something supposed to happen?"[165]
Friendship was as much as she could offer him. "Out of consideration of my
career, I decided then that marriage wasn't for me."[166]

Gibson committed to take the job at Lincoln University. Jefferson City was in the middle of Missouri, and Missouri was in the middle of the country, far away from the coasts, where the most important tennis tournaments, especially the grass court events, were played. Gibson's decision to take the job put her at odds with Dr. Eaton. He thought she should hold out for an offer from another Black college, preferably in Florida or North Carolina. Eager to assert and take care of herself, Gibson stood firm in her decision: "I feel that this is an opportunity that should not be pas[sed]-up, for I will have to start somewhere."[167] The distance ratcheted up the pressure to win. She decided it was time to make a major change: she would take a new coach.

Gibson had been working with Sydney Llewellyn informally during summer vacations from FAMC. Born in Kingston, Jamaica, in February 1911, Llewellyn was introduced to tennis while working as a ball boy at the city's St. Andrews Club. He migrated to New York when he was nineteen and thought little of tennis until 1946, when a friend invited him to a country club, likely Shady Rest, in New Jersey, for the Fourth of July and mentioned in passing that there were tennis courts on the grounds. Excited, Llewellyn made the trip and won the club's Independence Day tennis tournament. Impressed by Llewellyn's enthusiasm for tennis, his friends encouraged him to join the Cosmopolitan. Llewellyn, then thirty-five, went to the club immediately after the holiday and asked Fred Johnson for tennis lessons. Johnson was not enthusiastic about teaching him and, forty years later, his response still stung Llewellyn: "I'm not interested in teaching any old man tennis." It was, Llewellyn felt, "no way to speak to anyone." Still, he convinced Johnson to teach him. He also supplemented the lessons. "I read all the books there were. I went to every tournament I could go to," including Forest Hills. "Wherever there was a tournament, I was there. Many times I was the only black there. But I was studying my craft because I knew tennis could be my life." Yet Llewellyn could not rely on tennis for his livelihood. He gave lessons part-time, including at the Jewish resorts in the Catskills, and drove a taxi to make ends meet for himself and his wife, Leah.[168]

Gibson met Llewellyn at the Cosmopolitan in 1946. They saw each other occasionally on the ATA circuit, but they were not close contacts. Yet he felt that they were "on a collision course." Over the years, Llewellyn had tried to give pointers to Gibson, but she did not take him seriously. Few people at the Cosmopolitan did. "I was so intense in tennis that they call[ed] me Mr. T," as in Mr. Tennis, he remembered, "but it was Mr. T-ha-ha." Gibson, in contrast, was a star. Whenever she came to the club, "she used to have a little entourage with her," Llewellyn mused. "She played for her audience, and she'd leave." She "had everything but humility," Llewellyn thought. Still, they teamed in mixed

doubles in 1950 and had developed "a real good relationship" by 1951.[169] That
was when she came to him for help with her game. Gibson's friend Billy Davis,
a rising star in the ATA, was Llewellyn's first student. Davis, after seeing a frustrated Gibson at one of the tournaments that she played after returning from
Wimbledon, recommended that she seek Llewellyn's advice. She did, and
Llewellyn was pleased. He had long noticed that Gibson was "a great competitor" and "a very, very aggressive person" who "gave the men trouble . . . She
could beat [Davis]" as many as "two out of three" times. When Gibson asked
for Llewellyn's help, she showed a "display of humility" that he respected.[170]

Llewellyn took charge at once. He wanted to change Gibson's grip from
the Continental, which Johnson used by necessity to offset his disability
and taught to others, to the Eastern. Llewellyn's years of reading about and
observing tennis had convinced him that the Eastern grip was more effective, giving players the ability to make more powerful shots. She liked the
sound of more power, and committed to the adjustment. Llewellyn rented a
room at a YMCA and gave her lessons on its tennis court at night. He sometimes scheduled their lessons for early in the morning at a tennis court on
Seventh Avenue or even in the Bronx. The Cosmopolitan closed in 1951, but
there were other reasons to get Gibson away from the familiar environs of
Harlem, where she might be recognized. "I had to take her to a place where
there was no audience, because if there's any audience she becomes the great
Miss Gibson." Llewellyn taught Gibson his self-designed methods of court
strategy, "the theory of correct returns" and "the return of serve." He had her
practice hitting her serve to specific targets because, he felt, "to be a champion, you must have a great serve." Llewellyn told Gibson that "it would take
two years for my teaching to manifest itself" and that their real work would
begin once she "finish[ed] school."[171]

Graduating from FAMC gave Gibson more time to work with Llewellyn.
In later interviews, he pinpointed 1953 as the official start of their coaching
relationship.[172] She remembered the intensity of their workouts: "We would
have practice sessions every day, five days a week, eight hours a day." Davis
became her practice partner, a role he would have for years. "We would play
as if we were playing for our lives. . . . [W]e would have such great sessions,
practicing all day long," she recalled. They only took breaks "to have a snack,
and to relax, and continue."[173] In July, Gibson and Llewellyn teamed up
for mixed doubles at the ATA's Eastern (New Jersey) Open Championship
at Shady Rest. They did not win, but the tournament was a chance to
strengthen their bond. Gibson's immediate results in singles were further evidence that their alliance had potential. She competed in the Western Tennis

Championships, sponsored by the Miller Brewing Company, in Milwaukee at the end of the month. She was relieved to find that the ATA had paid for her hotel accommodations, or she might have withdrawn from the tournament. Instead, she finished second.[174]

———

Llewellyn had "urged" Gibson to take him as her coach in the summer of 1953 after seeing an issue of *Jet* magazine.[175] Produced by the Johnson Publishing Company, the firm behind *Ebony*, the palm-size *Jet* had been in circulation for less than two years and was having a deep impact on the Black masses, selling more than 300,000 copies every week. "The Negro's Bible," some called the popular and prevalent magazine.[176] The issue of January 1, 1953, the one that Llewellyn read, shot snark in Gibson's direction. A. S. "Doc" Young, the magazine's sports editor, "appraise[d] people and things in sports" for the previous year. Young listed "Althea Gibson, woman tennis player," as one of the two "biggest flops" in sports.[177]

In three words—"woman tennis player"—Young openly raised the topic of gender to question Gibson's singular representation in tennis of African Americans. No one else on *Jet*'s list, including Jake Gaither, recognized as "Negro college coach of the year," was identified by their gender. Gibson, the only woman featured, was.[178] It served as a reminder that Black America looked upon sports as a proving ground for manhood, and manhood was the vehicle for uplifting the race. Floundering, Gibson was failing to win the big events, especially Wimbledon and Forest Hills as well as important American grass court titles, and thus failing to prove the equality and even the superiority of Black Americans to Whites. Not so subtly, Young simultaneously implied that a Black man could do better and drew attention to Gibson's status as the leading and lone face of African Americans in the sport.

Focused on her own career, Gibson let the ATA guide the rest of its players, including the men and the boys. The association recommended players to the USLTA for consideration for Forest Hills invitations. In 1952, George Stewart, the reigning ATA men's national champion, and Reginald Weir, four-time past champion, were the first Black men to enter the tournament. Both lost in the first round, just like Victor Miller and Roosevelt Megginson, two Virginia teenagers whom Dr. Johnson entered in the annual National Interscholastic Tennis Tournament in Charlottesville in 1951. Dr. Johnson resolved to end his annual men's round-robin tournament and turn his home into a summer tennis camp to lead the ATA Junior Development program. He was determined to create a pipeline of players who would be competitive in USLTA tournaments and to locate and coach the Black boy who would win the National Interscholastic someday.[179] Dr. Johnson had called Gibson at their first meeting at Wilberforce in 1946 the "key to unlock the door" that kept Black players out of Forest Hills and the rest of elite amateur tennis.[180] Seven years later, the door was ajar, and it would take more than her to get those players beyond the first rounds. George Stewart, Oscar Johnson, and Ivy Cover Ramsey would also lose at Forest Hills in September, leaving Gibson—by default—to carry the banner for Black tennis as far as she could.

Jet was not the only Black news source to critique Gibson; criticisms cropped up in the newspapers that spring and summer. Journalists personalized their search for reasons for her struggles and stagnation. Cal Jacox of the *Norfolk Journal and Guide* accused her of being "difficult to handle," a charge that simultaneously denied her agency and harkened back to sportswriter Fay Young's intimation after her loss to Mary Hardwick in the exhibition match at Tuskegee in 1947 that she was arrogant and not sufficiently ladylike in temperament.[181] Jacox also wrote that she carried a "reluctance to take her tennis seriously enough," an accusation that ignored the difficulties of her circumstances, particularly her enrollment at FAMC and the realities of segregation.[182] In January, Jacox's wish list for the coming year in sports included his desire to see Gibson "coming down to earth and concentrating on her tennis."[183] In Philadelphia, Malcolm Poindexter of the *Tribune* reported that she was "very disagreeable away from public view," particularly in her interactions with the ATA, which itself received blame for the state of her game.[184] Journalists openly debated whether her inability to win more titles on the White circuit, including the most important ones, was because she faced comparatively mediocre competition in the ATA.[185] Still, Jacox kept his focus squarely on Gibson, as she was the one holding the racket and thinking her way around the court. "Althea Gibson's defeats in the finals of the National Clay Court and the Western Net Tournaments recently revealed that the young tennis star has, as yet, failed to develop the knack of winning the big ones," Jacox wrote in August as Gibson looked ahead to Forest Hills. "Until she conquers her inability to come through when the chips are down," he added, "she will be unable to advance higher in ranking among the nation's top net stars."[186]

Gibson was not oblivious to the talk. "I didn't advance in the game as fast as I had hoped I would, and certainly not as fast as a lot of people thought I should," she later admitted.[187]

Forest Hills, Gibson's last tournament of the 1953 season before she settled into life in Jefferson City, brought the absolute lowlight of her summer. She reached the quarterfinals, where she faced Connolly once again. Gibson started well, matching her opponent shot for shot. She broke Connolly's serve to even the match 2–2 in the first set. Connolly appeared to be buckling.[188] Spectators anticipated an action-packed match.

A lineswoman began to charge Gibson with committing foot faults. She racked up five charges in the third game alone. Breaking Dr. Johnson's commandment that his players never question officials' calls, Gibson asked the lineswoman for an explanation during the first set. "You are stepping on the line," the lineswoman told her, meaning that at least one of Gibson's feet touched the baseline or entered the court before she struck the ball.[189] Even after being told, she made the same actions with her feet. Gibson committed ten foot faults in the first set alone. She lost her concentration, her serve, and then her ground strokes before losing the set 6–2. Frustrated, Connolly spoke up during a break: "Althea, either play or default. I have never seen worse sportsmanship."[190] Undaunted, Gibson remained in the match and was charged with another five foot faults, for a total of fifteen. She lost the second set 6–3. The match, "a nightmare," in Connolly's memory, was finally over.[191]

But what had caused the nightmare? The accusations of the foot faults had the cast of racism, touching on perceptions of and questions about Gibson's ability to control her body, Black and five to six inches taller than Connolly's; the quality of her mind, specifically her aptitude for understanding and observing protocol; and the sheer needling by the lineswoman and her searches for errors. Even so, Gibson was nonchalant about the loss and refused to say that the lineswoman was prejudiced. "I wouldn't say that I was mistreated," she told Don Budge, who interviewed her on television after the match. "I couldn't see my feet. The line judges were there to watch for foot faults and to call them when they saw them." Gibson said the wind was the culprit, with gusts and swirls causing her to lose her serve and then everything else.[192]

Others cited poor officiating. "I think she might at least have been warned about her error," sportswriter Hamilton Chambers said after the match. Chambers thought that such foot faults were "often overlooked in other matches when they're recognized as unintentional."[193] Chambers and Danzig, who thought the spectators were on Gibson's side, argued that, without the distraction, she might have beaten Connolly.[194]

Days later, Connolly, eighteen, won her third straight women's singles title at Forest Hills, making her the first woman to achieve the Grand Slam in a single season. Switching to powerhouse coach Harry Hopman, the Australian Davis Cup captain, had helped. Connolly looked ahead to winning more titles in the fall and in the new year. Even so, she found the encounter with Gibson at Forest Hills hard to shake. Years later, Connolly still pondered the forces that had been driving Gibson that Saturday afternoon. "It is quite possible [Althea] felt she had been singled out and may have thought she had been a victim of over-officiating," Connolly posited. Otherwise, she was perplexed as to what had caused Gibson, twenty-six, to disintegrate. "I have no explanation of Althea's conduct nor do I know what stress she may have been under."[195]

6

Resurfacing

*Well, we've got a problem, as all countries and all states and
individuals have, but it's a problem that certainly can be
solved and that I firmly believe will be solved.*

—ALTHEA GIBSON, 1955–1956

BY SEPTEMBER 1953, Gibson was one of the nearly three hundred thousand Black people who lived in Missouri, fewer than the number who lived
in New York City alone. She was not in St. Louis or Kansas City, the "undisputed urban centers" of the state, where more than half of its Black population lived.[1] Jefferson City was, by contrast, the very small, and White, state
capital, plunked in the dead center of Missouri, separated from St. Louis
and Kansas City by more than 130 miles, several bridges, a narrow two-lane
highway, and clusters of communities of poor people. Just over twenty-five
thousand people made up the whole town.[2] "It wasn't exactly New York, not
by a long shot," she wrote ruefully.[3]

Known as the "Black Harvard of the Midwest," Lincoln University was
founded in 1866 as Lincoln Institute by Civil War veterans of the 62nd and
65th Colored Infantries of the Union Army, many of whom were former
slaves. Some White army officers also made financial gifts to support its establishment, the only public institution of higher learning for African Americans
in the state.[4] The university was both a scholastic oasis in a Jim Crow desert
and a last resort for Missouri's Black population. Lincoln acquired its schools
of journalism and law (the latter based in St. Louis) more than a decade
earlier, when the state legislature added them to keep African Americans from
enrolling in such schools in Missouri's other public institutions of higher education. Lincoln recruited and attracted Black scholars who, though educated
in the Ivy League, were overlooked by White institutions; invited intellectual
and cultural luminaries, Black and White, to campus for lectures and to receive awards; published the *Midwest Journal,* a scholarly review devoted to

African American history and studies; and enrolled students from around the world, including Nigeria, Liberia, Canada, Trinidad, and Bermuda.[5]

Athletics and the Health and Physical Education Department were part of Lincoln's commitment to excellence. When Gibson arrived, the campus was in love with its football star. Leo Lewis, known as "Mr. Touchdown," the "Minnesota Express," and the "Lincoln Locomotive," was in the midst of leading the team to a record season.[6] The P.E. department was in the early phase of a campaign to attract more top-tier athletes through a revitalized scholarship program. Gibson's singular position as the face of Black tennis and integrationist symbolism held cachet, contributed to her selection for the job, and brought publicity to the university. Like FAMC, Lincoln's name would appear in news stories about her, giving the university a type of celebrity endorsement.[7]

Lincoln, though, shortchanged Gibson. The university operated on a shoestring budget over which administrators had little control. Governors and legislators regularly thwarted presidents' leadership by interfering in university business and slashing budget proposals. Lincoln persevered like so many other Black institutions, which, in the words of Zora Neale Hurston, had to "throw up highways through the wilderness" of Jim Crow.[8] Acting with characteristic haste, Gibson accepted Lincoln's job offer without first seeing a contract. Raymond H. Kemp, the acting head of the P.E. department, decreased her starting salary by $100 ($1,110 in 2022) per month, allotting her less money than she had believed she would earn when she accepted the job. Kemp attributed the change to Gibson's "inexperience" as a teacher and to concerns that her new colleagues might harbor bad feelings if she were paid more money.[9]

Gibson, the only woman in the P.E. department, thus received an early lesson in the working lives of female faculty at HBCUs. Women in P.E. regularly received lower salaries than their male peers and were assigned more teaching responsibilities, while men were granted higher ranks and plum coaching positions. Lincoln's treatment of Gibson further destabilized her financial situation as she faced the rent on her apartment at 606 Marshall Street, a monthly car payment on her used Oldsmobile, and other personal expenses as well as those associated with tennis.[10]

Gibson was in a position of both prestige and peril as a P.E. teacher. On one hand, Black communities respected the teaching profession for doing work that would enhance the conditions of the race. Female P.E. teachers, a rarity, were seen as improving the health of African Americans, who had too often been experimented on when they were not being ignored. On the other hand, physical educators were sometimes dismissed on college campuses; P.E. teachers, the thinking went, were less important than other faculty because "they trained the body, not the mind."[11]

Gibson also navigated the fraught gender politics of her field. She was required to teach tennis and "all the other sports for women" to the "coeds," as female students were called.[12] Gibson was familiar with the expectations of refinement and femininity for Black women, intended to challenge stereotypes and thus improve the image of the race, and she was expected to teach a code that clashed with her personal outlook. She did not distinguish between sports for men and sports for women, nor did she think tennis should be played with any less vigor no matter who held the racket. This was not the outlook of a woman who was going to expect her pupils to take it easy, nor of one who cared to be seen as a paragon of femininity.

Gibson broke the rules of gender at Lincoln just as she did most everywhere else. She went straight to collegiate teaching at a time when most female educators began their careers at primary or secondary schools. She coached the men's tennis team, too, when coaching responsibilities, even for female athletes, most often went to men. Aside from the majorettes and cheerleaders, Lincoln, like other universities, had no sports teams for women. Gibson set her mind to being the best teacher that she could be. Soon after arriving on campus in September 1953, the enormousness of the transition from student to teacher struck her: "It seems that being a teacher you all-of-sudden rise to a level of full maturity which is so filled with responsibilities and hardships."[13] In her first season, she successfully led Lincoln's tennis team, the Tigers, to titles in singles and doubles in the Midwestern Athletic Conference, founded by Black schools in 1932, and to the team title in the Missouri Negro Interscholastic Athletic Association. Lincoln's student newspaper lauded her for "top notch directing."[14]

If any of the men on the team grumbled about being coached by a woman or questioned whether she had the athletic skills to lead them, Gibson squelched the talk with her racket. She once defeated the best male player from Concordia Seminary of St. Louis in a one-set exhibition match that turned out to be Lincoln's only victory in that meet, thus showing up the opposing team as well as her own. At the end of the season, she awarded varsity letters to two of her players, knowing full well that she could give those two plus the others on the team, and more than a few women on the amateur circuit, a sound thumping.[15]

Gibson also faced down another bugaboo of the female P.E. teacher and coach: the lesbian athlete stereotype. The long-standing lesbian stigma had become professionally and personally lethal by the early 1950s. Stoked by the federal government, Cold War hysteria over Communism disparaged gay men and lesbians as threats to national security and to the sanctity of families. Colleges and universities, including HBCUs, followed the lead of the federal government by terminating employees, including faculty, who were either discovered or suspected to be gay. Students were dismissed on the same grounds. Institutions used gender conformity as their measure of heterosexuality. To combat rumors of lesbianism, some women maintained feminine appearances and conduct while avoiding conspicuously close relationships with other women.[16]

And yet Gibson lived and worked through the paranoia and suspicion by flouting the rules of femininity, consequently drawing the attention of the Lincoln community. She played tennis, ping-pong, and badminton, "safe" sports for women. She also sought out opportunities to compete against Lincoln's men. Gibson wanted to join the sole faculty basketball team, which was composed entirely of men. Team members refused to have her, on the grounds that she "might get hurt." Of course, there was also the possibility that she would outplay her teammates. Shut out, Gibson practiced alongside the men's varsity team. Sure enough, she beat players in shoot-outs.[17]

Gibson joined the faculty softball team, where she was the only woman. Dwight Reed, the university's football and track coach, remembered, "You had to look two or three times at Althea to convince yourself that she was a girl. She played all the games so well. You couldn't tell she was a girl by the way she pitched or the way she shagged fly balls in the outfield."[18] Gibson dressed in shorts, pants, and T-shirts, shunning the requisite "feminine uniform" of dresses and skirts that sportswomen were expected to don in public.[19] Gibson wore a white blouse with a Peter Pan collar for her yearbook photograph, similar to the attire she wore for work every day, but she did not diminish her athleticism to satisfy social standards, dodge social stigmas, or make Lincoln's men feel better about themselves.[20] No matter the social climate, Gibson refused to order her life around what other people thought.

—◦—

In addition to working at Lincoln, Gibson faced the challenge of making a social life for herself as a single woman in the smallest town she had lived in since childhood. Jefferson City belonged to that special breed of American settings known as the small college town, rhapsodized by romantics as quaint but known by inhabitants as occasionally stifling and often riven with tension and division.

Segregation added to Gibson's challenge. She still loved going to the movies, but her joy was diminished since both of Jefferson City's movie theaters, the State and the Capitol, had segregated seating. The owners infrequently updated their offerings, leaving her to see the same film more than once and to sulk through each screening in a seat that she did not choose. Gibson said that Jefferson City "put out the lights and pull[ed] in the sidewalks at nine o'clock." Out of safety as much as choice, her social life revolved around Lincoln, whether on its "hill-top" campus or in "the foot" below, where the Black-owned businesses stood.[21]

Gibson once engaged in what she described as a "short experiment in sociological pioneering" to challenge recreational Jim Crow in Jefferson City.[22] Her effort carried overtones of compromise and conscience that reflected her years with Dr. Eaton, Dr. Johnson, and the ATA. Gibson and Donald William McMoore, assistant football coach and director of intramural sports, were frustrated that there was no place near campus where they and their students could bowl. Rejected by one bowling center, they negotiated with the second. One of the two White co-owners allowed the group to play in the morning but stipulated that they had to be gone by the early afternoon, "before his regular customers showed up."[23] Neither Gibson nor McMoore was thrilled, but they agreed and had fun during their visits, with Gibson striving to show off her 175 average. The arrangement ended abruptly when the man's business partner came to work one morning, saw Gibson, McMoore, and the students arrive to play, and met them with unadulterated hostility. "Not in this place. No colored allowed to bowl here. This is for whites only," he said.[24]

Gibson called the co-owner with whom she had made the original deal. He explained that the arrangement would have to end. "It's a matter of dollars and cents," he said. "If a couple of the leagues that use the place cancel out, we'll be in trouble. We can't afford to take the chance."[25] Gibson sensed that he was genuinely regretful. She also took his speech as a lesson in racism as a system, one that ensnared Whites who did not agree with segregation and who lived under and even struggled with its restrictions, albeit not with the same punitive consequences as African Americans.

The incident was another reminder that Gibson's experiences with integration placed her outside the norms of Jefferson City, and the rest of America. Just how far out she had been—and was—from Jim Crow as an outlook and a way of living was clear in February 1954. The National Broadcasting Company (NBC) aired an episode of *This Is Your Life* in which Gibson paid tribute to Alice Marble. The concept of the popular television series was simple: invite a group of people on the show to effectively eulogize a living person who had been an important figure in their lives but who had been given no advance notice that they were to be celebrated. As Gibson waited to emerge from backstage, Ralph Edwards, the show's producer and host, introduced her to Marble as "someone who benefited greatly in your efforts for democracy on the courts." Still offstage, Gibson spoke into a microphone. "My story is an example of how much Miss Marble has done for fair play in sports." Dramatically, she added that she would have quit playing tennis if not for Marble's support. The addition was untrue, but it made for entertaining television. Gibson then stepped before the cameras and told an abridged version of the story of how she came to play at Forest Hills, omitting the racial shadiness of the White tennis community. She concluded, "Miss Marble helped break down the racial barriers to give me and others like me a fair chance."[26]

At the end of Gibson's segment, she and Marble stood side by side onstage with their arms around each other. Gibson shared the stage with Marble and the group of friends and family there to honor her, including Dan Marble, her oldest brother; Mary K. Browne, her friend and mentor; and Eleanor "Teach" Tennant, her former coach. Gibson, well-spoken and elegant in a pale-hued dress and heels, was the only African American onstage. This radical display was transmitted directly into the homes of millions of Americans, where more White men and women than anyone cared to admit were uncomfortable seeing African Americans on the same social plane as Whites and not playing stereotypical parts.[27]

Gibson found that passing the time was easier after falling in love. She seems never to have named him publicly, describing him only as "a wonderful man" who was "a captain in the Army . . . in charge of the ROTC unit on the campus."[28] The description fit Dova L. Jones, a tall, lean man whose solemn face was decorated with a mustache. Jones joined Lincoln's faculty in the fall of 1953 as a professor of military science and tactics and leader of Lincoln's Reserve Officers' Training Corps program. A Tennessee native, Jones held a degree in mathematics, attended Officers' Candidate School, and did graduate work in math at the University of Chicago. He served in World War II, where he had tours of duty in France, England, and Japan, and as an officer in the Korean War.[29] Gibson fell madly for Jones and felt the hurts and pains of life ease when they were together. "Being in love, and being loved by somebody, was something brand new to me," she wrote in her autobiography. "Tennis no longer seemed like everything in the world to me; I was much more interested in going out on dates and having a good time."[30]

Gibson fell under Jones's influence, so much so that she prepared to make a major life change. In February 1954, Jones came to Bennett Hall, Lincoln's women's dormitory, and spoke to members of the senior class about joining the Women's Army Corps (WAC), the military service division. Gibson soon decided that she, too, should give the army a try.[31]

In the spring, Gibson applied for a position as a second lieutenant. Entering the WAC meant that she would move into yet another realm in which women were reputed to be gay, but she did not care much about that. Joining the WAC would, she thought, be beneficial "financially, and physically," suggesting that she was getting out of tennis shape.[32] The WAC would allow her to save money for herself and to send money to her family; it would also bring the prestige and ability to "live nicely" that came with being an officer, as well as a chance to flee Jim Crow society.[33]

Gibson was not the first woman who imagined the army as a springboard to stability and an escape hatch from society's restrictions. Enlisting would also enable her to prolong her relationship; her feelings for Jones grew serious enough that she imagined that they would be married by Christmas. She chose as references for her application to the WAC Dr. Eaton, Dr. Johnson, and Sydney Llewellyn; Llewellyn, who remained her coach, pleaded with her not to give up her tennis career.[34] The sheer swiftness with which Gibson took to the idea of joining the army was indicative of how easily persuaded she could be by others, particularly older men, and how desperately she wanted to begin her life anew.

—·—

Even before Gibson had accepted Lincoln's job offer, suspicions swirled that she was planning to give up tennis, at least the majors, where, according to some in the Black press, she had been "missing" since her debuts at Forest Hills and Wimbledon several years earlier.[35] After her first year at Lincoln, rumors emerged that she was unhappy and planned to leave and that she was going to give up both teaching and tennis so that she could join Count Basie's band as a singer. The chatter about her exit was so rampant that she and Lincoln officials denied it. Of course, only she, Captain Jones, Llewellyn, and Drs. Eaton and Johnson knew the truth.[36] Her return to the circuit gave the press another opportunity to be critical of her, and it gave her a chance to compete again after her longest hiatus from tennis.

Gibson started her three-month summer vacation in New York, where she did intensive work with Llewellyn. Llewellyn's influence on her was growing. Gibson considered him "the person closest to me of anybody outside my family." Llewellyn got her interested in astrology, one of his hobbies. He talked with her about the mental aspects of tennis. He believed in the power of self-talk and encouraged her to think only positive thoughts so that those would be the ones that would come to her in difficult moments during tennis matches. Llewellyn counseled Gibson to commit to working during competitions rather than having fun. He intervened in her off-court life, too, giving her a copy of Dale Carnegie's best-selling book, *How to Win Friends and Influence People*. It was all part of Llewellyn's program of being, in Gibson's words, "a psychologist" as well as a tennis coach.[37]

In July, Gibson competed in the New York State Tennis Championship, her first tournament in nearly a year, and won. Llewellyn's lessons on court strategy and knowing when to play cautiously worked. Instead of going for the forceful shots that she preferred but which sometimes wound up in the net or out of bounds, she bided her time and chose her placements carefully, enabling her to win many of the long rallies.[38]

Gibson was unable to keep up her form in her next tournament, the National Clay Court in River Forest. She was undone by poor planning. Instead of taking the train from New York to Chicago, she drove. The trip cost less money, but she arrived the night before her match fatigued and frustrated. She did not play with the patience and measured approach that had brought her the win in New York. She got caught between her old style and Llewellyn's new techniques. Too many of her shots against Lois Felix, a little-known player, were, according to the National Negro Press Association, "out of control, and, as a result, she lost 6–1, 6–1."[39] In August, Gibson secured what was essentially a guaranteed victory in women's singles, her eighth straight, at the ATA Nationals at Bethune-Cookman College in Daytona Beach, Florida. She beat Ivy Cover Ramsey, the only woman in the ATA who could give her anything close to competition.[40]

Forest Hills was the highlight of Gibson's August, but she had played so little in the past year that the tournament committee did not seed her. She arrived patently unprepared, too. Three events were not enough to get her in shape for the stiff competition. She lost in three sets in the first round, contributing to the *Amsterdam News*'s claim that she was "more or less past her peak."[41]

A slight pall and air of uncertainty hung over the women's singles at Forest Hills that year, reminding everyone that time and titles were guaranteed to no one. In July, days after winning her third consecutive Wimbledon singles title, Maureen Connolly was injured in a riding accident. A cement-mixer truck barely missed crashing head-on into Connolly and Colonel Merryboy, her gelding. The truck swerved and clipped her right leg, shredding her muscles and breaking her fibula. Instead of striving to win her fourth straight singles title at Forest Hills. Connolly was laid up in a hospital bed, recovering from surgery and fearing that she would never play tennis again. Connolly's tennis career turned out to be over at age nineteen.[42]

With the most dominant player in women's tennis out of competition, Doris Hart won Forest Hills for the first time in a tense, three-set battle with Louise Brough. It was Hart's sixth time playing in the final round of the tournament. She was twenty-nine and had finally won the career Grand Slam.[43]

Gibson had just turned twenty-seven and had yet to win any major at all.

———

As Gibson played at Forest Hills, a new opponent emerged. The August 5 issue of *Jet* referenced her in "The Truth About Women Athletes," a short article that played up the stereotype of the lesbian athlete only to disavow it.[44]

According to *Jet*, the "teacup gossip" about Gibson's sexuality had begun the moment she broke the color barrier at Forest Hills in 1950, and it centered around her tennis clothes and cohort. "This lithe, handsome tomboy . . . has been criticized for wearing trousers and having female friends," seemingly a reference to the preponderance of White women on the tennis circuit. An action shot of Gibson wearing tailored, belted white shorts and a matching open-collared shirt accompanied the article. Yet "the facts," as *Jet* discerned them, proved that she was heterosexual. "Her attire reveals a slim, voluptuous, eye-appealing figure and she has plenty of female friends of both races." *Jet* further stated that she "outgrew" her tomboy stage, an allusion to the widespread Freudian assumption that gay women were trapped in "an arrest of development," or as lesbian pulp writer Ann Aldrich wrote the following year, "The lesbian is the little girl who couldn't grow up" and develop a sexual attraction to men. Aldrich also wrote that "lesbians are good at sports; indeed . . . most gym teachers are 'lessies,' as are a majority of women athletes."[45] *Jet* concluded that Gibson, Negro League baseball player Toni Stone, and boxer Gloria Thompson belonged to the new corps of Black sportswomen who, while "hard-bitten, sexless and sensational afield, can make the lightning switch in personality that transforms them into the kind of women that make men turn their heads."[46]

The article was part of *Jet*'s strategy for hooking readers. By 1954, the magazine's weekly circulation was approaching 425,000, not counting copies passed through families and friends. Such rapid success had come in part by publishing ribald articles, many of which focused on homosexuality and perpetuated stereotypes of gay men and lesbians. There was a growing taste for such material as Americans, Black and White, consumed both Alfred Kinsey's bestselling studies and "pulps," mostly novels but also a few nonfiction titles about same-sex attraction between women that featured lurid cover art and were sold in pharmacies and grocery stores. Pulps introduced the public to the word "lesbian" and helped lesbians begin to craft their identities.[47]

The Black press had ensnared Gibson in its machinations once again. At the start of her career, she was co-opted into the pantheon of respectable race women, albeit as one who was young and novel in her tomboyish ways. "The Truth About Women Athletes" marked a shift in her usefulness to the Black media. It was among the first queer-themed articles that *Jet* published after *Brown v. Board of Education of Topeka* (1954), the public school desegregation case that gave hope to African Americans that integration was finally on the horizon and a prod that they must present themselves as ready. Ready meant straight. In the ensuing months, *Jet* and other Black publications wrote about homosexuality in unsympathetic terms and printed narratives of successful gay-to-straight conversions. "The Truth About Women Athletes" fit *Jet*'s aim of showing that Black women, including those who played sports, fit mainstream social conceptions of normal and modern. In the homophobic climate of the Cold War, that meant the women were heterosexual, the basis for advancing and representing the race. Certified as straight by *Jet*, Gibson remained in her tenuous position as a race woman a little while longer.[48]

———

Given Gibson's losing streak on the court, the Black press looked for someone to replace her as the race's leading tennis player. Pigtailed and left-handed thirteen-year-old Lorraine Williams, from the South Side of Chicago, appeared to be her successor. Like Gibson, Williams was the junior girls' champion of the ATA and came from a background that made tennis an unlikely pursuit. Williams was one of eight children raised by her widowed mother, a beautician. Williams was discovered and sponsored by dentist Willis G. Ewell and his wife, Dorothy Ann, a teacher and winner of ATA tournaments. The Black media billed Williams as a tennis prodigy who learned not only through consistent practice but also by watching and uncannily imitating the on-court actions of others, just like Gibson. Mary Hardwick, who lived in Chicago, gave Williams lessons and recognized her potential. "What Lorraine needs is the right kind of competition and constant practice. The lack of class competition early in their careers is what hampers good Negro tennis players," Hardwick noted. "She could be another Althea Gibson, or better."[49]

Others agreed. In 1953, Williams won a national tennis title at a USLTA event, taking the girls' fifteen-and-under title. She was "the logical successor to Althea Gibson," said the *New York Amsterdam News*, and her win "advanced the case of Negro tennis players a long way."[50] Gibson agreed that Williams had championship qualities. When asked about her in May, she rated Williams as an ATA junior player who demonstrated the potential to succeed in elite amateur tennis. Williams, she said, only needed to keep up her practice and on-court fitness.[51]

The outlook for Black men and boys in elite amateur tennis remained less auspicious, or at least there was no single figure on whom sportswriters felt they could pin their hopes. George Stewart won the ATA men's national title in 1951, 1952, and 1953, and Oscar Johnson won the title in 1950 and played in Milwaukee with Gibson in 1953. Both men, however, could only dream of winning USLTA-sanctioned tournaments.[52]

That the USLTA's fuzzy process for deciding which ATA players to invite to Forest Hills was questionable did not help matters. Gibson was not the only ATA player to get tossed in the first round in 1954. Ivy Cover Ramsey, Edgar P. Lee, a twenty-nine-year-old player ranked eighth in the ATA, and Dr. Eaton exited the tournament shortly after they took to their courts that year. Dr. Eaton's invitation was a most curious one, since he did not rank in the top ten of the ATA. He was summarily squashed by Tony Trabert, the defending champion, raising again the specter of rigged bracket pulls by the tournament committee.[53]

Joe Bostic pulled for Gibson from his column in the *New York Amsterdam News*, but he lamented the state of Black men in tennis and held out hope for their rise. In "These Are the Things I Hope for in '54," Bostic expressed that it was only "wishful thinking" that Black men—"our guys"—would figure in the top ten of the USLTA rankings.[54] Dr. Johnson was working to change the situation. He continued to train his band of juniors in Lynchburg every summer, traveled with promising ones to elite tournaments so that they could study the games of others, and brought boys to the Interscholastic Championships in Charlottesville and other USLTA competitions even as they were repeatedly defeated.[55]

—·—

Gibson tried to make the most of her time in Jefferson City. Two years earlier, when asked what she thought about Lincoln, she had replied, "It's beautiful and spacious."[56] After living there for several months, she felt as if the walls were closing in on her. Behind the wide and dimpled smile that Gibson displayed in her yearbook photograph, she was deeply unhappy. She faced, she said, "the problem of discontentment due to the environmental factors" and considered studying for a master's degree at New York University.[57] Jefferson City was as confining as its infamous landmark, the Missouri State Penitentiary. A riot in late September 1954 left four inmates dead, thirty-three people injured, seven buildings gutted by fire, and millions of dollars in property damage.[58] The prison was a half mile away from her apartment.

Gibson tried all manner of solutions to find happiness at Lincoln. She was charitable, joining the Dollar Club for the Polio Drive. She expressed her interest in music, singing two ballads and a blues tune as part of the College Women's Extravaganza, an annual faculty show. She sang with a five-piece band at a nightclub in town. She reconnected with Alpha Kappa Alpha, too, appearing as a special guest at a gathering of the Lincoln chapter at the conclusion of their recruitment rush activities in the winter of 1955. Seeking to be social and satisfy her hunger for games, Gibson joined two faculty-staff bridge clubs. An acquaintance from those days remembered her competitive spirit revealing itself. If Gibson's duo lost, the witness said, she grew visibly and audibly annoyed with her partner, on whom she would "blow up."[59]

Gibson's frustration was surely exacerbated by disappointment in her personal life. By the start of 1955, her relationship was over. The captain felt that the seventeen-year difference in their ages was too much. She was disappointed, but she was having second thoughts of her own. A "nagging doubt" about giving up tennis after "put[ting] so many years and so much sweat into it" had crept into her mind. Gibson was also conscious of "what other people had put into" her career, an oblique admission that the race work that undergirded the beneficence of Dr. Eaton, Dr. Johnson, and the ATA was not lost on her even though she did not play for the good of the race. However, that did not stop her from pinning her hopes for a better life on the army. In March she took, and passed, her physical examination for the WAC.[60]

Gibson resigned from the P.E. department at the end of the spring semester of 1955. She departed Lincoln at a moment when the university was in its own moment of transition. With the *Brown* decision the previous year, some White faculty were in classrooms during the 1954–1955 school year, and five White athletes played on the sports teams, one in basketball and four in football. News that as many as a hundred White students had enrolled for the following year raised pertinent questions about identity among the African Americans on the hilltop. Would Missouri close Lincoln and disperse students among the University of Missouri and the state's five other predominantly White institutions? Was Lincoln still a "Negro college"? If Lincoln remained open, would the Black faculty be let go and replaced, as was happening to Black teachers in elementary and high schools across the state?[61]

Gibson had firsthand experience with the trials that came with integration. Nonetheless, she left such questions for her former students and colleagues to puzzle over. Once the semester ended, she packed up her apartment and drove east in her Oldsmobile, letting the sight of Jefferson City fade away in her rearview mirror.[62]

———

Gibson retreated to New Jersey. Daniel, Annie, and her sisters still lived in the cramped apartment on West 143rd Street in Harlem, but it was not where she wanted to live. She stayed in Montclair with the Darbens. It was there that she waited for the WAC to call her up for officers' training school by late August.[63]

Montclair was the ideal place for Gibson as she devoted herself to getting back into shape. George Stewart, still among the top-ranked men in the ATA, was the director of physical education at the local branch of the YMCA. She and Stewart had daily rigorous workouts.[64] When Gibson won one set of a three-set match they played in June, she was overjoyed. She was also pleased that she was still able to meet the physical demands of three tough sets.[65]

Gibson applied her practice with Stewart and lessons with Llewellyn, who still opposed her decision to apply for the WAC, in tournaments that summer. In July, she won the Rose Taubele Memorial, a small event in the Bronx, and finished second in the women's doubles with Ivy Cover Ramsey. Next, Gibson was runner-up to Louise Brough in the Pennsylvania and Eastern States Tennis Tournament at Merion. She lost the last two sets 6–2, 6–1, but before that she charged into the match with confidence. She won the first set handily, 1–6, with a serve, ground strokes, volleys, and lobs that kept Brough, fresh from her fourth capture of Wimbledon, back on her heels and left Allison Danzig with the impression that Gibson had played her best tennis in five years.[66]

Gibson was playing with the thought that she was running out of time. She and Sarah Palfrey met for a "serious discussion" at the Eastern Grass Court Tournament in August. She trusted Palfrey as she trusted few people outside Dr. Eaton and Dr. Johnson, and she confided that she was planning to leave tennis. "She explained that she was already in her late 20s and had her future to consider," Palfrey remembered. "She didn't think she had many more years of tennis ahead, and felt she should be planning now for a secure means of livelihood."[67]

Forest Hills started in five weeks. Five years after making her debut there, Gibson prepared to make the tournament the site of her swan song.

———

August had long been a charged time for Gibson. The ATA Nationals, Forest Hills, the start of a new academic year, and her birthday all collided in that one month. Yet no August before or after would be as fraught with import as in 1955. Halfway through, she made her annual pilgrimage to the ATA Nationals, held yet again at Wilberforce in Ohio, and won the women's singles title for the ninth year in a row, handily beating her old junior rival Nana Davis (now Mrs. Quentin Vaughn) in two sets. Gibson and Dr. Johnson beat the Vaughns in the mixed doubles final. Her career was at least coming to a satisfying close on one circuit.[68] On August 25, she turned twenty-eight and prepared for what she expected to be her last run at Forest Hills. In the days that followed, dark and disturbing news came out of the South and upended her plans.

Overnight, on August 28, at least two White men entered a small farmhouse in Money, Mississippi, and kidnapped Emmett Louis Till, a fourteen-year-old Black boy from Chicago. Till was a guest in the home of his uncle and aunt. Days later, his body was found in the Tallahatchie River, held down by a cast iron wheel that weighed at least 150 pounds. He had been shot through the head and severely beaten. Roy Bryant and his half-brother J. W. Milam were arrested on charges of kidnapping and murder. Their crimes were believed to be acts of retribution against Till, who allegedly whistled at Bryant's wife, Carolyn, a White woman, during a visit earlier in the week to the grocery store that the Bryants ran.[69] What had happened to Emmett Till was precisely the sort of thing that disgusted Gibson about the South, and it was disgusting millions of other people around the world.

The Till murder made international headlines, riling the State Department. The agency had spent the better part of the decade after World War II trying to burnish the United States' image in the eyes of decolonizing countries in Asia and Africa and steering them away from Communism through its propaganda wing, the United States Information Agency (USIA). Reports of racial segregation and discrimination thwarted and complicated that work. The State Department tracked how media attention influenced worldwide perceptions of the country and found that "highly publicized incidents of racial strife" had the effect of "weakening" the United States' "moral position as the champion of freedom and democracy" while also "raising or reinforcing . . . doubts as to the sincerity and strength of our professions of concern for the welfare of others, particularly the non-white world."[70]

The State Department had wanted to send a team of tennis players to Southeast Asia for months. Only the "best—as players and as good representative Americans"—would do, said Harold E. Howland, the employee tasked with organizing tours.[71] "We need all the goodwill we can garner in India, Burma, Malaya, and other Southeast Asian countries."[72] Howland insisted to various American embassies in Asia that "an understanding and respect for America in that area of the world is most essential if we are to stop the spread of Communism there."[73] Tony Trabert and Vic Seixas, winners of both Forest Hills and Wimbledon, as well as Bill Talbert and Hamilton Richardson, a rising star in the amateur ranks, headed the short list of men that the department wanted to send abroad. Each man's personal and family obligations led the plan to fall apart. Still, Howland kept alive the hope of sending a team of two men and two women to Southeast Asia—specifically Colombo, Karachi, Kuala Lumpur, New Delhi, Rangoon, and Saigon—at the end of the year, especially since the president of the All-India Lawn Tennis Association had asked in January for just such a "first-class" team to compete in the Indian National Lawn Tennis Championships in New Delhi and the Asian Championships in Calcutta. The All-India group agreed to pay for the players' travel, board, and accommodations within the country and had made the same commitment to tennis teams that represented the United Kingdom and Australia, the two other countries with the most competitive tennis programs. The Till murder led the State Department to reconsider the complexion of the team best suited to carry out America's needs.[74]

Gibson was more than a thousand miles away from Money and nearly as far away from Chicago, where the world's attention shifted to Till's funeral in September, when the political fallout of the tragedy found her. Sometime around September 7, when Beverly Baker Fleitz put Gibson out of the tournament in the third round, Renville McMann, the president of the West Side Tennis Club, approached her with a proposition. "The State Department is thinking of sending a team of American tennis players on a good-will tour of Southeast Asia," he told her. "And they specifically said they would like you to be on the team." McMann asked Gibson whether she wanted to go. She was momentarily dumbfounded. "I couldn't figure out what the State Department might want with me," she remembered thinking. "I wasn't exactly the ambassador type."[75]

Maybe not, but Gibson was a good athlete in an upper-class sport, and she was Black—traits that the State Department saw as a boon in its hour of need.

Since the end of World War II, the department had been organizing international tours with the help of private organizations and citizens, including sports associations and athletes. Billed as goodwill initiatives, the trips were sheer propaganda. Many people regarded sports as apolitical, nothing more than fun and games that had some character-building components. The State Department knew better and regularly sponsored athletes, both individuals and teams, on trips abroad to display their athletic skills in competitions and interact with local communities. Officials prioritized getting the athletes to engage with young people, whom the department hoped to influence before they formed negative opinions about the United States. Black athletes were invaluable to the department's efforts, as their presence, officials thought, supplied visual evidence that America was progressing beyond its race problems.[76]

Nevertheless, the official State Department line was that the goodwill tours were not political. State Department staff fired back at anyone, including the president of the International Olympic Committee, who said that the athletic goodwill tours were political. "These sports ventures are not prompted by political motivation but rather by a sincere desire to enhance understanding in the world," Howland told *Sports Illustrated* in the summer of 1956. Excluding athletes from the "educational exchange program . . . would result in a distorted picture of our country."[77] Few would believe him.

The sight of Gibson interacting amiably with White teammates was intended to serve as proof of integration and to show that African Americans enjoyed social mobility. That she was a woman was beneficial, too. The department carried an interest in presenting American women as having opportunities that were unheard of in other parts of the world, including the Soviet bloc. Other leading tennis players, including Doris Hart, Dorothy Head Knode, Louise Brough, and Gussie Moran, had made similar tours abroad. Gibson's identity made her a veritable gift to the State Department, allowed her to enter elite company in tennis, and benefited her once again.[78]

This was not the first time that Gibson had been viewed as ambassadorial material. Her political symbolism had been mentioned in the American media, Black and White, since she broke the color barrier at Forest Hills in 1950. "How much more good is being done for the Negro race by the well-mannered and admired deeds of Jackie Robinson in baseball and Althea Gibson in tennis than by the radical rantings of [Paul] Robeson," a fan wrote to the *New York Herald Tribune* in September 1950.[79] Editorials in Black newspapers had compared her to real diplomats Edith Sampson and Ralph Bunche and touted her as a "top racial ambassador" and "an unofficial ambassador for better understanding between those who use color difference as an issue."[80] Tennis associations routinely contacted American embassies to request players to participate in tournaments after World War II. The State Department worked with the USLTA to accept the solicitations. Gibson seems not to have known it, but in 1951 the secretary of the Ceylon Lawn Tennis Association (CLTA) contacted the department after Wimbledon and asked for highly ranked American tennis players, men and women, to compete in the following year's Asian Tennis Championships. The CLTA secretary specifically asked for Gibson.[81] The State Department was ready to bet on her ability to appeal to and influence people of color around the world.

Gibson did not hesitate to accept the invitation. She put it together that the Till murder influenced the department's interest in her, but that did not lessen her eagerness to go. The Jim Crow system led Black people to make all kinds of leaps to better their individual situations. Gibson decided that the tour would surely be "interesting" and "a great honor," she told McMann.[82] Privately, she saw other compelling reasons to go. She excitedly told Dr. Eaton that this might be "the big break and opportunity that I have been waiting for." Gibson also saw the journey as a chance to restore herself after so many months, years even, of disappointments. "I do hope . . . remaining in Europe to play the circuit will help to improve me and my tennis playing." She was "so grateful for" the invitation and thought of herself as "lucky" to have been invited.[83]

True to form, Gibson soon made up her mind to bend that luck to her own benefit. In October, after competing in the Pan-American Games in Mexico City, she decided to try to remain in Europe after the State Department tour of Southeast Asia ended so that she might return to Wimbledon. Dr. Eaton suggested that she use the tour to build a professional network and enhance her appeal to corporations as a future public relations representative. Major American businesses were waking up to the existence of the so-called Negro market. Johnson Publishing Company was helping, too, by seeking to get the leaders of White-owned companies to advertise their products in the pages of *Ebony* and *Jet*.[84]

The tours were political for the federal government, but they were personal for the cultural ambassadors, many of whom used the excursions for their own ends. In this, Gibson was not unlike the other men and women the State Department sponsored. Federal sponsorship gave them credibility as important American cultural figures, steady pay, free travel, and the chance to hone and share their craft and passions with people around the world, an opportunity that some believed was genuinely beneficial to international relations.[85]

There was nothing to either stop or complicate Gibson's ability to go to Southeast Asia. The WAC still had not called her up and, according to a friend, once she decided to go to Asia, she simply skipped the interview; she did not bother calling or writing to explain. That she had applied at all had already been reported in a mainstream gossip column.[86]

Gibson did not have to think about the impact that being away would have on a relationship. Since returning from Jefferson City, she had started going out with William Darben again. Speculation swirled in Black gossip columns and in Montclair that their outings might mean that a "permanent love set" between the two was in the making.[87]

Yet Will still was not Gibson's romantic ideal, not in the way Dova Jones had been. She and Will had become "fast friends" after she refused his marriage proposal, but that was the extent of their relationship as far as she was concerned.[88] Over the summer, she had recruited players for the Southeastern Tennis Tournament, which Dr. Eaton helped to organize with the North Carolina Tennis Association. With misgivings and realism—and without romance—she entered Will in the singles and doubles competitions. "He is not the best," she said of Will's abilities, "but he does wish to participate."[89] A ringing endorsement it was not.

The State Department wasted no time in using Gibson in the Southeast Asian press. Following its long-standing propaganda strategy, USIA planted newspaper articles and pictures as early as September and October in Calcutta and Colombo to announce her pending arrival. Pieces billed her as "the prevailing young Negro tennis player."[90] Amid the fallout of the Till murder—and just days after Gibson committed to the tour—the *Daily News* in Ceylon published "Former World Tennis Champ Aids Negro Girl's Career." The profile recounted Alice Marble's support for Gibson's entry into the U.S. Nationals and even mentioned Jean Hoxie. None of the members of Gibson's Black network were mentioned. Similarly, the article mentioned FAMC and Lincoln, but omitted that they were Black institutions. The USIA erroneously depicted Gibson as a completely shadowy figure in America until Marble's editorial appeared in *American Lawn Tennis* and the *New York Herald Tribune* began to cover her, ignoring her fame in the Black press and her dominance of the ATA.[91] The State Department was whitewashing Gibson's biography to depict America as more integrated than it was.

In preparation for her departure, Gibson came to the Vanderbilt Hotel in Manhattan at the end of November to meet two of her three teammates.

Bob Perry, twenty-two, was a native of Southern California, a UCLA graduate, winner of the National Intercollegiate Doubles Championship for 1953–1954, and a member of the 1955 Davis Cup team. He planned to enlist in the army as a second lieutenant after the tour.[92] Gibson already knew Karol Fageros. Fageros, twenty-one, had introduced herself during the Pan-American Games to say that she would be a part of the team. A model and aspiring actress, she hailed from Miami and had won four tennis titles—the championships of Canada, Toronto, Hollywood, and Florida—in 1954. Tired of the hoopla that the media made about her looks, Fageros longed to be taken seriously as a tennis player. She was determined to win Wimbledon someday.[93]

Gibson had to wait a few days to meet team captain Hamilton Richardson, twenty-two, who was in England studying as a Rhodes Scholar. *Sport* described him as undercutting the popular image of the tennis bum. Richardson was a native of Baton Rouge, Louisiana, who had graduated magna cum laude from Tulane University and was a member of Phi Beta Kappa. The Junior Chamber of Commerce named him one of the outstanding young men in America in 1955. Ranked in the top ten every year since 1951 and third as the team toured Asia, he was predicted to be the next great American male champion, as he had already played on four Davis Cup teams. The State Department found heroic value in Richardson's childhood diagnosis of type 1 diabetes, which his biography treated as an obstacle that had not prevented him from "attain[ing] greatness" and had, instead, given "inspiration and hope" to youngsters and their families around the world.[94]

The State Department hand-picked Perry, Fageros, Richardson, and Gibson, who came to be known as the "U.S. Tennis Stars," to present the nation as youthful, attractive, successful, and ambitious, and officials prepared them to behave accordingly.[95] It was standard department procedure to advise cultural ambassadors on the dos and don'ts of representing the United States before tours began. Motion pictures, a television program, pamphlets, and lectures were part of the lessons designed to combat the image of the "ugly American" abroad.[96] The staff had a separate conversation with Gibson. They "warned me that I probably would be asked a lot of questions about the Negro's life in the United States," she remembered.[97] Pamphlets called "Americans Abroad: Spokesmen for the USA" and "The Negro in American Life" guided cultural ambassadors and citizens who lived abroad through discursive terrain made rocky by Jim Crow. Gibson did not recount that anyone tried either to influence her or to tell her what to say. Instead, staff left it to her to decide how to respond to queries or, worse, interrogations about race and racism. "All they asked was that I remember that I was representing my country."[98]

Of course, Gibson was representing herself, too.

———

On Tuesday, November 29, Gibson, Perry, and Fageros boarded Pan American flight 100 at Idlewild Airport. The next day, they reached London and picked up Ham Richardson. British Overseas Airways Corporation (BOAC) flight 912 carried the four to Rangoon, touching ground on December 3.[99] Gibson's journey had begun.

A British reporter who interviewed Gibson about the tour would later say that the schedule that the State Department put together for the team was "enough to kill a coalminer—or a carthorse"—and for good reason.[100] Spent in Burma (present-day Myanmar), the first week set the tone for the tour. The team's days began as early as 6:00 A.M. and involved playing exhibition matches against each other, teaming with local players as hundreds and even thousands of people watched, and attending social functions in Rangoon and Mandalay. The team was being sponsored to work, not to vacation.

Gibson complied. The team was entered in two tournaments for the tour, the Indian Lawn Tennis Championships, played December 10 through 17 in New Delhi, and the Asian Lawn Tennis Championships, played December 23 to January 2 in Calcutta. She quickly distinguished herself from her teammates by winning the women's singles titles in both tournaments, the women's doubles with Fageros in the Indian Nationals, and the mixed doubles with Richardson in the Asian Championships.[101]

More than forty years later, Richardson recalled the tour as a growing opportunity for Gibson. "A lot of the game of tennis is strictly confidence," he told an interviewer. Gibson "just really didn't know how to win." They discussed court strategy and maximizing points.[102] Gibson joined Richardson's suggestions with what she had learned on her own and from Fred Johnson, Dr. Eaton, Dr. Johnson, and Sydney Llewellyn. Gibson's take-charge ways amused Richardson. "She loved to just smack [balls] over the fence, particularly when she had a crowd of all men," he remembered. Whenever there was a chance to hit an overhead smash, she took it, telling him, "Out of the way, Hamball; this one's mine!"[103]

Both singles finals afforded Gibson an experience new to her in elite amateur tennis: she challenged another woman of color for the title. Sachiko Kamo was Japan's national champion, and her brother and doubles partner, Kosei, was a champion in his own right. Kamo battled her way to the final round of the Indian Nationals, where Gibson won easily, 6–2, 6–2. Two weeks later, Kamo gamely fought for the trophy in Calcutta. Kamo lost, but she earned respect for being tenacious in the 6–3, 9–11, 6–2 defeat. Gibson was impressed by her opponent's tenacity. "Miss Kamo has improved immensely since I played against her in Delhi only a fortnight ago," she said after the match.[104]

Gibson's abilities fascinated the media across Southeast Asia and earned her headlines and compliments, but coverage just as often emphasized her race, underscoring that she differed from Richardson, Perry, Fageros, and everyone else in the tournaments. She was, for example, "America's Althea Gibson," "the American star," and the "American lady."[105] Gibson was referred to as other things: "tall and dusky," "the American Negress Miss Althea Gibson," and the "dusky Cinderella" who had "gate-crashed into Forest Hills and Wimbledon."[106] The praise and the pejoratives followed her around the world.

Gibson noticed but was unfazed by the interest that South Asians took in her, stoked by the State Department. Proud of her victories, she mailed lengthy news clippings about her matches to Dr. Eaton. "I was obviously the principal attraction of the group. Inasmuch as we were traveling among dark-skinned peoples, that was completely understandable. I was played up everywhere we went," she boasted in her autobiography. "Because I was a Negro, the Asians not only were particularly interested in me, they also were especially proud of me. I can testify that they loved Karol, who not only played fine tennis but also looked like a Hollywood movie star, but they unquestionably got a special kick out of me because of my color."[107]

America's image was tarnishing rapidly during the team's tour, due to events in the South. In December, Georgia had global news wires humming shortly after Gibson and the team arrived in Burma: officials explored the possibility of selling state parks if authorities were made to enforce the new *Brown* decision. Governor Marvin Griffin created more buzz when he stated that the sports teams of state-sponsored universities should not have to play racially integrated opponents and voiced his opposition to Georgia Tech's bid against the University of Pittsburgh in the Rose Bowl. Alabama soon made headlines of its own. With Emmett Till and the *Brown* decision on her mind, Rosa Parks, a seamstress and longtime activist, refused to give up her seat on a bus in Montgomery. Her decision set off a bus boycott that African Americans in the city had long desired to challenge bus drivers' shoddy treatment. Before long, the Montgomery bus boycott was making headlines around the world, too. Then, in January, the *Pakistan Times* reported the arrest of seventy-two

African Americans in New Orleans for refusing to follow that city's segregation policy on buses.[108]

The climate was ripe for questions about what was happening in America
and why, but, Gibson, to her surprise, faced few. Some people approached her.
They had, she said, "read" things and wanted to "know what it really was like
for a Negro in the United States." Forewarned by the State Department, she
was prepared. "Well, we've got a problem, as all countries and all states and
individuals have, but it's a problem that certainly can be solved and that I firmly
believe will be solved," she told those who asked.[109] At other times, Gibson
chose to say that segregation was "a problem that's solving itself."[110] She tried
not to invite conversations about segregation and race. "I didn't see any point
in going too deeply into the matter. I answered all their questions honestly,
and I let them dictate how far the discussion should go."[111] Richardson was
impressed by Gibson's aplomb throughout the tour. She "was marvelous," he
said. "I mean she really made quite an impression. Frankly, she was an inspiration to all of us because she handled herself very well and spoke very well."[112]

Gibson knew more than she had ever wanted to know about Jim Crow.
She also knew that she had nothing to gain from elaborating on the system's
evils. She was consciously playing race as if it were a spectator sport.

—•—

The business and busyness of the tennis tour kept Gibson from being
preoccupied with problems back home. The State Department was so pleased
by the Southeast Asian public's enthusiasm for her and the team that officials
extended the tour by three days. The extension enabled more people across so-
cioeconomic classes to meet and see the team and gave the State Department
more chances to influence audiences, including in Bangkok, a new addition to
the schedule. The additional days meant more once-in-a-lifetime experiences
for Gibson.[113]

Tennis had long given Gibson chances to meet and interact with the social
elite, and this tour was no different. She met and entertained high-powered
figures from Asian society and politics. In Pakistan, the team played exhibition matches before a gallery made up exclusively of women at the prestigious
and private Dacca Club. In Hyderabad, an exclusive resort community, they
played before another audience of wealthy people. Only military officials,
event organizers and their guests, members of the local lawn tennis association, and USIA employees watched the exhibition matches that the team
played on an uneven tennis court in Karachi at the posh Gymkhana Club.
Some members of the Pakistani press were incensed by the class-based

segmentation of the events and further irritated that journalists were not allowed to attend despite having publicized the team for months.[114]

The privatization of events was purposeful and strategic for the State Department. The general public was not entirely cut off from meeting the team. Anyone could buy a ticket to the two championships in New Delhi and Calcutta as well as for three days of exhibition matches at Aung San Memorial Stadium in Rangoon. Still other events at which the team appeared were free and open to all. Young people and locals were not left out, either. In January, the team gave demonstrations to male college students at Karachi's N.E. Engineering College and played local players at the Gymkhana Club. The department, however, prioritized giving others more VIP exposure to the team, including opportunities to see Gibson. Staff knew from research that the wealthy and educated among Southeast Asians tended to be the most critical of segregation and the most concerned with the plight of African Americans.[115]

Courting the elite went beyond the tennis matches. Many lavish social gatherings made up the tour. In Mandalay, the government held a banquet for the team, and the Medical College in Rangoon held a cocktail party and dinner in their honor. A maharajah hosted the team as the guests of honor among thirty people at his palace. When the team arrived, Fageros was astonished to see a table a hundred feet long, filled with flowers and food. In Pakistan, they attended a dinner party that was hosted by one of the nation's wealthiest men. Gibson was taken by the display of food. The "Oriental buffet" was a delicious sight for the kid from Harlem who used to eat sweet potatoes roasted over fires fueled by wooden crates. "What a spread that was," she remembered, with "shark's fins, lamb, veal, chicken, rice, different kinds of curries, lobster, oysters and prawns." The prawns proved her undoing; she estimated that she ate as many as thirty. The next night, she overdid it during a meal at a lavish Chinese restaurant. Gibson was so sick with gastritis that she missed the next day's exhibition series.[116] In Calcutta the players sat for breakfast with officials at the South Club, the exclusive site of the Indian Nationals. Before the start of the Asian Championships, Gibson met the governor of West Bengal. These intimate social interactions, or "off-stage public relations work," were common features of goodwill tours that extended beyond the main events.[117]

Gibson reveled in the education that the tour gave her, becoming an amateur anthropologist. "The people's mode of living intrigued me," she said in 1984. "I considered it a great education to be able to travel around the world as I did, being the first black, female tennis champion of the world to have this privilege, and I enjoyed it tremendously." She learned about and observed purdah in Dacca. She was fascinated by the courtship rituals, saris, and food in India and Pakistan, too. In addition to culture, class matters were on her mind as she witnessed the similarities between the daily lives and concerns of most Indians and Pakistanis and Americans. Gibson considered it "great for someone to be able to travel, especially representing their country in a sporting event . . . to see how other people of the world live," but she was disturbed by some of what she saw, especially poverty.[118] "It's pretty much all or nothing" in Pakistan, she noticed, "and for most of the people it's nothing."[119] Years later, she told an audience that the conditions in India "turned my stomach." Perplexingly, Gibson believed that even with segregation Americans were "the luckiest individuals on earth because of the opportunities to advance and to make something of ourselves."[120]

The tour also gave Gibson an extended lesson in what life without Jim Crow could be. The excursion marked her most intimate and sustained contact with White people up to that point in her life. The teammates sat together in the same train cars. On train trips between Calcutta and Dacca, they slept together in the four beds crammed tightly into a single compartment, and shared a bathroom, too. Gibson, Fageros, Richardson, and Perry toured cultural sites together, in Mandalay climbing the famed thousand steps and standing in awe before the pagodas.[121] No one complained that Gibson had no right to be among them because she was Black. Richardson remembered their travels fondly, telling an audience in Shreveport, Louisiana, in 1966 that she was his "favorite" of the many people he met during his tennis career.[122]

Gibson socialized with Whites from other countries, too, and even made a new friend across the color line. She and Angela Buxton had first encountered each other in passing at the Pan-American Games in Mexico City. Buxton was part of the team that the British Lawn Tennis Association sent to the Indian Nationals and the Asian Championships, and in India they got to know each other better. Buxton was Jewish and, like Gibson, she had been a child migrant. Buxton's mother, Violet, moved her two children to Cape Town, South Africa, to seek refuge during World War II, while her businessman husband remained in England. In Cape Town, Buxton played with Black children, at least until Violet reluctantly bowed to apartheid and forbade it, worried for her family's own social position, already precarious because of anti-Semitism. Years later when Buxton made her way onto the amateur tennis circuit, she found herself on the margins of the tour by dint of her own very strong personality and the prejudice that pervaded the WASP-y tour, despite making the British Wightman Cup team in 1954 and 1955 and attaining a ranking of fourth. In India, Buxton invited Fageros and Gibson to practice with her when Pat Ward, her own doubles and practice partner, fell ill. Buxton got a close-up of Gibson's abilities at the Indian Nationals when Gibson and Fageros dusted Buxton and Ward mightily in the final round of the women's doubles. There were no hard feelings, though. Buxton was open-minded and kept an eye out for the future of Gibson's tennis fortunes.[123]

Meanwhile, Gibson and Fageros were forming a unique friendship. When Renville McMann had approached Gibson in the fall, she noticed that he knew Richardson and Perry would be on the team but said nothing about who the second woman would be. The thought crossed her mind that the USLTA and the State Department were searching carefully for someone who "would be friendly to the idea of going with me."[124] Contact between all the players had to be close. They would be doubles partners and share hotel rooms. Gibson found Fageros to be a game companion and one she liked very much. They stayed close to each other at social events, swam together in hotel pools—controversial by American standards no matter the region—and roomed together placidly.[125] In six weeks, only one matter divided the two women: hair.

Gibson set about washing and straightening her hair one morning early in the tour after swimming with Fageros at the Great Eastern Hotel in Rangoon. When she emerged from the shower, Fageros looked at her and laughed. When wet, Gibson's naturally curly hair rose straight up and out from the sides of her head rather than falling toward her shoulders as naturally straight tresses like Fageros's would. "Karol had never seen anything like it before and it just panicked her," Gibson remembered. Fageros "jumped on the bed and started rolling around and laughing."[126]

Gibson was conscientious about her appearance during the tour—no surprise given her conditioning by her middle-class Black patrons and mentors. Before she departed New York, Dr. Eaton told her to "remember that you are representing the United States. Take dresses with you and not slacks and try to put forth a special effort to be at your best at all times not only with regards to your dress, but with regards to your conduct in every way." That was, in his opinion, "the most important advice that anyone could give you at this time."[127]

Gibson took Dr. Eaton's instructions seriously, a sign of how deeply she wanted to succeed on the tour. She dressed conservatively for functions in a two-piece suit that was at least a size too large and had a skirt that fell below midcalf. She showed little flesh below her neck and carried a plain shoulder bag. Gibson saved her challenges to gender norms for the tennis court, where she continued to wear shorts, played with passion and power, and beat a man named Salam in a one-set exhibition match in Dacca. Away from the courts, she astonished her teammates, State Department staff, and locals with her pool skills. "Miss Gibson took on Ham Richardson and Bob Perry in a pool game in Pakistan, and this constituted something of a first," a department official remembered three years later. "Not only did she give them a sound lacing, but this was also the first time in the history of Pakistan that a woman had ever been seen in a pool room."[128]

Gibson brought the extensive tools that she needed to groom her hair all the way from New York: "a pressing comb, a curling iron, a can of Dixie Peach Pomade hair grease, and even an old soup can with the top cut off so I could make a fire in it and heat the iron," she said. She bought the material for the fire, "mentholated spirits," at a local drugstore.[129]

When Gibson heated the iron in the soup can and began straightening her hair, Fageros gawked. Gibson picked up her tools to do her grooming in the bathroom, where Fageros soon followed for more watching and more laughter. Fageros, witnessing for the first time this most private dimension of Gibson's life as a Black female public figure tasked with representing her race around the world, rendered her a spectacle in their hotel room, leaving her momentarily without sanctuary.[130]

Gibson found herself in the uncomfortable position of explaining her grooming process to Fageros, who, with her tanned White skin, straight blond hair, and buxom figure, checked all the boxes of Western beauty standards. In July 1954, *Sport* ran a full-length body shot of her standing with her head cocked just so and her chest thrust out. In the future, reporters would call Fageros "the blonde beauty," the "golden goddess of tennis," and "beauty queen of the courts," and liken her to a "Scandinavian movie queen." Fageros would find herself alternately frustrated by this attention and trying to decide how to harness it to her advantage.[131]

That day in the hotel in Rangoon, Gibson recalled saying to Fageros, "Don't laugh at me, honey, I can't help it. Us colored girls don't have hair like yours, that's all. This is what we got to do for it." Gibson had internalized the unkindness that American culture projected onto African American hair. "If I didn't press [my hair] with a hot iron, like this," she told Fageros, "it would be a mess." She and Fageros got through the tension: Gibson kept working on her hair and Fageros stopped laughing. Later, when Gibson was disappointed by the way that a hairdresser in India styled her hair, Fageros sympathized and offered to help her do the straightening the next time.[132]

Gibson and Fageros got beyond the situation because Gibson compromised and took the high ground, the path so often required of African Americans in otherwise all-White environs. She genuinely regarded Fageros as a friend, likely the first and one of the few that she had on the elite amateur circuit. "She wasn't being mean, mind you," Gibson recalled. "She was my friend" and simply lacked knowledge of grooming cultures other than her own. Fageros later said that she appreciated how much Gibson had helped her to improve as a tennis player. After weeks of practicing together in Southeast Asia, Fageros learned to adopt Gibson's more aggressive style on the tennis court and became more confident when she faced formidable opponents like Louise Brough after the tour. The following July, Fageros beat Brough in the third round of the prestigious Pennsylvania and Eastern States Tennis Championship. The press noted Fageros's "aggressive play at the net" and the "marked improvement in her service"—hallmarks of Gibson's game—and that the two had traveled to India together for the State Department.[133] For Gibson, leading, teaching, and, most of all, representing were endless. So was her reach.

———

The team gave its final exhibitions in Pakistan on January 17. The State Department was pleased by all that they had accomplished, especially Gibson. A Foreign Service employee wrote to her afterward to say that she was the focus of many of the "glowing letters" that locals sent to the American embassy in Ceylon, and added, "I'm most proud to say that you are an American."[134] Bill Lipper of the Public Affairs Office in Mandalay wrote to say that she was "still the most pleasant talk of the town" there. He was personally grateful to her for all that she had done "in the furtherance of American traditions and objectives" and in making tennis "Topic A" in the city.[135]

Gibson was proud of what she and her teammates had accomplished, too, judging that the tour was "an unqualified success."[136] Thousands of people had watched her play. Many were surely inspired to take up tennis or to get better at it no matter their level. Sachiko Kamo was a case in point. After winning the Japanese national tennis title eight times, she came to the United States in 1957 in search of new competitive challenges, including more varied and difficult court surfaces. Kamo won the Eastern Clay Court Tennis Championship and the New York State Open.[137] That same year, Ramanathan Krishnan, India's leading tennis player, thanked the State Department for bringing Gibson, Fageros, Perry, and Richardson to his country. During his own tour of America, Krishnan credited the team with creating "an interest that is getting stronger" among his fellow citizens.[138]

Gibson had gotten stronger, too, with four victories, more self-confidence, and a plan. During the tour, she told Buxton of her wish to play the European circuit and make it back to Wimbledon, but as the weeks passed she worried that her money would not last. Buxton had an idea. She encouraged Gibson to come to Europe, reasoning that she could survive on the novelty of her race and the ever-increasing solidness of her tennis skills. Gibson could live on the daily USLTA stipend of between $12 and $15 ($133 to $166) per day and coverage of her meals, laundry service, and hotel accommodations, plus under-the-table payments made to her by the tournament directors, who recognized that she was a draw and could fill seats. In effect, Gibson would put her status as a racial anomaly and spectacle to use to keep improving her game and, she hoped, to reach Wimbledon.[139]

Gibson packed her bags, pocketed her passport, and headed to Europe.

⸺

The next seven months were a blur of tennis, tennis, and still more tennis. Sydney Llewellyn had long thought he knew why her career had been stuck in neutral for so many years. "As a tennis player, [Althea] has the finest equipment of any woman who ever lived," he told a reporter. Her problem was that she had been confined to playing "vacation tennis," Llewellyn's term for competing mostly "between school semesters," whether as a student or as a teacher. As a result, Gibson "never played as often or as much as the other players on the circuit."[140] The year 1956 was her first chance to treat tennis as if it were a full-time job. Focused, Gibson became her own boss, her game her product. Tennis was a global sport, and she set out to make the indoor, clay, and grass courts of the world into her workplace, culminating, she hoped, in a decisive and triumphant meeting at Wimbledon.

Gibson began her self-guided tour in January in Stockholm, where she immediately shared a title and gained a rival. She and Sven Davidson of Sweden won the mixed doubles in the Scandinavian Indoor Tennis Championships. She reached the finals of the women's singles and doubles but was stymied in both by Angela Mortimer, the pride and hope of English women's tennis, the winner of the French Championships in 1955. Gibson had first met Mortimer in October of that year in the semifinals at the Pan-American Games and played in the style that was characteristic of her foundering midcareer matches. The first set was a dogfight, which Mortimer eked out 16–14. Then Gibson, exhausted and frustrated, wilted to lose, 6–1, in the second. After

Mortimer bested her, 4–6, 6–4, 6–3, in the title match of the Scandinavian singles, she and Ann Shilcock beat Gibson and Gudrun Johnson of Sweden to take the doubles, too.[141] Gibson racked up three losses in three months.

In her tenacity and background, Mortimer was something of a younger, English version of Gibson. Mortimer, too, had despised school and discipline. Between the war and her chores on the family farm in Totnes, she knew little joy or spontaneity in her childhood. Mortimer's father, distant and unyielding, "believed in encouraging me to fight my own battles . . . He expected me to fend for myself," she wrote in her autobiography. Like Gibson, Mortimer was also fiercely competitive and singularly focused. "What success I wanted, I wanted to win for myself. I was independent, and I didn't want help from anyone." After Mortimer discovered tennis at the age of fourteen, the game became her obsession. "There was one thing about tennis that appealed to me beyond any other game," she said. "I had to rely on no one but myself to do well." Within a decade, Mortimer could say that Teach Tennant had called her "the best young prospect in Britain," that she had won a Grand Slam singles title, and that she could beat Gibson, seemingly at will.[142]

Mortimer's respect for Gibson's game was riven with streaks of racism. She thought of her as "a tall darkie girl from America." She found her physically imposing, "a powerful girl, very tall," and considered her game "powerful," too, with "a good serve and volley." Mortimer felt a degree of intimidation and self-consciousness unlike anything she experienced when facing another competitor: "Playing against Althea, I looked small and insignificant, dwarfed by her tall, muscular power." Mortimer, however, also knew that Gibson appeared to give up "for some reason" during difficult matches. That was the difference that set the two women apart.[143]

When Gibson reached France in February, she reconnected with Angela Buxton. They teamed up for indoors doubles in the French Covered Courts Championships, beating Ann Shilcock and Susan Partridge Chatrier. Gibson and Hugh Stewart lost to Buxton and Torsten Johansson in the mixed doubles, but she beat Buxton to win the women's singles title. Gibson had come victorious to Paris from Cologne, where she won the women's singles and, paired with Frances Suzanne Schmidt, captured the doubles title in the West German International Tennis Tournament. Gibson won two more tournaments before she left France in February, the Cozon Cup in Lyons and the Gallia International in Nice, where she took down yet another English star, Shirley Bloomer.[144]

Gibson kept her streak going all through the late winter and into the spring. She won six singles titles in a row—Monte Carlo, Palermo, Naples,

Genoa, Florence, and Rome—along with several doubles and mixed doubles titles in the same events. Her momentum was halted in Egypt in March,
when she again faced Mortimer. Gibson managed to beat her in the doubles
and mixed doubles finals in the International Tennis Tournament in Cairo.
Mortimer, however, got the best of her in singles in the finals in Cairo, 6–0,
6–1, and in the Alexandria Lawn Tennis Championships, 6–3, 6–4. Gibson
was narrowing the gap, but she was still losing. She came to see Mortimer as
her "jinx opponent."[145]

Sportswriters agreed and favored Mortimer, as defending champion, to
win Roland-Garros, the French national title, at the end of May. They said
she held a "psychological advantage" over Gibson, the second-best player in
the field, because of those victories in Stockholm, Cairo, and Alexandria.[146]
In Paris, Gibson did not appear to have herself together—in one instance
quite literally. She needed two hours and three sets to beat Buxton in the
singles semifinals, where one of Gibson's bra straps snapped not once but
twice during the third set. Spectators whistled shrilly and clapped their
hands impatiently, while the umpire made a double entendre: "I'm sorry.
It's not my fault." Meanwhile, Buxton helped Gibson do the repairs with a
few safety pins in the women's dressing room. Writing for the London *Daily
Herald*, Clifford Webb mused, "It is a long time since I saw such an extraordinary mixture of good and bad tennis from two players."[147] Then Gibson
and Buxton played poorly together in the semifinals of the women's doubles.
They won, but Gibson's overall play was "lackadaisical" and she "overhit almost everything," according to Webb.[148] These were not good omens for the
final rounds.

Mortimer watched Gibson's doubles match with interest. With each of
Gibson's mistakes, Mortimer's confidence rose. She was already implementing
a practice regime that had been effective in her youth: spending at least a
half-hour each day hitting balls against a practice wall to gain control over
the length of her baseline shots. For Mortimer, seeing Gibson struggle with
Buxton affirmed that she indeed had the edge. Mortimer was even cocky
about it. "Althea Gibson and I have met five times during the past two years,"
she told Webb. "Until recently the results were very close." Mortimer went
on to recount the "marathon set" at the Pan-American Games. "I hope there
is nothing like that tomorrow—and," she added pointedly in reference to
Gibson and Buxton's doubles fiasco, "somehow I don't think there will be."[149]

Gibson saw the situation differently and got revenge. Going into the final,
she, too, remembered her history with Mortimer. "If I play her often enough,"
she said, "I'll get her in the end."[150] She regarded their previous meetings

as "such close matches" that she had reason to "[feel] very confident this afternoon."[151]

Then Gibson went out and saw to it that there was nothing close about this final. Relying on her serve and volleys, she took a mere eighteen minutes to wallop Mortimer, 6–0, in the first set. It was the type of on-court beating that Gibson meted out in ATA matches, not usually the stuff of Grand Slam finals. Mortimer fought back, trying desperately to push Gibson to a third set, but she could never do it. More than a full hour passed and "some of the finest tennis seen in a Paris women's final" was played by both, but Gibson took the second set 12–10.[152] Her arsenal—forehands, lobs, smashes, and serves—was not just sharp but diverse. She "played with much variety" in the second set, gushed one reporter.[153] Gibson's net game was so ferocious that Mortimer could not get anything past her. "She raced up to the net like a black wind-mill with all its sails whirling and bludgeon-smashed her way to match point," wrote Peter Wilson of London's *Daily Mirror* (so clever did his paper find the description that its headline the next day was "Triumph for the Black Windmill," praising, objectifying, and othering her all at once). She closed out the match with an ace down the center line.[154]

Gibson's upset victory at Roland-Garros sent a shock through the tennis world. Mortimer had been favored to win and was expected to give England its first back-to-back women's champion at the tournament since Peggy Scriven in 1933–1934. Mortimer was the player who was supposed to wrest the major trophies from America's grip, especially at Wimbledon. But Gibson disrupted the British fantasy of dominance.[155]

In the afternoon, Gibson and Buxton defeated Americans Darlene Hard and Dorothy Knode to win the doubles trophy. It was not the best match by Gibson and Buxton, whom Clifford Webb referred to as the "curiously-assorted pair," a sly reference to their being interracial together and in the minority individually.[156] They lost the first set, 6–8, and then fell to 3–4 in the second after Buxton erred on what should have been an easy return. Neither bothered nor annoyed, Gibson maintained the same aggressive out-look and strategy that had brought her victory hours earlier. "Don't worry about missing that one," she told Buxton. "We'll beat 'em up." They won the second set, 8–6, and the third, 6–1. Gibson delighted in playing with Buxton. "The stamina of Angela was what clinched the match," she said afterward. "It is wonderful to have a partner who is so strong in a final set."[157] That night, Buxton's father, Harry, treated the pair to dinner.[158]

Gibson's victory at Roland-Garros made people look at her differ-ently. Mortimer no longer thought of her as prone to giving up. "Althea was determined to win," she said after their match.[159] She also thought that Gibson had a real chance at Wimbledon. Others agreed, including Gibson herself. "When I defeated Mortimer that day in Paris," she told an audience in 1958, "I began to think that I had finally reached a point in my game that would lead me to the big victories."[160]

The French Championships also made people see Gibson as more than a novelty in the game of tennis. She was not just a Black woman who played elite tennis but the first Black winner of one of the four majors, which papers on both sides of the Atlantic noted. The day before the showdown with Mortimer, Peter Wilson had written her off as effectively a token in tennis. "Her game is not good enough" to either beat Mortimer or win Wimbledon, Wilson said. He dismissed her as only a Black "first" whose significance was limited to inspiring the dreams of some and changing the minds of others. "The entry of Althea Gibson, Negress, is now accepted in the tournaments of any truly civilised country in the world. One day, because members of her race are so often natural-born athletes, we shall have some Negro champions in lawn tennis and every other sport," he wrote, never entertaining the thought that she could be one of those champions. "That will be in part because of the pioneer work of the Gibson girl, which has spread beyond the confines of sport into a far wider and more important world—the world of human tolerance."[161] The next day, he admitted his mistake, confessed that he had been "a false prophet," and announced that "Althea had become the first Negro winner of a major title—and a worthy one."[162]

With only a sliver of hyperbole, Wilson noted, too, that prior to her tour of Europe the Continental tennis community "tended to forget that she was still playing" because she had not been back since 1951.[163] Five years later, with the French title in hand and Wimbledon on the horizon, how could anyone forget Gibson?

———

The English tennis season was as wide open in 1956 as it had been in a long time. The four tournaments at Surrey, Manchester, Bristol, and the Queen's Club at London gave the press and public alike the chance to gauge who the winner of Wimbledon might be. Americans had dominated the four events for decades, and they had swapped the women's singles title at Wimbledon among themselves without interruption since 1938. It had taken a world war to stop them—and the event—but they had returned to their winning ways when Wimbledon resumed in 1946. In 1956, though, none of the usual suspects could be counted on. Maureen Connolly had left competition after her accident. Doris Hart had turned professional after winning at Forest Hills in 1954 and 1955. Louise Brough was the defending champion at Wimbledon, but her injuries and performance anxiety increasingly made her game unpredictable. Margaret duPont could not be counted on, either. British journalists pinned their hopes on a new generation of Englishwomen, including Mortimer, Buxton, and Ann Shilcock, to bring Britain its first Wimbledon title since 1937, while others expected a member of the next wave of American women—Shirley Fry, Beverly Baker Fleitz, or Gibson—to break through.[164]

Within weeks, the British press was hailing Gibson as the best of the bunch. She was confident in her game and, after months of playing on all kinds of courts in all kinds of conditions, she had no trouble shifting from the clay at Roland-Garros to the softer grass courts in England. First, she beat Shilcock to win the Surbiton Championships at Surrey.[165] A week later, Gibson overcame Brough at Manchester's Northern Club. It took three sets, Brough never gave up, and Gibson was plainly nervous, particularly in the first set, but she won with her forceful serves, drives, and smashes. Forgetting the French Championships, the United Press called it "the biggest triumph of [Gibson's] career," and, given her early history with Brough at Forest Hills, in some sense it was.[166] Beating Brough made Gibson the favorite to win Wimbledon, and she backed up her status at Bristol in the West of England Tournament by beating Daphne Sweeney of Australia. The tournament committee at Wimbledon seeded Gibson fourth. Confident yet cautious, she skipped the women's singles at the Queen's Club to avoid pre-Wimbledon fatigue. Laurence Tingay of the London *Daily Telegraph* hailed Gibson as "the best American player which is the same as the best in the world."[167]

Gibson might have been the best player among American women, but she was left out of the competition reserved for the best players in the world. The Wightman Cup, the annual two-day competition between the top four players from the United States and the four best from Great Britain, was staged at Wimbledon in mid-June without her. She felt that "the people who picked" the American team, the USLTA, had deliberately snubbed her. Her argument was specious. Selection was based on records and rankings for the previous year, when her game had still been in the doldrums and she was ranked near the bottom of the top ten, rather than on the players' current form. Simply put, Gibson's timing was off. Nevertheless, she believed that she had been wronged: "There is no doubt in my mind that they meant to pass me up and they were just looking for an excuse."[168] That Buxton and Mortimer were on the British team likely added to the feeling that she should have been part of the most elite competition in women's sports. Instead, Shirley

Fry, Dorothy Head Knode, and Beverly Baker Fleitz joined captain Louise Brough in beating the British squad. Gibson did not say whether she blamed racial prejudice or opposition to her personality for her omission from the team. No matter the cause of her exclusion, "I didn't like it," she confessed in her autobiography, but she was powerless.[169]

———

Gibson looked good and played well as Wimbledon got under way. The stands surrounding Number 2 Court swelled with spectators as she marched all over Edda Buding, using drives, drop shots, and lobs to send the German-born Argentinian running wildly around the court. When it was over, Clifford Webb gushed that Gibson had "amazing dexterity" and the best overhead smash and serve in the women's game.[170] Tony Mottram, a former top player, offered a sexist compliment of Gibson's play, saying she played with "masculine power" as she "imitate[d] the net-rushing style of the men" and did so "with great success." Mottram saw Alice Marble, Margaret duPont, and Louise Brough—the greats of the game—in her every move.[171] Gibson, all business and unsmiling, then tore through Ann Shilcock and Pat Hird, sending a noticeable chill through the practically all-English galleries. When, for example, Gibson and Shilcock changed sides, most spectators applauded only the Brit. Some thought that nationality had nothing to do with the bias but race did. The press wrote up such occurrences, but, as one astute reporter noticed, Gibson could not have cared less about such niceties or slights: "coloured Althea Gibson . . . [who] never seems to be any crowd's special darling but who goes on winning just the same."[172]

Reporters dug out their backhanded racialized sobriquets, always a sign that Gibson had impressed them and even gotten under their skin. Suddenly she was the "cocoa-coloured throne-rocker" and "the Ebony Hurdle."[173] Predictions were that she could beat Brough in the semifinals.[174]

Not everyone was convinced. Gibson herself was not outwardly worried about living up to the pre-Wimbledon hype. "She always said she was the best in the world, even when she wasn't," Buxton recalled with laughter.[175]

The confidence had extended to Gibson's feelings about her singing. She had grown "serious" about pursuing a music career. Buxton asked a friend, singer Jerry Wayne, to organize a recording session. Gibson sang several songs and met the overseas representative for Louis Armstrong and Duke Ellington. "But that was all," she wrote later. "Nothing ever happened with those records," except she had something to play for friends when she returned home.[176]

Gibson was beginning to feel tired and as if her tennis game was becoming dull. In tennis, the difference between the best and the rest was scheduling. With their coaches, elite players planned schedules carefully to guard against becoming "over-tennised," fatigue brought on by playing too many tournaments and then entering a major with a game that was not "at a peak," as Maureen Connolly once described it, but instead "at the depths" or certainly at less than full tilt, which is what Wimbledon, Forest Hills, and the other majors required of champions.[177] Gibson felt that she "reached my peak in Europe about the time of the French Championships." That had been nearly two months earlier. Ever since, she felt that she "was going downhill," but she kept the feeling to herself.[178]

When Gibson lost to Shirley Fry in the quarterfinals, her fatigue was clear. The defeat, stunning to everyone except Gibson, happened on Centre Court. She won the first set 6–4, and some in the press and the gallery sensed an easy victory in the making. Fry, though, proved tenacious. She jumped out to a 4–2 lead in the second set and improbably reached for Gibson's wide—but fair—serves and volleys. Put off, Gibson lost her serve, and Fry won the set 3–6. Both Gibson and Fry made so many mistakes in the third and final set that it appeared that neither wanted to win, but, as Peter Wilson would say, for all the "unbelievably poor tennis" displayed in the set, "Althea was guilty of just a little more of it."[179] Tennis is a game in which players try to direct their opponent's movements, like a puppeteer pulling a marionette's strings. Fry began to control Gibson, getting her to come to the net when she wanted her to be there, not when Gibson chose to be there, Wilson noticed. Gibson, his "dark star," also bungled the basics, "missing the easy shots—the sign of a tired body and an uneasy mind."[180] Though she was the underdog, Gibson received little support from the crowd, according to reporter Scottie Hall. Hall sensed that the "atmosphere" on Centre Court was "tight-lipped, cold," and decidedly "anti-Gibson" in the silence that accompanied her winners. Hall thought about an ugly remark that he had overheard in someone else's conversation during lunch: "So Joe Louis became a champ. And what happened? Nigger boxers came out from under every stone. Same thing if Gibson walks away from here with a tennis pot." Hall deduced that most of the people in the gallery wanted to keep tennis as White as possible and that the best way to do that was for Gibson to lose.[181]

Gibson was clearly dejected after the match. She felt that she had not brought her A-game. Nevertheless, she certainly had not wanted her Wimbledon dream to end so soon. She could barely look Fry in the face, and instead of politely stopping at the net to congratulate her, Gibson merely shook her hand as they walked off the court on opposite sides of the net. It was an only slightly nicer rehash of her match against Helen Perez in New Jersey six years earlier. Gibson could have beaten Fry; in fact, she had at Manchester in the semifinals. Surely, Gibson felt what Wilson would write the next day in the *Daily Mirror*: that Fry was not an "indisputably better player" than she was.[182]

Fry, however, was a comparatively better-rested player who had placed little to no pressure on herself to win, unlike Gibson. She had played only a few tournaments in the preceding weeks and had low expectations for Wimbledon. "I didn't really mean to enter the tournament," she said later. "I did so only because I came here with America's Wightman Cup team." Fry won the French Championships in 1951, but she had even given up tennis for a time after 1952 on account of feeling inadequate in comparison to other players, in particular Maureen Connolly, who seemingly won Grand Slams with ease.[183]

Gibson's loss showed that she was not yet the elite player that she aspired to be. Back in America, that week's issue of *Life* magazine featured "Althea's Odyssey," an item feature that used two succinct paragraphs and seven pictures to show the highlights of her life and career, from paddle tennis in Harlem to her victory at Roland-Garros, as if anticipating her victory at Wimbledon. *Life* charged that Gibson "was not a first-class strategist" when it came to her game but that she had "learned how to follow her shots" and had "developed a steady backhand and a sharp volley," rather than relying solely on her "extraordinary power and big service" as she had in the past.[184] Perhaps the remarks were tinged with racism, leaning on the notion that Black athletes depended on physical prowess rather than mental acumen to succeed. Yet the fact was that all athletes had to grow and learn, and Gibson had not strategized her schedule to be at her best for Wimbledon. Instead, she had given her all in nearly two dozen tournaments around the world, tournaments that Buxton later called "slightly inferior" and that *Time* evaluated as "mostly provincial."[185] When push came to shove, except for Mortimer in France and the English tournaments afterward, none of the players Gibson beat with her new and improved game represented strenuous competition for her. For eight months, she had, to use a phrase, been jumping over the dollar to get the dime, and it finally dawned on her when she spoke to the press after the match: "It was easier to beat small fry elsewhere than big Fry at Wimbledon."[186]

Gibson settled for a consolation prize days later, when she and Buxton beat Fry and Brough to win the women's doubles championship. Fry had beaten Buxton to win the women's singles title earlier in the day. She won so decisively, taking only forty-five minutes, that the British newspaper *The People* headlined the article about the match "Angela Was Fry-ed!"[187]

Of course, Gibson had been, too, and in more ways than one as she played through her fatigue. With Fry ascendant and Forest Hills on the horizon, it remained to be seen whether Gibson, or at least her quest for a second major, would be again.

7

Press(ing) Matters

Having to contend with crowds hostile to me because of my color, with newspapermen demanding twice as much of me as they did of anybody else simply because my color made me more newsworthy, and even with powerful governments seeking to use me as an instrument of national policy because of my color, seemed to me to be more than anybody should have to bear.

—ALTHEA GIBSON, 1958

GIBSON COULD NOT beat City Hall. Perhaps she did not want to. Either way, coming to the grand white building in Lower Manhattan on July 11, 1956, at noon, five and a half hours after she returned to New York on a red-eye flight from London, was not her idea. Instead, politics was at play as she smiled and watched the mayor, Robert F. Wagner, grip a tennis racket while news cameras clicked, popped, and flashed.[1]

If others had had their way, Gibson would have received an even grander welcome upon her return to America. Since June, the editors of the *Amsterdam News* had lobbied for her to be honored with a ticker-tape parade, a reception at City Hall, and "a swank meal at the Waldorf-Astoria." She had "richly earned such a salute," and not simply because her string of tournament victories had "brought honor and glory" to the United States. Race made her a deserving candidate, too, the editors thought. "Negro Americans who conduct themselves in exemplary fashion while on foreign soil today are an effective propaganda weapon for this nation in the cold war with the Communist world," they said. "The State Department may give other reasons, but we know that this is the chief reason why Althea Gibson, Harlem's lanky tennis champion, is playing tennis on some of the most widely known courts in the world today."[2] The paper's prodding of Mayor Wagner and the New York City Council did not end with the editorial. The *Amsterdam News* published an illustration, too. "How About a Royal Welcome?" showed her waving to an unseen crowd as she sat atop the backseat of a convertible, while the mayor and Hulan E. Jack, Manhattan's first Black borough president, joined her for the ride. Soon, newspapers across the country were reporting the possibility that Gibson, either alone or with the other members of the tennis team, would be celebrated with a parade.[3]

New York's major Black politicians led a fight to garner recognition for Gibson as well. Earl Brown of the City Council introduced a resolution to acknowledge her singular performance abroad. Brown had a long-standing interest in integration and sports. He had pitched on the Harvard baseball team in the 1920s and actively worked to get the council to stop holding gatherings at Travers Island in New Rochelle because its owner, the New York Athletic Club, had neither Jews nor African Americans on its track team.[4]

Bertram Baker, ATA executive secretary, tried to pull even more powerful strings. In June, Baker wrote to New York governor Averell Harriman, Mayor Wagner, and none other than President Eisenhower "suggesting that a fitting reception be accorded" Gibson upon her return from London. Baker told Eisenhower about her selection for the State Department tour and her subsequent success, and noted that sportswriters considered her "the world's best tennis player and America's greatest goodwill ambassador in this field." Like the *Amsterdam News*, Baker tried to persuade with race. He told the president that Gibson was "a Negro girl" as well as "the first American Negro" to play at Forest Hills and Wimbledon. "Whether or not she wins the Wimbledon Championships," Baker wrote, "it is the general feeling that her accomplishments have reflected credit to our Nation and are worthy of recognition by our National, State and City government."[5] Baker, according to the *Amsterdam News*, supported having the entire team honored with a parade as a demonstration of "practical democracy."[6] Gibson's image was to be used yet again as the means to others' ends.

The overwhelming interest in Gibson by the politically minded was based in the dichotomy between her success abroad and the prevailing images and narratives about Black life in America that circulated in the domestic and global media. While she had been winning tournament after tournament and was named in one headline after another, each day brought reminders that revealed that liberty and justice for all was but a tagline in the United States. The civil rights movement was ramping up. Neither Emmett Till's mother, Mamie Till, nor Rosa Parks had gone silent after their public ordeals with Jim Crow. Both had traveled around the country for the NAACP. Back in Alabama, Martin Luther King Jr. was leading the Montgomery bus boycott. Inspired by Parks's stand, African Americans across the South launched bus boycotts in their own communities. Tallahassee joined the list thanks to Florida A&M students, a development that would have been unimaginable during Gibson's undergraduate years there.[7]

The burgeoning battle over school desegregation in the South had reinforced that African Americans were under attack in their own country and that Gibson was living a privileged life abroad to the benefit of the U.S. government. The gulf between Gibson's experiences and Alabama's response to its own pioneering Black woman, for example, was wide. In January, Autherine Lucy had become the first Black student to enroll at the University of Alabama–Birmingham (UAB). Lucy's enrollment ended after her third day of classes in February when an estimated one thousand people, including students, members of the Ku Klux Klan, and factory workers, rioted against her. The mob burned crosses, blocked traffic, and screamed heinous chants: "Where is the nigger?," "Lynch her! Kill her!," and "Keep 'Bama White!" Lucy retreated to a police car, where she lay on the floor and prayed. UAB's trustees deemed her presence disruptive to campus operations and expelled her days later.[8]

The *Atlanta Daily World*'s Marion E. Jackson had no qualms about the State Department's sponsorship of Black athletes like Gibson. Jackson considered the enthusiasm that people of color abroad expressed as they watched her, Mal Whitfield, Jesse Owens, and the many other African American sports figures who toured for the State Department in the 1950s "a glowing tribute to the recognition of the Negro as social force not only in the U.S. but the world."[9] Jackson remarked that there was "quite a contrast in the U.S.'s treatment of Miss Gibson and [what] Alabama was giving Autherine Lucy." Lucy was "a tragic starlet of trial by fire and the martyr of the mob at home," while Gibson was a "symbol of the democracy we seek to extoll to the world."[10]

Voices in the mainstream and Black media alike agreed that Gibson's symbolism was a boon to the State Department and found officials' statements to the contrary incredible. Harold E. Howland, organizer of the tennis team's tour, spoke to the significance of Gibson and other African Americans, including athletes, as goodwill ambassadors in an interview with Jackson. "They're not political propagandists," he said. "But in a quiet way, they serve as living refutation to Commie lies and distortions about life and opportunities in the United States."[11] The Associated Press would have none of it. "Miss Gibson, a Negro, and three white players . . . were sent to southeast Asia to counteract Russian claims that American Negroes are mistreated," the news agency reported in July in an article about her performance at Wimbledon.[12]

The State Department seems not to have sponsored Gibson's travels once the team's tour ended in January, though, given the surreptitious way in which the government turned to private organizations like the USLTA to secure goodwill ambassadors, the possibility was there. The press, especially Black newspapers, reported it as fact anyway.[13] That Gibson had burnished the American image on her own dime was an even bigger win for the agency. "The recent tour by tennis player Althea Gibson has elicited the praise and favorable comment for democracy from thousands despite the unfavorable publicity created by the Till murder, rebellion of the Southern states against the Supreme Court and Sen. James O. Eastland of Mississippi," Black sports scholar Edwin Bancroft Henderson wrote in a letter to the editors of the *Baltimore Afro-American*.[14] Henderson understood that news of Gibson's victories and smiling face, transmitted around the globe by newswires, had challenged stories about lynching, opposition to *Brown v. Board of Education*, and the rants of white supremacist politicians. "The State Department can never thank her enough," Bill Talbert wrote in *Sports Illustrated*.[15] The *Los Angeles Times* commented about the State Department, "You might say it issued her a visa to victory!"[16]

Nonetheless, recognition for Gibson on her return was a strictly municipal affair, limited to her "official city hall welcome" with Mayor Wagner.[17] The Democratic majority leader of the City Council, Joseph T. Sharkey, had refused to support Councilman Brown's proposal. Sharkey would not vote for any resolution for Gibson that did not also include Shirley Fry. "After an acrid debate," according to the *New York Times*, Sharkey got his way.[18] There was no ticker-tape parade, reception, or fancy banquet. The council decided that the entire State Department–sponsored team should be recognized, not just Gibson. Since the other players were unavailable, the White House decided in an internal memorandum, there was "no reason" to send Gibson a personal message from the president.[19]

Eisenhower's aides were not completely opposed to recognizing Gibson. Max Rabb, the president's cabinet secretary, judged her "a very fine symbol of character and determination." He and Jacob Seidenberg, who headed the President's Committee on Government Contracts, briefly considered appointing her to the newly formed National Physical Fitness Commission headed by Vice President Richard Nixon but decided that it was too late to make such a move. Seidenberg followed the Black press and was sensitive to the *Amsterdam News*'s observation that plenty of White people "under dubious credentials" had been given ticker-tape parades.[20] Black people, it was implied, had to work at least twice as hard for the same honor. Rabb,

Seidenberg, and Ann Whitman, the president's personal secretary, decided it would be best to acknowledge Gibson at a different time. Whitman worried about Eisenhower, who was convalescing from a heart attack, doing anything that "smacks of politicking too much" in the forum of public opinion. "If she wins at Forest Hills, maybe."[21] Eisenhower was also up for reelection in the fall and needed every (White) vote he could get.

For eight months, Gibson had created a counternarrative—or at least a distraction—about what was possible for Black people in America. She had, according to *Sports Illustrated*, "brought an electrifying quality back to tennis which has been sorely missing in recent years."[22] Race, combined with her athletic abilities, made her "an unusually good envoy for her country," while her work ethic and persistence made her "part and parcel of the real America that works for what it gets and plays hard and well to win," said the *New York Times*.[23] Yet more than a few American politicians did not know how to respond to her success. Others considered her a means to achieve their ends. Race made Gibson a political paradox, a godsend, and kryptonite all at once.

When Gibson was abroad, she likely knew little about the specific machinations over her career happening at home. She did know, however, that others—the State Department and the media, Black, White, and international—were politicizing her career in the name of race. She did not like it. While she was in London, several British newspapers erroneously printed that she was from Alabama, further connecting her to segregation and the rapidly deteriorating American image.[24] Gibson also knew that she wanted to win, and so, even before she returned to America, she set out to take charge of her own image.

On the eve of Wimbledon, Gibson met the press pool in London and revealed just how far she was—or wanted people to believe she was—from discrimination and segregation. "Miss Gibson said that she had encountered no color barriers on her climb through the ranks of championship tennis," Kennett Love, a *New York Times* reporter, wrote. "The tournament matches were arranged for her, she said, adding, that she 'just played.' None of the players she has encountered in the amateur circuit have ever been rude, she says."[25]

Gibson was rewriting her personal history while also holding firm to her long-standing assertions that she had never experienced hostility on the circuit. She overlooked the saga of her entry at Forest Hills. She also ignored what others knew: that some of the women did not like her presence on the circuit. "They wouldn't even talk to her let alone play doubles with her," Angela

Buxton said nearly sixty years later of some of the White women in tennis, singling out as exceptions Karol Fageros and Darlene Hard (who replaced Buxton as Gibson's doubles partner).[26] Gibson's body type and gender expression raised eyebrows among some players, too. Australia's Mary Hawton admired her abilities as a tennis player, though with a racist cast. Hawton described Gibson as a "negress" and "loose limbed" with a "wonderful service, overhead and volley" that were indicative of a "well produced game" that "Australian juniors" would benefit from emulating. Hawton, however, was less enamored with Gibson's garb. Gibson and Suzy Körmöczy had worn "tailored shorts and plain shirts" in the final of the Italian Championships in the spring. "Watching from a distant court," Hawton sniffed, "one would hardly know them from men." Their ensembles, Hawton thought, did not "look nearly as nice on the courts as frocks."[27]

Fred Kovaleski met and socialized with Gibson in Egypt in the spring of 1956 and remembered her interactions with the other players as she did—or as she chose to. "Look, she was part of the group," Kovaleski said in 2014. "I remember her as being a rather happy person in those, the limited years, or times I was with her. And she'd take part in our evenings if we had a free night off somewhere." Kovaleski remembered Gibson joining the band on the stage at a nightclub and in the bar of the Gezira Palace Hotel in Cairo to sing. "She was certainly welcome by the players. There was no kind of feeling, 'Hey, this is an African American,' and somehow we were uncomfortable being with her. Not at all. She was a tennis player and part of the group. That was it."[28]

Kovaleski's account may be accurate, but it raises the question of the terms under which some of the players were "comfortable" with and willing to accept having Gibson around. Sharing a hotel room with a Black person and spending hours in close contact with her as a teammate were one thing. Sitting at a remove in an audience while that same person provided entertainment from a stage was something else entirely. The latter, in fact, was one of the few and consistent ways in which Whites had been willing to accept African Americans for centuries.

Told of Kovaleski's assertion, Buxton was incredulous. She suggested that many of the White players likely looked upon their relationships with Gibson as transactional and changed their attitudes toward her in the spirit of self-gain. Once Gibson proved herself "one of the best players around in these slightly inferior tournaments, trying to make ends meet," Buxton said, they were willing to play with her for the chance to win, spend time in exotic places like Cairo, and possibly get an under-the-table payment, too.[29] Players' attitudes toward Gibson were different on American soil, too. In 1984, Gibson reluctantly admitted that she was not always invited to attend "parties," "cock-tail affairs," and other occasions for "hanging out" with her colleagues. Yet she was adamant that the exclusion "didn't bother" her. "I ignored it," she said, just as she ignored the "prejudice" that surrounded her. Being "so intense in my tennis" and "antisocial" in the fifties "saved me," she asserted. She often returned to her hotel room, ate dinner, and called her coach to discuss her next match. It was a way to survive. It was also lonely.[30]

Others, looking back, remembered more tension than Gibson divulged. "Playing against Althea was not terribly pleasant," Louise Brough told an interviewer in the 1980s. "She had a way of stalling and doing things [on the tennis court] that she perhaps was not aware of, but we all thought she was doing it on purpose."[31] Gibson denied Brough's charge when confronted, saying, "That's their version. I don't believe I ever stalled in a match."[32] The hold-ups that Brough and others thought of as a gamesmanship tactic might have been Gibson's way of steadying her nerves, a trait that many sportswriters noticed. Doris Hart admitted that many players were not warm toward Gibson and that they knew she had a harder time than they did. "We all knew the discrimination she was facing. I accepted her just as she was," Hart said vaguely. "I wouldn't say she was a friend. She was a little cocky, arrogant, and that rubbed many of us the wrong way, but I'm sure things were not easy for her and she had reasons for being how she was."[33] Hart had firsthand experience with Gibson's competitive self-confidence. She beat Gibson in each of their tennis matches. After one of those losses, Gibson shook Hart's hand at the net and audaciously said, "Tell me: how come you won? I'm much better than you."[34]

Gibson's desire to win explains her decision to be less than forthcoming about strife on the tennis circuit. It was her version of the maxim that great athletes have short memories. Sydney Llewellyn, whose coaching was geared as much toward strengthening her mental game as her on-court tactics, supported and replicated her approach. "She has been treated magnificently by everybody," he told Gussie Moran in an interview published in the fall of 1956.[35]

Gibson was not a Black woman in an ordinary line of work. She did, however, occupy White-controlled spaces—country clubs, stadiums, and little rooms or sidelines where she met the press. Dissembling about prejudice and unpleasantness, as generations of Black women did before and after her heyday, was a survival strategy. It enabled her to maintain a modicum of control over her circumstances and to keep at least some of the negativity at bay, allowing her to focus her mind as much as possible on practicing, playing, winning, and generally having peace.[36]

Gibson could not control everything, of course. Even Love, with his Ivy League sophistication, would write insultingly of her, "She is as much in her element on a fast lawn court as a panther is on an Arizona mesa. As she waits, half crouching, for a serve the comparison comes naturally to a spectator's mind."[37] More likely, though, the comparison came to the minds of White spectators who were not accustomed to Black bodies in their midst. Appearing satisfied and oblivious to prejudice mitigated at least some questions that the press asked her about race. Denying both tension and racism also allowed her to continue to have opportunities to play. Gibson wanted the State Department to arrange another competitive team tour, and she wanted to be part of it.[38] Speaking openly about Jim Crow was not the way to receive a second invitation from Uncle Sam. If she could not play, she could not win. It was as simple as that.

Gibson disavowed that she was a pioneer, too. Throughout her career, sportswriters, Black and White, wrote some variation on the idea that she actively tried to become the first Black winner of Forest Hills, Wimbledon, and other events. The Associated Press called her a "trail-blazer for her race."[39] Fay Young of the *Chicago Defender* imagined that she considered herself "an evangelist whose skill with the tennis racquet, and her sincerity, is breaking the colour barriers."[40] Yet Gibson came across as ambivalent and even disinterested in such a role by the summer of 1956. "Whatever trails she may have blazed in behalf of her race have been incidental to her career, as far as Miss Gibson is concerned. Although she is gratified if they have, in fact, been blazed," Love wrote, and quoted Gibson: " 'I am just another tennis player,' she said, 'not a Negro tennis player. Of course, I am a Negro—everybody knows that—but you don't say somebody is a white tennis player, do you?' "[41]

The display of Gibson's candor about race, identity, and representation carried over into July. Like many tennis players, Buxton tried her hand at journalism. That month, *British Lawn Tennis and Squash* published her essay "My Friend, Althea," an attempt to tell the world about the person that Buxton knew: "Althea the woman" who enjoyed sherry and the occasional cigarette, talked with her about men, and took long baths, rather than "Althea the tennis star" who was then "the focal point of hundreds of newspaper reports, magazine features, radio and television interviews." From her self-described perch as "confidant," Buxton revealed that "Althea is determined to make the grade in her own way, and no longer sees herself as the leader of any special cause." Buxton herself believed that Gibson's presence in tennis was weapon enough for civil rights. "Her personality cannot fail to be the finest propaganda against racial discrimination. Althea has already joined the legions who have battled for tolerance, justice, equality, and the banishment of all prejudices. In tennis she has triumphed over countless obstacles to set a mighty precedent."[42]

Gibson found herself wishing that no one cared either way about whom or what she did or did not represent, but that was unrealistic for a transnational Black public figure. In many ways, getting out of the United States had given her refuge from race. When it came to the media, though, her status as a racial anomaly was too obvious for the international media to ignore.

The pernicious effect of the racism of the English press had emerged on the eve of Wimbledon. During the Northern Manchester tournament, Gibson submitted to an exclusive interview with the London *Daily Mail*. Before the two-part piece was published, the newspaper promised its readers that she would give a first-person account of her life and career in the article, which was titled "Harlem to Wimbledon." Yet much of part one sounded nothing like Gibson. Some things rang true, such as that she sometimes felt "bad" about the gap between the luxurious lifestyle she enjoyed on the tennis circuit and the life that her parents and siblings lived. "I'm determined to make good for my family," she said. She gave the article credence, admitting in her autobiography that had she let her guard down with reporter Ralph Hewins to discuss her meager background and the impact of having little money, including fewer nights out than she might have liked and spending less money on clothes than she might have wished. She was, however, unlikely to have described herself as a "Negress," as part one claimed repeatedly. The piece was also filled with factual errors, saying that she had five siblings instead of four, calling Buddy Walker "Bunny," confusing Sydney Llewellyn for Fred Johnson, and insisting that she sang neither blues nor jazz.[43] The piece, in many ways, justified her growing wariness of the press.

"Why She Aims to Reach the Top," the second part of the *Daily Mail* series, so diverged from the first installment that it raises the possibility that Gibson, or others, complained. Authorities from the British Lawn Tennis and Squash Association, which ran Wimbledon, reportedly judged "Harlem to Wimbledon" controversial and asked Gibson not to be interviewed unless someone from the association was with her. There were concerns that she had written "Harlem to Wimbledon" and that the *Daily Mail* paid her, in violation of the rules of amateurism.[44]

No matter what happened, the change was obvious. The as-told-to style was gone, replaced by Hewins as the third-person narrator who quoted Gibson. "Negress" disappeared, too, as did the factual errors. Readers learned that she was from South Carolina, not Alabama. The Gibson of part two admitted her wariness of speaking openly about almost anything. "I don't care to say too much about my inner thoughts for publication as I am one of those people who don't like to be invaded. It's not my habit to let people get on the inside of me," she told Hewins, being paradoxically open about her habit of dissembling. She spoke of her pleasure in the State Department tour, saying of the youngsters who watched her play and whom she coached, "As they flocked around me and often showed extraordinarily rapid improvement I felt that I was serving a really useful purpose in bringing different peoples together in friendly sporting rivalry." This was textbook State Department messaging, but Gibson did genuinely enjoy sharing her love of tennis with children. Two weeks earlier, on the eve of the North of England Championships, she joined Lew Hoad, Jaroslav Drobny, and Thelma Long to give demonstrations for juniors in Bradford.[45] Gibson allowed Hewins to believe that she had not encountered prejudice in the United States, Europe, or any other country. Hewins did report, however, that "she is sensitive to atmosphere and in some places she has felt uncomfortable." Gibson had concluded that the discomfort and the feeling that she "didn't somehow belong" and "was different" had "undermine[d] her self-confidence and her play" at times over the past decade. It was also clear that she felt that she had to overcome such feelings. It was a candid admission. She felt that her success in 1955–1956 meant that she had "conquered" the feeling that she was an outsider in tennis.[46]

Gibson, displaying nuanced thinking and an openness to finding her own way of improving the social problem of race, expressed what she hoped her tennis career might do for African Americans. She did "feel" as if she were "a sort of ambassadress for my people, and am spurred on to greater efforts by that sense of responsibility," she said. Yet the responsibility did not involve winning exclusively: "I seek to prove by my own performance that we are equals of anybody." Gibson took an expansive view of "performance" in her desire that African Americans would do what they could to give themselves the best chance to succeed. To Gibson, that meant taking stock and ownership of their emotions and sense of self. "It's wrong that we should so often get that feeling of not belonging and uncomfortableness, whether it is justified or not. I am striving to help break down that old feeling of uneasiness. My own progress doesn't seem so far to have fired any noticeable number of young

American Negroes to take up lawn tennis seriously," she added. "But I hope that may happen if I get right to the top."[47] Gibson used the *Daily Mail* interview as her chance to say that she hoped that her presence in tennis could inspire other African Americans not to hold themselves back from entering similarly all-White realms. That, she implied, was more important and could have a greater social impact than simply getting more Black youths to play tennis. It was also a message that derived from what she learned and observed from Dr. Eaton, Dr. Johnson, and the well-off and striving members of the ATA who loved tennis as much for its character-building, future-making elements as for its competitive dimensions.

The second installment of the *Daily Mail* series was a rare opportunity for Gibson to control when and how she became part of discourses about race. That summer, her name was dragged into two discrimination scandals. Following Georgia's lead, Louisiana passed an interracial sports and games ban, a move that threatened the playing of college football's Sugar Bowl in New Orleans. "The world of sport has given the American negro the chance to score highly in his struggle for equal opportunity," English journalist Barent S. Meier wrote in an installment of his syndicated "Letter from America." "He has won undisputed points in many national and international contests." Gibson was the first (and only female) athlete that Meier named as an example, alongside Joe Louis and Rafer Johnson. Newspapers even published a picture of Gibson beside the essay, which was published in some cases under the title "Coloured People Are Barred from Sport."[48]

Gibson was particularly perturbed when she learned that she was being linked to the racial and colonial conflict between England and India. The article "Althea Center of British Rhubarb" opened by quoting an unnamed British newspaper's report that England was obligated to "show by our actions that we are free from race and colour prejudice of every kind" to retain India and its 368 million people as part of the British Empire.[49] The same report used Gibson's match at Wimbledon against Ann Shilcock to demonstrate the chasm between that ideal and the British reality. The writer accused spectators of showing bias for Shilcock by applauding for her during a changeover but disrespecting Gibson by remaining silent when she switched sides of the court. "Being considered an adjunct of U.S. State Department policy, as had been the case off and on during our Southeast Asia tour, was bad enough," she said in her autobiography, "but having to bear the responsibility for England holding on to 368,000,000 citizens of India was definitely more than I could manage."[50] The situation, Gibson felt, was an example of her involuntary role "as an instrument of international policy." As much as

Gibson had enjoyed the tour with Fageros, Richardson, and Perry and the victories that followed, she disliked the political implications, including the symbolism, that came with her travels.[51] She was also frustrated by the ways in which race saddled her with labor unknown to her White colleagues on the tennis circuit. "Having to contend with crowds hostile to me because of my color, with newspapermen demanding twice as much of me as they did of anybody else simply because my color made me more newsworthy, and even with powerful governments seeking to use me as an instrument of national policy because of my color, seemed to me to be more than anybody should have to bear."[52]

Gibson's public statements and private thoughts during this time showed that she definitely was not the Jackie Robinson of tennis, politically speaking. One could not imagine Robinson resisting the label "Negro ballplayer" or believing that his visibility and athleticism alone were sufficient for changing the status quo for African Americans. As it happened, the NAACP had announced in June that it would award Robinson its distinguished Spingarn Medal. Robinson's "civic consciousness," according to executive secretary Roy Wilkins, had only grown in the almost ten years since he had entered Major League Baseball.[53] For years, Robinson had been refusing to remain silent in the face of umpires' bad calls and instead challenged them as many White players did. He also called out other teams for integrating at a snail's pace, and pushed the Dodgers not to use the services of hotels that practiced Jim Crow. He increased his involvement with social justice organizations like the NAACP and the Anti-Defamation League. Gibson's perspective was more in line with that of some of Robinson's younger colleagues in baseball, namely Roy Campanella and Willie Mays, both of whom Robinson looked upon with irritation for, he thought, sitting passively in the bleachers as far as civil rights were concerned.[54]

It did not take long for a leading Black newspaper to chide Gibson for saying that she was a tennis player, full stop, no reference to race required. The editors of the *Pittsburgh Courier* took notice of the *New York Times* article and devoted space to schooling her on race and identity. "Well, if Miss Gibson does not know it, the tendency to identify participants in competitive sports by race, nationality or color is as old as history. That is what gives the competition its spice and flavor." The editorial board was correct that the press and public had long pitted races and nations against each other as matters of pride and entertainment. Such a way of seeing sports was so intrinsic, so deliberately constructed, that even the editors were unable, or unwilling, to see other possibilities. "Whether Miss Gibson likes it or not, she will be an American

Negro tennis player as long as she wields a racquet. Whether she wants to be identified as a Negro tennis player or not she will be, and her victories will reflect credit upon all other Negroes."[55] They called the editorial "Orchids to Althea," but it might just as well have been called "Raspberries." No less than the *Courier*, one of the leading and legendary instruments of civil rights, was denying Gibson what she wanted most of all—the right and the power to choose.

Not every major Black publication took issue with Gibson's desire for stark labels and distinctions around race to disappear. *Ebony* embraced her perspective in practice and implied that whatever she was doing was working, so she should keep on doing it. In August, the magazine published "Althea Has Finally Arrived." Like its first treatment of her in 1950, the magazine again defined success in terms of her proximity to Whiteness. *Ebony* contended that Gibson, "the Jackie Robinson of women's tennis," had matured since her debut at Forest Hills in 1950 and that her maturation led Whites to accept her without reservation. *Ebony*'s pictures and captions made the point. She was shown either alone on the tennis court or with White players. None of the people who accompanied her in the pictures were Black. Without judgment, *Ebony* pointed out that her doubles partners "always were white" and that she "seldom runs into racial incidents [and] is highly respected by opponents." The magazine praised Gibson for her navigation of the color line. It recognized that the class dimensions of tennis made her "unique among today's Negro sport stars," as she was the only one in a game popular among the "smart set," which included "snobbish people." She had "made good in this society" and, in so doing, "reached over the masses to win the support of the few who frequently influence the masses."[56]

Unlike the *Courier*, *Ebony* found nothing of concern in Gibson's approach to race. Instead, true to its approach, the magazine saw her as a Black woman to emulate, even if she did, "occasionally, smash a racquet to the court in disgust." Sure, she "wore her hair in a boyish bob." Nevertheless, *Ebony* claimed, almost strainingly so, that she was "graceful" and carried "poise . . . [of] such depths that she can be trusted with a goodwill ambassadorship."[57] Gibson, according to *Ebony*, was a queer hybrid of race, gender, class, and conduct, and an example of, rather than a threat to, the social advancement of Black people.

Across the Black media, expectations for Gibson ran high. Nationwide, a deep and long swath of pride had run through coverage of her international tour. The comparisons with Robinson were revived, and even though her loss to Fry in the quarterfinals that year "dashed" the "hopes" of millions that "a Negro would wear the Wimbledon tennis crown," many took pleasure in knowing that with the doubles title that she shared with Buxton, Gibson had "[written] her name in the history books as the first person of color to win a trophy in the world series of tennis."[58] Yet her status brought heightened intraracial scrutiny. Writers still took issue with her personality, accusing her of having "egotistical ways" and a "temper that earned her the title of 'bad actor.'"[59] Unlike male athletes, she continued to be critiqued for her appearance. In June, the *Baltimore Afro-American* ran a picture of Gibson hoisting a trophy in Europe, during one of the spans in which she had given up relaxers. "No Apex until after Wimbledon for 28-year-old Althea Gibson," said the caption, referencing the Apex Beauty Products Company, a Black-owned business that sold popular hair-straightening products. Gibson "has been so busy collecting tennis trophies all over Europe she hasn't had time for hairdressers." This, according to the writer, was a "big problem."[60] It was the *Afro-American's* way of saying that Gibson did not conform to the standards of the time for a model Black woman.

Gibson's private life was scrutinized, too. She generally kept her career and her family life separate. Daniel and Annie still had not seen her play. *Ebony, Jet*, and the major Black newspapers regularly featured and reported on the family lives of Black athletes, practically all of whom were married and fathers. Gibson, single and without children, was different, and reporters noticed. The *Afro-American* ran a picture of her with Daniel and Rosemary Darben that was taken on Gibson's first day back in New York after returning from London. The picture was snapped at Daniel and Annie's apartment. The newspaper called it "one of the rare family photos involving . . . the tennis star."[61] The caption read as a snide rebuke of Gibson for keeping her family away from her public image.

Then there was the Black media's interest in her relationship with Will Darben. The two had resumed seeing each other for the brief period that she was back in America, though she considered him only a friend. Misidentifying Darben as "Bill Barden," an Associated Negro Press gossip columnist wondered whether she "has finally found the right guy."[62] The statement said as much about the social values of the era as it did about Gibson.

Gibson was, in fact, still in no hurry to settle down. She was having the time of her life traveling the world, chasing tennis balls and tennis trophies. "Tennis has been a magic carpet for me. I wouldn't have missed these experiences for anything in the world. Life is wonderful," she had told British reporters in May.[63] The remark was at odds with all the news of the downtrodden and oppressed status of Black people and hardly suggested that she felt she was missing anything by not giving up her career and settling down to marriage and motherhood. Instead, Gibson kept her options open. She had a brief fling with a man, a swimmer who was a native Egyptian, when she played in the tournaments in Cairo and Alexandria.[64] In intimate talks with Angela Buxton, Gibson suggested that she "had her suitors."[65] Fred Kovaleski surmised that she was open to other relationships, and just relations, too. Recalling one of those evenings in the nightclub in Cairo, he said, "I think Althea was game to end up in your room in the hotel if that just happened to happen," he said. "She was game, I think. In fact, I'm pretty sure."[66] When it came to intimacy, Gibson was not following the traditional playbook.

Gibson was a reluctant political figure, and she acted accordingly. Though irritated by others' attempts to connect her with social and political matters, she knew she was a public figure whose voice and presence meant a great deal to many people. She had her own ideas about what African Americans could take from her rise. Even if she was not playing for them, Gibson hoped observers would realize what she did represent was a willingness to face, get defeated by, and thus learn from challenging opponents, which she saw as the only way to get better. "As far as tennis is concerned, it is my personal feeling that my success may help produce finer and better Negro players," she told the English press pool. "You need top-flight competition to reach the top. My own development this year was greatly enhanced by the players I was pitted against." She also struck an optimistic tone about sports integration. "In the field of sports you are more or less accepted for what you can do rather than what you are. That's been true since Jackie Robinson's time. They've"—presumably White sports administrators—"discovered there were other Negroes who could perform as well," she said. "In tennis there will be others, too."[67] While she did not think that there absolutely had to be others, she did think discrimination should not stop any who tried.

Yet for all her independent and creative thinking and her public denials, race and racism were taking a toll on Gibson. She had sometimes felt "painfully lonesome" as she traveled alone in the months after the State Department tour, particularly after she left Egypt. The feeling stemmed from the isolation of being the only Black person in so many of the spaces in which she found herself and the knowledge that as a result of her singularity she was, in the minds and eyes of others, a representation of all Black people. "No matter how hard I tried to think of myself as just another person, I was constantly being confronted with proof that I wasn't, that I was a special sort of person—a Negro with a certain amount of international significance," she told Ed Fitzgerald, her editor and ghostwriter. "It was a strain, always trying to say and do the right thing, so that I wouldn't give people the wrong idea of what Negroes are like." She longed not to be the Black representative. She also yearned for a companion, maybe romantic or perhaps just a good Black friend, "someone of my own, someone I could completely relax with and let my hair down with."[68] Focused on her future and wary of the press, she would not admit this for two years, until *I Always Wanted to Be Somebody* was published.

Gibson had no time to wallow openly, not with Forest Hills, the last major of the season, looming in the summer of 1956. The news media were segregated but, Black or White, outlets agreed that focusing on her as a racial representative and little else would be their approach. That approach made Gibson's navigation of her career harder because of the wide chasm between public perceptions of her as a Black woman in White tennis and the way in which she saw herself.

Gibson would conduct her career as she chose. She would be honest or withholding, nuanced or definitive, and just plain ambivalent when it came to talking about race and what she represented, symbolized, or aspired to. Whatever Gibson said or did, she would do so in her own way to fit her beliefs and with her own best interest in mind.

8

Changeover

The player of [1956] was undoubtedly Althea Gibson, who won the French Championships and almost every tournament in which she competed.

—*DUNLOP LAWN TENNIS ANNUAL AND ALMANACK*, 1957

GIBSON HAD NO intentions of letting up. "I don't want to be stale for the Nationals," she told the press at City Hall in July 1956. She also admitted what everyone knew: Shirley Fry was her new rival. Her great "hope" was to "reverse that loss to Miss Fry."[1]

The only way Gibson could think to do it was to play as much as possible in the six weeks leading up to Forest Hills. Stubbornly, she held to the mindset that had contributed to her loss at Wimbledon. Then she had, by her own admission, "overtennised" herself by playing week after week, neglecting to add strategic breaks to her schedule. Back in America, she made the same mistake. "I'll try to take a week's rest in there somewhere," she told the *New York Times* in mid-July.[2] Four days later, she was back on the tennis court.

The results were mixed. Fry beat Gibson 7–5, 6–1 in the final round of the National Clay Court singles in Chicago. From the score, it looked like one of Gibson's early matches, when she was routed after falling behind and inexplicably giving up. It was actually worse than that. She had led the first set 5–2 before Fry rallied to win five games straight.[3] The following week, Gibson was back on form, winning the Pennsylvania and Eastern States Tennis Championship, beating Margaret Osborne duPont, past winner of the French Championships, Forest Hills, and Wimbledon, in the title match. The convincing win, 6–1, 6–4, declared Allison Danzig, was Gibson's "most notable achievement on an American turf court."[4] She quickly followed the victory by at last taking down Louise Brough in August at the Eastern Grass Court Championships in South Orange. DuPont was nearly forty and Brough was on the back end of her career.[5] The win affirmed that Gibson was the exciting future of American women's tennis.

So was Shirley Fry, and she was wiser than Gibson. Ahead of Forest Hills, Fry followed the same formula that had won her the trophy at Wimbledon, playing a light tournament schedule. Gibson, meanwhile, went to Grossinger's, the resort in the Catskills, in mid-August. The time out of the city was a vacation, but it was work, too. Gibson played exhibition tennis matches, including with Angela Buxton, and gave clinics with head pro Eli Epstein. Then she went down to Ohio for the ATA Nationals.[6]

The trip to Wilberforce was an obligation, not a priority or meaningful preparation for a major. When, for example, Gibson outlined her tournament schedule at City Hall to the press corps, she named Chicago, Merion, Orange, and Forest Hills. She said nothing of Wilberforce. Perhaps it was a mere oversight or an indication that she was not sure she would participate. Gibson told the press several times that playing against challenging players in Asia, Africa, and Europe had improved her game. She had long ceased to face such competition in the ATA.[7] And yet there was no gracious way to get out of the trip. To skip the tournament was to risk hurting the feelings of people who had supported her in the past and to elicit accusations that she had grown too big for her britches with the State Department sponsorship and dozens of titles.

There was no question that Gibson would win the ATA Nationals. She beat Nana Davis Vaughn, 6–1, 6–1, in the title match and lofted the trophy for the tenth straight year. Six days separated that final and the start of Forest Hills. There would soon be reason to question whether playing in the ATA Nationals was still worth it.[8]

When Gibson returned from Wilberforce, she was given a chance to reflect on her earliest origins in the game. The United States Paddle Tennis Association (USPTA) held a luncheon for her at the Advertising Club and presented her with a plaque in recognition of her international success. Gibson reminisced about her days of dominance on the chalk-outlined courts on 143rd Street and spoke of how far she had traveled since then. "I owe the game a lot," she told the group. "From paddle tennis I moved to the game I am playing and I hope that I can, and am confident that I can, bring the paddle-tennis-to-tennis career to a peak by winning the national championship at Forest Hills in a few days."[9] It was something else, not necessarily defined by race, that she was playing for.

Forest Hills gave the world the chance to see that American women's tennis had reached a turning point. For the second time in three years, there was no defending champion. Doris Hart had turned professional after winning in 1955. Brough and duPont had four Forest Hills singles titles between them, but neither was as formidable and consistent as they had been in the past. The changing of the guard was fitting, as 1956 marked the diamond jubilee— seventy-five years—of the tournament.

Shirley Fry and Gibson did not exactly represent fresh newcomers. They were late bloomers who were overcoming their pasts. Both were twenty-nine. Fry had reached the Forest Hills final in 1951. The pre-tournament talk centered on Gibson and Fry, and the USLTA catered to their rivalry and to public interest in Gibson. The tournament committee placed them on opposite sides of the draw and selected Gibson, Fry's "most dangerous challenger . . . for the women's title," as the *New York Times* put it, to "open 'the show'" that was Forest Hills. She would meet Nell Hopman, the wife of the Australian Davis Cup captain, in the very first match of the tournament, and in the stadium no less. Nature got in the way, as rain pushed the start of the tournament back by a day. The delay only ratcheted up the anticipation.[10]

Like the storm that fell on Queens that first day, Gibson pelted her opponents one by one on her way to the final round. She never lost a set against Hopman, Lois Felix, Karol Fageros, Darlene Hard, or Betty Rosenquest Pratt, but that did not mean the wins came easily. Allison Danzig, always a studious analyst of Gibson's game, thought she "looked shaky" against Felix.[11] Hard, nineteen, was tenacious and fearless, forcing Gibson to win the first set 9–7. Gibson controlled the second set, 6–1, but Hard had given her a reminder that the next generation of stars was coming up fast. In the semifinals against Pratt, Gibson won the first set 6–1, and got up to a 4–1 lead in the second set. Pratt then won three straight games, bringing herself into a tie and shifting the tenor of the match. A presumed cakewalk for Gibson suddenly turned into a surprise dogfight. Pratt, after all, had beaten her years earlier. Then again, Gibson had beaten Pratt, too, and after steadying herself she did it again, taking the set 10–8.[12]

By the time Gibson met Fry in the final match, she was spent. Fry rifled volleys at Gibson in the first set and drilled her with groundstrokes in the second. Fry's serve kept Gibson back on her heels, too. After weeks of play, intense concentration, and trying as hard as players did at majors, Gibson found her arsenal depleted. Her overhead and lob lacked the firepower and accuracy that she needed, a sure sign of fatigue. Gibson's serve, effectively the engine of her game, failed, too. After she accrued some half-dozen foot faults,

Gibson became cautious, standing as much as two feet from the baseline. Her serve, considerably weaker than if she had stayed in position, became easier for Fry to return. The match was over in fifty-four minutes, with Fry winning, the United Press said, with "ridiculous ease."[13] Watching from the stands, Sydney Llewellyn made his own assessment: "Fry beat her like a mother beats a child."[14] Daniel, watching his "Al" play for the first and only time, wanted a rematch. Gibson had not lost a single set against her five previous opponents, but against Fry she went down 6–3, 6–4. Gibson decided that she had lost because she was "overcautious in the first set and overly reckless in the second."[15] This time, hybridity of the wrong kind had killed her chances.

After the match, Gibson was more gracious than she had been after losing to Fry in the quarterfinal at Wimbledon. The pictures certainly looked better. Gone was the sullen expression, the limp handshake, and the body turned away from Fry's at the net. Gibson accepted the plate for second place and laughed and smiled jocularly alongside the victor. She went to the locker room and left the stadium to put the day's events behind her.

Fry, meanwhile, faced the champion's obligations to meet the press. She spoke frankly about what had been driving her all season. After Doris Hart's retirement, Fry had unofficially vaulted to the number one ranking. "Some people thought I hadn't earned it, so I decided to go out and win this year." Fry was unperturbed that she faced her ninth attempt at Wimbledon and her sixteenth at Forest Hills. She had been playing the game since she was eight or nine and no longer lived or died by the scoreboard. At one point she had thought about giving up tennis, but instead decided to stay in the game and take a different tack. She chose her schedule selectively with a newfound self-knowledge that allowed her to relax. "I play better when it doesn't matter if I win or lose," she said. Fry also made a pledge to herself before the press corps: "No more tennis this year."[16]

It was a freedom, and an approach, that Gibson had yet to know.

———

The naysayers quickly pounced. Questions swirled about whether Gibson would ever—indeed, could ever—win Wimbledon or Forest Hills. *Sports Illustrated* alleged that she had a "block" against winning them.[17] Within weeks, *Sport* printed an article with the title "Can Althea Gibson Make It?" The author, Gussie Moran, posited that Gibson was running out of time. Age was "militating against her."[18] Moran quoted Maureen Connolly, who had become a well-regarded tennis correspondent since the end of her playing career, as saying that Gibson "doesn't think. She lacks the killer instinct."[19] The quote was a year old, and Connolly had become more enthusiastic about Gibson's abilities since then. She believed that Gibson had become expert at reading the condition of her opponents. Still, the comment captured the rising and inevitable perception that there was something faulty inside Gibson that held her back. Some thought she faded in the last two majors of the year because of the "center-court jitters" or her "faulty backhand."[20] Everyone, it seemed, either was looking for an explanation for her near-misses or else had one and was trying to back it up.

Gibson's own reaction to the loss was neither panicky nor maudlin, nor was it filled with self-blame. She was "disappointed," she said later. She was, after all, a highly competitive athlete. Yet she also possessed maturity and perspective born from recognition of how far she had come in a year, from on the verge of giving up tennis to becoming the third-ranked woman tennis player in the world and, after Roland-Garros, a major champion. "I was certain now that I was capable of playing on even terms with the best amateurs in the world, and even if I hadn't been able to beat them as often as I could have wished this year, I would get them the next time around."[21]

Gibson kept up her intense schedule, still believing that playing as much as she could was the only way to get better. Four days after the Forest Hills final, she beat Shirley Bloomer to win the singles of the O'Keefe International Invitation Tennis Tournament in Toronto and shared the doubles title with Karol Fageros. The twin victories—and on clay after playing on the much faster grass of Forest Hills—were signs that she was neither slowing down nor feeling sorry for herself.[22]

Then Gibson went to Los Angeles for the Pacific Southwest Tennis Championship, the premier tournament on the West Coast. With its list of international players and exclusive setting at the Los Angeles Tennis Club, the Pacific Southwest was as close to a major as a tournament could get without being a Grand Slam. In the final, Gibson beat Nancy Chaffee Kiner, who had bested her at the National Indoors six years earlier. The victory was satisfying, too, because Gibson added her name to the broad silver plate with Dorothy May Bundy, Sarah Palfrey, Pauline Betz, Louise Brough, Margaret Osborne duPont, Maureen Connolly, Doris Hart, and Alice Marble, further proof that she was among the best to play the game. Marble watched the match, escorted Gibson from the court after the trophy presentation, and posed for pictures with her afterward.[23]

Gibson's status as an outsider was undeniable during her time in Los Angeles. The racial dynamics of the L.A. Tennis Club were abundantly clear in the tournament program. At first glance, she was given a place of honor in the booklet. Shown in a simple white tennis dress, she was the only person pictured on the page devoted to praising the international diversity of the players. Gibson, however, was the only Black player in the tournament. She was also the only Black person shown in the picture-rich program aside from two unnamed club employees who, wearing their crisp white servant's uniforms, tended to four White women seated at a table on the club's lawn.[24]

Gibson seems not to have attended the Tennis Ball in Los Angeles. She did not lack for entertainment, however. The city had its own thriving Black community whose elite leaders were not going to allow her to go unrecognized. The women of the Turnabout Charity Club and the men of the Pacific Town Club held a reception in her honor the night before the Pacific Southwest final. Gibson came to the Town Club dressed to the nines with freshly styled hair and hoop earrings. Attendees celebrated her status as the "First Lady of the Tennis Court" and watched as Nat "King" Cole and his wife, Maria, posed for photographs with her. The Coles were intimately familiar with the bitter ironies of the color line. Cole was among the most popular singers in the country, but just a few years earlier, residents of Hancock Park, among the city's most sophisticated neighborhoods, had complained when the couple bought a house there. Cole presented Gibson with a 35 mm camera as a memento of her time in the city. Tennis players enjoyed coming to Los Angeles in part because of the Hollywood celebrities who came as spectators to the Pacific Southwest. Some even invited players to visit them on the sets of their movies. Gibson appreciated the gift and the chance to meet Cole, the king of Black entertainers, at the warm reception put on especially for her by people of her own color in an otherwise strange town.[25]

After Los Angeles, she played the Colorado State Championship in Denver. Gibson won the singles, never losing a set, and teamed with Gardnar Mulloy to win the mixed doubles, too.[26] She was just as dominant and consistent in her public remarks in the fall as she had been earlier in the season, holding firm to her intention to define herself—and her life and career—rather than allow others to do it for her. Whenever possible, she fended off the intrusive inquiries and negativity in the press. In Denver, she was gracious in praising Fry for her play at Forest Hills but refused to accept the premise that "nerves" had led to her loss: "Fry was a champion that day. I couldn't handle her and so she had to win." Nervousness was neither unusual nor specific to her, she explained. "Of course, you're always nervous when you play center court at Wimbledon or Forest Hills—everybody is." Choosing to be combative for the sake of it, Gibson disagreed when a reporter, following a long-standing trend in the press, compared her style of play with Alice Marble's. "She was my idol," Gibson explained, but said that "I didn't pattern my game after her and I only saw her play once." Yet soon, and for years afterward, Gibson would say the opposite, that she had indeed modeled her game on Marble's. To the predictable questions about marriage, she responded simply, "I haven't given it any thought."[27]

Gibson's steadiness extended to her statements about race. When a reporter asked again about her encounters with discrimination on the circuit, she said that "tennis just isn't that kind of game."[28] Ahead of the final, Gibson was mobbed by several children—all of them White—who wanted her autograph. They did not care about her color, only that she was a star.[29] Before the Pacific Southwest, she spoke with the *Los Angeles Times* and reiterated her belief that changing her attitude about race had improved her game considerably. "By now I'm not as conscious as I was of being the only representative of my race in big-time tennis. I used to think about it constantly," she said. "I had the well-wishes and desires of so many people behind me. Nowhere have I encountered discrimination. I'm still aware of representing my race, but I play tennis more for myself."[30] During the trophy presentation, Gibson told the overwhelmingly White crowd, "Everyone has been swell to me and I hope to return soon."[31]

Yet plenty happened after Forest Hills to belie Gibson's rosy assertions. Acting on the wishes of members of the Denver Country Club, the tournament site, Mulloy had invited her to play in the Colorado State Championships. The club accurately thought she would drive up ticket sales, and she was the highest-ranked player in the field and "the designated star," Mulloy later said.[32] The club's tennis courts, however, were as far on the grounds as some of those same members wanted her to go. Typical of most tournament sites, the club hosted a gala during tournament week, where Gibson mingled sociably among the other tennis players and guests. When Mulloy arrived, a group of members homed in on him. "I was cornered by several slightly inebriated members who wanted me to discreetly escort Althea from the premises," Mulloy recalled in his 2009 autobiography, *As It Was*. Their insistence made Mulloy "livid," but he also sought to "avoid an embarrassing situation." Mulloy asked the band to play "Moon over Miami." Then he "dragged a reluctant Althea on stage to sing." She stayed on the bandstand for a long time and the club members, willing to enjoy her labor to enhance their leisure, were satisfied.[33]

Mulloy, a Miami lawyer, came face-to-face with racist hostility toward Gibson another time. Standing on the steps of the courthouse in Dade County, Florida, with a group of attorneys, he talked about his summer on the tennis circuit. Suddenly, one of the group asked, "Gardnar, how come you played doubles with that nigger?" Mulloy refused to either make light of the question or let it go. "Oh, I didn't know she was a nigger," he said. "I thought she was a brilliant tennis player."[34]

———

An incident that took place soon after Gibson's visit to Denver underscored her paradoxical position as a Black celebrity. In October, she flew to Mexico City for the Pan-American Games. The pilot was forced to land the plane somewhere in Texas. Airline agents arranged for each passenger to get a hotel room. Gibson was placed in "a flophouse. The lock on my room door had been broken and there was a big gaping hole where it used to be." Recounting the incident in 1975, she acknowledged that the airline and the town's hotels were subjecting her to prejudice. She also pointed out that she deliberately chose not to use her celebrity identity to try to get a safer room somewhere else. "I can't do things like that," she said. "Why blow your own horn." Going public would have forced her to contend with negative publicity. It also would have displeased the State Department. Gibson, once again, made careful calculations. She chose to pass the night alone without sleep and on edge: "I had one eye closed and one eye open."[35]

When Gibson finally made it to Mexico, she got to know her doubles partner, Darlene Hard, better. Writing for *Sport* several months earlier, Maureen Connolly had placed Hard on her list of "Tennis Girls of Tomorrow." Hard's style of play was like Gibson's. She, too, had the "big game," Connolly observed, "a hard serve and volley reminiscent of Alice Marble."[36] Connolly thought Hard could win Forest Hills or Wimbledon by 1958, but first she needed to develop her confidence and skills of concentration. Playing with Gibson was sure to help both. Gibson was not known as either a natural or great doubles partner. Buxton thought that in the beginning of their partnership they had played as "two singles players rather than as a coordinated pair."[37] Gardnar Mulloy thought Gibson was "perhaps unwilling to concentrate on the doubles" in a tournament because "she feels she must devote her attention to winning at singles," which, he insisted, was a trait shared by some of "the best [players] in the world.[38] With Hard, Gibson indeed concentrated. After Gibson beat her to win the Pan-American singles championship, they won the doubles titles.[39]

The Pan-American also gave Hard a chance to see what Gibson's life among the other women on the circuit was like. Hard came to admire her. Long after their careers were over, she spoke about what Gibson had faced and the ways she responded. Hard understood that Gibson was under a great deal of pressure as the only African American on the circuit and thought she "was pushing" to succeed. She also acknowledged that there had been problems between Gibson and the other women. Gibson "sometimes caused the trouble. Sometimes she didn't. How do you know? It's hard to step back and objectively say this happened or that happened, because I think we all have problems in communicating. Althea worked through it."[40] It's unclear what Hard meant by "trouble," but it is certain that all was not as placid as Gibson led the press and, by extension, the public to believe.

Gibson was unconcerned about the gap between fact and fiction. Her methods—consistently good play, careful rhetoric about race, and public plaudits for the State Department—were working. She had said in the press that she hoped to be invited to represent the United States abroad again. Officials, it seemed, were listening. She formally committed to a second invitation to serve as a goodwill ambassador on a tour sponsored by the federal government and the Australian Lawn Tennis Association. When Gibson went Down Under, her rival Shirley Fry would be coming, too.[41]

As Gibson crossed from the Northern to the Southern Hemisphere in the fall of 1956, she made a major move across the color line in the American media. *World Tennis* used a solo portrait of her for its November cover, her first for an American magazine. She had been a regular presence in White newspapers and magazines during the tennis season, the subject of blurbs, full articles, substantial profiles, and editorials. She had appeared regularly in articles and photographs in *World Tennis* throughout the year. Giving Gibson the November cover was a natural and unsurprising choice, since she had won each of the tournaments—Toronto, Denver, and Los Angeles—that the issue covered at length.

Yet the portrait was significant, too. White publishers rarely placed African Americans on magazine covers, and when they did, the images could be riddled with stereotypes, which made *Ebony, Jet, Negro Digest*, and all the rest of Johnson Publishing Company's output so important to Black people. "The white folks sure think they're beautiful," Bob Jones, Chester Himes's beleaguered Black everyman, says "sardonically" in *If He Hollers, Let Him Go* as he stops to "look at the rows of white faces on the magazine covers at the book stand."[42] Narcissism and Eurocentric beauty standards were not the only factors that influenced publishers' decisions. Profits and assumptions about tastes and politics played a major part, too. To put a Black face and body on a magazine cover risked turning off White consumers who might see Black not just as unattractive but as inherently suggestive of a publication's liberal attitude, especially amid the rising racial turmoil of the day.

Gladys Heldman, *World Tennis*'s founder and editor in chief, was indeed progressive. Audaciously leading her own sports magazine was one outward manifestation. Lending Gibson a tennis racket at the Good Neighbor in Miami in 1951 after the restringing debacle had been a comparatively minor one, though not something every competitor would have done. *World Tennis* framed Gibson's cover portrait in bright red, making sure the issue would stand out on magazine displays and end tables coast to coast. Heldman was committed to putting out a strong magazine every month that covered the most notable and successful figures in tennis, which were sure to get people talking and reading. Gibson was one such person.

The *World Tennis* cover was a welcome change in mainstream media coverage of Gibson that fall. It came on the heels of "Can Althea Gibson Make It?," Gussie Moran's article for *Sport* that portrayed her as troubled. Moran had not interviewed Gibson, but she did talk with Sydney Llewellyn. Llewellyn was honest, and some of his comments did not help her image. "Althea has been a mixed-up girl all her life," he said. "As a tennis player, she has the finest equipment of any woman who ever lived. As an individual, she has personality problems so deep and enveloping that they are constantly interfering with her career. But I think she is cutting loose from them. When she does, no woman tennis player will be able to touch her." Llewellyn added, "Her trouble was that she simply didn't mind hurting people. But she has changed a great deal, I think, and she is a better player for it."[43]

Moran's angle was to focus on the ways in which Gibson made it impossible for the media to touch her, too. Moran gave a litany of Gibson's less-than-generous interactions with the media: telling a photographer not to take close-up pictures of her, standing up Australian media for an interview, telling an English writer to simply reprint a past story on her rather than interview her for a new one, and being particularly rude to a young female reporter for a major New York paper's magazine section. Gibson, according to Moran, was not afraid of directly confronting members of the press, either. After a sportswriter criticized her backhand in Europe, she supposedly tracked him down on-site and said of her backhand, "It's doing just fine, thank you."[44] Without citing a source, Moran claimed that Joe Louis no longer held Gibson in high esteem because of her behavior. Sugar Ray Robinson, though, defended her: "Althea isn't talkative. She's shy around people, which is sometimes misinterpreted."[45]

Sport and Moran simply printed what reporters had been saying among themselves for years. The murmurs dated to Fay Young's upbraiding of Gibson after she had lost the exhibition match to Mary Hardwick at Tuskegee almost a decade earlier. In September, the *Los Angeles Times* openly acknowledged media displeasure with Gibson's disposition. "Althea has been pictured as a difficult interview. But," the reporter observed, registering her own surprise, "she was completely cooperative in her first appearance at the Pacific Southwest."[46] All of it reflected two unavoidable aspects of sports celebrity. First, no matter how well an athlete played, the press wanted him or her (especially a her) to be likeable. Second, likeableness was measured by perceived approachability. These represented still more expectations that Gibson had to figure out how—and whether—to manage as she led her career.

The State Department found Gibson plenty suitable for its purposes in Australia. Staff arranged her tour with Shirley Fry to coincide with the Olympic Games being held in Melbourne. At the request of the Australian Lawn Tennis Association, Gibson and Fry played in the country's four most important tournaments. Gibson won their first two events, the New South Wales Championship in Sydney and the South Australian Championships in Adelaide.[47] Fry beat Gibson in the two events in Melbourne, the Victorian Championship and the Australian National Championship, another major. Together, they won doubles titles, too, including at the National.[48]

Gibson more than held her own when paired with Fry as thousands of Australians watched. "She sent down cannon ball services at the Australian pair and rocked them with sizzling smashes," reported *Argus* after Gibson and Fry beat Mary Hawton and Fay Muller, local favorites, in the Victorian women's doubles final. "Play against Althea is like playing against a man," Muller said afterward, joining the long list of people who could not accept that a woman could play with the kind of power that Gibson did. "I've never come up against such a hard woman server or smasher."[49] Gibson and Fry's games matched, but Fry still held the upper hand. Like Gibson, she had powerful strokes but also the discipline to keep the ball within the lines, a sense of control that occasionally eluded Gibson. Their meets were riveting, and the press quickly dubbed them "the finals twins," a cute name that underscored their national kinship.[50]

Yet the breezy nickname belied the hardships that arose on the tour. Aspects of the trip to Australia explained why Gibson liked international travel—"just enough to make life interesting."[51] The trip was long, stretching from the middle of November through the end of January and designed by the State Department to maximize Australians' exposure to Gibson and Fry, who represented the Black-White tandem that officials prized. When they were not playing, the pair, like all goodwill ambassadors, were obligated to attend social functions, where Gibson carried the unspoken knowledge and feeling that the other attendees and State Department staff were watching her. The competitive schedule was grueling. Gibson and Fry played exhibition matches on top of the four tournaments plus the Seaside Singles in Sydney during the first week of January, which Gibson won by dramatically coming back from losing the first set 0–6. In addition to practicing and playing in the singles and doubles, she played mixed doubles with Neale Fraser, an Aussie, in Victoria, too.[52]

Some of Gibson's toughest opponents in Australia proved to be the spectators seated in the grandstands and the line judges and officials who oversaw her matches. She was repeatedly called for foot faults. She reverted to her habit of defensive nonchalance when a linesman in the women's doubles final at the Victorian charged her with five. "It didn't upset me—nothing upsets me on the court," she told reporters after the match. "If the linesman called against me, then I must have footfaulted." She could afford to be congenial about the situation because she and Fry won the match.[53]

Two days later, Gibson's affability disappeared in the disastrous women's singles final as linesmen called twenty-one foot faults against her. A United Press reporter noticed that "whenever she could get her first service in without a challenge from the linesman, Miss Fry was unable to cope with it."[54] Gibson did not accept the decisions. She pushed back repeatedly and at one point asked, "Why don't you stop this and let's get on with the game?" It was a plea of annoyance veiled as a question. Twice Gibson whacked tennis balls into the grandstand with her racket, with one landing in the official box where Australian prime minister Robert Menzies sat. She chopped fiercely and frustratedly at the net cord, too. When a rainstorm struck late in the second set, Gibson, already battling a cold and searching for equilibrium, cocooned herself in the women's locker room, where she refused to speak to anyone. Jenny Hoad, wife of one of the country's tennis heroes, Lew Hoad, and a fine player in her own right, acted as her protector. "Don't try to talk to Althea now," Hoad told reporters who gathered nearby hoping for a comment. "She's more than a bit mad over all this."[55]

The crowd added to Gibson's irritation. Most were on her side, or at least found the penalties annoying enough that some called, "Change the umpire." Indeed, an additional judge joined the match. At one point, Gibson led the third set 5–1. As she held match point at 5–3 in the third set, one of the eight thousand spectators at Kooyong Stadium shattered the silence before her serve, shouting, "Let your hair down, Althea." It was a loaded comment. Did he mean that Gibson should relax, or was he making a dig at her hair type and style? Either way, the outburst was rude, inappropriate, and disruptive. Gibson, alone, perturbed, literally surrounded, and on display in one of the "White men's countries" of the world, lost the game.[56] Watching but in no way pleased, Fry battled back from almost certain defeat on the rain-slicked grass and won the match.

Gibson did not leave the stadium any more quietly than she had played in it. "If they'd only be consistent, I'd have no quarrel with them," she told reporters after the match. "In this game, your service is a mechanical thing. You go through the same identical motions all the time, unless you're in the process of experimenting with something new." She took issue with the officials in Melbourne. "How can it be that you serve properly in two cities in Australia and suddenly, doing the same thing, you are wrong in Melbourne? . . . [T]his inconsistency is what gets me down."[57] The story of Gibson's loss quickly spread. Wire services reported on her conduct, and newspapers across the country carried articles with headlines and text that described her as "irate," "in a rage," and having "burst out angrily" with her question to the linesman and shown "fits of temper."[58]

Gibson drew heavy criticism in the Australian press, even as another possible reason for her irritation was revealed: sexism. The women's singles final had not been the only one scheduled for that afternoon on Kooyong's stadium court. So, too, was the men's matchup. Officials knew that the forecast called for intermittent rainstorms followed by clear weather in the evening. The tournament committee, according to Alan Stewart of the Melbourne *Herald*, "asked" Gibson and Fry to play first, believing that their match "would suffer less from interruptions." The committee "decided that the public would want continuity in the Lew Hoad–Ken Rosewall match because the clash was a vital one to both players." It seemed never to have occurred to either the committee or Stewart, who commended the group for doing a "fine job," that the women's final was vital to its competitors.[59]

The decision reeked of the widespread notion that men's tennis was more important and entertaining than the women's game. It harkened back to the semifinals of the French Championships in 1948, when Patricia Canning Todd, the defending champion, was defaulted for refusing to play on a far-off side court with little room between the fencing and the baselines, rather than Roland-Garros's commodious No. 2 Court, the previously planned location, to accommodate the men's schedule. Such things happened in America, too. Writing in her autobiography, Doris Hart, who toured Australia with Louise

Brough in 1948 and 1949, noted an upside to the military enlistment of America's top male tennis stars during World War II: "For once [the women] were the feature attractions and played on the front courts instead of being relegated to the 'pasture'!"[60]

Stewart blamed Gibson—her cold, the foot faults, and that she "moved around the court like a tortoise in the intervals between play"—for the nearly three-hour women's final and the subsequent delay in the start of the men's final. Adrian Quist, Stewart's colleague at the *Herald*, agreed. Quist accused Gibson of making "leisurely changeovers" that, in addition to the rain, "strung out the women's match." Gibson might have been calming herself or trying to get the match delayed for the next day and better weather. In any case, neither woman, Quist wrote, played "great" tennis, and their match "ruined the Victorian men's singles," which, he added, "the spectators . . . really came to see."[61] Why Quist and Stewart did not also blame Gibson and Fry for the rainstorm is unclear.

The Victorian Championship underscored sexism as an issue Gibson faced that no one talked or wrote about. She likely had her dreadful experience in Melbourne in mind when she told *British Lawn Tennis and Squash* weeks later, "Australia would probably produce many fine women players, but women are simply not encouraged by the Australian Association. Even good matches are pushed away to outside courts."[62] Media around the world reported on Gibson's success amid racial prejudice and clamored to ask her what she thought about race. No one discussed her experiences with sexism and gender discrimination, though she could have schooled the press and the public on those topics, too.

—·—

Discounting the Melbourne officials, Gibson enjoyed the trip. Australians were "easy-going and as naturally hospitable as any people in the world," she wrote. That they also "love[d] tennis" made matters easier. "We really loved the country."[63]

Australia was a rare tennis trip, international or domestic, in which Gibson could speak in the plural. Fry made the Australian tour better. She was Gibson's roommate but also "good companionship."[64] They talked at the end of each day. Fry spoke in what some considered a "heavy, drawling twang" that blended the Akron, Ohio, of her upbringing with the St. Petersburg, Florida, necessary for her tennis career.[65] Fry had a reputation on the circuit for being down-to-earth, generous, and sincere in her praise, even to opponents who beat her, traits that belied her enviable pedigree and status in the "It" crowd of

American women's tennis for more than a decade.[66] It was easy for Gibson to pal around with Angela Buxton and Karol Fageros; she—and everyone else—knew that she could beat them, left-handed if she wanted to. This was different. In Fry, Gibson found for the first time a White contemporary whose game was better than hers but with whom she could get close and not feel intimidation or unease.

Gibson finished the State Department tour alone. Fry stayed in Sydney after January, leaving Gibson the only American entered in the Asian Championships in Colombo. Before reaching Ceylon, she passed a two-day layover in Singapore, where she played golf with an airplane steward and a horse jockey. It was, she said, "better than just sitting in a hotel room, reading." Though glad for the men's company, Gibson was self-conscious about what they would think of her if they knew the extent of her abilities. She played well and set out to "show off" her skills, but when the men called her a "natural-born golfer," she deliberately stayed silent about her other abilities. "I didn't bother to tell them that I'm also a natural-born basketball player, baseball player, football player, bowler, boxer, and that I shoot a pretty fair game of pool, too. I didn't want them to think I was a tomboy."[67] Thousands of miles from home and in the company of strangers, she was careful about precisely what she revealed to others. The silence spoke for itself—namely, that she knew her adeptness at sports suggested lesbianism in the minds of many.

The State Department had put Gibson's image to work weeks before she arrived. In January, USIA ran an illustration of her in the Ceylon *Daily News*. "Althea Gibson . . . A Leading World Tennis Player" touted the singles titles she had won in 1956 and announced that her "big goal" for 1957 was to win Wimbledon and Forest Hills. It also featured three images. Gibson smiled as she returned a drop shot in the middle and largest. On the left, three women lifted hand weights as a caption described Gibson's short career as a P.E. teacher at Lincoln. On the right, she was drawn reading while surrounded by a stack of books. "She reads a good deal," a caption said. "Her literary preferences are the Bible, autobiographies, and detective novels." USIA took a liberal approach to the illustration, describing Europe as part of "her goodwill tour," again raising the possibility that the State Department had paid for part of the tour through the USLTA in addition to the sponsorship provided by the national lawn tennis associations in the countries she visited between January and July.[68]

Decked out in a smart two-piece skirted suit and a white blouse that set off the glowing tan she had picked up in Australia, Gibson exuded confidence as she stepped off the plane. With a broad smile and a warm salutation of

"Hi there!" she heartily greeted the officials and reporters who stood on the tarmac waiting for her.[69] The Ceylonese had been anticipating her arrival for weeks. The local press touted her entry in the tournament and billed her as "ever popular" and "sure [to] . . . thrill the fans even more than she did last year."[70] Still smarting about Melbourne, she commented on the state of tennis Down Under ahead of the Asian Championship and Wimbledon: "Where women are concerned I don't think there will be any serious challenge from Australia. English women players compare well with those of America. All the same I have a good chance of winning the Wimbledon title this year."[71]

The CLTA placed Gibson's matches on Centre Court, and local women streamed into the stadium to see her play. Gibson attended the dinners and other social functions that had by then become routine. She sang a noontime blues concert in the USIA library and at a private party. "Althea has entertained music lovers all over the world with her husky-voiced 'Blues' singing," the *Daily News* reported on its "ladies' page." "We heard her sing at a party the other night and the guests were kept spellbound with some of her favourites."[72] Away from the stage, Gibson had to settle for two legs of the triple crown in the Asian Championships. Playing in all three finals, she defended her women's singles title and, teamed with Jaroslav Drobny, captured the mixed doubles, too, but lost the women's doubles with her partner, a local Ceylonese player remembered only as C. Fonseka, against Pat Ward of England and a Mrs. K. Singh of India.[73]

Then Gibson packed her rackets and headed home. She was finished with following the sun and the invitations to enter more tournaments. Free for the first time to play more than the "vacation tennis" of her early career, she had binged competitively all through 1956, only to find that she had no capacity for what mattered most, Wimbledon and Forest Hills. "All the way back to New York, between catnaps, and with the comfortingly steady roar of the four engines in my ears," Gibson recalled later, "I thought about what I could do to make 1957 Althea Gibson's year."[74] She knew the answer. She had to stop jumping over the dollar to get the dime.

9

Finding Fault with a Winner

*I tried to feel responsibilities to Negroes, but that was a
burden on my shoulders. If I did this or that, would they
like it? Perhaps it contributed to my troubles in tennis. Now
I'm playing tennis to please me, not them.*

—ALTHEA GIBSON, 1957

GIBSON STRETCHED LANGUIDLY on the couch and watched as the
images passed across the television screen at the Darben house in Montclair.
No matter the quality of the program, the surrounding decor made looking
at the set a pleasure, at least for her. Some of her trophies sat across its top,
making it impossible not to think of her career, her successes, and, competitor
that she was, her hunger for the next ones she wanted to win. The Wimbledon
plate and the Forest Hills cup would look awfully good beside the Lenglen,
her favorite so far, the prize for winning the French Championship—if only
she could get them.[1]

A reporter soon interrupted Gibson's rest and reverie. Samuel A. Haynes,
representing the *Afro-American*'s chain of newspapers, knocked on the door.
Will answered and, before she could stir from the couch, Gibson found herself facing Haynes. Armed with pen and notepad, Haynes asked impertinent questions about whether the rumor, published days earlier on the front
page of the *New York Amsterdam News*, that she was engaged to marry Will
was true.[2]

While Gibson had been traveling across the country and around the
world building her arsenal of tennis skills and adding to her trophy collection, "family fever" had continued to sweep the nation.[3] Since the end of
the war, Americans across racial groups had been marrying and having children at rates higher and ages younger than in previous decades. Millions
submitted to the postwar prosperity and optimism, portrayals in popular
culture, and programs and messaging of the federal government that settling

down and raising a brood were the thing to do personally and as a matter of good citizenship—the sooner, the better. African Americans succumbed, too, urged on by their media and the ministerial civil rights leaders who posited that marrying and having children—in that order—was another form of adhering to gender norms and a vital way to show that Black people could attain the White middle-class ideal, proof of their preparedness for integration. Marriage and parenthood had in effect become greater racial duties for Black people than they had been even a few decades earlier.[4]

Gibson's colleagues on the tennis circuit joined the matrimonial parade. In June 1955, twenty-year-old Maureen Connolly married Norman Brinker, a member of the United States equestrian team. The caption to Connolly's wedding portrait published in the *New York Times* bleated the notion that women could not—and indeed should not—blend marriage, motherhood, and careers. " 'Little Mo' Gives Up Tennis,' " the *Times* said, explaining that she "would play tennis in future only as a pastime."[5] By early 1957, Connolly was expecting her first child. Shirley Fry had stayed behind in Australia to plan her wedding to Karl Irvin, an American advertising executive based in Sydney. They married there in mid-February, and Fry immediately abandoned her career. Haynes assumed that Gibson would "soon follow in the footsteps" of Fry.[6]

Domesticity was thus yet another trend Gibson bucked, and the press, Black, White, domestic, and international, noticed, leaving her to respond repeatedly to questions about her present and future. Gibson's reactions to inquiries about her romantic life were as varied yet consistent as those that she gave about race. When a reporter dared to ask her the previous year whether she had a beau, she gave a curt response: "That's my business."[7] Another asked her at the press conference held before the Colorado Open whether she planned to marry anytime soon. Gibson's mind was firmly set on the tournament: "I haven't given it any thought."[8] During a layover in London on her way back to America in February, Gibson visited the office of *British Lawn Tennis and Squash*. She led the interviewer to believe that she would be married and listed in the Wimbledon program as "Mrs.," though she did not say either what her new surname would be or when the wedding ceremony would take place.[9]

Gibson's comments to Haynes were direct and cool, made even more so by the presence of Will, who had positioned himself awkwardly beside her on the couch. Will's sight was trained on the television, but his hearing, Haynes thought, was attuned to every word Gibson uttered. "I have no comment to make," she said over and over when Haynes asked whether the report was true. She was more voluble, if still repetitive, when addressing her immediate plans for her career. "All I plan to do is to rest and prepare for the 1957 Wimbledon matches," she said. "My only concern right now is to prepare for the Wimbledon championship." So unwavering was Gibson that she struck Haynes as sounding "like a woman possessed."[10]

When the marriage rumor spread, Gibson was in the middle of carrying out the plan that she thought would lead her to victory at Wimbledon. She was, she said, taking "a complete rest" stateside before starting her season abroad.[11] She was even willing to defy the desires of the State Department and the USLTA. "Wimbledon is the thing I really want to win and I feel this is my year," she told *British Lawn Tennis and Squash*. "I expect they will put pressure on me to go to France, but I want to begin my European tour at Manchester and not play on hard courts."[12] It was a wise and strategic decision that showed her evolving attention to her own body and its capacity to withstand the rigors of tournament tennis, as well as the impact, subtle but profound, that shifting from hard court to grass could have on her chances at Wimbledon. The Associated Negro Press, however, did not grasp that Gibson was arranging her schedule to suit her career goals. Instead, it connected her time off, a "good rest from tennis," with her supposed plan to marry.[13]

The highlight of Gibson's remaining weeks in America was not a proposal but a party. The Women's Guild of the ATA's New York chapter celebrated her with a lavish bon voyage send-off at the famous Birdland Cafe. It was an interracial affair, just like the association's aims and Gibson's career. Comedian Sam Levinson and Sammy Davis Jr., "Mr. Wonderful" himself, entertained Gibson and the three hundred guests. Renville McMann from the USLTA and Frank Peer Beal, the president of the U.S. Paddle Tennis Association, came, too. Proceeds went toward the ATA's junior development ambitions. The guild presented her with a 16 mm projector and a scrapbook filled with pictures and newspaper clippings that covered her rise. Dressed in a long, light-colored flowing skirt and a dark, fitted short-sleeved blouse, Gibson was touched, as she so often was when people honored her. She also demonstrated her flair for the dramatic and her refusal to let an opportunity go to waste. Immediately after declaring herself "too thrilled by everything happening today . . . to talk," she launched into a song, "I'll Be Seeing You (in All the Old Familiar Places)," a wise move given the venue and her rapidly growing seriousness about becoming a professional singer. The guild gave each guest a copy of the November issue of *World Tennis* with Gibson on the cover as a memento.[14]

Gibson soon appeared on the cover of another magazine, but the coverage was neither laudatory nor of the type that any respectable organization would distribute. *Hep*, a tabloid published out of Fort Worth, Texas, placed a picture of her on its June cover alongside the words "The Strange Case of Althea Gibson." "Strange" was an operative word that connoted "gay," thanks to its presence on the covers of popular lesbian pulp fiction paperbacks.[15] If anyone missed the insinuation about Gibson, they need only to have opened the magazine.

"This is a great tennis player named Althea Gibson," the first page of the article blared. "A lot of people talk and whisper about her. . . . Why do they do her like they do?" *Hep* asked. "'Cause she ain't got a man." Readers intrigued enough to turn the page saw a picture of Gibson finishing a backhand stroke, wearing long belted shorts, a polo-style shirt buttoned to her throat, and neither makeup nor jewelry. Her limbs, taut and muscular, showed, while her hair, un-straightened and uncurled, looked even shorter than it was, matted and drawn up by perspiration and heat.[16]

"The athlete as beauty queen" had become the preferred image of sportswomen in the mainstream. Many played to it. The Bauer sisters, Marlene and Alice, of the Ladies Professional Golf Association Tour, and even Gibson's colleagues in amateur tennis, such as Karol Fageros, complied. In school systems nationwide, cheerleading squads and pageants organized around homecoming and bowl games were as close as girls could get to athletics. Black sports groups were not immune. Ed Temple, the coach of Tennessee State University's famed women's track team, the Tigerbelles, did not allow photographers to snap pictures after races until after squad members had combed their hair and applied makeup. Leading industry magazines *Sport* and *Sports Illustrated* set up photo spreads of sportswomen to look like pinup displays rather than serious portraits. Golfers, tennis players, and swimmers were among their favorite subjects.[17] *Hep* deliberately published an image of Gibson in which she looked like the masculine-presenting woman that Rhoda Smith, the Eatons, and Dr. Johnson had sought to change a decade earlier. "Althea Gibson," said the caption in bold type and all caps, "has given a strong backhand to romantic swains."[18]

Hep's writer, St. Clair Johns, told of Gibson's athleticism and long-standing love of sports; her interest in other male-associated pursuits, including her self-professed "tomboy tendencies"; the fact that the other members of the Mysterious Girls had supposedly married by the time they were twenty; and the observations of unnamed sources that she "wasn't interested in boys" or "moon-eyed Lotharios" when she was a teenager. Giving in to contemporary pathologies that homosexuality stemmed from childhood troubles and faulty parenting, *Hep* asked, "Could her childhood have had anything to do with her spurning boys?"[19] Gibson's feelings had left her unmarried as she neared thirty, Johns claimed. Her "consuming passion to win 'em all," exemplified by her "blowup" at the Victorian Championship in Australia, "is believed the reason for her still being single at 29."[20]

A public relations challenge loomed as Gibson packed for England. *Hep*'s publisher was owned by Whites. Nevertheless, the tabloid, which billed itself as giving "the lowdown on Sepia, U.S.A.," had tapped into a gossipy discourse about Gibson that was circulating among African Americans.[21] Her status as a maverick of gender and race was taking on associations that could threaten her image, popularity, and post-amateur marketability. *Hep* did not directly apply the word "gay," "lesbian," or "homosexual" to her, but it did not have to. The dreaded stereotype of the lesbian athlete ran throughout "The Strange Case of Althea Gibson."

———

Gibson was a grown woman, but she still had her "boon coons." On May 23, Sydney Llewellyn, now firmly established as her coach, drove her to Idlewild, and Buddy Walker joined them. Edna Mae Robinson met the trio at the airport and discreetly passed her twenty dollars "for extra spending money."[22] Not that she needed much, for once. The USLTA had named Gibson, along with Ham Richardson, Herbert Flam, and Louise Brough, one of America's four official representatives at Wimbledon and was paying for her airfare, room, meals, and incidentals. The decision pleased Gibson as a reflection of the way that her fortunes, and perceptions of her, had changed since 1950. "We have come a long way," she wrote to Dr. Eaton when she learned the news.[23]

The money would stretch further than usual, too. Angela Buxton, out of the tournament with a lingering wrist injury and working at a department store, Lily Whites (a name that gave Gibson a big kick), met her at Heathrow Airport in her Austin convertible and brought Gibson to her home. Gibson would stay at Buxton's two-bedroom flat for her time in the London-area tournaments: Beckenham, Queen's Club, and, of course, Wimbledon. With Buxton's company, Gibson would have the friend with whom she could let her hair down, as she had so often wished for the year before. Her friends knew how much the trip and the tournament meant to her. "Since I've been trying for two years, maybe it'll be third strike in at Wimbledon," she reasoned hopefully.[24] Llewellyn, Buddy, Edna Mae, and Angela wanted her to feel as if she were royalty.[25] Gibson's friends Katherine (Kay) Landry and Dorothy (Dot) Parks did, too. ATA members and WAC captains, Landry and Parks saved their leave time so they could come to London from their base in Germany to support her during the fortnight.[26]

Gibson was a study in confidence, strategy, and caution as she prepared for Wimbledon. Rather than check her three tennis rackets with the rest of her luggage, she had carried them with her on the plane. "I didn't want anything to happen to them," she said.[27] She was so optimistic about her chances of winning Wimbledon that during her first week in London she went to Lily Whites and bought an evening gown for the Wimbledon Ball. She even started drafting her speech for the event, spending days on it with Landry and Parks. Focused on getting what she came for and nothing less, Gibson was unabashedly self-centered. She entered and won with Darlene Hard the women's doubles title at the Queen's Club tournament, the last event before Wimbledon, but passed on the singles, where she would have been the favorite and a top draw for ticket sales, because she did not want to be "all tired out" before the start of the major.[28] A year earlier and even in Australia, Gibson had accepted virtually any invitation to play an exhibition match or attend a social event as a guest. This year, however, when the International Lawn Tennis Club invited Gibson to its garden party in Hurlingham, she declined in favor of rest and giving attention to a finger on her right hand that she injured during the Kent Championship at Beckenham.[29]

Gibson was unafraid to both show and tell anyone who would listen what her priorities were. When rain began to fall before the start of her semifinal match at the Northern Lawn Tennis Tournament at Manchester, she refused to play. "I am sorry to disappoint everybody," she said. "But it is Wimbledon I'm really here for. The court is very slippery and I dare not risk falling and spraining or breaking a limb. If it comes to the worst, I shall have to default."[30] Thelma Long, her Australian opponent, agreed, and officials postponed the match and called for the court to be covered to protect it from the overnight rain. Gibson's stance proved prescient. The next day, during the first set of the postponed match, Long slipped on grass left uncovered overnight on the perimeter of the court, injured herself, and was forced to withdraw.[31]

A week later, Gibson had a scare of her own. She took a serious fall in the semifinal at Kent. She rose with a limp, a cut and bleeding knee that required first aid from two nurses, and the eyes and silence of thousands of shocked spectators surrounding her. More than a few wondered whether they had just witnessed the beginning of the end of her Wimbledon hopes. She beat her opponent, Christine Truman, 6–0, 6–3. The fall reminded Gibson that she could not control everything, but what she could, she would to great effect.[32] Playing three weeks straight, she won the women's singles titles at Surbiton, Manchester, and Kent, consistently backing up her assertion that she was "playing better than ever."[33]

Yet the British media were neither convinced nor impressed by Gibson's performances. They battered her with criticisms despite her three victories and the fact that across all those matches she lost only one set. Writers excoriated her for supposedly taking too long, seventy-five minutes, to beat Long in the Surbiton final and for not playing at full tilt. "It was not the real Althea," said Stanley Doust of the *Weekly Dispatch*. "Only occasionally did she show her power tennis."[34] She received limited understanding when, forced by rain to compete in the semifinal and the title match at Manchester in the same day, she again moved and played cautiously rather than with abandon. "Miss Gibson did not impress in either match," Doust wrote. "But she appeared to be taking matters quietly on the slippery court."[35] She was accused during the Kent Championships of "play[ing] just well enough to win."[36]

Gibson raised anticipation—and angst—with each victory that there would soon be a "coloured Wimbledon queen." A media chorus arose to chant that the competition she faced was less than keen, as if preparing early to delegitimize her likely historic success.[37] *World Sports*, the official magazine of the British Olympic Association, placed Gibson on its cover for June, the Wimbledon issue. In the striking portrait, Gibson held her tennis racquet and stood straight and tall, dressed in her tennis whites—flat-front shorts and simple collared pullover—with her hair brushed back in a natural bouffant that suggested the ongoing distance between herself and straightening products. Wearing bright red lipstick, she posed with her head turned and her gaze fixed away from the viewer as she stared up to the left, as though to look at the title of the magazine. Taking over the world of sports, the gaze implied, was her aim. The cover story, however, dismissed women's tennis and their draw at Wimbledon.[38] "Women's international lawn tennis is still at low ebb; there is plenty of room at the top, but no one fully competent to fill it," wrote Susan Noel, who declared the year as "mediocre 1957," just as the previous year had been "mediocre 1956." Noel viewed "dusky Althea Gibson" as a champion by default, the "best of the 'old-stagers'" who was neither a "great champion in her prime," as Brough and Hart had once been, nor a young player "on the threshold of greatness."[39]

Others, too, described women's tennis as having reached a "lean period," a "low standard," a phase without a "'bumper bundle' among the lot of 'em this year," and a "non-vintage year" at Wimbledon.[40] Age and time affected the field. Many years on the circuit had weakened Brough and Dorothy Knode, who still played, and led Hart to retire, but comparatively less experience had left several younger players, mostly British teens and those in their twenties, with little chance of holding their own. Marriage and motherhood had taken away not only Connolly but also Beverly Baker Fleitz who, though she still competed, was not the force that she had once been. Gibson was simply "the best of the poor bunch."[41]

Gibson did not fit the British press's dominant image of a Wimbledon queen. Not since Dorothy Round Little in 1937 had a British woman won the singles tournament, and insecurity had set in about the state of their countrywomen's game. Several Englishwomen came to mind as desired contenders, but illness or injury held back Angela Buxton and Angela Mortimer. Pat Ward had been among Britain's best for years, but her conditioning and consistency were suspect. Christine Truman was a dark horse. Nearly six feet tall, she possessed the kind of power game that many hoped could stand up to Gibson's, but, at sixteen, she was comparatively inexperienced.[42]

None of those players carried the nation's burden to win as Shirley Bloomer did on the eve of Wimbledon. Bloomer had the best record of any British woman that season, having won hard court titles in Britain, France, and Italy. She was tenacious and could beat back players with attacking styles, including Darlene Hard. Bloomer's ground strokes, however, could be erratic and, like Hard, her attitude was painfully dodgy. "I've never yet beaten Darlene on grass," Bloomer said before they faced off in their semifinal match at Kent. "The way I'm playing it does not look as if I'm going to succeed tomorrow."[43] It was a self-fulfilling prophecy, as Bloomer indeed lost. Bloomer's attitude earned her fans, who saw her outlook as quintessentially appropriate for a female athlete. The blue-eyed blonde joked about "concentrat[ing] on" her tan rather than her tennis in the Caribbean at the start of the season, bought into the idea that the caliber of the women's game had indeed fallen, and, though only twenty-three, already envisioned the end of her career. "Yes, I know it's not a good year for women's tennis," she told Peter Wilson of the *Daily Mirror*, "but the moment the game begins to be more serious than the important things in life I should like to give it up." Wilson ate up her comment, declaring that Bloomer "has exactly the right outlook on the game" and "is as good an ambassadress as we [the British] could have in sport."[44]

Gibson did not fit Wilson's idea of a tennis ambassadress, nor did she care to. As Wimbledon loomed, she was a fount of self-confidence and sensibility, never uttering the type of self-defeating, undermining talk that made Bloomer palatable to so many in the public and press.[45] Gibson insisted that she was not taking it easy in her matches, as she had been accused of doing. It was true that she was not playing every match as if it were the Wimbledon final, but that was because she had learned that such an approach was not the way to reach the Wimbledon final. Still, that did not mean that she was coasting. Gibson even saw threats in the players who faced off on other courts. At Kent, she applied Dr. Eaton's advice that she study the techniques and tendencies of other players. After winning her own second-round match in eighteen minutes, she hurried to a nearby court to study Bloomer, whose match was scheduled at the same time. Gibson was taking nothing for granted.[46]

Unlike Bloomer and the press, Gibson did not bemoan the quality of women's tennis. Speaking to a reporter at Kent, she conceded of the field for Wimbledon, "I think the general standard this year is a little lower, and I believe I am playing at my peak."[47] There was still a Wimbledon to be played, and Gibson intended to win it.

The unflattering and blatantly sexist talk that circulated about Gibson in the British press served to underscore that she was not many people's idea of a women's tennis champion. Some of the worst appeared in the *Daily Mirror*. Jack Peart was of the ilk who believed that women tennis players were to be dismissed, even at Wimbledon. "No serious tennis enthusiast regards the ladies as being in the tourney for any reason other than decoration," he wrote. Peart deemed Gibson the most likely woman to win, yet he complained in all caps, "BUT SHE SURE TAKES HER TENNIS SERIOUSLY," and he maligned her as "long-legged Althea with a lithe, boyish figure and old-fashioned shingle."[48]

Reporters scrutinized Gibson's facial expressions, bothered that she did not wear a perpetual smile to please others. Her face was supposedly "a coffee mask" as she analyzed Bloomer's play. She was repeatedly criticized for being "unsmiling" and "stern," a woman who played a game for a living but who, to the disappointment of those who preferred women to be decorative, did not play around.[49] Peter Wilson posited that her demeanor, unfeminine in his estimation, made it hard for the public to root for her. "Lawn tennis for her isn't a game. It's a fight, a career—HER LIFE," he wrote. "Her strong face, moulded in brown clay like the rough cast of a sculpture, remains almost impassive save for the occasional scowl of self-impatience when she has made a really bad shot." The way that Gibson played did not win her fans, either, at least not Wilson. "Her game is an imitation of a man's game. And because she is not a man, it is only a second-best version. . . . Strange, aloof Althea plays a man's game badly and a woman's game disinterestedly."[50]

Of course, no one leveled such criticisms and expectations at men in sports or in any other field. Gibson knew what the press was saying about her. Simply yet assertively, she brushed back the double standards. "Everyone I face across the net is dangerous until I've played the match-winning shot," she told the *Daily Mail*. "This tennis game is a serious one. I play it that way."[51]

———

Fourteen thousand people gathered at Centre Court on "Ladies Day," June 25, to watch Gibson face off against Suzy Körmöczy of Hungary in the second round of the seventy-fifth playing of Wimbledon. Gibson had been given a bye in the first round, the traditional show of respect from the tournament committee for number one seeds. Unintimidated and playing with low expectations, Körmöczy nearly staged an upset with her backhand, speed, and retrieving skills. The crowd buoyed her. Later, some explained that the support was natural, given that Körmöczy was the underdog. Her 5'2" height, they said, made it inevitable, too. Gibson, eight inches taller, thought they looked "like Mutt and Jeff" as they entered the court side by side.[52] Others thought the blatant partisanship was unbecoming to and incongruous with Wimbledon's reputation. The support for Körmöczy went beyond cheering for her—it extended to openly clapping when Gibson made a mistake.[53]

Refusing to be distracted or denied, Gibson responded by focusing more intently on the match. She defied the predictions of those who forecasted that her attitude might take her out of the tournament. "In skill she is unmatched," said one, "but flaws in her temperament may prove her undoing. She does not take kindly to the 'rubs of the green' and when she is upset, her concentration tends to desert her."[54] Gibson relied on her serve, short shots that drew Körmöczy to the net, and lobs. When the match was over, she spoke with the same calm and confidence that got her the win, 6–4, 6–4. Unlike the media, who tried to raise her hackles by stressing that she was nearly ousted in her first round, Gibson chose to be upbeat: "Suzy is the bravest little player I have ever met. I'll never know how she got some of my shots back."[55] Resisting the alarm bells that others tried to sound, she added, "It was the ideal workout for me. I am confident that my game will be raised more and more as the tournament goes on. I have never felt better." She batted away questions about the gallery's bias, too. "I heard the crowd rooting for Suzy, but it didn't worry me a bit. She played some fine shots which deserved to be appreciated."[56]

Gibson's no-nonsense outlook and positivity served her well as the fortnight ramped up. She weathered criticism that she was neither "impressive" nor "show[ed] the form of a potential champion" by beating Australia's Margaret Hellyer, Britain's Gem Hoahing, and South Africa's Sandra Reynolds.[57] Through it all, spectators continued to jeer her. Gibson continued to keep her eye on Bloomer, too. She attended Bloomer's first-round match against Pat Ward, searching for any weakness she might exploit. The reconnaissance mission proved unnecessary. Christine Truman beat Bloomer in the fourth round, positioning herself as the last Brit, male or female, standing in the singles. When she beat Betty Rosenquest Pratt in the quarterfinal, Truman set up a semifinal showdown with Gibson.[58]

The media embraced Truman as its darling. A native of Essex, she was the daughter of an accountant father and a stay-at-home mother who chaperoned Christine to tournaments. The comparisons to Maureen Connolly were inevitable. Reporters christened Truman "Britain's Little Mo,'" the "toast of Wimbledon," and "Wimbledon's wonder girl."[59] Truman, though, remained level-headed through all the excitement, betraying a maturity beyond her years and a respect for Gibson that exceeded the capacity of some of the adults on the grounds. During the press conference after her defeat of Pratt, Truman learned that Gibson was her next opponent. "She's not playing well," someone gleefully interjected into the proceedings. Truman said only, "I'll find out soon enough."[60] She was just sixteen, playing in her first Wimbledon, and stood on the cusp not only of reaching the final but of receiving the trophy from Queen Elizabeth II. All bets were off where British respect for an American was concerned. That the match would take place on July 4— the American Independence Day—on Centre Court intensified the national drama.[61]

Gibson met the semifinal match against Truman as a make-or-break moment. "Guess I've got it all to lose," she said the night before, as she thought about her paddle tennis matches in Harlem, where her reputation in sports had first been on the line. The prospect of seeing the adolescent Truman only made the connection stronger. The next morning, Gibson paced herself. From the balcony at Buxton's apartment, she stopped her ablutions to listen as a clarinetist practiced somewhere in the distance.[62] Then she drove herself to Wimbledon in the Austin that she had rented for her stay in England. Secluded in the ladies' dressing room, Gibson read her mail and watched doubles matches. Two hours later, an attendant called her and Truman to prepare to enter Centre Court. Gibson complied with the officials' instructions to curtsey toward the royal box, where the Duchess of Devonshire sat. Then, calling to mind one of her long-ago realizations from the Cosmopolitan— "that you could walk out on the court like a lady all dressed up in immaculate white, be polite to everybody, and still play like a tiger and beat the liver and lights out of the ball"—she quickly and precisely set about dashing hopes across England.[63]

Her work did not take long. Point after point, game after game, Gibson showed that there was a reason that some called her "the mighty Althea Gibson" as she smashed overheads, served ferociously and accurately, and charged from the baseline to the net, demolishing any idea Truman had of starting rallies and placing shots around the tennis court.[64] In only ten minutes, Gibson was up four games to none. She needed just six more minutes to win the set 6–1. Seventeen thousand people watched in almost complete silence as she won the match in forty-one minutes.[65]

Spectators, downhearted and shocked, filed out of the stadium, taunted by the day's souvenir program booklet, which featured Gibson on its front. She still had to face reporters in the post-match press conference, where she held fast to the businesslike mien that was getting her through the fortnight. Her performance against Truman, the girl who was supposed to represent Britain's best, had answered—at least momentarily—the media assessments of the state of her game. She used the rap session to offer gracious praise for her vanquished opponent. "Miss Truman obviously has got what it takes to make a future champion," Gibson said.[66] "How long? I shouldn't like to say. But she'll be a champion all right, in due course."[67] Her competitor's presence across the net led Gibson to reflect on her own rise in the game. Truman, she said, "reached the Wimbledon semi-finals at an age when I was playing in all Negro tournaments against nobody of importance. And look how long it took me to reach Wimbledon's last four. Why I am all of 29 years old!" Magical runs for juniors in the adult divisions of elite tennis tournaments were rare in those days. For the first time, three juniors were playing in the women's ranks that year. As Gibson alluded, segregation made the possibility that up-and-coming Black tennis players would be the wunderkinds of such events virtually impossible.[68]

Truman was as gracious in defeat as Gibson was in victory. She was disappointed, not so much because she had played poorly but because Gibson's dominance during the match had stymied her ability to play at all. "I don't let these things worry me," she said. "At my age one must expect to be beaten and benefit from lessons learned. I suppose I was a bit nervous, but that's no excuse. Maybe if I could have played three or four sets more against Althea, I would have found out more about her game, and been able to do better." She was able to smile at the thought. Showing deference for Gibson as a competitor, Truman added, "There is never anything to be upset about in losing to a top-class opponent."[69]

Such class continued to elude more than a few members of the British press. Some lauded Gibson's play. As if regarding her as a schoolmaster and Truman as a pupil, the *Western Mail* cited Gibson for having "laid down the lesson kindly, but firmly," that she was the better player.[70] Yet the same writer was among those who resorted to animalistic prose about Gibson's masterful performance. Truman suffered "a severe mauling" from Gibson, "a particularly fierce tigress of a lawn tennis player."[71] At the net, she "resembled a gigantic spider hovering over its web" as she "gobbled up" Truman's shots, said Wilson in the *Daily Mirror*.[72] The *Daily Express*'s Roy Ullyett, one of the most famous and esteemed cartoonists of the era, produced a uniquely racist work. Ullyett illustrated Gibson by drawing on the tradition of racist caricatures. He exaggerated the size of her lips, which he pushed forward into a pout, and drew her eyes as shifty and focused to one side. Standing at the net and shaking the hand of her otherwise bodiless White opponent, Ullyett's Gibson spoke in dialect and betrayed both her awareness of the animosity from the men and women in the stands and ignorance about tennis etiquette: "Do I shake hands with the 17,000 spectators?" she asks. "Ah sure was playin' against all of them too."[73] It was yet another example of how some members of the press could not simply acknowledge that Gibson was a good player but had to blend insults with praise and distasteful references to her perceived racial differences.

———

Gibson's friends Landry and Parks, the WAC captains, watched her matches from the stands throughout the fortnight and were likely among the few in the stadium who wanted her to win. (Another was possibly the Black ball boy, a first at Wimbledon, who chased down the Slazengers that she denapped with every wallop.) Landry and Parks celebrated Gibson's victory in the semifinals by having dinner with her at Le Couple, her favorite French restaurant in London. Then they brought her back to Buxton's apartment, prepared a hot bath for her, and read to her until she fell asleep. Gibson savored the company. Landry and Parks were her "lady's maids," she said. Even more, they were trusted Black companions with whom she would "never have to be on guard."[74] They were everything she had missed the previous year when she had been on the road for the State Department, and they had become part of her systematic plan to win.

The strategy culminated on Saturday, July 6. Buxton gave Gibson a good-luck kiss before leaving the flat to call the match for television. Landry and Parks rode to Wimbledon with Gibson. In the locker room, Gibson dressed with care. She thought that her new tennis duds—one of the short-sleeved Fred Perry pullovers that she preferred and pleated shorts designed by Teddy Tinling—were "pretty."[75] Others considered her attire to be merely "no-nonsense," the opposite of what the fashion industry had long insisted that women's apparel was supposed to be.[76] Yet no-nonsense was precisely what Gibson preferred, as it matched her approach to her career. The buzz of voices chatting about Queen Elizabeth's attendance at the match, her first final as monarch, filled her ears with a pleasant ambient noise that added to the specialness of the day. Gibson headed to a side court for a warm-up session with Shirley Bloomer, proving that those scouting missions had yielded an innovative result, then headed back to the locker room to put on a fresh shirt before the start of the match at 1:15.[77]

Dressed all in white and satisfied with her preparations, Gibson was enveloped by calmness. As she waited to enter the tennis court, she fell silent and said a prayer, as she did before each of her tennis matches. Each prayer was the same: "Not to win specific points or matches but definitely to inspire me to give of my best on court. If, with His help, I cannot beat my opponent I accept defeat as something that was ordained." Quiet and still on the edge of Centre Court, Gibson "felt everything was just the way it should be."[78]

And it was. Darlene Hard, her opponent, crumbled as the barrier that many longed for to keep Gibson from grasping the trophy. In the spring, some had cast Hard as the "White hope" who could stop Gibson's race-defying, historic win at Wimbledon. Hard, however, was personally disinterested in the role and competitively ill-equipped to comply. In her painfully self-deprecating manner, she had discounted her chances of reaching the Wimbledon final as a "lark" in the spring. "I figure I can only win Wimbledon if about six other leading competitors retire with broken arms or something!" she told an amused reporter in April.[79]

Hard lacked the skills, mental as well as physical, to match Gibson's curated dominance, persistence, and self-belief. Gibson hammered her serve into Hard's backhand in game after game. When Hard rushed to the net, Gibson hit passing shots to the back of the court and, in command of the tennis ball, kept them inside the lines. When Gibson ran to the net, Hard faltered further, left to watch Gibson return the volleys. Throughout her career, the press, British and American, described Hard's weight in unflattering terms, and she appeased them with jokes of her own. By the second set, her conditioning appeared to be failing her. Gibson felt the heat, more than ninety-six degrees in the shade. "It was the hottest final I've ever played in," she said later, but Hard seemed to feel it more acutely and began to falter, the sun's rays intensifying her headache, her nervousness, and the misery of losing.[80] Yet Hard was roused by the poor sportsmanship of some among the sixteen thousand spectators who cheered and clapped when Gibson made mistakes. Hard, already a spectator to her own demise, responded to their untoward conduct by smiling and clapping when Gibson hit a winner.[81]

Gibson won 6–3, 6–2 in fifty minutes. She had not lost to Hard. Nor had she lost to her emotions, either her temper or her anxiety, as many in Britain and America thought possible.

"At last! At last!" she said over and over before running to the net to shake Hard's hand and to praise her play. Within minutes, the trophy presentation had begun. Gibson was composed yet moved as Elizabeth II approached atop the red carpet unfurled onto the green turf by attendants. Gibson was proud of herself for curtseying successfully. The queen was gracious, asking Gibson with polite concern how she fared in the heat. Dressed in a frock of red and white silk printed in flowers, she was lovely, Gibson recalled. She "looked exactly as a queen ought to look, except more beautiful than you would expect any real-life queen to look." As Elizabeth presented Gibson with the Venus Rosewater dish, the women's trophy, the stadium erupted in a roaring ovation. Gibson thought the response was "splendid."[82] She had noticed the shenanigans in the stands during the tournament but kept her thoughts to herself. "I guess my manner of play irritated the crowd," she told a Black American reporter when Wimbledon was over. "I guess I didn't have the graciousness of the run of the mill women tennis performers."[83] With the queen present, the crowd was like a bunch of schoolkids suddenly remembering their manners when the teacher stepped back into the classroom.

One of the world's leading symbols of white supremacy and White womanhood had presented a sterling silver salver to a Black woman, a descendant of slaves, while a stadium filled with colonizers cheered. These were role reversals for the ages. Then Hard, overwhelmed by emotion, reached up onto her tiptoes, pulled a beaming Gibson toward her, and planted a congratulatory kiss on her cheek.[84]

—·—

Gibson had gotten what she came for—the Wimbledon singles title—but she still faced tournament obligations. First, there was the women's doubles final, which she and Hard won, 6–2, 6–1, over the Australians Long and Hawton. Then she played the mixed doubles final with Neale Fraser and lost, 6–4, 7–5, to Hard and Mervyn Rose. By the third match of the day, her poise had begun to slip amid the heat and the emotional excitement. She first lost control of her serve and then of her temper, which, one writer observed, "looked like [it was] getting the better of her."[85] Gibson was the new queen of the tennis world, but she remained herself, an intensely competitive and passionate perfectionist with sometimes mixed feelings about playing doubles. Mixing of another type took place in the evening, when Gibson, dressed in her new floral evening gown and accompanied by Dot Parks, Buxton, and Buxton's boyfriend, attended the annual Wimbledon Ball. She sat at the head table, dined between the Duke of Devonshire and Lew Hoad, the men's singles champion from Australia, and waited patiently for her return to the spotlight.[86]

The moment arrived after dinner. Gibson delivered her speech to the nine hundred men and women who filled the ballroom. She quoted Winston Churchill's famous address to Parliament during World War II, calling the occasion her "finest hour." The ball was "the crowning conclusion to a long and wonderful journey," she said, before thanking Buddy Walker, Dr. Eaton and Dr. Johnson, Sydney Llewellyn, the ATA, the USLTA, Angela Buxton, and "the many good people in England and around the world" who had encouraged her. She did not mention her parents, a strange omission for a speech written days and even weeks in advance. Gibson acknowledged that "the victory is not mine alone" but was a "profound salute to my most worthy court opponents whose outstanding ability and invincible courage and determination aroused a challenging response in me." It was also a "total victory of many nations" and "a collective victory of many champions." She concluded by accepting "the responsibility" that came with being the Wimbledon champion and symbolically "wearing" the tournament's "crown." Exhibiting her flair for the dramatic, she ended with a prayerful oath in which she called on God to "grant that I may wear [the Wimbledon crown] with dignity, defend it with honor, and, when my day is done, relinquish it graciously."[87]

The speech was as fascinating for what Gibson left out as for what she included. She had struck the tone of a gracious and thoughtful internationalist. Attendees praised the speech as "heartwarming" and "accomplished and sincere."[88] It was also colorless and devoid of controversy. Back in America, Olin D. Johnston and Strom Thurmond, the two senators from South Carolina, her birth state, had positioned themselves in staunch opposition to the Civil Rights Act of 1957, which was being weakened as it wended its way across Capitol Hill, but she said nothing about it. Nor did Gibson make any references to either segregation or sexism in her career. Later, in *I Always Wanted to Be Somebody*, she was more forthright. Meeting Queen Elizabeth "was a long way from being forced to sit in the colored section" of the Wilmington buses, she said, and dancing with the Duke of Devonshire, as she did that night, "was a long way from not being allowed to bowl in Jefferson City."[89] She knew deeply the contradictions of being a Black pioneer, experiencing the highs of life among White elites yet being denied entry into the most mundane of social spaces, but she chose not to say such things at the ball. The omissions were indicative of her very human desire to think only of pleasant things during one of the happiest nights of her life, her continued devotion to the positive thinking that had contributed to her victory in the first place, and her politics—integrationist and individualist but never militant—where race was concerned.

That Gibson's outlook differed from that of so many people was apparent as the evening wore on and as race, gender, and recreation collided in disconcerting ways that in her joy and persistence she either did not see or chose to ignore. Following Wimbledon tradition, she and Hoad opened the ball after dinner with the first dance. Interracial marriage was illegal in most American states and the British were hardly keen on mixed marriages either, but there were Gibson and Hoad, smiling and moving across the dance floor as the first mixed-race pairing of singles champions in Wimbledon history. Snark circulated among some of the attendees who judged Gibson for her lack of "confidence" on her feet. "By general consent their performance was not up to previous standards," the *Birmingham Post and Gazette* reported after the ball in at least a partial shot at Gibson's feminine bona fides.[90]

Then, well into the evening, Ham Richardson, Gibson's teammate from her first State Department tour, and Vic Seixas, Wimbledon champion of 1953, led a push for her to sing with the band. She did not need much cajoling. Singing suited her ebullient mood as well as her aspirations to launch her singing career. The ball and the subsequent newspaper coverage offered an opportunity for a showcase. And so, in another Wimbledon first, a champion sang at the ball. Gibson performed two songs, "If I Loved You" from Rodgers and Hammerstein's *Carousel* and "Around the World," as the other attendees, practically all of them White, danced and applauded their approval.[91] The scene was an eerie replication of the Tennis Ball in Colorado. She had started the evening as the queen of the ball but finished it as the entertainment.

—

"Quite a difference from the day I left," Gibson said through a smile.[92] The throng watched and cheered her arrival at Idlewild at 6:30 A.M. on Tuesday, July 9. Yet some things had not changed. During a press conference at the airport, a reporter asked whether she "found in getting to the top of the tennis world that you had any real great obstacles because of your race?" Gibson denied it: "No, I don't think there were any obstacles as far as race was concerned." Win or lose, she was still dissembling.[93] Among the well-wishers were Fred Johnson, Edna Mae Robinson, and Buddy Walker as well as Annie, who, seeking to look her best for her oldest child, was just hours removed from a special trip to the beauty parlor and was wearing her Sunday best topped with a hat. Spotting Annie at the head of the crowd, Gibson bellowed, "Hi, ya, sweetie pie."[94] Gibson's younger sister Mildred, married with two daughters of her own, and Daniel Jr. were there, too.[95]

So was Will. Gibson had won one of the most coveted prizes in sports, but many in the media were still fixated on her plans for marriage. New rumors circulated that she was going to marry him either immediately after Wimbledon or later in the year. "I have a boy friend, but I am not engaged to anyone," she had told reporters at Heathrow before boarding the plane back to America.[96] Between Idlewild and Harlem, Will, considered a handsome, debonair, and quiet catch by the Black society and gossip columnists, found himself fending off assumptions about his presence in Gibson's life. He followed her lead, but with a slight difference: he told anyone who asked, "We are not yet engaged," inserting a little word that carried a great deal of hope, like the letters they exchanged when she was abroad.[97]

Daniel Sr. was missing. His overnight shift at the garage ended at 7:00 A.M. and no other employee could, or would, relieve him. Like his line of work, Daniel's absence was a reminder of how hard and different Gibson's background was in comparison to the image of elite amateur tennis and the rarefied world of Wimbledon she had just conquered. After the celebration moved from Idlewild to a breakfast party at Bertram Baker's brownstone in Brooklyn to the Gibson family's apartment on West 143rd Street, Gibson finally saw her father. Home from work at last, he hung out the third-floor window, yelling his pride down to her for the whole block to hear, "taking it big," she thought.[98] When a reporter caught up with Daniel and Annie at the celebration, they offered their own candid and poignant statement about their place in their daughter's tennis pursuits. "She never cost us any real money," they agreed, "because we had none to give her."[99] The day after Gibson won, Annie confessed, "I didn't think a Negro girl could go that high."[100] The problem was not so much that she did not believe in her daughter. It was that the accomplishment was such a radical departure from the opportunities available to Black women that she found them difficult to reconcile.

Gibson soaked up the homecoming. Blending her urban roots and the gentility of the game that she played and reflecting her own gender hybridity, she wore a brown leather jacket over a white tennis dress. From around the neighborhood, more than one hundred children, all of them Black, gathered on the street and the sidewalk in front of the apartment building. "They remind me of my own youth," she said wistfully. She posed for pictures with them, allowing them to hug, touch, and kiss her. She exalted paddle tennis and play streets, praising their impact on her life. "My victory was your victory," she said to everyone on the street. The children had been on her mind at Wimbledon, alongside thoughts of her coaches, her family, and her friends: "Actually, I played for them."[101]

Asked to share advice with the youngsters as the local girl who had made good, Gibson, unsurprisingly, suggested tennis, but at least part of her reasoning was unusual. The game was a panacea for "juvenile delinquency," she said, using the language of the era to describe the rapidly growing concerns about gang membership and crime among children and teens. She also recommended tennis to build toughness. "A lot of kids think tennis is a sissy game. I wish they wouldn't," she said unselfconsciously, adding, "Tennis is as rugged as football. In fact, it is the most strenuous game in the field of sports."[102] Her message was at odds with the time. It ran counter to the popular notions that male tennis players were less manly than other sportsmen and that tennis was wholly acceptable for women because it was a game they could play and still retain their femininity. The remark also revealed Gibson's image of herself as being as tough as the men who played the reputedly most masculine sport. Given the rumors and innuendo about her own sexuality, the comment was gutsy.

Two days later, Gibson was the picture of American ladyhood as New York celebrated her with a ticker-tape parade at last. She accessorized her silk dress of red and blue checks with a white orchid. With ten thousand people lined along the parade route and her family ensconced in cars that trailed behind, a long beige Chrysler convertible was Gibson's chariot, ferrying her smoothly through the storm of confetti and ticker tape that poured down on her as she waved and blew kisses to the crowd from Broadway to City Hall, where the mayor waited outside to congratulate her. Bands from the navy and the fire department played, while police officers on horses and color guards from the army, air force, and coast guard led the way. No one had ever seen anything like it for a Black woman, even in sports. Practically all the women on the 1956 Olympic track and field team were Black. They had been given their medals in Melbourne the previous fall and then were sent back to their respective hometowns, where their Black friends and neighbors threw down red carpets and threw up hosannas for them. With her state-sanctioned and state-supported ticker-tape parade, Gibson was bucking still more trends.[103]

At the banquet that followed at the Waldorf-Astoria, speaker after speaker, all of them men who represented either a tennis organization or the municipal government, praised Gibson as a proud symbol of the nation and of American women. Richard C. Patterson, the commissioner of the department of commerce and public affairs, hailed her victory as representing that American women were "endowed with great courage and powers of physical endurance which often exceed those of the so-called stronger sex."[104] Renville McMann, the president of the USLTA, praised her as a "wonderful ambassador . . . a saleswoman . . . for America." She did a "grand job" on the 1955–1956 international tour and by continuing the dominance of American women by going to England and winning Wimbledon. "In those trips, in my humble opinion," said McMann, "you have done more to spread the American gospel and create goodwill for America than the great majority of ambassadors abroad today."[105]

Hulan E. Jack, Manhattan's first Black borough president, was the only speaker who ventured to discuss the significance of her victory in the context of the racial struggle unfolding across the country and around the world. "What you have done is added strength and meaning to 'The Star-Spangled Banner' and is as truly American as the Stars and Stripes," said Jack in his St. Lucian accent. "How you reached that goal is an inspiration to all Americans. What you came through to sit here today, honored by your fellow citizens of all races, creeds, colors, and religions is ample proof that in our democracy we take the leadership in emphasizing human achievements as we move ever forward in our vigorous crusade toward full, equal opportunity."[106] Presenting her with the city medallion, Mayor Wagner praised Gibson as "a great champion in tennis" and "a great representative of this country we love so much." She was a local heroine, too, he said, an "example" to the city's children and the first woman from New York to win Wimbledon. "I suppose it's a long way from . . . West 143rd Street to the Center Court at Wimbledon, but you made that march in a dignified and fine way," Wagner said, steering clear of discussing the inequalities that had made her march longer than that of so many others. The ceremony had all the trappings of a slick and colorless piece of State Department propaganda.[107]

Gibson went along with the program. She gave gracious thanks to many, including her parents this time. She was jovial, laughing at her onetime thought of giving up tennis for the WAC, and ended her speech with a joke that alluded to her well-known troubles with officials on the tennis court from Melbourne to New York. The joke went as follows: To God's surprise, Satan invited him to stage a tennis match. Perplexed, God asked how Satan dared think that he could win, given that the heavenly team included such players as Trabert, Mulloy, Seixas, and Hoad. "Well, you may have all the best tennis players in the world," Satan replied, "but I got all the umpires and the linesmen down here."[108] The Palm Room erupted in laughter and applause. From their tables, Sarah Palfrey, Bobby Riggs, and Jackie Robinson joined in; so did Dr. Johnson from his seat on the dais.[109] The quip was as close to controversy as Gibson, the state-appointed lady of the hour, wanted to get.

———

"She must be dog tired," Daniel said between chomps and puffs on a fat cigar as he sat in his favorite chair in the apartment, "but," he concluded, "if she can walk, she'll play."[110] This time father knew best. Gibson was exhausted after the emotional week. She had also given a bevy of interviews—never her favorite thing. There was one with a radio call-in show in Montclair; another with the model, actress, and amateur tennis player Jinx Falkenburg; a session with a local evening news program; a visit with Ed Sullivan on his show, *The Toast of the Town*; the press conference at Idlewild; and a conversation with the reporter that the *New York Times* had sent to the airport and then to her parents' block the day she arrived.[111] Still, Gibson refused to slow down. The National Clay Court Championship started on Saturday in the Chicago suburb of River Forest. By Friday, she was gone.

She was determined, too. Gibson intended to maintain her winning form for Forest Hills. She wanted to win to satisfy herself, of course, but there was an added benefit: victory could countervail the talk on both sides of the Atlantic that despite winning every set in each of her matches, she was the Wimbledon champion by default and with caveats.

Winning Wimbledon had not changed that Gibson was Black and that the greater Chicago area was a veritable playground for Jim Crow. The Pump Room at the Ambassador East, one of the city's landmark hotels, would not accept reservations for a luncheon in her honor. The other hotels were no better. There were three in River Forest, but none would give her a room. Neither would any of the hotels in nearby Oak Park. It would have been more surprising if she had been accommodated. Well into the 1960s, Black members of integrated sports teams, collegiate and professional, were frequently housed separately from their White teammates on the road. The situation was so normal that occasions when Black athletes could board in White-owned hotels were newsworthy.[112] Gibson stayed at a motel twelve miles away from the River Forest Tennis Club, the nearest that tournament organizers could find for her. She had to factor the distance and additional travel time into her daily plans for practice and play, labor and preparation that her White colleagues did not have to perform, but she did it and, characteristically, said nothing about the segregation to the press, including the Black newspapers.[113]

Gibson hardly felt that the Black press was on her side that week. According to Russ Cowans, whose syndicated column the *Defender* published, the trouble started on Monday when she was dismissive of a "girl reporter" who asked "if she felt her recent achievements had helped her race." Gibson supposedly replied, "I'm trying to help myself."[114] Wendell Smith described a similar event. A reporter in Chicago asked her whether she "cherished" being compared with Jackie Robinson. "No, I don't consider myself to be a representative of my people," she was presumed to have said. "I am thinking of me and nobody else."[115] The next day, according to Cowans, Gibson, citing fatigue, delayed for more than eight hours a prescheduled interview with a magazine writer from New York. Cowans accused her of ignoring the spur-of-the-moment requests for interviews and pictures from reporters and photographers who turned up unannounced to speak with her at the tennis club. "No pictures," she supposedly repeated. Cowans said that he approached Gibson twice for short interviews and she rejected him each time, first with the explanation that she had "business" to discuss with a tournament official and later by telling him, "I'm leaving," though she stayed on-site for fifteen minutes more.[116] The Chicago press reported on Gibson's behavior for the entire metro area to see. Nonplussed by the kerfuffle, she focused on the tournament and won, convincingly beating Hard in the final 6–2, 6–3, before a pro-Darlene crowd of five thousand. Gibson celebrated her triumph in grand style that night, joining a group of friends as they club-hopped from the Blue Note, where they listened to Duke Ellington and his orchestra, to the Black Orchid to hear jazz singer Sallie Blair.[117]

Cowans's and Smith's diatribes against Gibson appeared in the Black press days after the tournament ended. Cowans was so incensed by her "arrogancy" that he wrote two pieces about it. "I admire Althea's ability on the [tennis] court. Her achievements . . . throughout the world attest to that," he wrote in one. "But you can't make a silk purse out of a sow's ear, and you can't make a gracious person out of Althea."[118] In his column, "Russ' Corner," Cowans crudely called her "as ungracious as a stubborn jackass" and "the most arrogant athlete it has been my displeasure to meet." She lacked "graciousness and affability," he said, comparing her unfavorably to several male athletes and some of the most popular women in golf—the late Babe Zaharias and sisters Marlene and Alice Bauer, all of whom were White.[119]

Smith agreed. To his mind, Gibson was no longer the modest girl he had met in her debut at the National Clay Courts seven years earlier. "Has Net Queen Althea Gibson Gone High Hat?" his article asked in its title, accompanied by a picture of Gibson with her nose in the air. Smith answered affirmatively. She had "become so obsessed with herself" that she could talk with English royalty but not to "friendly writers" in Chicago, who had taken to calling her "Tennis Queen and Bum of the Court" because of her "arrogant, despicable treatment" of them. Smith also took pot shots at Gibson that were patently false. Ignoring her speeches at the Wimbledon Ball and after the ticker-tape parade, he claimed that she "does not recognize [her] benefactors," Dr. Eaton and Dr. Johnson. She had won Wimbledon "solely because of their benevolence," he averred, saying nothing of her own diligence and sacrifices. Smith also erroneously reported that Florida A&M had allowed her to "'skip' through" her studies. "She is neither scholarly nor smart," Smith wrote. Making an oblique reference to her class background, Smith penned, "It might be wise for Althea to take stock at this time and realize that while she wields a mighty racket, she is still only a tennis player and nothing more."[120]

The attacks were jarringly anomalous in the post-Wimbledon coverage of Gibson in the Black media. Coast to coast, her life story was likened to a Horatio Alger tale, and front pages featured pictures and articles about the ticker-tape parade. She was compared to Jackie Robinson for achieving another long-shot first in sports for African Americans and to Booker T. Washington for being a model of perseverance. According to some, in her continued persistence at tennis despite having lost so many times, Gibson symbolized African Americans' battles for civil rights. She demonstrated the resolve required of the race. "If the Negro can be Gibson-hearted in his fight for his rights his triumph is only a matter of time," Gordon B. Hancock, sociologist, pastor, and civil rights activist, wrote for the Associated Negro Press, ironically imploring the race to employ the tactics of a woman.[121] The National Council of Negro Women (NCNW) had issued a statement praising Gibson for the social significance of her triumph at Wimbledon. "This feat of skill, technique, endurance, idealism and will should be a lasting spring of courage for youth everywhere and especially Negro youth," said the group's president, Vivian Carter Mason. "Miss Gibson's triumph brings joy to women, to America and to the world of sports, for here is again demonstrated that given the opportunity—even the edge of opportunity—those who have it in them can make good." Like Hancock and many others, Mason ascribed political importance to Gibson and her success: "America is universally in-debted to Miss Gibson for she is proof that all America cannot be judged by the irrational, spiritually and socially impoverished south whose frantic efforts to stay progress are pitiable in this time of the nation's struggle for world survival."[122]

After the debacle at the National Clay Courts, Black journalists across the country came to Gibson's defense. The *Pittsburgh Courier* published several pieces that challenged Smith, its former star reporter. Bill Nunn, who wrote the paper's sports column, reported that Gibson was not "big-headed," as Smith and Cowans alleged. "You have to remember she's a woman who has been under a lot of pressure," Russell Jacquet, jazz trumpeter and Gibson fan, told Nunn. "Her reactions under such circumstances don't necessarily show her as she really is."[123]

The *Courier's* Evelyn Cunningham, one of the most prominent Black women journalists of the era, agreed. Years earlier, Cunningham had described Gibson as "impenetrable" and compared her personality to "icicles."[124] After Wimbledon, Cunningham saw her as a "complex personality" who was "misunderstood," and she believed that Gibson was adjusting to the pressure and "tremendous responsibility" that came with her elevated status as the "heroine of Negroes throughout the nation" after winning the tournament. "Opportunists" and "high-class hustlers" suddenly vied for Gibson's attention and tried to edge out the friends, like Buddy Walker and Edna Mae Robinson, who had stood behind her before she even had a tennis career. Gibson was, Cunningham believed, "leery and skeptical about [the] new faces" who sought to curry her favor, some of whom were members of the media.[125]

Walker and Edna Mae backed Gibson in an interview with Cunningham. Leaning on stereotypical preferences of femininity, they called her "sweet, gentle, down-to-earth, witty, [and] easy-going." Edna Mae went further. Sounding like the highly feminine woman and model that she was, she directly challenged what she saw as the tendency of the media to read Gibson's body type as suggestive of her personality. "Althea is a very feminine person, despite her masculine build," Cunningham deduced from her conversation with Edna Mae. She "will cry or blush at the drop of a hat."[126]

The *Los Angeles Sentinel* published a thoughtful essay saying it was "unfortunate that . . . Althea must be judged as much for her personality as for her athletic ability." She was not "blameless" for the negative coverage, the paper decided, but there was no reason for her to "pretend" that she was of the "hail fellow, well met" variety, either. "After all, if she weren't the way she is, she wouldn't be a champion, and nobody would want to interview her anyway!"[127]

––•––

Gibson arrived in Pittsburgh in mid-August for her next competition, the Wightman Cup matches, where she was the center of attention. That was normal for the Wimbledon champion and the number one player in the world. Yet the firestorm from Chicago heightened scrutiny of Gibson. The surveillance happened socially. The American and British teams gathered at the clubhouse of the Edgeworth Club, the tournament host site in the suburb of Sewickley, for a reception and cocktail party followed by a buffet dinner with club members, tennis officials, and local dignitaries. Society columnist Hazel Garland covered the event for the *Courier* and, joining the ranks of Gibson's media defenders, observed that "most eyes at the reception were on Althea," who impressed Garland with the way that she carried herself that evening. "Looking very attractive in a pretty cocktail dress, Althea was poised, gracious, and very easy to converse with," Garland reported, contrasting her more feminine persona "in a social setting" to how she appeared "on the tennis courts," where she was "all business."[128]

During practice sessions at Edgeworth, she was calm and focused. One observer was struck by the way Gibson moved with "fluidity and discipline" and walked with "the relaxed unstudied grace of a lean lithe boy."[129] The latter point was intended as a compliment. It also showed the continued feeling among many that she blended perceptions of masculinity and femininity.

Gibson felt that her team was behind her. She was elated to represent the country. Sarah Palfrey had played on and assisted American Wightman Cup teams since 1930, and she was convinced that she had never seen a prouder American team member. Gibson's pride showed the day she received her white blazer, the gift given to all team members. Standing in captain Margaret duPont's room at the team hotel, she slipped on her jacket as Palfrey and duPont watched alongside teammates Brough, Hard, and Dorothy Head Knode. Gibson studied her reflection in the mirror. "Her expression and her manner verged on exaltation," Palfrey recalled.[130] Suddenly, Gibson's face turned quizzical. "I don't want to seem fussy," she said to the others, "but don't you all think the sleeves are too short? You see, this is the first one of these I've ever had, and I want it to be just right." Her words reflected her unusual physical stature. At 5′10½″, she was the tallest member of the team. She was not ashamed of her size despite being neither petite nor buxom, among the standards for beauty in the decade. She considered it "an advantage to have some height" in tennis, but this time her long arms were an inconvenience.[131] Her past colored her comments, too. Gibson did not tell the group, but she had spent her lifetime receiving hand-me-downs as well as dresses and skirts that other people thought she should have whether she liked them or not. The blazer was different. Menswear-inspired, it symbolized her place at the top of women's international tennis; the garment was the ultimate for Gibson. Everyone in the room laughed, but they agreed with her about the sleeves and made suggestions about fixing them. Their input moved her. In that moment, she did not feel like the lone Black member of the team: "I really felt as though I belonged."[132]

Still, Gibson had to meet the press, and the lingering questions about Chicago, alone. Seated on a patio chair outside the clubhouse for a press conference, she confessed that she knew she had problems with the media. "Everywhere I've traveled stories about my bad relationship with the press have followed," she said. She read what was written about her and disagreed. "They say I'm ungrateful to those who have helped me. Unflattering insinuations have been written about my being uncooperative when it comes to giving interviews." The situation left her frustrated. "A lot of these stories have me on my guard. I've been in a constant state of confusion. Most of the time," she confessed, "I can't help wondering what they want of me."[133]

Gibson offered her side of the story about Chicago and revealed details that neither Cowans nor Smith had written as well as the sophistication and acumen that Smith denied her. "They said I was hostile and wouldn't cooperate," she said. "I say I wasn't given a fair opportunity to be helpful." She recounted that a photographer had disrespected her at the River Forest Tennis Club as she left the court. He "grabbed me by the arm and demanded that I come over for a picture." The gist of the criticisms from Cowans and Smith was that Gibson was no lady. She responded with a savvy retort. "No gentleman would have snatched me the way he did," she said. "Yet, when I refused his command, he seemed to think I had committed one of the worse sins in the world."[134] She described having a similar encounter earlier in the week at the Edgeworth Club. A reporter approached her for an interview. "'Just a minute. I'd like to talk to you.' I said, 'Just a moment. I'd like to get some water first.' He became peeved and wrote that I was becoming impossible."[135] The *Pittsburgh Press*, a White paper, reported that she simply said "no" when two sportswriters asked, "Do you have a few minutes, Althea?" The story was a twenty-three-word news brief, but the *Press* published it under the large headline "Althea Has No Time to Spare."[136] Her "sin" was the same in both instances. She had refused to acquiesce and inconvenience herself to suit the needs and interests of men.

Gibson was adamant that going forward she would not change her ways with reporters. "I don't stop every time they bark," she said.[137] Effectively dismissing the press as leeches, she told the pool, "It seems when a person gets to be a champion or reaches some high station that's when they start chopping away."[138] Further revealing her nonconformity and awareness of the double standards that she faced as a woman, Gibson announced that she planned to imitate a man in her future dealings with the media. She was a long way from Harlem, but Sugar Ray Robinson remained her idol. She had fought like him as a kid on the streets and she would deploy his tactics as an adult, she said. Robinson "didn't scrape and bow" to the press, even after reporters "cut him to bits," and neither would she. Gibson promised to "do what I think is right and not worry about what some people who don't mean a thing to me say. Then when I get mad, I'm going out on the tennis court and take it out on whoever's across the net."[139] "All of this stuff is just making me meaner on the tennis courts," she concluded.[140]

The Wightman Cup tested Gibson's resolve. There was no other sporting event like it for women. Some called it "the World Series in women's sports," a testament to the primacy of tennis in women's sports. Outside of the Olympics and the tennis and golf majors there were few truly international athletic competitions for women.[141] Gibson played with the pressures of being a rookie, the first Black member of the team, and the Wimbledon champion, which made her the team's unofficial leader and, as a result, the player that the captain, Margaret duPont, chose to play in the first match. Like the other competitors, Gibson was also playing on a slow, composition hard court that gave the ball a high bounce unlike anything she ordinarily encountered. Her nerves showed the first day. For the first time since the war ended, tickets sold out. The capacity crowds, two thousand people each day, were substantially smaller than those who had watched her at Wimbledon, but the Wightman Cup was different. Gibson took seriously that she was playing not for herself but for her country. She committed ten double faults and a few untimely foot faults in her first singles match, a meeting with Shirley Bloomer.[142]

Gibson was not the only one who was nervous. The *Courier* estimated that as many as five hundred African Americans, several of whom had never attended a tennis tournament, came to the Edgeworth Club just to see her play. They were proud of Gibson and felt that her success elevated the image of African Americans. "Even the domestics took on an air of aristocracy," noted a reporter for the *Pittsburgh Courier*. Yet self-consciousness pervaded the crowd. Many of the Black spectators wanted to express vocally and loudly their jubilation over her success. Surrounded by the centuries-old trees and the English-manor-style clubhouse, and outnumbered by White men and women, they restrained themselves so as not to either embarrass her or give credence to racist stereotypes of Black boorishness.[143]

Gradually, Gibson steadied herself. Hazel Hotchkiss Wightman, four-time singles champion at Forest Hills and the donor of the cup, rooted her on. Between matches, Wightman stood behind her, put her arm around her back, and gave her smiles and pep talks. Gibson responded to the challenge and to Wightman's attention, though whether she grew comfortable enough to call the older woman "Mrs. Wightie," as the others did, is unknown.[144] Wearing a traditional tennis dress, she scored two points for the team on the first day, one by beating Bloomer and a second while paired with Hard against Bloomer and Sheila Armstrong in doubles. On the second and final day, she faced Christine Truman, who attempted vindication after the shellacking that Gibson had given her at Wimbledon. Insecurity proved Truman's downfall. Rather than playing to her strengths, she tried to replicate Gibson's game. Gibson, "poetry in motion" according to Mary Hardwick, who reported on the competition for *World Tennis*, won 6–4, 6–2 in thirty-five minutes, earning her third point of the competition, half of the team's tally in beating Great Britain 6–1 to give America its twenty-first straight Wightman Cup victory since 1930. Gibson had more than delivered on her promise at the press conference.[145]

With Forest Hills looming, Gibson's Wightman Cup teammates became her rivals again. DuPont, Brough, and Hard pushed her to prove that she was indeed the best player in the world. For two weeks, however, she did not look like the best player even in Massachusetts.

Hard stretched her in the semifinals at the Essex County Club women's tournament in Manchester, forcing her to three sets before Gibson could look up at the scoreboard and see that she had eked out victory at 6–4, 2–6, 8–6. The next day, she beat Brough in the final, but her performance was hardly dominant. A week later, in Brookline, Gibson and Hard lost 6–2, 7–5 to duPont and Brough in the final round of the National Doubles Tennis Championship. It was the twelfth national doubles title for Brough and duPont, among the most dominant doubles teams in tennis history.[146]

Yet instead of praising Brough and duPont's excellence, some chose to criticize Gibson. The *Boston Globe* reported that many people were "disappointed" in her performance. Hazel Wightman disagreed. Wightman thought that "people expected too much of" Gibson, who, she said, was "nervous" but still "stood up very well" during the match: "I don't think Althea played as well as she is capable of doing. But I think she is greatly improved over a year ago." Wightman implied that it was unfair not to critique Hard's play, too, as the pair were a team. "Doubles depends too much on the partner," Wightman reminded the reporter. "Both she and her partner, Darlene Hard, were nervous under pressure." Ralph Chambers, the tennis pro at the Longwood Cricket Club, disagreed. "She doesn't have enough doubles sense," Chambers said of Gibson, offering a take that questioned her intelligence. "Maybe that's because she hasn't played enough doubles," he added before allowing grudgingly, "She has one real good point—her overhead."[147] The statements got to the heart of Gibson's individualist and power-centered outlook. They were also in sync with the thoughts of both tennis diehards who disliked the power game and the prejudiced, who were disinclined to praise her for anything. In Boston, both camps were legion. "Althea Gibson, who won at Essex but lost at Longwood, convinced the local tennis set that she is a good but not a great player," the *Globe* reported.[148]

Good or great, Gibson was an attraction. Essex had its biggest crowds since 1938 and the final three days sold out entirely, a rarity in a women's-only tournament and an outcome that had everything to do with Gibson's fame. African Americans were drawn to the event, too. Before becoming as famous for his bespoke outfits as he was for his tennis journalism, Bud Collins was a young reporter in Boston who attended tournaments across New England and the mid-Atlantic. Collins was taken aback at Essex, where he saw White fans mostly filling the five hundred seats in the bleachers and as many as a hundred Black women, whom Collins assumed were maids to White families in the Boston suburbs, in folding chairs put out as overflow spots.[149]

With the possibility of Gibson winning Forest Hills on the horizon, *Time* and *Sports Illustrated*, among the most popular periodicals in the country, placed her on their covers. With its selection of Gibson for its September 2 issue, the preview for Forest Hills, *Sports Illustrated* made her the first Black woman so featured. Photographer John G. Zimmerman captured Gibson, hair coiffed in her preferred short and salon-treated curly style, in close-up from the shoulders up as she smiled through lips painted a medium shade of red and looked straight into the camera. It was a warm and substantive portrait devoid of stereotypes and conveyed the magazine's message: "Althea Gibson Meets Her Biggest Test at Forest Hills."[150] Boris Chaliapin, *Time*'s famed portrait artist, drew her looking older than her years from the neck up and surrounded by a clay tennis court as if she had quite literally broken the mold with her emergence in the game. She was the first Black sportswoman to appear on a *Time* cover—"the Mount Everest of international acclaim," one Black sportswriter wrote with pride.[151] Indeed, the iconic, red-bordered space was cultural real estate most often populated by politicians, royalty, and entertainment legends. Both Jackie Robinson and Sugar Ray Robinson had been there in 1947 and 1951, respectively, and Gibson joined a long list of White women tennis players who had been there, including America's Helen Wills (twice), Helen Hull Jacobs, Pauline Betz, and England's Betty Nuthall.[152] Readers could judge for themselves which portrait of Gibson they preferred, but each was, like the woman herself, a stark divergence from the norm. It was rare for national magazines to make Black people the subjects of general human-interest stories as opposed to coverage of crime or segregation strife, and yet there was Gibson smiling and peering out at America.

Nonetheless, racism and sexism lurked within each historic treatment and portrayed Gibson as a social aberration. Across more than three thousand words, *Time*'s Serrell Hillman gave White America its most substantive treatment of Gibson since the *American Lawn Tennis* profile in 1950. Hillman interviewed Daniel, her sister Mildred, Dr. Eaton, and Gibson herself. He wrote about the Cosmopolitan, FAMC, Lincoln, and the transformative effect of the State Department tour on her game, and praised her impact on her sport: "Behind Althea Gibson, women's tennis curves off into mediocrity: with her, the U.S. Lawn Tennis Association would not have much of a show."[153] Yet Hillman also portrayed her as a lifelong gender anomaly. Mildred told him that Gibson had cared more about stickball than lipstick as a girl. Daniel reported his ambitions to make her into a boxer. Dr. Eaton described her table manners and difficulty being "a lady on the court," noting, too, that she had not owned a dress when she arrived at his house more than a decade earlier.[154] Nana Davis Vaughn, her rival from her junior years, said Gibson "was a very crude creature" in those days. According to Hillman, her personality had improved slightly, reaching a state of "defensive truculence." Her game displayed "a champion's unmistakable power and drive," but she "is not the most graceful figure on the courts, and her game is not the most stylish." Hillman even worked in the stereotype about African Americans and their supposed affection for chicken. Gibson told of her short-lived job at the poultry plant. "I used to have to take out the guts and everything, but I still like chicken," he quoted her as saying.[155] *Time*'s message was clear: Gibson was the best woman tennis player in the world and the best Black one, but genderwise and in terms of tennis skills, she was flawed, rough around the edges, and not like the White girls.

Sports Illustrated treated Gibson better, but the suggestion of difference was still there. Written by Sarah Palfrey, the one-page feature amounted to a short essay based on their overnight drive from Sewickley to New York after the Wightman Cup. The story had its intimacies and came across as intended to address some of the controversies about Gibson. She praised Dr. Eaton ("the guy who took such good care of me . . . when I was a kid"), stated that she had not been offered a contract for professional tennis and had no plans to turn pro, and spoke of marriage. "I'd like to get married, if I could have a career too," she told Palfrey. "I think this is possible if the man is understanding and if the girl doesn't get swell-headed like some movie stars who start believing their own press reports."[156] That the magazine saw Gibson as different from other women in tennis showed in the pictures. On the opposite page, she was shown during a changeover. One foot on the ground and the other raised up on a step at the umpire's chair, she looked down in concentration. The subdued image and the side view highlighted the leanness of her frame.[157]

On the next page, Karol Fageros, Shirley Bloomer, and Darlene Hard posed and smiled at readers in bright portraits taken on sunny days that showed off their golden tans and bosoms. Captions that had little to nothing to do with the women's tennis abilities introduced them to readers: Fageros "contribute[d] high fashion and glamour," Bloomer, who lifted her dress to reveal more of her thighs, was a "small and attractive blonde," and Hard had "a vibrant personality."[158] Together, the tableau reinforced the image of a game played by sexy young White women who gave sensual pleasure to spectators, especially men. Bill Talbert predicted that Gibson would win Forest Hills. "Apparently there is no female player who can press her," he wrote for the magazine. "It's Althea's year."[159] She dominated the world of blond White women in tennis, but, brown-skinned and hardly voluptuous, she existed outside their orbit, too.

In *Time*, Gibson made clear that she also existed outside the orbit of Black people in terms of her imagination. She revealed her wariness of glad-handers who had emerged, or reemerged, since Wimbledon. Like most people, she had accepted the help, great and small, of people throughout her career, but, she reasoned, that did not mean that she owed something to everyone. "No matter what accomplishments you make somebody helps you," she said, aware of the press reports that told of the support she had received for years, especially from African Americans, and seemingly needed to repay. Her career and her achievements were public, but they were also her own and she wanted to keep them that way. "People saw me going up there, and now they want to ride on the wagon. Whenever I hear anyone call me 'Champ,' I think there's something behind it."[160]

Most daring of all, Gibson repudiated the expectation that she carry out her career as anything but a personal endeavor. "I tried to feel responsibilities to Negroes, but that was a burden on my shoulders," she told Hillman. "If I did this or that, would they like it? Perhaps it contributed to my troubles in tennis. Now I'm playing tennis to please me, not them."[161] It was a bold statement that belied the countless articles and editorials that claimed she had made it her mission to play for and to represent African Americans in tennis.

Gibson's words also put her at odds with historical and contemporary civil rights messages. Amid the gradually growing civil rights movement, Black media, ministers, and social reformers were intensifying the message that she had learned long ago, beginning at the Cosmopolitan: that Black people should devote their efforts and energies to being the best they could possibly be in all they did as a commitment to improving the standing and future of the entire race. Each African American, these figures and cultural groups argued, was to be guided by the goal of representing and advancing the fortunes of the other members of the race. Gibson disavowed that demand in the interview with Hillman. She had said as much the year before in the *Los Angeles Times*, and Smith and Cowans had mocked her thoughts on the matter in July. Now *Time*, a mainstream, bestselling weekly newsmagazine, had her on record as saying that she played, and won, for herself, and the entire country could read it.

Gibson was also running afoul of Black tennis aficionados as well as reformers who took no particular interest in the sport but were zealous about traditions. Since Wimbledon, Black sportswriters had returned to airing their worries about the future of Black tennis. "Will Another Tennis Champ Come from the ATA?" asked a headline in the *Amsterdam News*.[162] "Where are the tennis players who will step into [Althea Gibson's] shoes in the future?" Cal Jacox asked at the Norfolk *Journal and Guide*. His answer: "If current reports are correct there are none."[163] A chorus had risen within the Black media to say that her victory gave her a responsibility to see that the integration of tennis did not end with her success. P. L. Prattis of the *Pittsburgh Courier* invoked the rhetoric of the Wimbledon women's champion as the queen of tennis and the example of Jackie Robinson to imagine Gibson's future of service to African Americans. Robinson "walked through the doors of organized baseball (due to the efforts of others) and kept the doors open for scores of others. What will Queen Althea do?" Prattis had ideas. He suggested that she could act as a talent scout and motivator who focused exclusively on Black tennis players and secure sponsorships for them. "If Miss Gibson will recognize and accept this as part of her new responsibility as queen, I am sure that she will not only find the girl who will some day wear her crown, but also the boy who will some day win the singles title at Wimbledon for the United

States," Prattis wrote. "May the reign of Queen Althea be a long one and may she find her own successor."[164]

The idea held no appeal to Gibson. She showed her seriousness about doing as she pleased where tennis was concerned at the ATA Nationals, where she did not defend her title. She did not skip the tournament entirely, but she was creative in her visit to Wilberforce. She and Hard played, and split, a two-set exhibition match before an integrated audience, including Ohio's secretary of state and treasurer, with two ball boys, one Black, the other White. Anna Arnold Hedgeman, a special assistant to Mayor Wagner, the first woman and first Black woman to hold a position in the cabinet of a New York mayor, was suitably impressed. "This was integration—not meetings—no manipulated decisions—just two capable people meeting each other on terms of equality," she wrote to the *Amsterdam News* after watching the match. "The rules of the meet were set by the game, and not by color or lack of it. This was a great day. All American Youth would have loved it."[165] The compromise met the ATA's tradition of interracial competition. It also helped Gibson. The match showed her growing the game of tennis among Black youngsters, including the boys whom the ATA and the Black media desperately wanted to see gain a foothold in the game. It also gave her at long last genuine competition against whom she could test and measure her own skills in the lead-up to Forest Hills, the only national tournament that mattered in her mind.

Forest Hills was a home game, but Gibson treated it with the same studied care that she had applied to her time in England. She stayed at the Vanderbilt Hotel on 34th Street and Park Avenue with the other tennis players, guaranteeing herself the space, privacy, and peace that she needed to be at her best but which would have eluded her in Harlem. Cars shuttled the players between the hotel and the tennis club each day. It was all so convenient, she thought, so easy, unlike the way things had been when she played at Forest Hills for the first time in 1950.[166]

For the next two weeks, Gibson mostly made tennis look easy, too. Her biggest struggle came early. Karol Fageros, her old buddy from the first State Department tour, gave her a tougher time in the first round than anyone expected. Fageros had long since grown tired of being seen as only a pretty young thing. She wanted to win major titles. Playing with a now-or-never spirit amplified by meeting Gibson, the tournament favorite, in a do-or-die match, Fageros came out fighting. She produced forehand drives, volleys, and drop shots that few had ever seen her unleash, and she scrambled and retrieved from the corners with gusto. Gibson was "never in serious jeopardy" of losing, thought Fred Tupper, who covered the match for the *New York Times*, but she refused to relax.[167] The "Golden Goddess," as Fageros was sometimes called, might very well have been the "black sheep" whom Gibson thought could beat her if she allowed herself to become "overconfident."[168] Gibson prevailed, 6–4, 6–4, but she left the stadium with "mixed emotions" about winning against her friend and taking her out of the tournament. She knew, though, that it was necessary if she was going to win the title.[169] Fortified by staving off Fageros's attack, she mowed down the next four players she faced without losing a set, just like at Wimbledon. After dispatching Dorothy Head Knode in the semifinals, she said with verve, "I feel I am reaching a crescendo."[170]

Gibson rose early on Sunday, September 8, the day of the final, with much on her mind. She was to face Louise Brough, leading her to remember their dramatic first encounter at Forest Hills. She thought, too, of all that was at stake. "If I could just win this one match," she mused grittily, "nothing under God's blue sky could keep me from being ranked No. 1 next year." She also nursed a more immediate thought: driving herself to Harlem for a prescheduled appointment with a hairdresser. The Vanderbilt boasted an array of modern amenities, including a beauty salon, but, besides the fact that it was closed on Sunday, Gibson could not be sure that the White-owned hotel had stylists with either the training or the inclination to work with her hair. She wanted to look her best for one of the biggest days of her life, and so she slipped off to Pat Hicks's shop on 125th Street.[171]

Gibson and Brough played as if each knew what was on the line, but that did not mean they played well. On Gibson's mind was the potential number one ranking and the opportunity to silence naysayers, while Brough, thirty-four, was two years removed from her last major title, Wimbledon, and eager to win one more in her career. Brough took a 2–3 lead in the first set, helped by Gibson's errors, including double faults. For a time, it looked as if Gibson's old habit of giving up after falling behind had returned. Then she regrouped and won the next four games and the set. In the second set, Brough lost confidence and began to play cautiously but still racked up mistakes of her own; Gibson, thinking strategically, let her. "I didn't very often try to hit the ball as hard as I can because I felt that it was smarter to let Louise make the error, and that's pretty much the way it went."[172] Gibson kept pounding her serve, reaching for Brough's wide shots, and running for the net to cut off the others. It all wore Brough down. At set point, Brough double-faulted, hitting the ball into the net. At 6–2, the match was over, and the American national title belonged to Gibson.[173]

In both her words and appearance, Gibson was humble and honest after the match. Richard Nixon, the vice president who desired Black votes as he looked ahead to the 1960 presidential campaign, awarded her a silver plate and the winner's trophy decorated with red roses and white gladioli. Gibson posed for photographs with unseeded Malcolm Anderson, the cowboy on his father's cattle ranch who won the men's title in a three-set upset over his fellow Australian Ashley Cooper. They looked alike, with their trophies, short hair, collared white jackets, and crisp white shorts with pockets.[174] In her victory speech, she praised Brough's "excellent play and fine sportsmanship." She thanked God for the "USLTA officials, distinguished guests, and tennis friends" as well as the eleven thousand people in the stands because, she said, "without the united help of all of you, this victory would not have been accomplished." She ended by repeating her pledge at Wimbledon to "wear this title with dignity and humility."[175] The stadium erupted with the sound of applause the likes of which, *Life* and others reported, had not been heard at Forest Hills in years. Gibson celebrated her triumph by having dinner at Frank's Restaurant in Harlem with Llewellyn, Bill Davis, her practice partner, and Tom Giangrande, the owner of Harry C. Lee, her racket sponsor. They were served by White waiters, the only kind that Frank hired because he believed "there ought to be at least one place where a colored man can have his meals served to him by a white man," a necessity that Gibson doubted. After dinner, she and the group returned to the Vanderbilt for a party with more friends and her family.[176]

Speaking to the press afterward, Gibson shared insight into the way in which her competitive philosophy had changed in the preceding two years. Tennis is "only a game," she said, "and games are competition. You are out there to compete and if you go out there with the idea of enjoying it, you become relaxed and you can control it. It won't control you."[177] True to her self-imposed program of interacting with the public and the press, she said nothing about the latest social controversy involving race, even as others tried to pull her, and her symbolism, into it.

—

While Gibson had been moving through her rounds at Forest Hills, trouble had been brewing in a locale far away. Dispatched by Governor Orval Faubus, the Arkansas National Guard blocked nine Black students from entering Central High School in Little Rock, the state capital. More than three years had passed since *Brown v. Board of Education* (1954), but, like most school districts across the South, the city's school officials defied the court ruling, giving in, like Faubus, to white supremacist leanings, both their constituents' and their own. The process of integrating Central High resumed more than three weeks later, when President Eisenhower federalized the state's National Guard troops and assigned another thousand members of the Army's 101st Airborne Division to circle the school's grounds and protect the Black students, who came to be known as the Little Rock Nine, from the angry mobs of White students and adults who were prepared to use violence to keep them out. It marked the first time since Reconstruction that the federal government had deployed the military to enforce the civil rights of African Americans. Reports and pictures of the intransigence and hostility of the White Arkansans to school integration circulated in newspapers and magazines and on television screens throughout the month of September.[178]

The world was watching Little Rock, too, and the president knew it. "It will be a sad day for this country—both at home and abroad—if school children can safely attend their classes only under the protection of armed guards," Eisenhower told the American people in a national address as he federalized the Arkansas guardsmen.[179] Citing the perceived global threat of Communism, Eisenhower declared that Little Rock's segregationists, in their defiance, were dealing tremendous "harm" to America's "prestige and influence."[180]

Little Rock scotched the likelihood that Eisenhower would meet Gibson at the White House. Presidents had greeted athletes there since after the Civil War. Eisenhower, who personally opposed integration but supported the rule of law, sent her a congratulatory letter after Wimbledon, and Nixon sent one of his own after Forest Hills, but the type of formal meet-and-greet with Gibson that the president's associates had imagined in 1956 never happened. The Executive Mansion instead relayed to her through the press that she could drop by if she happened to be in Washington. Eisenhower believed in "racial symbolism" more than genuine acts of change, but formally inviting her to the seat of the American government was something he chose not to do.[181]

The State Department, on the other hand, moved quickly to co-opt and deploy Gibson's image to limit the damage done in Arkansas to the American brand abroad. USIA commissioned Walter de Hoog of the Hearst Newsreel Service to direct and produce *Althea Gibson, Tennis Champion*, a short propaganda film that idealized her adolescence in Harlem and showed her receiving respect from White people, famous and ordinary. The poverty, gangs, and near total Blackness of her Harlem were nowhere to be found. Instead, viewers saw contemporary footage of public streets, parks, playgrounds, and tennis courts where Black, White, Latino, and Asian children amused themselves together as they supposedly had in "the New York of 15, 20 years ago." Fred Johnson appeared as himself in a silent cameo. In a scene intended to represent both Gibson's youth and racial integration in American life, Johnson gave lessons to a young Black woman, who resembled Gibson, and three White male students at a public tennis court. Over moving pictures of her tennis career from 1950 to 1957, the film's narrator described her persistence in improving her game to become the champion of Wimbledon and Forest Hills. USIA incorporated a series of images of Gibson enjoying amiable relations with Whites, from children who asked for her autograph or received lessons from her, to crowds cheering during matches and at the ticker-tape parade, to Queen Elizabeth and Richard Nixon awarding her trophies. The State Department had already made similar films about Marian Anderson and Ralph Bunche, and in the next few years would also produce films about track and field stars Rafer Johnson and Wilma Rudolph. The message in each installment was clear: America was more than the racism that Little Rock and other events revealed.[182]

African Americans watched and commented wryly that the same country could produce both the hatred of Little Rock and the historic events of Gibson's career. Hazel Garland, the society columnist who had covered Gibson at the Wightman Cup, was dumbfounded by the different responses to Black progress in New York and Arkansas. Garland experienced pride in her heart and tears of joy when, flipping television channels one afternoon, she happened upon footage of Gibson receiving applause from the crowd at Forest Hills and the winner's trophy from Nixon. Garland's emotions shifted moments later when she saw a report about Little Rock. "There were tears a few minutes later, but not for the same reason," she recalled, and she felt "no pride," either.[183]

Closer to Harlem, others found Gibson's treatment at Forest Hills and the abuse of the Little Rock Nine at Central High School a disturbing "study in contrasts," too.[184] The *New York Age* devoted a page to each in its September issues, positioning Gibson prominently amid coverage of the school desegregation crises, a considerable investment for a biweekly newspaper. On September 14, the editors published a sizable picture of her smiling with Nixon and Anderson at Forest Hills beside a long list called "On the Integration Front" that outlined the violence, resistance, and arrests that had come with efforts to bring Blacks and Whites together in public schools. Two weeks later, the *Age*'s front page read "IKE ACTS!" in huge letters, showed a picture of a White man chasing a Black man in Little Rock, and promised stories inside about the National Guard in Arkansas and "New York's Jim

Crow Schools." The page's only other item was a picture of Gibson receiving the city's medal of honor from Mayor Wagner after the ticker-tape parade in July.[185]

In her public silence about Little Rock, Gibson was unlike other Black celebrities. Louis Armstrong, her fellow State Department ambassador, broke from his reputation among younger jazz men as a trumpet-playing, handkerchief-holding, grinning Uncle Tom who played for segregated audiences to express his ire about the situation. "The way they are treating my people in the South," he told the press, "the Government can go to hell." Faubus was, to Armstrong, "an uneducated plow-boy" and Eisenhower was "two-faced" and weak for letting the Arkansas governor "run the government." "It's getting so bad a colored man hasn't got any country."[186] Armstrong, who had toured Ghana in 1956, threatened not to move ahead with a planned goodwill tour of the Soviet Union, though he changed his mind after Eisenhower intervened in Little Rock. Eartha Kitt, "never a great race woman" according to a columnist for the *Los Angeles Sentinel*, surprised many when she told reporters in Chicago that she agreed with Armstrong.[187]

Meanwhile, Gibson, brimming with confidence and willing to tell anyone who would listen about her newfound self-assurance, kept her attention on her career. It was part of her preference, which she later described, to "steer clear of political involvements" and "make my way as Althea Gibson, private individual."[188] Increasingly, reports of displeasure with her assertiveness surfaced in the media. The chairman of the Toronto International Tournament castigated her for, he said, giving him the runaround about her plans to enter the event. "Althea was always hard to handle, being one of the most temperamental players," Doug Philpott told the Associated Press, "but now she's turned into a prima donna. It wasn't money that was involved, it was just her temperament." Asked about it at Forest Hills, Gibson described herself as "flabbergasted," insisted that she had told the necessary figures that she would not defend her title in Toronto, and, refusing to get caught in a controversy, kept the focus on Philpott. "He must have a grudge against me or something. I don't know why." She dismissed the matter as "commotion."[189]

Reports of more trouble followed as Gibson defended her title at the Colorado Open in Denver, where she reprised her role as chanteuse for the White attendees at the Tennis Ball, and then headed to California for an extended trip combining business and pleasure. She arrived in Los Angeles later than expected for the Pacific Southwest Championships, where she was to defend her title with Sydney Llewellyn watching. Perry T. Jones, the deceptively cherubic-looking president of the Southern California Tennis

Association and the chairman of the tournament and reception committees, had displeased her. Jones, who had actively worked against allowing African Americans to enter the Southern California Tennis Championships in the 1940s by limiting their access to entry forms and once wrote a letter to the USLTA president asking for advice on ways to "effectively and legally prohibit Negroes from participating in [Southern California Tennis Association] tournaments," had not secured accommodations for Llewellyn.[190] The conflict was curious and raised the specter of a show of power by Jones, Gibson, or both. By delaying her arrival in Los Angeles, Gibson gave the impression that she was not going to come at all. What is more, the weekend was occupied by Davis Cup exhibition matches at the tournament site, the Los Angeles Tennis Club, buying still more time for everyone involved. Instead, Gibson remained in Denver until the matter was sorted out. Once she arrived in Los Angeles, she stayed as planned at the home of ATA friends Eoline and Spot Thornton, while Llewellyn took quarters at the Black-owned Watkins Hotel. *World Tennis* took note that some in the White tennis community were growing exasperated with Gibson. Members of the Pacific Southwest tournament committee "had decided it was 'not worth the expense'" to have invited her.[191] In an interview with Jeane Hoffman of the *Los Angeles Times*, Gibson revised the story of her career, saying, "I always had the strokes; now I have the confidence to go with it." Gibson explained that becoming "more relaxed" had also led to her success.[192] She played some of her best tennis on the tennis club's hard courts and beat Louise Brough 6–3, 6–1 to win the title for the second straight year. She also defended her doubles title with Hard, giving yet another largely White crowd more than their money's worth.[193]

Gibson's growing reputation for conceit preceded her in Black Los Angeles. During the tournament, the 100% Wrong Club, a group of Black sportswriters, feted her with a formal dinner at the Milomo Club on Western Avenue, the capital of Black Los Angeles. When a reporter asked her about the bad press that she had received about her "attitude," Gibson replied, "Thank you, Mike Wallace," eliciting laughter from the room. She then candidly responded that heightened scrutiny was the price she paid for being the best in her field.[194]

The audience accepted the response and Gibson. The sportswriters gifted her with a necklace selected by actress Dorothy Dandridge in recognition of her achievements. With or without the jewelry, she charmed and dazzled the audience, in contrast to the stories that ran rampant about her in the press.[195] "I found her to be quite some chick," L. I. "Brock" Brockenbury, the sports editor of the *Los Angeles Sentinel*, reported with more than a few notes of surprise. "She is charming, and bubbling over with personality," he told his readers. She gave a "brilliant talk" and displayed her "modesty and humility" as well as her quick and easy sense of humor.[196] Enchanted, Brockenbury found Gibson physically attractive, too. *Ebony* had just released its October issue, which featured her on the cover in a patriotically themed pose that many agreed made for a flattering portrait: she leaned against the net on a tennis court while wearing a white jacket and pleated tennis skirt and holding two racquets, one sheathed in red and the other in blue. Seeing Gibson in person with her makeup, elegant evening attire, and freshly styled hair, Brockenbury did not think *Ebony* had done her justice.[197]

Gibson was in top form and good spirits for the entire trip. The operators of the Olympic Auditorium and Brad Pye, a writer for the *Sentinel*, arranged for her to be a special guest during the light heavyweight championship fight, where she watched Archie Moore defend his title, knocking out Tony Anthony in the seventh round. In Berkeley, she beat Brough again, this time in the final match of the Pacific Northwest Championship. Days later, she returned to Los Angeles to present trophies to the winners and runners-up in the all-Black Arlington Racquet Club's fourth annual tournament. Gibson had practiced on the tennis court of tournament chairman Dr. Walter Davis and his wife, Eloise, throughout her run in the Pacific Southwest. On her return trip, she relaxed with the guests, including entertainer extraordinaire Cab Calloway, in the Davises' spacious home and sang a few songs, to their delight. She sang the next night, too, when Alpha Kappa Alpha members in the city honored her during a program at the local YWCA. For nearly three weeks, she luxuriated in the spoils granted her as a sports star.[198]

Gibson avoided, however, the hard topic of race. Publicly, she still said nothing about Little Rock, at least nothing that ended up in the papers. Privately, she supported the idea of school desegregation, but she did not come forward in the fall of 1957 to say as much.[199] Speaking up for integration and against Faubus and white supremacy might have lifted the spirits of some African Americans and their allies. Yet doing so carried risks—namely, of alienating the White-controlled tennis community and jeopardizing her standing with the State Department. Her words might also have further enraged the dyed-in-the-wool white supremacists who loathed her. The hate mail that *Time* received after putting Gibson on its cover showed that such people did not care if their names were known. "I'll accept Kim Novak, Khrushchev, and even Chief Justice Warren on your covers, but I'm afraid I couldn't stand your Althea Gibson cover around the house," wrote John E. Meeks of Baton Rouge, Louisiana.[200] The hostility did not just come from the South. "I must protest your Aug. 26 issue of TIME with Althea Gibson on the cover," wrote R. M. Shaw of Philadelphia. "We have enough trouble with these people without paying for a magazine which carries such news."[201]

Back in Los Angeles, Brockenbury remained impressed with Gibson, but he stewed over the one topic on which she had disappointed him. It had nothing to do with Little Rock but everything to do with desegregation. "My big criticism of Althea is that she doesn't seem to have much interest in finding and developing a successor from among the colored players," he lamented. Like P. L. Prattis of the *Courier* and others, Brockenbury wanted Gibson to be an agent of sustained integration and change in tennis, not just a player. Seated beside her at the Milomo Club, Brockenbury had confronted her with his complaint and asked her what she thought about being compared to Jackie Robinson. Days later, her response still rang in Brockenbury's ears. Jackie was in a "class by himself" and had "made her road much easier," he remembered her saying in her impressive and measured tones of modesty and humility. Yet Gibson asserted she was "not the 'Jackie Robinson of tennis.'"[202]

Game Over

*I was only thirty years old and I had the best part of my life
still to live. I had to think about making enough money to
support myself, about fitting myself, a Negro girl, into the
larger world that I had come to know and to enjoy, and
about whether or not I wanted to get married—and if
I did, what was I going to do about it?*

—ALTHEA GIBSON, 1958

"HECTIC," GIBSON CONFESSED when the reporter from the *Los Angeles Times* asked how her life had been since winning Wimbledon and Forest Hills. Gibson's response had nothing to do with her tournament schedule. "The phone rings all the time. Requests for personal appearances, television shows, [and] magazines" flowed in, she said. A deluge of mail arrived daily, too, with announcements of awards and invitations to be a guest of honor at swanky banquets, many of which she attended.[1]

In November, Gibson was a guest of honor at the elegant World Fellowship Luncheon hosted by the National Council of Negro Women in New York. Weeks later, she went to Montreal to play exhibition matches to open the Canadien Tennis Club at St. Laurent College. Gibson surprised her hosts by speaking French without an American accent and beating Quebec's fifth-ranked male player 8–3. Fans shouted questions to her as she signed autographs after the set. One fan asked Gibson whether she could cook. It was typical of the kind of sexist questions and comments hurled at women in sports. Gibson handled the ridiculous inquiry with a smile and an evasive response: "I can't answer that one because it might incriminate me."[2] On Thanksgiving Eve, she joined boxer Floyd Patterson and Phil Rizzuto of the New York Yankees in Newark for the department store Bamberger's annual "Parade of Light," waving at the two hundred thousand people who lined the route. December brought the greatest honor of all. She attended the Orange

Blossom Classic, the most prestigious event in HBCU football, in Miami as
Florida A&M's guest, watching the Rattlers win to complete an undefeated
season.[3]

Becoming the first Black champion at Wimbledon and Forest Hills and
being one of the most famous Black women in the world brought numerous
opportunities. Each was given because of the singular talents that had made
Gibson famous. Yet all too often those opportunities also revealed people's
judgment of her as a woman who lived with little regard for ideas about what
was normal for a person of her race and gender and in the rarefied country-
club sport that she played.

The magazine coverage was a case in point. The Johnson Publishing
Company covered Gibson in its two most important enterprises, *Jet* and
Ebony. Yet the feature stories reminded readers of her reputation as a less-
than-ideal heroine. Borrowing from the 1956 *Ebony* feature, *Jet* argued that
Gibson had "conquered herself" and reached the top of the tennis world
through persistence despite her many losses after debuting at Forest Hills in
1950. The writer, A. S. "Doc" Young, who had dubbed her a "flop" in 1953,
noted that she ignored "people who mistook her dedication for aloofness."[4]

Ebony's coverage later that year continued in the same vein. Gibson's portrait on the October 1957 cover of *Ebony* was beautiful, perfectly illustrating
the accompanying story, "Tennis Queen from Harlem." Inside the issue,
though, the magazine presented her as the opposite of queenly. "Althea sometimes seems to feel out of place in the dainty, feminine world," said *Ebony*. She
was also no race woman in the magazine's estimation: "A mixed-up kid most
of her life, she simply wasn't ready to assume the public relations demands
of her Jackie Robinson–like pioneering role" in tennis. Russ Cowans's insult
that she was "as ungracious as a stubborn jackass" appeared, too.[5]

Gibson received little better treatment from White media. A reporter
for the *Los Angeles Times* paid her a backhanded compliment, writing that
Gibson was "easier to talk to this year."[6] *Look* made her the subject of a feature
in November. "Althea Gibson . . . Tragic Success Story" chronicled her life as
a cautionary tale complete with the overtones of nonconformity to standards
of class, gender, and race. She "had no home of her own" and depended on
others "for everything from lessons in tennis to instructions in manners,"
wrote author Christy Munro. Calling Gibson "a girl with raw edges and
wounds," Munro remarked that "the genteelness of tennis has never been easy
for Althea," that her "tennis manners" were hardly impeccable, and that "some
of her benefactors say that she isn't living up to her obligations to her race."[7]
The pages of fashionable media outlets were not unlike the exclusive world of

amateur tennis: Gibson could appear within them, but her presence was still treated as a problem.

Gibson was the most accomplished woman in sports. The Associated Press named her the Woman Athlete of the Year in a landslide, with sportswriters casting 420 out of 516 first-place votes in her favor. She was the first Black woman to win the award since its inception in 1931, but race did not drive her feelings about the distinction. Gibson was thrilled. The award came with two trophies and two separate trophy presentations. At the first, in February, she called the award "my greatest honor" because it "covers women in all sports."[8] Yet, as an amateur, she had no money to show for it.

The financial incentives for Gibson to remain a tennis player were few. She was not interested in teaching tennis at a private club, but no club had offered her employment anyway. Race was the reason, she thought. "To hail my talents in public doesn't cost anything, but to hire a Negro—and a Negro woman at that—to teach white club members called for a bigger expenditure of courage than most club owners were willing to make."[9] Gibson hoped she might "have some connection with some sort of tennis academy or school where children can come and be taught the proper way to play, at little or no cost," but no such offers came, as tennis largely remained the game of the social elite.[10] She continued to represent Harry C. Lee, playing the company's rackets in exchange for a fee of $75 ($791 in 2022) each month, but no other firm reached out to her about endorsing their wares.

The rarest and most profitable option of all—touring while under contract to a professional tennis group—did not come Gibson's way after she wrapped her season in October 1957. When people were not predicting that she would leave amateur tennis to get married, they speculated that she would leave to turn professional. Gibson continued to address the former topic bluntly. "Is she getting married, as reported elsewhere?" the *Los Angeles Times* asked in September. " 'No,' said Gibson, flatly. And that was that." Regarding her career, she had a ready reply: "You have to have an offer before you consider it."[11] Jack Kramer, the man who held a virtual monopoly on the business of professional tennis, neither called her nor wrote a letter.

Defenders of amateur tennis looked upon Kramer as a pirate who was leading "the pro raid" on their sport and threatening its future.[12] They were not entirely wrong. After winning the men's singles titles at Wimbledon and Forest Hills in 1947, Kramer had turned professional, competing against Bobby Riggs on a tour led by Chicago businessman Jack Harris and in the process earning $87,000 ($917,296 in 2022). By 1953, he had become a full-fledged promoter with his own company. Kramer's World Tennis, Inc., almost single-handedly wooed amateurs who either were popular showmen or had reached the top of the sport by winning Wimbledon, Forest Hills, or both and wanted to be paid for it, leaving critics to claim that the best players were in professional tennis, not the amateur game. Kramer offered salaries, percentages of ticket sales, and performance-based bonuses. Pancho Segura, Pancho Gonzales, Frank Sedgman, Ken Rosewall, and Tony Trabert were all part of his stable. Immediately after Wimbledon 1957, Kramer signed twenty-two-year-old champion Lew Hoad to a contract worth $125,000 ($1,317,945 in 2022) for a round-the-world tour of twenty-five months. His players were indisputably the best in the world, and people across the United States, Australia, Asia, and Europe flocked by the thousands to arenas and auditoriums to watch his troupes play matches for a few nights before moving on to another city or town. The tours were not glamorous, but they made money and got more players, journalists, and members of the public to take seriously the idea of open tennis—professionals and amateurs meeting in tournaments, including the four majors.[13]

Gender excluded Gibson from what *Sports Illustrated* called Kramer's "small green empire."[14] "I'm not against women's tennis," he would say in the 1970s. "I'm only against losing money in women's tennis."[15] Except for his mother, who cashed and mailed checks for World Tennis, Inc., Kramer's business model did not include women. "All they do is cut the take for the boys," he told the press.[16] Kramer insisted that his stance was based on fan interest. "The only prejudice practiced in tennis against women players is by the fans, who have shown repeatedly that they are prejudiced against having to watch women play tennis when they might be able to watch men play," he wrote in his autobiography, *The Game*, in 1979. "People get up and go get a hot dog or go to the bathroom when the women come on."[17]

Kramer pointed to experience to explain why he considered women's professional tennis a losing proposition. In 1951, he and Riggs signed Gussie Moran to a contract worth $35,000 ($398,833 in 2022), thinking that the fame that followed her for having worn lace-trimmed panties at Wimbledon in 1949 would enhance ticket sales for an uncharacteristically flagging tour. To face off against Moran, they signed Pauline Betz, the four-time winner at Forest Hills. From Kramer and Riggs's point of view, the Moran-Betz tour quickly went from promise to "disaster." Moran was no match for Betz, and ticket sales plummeted. Kramer deduced that people wanted to see a competition, not a foregone conclusion, though he had not thought that way a

few years earlier when he beat Segura, Gonzales, and others before enthusiastic crowds. Kramer blamed Moran, who, in addition to losing night after
night, did not live up to the purpose of her hire. "The lace-panty publicity was
worthless," Kramer complained. "Then on top of everything else, Gorgeous
Gussy just wasn't as gorgeous as people were expecting," even if she was, in his
opinion, "far more beautiful than the rest of the dames in tennis."[18] Kramer's
chosen lesson from the experience was simple and not uncommon: women
had to be both good athletes and sexy if they were going to be popular with
the public and profitable in sports.

By 1958, Kramer's interest in Gibson mostly had to do with the free publicity that came with dropping her name. He sometimes mentioned her
in interviews, floating the fantasy of a Connolly-Gibson tour, which he
knew was impossible because of Connolly's career-ending injury. Kramer
even teased the possibility of signing Christine Truman, a spiel that made
headlines, kept his name in the papers, and chagrined her parents. Predicting
a redux of the Betz-Moran affair, however, Kramer had no real intention of
signing Gibson. He did not think any of the women on the amateur circuit
could give her stiff competition that would consistently attract the public and
make money. Kramer expressed himself in harsh generalities that perpetuated
stigmas about women in sports. "They are just not good enough," he said of
women as professional tennis players.[19] And so just as being an outsider had
cost Gibson opportunities to compete at the start of her career, she became
a major-winning veteran only to see her status as the best in the game cost
her money.

Publicly, Gibson maintained a necessary posture of opposition and ambivalence about turning professional. She knew that she could lose her amateur status if she betrayed even the "intent" of going professional, the grounds
upon which the USLTA had expelled Betz and Sarah Palfrey a decade earlier.
Gibson trod carefully when reporters inquired about her future in the sport.
"I haven't been asked" to turn pro, she told *Sports Illustrated*, adding for emphasis, "Honestly not." "I'm still an amateur (with no offers or plans to turn
professional)," she told the *Amsterdam News*. She still enjoyed the competition and winning majors. She imagined that she could remain an amateur
while making money from other pursuits—namely, writing and singing. She
was also clear-eyed about her prospects of achieving lucrative and long-term
success in professional tennis. "From what I understand, women professionals
never have done well on tours compared to the men," she told Palfrey.[20]

Still, it was hard for Gibson not to ponder the life-changing money that
could accrue from going pro even if it was less than the men received. After

years of living on the road and in Montclair with the Darbens, she wanted an apartment of her own, a clear signal that her denials of an interest in marriage were true. Gibson appreciated the continued financial support of Dr. Eaton and Dr. Johnson, but she wanted to sustain herself beyond the monthly Harry C. Lee money and savings that she squirreled away from the per diems the USLTA doled out to players for tournaments. She was thinking more seriously, too, of providing for her family. Kramer and other men justified under-the-table payments to amateurs on the grounds that men had to look out for their wives and children.[21] She understood. Learning of Hoad's contract, she said, "He's got a wife and family and no one is going to look after them if anything happens to him in the amateur game." But she had a family to think of, too, and Jane Crow, like Jim Crow, was in her way.

Daniel and Annie thought about Gibson's financial future as well. Annie openly spoke her dream that Gibson would turn pro, make a significant amount of money, and buy a house to get the family out of the apartment in Harlem. Lillian, seventeen, and Daniel Jr. still lived there, along with Mildred and her two young children. All the better, Annie thought, if the house came with enough land for her to have chickens. Daniel's dreams were not nearly as vivid, but, facing another decade at the garage, he thought about what a check in the high five or low six figures could mean. "It's the one thing we've been waiting for," he admitted to the *New York Post* after she won Wimbledon. "We never bothered her one way or another about money, but it wouldn't hurt if she could make some."[22]

Gibson agreed. She wanted to move her family to the suburbs, but that would take time. She also wanted to support her brother Danny's ambitions to be a singer and her sister Lillian's interest in becoming a dancer. Finding satisfaction beyond tennis was top of mind for Gibson, too, but she was not certain that she wanted entirely to leave the game—competition, really—behind. Surely it was possible, she thought, to do it all. The desire to explore the possibilities was great, but so was the pressure, external and internal, to capitalize on her fame. She knew that name recognition did not last forever. "I've gotta make good while the iron's hot."[23]

———

Gibson soon made her first stab at securing her future. Book contracts were a privilege that female tennis players enjoyed over their counterparts in other sports. Since the 1920s, it had become something close to a tradition for women who reached the number one ranking in tennis to write autobiographies. Helen Wills, Helen Hull Jacobs, Alice Marble, Pauline Betz,

Althea Gibson in 1944. Looking back on her youth, she called herself "the wildest tomboy you ever saw." Bob Davis, Black Tennis History.

Fred Johnson, Gibson's first tennis coach, gave her lessons at the Cosmopolitan Tennis Club in Harlem in the early 1940s. As a teen, she resented his devotion to discipline. Thirty years later, she confessed what others knew: "I can truthfully say he started me on my way to become the champion that I became." From *Althea Gibson, Tennis Champion*, film by the U.S. Information Agency (1957). National Archives.

On the Eaton family's tennis court, c. 1946. Gibson's transformation from "tomboy" to "lady" had begun. Center for Southeast North Carolina Archives and History, William Madison Randall Library, University of North Carolina at Wilmington, Wilmington, North Carolina.

Gibson enjoyed practicing with men and did not shy away from competing against them. She participated in the women's division of the Southeastern Open Tennis Championships, a tournament of the American Tennis Association (ATA), in Durham, North Carolina, in 1948 and posed for pictures with men who also entered the tournament. Pictured (left to right): Dr. Lewyn E. McCauley, John Hervey, R. D. Russell, Dr. R. Walter Johnson (Gibson's mentor and coach during her training visits to Lynchburg, Virginia), Gibson, Nathaniel Jackson, Dr. Richard Cohen, Dr. Hubert Eaton Sr. (the mentor and coach with whom she lived in Wilmington, North Carolina), and W. L. Cook. John H. Wheeler Collection, Kris Ford and the Archives Research Center, Atlanta University Center, Robert W. Woodruff Library.

Three-Star Performer--By Ric Roberts

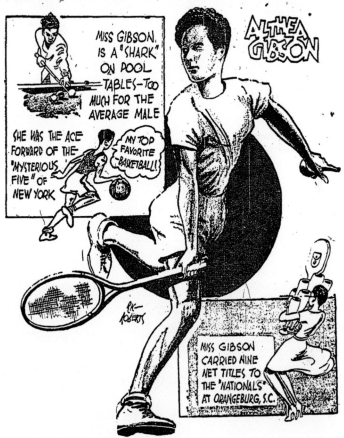

Gibson's athleticism made her a celebrated figure in the African American press long before she began to compete in White tennis tournaments. She was a novelty to journalists, thanks to her skills in multiple sports. Sportswriter and illustrator Ric Roberts drew Gibson as an exception to the notion, popular in the 1940s, that playing sports undermined a woman's ability to be feminine. "Three-Star Performer" by Ric Roberts, *Pittsburgh Courier*, August 21, 1948.

Dr. Eaton encouraged Gibson to study the games of other tennis players as a way to devise a strategy for her matches against them. She often visited the matches of potential opponents to assess their strengths and weaknesses. New York City, c. 1950. Gordon Parks/The LIFE Picture Collection/Shutterstock.

Gibson's victory in the Eastern Indoors Tennis Championship at the Kingsbridge Armory in the Bronx, New York, in March 1950 put her in the spotlight and under tremendous pressure. Gordon Parks/The LIFE Picture Collection/Shutterstock.

Wearing her signature shorts and collared shirt while competing at River Forest, outside Chicago, in the summer of 1950, Gibson sports the look that *Jet* later linked to gossip about her sexuality. Gbf/AP/Shutterstock.

Sarah Palfrey, U.S. National tennis champion of 1941 and 1945, brought Gibson to the West Side Tennis Club to practice in July 1950. Palfrey became a friend and confidant despite their vastly different backgrounds. AP/Shutterstock.

After her debut match at Forest Hills in August 1950, Gibson walks with Alice Marble, four-time U.S. National tennis champion and winner of Wimbledon in 1939. Published in *American Lawn Tennis* in July 1950, Marble's op-ed in support of Gibson's participation in the national championship drew international attention to the issue of segregation in tennis. Mary Hardwick, an active supporter of integrating tennis, stands in the background on the left, holding a rolled program in her hands. Several of Gibson's Harlem mentors are in the crowd, too. Buddy Walker, tall, hatless, smiling, and wearing a mustache, stands several feet behind Marble. Distinguished by a wide-brimmed hat, Rhoda Smith watches from the middle. Fred Johnson, wearing sunglasses and a hat, stands a few feet behind Gibson. National Archives, RG306-PS-B.

Gibson with Louise Brough, reigning champion of Wimbledon, after their dramatic match in the second round at Forest Hills in August 1950. Brough said afterward, "The rain was probably the only thing that saved me." West Side Tennis Club Archives.

With Jackie Robinson at a celebrity fundraiser in New York City in 1951. Gibson did not like being compared with the baseball legend, but she never denied that his entry into Major League Baseball allowed her to cross the color line in tennis. Everett/Shutterstock.

Charismatic and commanding, Gibson could spellbind audiences with her speeches and, later, "chats." Here she speaks at Florida A&M College, her alma mater, during a gathering of the New Homemakers of America, c. 1951. Meek-Eaton Black Archives Research Center and Museum, Florida A&M University.

Gibson looking her sophisticated and feminine best as she returns to Wilmington, North Carolina, to visit the Eaton family in 1952. Center for Southeast North Carolina Archives and History, William Madison Randall Library, University of North Carolina at Wilmington, Wilmington, North Carolina.

Gibson graduating from Florida A&M on June 1, 1953, at the age of twenty-five. Completing high school and earning her bachelor's degree were among her proudest achievements. Center for Southeast North Carolina Archives and History, William Madison Randall Library, University of North Carolina at Wilmington, Wilmington, North Carolina.

At the West Side Tennis Club, c. 1953. Gibson's blistering serve was considered the pièce de résistance in her arsenal. West Side Tennis Club Archives.

Playing at the West Side Tennis Club, August 1953. This was one of the few times Gibson got the better of Maureen Connolly, the teenage phenom who was the first woman to win the calendar year Grand Slam. Gibson never beat her in a tournament. United Press photo. West Side Tennis Club Archives.

Gibson enjoyed sightseeing during her travels abroad. In May 1956, while competing in the French Championships, she took pictures in front of the Hôtel National des Invalides in Paris. Thomas D. McAvoy/ The LIFE Picture Collection/ Shutterstock.

Gibson and Angela Buxton receive the women's doubles trophy from the Duchess of Kent at Wimbledon in July 1956. Buxton was a close friend to Gibson through thick and thin. AP/Shutterstock.

Gibson loved to sing and often performed for audiences when she traveled abroad. Here she sings for students in Sri Lanka in 1956–1957 while touring for the State Department. U.S. Embassy in Sri Lanka, Colombo, Twitter, https://twitter.com/usembsl/status/700 284176830984192.

Gibson visited the offices of *British Lawn Tennis and Squash* before returning to the United States in February 1957 after spending several months competing in tennis tournaments in Australia and Sri Lanka. She learned that getting more rest and playing fewer tournaments were the keys to winning Grand Slams. The Museum of the International Tennis Hall of Fame, Newport, RI.

Althea Gibson and Karol Fageros, c. 1957–1958. Gibson and Fageros developed a friendship while traveling together as part of a four-person tennis team organized by the State Department in 1955. Fageros credited Gibson with improving her game. The Museum of the International Tennis Hall of Fame, Newport, RI.

Gibson won many friends in the State Department between 1955 and 1959. Officials enthusiastically used her image and success to push back against news stories about racial discrimination in the United States that circulated in the international media. To the delight of the agency's leaders, she also encouraged its female employees to take up tennis. Collection of the Smithsonian National Museum of African American History and Culture.

ALTHEA GIBSON of New York City, U.S.A.
A LEADING WORLD TENNIS PLAYER

DURING HER GOODWILL TOUR OF ASIA AND EUROPE.
ALTHEA, 29, WON 14 SINGLES TITLES. HER BIG
GOAL IS TO WIN THE 1957 WIMBLEDON AND U.S.
WOMEN'S SINGLES TITLES.

BEFORE MAKING HER GLOBAL TOUR,
ALTHEA, WAS A PHYSICAL EDUCATION
INSTRUCTOR AT LINCOLN UNIVERSITY
IN MISSOURI.

SHE READS A GOOD DEAL. HER
LITERARY PREFERENCES ARE THE
BIBLE, AUTOBIOGRAPHIES AND
DETECTIVE NOVELS.

The State Department capitalized on global interest in Gibson during the Cold War. The agency sponsored her on several tennis tours and even made a short film, *Althea Gibson: Tennis Champion*, about her rise from the streets of Harlem to victory on Wimbledon's Centre Court and at Forest Hills. Federal officials saw Gibson's success as an effective tool to counter Communist propaganda about racial discrimination in the United States. Created in the fall of 1956, this illustration was one of numerous drawings of athletes that the United States Information Agency (USIA), the propaganda wing of the State Department, bundled in so-called "youth packets" and published in newspapers abroad. The illustration ran in the Ceylon *Daily News* on January 16, 1957, just as officials were arranging for Gibson to compete in the Asian Tennis Championships in Colombo, the country's capital city. Like sports, drawings of this kind were part of the State Department's strategy to covertly influence young people's ideas about America. National Archives, United States Information Agency (USIA) Records.

Gibson leaves New York's City Hall in July 1956 after a photo op with Mayor Robert F. Wagner. She is accompanied by Will Darben. Darben had long wanted to marry her, but she was less sure. Photographs and Prints Division, Schomburg Center for Research in Black Culture, The New York Public Library.

Darben and Gibson attended a farewell party at New York's Birdland Jazz Club before she traveled to England in May 1957 in pursuit of an elusive Wimbledon singles title. Darben's presence in Gibson's life sparked questions, rumors, and speculations about whether and when they would marry. *World Tennis*, October 1957. The Museum of the International Tennis Hall of Fame, Newport, RI.

The State Department sponsored Gibson and Shirley Fry during a tennis tour of Australia in 1956–1957. Here they arrive in Adelaide for the South Australian Championships, which Gibson won. Fry's victory in the Australian Championships prevented Gibson from achieving the career Grand Slam. The Museum of the International Tennis Hall of Fame, Newport, RI.

Gibson and Fry met in the finals of every tournament they played during their visit to Australia. The press dubbed them "the finals twins." Off the court, they got along well, too. Here they play at Milton, Queensland, Australia. Brisbane John Oxley Library, State Library of Queensland.

Gibson went to England in the spring of 1957 focused on winning Wimbledon. Here she plays the ladies' singles quarterfinal against Sandra Reynolds of South Africa. *Jet* published the picture on the cover of its August 1st issue. AP/Shutterstock.

Queen Elizabeth II presented Gibson with the winner's plate at Wimbledon in July 1957 as Darlene Hard, runner-up, looked on. The queen made a deep impression on Gibson: "She looked exactly as a queen ought to look, except more beautiful than you would expect any real-life queen to look." AP/Shutterstock.

Despite losing badly to Gibson in the Wimbledon final in 1957, Darlene Hard gave Gibson a congratulatory kiss after the trophy presentation. Later that day, the pair won the women's doubles title together. AP/Shutterstock.

Gibson and Lew Hoad dance at the Wimbledon Ball in 1957. Tradition dictated that the men's and women's singles champions had the first dance. As early as 1951, when Gibson made her debut at Wimbledon, anxiety surfaced over the possibility that she might win someday and dance with a White champion. "Wimbledon Ball," *The Australian Women's Weekly*, July 31, 1957. Trove/ National Library of Australia. https://trove.nla. gov.au/newspaper/article/ 48076430

Seldom at a loss for words, Gibson was overwhelmed by the crowds who greeted her during the ticker-tape parade in New York City after she returned from Wimbledon in July 1957. The *New York Amsterdam News* had pitched the idea for the parade more than a year earlier. Bertram Baker, executive secretary of the ATA, is seated behind the driver. Everett/Shutterstock.

After the ticker-tape parade, Gibson was the guest of honor at a banquet luncheon held at the Waldorf-Astoria Hotel. Mayor Robert F. Wagner presented her with the city's medal. Her parents, Annie and Daniel, joined the celebration. Later, Gibson recalled that they saw her play tennis only once. Harry Harris/AP/Shutterstock.

Ugly caricatures of Althea Gibson, like the above, were published in English newspapers while she was fighting to win the tennis crown at Wimbledon.

Spectators at Wimbledon were noticeably cold toward Gibson as she defeated opponents, including local favorite Christine Truman, on her way to winning the singles title. Famed British illustrator Roy Ullyett used racist caricature—exaggerations of Gibson's features and stereotypical dialect—to capture the tension. The *Pittsburgh Courier* reproduced the cartoon to show readers the layers of animus that surrounded Gibson in the British press and public. *Pittsburgh Courier*, July 13, 1957.

The State Department used footage of Vice President Richard Nixon presenting Gibson, the first African American winner at the U.S. Nationals, with the winner's trophy at Forest Hills in September 1957 in the propaganda film *Althea Gibson, Tennis Champion*. (Australia's Mal Anderson, winner of the men's title, stands on the right.) To the filmmakers, Nixon's presence could convince global audiences that the American government and prominent White leaders respected African Americans. West Side Tennis Club Archives.

When Gibson successfully defended her singles title at Forest Hills in September 1958, Secretary of State John Foster Dulles presented her with the trophy. Her coach, Sydney Llewellyn, right, shakes Dulles's hand. Collection of the Smithsonian Museum of African American History and Culture. Gift of Donald Felder and family.

Gibson gives a tennis clinic for students at Midwood High School in Brooklyn, New York, in December 1957. Throughout her life, she enjoyed teaching the game of tennis to others, though she did not want to become a full-time instructor. She gave lessons and clinics around the world. *World Telegram & Sun* photo by Ed Ford. Library of Congress Prints and Photographs Division, LC-DIG-ds-04399.

Gibson would teach tennis to anyone who was interested. She derived special pleasure from engaging with children, a positive outcome of her turbulent childhood. From *Althea Gibson, Tennis Champion*, film by the U.S. Information Agency (1957). National Archives.

Gibson calling lines during a tennis match at the Caribe Hilton in San Juan, Puerto Rico, in early 1958. The Museum of the International Tennis Hall of Fame, Newport, RI.

Gibson with Eddie Herr, director of the Good Neighbor Tournament, in Miami in 1958. Herr defended her amid mounting media criticism. When Gibson debuted in the tournament in 1951, he paired her with his daughter, Susan, in doubles. Private collection.

Gibson drew deep pleasure from beating Angela Mortimer to retain the Wimbledon singles title in July 1958. Just a few years earlier, Mortimer had been her "jinx opponent." *Illustrated London News*, July 12, 1958. British Newspaper Archive.

Gibson won Wimbledon doubles titles with three different partners. Maria Bueno was the last one, in July 1958. Here their smashes and serves were not enough to win the National Doubles Tennis Championship in Boston in August. *British Lawn Tennis and Squash*, October 1958. The Museum of the International Tennis Hall of Fame, Newport, RI.

THE LADY CHAMPION SMASHES WITH GUSTO, HER PARTNER WATCHES WITH GRACE

Althea Gibson and Maria Bueno in action at Boston

Reception for ALTHEA at New York Mayor's residence in 1958. FAMU faculty members are (from Left) Rebecca Steele, Sadie Gaither and Annette Thorpe

On July 16, 1958, New York mayor Robert F. Wagner and his wife, Susan, hosted a reception for Gibson at Gracie Mansion after she successfully defended her Wimbledon singles title. The mayor proclaimed it "Tennis Day." Gibson poses with Florida A&M faculty members Rebecca Steele, Sadie Gaither, wife of football coach Jake Gaither, one of Gibson's mentors, and Annette Thorpe. State Archives of Florida, Florida Memory, https://www.floridamemory.com/items/show/263820.

Gibson's portraits on the covers of African American magazines reflected her celebrity. This was her second *Jet* cover in two years. Ambivalence, admiration, and animosity all permeated coverage of her career in the pages of the Black press. Google Books.

"...with God's help I hope to win the crown with honour and dignity. —Althea Gibson"

Gibson impressed tennis fans and others in India when she played in tournaments and exhibition matches there in 1955–1956. She was still the toast of the country, as her portrait on this cover of *National Sports*, an Indian magazine, attests. Collection of the Smithsonian National Museum of African American History and Culture. Gift of Donald Felder and family.

As the first African American to enter and win the U.S. National Tennis Championship at Forest Hills and Wimbledon, Gibson was a global media sensation, appearing in newspapers and magazines and on radio and television broadcasts consumed by people fascinated by her story of overcoming improbable odds to become the number one tennis player in the world. Here she is on the cover of Argentina's *El Gráfico* after receiving the Venus Rosewater Dish for winning Wimbledon in 1958. Wikimedia Commons.

Gibson with the other members of the American Wightman Cup tennis team for 1958: Margaret Osborne duPont (captain), Janet Hopps, Mimi Arnold, Karol Fageros, and Dorothy Head Knode. Neither Gibson's stardom nor her pride in representing her country were enough to lead the team to victory. Collection of the Smithsonian Museum of African American History and Culture, © D. R. Stuart.

Althea Gibson, jet-setter, c. 1959. She was accustomed to "living with a tennis racket in one hand and a suitcase in the other." Collection of the Smithsonian National Museum of African American History and Culture.

Harper & Row published Gibson's first memoir, *I Always Wanted to Be Somebody*, in November 1958. Many in the Black press took issue with her views on segregation and her attitude about being a racial symbol. Private collection.

When Gibson published *So Much to Live For*, her second memoir, in 1968, she presented herself as moderate and willing to confront racial prejudice when it undermined her new career pursuits. Private collection.

After years of singing among friends and in intimate settings, Gibson recorded an album, *Althea Gibson Sings*, in the winter of 1958. Gaining a foothold in the music industry proved harder than she thought it would be. Private collection.

Gibson went to Hollywood in the fall of 1958 to make *The Horse Soldiers*, a Civil War Western starring John Wayne and William Holden and directed by John Ford. She worked behind the scenes to improve her part, a house slave named Lukey. RGR Collection/Alamy Stock Photo.

Gibson, Karol Fageros, and Abe Saperstein, owner of the Harlem Globetrotters, announced their partnership in professional tennis at New York's 21 Club on October 19, 1959. Gibson and Fageros played exhibition matches before Globetrotters games and during halftime. Harry Harris/AP/Shutterstock.

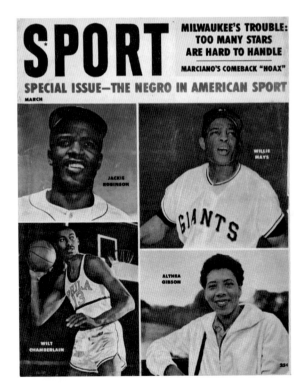

Gibson's appearance on the cover of *Sport* for March 1960 with Jackie Robinson, Willie Mays, and Wilt Chamberlain symbolized her unique standing as a Black woman in sports. Unhappy to see serious coverage of African American athletes in a mainstream magazine, some readers wrote hostile letters to the editors. Private collection.

Product endorsement deals proved elusive for Gibson as a professional athlete. Racket maker Harry C. Lee, which she represented as an amateur, used Gibson and Fageros in an advertisement in *World Tennis* in 1960. The Museum of the International Tennis Hall of Fame, Newport, RI.

Gibson worked as a community relations representative for the Ward Baking Company from 1960 until 1965. Engaging with predominantly African American audiences, she pitched Ward's Tip-Top bread. Though often monotonous, the work could be fun. Here Gibson poses with her "Tip Top Toaster" team after a charity basketball game in New York in 1961. University of Minnesota Libraries, Kautz Family YMCA Archives.

Gibson's work for Ward extended her presence in the public eye. The company placed advertisements like the one seen here in Black newspapers, which it hoped would increase sales among Black consumers. Photograph by M. Associates. Photographs and Prints Division, Schomburg Center for Research in Black Culture, The New York Public Library.

Along with blazing trails, Gibson and Jackie Robinson shared a passion for golf. In February 1962, they shared top honors in the Ray Mitchell North-South Winter Golf Tournament held at the City of Miami Country Club in Miami Springs, Florida. AP/Shutterstock.

Gibson competed in several tournaments organized by the United Golfers Association (UGA), which was founded by African Americans. Here she talks with sports reporter Milton Greenglass at the Hotel Statler during the UGA Championship at Ponkapoag Golf Course in Canton, Massachusetts, in August 1961. Brearley Collection, Boston Public Library. Digital Commonwealth, https://ark.digitalcommonwealth.org/ark:/50959/xs55nd16c.

Gibson joined the Ladies Professional Golf Association (LPGA) Tour in 1963, but she did not achieve the same success in golf she had in tennis. August 5, 1966, brought one of the highlights of her golf career. She shot 68, setting the women's course record at Pleasant Valley Country Club in Sutton, Massachusetts. The next day, she scored 88. Bill Chaplis/AP/Shutterstock.

Gibson has fun guiding Dinah Shore on the golf course. The singer, actress, and television personality was an avid golfer and supporter of the LPGA Tour. While playing in the professional tournament that Shore hosted in Palm Springs, California, in April 1973, Gibson won a new Mercury sedan. She drove it for years. Photo by Martin Mills/Getty Images.

In 1973, Pepsi-Cola appointed Gibson as the national director and technical advisor for its Mobile Tennis Program. The job gave her the chance to share the game she loved with young people in urban communities. Bettmann/Getty Images.

Gibson's various jobs for the state of New Jersey in the 1970s brought her into closer contact with children. Here she meets Kyla Johnson (left) and Tawanna Choice (right) as part of the Newark Summer Fun Club. Newark Public Library.

In 1975, Governor Brendan Byrne appointed Gibson as the state athletic commissioner of New Jersey. In March 1976, she addressed a committee hearing focused on bringing prizefighting back to New Jersey and learned that politicians did not always play fair. Bettmann/Getty Images.

Arthur Ashe, Dr. Johnson's other famous protégé, was the superstar Black tennis player in the 1970s. Ashe and Gibson were allies for charitable causes during the decade. Here they encourage Derek Irby at a tennis tournament sponsored by the United Negro College Fund in October 1976. AP/Shutterstock.

In 1979, Gibson went to Dorchester, Massachusetts, to serve as a guest coach for the Franklin Field Tennis Center, now known as Sportsmen's Tennis & Enrichment Center. She worked one-on-one with Zina Garrison, Andrea Buchanan, Leslie Allen, and Kim Sands (pictured here from left to right). Sands said of Gibson: "She knows tennis and she cares." Courtesy of Sportsmen's Tennis & Enrichment Center.

In 1990, Zina Garrison reached the title match at Wimbledon, making her the first Black woman to compete in a Grand Slam final since Gibson won at Forest Hills in 1958. The All England Club flew Gibson to Wimbledon to watch the match. Ashe covered the tournament for HBO. Carol Newsom Collection. The Museum of the International Tennis Hall of Fame, Newport, RI.

The All England Club invited past champions to Wimbledon for the tournament's one hundredth anniversary in 1984. Gibson brought Sydney Llewellyn, her new husband, to the event. John Russell Collection, The Museum of the International Tennis Hall of Fame, Newport, RI.

Later in 1984, Gibson reflected on her tennis career in a wide-ranging interview with film-maker Bill Miles as part of his Black Champions series. Asked to describe her style of play, she responded, "Aggressive, dynamic, and mean." Washington University in St. Louis University Libraries.

Brian Lanker photographed Gibson for his book *I Dream a World: Portraits of Black Women Who Changed America* (1989). Interviewed for an essay that accompanied her picture, Gibson was direct in describing how good she had been in her prime: "I had the best serve in women's tennis. I had the best overhead in women's tennis. I had the most killing volley in women's tennis." Harvard Art Museums/Fogg Museum, Schneider/Erdman Printer's Proof Collection, partial gift and partial purchase through the Margaret Fisher Fund, © Brian Lanker, Photo © President and Fellows of Harvard College, 2011.348.

In 2019, a statue of Gibson was unveiled on the grounds of the USTA Billie Jean King National Tennis Center in Queens, New York. Sculptor Eric Goulder calls the work a "monument" and hopes it will inspire viewers to learn more about the life and legacy of its subject. Photo courtesy of Eric Goulder.

Althea Gibson serving at the U.S. Nationals at Forest Hills in 1957. Photo taken by Bob Cox. West Side Tennis Club Archives.

Doris Hart, and Maureen Connolly had all told their life stories. In the fall of 1957, Gibson decided to join them.

Ed Fitzgerald, the editor of *Sport* magazine, initiated the project. Driven and seemingly indefatigable, Fitzgerald had gotten his start in journalism in high school, covering the local sports scene in his hometown, Yonkers, New York, where he had returned after serving in the army in World War II. Eschewing college, Fitzgerald landed a job as a writer for the newly created *Sport* in 1946 and earned a reputation as a hard and agreeable worker for whom no project (or celebrity) was too difficult and no deadline too tight. By 1951, he was editor of the whole enterprise. Fitzgerald had written young adult sports novels and ghostwritten *Tennis Is My Racket*, Bobby Riggs's 1949 autobiography. Seeing in Gibson a chance to write about another interesting tennis personage, he reached out to Sydney Llewellyn, who had firmly positioned himself as her trusted advisor in addition to being her tennis coach.[24]

Gibson and Fitzgerald's collaboration was unusually intimate, a sign of her desire for the book to succeed. She spent weekends in Yonkers at Fitzgerald's family home. Fitzgerald and his wife, Libuse, poured Gibsons for her and listened as she claimed that the cocktail had been named for her. As if transported back to Williston Industrial, she played football with a group of high school boys and shocked Fitzgerald by throwing the ball "the length of four full backyards." When Eileen, the Fitzgeralds' ten-year-old daughter, was sick, Gibson brought breakfast to the child's room, adding with a flourish, "This may be the only time in your life you'll ever be served breakfast in bed by the Wimbledon champion." Each word and action amused Fitzgerald and added to his impression that there was no one quite like her. "Althea," he would remember three decades later, "was an original."[25]

Fitzgerald found that Gibson "didn't talk about race much," and her silence on the topic fascinated him. To accommodate their schedules, the pair sometimes had business meetings over meals in Manhattan. Fitzgerald knew that he had to be selective about where he took Gibson, as New York's dining scene was not free of racism. "She never said a word about where I took her to eat when we met for working dinners in the city," he recalled, "although she knew perfectly well that some places I liked wouldn't have let her in." Fitzgerald was struck by Gibson's lack of a visceral, personal response to racism even as it was all around them and a regular feature of her life.[26]

In the 1980s, Fitzgerald claimed to have based the book entirely on his one-on-one sessions with Gibson, but comparisons between the autobiography and other primary sources show that he also used interviews she had given to other reporters around the country and in England, particularly

between 1956 and 1958. The resistance to the Jackie Robinson comparisons
that she had displayed in interviews with the *Los Angeles Sentinel* and the
Miami News appeared in the book, as did her insistence that she was "an individual." Gibson's statement to the *New York Times* in 1956 that "I'm not a
racially conscious person. I can't help or change my color in any way, so why
should I make a big deal out of it? I'm a tennis player, not a Negro tennis
player" also appeared in the book. Fitzgerald inserted quotes from Gibson's
April 1958 interview with the *Miami News* in which she said that she, unlike
Robinson, did not see herself as "a Negro battling for equality" and did not
"possess" the "feeling" that would lead her to social activism. She also told
of the abusers in her family, Daniel and Uncle Junie; her years as a truant
fighting on the streets; her gender nonconformity first in Harlem and later in
Wilmington, along with the Eatons' efforts to correct it; and the squabbles in
the ATA over her career. Gibson, in her candor, revealed that she lacked a traditional Black middle-class upbringing and that, as an adult woman, she did
not believe in one of its leading tenets: not to reveal any personal information
that gave fodder to White people's stereotypes of African Americans.[27]

Independence facilitated Gibson's openness. Fitzgerald noticed that she
had no spouse, partner, or lover to influence her—or him. He surmised that
Llewellyn "liked to cast himself" as Gibson's "Svengali," but she was, in her
interview sessions with Fitzgerald, either operating without his influence or
ignoring it. "She just did it her way," he remembered. Tentatively titled "The
Grass Is Greener," the book was to be released by Harper and Row at the
end of 1958, with pre-publication serialization in the *Saturday Evening Post* in
the late summer. The venues were decidedly mainstream, putting Gibson's life
story before millions of Americans, Black and White. The story they were to
read was to be "all Althea, not glamorized, not bowdlerized, not a cop-out,"
according to Fitzgerald. He, a White man, had come to see the project as
"more of a race book and a book about aspiration than it is a tennis book."[28]
Indeed, unlike memoirs by other tennis players, there were no chapters devoted to playing the game.

Something else was missing, too. No one else had been present at the
dinner meetings and sessions in Yonkers. No one close to Gibson—and
Black—with media savvy and foresight had been there to ask her whether she
wanted to rethink or rephrase anything she had said.

———

The thought of a singing career captured Gibson's imagination more than
anything else. If she could be a professional anything, she thought, it would

be a singer, not a tennis player. Hungry to compete and to perform, Gibson dreamed of playing amateur tennis in the summer and singing in winter. Her ideal scenario was to have steady engagements, preferably at an established club, during the off-season. She would not consider singing "in small dives. It's the big thing or nothing with me."[29]

Gibson took major steps toward her dream in the fall of 1957. Believing that "you have to work at it," she started taking vocal lessons with James Scott Kennedy, a speech and voice professor at Long Island University.[30] Fortified by their work together, she accepted when Abbe Niles, a member of the West Side Tennis Club, presented her with an opportunity. Niles was a member of a committee tasked with organizing a gala birthday tribute for W. C. Handy that would raise money for the famous blues composer's Foundation for the Blind. Niles invited Gibson to perform at the celebration in November at the Waldorf-Astoria. Pre-event publicity touted that Milton Berle, Tallulah Bankhead, and Lena Horne would be entertaining, but Gibson's performance was a "great surprise," according to Ruth Ellington, a society columnist who was there. Gibson took to the stage in a room filled with famous people, including Ed Sullivan, Ralph Bunche, Congressman Adam Clayton Powell, Oscar Hammerstein, and novelist Fannie Hurst. Ellington remarked on Gibson's "lush contralto" and characterized her as a "very gifted gal"—though not specifically for the quality of her voice but because she both sang and played tennis.[31] Henry Onorati, a music executive, was in the audience, and when he invited Gibson to make an album with his company, Dot Records, she said yes and allowed herself to think that her dream of singing in theaters and nightclubs and on television was about to come true.[32]

Gibson got a rude awakening at the turn of the year. Dot gave her a week's notice about the date of the recording session and allotted only a single day for her to record twelve songs. Gibson knew that she was not on the same level as Ella Fitzgerald or Peggy Lee, but, she reasoned, such brisk treatment made it much less likely that she would ever have the chance to be in their company. She had seven days to choose her songs, practice on her own, and rehearse with her assigned band, the Doles Dickens Quartet. Making matters worse, she came down with the flu.[33]

Dot disrespected Gibson and got away with it because she was a wide-eyed outsider in the music industry. The company preyed on her fame, her name, and her naiveté. Dot was Gibson's only option. Fatigued, "full of tea and lemon and medicine," and with her voice lower than usual, she went through with the recording date. The day made for "a grueling experience" and, she admitted, the "conditions were far from ideal."[34] When it was over, she tried to console herself with the positivity that Llewellyn encouraged, but it was hard.

———

In late January, Gibson made her first trip to Minnesota to play singles and mixed doubles exhibition matches with local players at the Minneapolis Armory as part of a sports program to celebrate the centennial of the state. The governor made her an honorary citizen and she stayed at the Leamington, the finest hotel in the city. The two-day visit was a smashing success, as Gibson impressed both on the tennis court and away from it. She beat Bill Moore, a celebrated former member of South High School and the University of Minnesota's football teams, 21–3 in table tennis and 225–190 in bowling. Twice outdone, Moore could only stand back in wonder at Gibson's superior skills, telling onlookers, "Man, it's a good thing that she didn't go out for football at South. I'd have never made the team."[35] On the night of the exhibition series, Gibson won both her matches, including her singles match against Jeanne Arth, who played the amateur circuit, and she made the more than twenty-three hundred spectators—a record for a tennis exhibition with amateurs in Minnesota—laugh as she clowned and made jokes during the night. After her partner, Kenny Boyum, hit a low-flying winner, Gibson stopped the match and measured the height of the net. When Arth's teammate, Wendell Ottum, hit a drive deep into the backcourt, she again stopped the match and encouraged the spectators to applaud him. Charity was part of the trip. Proceeds from the sale of the five hundred tickets set aside for students were donated to a scholarship fund for Black college students.[36] Relaxed, in good spirits, and supporting philanthropy, Gibson came across as different from her reputation in the media.

That did not mean that she missed an opportunity to use the engagement, or others like it, to promote herself. "I've achieved all there is to achieve in amateur tennis," she said as she stepped off the train in Minneapolis. "I realize there are some who do not rank me with the best women tennis players in history. My goal is to prove that I am that good—and I think I can accomplish that within a year." The rhetoric and the theatrics called to mind either the antics of a boxer or Hollywood's portrayal of a gunslinging bully announcing himself upon arrival in some little town in the Old West. Gibson continued, "I definitely feel that I am the best woman tennis player in the world. I have reached my peak. I do not have any weaknesses in my game."[37] She denied that the press influenced her outlook on her abilities. "I read the criticisms all right, but I never permitted it to penetrate my mind. No, and I didn't take an 'I'll show them attitude' either. . . . If I had paid any attention to the criticism I would still be losing."[38] But days later, while receiving an award from the B'nai B'rith Sports Lodge in New York, she showed that the criticisms did matter to her. "Some people still don't believe I'm the world's best women's tennis player and I'll prove it by winning both the Wimbledon and Nationals crowns," she told the audience. "That's not conceit. That's confidence, and then maybe I'll think of turning pro if the right offer comes along."[39]

Llewellyn believed that Gibson was the best woman tennis player in the world, but he worried about her devotion to music. The Coach, as she sometimes called him, was skeptical of her ability to craft a singing career. He told her more than once that she was a "ham" and and that she "couldn't sing [her] way out of a paper bag."[40] He was concerned as he watched her devote more time to her voice work than to her tennis game, especially as she shifted from practicing on the wooden boards of indoor courts in New York to the clay at the site of her first tournament in Colombia and began to experiment with playing from the backcourt rather than sticking to her usual serve-and-volley game.[41]

Playing in the Barranquilla Tennis Tournament in March, Gibson lost to twenty-three-year-old Janet Hopps of Seattle in three sets in the semifinals. It was Gibson's first singles defeat in more than a year. She blamed her loss on the lights of the night match, the high altitude, and the wind. A week later, the conditions were more to her liking. At the Gran Toreno Tournament in Caracas, Venezuela, she beat Hopps in the semifinals before getting the best of Maria Bueno, the eighteen-year-old sensation from Brazil, to win the title before a sell-out crowd.[42]

Gibson tried to recover her old form in her next events, but the efforts proved uneven according to her own high standards. She reached the final of the Caribe Hilton Championships in San Juan, Puerto Rico. Determined to seize every advantage, she watched the semifinal match between Bueno and Beverly Baker Fleitz. When she and Fleitz met in the final, Gibson was unable to execute her plan of winning by staying in the backcourt. Her groundstrokes faltered, banging into the net or going out of bounds, and Fleitz won. Reporters and photographers gathered around Fleitz, always a darling of the press with her red hair, upturned nose, nipped waist, and pedigree in the game; before she married and started a family, many assumed that she would be the breakout player to win grand slams when Brough and Hart faded away. Defeated, Gibson could only trudge heavily off the court, resenting the "noisy hand" that the gallery gave Fleitz on the final point.[43] *World Tennis* wryly noted of Gibson's exit, "There was a certain sadness in seeing 'Big Al' walk off the court the loser."[44] The masculinized nickname underscored perceptions that she was Fleitz's unappealing opposite.

The loss to Fleitz spoiled Gibson's fun. She had chosen to play in South America because she had never been there, and she was suitably enchanted, beginning with the travel arrangements. Eddie Herr, who had invited her to compete at the Good Neighbor Tournament in Miami in 1951, gave her information about the tournaments played on the continent and in the Caribbean and handled the details. It was the kind of special attention that gave Gibson enormous pleasure. "That's the best part about being an internationally ranked amateur tennis player," she told Fitzgerald. "It's the next best thing to having a travel agency send you a whole bunch of colorful brochures and invite you to pick whatever trips you would like to make, free."[45]

Across her weeks in the Southern Hemisphere, Gibson was "content to live the good life." She slept and ate late, swam in the pools at expensive seaside hotels and resorts, sunbathed, and lunched and dined at the tennis clubs with her fellow players. Gibson sang for the four hundred guests who attended a gala in Caracas. In San Juan, she was the only Black guest at the Caribe Hilton but felt neither isolation nor animosity and, joining the other players, relaxed in her cabana on the beach. "I couldn't possibly have been treated more cordially or with more consideration," she told Fitzgerald. "I couldn't have lived it up anymore if I had been a millionaire in my own right. A millionaire with a white skin, at that."[46] America remained in turmoil over civil rights, but Gibson enjoyed luxuries few people knew, certainly few African Americans, and she was determined to get all that she could out of her self-described spot as "a Negro with a certain amount of international significance."[47] Plenty of other people had surely profited from it.

But lonesomeness weighed upon her, too. Although Gibson loved the adulation, the competition, the amenities, and the sights, she loathed being on her own. The trips were especially tough, she told Fitzgerald, "when there is nobody in the company to whom you feel close."[48] Socially and romantically, Gibson often felt isolated. She was with the crowd and a more accomplished player, but she was not genuinely one of them. The amateur tennis circuit was infamous for the constant swirl of couplings and splits that happened among the young White players. By self-admitted choice, and possibly because of the de facto racial protocol, both spoken and silent, that governed recreation, romance, and the color line, Gibson lived on the edge of that cycle. She was decidedly alone. Sometime after the fall, her relationship with Will had come to a halt. Her devotion to her career, be it in singing, tennis, or both, was the deciding factor. "Most fellows I know want their women around most of the time, where they can see and talk to them. In my case I'm never in one place long enough," she told *Jet*.[49] In Minneapolis, a reporter asked Gibson about the persistent rumor that she was going to marry Will. "Nope," she replied. She had "no one man," adding, "I've got several boy friends."[50] Never once did she reveal their names, and she was not publicly associated with any man other than Will.

In Caracas, Gibson found herself attracted to a Venezuelan whom she saw playing in the men's doubles. "I made it my business to speak to him," she recalled. They met for a drink, chatted amiably, and suddenly, overtaken by her feelings, Gibson "blurted" out that she "liked" him. The player, whom she did not name in *I Always Wanted to Be Somebody*, admitted to being flattered but told her the next day that he could not reciprocate. The whole experience, the spontaneity of her admission and the matter-of-factness of his reply, hurt. "I felt," she said, "like a fool." Self-deprecatingly, she told Fitzgerald that the encounter "served to convince me that I hadn't lost my old touch when it came to relations with the opposite sex." From start to finish, the anecdote suggested that Gibson, not unlike many people, could be clumsy when it came to courtships and hook-ups. "I'm no authority on the boy-girl bit," she said.[51]

—•—

Gibson's early-season pleasure tour ended on a sour note. She beat Bueno again to win the Caribbean Championship in Kingston. Then, at the Good Neighbor, in Miami Beach, Gibson, the tournament headliner, lost to Hopps again in the semifinals, 8–6, 6–2. Hopps played what she called "dinkus," getting the ball just over the net to drop into the forecourt, thus forcing Gibson to run from the backcourt, where she had stationed herself. The Associated Press called the defeat "the biggest upset" of the tournament and "startling."[52] The ninth-ranked player in the country, Hopps was unfazed by Gibson's tactics. "When you play Althea you have to beat psychology, too," she said after the match. "She tries to intimidate you, get you nervous and make you beat yourself. She'll make a good shot and stare at you as if to say, 'want some more like that?' "[53] Hopps detected a change in her opponent's attitude and approach to the match when Gibson realized that the tactics were not working. "She seemed to get discouraged when I wouldn't fold and she began pressing."[54] Struggling with her racket, Gibson was not above applying gamesmanship and mind games in her attempts to win.

There was fallout from the loss. Gibson found herself in another dustup with the press. During the match, she was demonstrably frustrated as she saw her 5–1 lead in the first set disappear and spectators turned on her. Afterward, she ignored one reporter and brushed off a second. Citing illness, which Llewellyn later confirmed, she refused to stand for interviews. "I didn't feel good," she told reporters as she walked off the court. "Anybody could have beaten me today. [Hopps] just beat me period." With that, she was gone.[55]

The next day, when Gibson and Bueno won the doubles title, she was more talkative, though she did not tell the press pool that she was experimenting with her game to improve her groundstrokes and passing shots. It hardly would have mattered. Gibson was like a general who refused to divulge war strategies to the enemy. "Everybody seems to expect a person who's called a champion to win all the time," she explained. "But sometimes a champion has an off day, you know. After all, a tennis player never plays the same game twice. Every day is different." In a jarring departure from her all-or-nothing approach to competitions in the past, Gibson dismissed the seriousness of the events that she had lost. "These tournaments didn't mean anything. In fact, they were a test. I played the circuit to see if I was lacking anything. I find nothing particularly lacking."[56] Sensitive about her third loss in five matches, she resorted to defensive braggadocio, the kind of talk deemed "unladylike" and unsportsmanlike.

Gibson's reserve toward the press after the tournament matched her attitude toward them during it. Edwin Pope, the assistant sports editor for the *Miami Herald*, had interviewed her days earlier as she watched a men's doubles match and found her paradoxically open in reserving the right to be less than forthcoming. "Go ahead, ask questions," she said. "I may not answer them all." Pope led by asking her about race. "Has it been tremendously difficult to be the world's first outstanding Negro tennis player?" Gibson gave a single-word response: "No." Following up, Pope asked whether she had encountered "any problems" or "personal difficulty" in tennis where race was concerned. "Most of my problems have been handled by the American Tennis Association," she replied. As for personal encounters with racism, she gave a response that reflected the way she chose to see her place in the country and her mindfulness of the backlash she could face if, as a visitor in Florida, she said anything perceived as critical of Jim Crow in the South. "Listen, I was brought up in New York. I never had to worry about discrimination. I think of myself as an individual. I've always considered myself as good as anyone else." Gibson's response shut down Pope's questions about race, but she soon found herself cutting off still more interrogations. Asked about the Canadian tournament official who had called her a "prima donna," Gibson replied, "Those things are minor with me. I don't have to explain myself to people who know me." She refused to state her age, saying it was "an artist's privilege" to keep such information private. She also refused to discuss any aspect of her tennis game. "I don't talk about my game. If I do, I tell my weaknesses and my strengths." Pressed, she grew, in Pope's recollection, noticeably annoyed. "They have an IDEA," she said. "They don't KNOW. I'm not going to tell them." She also refused to name her favorite song on the forthcoming album. "If I told you that, I'd be telling what is in the album. I don't want to do that." When Pope asked about turning to professional tennis, she explained her secrecy. "That's one subject I can't talk about—turning pro . . . I might get chewed out if I did."[57]

Gibson had reason to be on guard with Pope. She had no way of knowing his intentions and motivations. Pope, who was White, might have set out to write an attention-grabbing piece about race that was intended to get readers talking, regardless of the stress and distractions that honesty would cause her. He might have been out not only to get a story but to make one. In the year after the kerfuffle in Chicago, journalists reported on Gibson's demeanor and alluded to her reputation for obstinacy, no matter how generous and candid she was in interviews. Gibson's caution and suspicions about Pope proved founded. He joined the parade of White journalists who likened her to an animal, writing that she "had the look of a brown tigress," and linked her stand-offishness with him to her reputed disdain for the press.[58]

People at the tournament who knew Gibson tried to defend her. Herr, the tournament chairman, explained, "I've known her a long time and she's a nice person. She's isolated so she clams up." An unnamed player, likely Karol Fageros, agreed: "She's just slow to trust people. Once you have her confidence, she's as nice a person as you'd want to know—off the court that is. She went to college, but she went to no finishing school. She had to come up the hard way. Despite her outward show of confidence, I don't think she's quite sure of herself." Some people would not change their minds, though, no matter what anyone said. "Smart-alecky. Cocky. Big-headed" was, according to another Miami writer, what people thought of Gibson after she left town.[59]

The vigorousness of Gibson's reactions to her losses to Hopps and Fleitz belied her claims that she was unworried about the likelihood of successfully defending her title at Wimbledon. Since her landmark wins in 1957, an uneasiness had come over her. She increasingly saw herself as prey rather than predator, a Goliath in a field full of Davids. Llewellyn sometimes told her to "keep looking over your shoulder," a reminder to make a full turn when she made a tennis stroke.[60] The phrase also applied to how she increasingly looked upon her place at the top of the tennis world. Gibson told the *Los Angeles Times* in September, "Anyone . . . can come along and beat you, even if they're not expected to. They say, 'uneasy lies the head that wears the crown,' and in a sense that's true, because you're always a target."[61] In Miami, she had the same idea. "I met some good opponents and they all seemed 'up' for the match when they beat me. Everybody wants to beat a champion. I felt the same way when I was coming up."[62] Publicly, Gibson held fast to her confidence about her place in tennis even as she began to think that her prime was closer to the sport's past than its future.

—

Dot's release of the album placed Gibson under an even brighter and harsher spotlight. Previous Mays had brought speculation about her chances at Wimbledon. In 1958, those questions—more intense after her losses to Hopps and Fleitz—combined with scrutiny of her abilities as a singer.

Called *Althea Gibson Sings*, the album consisted of a dozen standards with lyrics characterized by longing, loss, fears, and unrequited love. The collection was a blend. Some songs, like "Don't Say No" and "Around the World," were upbeat, while others, including "A Cottage for Sale" and "September Song," were somber. Gibson's range was limited. She seldom reached for high notes. Singing with control, discipline, and precise diction, she never let loose as most of the pop and jazz singers of the era did. The tunes had none of the catchiness of rock and Motown, which were attracting young listeners and changing the music industry.[63]

The album presented Gibson as a female crooner, her sound belying the picture of her on the cover—with bare shoulders, shiny close-cropped hair, and bright red lipstick—that made her look like the quintessential sexy girl singer. Australian Mary Hawton, Gibson's frequent opponent during the international tour of 1956, had once observed that she had a "magnificent crooning voice," while Llewellyn thought that she "mimicked Billy Eckstine," one of the most famous pop singers of the decade. It was an apt comparison. While singing to herself as a teen in Harlem, she had imitated the styles of popular male and female singers.[64] But crooning was not supposed to be the stuff of women. Men, most famously Bing Crosby and Rudy Vallee, crooned, delivering love songs softly and silkily in a style that was a few steps above talking, making millions of women swoon, while triggering angst from social critics who interpreted the men's vocals as insufficiently masculine. Gibson thought her voice was "pretty deep for a woman" and privately harbored "a fear that the quality of my voice—the low tone—would not be accepted."[65]

Positioned outside musical gender norms, Gibson readied herself for public opinion. *Variety*, the leading source on the entertainment industry, judged that she had "a good vocal forehand," was "not overpowering," and "hits with a bluesy voice and a swinging beat that bespeaks of musical savvy and confidence."[66] Others were less enthusiastic. "Althea's Voice Not as Good as Tennis Playing," headlined an article in the *Chicago Defender* that concluded, "As a singer, she is not outstanding."[67] According to another writer, Gibson looked "'like a two-fisted Carmen McRae' when she turns on her singing talent."[68] It was another way of disparaging her as manly.

Gibson persevered and thought she had caught another break when Ed Sullivan invited her to appear on his variety show for two dates, beginning with May 25. The bookings offered invaluable exposure. A staple of American life on Sunday nights, *The Ed Sullivan Show* was the most-watched national television program. Her visit fit the host's interests in integration, entertainment, and sports. As a teenager, Sullivan had played high school baseball in New York's Westchester County and was accustomed to, and unfazed by, competing against mixed-race teams. Three decades later, Sullivan regularly booked athletes, men and women, as well as Black performers as guests on his show. He believed that television, streamed into the living rooms of millions of White households, was a vehicle through which African Americans could win social acceptance.[69]

Acceptance, however, proved elusive. The Black press and the NAACP lobbied for the three networks (the only ones in existence at the time) to feature more Black actors, actresses, and entertainers on their programs, but television executives were reluctant to act. White viewers and advertisers were content to see images of themselves—typically idealized—reflected on-screen. When African Americans did appear on programs, they mostly played servants or other physical laborers and seldom any part that put them on equal standing with Whites. Variety shows were an exception. Black entertainers like Ella Fitzgerald, Lena Horne, Harry Belafonte, and Nat "King" Cole sang, performing the supposedly natural skill with which Black people were most likely to be associated and well received. Still, there were limits to what even crossover entertainers could do. In 1957, NBC canceled Cole's variety show. *The Nat "King" Cole Show* was a hit with critics, but advertisers were wary of backing a program led by a Black entertainer, and many southern stations refused to air it. Sullivan knew the situation well. Sponsors, including Lincoln-Mercury dealership owners, complained that he was too friendly with his Black guests, including women, but he kept on treating them warmly, holding and shaking their hands.[70]

When Gibson took to Sullivan's soundstage, she was Sullivan's only Black guest; the other entertainers, the actors in the commercials, and most of the audience were White. She was noticeably nervous as she walked stiffly onto the stage in her gloves and long, fitted evening gown. Gibson later confessed to Sullivan, "I've had a lot of tough tennis matches, but the toughest match of all was coming on TV on your stage the first time and then continuing as a singer."[71] Steadying herself, she sang "So Much to Live For," the sentimental ballad that Kennedy, her vocal coach, had written especially for her and that was the finale to *Althea Gibson Sings*. She opened with a prelude—"Though life seems dreary and blue / You know there's someone who cares for you / Though the heart of man be gone / His soul will carry on"—before launching into the lyrics.

> *We have so much to live for*
> *To work and to play*
> *So much to live for*
> *As we go on our way*
> *To love one another*
> *To banish all drear*
> *To work with each other*
> *To satisfy needs*
> *We have so much to live for*
> *To laugh and to smile*
> *So much to live for*
> *Before that last mile*
> *So why not be happy*
> *And thank God above*
> *For all He gave us*
> *And make a world filled with love*
> *And make a world filled with love.*[72]

The song was inspirational and inoffensive, saccharinely making a vague gesture to integration but mostly using Christianity to reach the audience. When Gibson finished, she looked relieved. Then Sullivan presented her with the Babe Didrikson Zaharias trophy, so cartoonishly large that it had to be wheeled onto the stage atop a cart, as the second trophy for her selection as the AP Woman Athlete of the Year. Gibson left the studio believing that all had gone well. "What was that you said about me not being able to sing my way out of a paper bag?" she said to Llewellyn, who was waiting for her offstage.[73] Afterward, they celebrated with champagne at Lindy's on Broadway. Gibson felt that she had been "in good form" onstage and that the "very big round of applause" from the audience meant that she had succeeded.[74]

Television viewers and critics were in nearly unanimous agreement that Gibson had not served herself well. She later heard that viewers at home felt that her voice was "overpowered by the musicians" in the orchestra. The criticisms, though, went beyond just the "bad mix."[75] *World Tennis* surmised that "So Much to Live For" was the wrong song for her: The "semi-religious ballad . . . did not do justice to her talent."[76] *Variety* assessed that she had "a simple, resonant voice, almost manly and not always well controlled." To her credit, the weekly continued, she possessed "professionalism in her demeanor and her style."[77] John P. Shanley, the television critic at the *New York Times*, was less impressed, calling her performance on Sullivan's show "much less exciting than her achievements at Forest Hills, Wimbledon and other tennis arenas."[78] In Atlanta, the *Daily World's* Marion E. Jackson judged Gibson's act "something less than sensational" and advised her to "stick to tennis."[79]

Two days later, Gibson was in England. The strategy and care with which she had approached the pre-Wimbledon tests in 1957 were gone. This time, she boarded an overnight plane at Idlewild, arrived at London's Heathrow Airport, and settled into Angela Buxton's flat for a short rest. Six hours later, she won her first match in the Surrey Championships. Asked afterward about her odds at Wimbledon, Gibson continued to press her case. "I am playing better than last year so I cannot see why I should not win the title again."[80]

Gibson backed up her talk. She won the Surrey title after trouncing Mimi Arnold, a nineteen-year-old fellow American, 6–1, 6–0, in thirty minutes. The next week, she won Manchester. Facing Maria Bueno in the final, Gibson paced herself between points, and for good reason. Bueno played Gibson's brand of power tennis. Many saw her as the biggest threat to Gibson's defense at Wimbledon. Focused, she refused to give Bueno any early hope. Gibson won the first set 6–1 and squeaked out the second 8–6, relying on her "masculine service," observed one writer, to squelch Bueno, who could only stick out her racket and pray for contact.[81]

After the match, Gibson waxed uncharacteristically sentimental. Tennis tradition held that players who won a tournament three times kept the trophy, but Northern Club officials, hoping to keep their silver tray, offered her a larger and more valuable gift if she would return it to them. Gibson refused. "Not even if [the tournament chairman] offered me several thousand pounds. No money could buy the toil and tears and sweat which went into

the winning of that Cup," she said. "I want to have it to look at when things
go wrong, and maybe I will be able to show it to my grandchildren one day."[82]

Life after tennis was clearly on Gibson's mind. Unknown to all but Buxton,
a man was, too. Dova Jones, her old beau from her days at Lincoln, dropped
by the flat. They spent two days in Gibson's bedroom.[83]

———

The London press continued to exist as a lion's den for Gibson. Before her arrival, writers feasted on her losses in the spring. Peter Wilson, who had spent
1956 and 1957 churning out racially insensitive one-liners about "the big girl"
who was "as prickly as a dusky cactus" and finding new ways to compare her
to tigers, salivated with the thought that her misfortune offered "a ray of hope
for up-and-coming [English] youngsters."[84] Gibson remained the favorite for
Wimbledon, but reporters still considered her merely the "best of what must
conscientiously be admitted to be a poor lot," foresaw a second straight "lean"
championship, lamented again that women's tennis had dropped to its "lowest
standard since the war," and recalled nostalgically the days of Connolly,
Brough, Hart, and duPont—the period when she was not a factor.[85]

The Wightman Cup revealed the depth of the pressure that Gibson
was under as the number one player in the world. The Americans came to
Wimbledon, the host site of the matches, with their least experienced team
in decades. With Louise Brough deciding to give up Wimbledon in anticipation of her marriage and Darlene Hard running out of money for tennis,
Karol Fageros, Mimi Arnold, and Janet Hopps, Wightman Cup newcomers
all, made the trip. Playing in the series opener, Gibson beat Shirley Bloomer
to give the Americans their only victory in three matches on the first day.
Gibson was expected to win, but the score, 6–3, 6–4, was closer than most
people expected and led to criticism that she was "making more mistakes in
the second set than a Wimbledon champion should have made," according to
the *Liverpool Echo*, and playing with a game "as full of errors as a colander is
full of holes," thought Wilson.[86]

After losing to Gibson each time they met in 1957, no one expected
Christine Truman, seventeen, to win the next day. But the three straight
losses to Gibson had fueled Truman to train harder in the off-season. Using
exercises custom-made for her by Geoffrey Dyson, one of England's premier
coaches, she worked on her physical fitness and became, she said, stronger,
faster, and more agile on her feet. Truman also studied Gibson's tactics with
the help of her coach, George Worthington. Worthington broke down
Gibson's game, shot by shot, and advised Truman on the correct returns to

make. He practiced with her and replicated Gibson's blistering serve. It was just the kind of methodical, strategy-based approach that Llewellyn took to tennis, and it worked.[87]

Gibson closed out the first set at 6–2 in nineteen minutes, but Truman refused to give up. She jumped out to a 3–0 lead in the second set. Gibson fought back, nailing Truman's backhand. Otherwise, she continued to play cautiously, relying on veteran consistency. She was caught between two types of play, the backcourt experimentation and the serve-and-volley style that was her trademark. Truman, the upstart, played as Gibson once had—as if she had nothing to lose. She applied the plan of attack she and Worthington had devised. Following his advice, she returned Gibson's serves, "masculine severity" and all, according to Peter Wilson, with forehands that dropped to Gibson's feet, forcing her to bend lower than she expected or wanted. With another forehand, this one hit crosscourt and returned with an errant volley by Gibson, Truman won the set 6–3, evening the match. Truman kept going in the third, meeting Gibson game for game, until Gibson led 4–3. The advantage could have dealt a psychological blow to Truman; Gibson was, after all, just two games away from what she and most everyone else had come to Centre Court thinking was certain victory. Truman had proven her point that she was an improved player, but that was not enough for her that Saturday afternoon. Reaching into her Gibson-inspired bag of tricks, Truman rode her own harsh serve, heavy forehand, and dominant overheads to victory, 6–4. *World Tennis* called the bout "one of the great matches in tennis history," a "spectacular upset," and "the key match of the Wightman Cup."[88] It was also a replay of Gibson's spring. "The child," said the *Sunday Dispatch*, "had beaten the champion."[89] Gibson and Janet Hopps won their doubles match against Ann Shilcock and Pat Ward later in the day, but it did not matter. At 4–3, the Americans lost the cup for the first time since 1930.[90]

British sportswriters rejoiced, celebrating Truman's victory and reveling in Gibson's defeat. Papers reprinted her confident boasts about her prospects at Wimbledon and retorted that she had been proven wrong. Truman became a national heroine and was promptly seeded second for Wimbledon, adding to fervent hopes that an Englishwoman would win the tournament again at long last. In taking down Gibson, Truman had become, said the *Sunday Dispatch*, "the white hope of British tennis."[91]

In the aftermath, Gibson was gracious in defeat. She congratulated Truman at the net after the match and, during the teams' party at the Dorchester Hotel that evening, met up with her vanquisher, embraced her, and praised her play. "Why did I lose? It was just one of those things," Gibson reasoned. "Christine was playing inspired tennis. I played well, but it wasn't enough. It was a great game and a good defeat."[92]

Inside, though, Gibson was "miserable" over the loss, and the defensive side of her nature soon emerged. When a reporter for the *Daily Mail* brought up the Wightman Cup at a garden and tennis party in London's Highgate suburb, she cut off the conversation. "So what? I'm still the Wimbledon champion. Besides, that's the first time Christine has ever beaten me, and I intend to make sure it's the last."[93] On the eve of Wimbledon, she was even more defiant. "Make no mistake. I shall win the next time I play Christine Truman. That's all I've got to say. I shall win. You may say that my confidence is pretty good. Don't expect me to go into any match in this tournament reckoning to lose."[94]

Leverage and legacy were on Gibson's mind. Thoughts of heightened esteem or status for other African Americans were not. A second Wimbledon title would be "an important asset" for her future, she reasoned, giving her another rare standout achievement that could be used to get more money, opportunities, and positive publicity no matter what she chose to do. She also viewed the successful defense at Wimbledon as a way of making a case about her place in sports generally and in the annals of tennis history specifically. "In sports, you simply aren't considered a real champion until you have defended your title successfully," she told Fitzgerald. "Winning [Wimbledon] once can be a fluke; winning it twice proves that you are the best. I was passionately determined that there would be no 'one-shot' tarnish on my Wimbledon Championship."[95]

—-—

Once the fortnight of play at Wimbledon began, Gibson got to work. She did not have to worry about Truman, who lost in the third round. For two rainy weeks, Gibson reasserted her dominance. One by one, she beat Australia's Margaret Hellyer, Mexico's Yola Ramírez, and England's Shirley Bloomer and Ann Haydon. Bloomer put up the toughest fight of them all. After losing the first set, Bloomer won the second, 6–8, and jumped out to a 2–0 lead in the third, but Gibson shut down any possibility of an upset by winning the next six games in a row.[96]

Some writers dinged Gibson for not playing as well as she had the previous year, but she stuck to her strategy, physical and mental, in match after match. Jettisoning her experimentation with backcourt play, she committed to her dominant serve and ran to the net for volleys at every opportunity. Gibson also devised ways to approach each opponent based upon her knowledge and observation of their games. The semifinal match versus Haydon proved a case in point. She did not go easy on Haydon just because she was nineteen, comparatively inexperienced, and playing on Centre Court for the first time. Gibson also came to the match forearmed with the knowledge that Haydon was left-handed, a fact that "her opponents sometimes forget," Gibson thought, but which she did not. "I had a plan for defeating her and it worked just as I planned it."[97] She insisted that, contrary to what so many said, her game was not based exclusively on brawn. Wilson of the *Daily Mirror* agreed and praised her victory over Haydon as evidence that Gibson "won with brains instead of just muscles" and "proved she is a COMPLETE player by winning the points which really mattered with gentle shots instead of using mere blasting speed."[98]

Angela Mortimer might have fared better if she, too, had let go of the idea that Gibson was an ogre. Mortimer shocked the nation by beating Suzy Körmöczy to reach the Wimbledon final. Mortimer was in the middle of a comeback that had begun in January, when she won the Australian Championship, a breakthrough after the havoc that illness had wrought on her stamina and strength for the past two seasons. At Wimbledon, Mortimer was the first unseeded player to reach the women's final, and madness ensued. Sportswriters hurried to file their stories about the historic feat and the match to come, casting Mortimer as "Miss Sport" and the "forgotten girl" who faced the challenge of overcoming Gibson, the "Black Queen of Lawn Tennis."[99] Fans cheered, reached out to touch Mortimer on the club's grounds, and lined up eighteen hours before the match to get tickets.[100]

On match day, Saturday, July 5, the crowd was behind Mortimer, but she could not depend either on the hopes and dreams of her compatriots, who ringed the stadium and cheered wildly for her, or on the dubious work of the officials, who called Gibson for eleven foot faults during the match, raising questions in the minds of even her toughest British critics about their intentions and their integrity. Mortimer charged to a 2–0 lead in the first set and then to 4–2, gaining strength from Gibson's inconsistent forehand drives and keeping her from coming into the net. Gibson held on, winning games when she was on serve and holding steady in the rallies that were part of Mortimer's game plan. In the end, it was Mortimer who faded. "Playing Althea, I felt tiny and overpowered . . . under-sized and frail," she said years later. Mortimer reached 5–4 and set point in the first, but Gibson batted away her and the crowd's hopes when she set up and struck a forehand that whizzed by Mortimer, hit the baseline, and sent chalk floating through the air. "After that," Mortimer recalled in her autobiography, Gibson "never looked back."

She won the first set at 8–6, and though Mortimer won the first two games of the second set, Gibson dug in, hit serves that one writer likened to a "cannonball shot," and won the next six straight games to seize the match.[101]

When it was over, Gibson was satisfied. The Duchess of Kent presented her with the Venus Rosewater Dish as seventeen thousand spectators watched. Gibson praised Mortimer, confessed to having a case of "finals jitters," and brushed off the officiating. "These decisions didn't really upset me, even though I didn't think I was at fault," she said.[102] Gibson did not, however, say one thing that was on her mind. She thought she might have just played her last Wimbledon, making her doubles victory with Maria Bueno even more special. For good measure, she gave the press corps one more confident boast to report. Of falling behind early in the second set against Mortimer, she said, "I knew I would get the upper hand sooner or later."[103]

———

Gibson rightly observed that her victory silenced the critics. She knew the discourse: that she was merely "the best of a poor lot."[104] After she beat Mortimer, though, British and American writers conceded that Gibson was the best player in women's tennis after all.

With her name engraved twice on the Wimbledon trophy, Gibson felt that she had "answered the big question" about her tennis abilities.[105] Yet the questions about her future lingered. With Forest Hills weeks away, she set out to control her destiny and her public image one more time.

Gibson began by getting an apartment. Unit 3J of 461 Central Park West was the first place that she could call her own since her stint in Jefferson City. She settled in during the summer, once she began to make money from her appearances at public events and on television. The book brought an advance, too. The monthly Harry C. Lee earnings helped, as did the money that she had managed to save from her USLTA expense allowances. Given her self-confidence, Gibson likely exercised her prerogative as the best woman tennis player in the world and received appearance money. Like her earnings, the apartment was not much. She had little furniture and little time to find any, but she had peace and privacy at last.[106]

The most often asked question was whether and when Gibson would give up amateurism for professional tennis. When asked after Wimbledon whether Jack Kramer had contacted her, Gibson answered honestly and assertively. "Mr. Kramer has not spoken to me and I have not spoken to him," she said. "I don't know what's in his mind and he doesn't know what's in mine."[107] It was an empowered response that emphasized her agency.

Indeed, Gibson was hardly sitting on her hands. With Llewellyn's help, she secured a lawyer, Earle Warren Zaidins, to review her business opportunities and contracts. Zaidins, thirty-three, specialized in entertainment law and had previously represented Billie Holiday, the renowned and troubled jazz singer. Together, Gibson, Llewellyn, and Zaidins founded a corporation, Althea Gibson Enterprises, to handle her work in television, publishing, and music, among other things. "The three of us were to bear all the expenses and, if the Good Lord were willing, to reap all the profits of enterprises in which I got involved," she later wrote.[108]

Gibson kept her game sharp but also staved off fatigue and minimized distractions in preparation. She skipped the National Clay Courts—and the Chicago media—in July, and in August she declined to return to Boston for the Essex women's tournament, citing concerns about getting "overtennised" before Forest Hills.[109] Gibson won the Pennsylvania and Eastern championships, respectively, but each time narrowly missed losing to yet another up-and-coming player. Called a "heady, courageous and aggressive competitor with [a] powerful all-court attack," Sally Moore played in a style not dissimilar to Gibson's.[110] Moore, the Wimbledon junior champion from Bakersfield, California, gave her scares in the finals of both events, further reminders that the next generation was coming.

The brushes with defeat gave Gibson even more reason to invest in her singing career. She publicized her album every chance she could get. Mayor Wagner proclaimed July 16 "Tennis Day" and hosted Gibson, Daniel and Annie, city officials, and members of the local tennis communities for a reception at Gracie Mansion. Gibson, the guest of honor, presented Wagner with a copy of *Althea Gibson Sings* as photographers snapped away. Weeks later, she appeared on the *Today* show with Dave Garroway. After winning the Eastern, she made a beeline to New York to appear as the mystery guest on the CBS game show *What's My Line?*, where she would have a chance to talk up the album and her next appearance on *The Ed Sullivan Show*. Wearing a trendy sack dress, she confronted the impish impertinence of panelist Bennett Cerf, the publisher and co-founder of Random House, who asked how she would "make out against one of the ranking male tennis players." Gibson called the question "unfair" and, when Cerf pressed, she parried, "I dare not say because there are so many males in the house." Then she demurred: "Well, maybe I can get a point or two. I wouldn't know about the game." Host John Charles Daly joked that Gibson had a future career in "diplomacy," but it was the singing career that concerned her, and her mood was noticeably less buoyant when the album was the topic of discussion. She hesitated, cast her eyes downward, and allowed her lips to fall before glumly answering, "I hope it's doing well."[111]

It was not. Privately, Gibson blamed Dot. The company committed to promote the album for only six months, rather than the full year that she preferred, and sales, like the reviews, were low. Reports surfaced about Gibson's unhappiness and that she wanted to switch labels. It was unclear, though, that any other company wanted her.[112]

Gibson was determined to sell the record, regardless of the ill will that she might stir up. She chose to leverage her status as a gate attraction and Wimbledon champion to give herself a chance to both return to *The Ed Sullivan Show* and win another national title. She committed to compete in the National Doubles Championship at Longwood Cricket Club on the condition that the tournament committee agree to move the women's final up by a day, to Saturday, if she and Maria Bueno, her partner, made it that far, to make it easier for her to appear on the show. The committee agreed. Gibson and Bueno indeed reached the final, where they were to face Jeanne Arth and Darlene Hard. The committee then reneged on their promise. They suggested that she play the match early on Sunday, August 24 and then fly to New York to do the show in the evening. She refused and explained that she needed to rehearse on Sunday afternoon. Practicing self-interest, Gibson fueled the entrenched perception that she was difficult. The committee went through with the arrangement but was annoyed. "Wimbledon wouldn't have permitted her to do this," one committee member told the *Boston Globe* on condition of anonymity. "There the tennis comes first, not a TV show." Chillingly, the newly appointed USLTA president, Vic Denny, suggested that the association's rules committee be consulted about Gibson's amateur status, even though she had secured their approval before she made her first appearance on the show in May.[113]

Brimming with confidence, Gibson rose at Mrs. Wightman's the morning of the doubles final. Arth, another of the player-guests in the elegant Chestnut Hill house, found Gibson in the kitchen pouring honey into a glass of milk before drinking the concoction. Arth, who admired her, asked why. Gibson, again playing her game of secrecy with an opponent, said only, "You will find out on the court!"[114] Hard and Arth, the unseeded team, won the final in an upset, giving committee members and others with bad impressions of Gibson reason for schadenfreude.[115]

Gibson got her wish to reach New York a day early, but her second appearance on Sullivan's stage showed that she remained a work in progress as a performer. The first guest and, again, the only Black one, she strode confidently to center stage wearing a light-colored, short-sleeved, sequined high-waisted dress and long white gloves. Framed by two bongo players, she sang "I Should Care," another song from the album. Everything went as expected until the end, when, seeming to run out of air, she did not reach the high notes. She spoke rather than sang the last three words. The mistake registered on Gibson's face. She stiffly bobbed her head and shoulders as the music faded, but so did the brightness and wideness from her eyes. When she finished, the guest co-host, Canadian comedian Johnny Wayne, offered neither praise nor comment, saying only, "Althea Gibson!"

The critical reviews that followed were just as mixed. "She indicates a warm voice, but a cold manner," *Variety* judged, and "got passable results." The critic found the close-ups of her face "too severe."[116] *Boston Globe* television critic Elizabeth W. Driscoll appreciated that Gibson was "agreeably unaffected in [singing] style" and thought the performance was "very pleasant and acceptable," but it "wasn't spectacular . . . she obviously needs a little more professional training for the microphone circuit." Driscoll was less generous in her praise of Gibson's wardrobe. "Whoever is picking her costumes isn't doing right by our champion. The sequin-topped dress and the gloves didn't do a thing for her," Driscoll wrote, joining the long list of people who took issue with Gibson's expressions of femininity.[117]

In her title defense at Forest Hills, Gibson played to please no one except herself. In the early rounds, she easily staved off three young challengers, including Christine Truman in the quarterfinals. When the gallery bristled as she took her time between points and games, she showed no intention of speeding up. Gibson's conquering of Beverly Baker Fleitz in the semifinals was particularly satisfying. For nearly a year, reporters had pointed out that she had never beaten the famous redheaded tennis player, who some audaciously called "the world's best woman amateur player."[118] Gibson ended that talk at 6–4, 6–2.

Gibson had a cold and faced a refreshed Darlene Hard in the final. Playing only her second tournament of the year, Hard was noticeably more mature than she had been when she lost to Gibson in the Wimbledon final in 1957. Gibson, on the verge of realizing her dream, was out of sorts. Hard outwitted her, climbing to a 3–1 lead and then winning the first set 6–3, with a strategy that caught her off guard. Hard "was cutting my serve off, coming in, and catching it right on the rise, therefore beating me to the net," Gibson told an interviewer in 1984. "I was totally confused."[119]

Gibson might have been further thrown by an altercation with the referee, Dan Johnson. Before the start of play, Johnson told her that she could not sit down at any point during the final, that to do so—as she had done during the semifinal match—was against the rules of continuous play. The intervention called to mind the over-officiating at Wimbledon in July, the foot faults in Australia, and the many similar moments from her career. Gibson looked Johnson square in the face and made him a promise: "I will sit down."[120]

Gibson fought back and won the second set. During a break before the start of the third, she struggled to devise a strategy that might lead to victory. Reflecting on the match with the interviewer, she recounted her thoughts. "I said, 'Now here I am the defending champion about to lose.' I said, 'No, I don't want this to happen.'" Gibson made eye contact with Llewellyn, who sat in the marquee. "He gave me one signal, and I proceeded to obey that signal and started pulling a shot on Darlene that surprised her. And that was the lob."[121]

Stunning the eleven thousand people seated in the stadium, Gibson took control of the match. When Hard ran to the net for volleys, Gibson hit moon balls over her head. Sometimes the ball landed within only two inches of the baseline. Time and again, if Hard returned the shots at all, she did so with awkward backhands that slammed into the net. Running from net to backcourt and back again, she grew exhausted and confused. But Gibson only got stronger. She played through the pain of spraining two fingers on her right hand during a fall in the third set. She mixed up her shots but never completely let go of the lob, leaving Hard unsure what to do and where to run or stand, in the backcourt or at the net. Gibson won the last two sets 6–1, 6–2.[122]

Forest Hills was Gibson's again. She—not Hart, not Fry, and not Brough—was the first player to win Wimbledon and Forest Hills back-to-back twice since the beloved Little Mo in 1952–1953. Gibson had answered the critics who doubted that she belonged at the top of the world rankings, said she folded when the chips were down, and insisted that she was not among the best women to play the game.[123]

After the match, Gibson at last said what was on her mind. John Foster Dulles, the secretary of state, presented her with the trophy, providing the State Department with another photo op. At the press conference following the trophy presentation, Gibson announced her intention to leave amateur tennis for a year to focus on her singing career. Llewellyn and Zaidins stood beside her. Gibson called it a "sabbatical," but she admitted that the hiatus might be permanent. "Right now I will be out of tennis a year. I don't want to predict what will happen after that. But soon I will begin to slip back and that won't be pleasant. I would prefer to quit at the top." She also wanted to make money.[124]

II

New Frontiers

It's a hard thing to keep coming back time after time in the face of defeat. . . . If you are convinced of the merit of your goal, and if you want to reach it badly enough, paying the price of embarrassment is not so hard. . . . When you feel that your goal is worth the price, you can stand an amazing amount of embarrassment, defeat and fatigue.

—ALTHEA GIBSON, 1960

GIBSON'S SABBATICAL FROM tennis further marked her as a social outlier in the 1950s. She was not retiring to get married and start a family, nor was she leaving amateurism to become a professional tennis player or to take up a definite and stable career. In fact, uncertainty and exploration were the only definite features of her departure and the way she would spend her time away.

Gibson later admitted that she had "no specific line of work in mind" when she left amateur tennis. She had only "prospects on the horizon," and while in her estimation they were "many" as well as "exciting and profitable," they all turned out to be short-lived opportunities that began with promise and ended with disappointment and failure. They were indicative of the multitude of ways in which she did not fit American society and culture in the late 1950s and where they were headed in the 1960s and beyond.[1] Again and again, Gibson found herself either ahead of or behind the times as well as failing to meet other people's ideas of where she belonged, what she should say, and what she should do as a Black woman, a sports amateur, and an athlete who was steadily moving past her prime.

Her finances had become a constant source of interest in the media. "Is Althea Gibson really broke?" asked the *Pittsburgh Courier*.[2] "Her life sounds like the typical rags-to-riches success story—but Althea has no riches," *Look* asserted.[3] Ignoring her salary at Lincoln, *Jet* reported that she had "never had an income" and that the tax returns she filed for 1957 and 1958 were her first.

The press was curious about a woman who would "sacrifice" so much for a sport and pay a "high price . . . [for] proving she can swing a racquet better than any woman alive."[4]

Seldom, though, did she care. Gibson embarked on her post-amateur phase intent on achieving her own personal goals and getting as much pleasure and satisfaction out of life as she possibly could. She would make her own decisions about whether, how, and for whom to engage in battles for fairness and equality. She would figure out how to make money, too.

Gibson remained a magnet for criticism. Before its publication in book form, her autobiography was serialized in the *Saturday Evening Post*. The placement showed the breadth of her celebrity. Two decades earlier, the magazine had serialized the autobiography of Helen Wills, one of the best players in the history of tennis. Some readers griped that the magazine gave Gibson an extended and special platform. The editors printed six letters from readers who had written to express their thoughts about the series. Five were negative. A former member of the Cosmopolitan took umbrage with Gibson's portrayal of its club members: "Althea's success has been rooted for since we were members of the old Cosmo Tennis Club in Harlem. Although she may be Somebody, she appears not to have found herself." A minister in Chattanooga was incredulous that "the honored Post" had "roll[ed] out the red carpet for "a lying, deceiving, drinking, pool-playing, philandering, street-fighting, egotistical, loud-mouthed, long-legged, strong-armed screwball." Margaret Makin from New York similarly called Gibson out for not being respectable. "The first article by Althea Gibson (and the last I shall ever read) will set the Negro people back 100 years. I hope it does as much for SEP circulation." Mrs. Wayne B. Vinson of New Orleans disliked that the magazine published stories about prominent African Americans, period. In July, Roy Campanella had been the subject of a feature article in which he discussed his recovery from the car accident that left him paralyzed. Vinson was unmoved by the former Dodger's misfortune and disturbed by a photograph from the 1957 Wimbledon Ball: "I'm certainly not interested in Campanella and whether he walks again and I especially think it's a disgrace to publish a picture of this Althea Gibson dancing with Lew Hoad, who looks like a white man. . . . I wish you would be a little more considerate of your white southern readers."[5] Each letter reflected the bigotry and bitterness that surrounded Gibson.

Gibson's foray into acting was the first in a series of impromptu engagements in her improvised journey. In the late summer of 1958, the independent

Mirisch Company was casting roles for *The Horse Soldiers*, a film based on Harold Sinclair's Civil War novel, which had earned rave reviews upon its publication in 1956. Like the book, the film was an action-packed account of Grierson's Raid of 1863, when Colonel Benjamin Henry Grierson of the Union Army led a brigade of seventeen hundred cavalry soldiers nearly five hundred miles from Tennessee through Mississippi and into Louisiana, destroying rail and telegraph lines, roads, bridges, and Confederate supplies over a period of more than two weeks, during which the unit imprisoned Confederates and released and took on enslaved people. Mirisch hired John Wayne, America's favorite cowboy, to play Colonel John Marlowe, the character based on Grierson, and negotiated with Paramount Pictures to acquire the Academy Award–winning heartthrob William Holden for another major part. John Ford, who had won six Academy Awards, signed on to direct.[6]

Mirisch was interested in Gibson, too. An agent, Aleck Alexander, and the Music Corporation of America, which represented Gibson, arranged for her to do a screen test for *The Horse Soldiers*. She was thrilled. A career in show business had been her first desire, dating back to her early days of skipping school to see movies. Gibson saw more similarities than differences between acting and athletics. She had spent much of her life performing her craft in front of cameras, and whether on a tennis court or a soundstage, she intended to do her best. Within two weeks of her sabbatical announcement at Forest Hills, she quietly flew to Los Angeles and refrained from telling reporters that she was there for a screen test. Yet she took great satisfaction from the experience and savored the reaction of those who had watched her preliminary performance. "After the test was over, the cameramen, the light men, everyone in the crew spontaneously applauded," she told a reporter five years later. "John Ford, the director, told me, 'When the crew applauds, that means you're really good. It just about never happens.'"[7]

When limited news of the screen test emerged, the Black press greeted it with interest and high hopes. Gibson stood to win her first part in a motion picture—no mean feat—which some thought could lead her to make her sabbatical permanent. Though still unsold on her talents as a chanteuse, entertainment columnists were willing to give Gibson a chance as an actress. "Combined with her fine speaking voice and determination to succeed she should do okay as a newcomer to the field of movie acting," said one.[8] Yet, like Gibson's tennis career, her possible entry into the film industry was about more than herself alone. It was about race and social progress.

Hollywood had reached an inflection point where portrayals of African Americans were concerned. Since the film industry's inception, Black actors had mostly been cast in movies as servants, criminals, and the indigent, seen primarily in the background and with little screen time, much of which was devoted to lending comic relief rather than gravitas or romance. The late 1950s marked an exciting moment of change, impelled by the wartime and postwar activism of civil rights groups. Hollywood released so-called message movies that preached, creatively if sometimes unevenly, the wrongheadedness of racism, and films with all-star, all-Black casts hit theaters, too. Building off the work of actress Lena Horne in the 1940s, a new generation of Black entertainers bolstered the hopes and dreams of millions of African Americans. Ruby Dee, Ossie Davis, Sidney Poitier, Dorothy Dandridge, Diahann Carroll, Harry Belafonte, Eartha Kitt, and Sammy Davis Jr. catapulted to stardom and cultural heroism by winning leading roles and portraying characters that were multidimensional, modern, and as close to equals—narratively and socially— with their White co-stars as Hollywood had ever allowed. Like sports, the film industry appeared to be a cultural site where African Americans were getting over racial barriers to stride toward integration. When rumors began to circulate in October that Gibson had won a part in *The Horse Soldiers*, she seemed poised to add her name to the roster of athletes who also acted, including Ty Cobb, Babe Ruth, Jackie Robinson, Woody Strode, and Archie Moore.[9]

Yet Gibson herself remained at a curious distance from the production. She said nothing to the press about her screen test or the part, in a marked departure from her volubility all year long. By late October, Ford and the rest of the cast and crew had begun filming on location in Natchitoches, Louisiana, but Gibson was not there. Told by his son, Pat, who acted as a location scout, that "segregation is still complete" in the region, Ford decided not to have her make the trip.[10] A stunt double went instead. Famed entertainment columnist Walter Winchell reported that Wayne and Holden were "furious" that Jim Crow kept Gibson apart from her colleagues. Fury alone, though, did not change the law, and Ford and Gibson agreed that she would shoot her scenes in Hollywood.[11]

Gibson passed the fall fulfilling obligations that burnished her image as a Black icon. She went to Washington, D.C., as a guest of honor for the annual awards banquet hosted by the Pigskin Club. The black-tie affair raised money for the NAACP's Freedom Fund, which was building a war chest for the civil rights struggle in the South, the United Negro College Fund, and Big Brothers of America. Lawrence Oxley, the club's president, proffered the invitation to her through Dr. Eaton, a member. In his role as manager, Sydney Llewellyn coordinated the details. Gibson received a plaque for making an outstanding contribution to sports, the first time in the club's twenty-one-year history that it recognized a woman for sports achievement.[12]

On November 20, she made good on her commitment to Carl Van Vechten. Once among the foremost White patrons of the Harlem Renaissance, Van Vechten had spent the past two decades photographing the preeminent Black cultural figures of the twentieth century for a photography project that he had promised to the archives of Yale University and months trying to get Gibson to pose in his studio at 146 Central Park West. "I have spent more time on Althea Gibson already than she has spent on her tennis career," he wrote exasperatedly to Langston Hughes. In the unctuous, racialist style that made so many Black people distrust him, he wondered, "Why is it that only cullud are so difficult to line up for photographs?"[13]

The results turned out to be worth the wait. Earle Warren Zaidins, Gibson's attorney, wrote to Van Vechten, telling him that she was "anxious" to see the results and was particularly interested in "a glamour shot" from the session.[14] Van Vechten's work went beyond glamour. He captured Gibson as no one else had. Under his lens, she was multifaceted, confident, and un-guarded in some shots yet vulnerable in others. She posed in an evening gown for one series, visually playing the part of the lady that she was actively making part of her persona during her break from tennis. In another set, she wore her tennis togs—shorts in some photographs, a skirt in others—and alternated between demonstrating movements that she might take on the tennis court and holding her racket as if it were a harp. In Gibson, Van Vechten saw a free-spirited, artistic athlete of the highest caliber who delivered with her tennis racket joy and originality to all, including herself.

Gibson would soon find it necessary to draw upon the imagination and resolve that Van Vechten saw within her. After her arrival in Hollywood on December 1, she faced reporters' seemingly obligatory questions about mar-riage with her characteristic blend of candor and enigma. Asked whether she was going to marry Will, she said, "No, I have no plans." Asked whether she planned to marry anyone at all, she replied, "Well, let's put it like this. I am . . . not seeking or looking—but—well, I suppose I'm available."[15] Straining credulity, Gibson insisted that she had come to California with no knowledge of her part in the film. She only knew, she said, that she would not play an athlete of any kind. This was false. In a speech that she prepared after her work on the film was completed, she wrote, "The scene that I did for Mr. Ford was from the script of 'The Horse Soldiers.'"[16] Within days, details about Gibson's role, and a possible explanation for her reluctance to talk about it, emerged. *Variety* reported that she was to play a "slave girl," while United

Press International said she would be a "housemaid in a southern mansion."[17] No matter what anyone called the part, the implications were unambiguous. Gibson, the Black woman who had been presented with sterling silver salvers at Wimbledon by White royalty, who had served aces against White women on tennis courts around the world, and whose life story some people thought should be made into a movie, was taking a major step backward.[18]

The timing could not have been worse. That fall, questions about Gibson's loyalty to and self-identification with African Americans rose in the Black media. Her book was to blame.

Harper and Row published *I Always Wanted to Be Somebody* in November and printed abridged excerpts in the December issue of *Reader's Digest*, putting Gibson's candor with Ed Fitzgerald out in the open at last. Three passages rubbed some Black reviewers the wrong way. In one, Gibson described her disinterest in social justice efforts. "I have never regarded myself as a crusader," she said. "I'm always glad when something I do turns out to be helpful and important to all Negroes—or for that matter, to all Americans, or maybe only to all tennis players. But I don't consciously beat the drums for any special cause, not even the cause of the Negro in the United States, because I feel that our best chance to advance is to prove ourselves as individuals." She continued, "That way, when you are accepted, you are accepted voluntarily, because people appreciate you and respect you and want you, not because you have been shoved down their throats." Gibson was clear that she was not "opposed to the fight for integration of the schools or other movements like that." She was just as clear, though, that she did not feel a responsibility to get involved. "It simply means that in my own career I try to steer clear of political involvements and make my way as Althea Gibson, private individual. I feel that if I am a worthy person, and if I have something worth while to contribute, I will be accepted on my own merits, and that is the way I want it."[19] Gibson's definition of politics was decidedly limited; she omitted that her tours for the State Department were politically and racially motivated.

A second passage showed Gibson appearing unmoved by the segregation that Black southerners faced. She felt "no feeling of exclusion any more" in her own life, she said. Ensconced in New York and welcomed in prestigious spaces around the world, Gibson was not troubled by her inability to "stay overnight at a good hotel in Columbia, South Carolina," or to play tennis against a White player in Louisiana because of the state's Jim Crow laws. "There is, I have found, a whole lot of world outside Louisiana—and that goes for South Carolina, Mississippi, Georgia, Alabama, and all the other places where they haven't got the message yet." Applying her training from the State Department, Gibson concluded that "there has been a lot of good will shown on both sides lately" and that "we're making progress."[20] She did not address the violence and trauma, physical and emotional, that Black southerners encountered daily.

Gibson's most provocative statements concerned Jackie Robinson and the Black press. For years, she had told reporters that she disliked being compared with Robinson. In the book, she explained the differences between herself and the man who she admitted had "paved the way" for her career. Robinson "thrived on his role as a Negro battling for equality whereas I shy away from it. . . . I shy away from it because it would be dishonest of me to pretend to a feeling I don't possess." Gibson credited Robinson as a voluntary change agent for African Americans. Unlike herself, he "always saw his baseball success as a step forward for the Negro people," she said. There was something else that separated Gibson, an amateur athlete, from Robinson, a professional. It was money, and she gave an unvarnished assessment of it. Robinson's earnings from baseball and his many endorsement deals had enabled him to build a custom home on property that he and his wife had bought in the Connecticut suburbs, though not without their own extended bout with housing discrimination. Robinson, she averred, "aggressively fought to make his ability pay off in social advances as well as fat paychecks," something amateurism would never allow her to do.[21]

Gibson asserted that any activism she engaged in would have to be done "my way." She acknowledged that many African Americans disagreed with her point of view and noted that "[a] lot of those" who did were in the "Negro press." She had had tense exchanges with reporters on both sides of the color line and around the world, but in *I Always Wanted to Be Somebody*, she focused her irritation on Black journalists. "Members of the Negro press . . . beat my brains out regularly. I have always enjoyed a good press among the regular American newspapers and magazines," Gibson said, ignoring the profiles that *Sport*, Fitzgerald's own magazine, had published about her in October 1956 and July 1958. Alluding to the imbroglio in Chicago after her first victory at Wimbledon and the homophobia-tinged coverage that had followed her for years, Gibson explained that she felt that she was "uncomfortably close to being Public Enemy No. 1 to some sections of the Negro press."

I have, they have said, an unbecoming attitude; they say I'm big-headed, uppity, ungrateful, and a few other uncomplimentary things. I don't think any white writer has ever said anything like that about me, but quite a few Negro writers have, and I think the down-deep reason for it is that they resent my refusal to turn my tennis achievements into a rousing crusade for racial equality, brass band, seventy-six trombones, and all. I won't do it. I feel strongly that I can do more good my way than I could by militant crusading. I want my success to speak for itself as an advertisement for my race.[22]

The only part of the race that Gibson was concerned about, it seemed, was tennis players, and she felt she had done all she could do to help them. She was aware of the Black media discourse that Black men and boys deserved a place in amateur tennis. She agreed but felt that they had to earn it either alone or through the combined efforts of the ATA and the USLTA rather than with her assistance. "I modestly hope that the way I have conducted myself in tennis has met with sufficient approval and good will to assure that the way will not close behind me." That some Black men had competed at Forest Hills in 1957 was "heart-warming," she said. "Their presence there, I feel, is the best answer I could possibly make to the people who criticize me for failing to do as much as they think I might do to help my people move forward."[23]

Reviews of *I Always Wanted to Be Somebody* in major White venues had no trouble with Gibson's comments. Allison Danzig of the *New York Times* simply noted that she was "no woman on a mission" and quoted her line about crusading as evidence.[24] Robert E. Lee Baker, the reviewer for the *Washington Post*, assessed the book along with others that dealt with African Americans' lives and published a group review under the headline "Race Relations' Brighter Side." To Baker, part of the supposed brightness of Gibson's life story was that she had "not taken the role of crusader for her race," and, quoting her book, he pointed to her belief that "our best chance to advance is to prove ourselves as individuals."[25] *Kirkus Reviews* called the book "[a] must for tennis fans" and opined that Gibson had given "a firm reply to the critics who condemn her reluctance to assume the role of professional Negro," a phrase that captured White Americans' preference for African Americans who did not either address or challenge the racial status quo.[26] Through Fitzgerald, Gibson appealed to both dyed-in-the-wool white supremacists and Whites who might have disagreed with segregation but who enjoyed the comforts of not being confronted with—and made uncomfortable by—racial prejudice.

Leading Black voices, however, were appalled. Most reviews of the book in the major Black metropolitan weeklies were neutral or even generic, but in notable cases the backlash against Gibson was swift and direct. The Cleveland

Call and Post charged that she had committed a "foot fault" in the sense that she had "literally put her foot in her mouth" in her remarks about not being a "crusader" and in her sense of herself as "an individual." "She demonstrates that in the years she has been in the public eye she has learned practically nothing about the basic problems of her own people," wrote the editors. Gibson credited many people—Buddy Walker, Fred Johnson, Dr. Eaton, and Dr. Johnson—for her success in tennis, but the *Call and Post's* editors chafed at her perception of herself as someone who had made it over the color line yet owed nothing to anyone (least of all anyone who was Black), carried no responsibility to help other Black people, and would never need a helping hand again. "Miss Gibson will be in for a rude awakening when she finds that her ability as an individual isn't going to mean much in getting her a job outside the categories where Negroes are traditionally employed." In a classist dig, the editors added, "If she thinks otherwise, she will soon be back where she started, a Harlem delinquent."[27]

Sam Lacy, in Baltimore, was equally disturbed. Lacy, who had cheered Gibson's accomplishments on the tennis court for a decade as often as he had been critical of her, could not abide either her comments about the Black press or, he felt, her self-important idea that she was able to "crusade" for African Americans at all. Biased, Lacy accused "the WHITE press" of "lampoon[ing] her as 'arrogant and uncooperative,'" while he and other Black writers had, he insisted, sought to defend her. Lacy disagreed, too, with the book's advertising campaign comparing Gibson to Jackie Robinson and Marian Anderson for achieving cultural firsts previously denied African Americans. "Much as I like the champ, I'm afraid she has neither the moral courage of Robinson nor the quiet dignity of Miss Anderson."[28]

—————

Back in Hollywood, courageous was hardly the word to describe the character the writers had imagined for Gibson in *The Horse Soldiers*. She played Lukey, the house slave to Hannah Hunter (Constance Towers), a White plantation owner in Mississippi loyal to the Confederacy. Marlowe (John Wayne) is forced to take Hannah and Lukey along on his mission after Dr. Curtis Kendall (Holden) discovers that the two women have eavesdropped on Marlowe as he discussed the cavalry's plans. Like Hannah, Lukey was a figment of the White screenwriters' imaginations. Martin Rackin and John Lee Mahin, who were also the film's producers, added the character, who did not appear in Sinclair's novel, and created an unflattering fantasy of how an enslaved Black woman would look, speak, dress, and carry herself during the Civil War. In keeping with Hollywood's history of making the servant Black woman the polar op-posite of the lead White woman onscreen, Rackin and Mahin envisioned Lukey, masculinized in name, as "guzzy haired" and "homely." Hannah talked in the sweetly accented tones associated with upper-class White southerners, but Lukey spoke in dialect. "Sojers 'em whut," Gibson was to say as her first line. "Lawd" was another keyword, and "Da's the trufe" appeared, too.[29]

The indignities and differences extended to gender. The script called for Hannah and Lukey to ride across the rough southern backcountry with Marlowe's troops. Hannah was to be "mounted on a horse, riding side saddle," the "ladylike" way for women in the nineteenth century. She was to wear "a work riding skirt and non-matching jacket" with a straw hat and a scarf as accessories. Rackin and Mahin planned for Lukey to make the excursion "on a mule, riding astride" in comparatively masculine attire: "apron jeans, too big for her, and a turban."[30] Lukey's original backstory added to her queerness. Rackin and Mahin imagined that Hannah's unnamed mother had died while giving birth to her. Lukey's mother, enslaved on the Hunter family's plan-tation, nursed the motherless Hannah and her own child, too. "We's breast close," Lukey was to tell Marlowe to explain her devotion to Hannah and her refusal either to inform on or desert her owner-mistress in favor of freedom. Lukey was also to say of Hannah, "Ah loves her." The scene called for Gibson to play along with the plantation-school trope of the faithful slave and to mouth lines that carried homoerotic overtones.[31]

The entire situation made Gibson nervous. The screen test was one thing. Getting and performing the part was another. "I had a serious problem with this role of 'Lukey,'" she wrote once production was finished. She again claimed falsely that she had "never had too much personal experience with discrimination or anti-Negro feeling," but she recognized the drawbacks of the role. "Very naturally, I did not want to expose myself, or my people, to implications of slavery."[32] Elaborating in her second autobiography, *So Much to Live For*, published in 1968, she explained, "I was resolutely determined not to utter lines that reflected so negatively and distortedly the character of a colored woman. I felt that my own dignity and the dignity of the American Negro were on the line." Gibson's salary—which some estimated to be as much as $10,000 ($102,518 in 2022)—was at stake, too. Yet she was willing to risk losing it, and the part, she claimed, if that were "necessary to illustrate my sincerity."[33] It never came to that.

Gibson set out to change the part and enlisted Ford and the screenwriters, Mahin and Rackin, to help. She wore the servant's costume, "right up to the handkerchief on my head," she wrote, but she drew a line at the dialect, which she found "offensive and unnecessary" as well as "unnatural" to her own proud and precise speech pattern. All three men consented to make alterations in Lukey's characterization. Gibson led a "protest" that was "quiet," she said. Realizing her seriousness—and likely fearing public embarrassment—Mahin and Rackin "deleted the obnoxious lines."[34] Gibson also learned a lesson about compromise and the world of acting: "I came to understand that one did not have to be a slave to portray a slave, anymore than you have to be a bad apple yourself to portray 'the bad guy' in a movie."[35]

Vestiges of the old Lukey remained. In character, Gibson still spoke in strange syntax and incomplete sentences, and she spent most of her screen time looking perplexed or disapproving as she stood in the background or off to the side. But comparisons between the script and the final cut of the film show that more than a few lines changed. The "breast close" scene and one in which Gibson, in dialect-ridden dialogue, was to play Cupid, another trope that Hollywood assigned to Black characters, were excised. Nor did she wear jeans or straddle a mule. Like Towers, Gibson and her stunt double wore a skirt and a hat while riding a horse sidesaddle. Tall and lean, Gibson made for an unusually fit and athletic-looking mammy, to be sure. Hers turned out to be a learned one, too. In one scene that does not appear in the script but is in the film, Lukey upbraids Hannah for "talking like a field hand."[36] Gibson was left to hope that the changes made the part appear more dignified on film than it did on paper.

Gibson relished her three weeks in Hollywood. The cinema had been her escape hatch wherever she had lived. Finding herself in the moviemaking capital of the world, she was awestruck and soaked up the newness and excitement of her temporary home. Without complaint, she rose early to begin shooting at seven, even when work was delayed for hours. Gibson came to the set on days when she did not have to work, just to see the "complex technical and human elements" that went into making motion pictures. She met Edward G. Robinson and Gregory Peck, among the stars she "had always worshipped."[37] She experienced neither tension nor strife on the set, she remembered, including from Ford. Understanding that she was a newcomer, the legendary directory treated Gibson with patience and kindness. She called him by his nickname, "Pappy." (The others called him Mr. Ford.) He generously told reporters that Gibson gave a "magnificent performance." She was among the few Black women in Ford's oeuvre. Hattie McDaniel was another, and some of Gibson's traits in the film—the disapproving sidelong glances and fussing at Hannah in one scene and at two Black men in another—recalled McDaniel's Mammy in *Gone with the Wind*.[38]

The rest of the principals let Gibson be herself, too. When photographers came to the set to take pictures of Gibson for the Black press, Wayne, Holden, Towers, and Ford posed with her. Along with Ford, Holden and Wayne hosted a welcome luncheon in Gibson's honor after her first week on the production.[39] She took a liking to Wayne, whom she found "tremendously helpful." Using one of her favorite phrases, and perhaps exaggerating, she wrote that Wayne "made it his personal business" to give her tips. His advice was minimal, boiling down to "be natural, be yourself." As Gibson, a college-educated and well-traveled woman, was playing a part originally conceived as menial and devoid of pride, the tip was puzzling.[40]

Then again, Wayne's interest in Gibson was curious. Within a dozen years, he would publicly become the voice of white supremacist rhetoric. "I believe in white supremacy until the blacks are educated to a point of responsibility," he would say in *Playboy* magazine in 1971. "I don't believe in giving authority and positions of leadership and judgment to irresponsible people."[41] Gibson, a neophyte actress, posed no threat to Wayne or his privilege, so they had no trouble. She had survived a short lifetime of sharing space with White people who held such views but who kept the ideas to themselves, more or less. When filming ended in December, Wayne gifted her a coffee mug. She loved it.[42]

⸺

Gibson had few activities to occupy her time as she waited anxiously for the release of *The Horse Soldiers*. In January 1959, she played a charity basketball game for the Harlem YMCA. Jackie Robinson was a referee and Ruthe Campanella, who had been an all-around athlete before marrying Roy Campanella, the Dodgers' former catcher, was the star of the opposing team. Gibson led her squad, sponsored by fashion model Dorothea Towles, to victory by scoring nearly all their points. That was unsurprising. The team uniform was another matter. Like her teammates, she wore a skintight red leotard that revealed her bra and clung to her rear end. For jackets, Towles outfitted the team with "pink net trapezes bedecked with hundreds of red and pink roses," Gibson recalled.[43] Even in a charity basketball game, female athletes were expected to be sexy and alluring, and Gibson complied, trading her preference for sensibility in athletic wear for sex appeal. It would not be the last time she had to compromise in her new public image as she shifted uncertainly into her future. Around this time, she underwent dental work to improve the appearance of her top front teeth.[44]

New or old, Gibson's image remained valuable to the State Department, and in February she embarked on a three-week tour of Latin America. She went to Guatemala City, Barranquilla, Bogotá, Lima, Santiago, Rio de Janeiro, and Caracas. Government officials judged that she "superbly refutes racial bias propaganda of Soviets in all contacts."[45] Thrilled by her effectiveness as a propagandist, they worried that her new focus on singing would disrupt their plans for her. State Department staff needed her skills and presence in the Southern Hemisphere, particularly in Venezuela and Haiti, where anti-American sentiment was high. In May, protesters in Caracas viciously attacked the limousine that carried Vice President Nixon and his wife, Pat. Crowds spat on and threw rocks at the vehicle, unleashing their rage over the United States' decision to grant exile to Marcos Pérez Jiménez, Venezuela's unpopular, dictatorial president, who had been deposed in January, and Pedro Estrada, the former national security director. Gibson endured an intense schedule of media obligations, demonstrations, face time with politicians and the public (especially children and teenagers), and tennis exhibitions. She personally handed out tennis rackets in Caracas and Port-au-Prince, "an effective goodwill device," judged public affairs officer Hewson A. Ryan. Each act seemed to win more positive opinions of America. Gibson's "visit is considered to have been highly successful from the country program point of view," assessed Ryan, who was particularly pleased that her trip allowed the agency to further cultivate relationships with the Latin American sports media and members of the tennis community that could be exploited later.[46]

The State Department's pleasure came at a price for Gibson. Her itinerary had given her more personal time than she had previously known on her federal tours. In Chile, for example, she shopped, went to the movies, took horseback rides, swam, and basked in the sunshine. She promoted her album during interviews and, as usual, enjoyed interacting with children. "We need to help them in their physical program and provide facilities for them to play with and to accomplish something in sports themselves," she told State Department personnel upon her return to the States. Yet unhappiness again found Gibson while she was abroad. For one thing, she was frequently alone. Staff gave her "a great deal of personal attention," but it was not enough. When the "extensive and tiresome" trip was over, Gibson regretted that she had not asked the department to send a travel companion along with her. The loneliness reminded Gibson yet again that she had no significant other. "That's the bad thing about a woman who travels," she lamented to staff. "You . . . have no dates. No one to take you out. You have to do it by yourself. Entertain your own self, and that can be very boring." It was a rare, candid confession from Gibson about the hard reality of her life as a woman on her own.[47]

Gibson was also coming to resent living under constant watch. Ryan, the public affairs officer, reported on her activities to State Department headquarters in Washington. He observed that she carried herself with "warmth and intelligence as a person both on and off the courts." She committed "a few minor breaches of etiquette" that Ryan did not name but which he blamed on "her fatigue."[48] Overall, Gibson acted with "equanimity and poise" even when besieged by crowds. Ryan's scrutiny was favorable, but it was still scrutiny. That State Department staff wrote confidential reports on all their cultural ambassadors was of little consolation to Gibson, whose temperament was being monitored yet again, this time by her so-called friends in the federal government.

Gibson disliked the prying eyes, but she could make light of the situation, too. Upon her return to the United States, the State Department invited her to Washington to discuss her travels and to encourage staff, especially the women, to take up tennis. She opened the question-and-answer session with humor and bite: "I'm sure that most of you know more about me than I know of myself." The assembly of nearly six hundred laughed, just as they did to her response when a man in the audience asked whether she planned to get married soon: "Are you available?" The personnel were just as amused by another of her lines. "I wasn't involved too much with the politics," Gibson said of her trip. "I am not a politic . . . I don't go into that field. I stick strictly to tennis and trying to help those who want help."[49] She was sincere, and the audience, knowing the truth behind their use of her, was sincere, too, in their laughter.

Gibson remained a visible public figure in the spring, but she was plainly adrift. Days after she announced her sabbatical, Bob Addie, a sports columnist for the *Washington Post*, wrote that Kramer was "trying to get" Pauline Betz to tour with Gibson.[50] Addie was in a position to know: Betz was his wife. The head professional at the Edgemoor Tennis Club in Bethesda, she had beaten Doris Hart twice to retain her title as the women's world professional champion. Since leaving amateur tennis, Hart had become a club pro in New Jersey and Miami and traveled to several states to give tennis clinics as a representative of Spalding, the sporting goods firm. Gibson said she would "listen if Jack Kramer made an offer."[51] But he did not. Lacking definite plans for turning professional, she told her fellow guests at a reception held at the Peruvian embassy in Washington that she was considering returning to amateur tennis in 1960. Gibson's music career had cooled, too. Aside from a return to *The Ed Sullivan Show* in the summer, she had no bookings to sing.

She admitted that the album was "not doing too well" but hoped to make a second one for Dot in the spring.[52] The session never happened, and she was coming to believe that the company was dishonest. "I certainly believe my record would have a far better chance on its own, if it didn't have to compete with payola practices," she concluded.[53] In April, she used an appearance on Edward R. Murrow's *Person to Person*, a show designed to give television viewers an intimate look into the lives of celebrities, to promote her recent activities and to try to net new opportunities. As a television crew followed Gibson around her apartment, which Murrow called "small," she discussed her past in sports and talked of her new ventures. She showed off copies of her book and the album, which were strategically placed nearby as props, and played a sample from the record.[54]

Gibson got a boost, emotional if not financial, weeks later in Philadelphia, where the Ladies' Auxiliary of nearby Lincoln University gave her an award at its annual tea. Roy Wilkins, the executive secretary of the NAACP, received a citation, too. Gibson was a person of significant interest to the association. In the summer of 1958, the Curtis Publishing Company, which owned the *Saturday Evening Post*, had sent the association's New York office abridgments of each of the three serializations of her autobiography. Months later, Wilkins or someone from his office wrote "Love Althea!" on the letter in which the auxiliary's president, Mrs. I. J. K. Wells, informed him that Gibson had been invited with the promise of an honorarium and all travel expenses and asked him to "encourage her to accept." Gibson's presence, the president wrote, would "only add to the bigness of the occasion."[55] When Wilkins addressed the audience of one thousand, he paid special tribute to Gibson, who "contributed immensely to the Negro's battle for civil rights by excelling in her sport and by being a representative of American Negro Womanhood."[56]

The release of *The Horse Soldiers* in June showed the limits of Gibson's representation and the duality of her life. She received some praise for her part. *Variety* called her "effectively dignified" as Lukey, and Harry Levette, a reviewer for the Associated Negro Press, agreed.[57] Levette took special notice of Gibson's speech, lauding her "perfect and distinct enunciation" and the absence of dialect, except for "what is natural with both whites and Negroes in the south."[58] He downplayed the servile nature of her role, too. Lukey was the "constant companion [and] confidante" of Hannah, according to Levette, who judged that Gibson had successfully portrayed Lukey as "an advising friend" rather than as a servant.[59] A writer for the Black *California Eagle* found Lukey "courageous" because she "faces every hardship her mistress does, even though at the end she must die for it," a line lifted from the promotional materials that Mirisch distributed to the press.[60] Gibson, though, would not experience the adulation and excitement that Towers, Wayne, Holden, and Martin Rackin did at the film's world premiere, in Shreveport, Louisiana. She was not there, just as Mirisch used her minimally in promotional materials. Lines had to be drawn on invitations to the cast for the festivities. The color line was an easy one.[61]

Gibson simply moved on and said nothing about the exclusion. She went to Washington, D.C., to play exhibition tennis matches with Vic Seixas, Shirley Fry, and Ham Richardson on the courts at the Sheraton Park Hotel. Gibson beat Fry in singles and teamed with Richardson, her old chum from her first State Department trip, to win the mixed doubles match, too. Neil McElroy, the secretary of defense, and Earl Warren from the Supreme Court were among the fourteen hundred people who came to watch. Gibson did not have complete liberty in America, but she did have the attention of a chief justice.[62]

———

Two days later, Gibson flew to London. She was obligated to promote *I Always Wanted to Be Somebody*, which W. H. Allen and Company had published in England, and then there was Wimbledon, which she covered through a ghostwriter for the London *Evening Standard*. For decades, newspapers and magazines had hired the best women in tennis as reporters and writers. Gibson's selection signaled that she was among them. She watched as Maria Bueno and Darlene Hard, her two young former doubles partners whose games she had influenced, battled in the final for the women's singles title. Bueno, Brazil's "Little Saber," won, slashing America's fourteen-year hold on the title. Asked what it had been like to know for more than a year that she had been the best in the world at her craft, Gibson simply replied, "It was very satisfying."[63]

The sense of peace dissipated abruptly, shattered by another story about racial discrimination in America. This time, the South was not the culprit. Forest Hills was.

Ralph Bunche, the undersecretary for special political affairs for the United Nations, revealed to the press that the West Side Tennis Club had a discriminatory membership policy. Bunche's fifteen-year-old son, Ralph Jr., had become interested in tennis. The Bunche family lived in Kew Gardens, Queens, a short walk from the club, where some of Ralph Jr.'s friends were members and where he had taken lessons with the club's teaching professional, George Agutter, since April. Both the friends and the pro thought young Ralph should become a member, too. Agutter, in his early seventies, admitted later that he had met Bunche Sr. years earlier and assumed that he was "French or South American," not African American. Ralph Jr., with light skin and hair that was straight and sandy, could easily have passed for White, and Agutter assumed that he was. Desiring to support his son's interest and rapidly developing game, Bunche called Wilfred Burglund, the club president, to inquire about a junior membership. Burglund was pleasant enough, speaking, Bunche said, "with a tone of 'some of my best friends are Negroes,'" but he was also clear: membership was by invitation only. The club was like a private home, "where you invite whom you want," Burglund said, invoking the rhetoric that had undergirded the exclusionary membership policies and practices of American country clubs since their start. There were, "to [Burglund's] knowledge, no Negroes or Jews in the club" and "there were not likely to be." Mass resignations would ensue, Burglund predicted, if an African American became a member.[64]

Bunche, among the most admired Black men in America thanks to his Nobel Peace Prize, made the incident public as a matter of conscience, his own and others'. "I deliberately revealed this experience only because I find it to be rather shocking in New York City and think citizens of the city and of the country are entitled to know about it." The policy was not tantamount to Jim Crow in the South, with its "disenfranchisement, deprival of other rights, segregation and acts of intimidation suffered" by African Americans, Bunch pointed out. Nor was it like Jim Crow in the North, where discrimination in housing and employment was the norm. The club's rule, though, "flows from the same well of racial and religious bigotry."[65] Bunch was under no illusions that his accomplishments shielded him from prejudice, and he felt that his position gave him a responsibility to speak up.

Gibson held a different view and found herself drawn into a story that rapidly escalated into controversy. As the African American most closely identified with the West Side Tennis Club, her name was dropped into news stories about the matter and its fallout for weeks. Reached in London, where she visited the newly married Angela Buxton Silk, Gibson first expressed surprised incredulity. "How ridiculous. Are we living in the twentieth century or not?"[66] The next day, she refused to reject the club. Reporters met Gibson at Idlewild shortly after her plane landed. Asked whether she would play at the club again, she reminded them that she would not compete at Forest Hills later in the summer because of her sabbatical. She added that she would still practice at the club "if they invite me" and "as long as they treat me as a person and a guest, I'll play." She still found the club's exclusion of Bunche "very ridiculous" but expressed confidence that "within time these things will change."[67]

Gibson's willingness to associate with a place that practiced discrimination reflected her realism and moderate race politics. The West Side Tennis Club was hardly the only exclusive American setting where being a WASP was virtually a membership requirement. The truth was that most country clubs barred African Americans, and many ignored Jews; they simply did not advertise their prejudice or codify Jim Crow in their bylaws. Unspoken habit sufficed. If the ATA had been unwilling to enter Gibson into tournaments at clubs that practiced discrimination, she would not have had a tennis career across the color line. Bertram Baker, who had led the ATA with moderation for more than a decade, agreed with Gibson and sent her a letter of support in which he praised her "forthright statement to the press [as] a demonstration of courage, clear thinking and an indication of your sense of fairness."[68] Dr. Eaton understood her point of view. He believed that protests and withdrawals would harm "colored tennis" by limiting the opportunities available to the next generation of Black players.[69]

Two revered Black sportsmen were on Gibson's side but kept their nuanced opinions to themselves. Jackie Robinson and Larry Doby believed that accepting invitations to venues that did not otherwise admit African Americans was the only way to change Whites-only policies. At the year's end, Doby told *Sport* magazine that "class and characteristics would show" among upper-class Black guests and thus lead Whites to drop their belief in stereotypes of African Americans.[70] Robinson had a visceral reaction when he learned of the club's refusal to have Bunche as a member. "I couldn't help but tighten up deep inside," he told the *New York Post* when the news broke.[71] Robinson did not, however, criticize Gibson for her stance. He shared it. "There was a time when I disagreed violently," he said in the roundtable, but conversations with other African Americans had changed his mind. "If you don't go, then how will we ever be able to go?" they told him. "Somebody has got to be first."[72]

Many in the Black media and elsewhere did not see it that way and put Gibson in their crosshairs. Her comment, they alleged, was more than a "verbal goof" or a comment made in haste.[73] It was a sign of her selfishness, her disloyalty, and her ingratitude to African Americans. Some ATA members spoke against her. College professor Arthur Chippey, long involved in the association's activities in South Carolina, held nothing back when Sam Lacy interviewed him for a story about Gibson's response: "It is unfortunate that Althea doesn't realize that there is more at stake than her own personal pleasure." Chippey found it unfathomable that she would align herself with a place that, he felt, used her. The USLTA rented the club's facilities for the national championship and received a percentage of ticket sales. From the start, Gibson's matches had drawn large crowds. Yet money was not Chippey's only point of concern. Her mentality bothered him. "I have reason to believe that Althea now prefers to divorce herself from the race," he told Lacy. "Her attitude for some time now has seemed to be that she doesn't need us any more."[74] Chippey's "us" could have meant either the ATA or African Americans. Either way, he was not alone in thinking that Gibson was enabling segregation. "They can find one every time," the *New York Amsterdam News's* Jimmy Booker said of Whites who, drowning in charges of racism, searched for the public support of a Black person. Gibson, in Booker's opinion, had thrown out a lifeline to Berglund and the club. "Now, Miss Gibson. Tsk, tsk."[75]

The Horse Soldiers, in wide release in July, was swept into the maelstrom as critics began to pan Gibson's role. "Anyway you spell it, from champion to companion to 'Miss Ann' is quite a comedown—even if it is not for real but for reel," said a reviewer for the Associated Negro Press. "Is it good a tennis champion—the winner of numerous awards which no other member of her race has obtained—[has] to lose her identity???"[76] The *Courier's* P. L. Prattis resurrected Gibson's infamous statement that she was "not a Negro tennis player." Coldly, Prattis scrawled that her "menial" part in the film proved that "the whites know what she is [even] if she doesn't."[77] Sam Lacy thought she was willing to stoop to any level to get close to Whites. "In view of her 'bandana' stand" in support of the West Side Tennis Club, Gibson was, Lacy thought, "perfectly cast" as a maid in the film. "From her actions, the obvious conclusion one has to draw is that Althea's book is aptly titled.... She calls it 'I Wanted to Be Somebody' [*sic*].... [S]he might have added 'even if wearing a bandana.'"[78] Gibson even became a topic of discussion at the annual convention of the NAACP. Meeting in New York City, the group celebrated the accomplishments of its first fifty years and pondered the ills of race that remained, including stereotypes. With Roy Wilkins seated nearby, Charles Wesley, the president of Wilberforce College, the longtime host of the ATA Nationals, stood before four thousand attendees and specifically decried Gibson's participation in *The Horse Soldiers* as a "sad commentary on a brilliant career."[79]

Gibson let the news cycle run its course and went through with her plans for the rest of the summer. In August, she attended the ATA Nationals at Wilberforce and beat Karol Fageros in another integration-minded exhibition match. Then, the day after her thirty-second birthday, Gibson came to the Loew's Victoria Theater on West 125th Street, where its owner, Bob Solomon, feted her as part of the opening of *The Horse Soldiers* in Harlem. Solomon gave her top billing on the marquee, with her name in lights above Wayne's and Holden's. The old neighborhood had not snubbed her, even if Hollywood—and Shreveport—had. "Few things move me, but that evening really touched me," she told Solomon in a letter.[80] Gibson needed the lift. Three days earlier, she had made her third and final visit to Ed Sullivan's show. Her performance was as uncompelling as the others had been, but with one difference. Crooning Billy Eckstine's "Jelly, Jelly," she sang the blues.[81]

There was nothing left for Gibson to do except play tennis. She had no bookings to sing. *The Horse Soldiers* taught her that acting could become her new passion. "If God is as good to me as He has been up to now, I hope I will do some more of it," she wrote in a speech called "How I Feel About Being 'On Stage.'"[82] And though there was a rumor that she was going to appear on Broadway, it was not to be.

Saying that she could not "refuse to play for my country," Gibson accepted an invitation to join Dorothy Head Knode, Mimi Arnold, and Karol Fageros on the US team bound for the Pan-American Games in Chicago.[83] She came from behind to win the women's singles title, but she nearly lost her amateur status.[84]

Speaking off the cuff was to blame. Rumors were flying that Gibson planned to turn professional imminently. One piece of gossip raised eyebrows from coast to coast. Gibson, it said, was forming a women's professional tour. Darlene Hard, Fageros, and Christine Truman were said to be attached. Faced with questions after her semifinal match, she refused to either confirm or deny the reports. Instead, Gibson offered her assessment of amateur tennis and intimated that she regretted the decisions she had made. "You can play your best, give sweat and tears, and not make a dime," she said.[85] Gibson added that she would "turn pro tomorrow" if "an attractive offer" came her way. "I've got to eat," she said. "It seems a shame when one spends an entire lifetime doing something only to find in getting older that you have to do something else in order to keep on eating."[86]

For months, Gibson had dispensed with caution in talking about professional tennis and amateurism. Her sabbatical was about putting "potatoes on the table," she told the *Los Angeles Times* in January. "I have to earn a livelihood and I can't live on amateur tennis."[87] To others, she pointedly remarked, "You can't eat a crown."[88] She had grown fed up with the financial restrictions

of amateur tennis, which, she told *Jet*, had forced her to turn down an opportunity to "endorse a line of women's sports clothes" and prevented her
from accepting a new car. The murky rules of amateurism prohibited players
from receiving compensation based on their athletic achievements, including
"reputation."[89] The Pan-American Congress decided that she had at last gone
too far in Chicago. Its Commission of Statutes and Rules issued a statement
calling for an investigation into Gibson's post-match comments with the possibility of public censure. The USLTA hardly came to her defense. While
the vice president, George E. Barnes, was "surprised" by the Pan-American
Congress's reaction given Gibson's patriotic entry in the Pan-American
Games, a member of the association's executive committee had harsh words
for her and anyone else who rued their post-amateur fortunes—or lack
thereof.[90] "We certainly do not feel any responsibility for providing an eventual livelihood for tennis stars," said James Barnes, a former USLTA president.
"We expect they come to the sport originally because they like it, and not as a
career training ground."[91]

With the winds of another controversy swirling around her, Gibson
returned to New York to watch the matches at Forest Hills. Maria Bueno
won the women's singles title and Arthur Ashe, Dr. Johnson's protégé, made
his debut. Ashe was sixteen and slotted at fifth in the USLTA's boys' singles
rankings. He lost to Rod Laver in the first round, but he impressed the gallery
and, in pushing the Australian, five years his senior, to 7–5 in the second set,
stirred talk that he might have a bright future in the game. Gibson, meanwhile, could not escape her past. Confronted by reporters, she refused to
make a verbal retreat from her statements in Chicago. "All I said was that I've
got to start making some money. I didn't take a slap at amateur tennis. It's a
sad day when a person can't express an opinion. It's no secret to anyone that
I'm open to the right pro offer."[92] Weeks later, she thought she had found it.

On October 19, Gibson joined Fageros and Abe Saperstein, the owner of
the world-renowned Harlem Globetrotters, at New York's legendary 21 Club.
She and Fageros would tour nationally with the Trotters, as the basketball
team was known. Gibson was going boldly where few women in tennis—
none of them Black—had gone before and where none had found lasting,
lucrative success. According to Saperstein, she was to be paid handsomely.
Fageros was to receive $30,000, while Gibson would earn "near $100,000"
to play ninety single-set exhibitions in four months ($305,439 and $1,018,131,
respectively, in 2022). "The money Miss Gibson will earn on this tour is by
far the most ever paid to a woman athlete, and is very near the tops for any
performer in the field of international sports."[93] Photographed with Fageros,

a basketball, and a tennis racket in kitschy publicity stills at the restaurant, Gibson smiled with delight.

——

On November 17, 1959, in San Antonio, Texas, Gibson began her career as a professional tennis player.[94] She learned at once what the men and women who had gone before her already knew: leaving amateur tennis brought a salary as well as a price. For Gibson, that price would prove exceptionally high.

With Fageros at her side, Gibson encountered all the conditions that gave professional tennis a seedy air. They played in poorly lit gymnasiums and civic auditoriums and risked injury running across varnished floors and dodging the limbs of people who sat around the makeshift tennis courts. Noisy spectators and concessions workers, who hawked snacks and beer whenever they felt like it, were the norm, replacing etiquette-conscious galleries that stayed still and silent until the end of each point. Gone, too, were tournament weeks or, in the case of the majors, fortnights spent in a pleasant suburb or a happening city where a social committee organized cocktail parties, moonlight soirees, and balls that brought mingling and networking. Instead, the one-night engagement was the hallmark of the professional tennis player, and Gibson and Fageros had them in spades until April 1960.[95]

In interviews, Gibson cast her choice to turn professional as an act of altruism and leadership for teenagers and women. "I wanted to meet the young people," she said weeks into the tour. Aware of the discourse about juvenile delinquency and gangs, she elaborated: "The teenagers that everyone seems to think are going to the dogs. I have found our young people smart, honest in their opinions, and want[ing] straight answers to the questions they" ask.[96] Gibson also saw the tour as a chance to change perceptions of women's tennis and to open doors for women who were interested in joining the professional ranks but worried there was no lasting place for them. "Traveling with the Globetrotters will bring us into many cities that haven't seen much women's tennis," she said. "I am sure we will be breaking the ice for other women to turn pro with us, and I know several of them who want to. They've never had the way shown to them."[97] The way, though, proved hard.

First, there was the money. She played for it, and Gibson did not mince words on the subject: "I like money. It will give me the things I have always prayed for."[98] Many oohed and ahhed over Gibson's reported salary. "Good Luck, Al!" the *Amsterdam News* editorialized days after the announcement luncheon at 21, and wished her a future in which she made "a cool million."[99] Sportswriters and people in tennis, though, were skeptical that Saperstein was telling the truth. Jack Kramer was among them. A promoter could not pay $130,000, including Fageros's contract, and "remain solvent," he and his people reportedly thought.[100] Sam Lacy thought the pair were making "closer to" a combined $50,000, with $35,000 going to Gibson and the rest to Karol.[101]

Kramer and Lacy were on to something. Years later, Gibson admitted that Saperstein paid her "about $80,000" ($814,504 in 2022). It was a "stupendous amount of money," but that, she confessed, was not her take-home pay. Gibson, Saperstein, and Zaidins, her lawyer, agreed in their contract negotiations that she would head "a road company" that was "independent of the Globetrotters." Gibson and Fageros played their exhibitions as part of the basketball team's show and were featured in its advertisements, but that was the extent of Saperstein's responsibility to them. As the principal of the road company, Gibson's second corporation, she was responsible for all the expenses associated with the tour. She paid a salary to Fageros, who later said that she banked $22,000 ($223,990 in 2022), and undisclosed amounts to the crew. Llewellyn came along as business manager, Bill Davis, the ATA men's national champion, acted as road manager and his assistant, and Gibson hired a woman to act as her own secretary and assistant. In addition, she paid for the troupe's station wagon and tennis court equipment as well as "a percentage" of their travel accommodations. Taxes, to New York State and the federal government, awaited, too.[102]

Gibson worked hard for her dwindling fortune. She and Fageros soon found the touring experience "a grind" and "grueling."[103] Like Gussie Moran on Kramer's long-ago tour, Fageros's function was to attract audiences with her femininity and sex appeal, traits that some thought were beyond Gibson. "Althea Gibson seems to feel that pro tennis is waiting for her with arms wide open," Dan Burley wrote in the *Chicago Defender* before she turned professional, predicting failure. "Female net pros have to be pretty . . . for them to be big boxoffice."[104] The Globetrotters' organization publicized Fageros as the "Golden Goddess." Reporters referenced the gold lamé tennis panties and twenty-five different tennis costumes that she wore. Within weeks, Fageros developed bursitis, a very unsexy repetitive stress injury, making it even harder to give Gibson any semblance of competition. When Fageros was too ill to play in St. Louis in February, Gibson played a set against Davis and won, 6–4, leading to a blaring headline in the *Los Angeles Sentinel*: "Althea Gibson Beats Man in Tennis Battle."[105] Unable to return Gibson's serve with consistency or exploit the few errors in her steady game, Fageros had never beaten Gibson during their amateur days and, as a professional, she would do little better, winning only five times in their approximately 120 matches.[106]

Winning so much did not addle Gibson, who—in contrast to Fageros's numerous outfits—stuck to seven "strictly tailored white togs, all drip-dries," but she found herself wondering whether associating with the Globetrotters diminished her image as a serious sportswoman.[107] "I am an athlete above all else," she proudly told a writer in Lincoln, Nebraska.[108] Self-consciousness drove her declaration. Saperstein was a competitive businessman intent on keeping the money flowing, especially after losing Wilt Chamberlain, the team's star player, to the Philadelphia Warriors of the NBA. Gibson and Fageros were the latest "something new" that Saperstein had chosen in order to turn a profit.[109] He was forthright that he neither intended to stay in the tennis business for long nor planned to compete with Jack Kramer, whom he considered "a friend." Kramer "had no place in his troupe for the gals, and we can use them on our Globe Trotter basketball cards," Saperstein said on the eve of the tour. "We'll just replace our preliminary game with the tennis exhibition."[110]

Positioned as pregame and halftime entertainment, Gibson and Fageros gave people who did not follow tennis an entry into the game, but they also fit Kramer's belief that women's tennis was a break from the supposedly more entertaining and legitimate event of anything men did. Gibson stifled her misgivings but, stationed amid the panoply of antics that filled the time before the games and between the halves—table tennis rapidly played, tumblers, a ballerina on a bicycle, and people who balanced on their hands and heads—she sometimes worried that she looked like just another "act." By the end, she made concessions. "This is show business," she would say, or "It's a living."[111]

Undoubtedly, Gibson and Fageros were a spectacle, even if they were loath to admit it. Black and White women still were not fellow travelers in the cultural imagination in the late 1950s, and the former was never supposed to have the upper hand on the latter. Yet there she and Fageros were, facing off on the tennis court, their friendship, business arrangement, and Gibson's athletic superiority obvious for all to see. The anomaly extended beyond their tennis matches. When she and Fageros were not playing tennis, they were traveling to the site of their next contest with Llewellyn, Davis, and the assistant. They were a strange group in those pre-integration days: four African Americans—two men and two women—and one very blond White woman, navigating the highways and back roads of the country in a yellow station wagon with a U-Haul trailer filled with tennis paraphernalia attached.[112]

The issue of race was always present, even if the group rarely discussed it. Relying on a wire service, small-town newspapers published articles that described Gibson as "sepia" and "dark-skinned."[113] Local reporters mentioned race, too. In Corpus Christi, for example, Gibson was "the tall Negro gal."[114] Except for a two-day visit to Miami, Fageros's hometown, the troupe deliberately dodged the Deep South. When the Globetrotters spent ten days there in early March, beginning in New Orleans, Gibson, Fageros, and the crew went to Pennsylvania and Ohio instead.[115]

For the entire four months, the five made their expedition as a family, eating together, staying in the same hotels, and spending alternate shifts in the bed space jerry-rigged in the station wagon. They shared the ever-present threat of violence and humiliation from White motorists, police, and business owners; Gibson admitted they had embarked on their journey aware that Jim Crow was to be their sixth companion in "food and housing accommodations."[116] Nearly thirty years later, Fageros recalled the prejudice. "They treated Althea horribly," she said. Owners of restaurants and hotels refused to serve her, Wimbledon, Forest Hills, State Department sponsorship, and global celebrity be damned. Fageros did not escape hostility. She had joined the tour to gain "financial independence" and have money of her own before she married.[117] An unabashed "status seeker"—not, she said, to be confused with a "social climber"—Fageros wanted money to support her family and to invest in the Florida real estate market.[118] When the tour ended, she faced backlash from members of a Miami-area country club who proposed blacklisting her from employment as a teaching professional because she had been part of Gibson's tour. Gibson spoke guardedly about her own encounters with racism during the tour. A reporter for San Francisco's *Examiner* asked her about her "acceptance in tour towns, some of them 'Jim Crow.'" "They still make a point of my being a Negro," she responded. "Personally, I prefer to do my battling for racial equality by setting a good example as a professional and as a person. But I will speak out when I feel I should."[119]

The feeling struck Gibson on December 20. Norfolk, Virginia, was the penultimate stop before she and the others took a long-awaited five-day vacation for Christmas. Stepping onto the floor of City Arena, she scanned the audience, nearly three thousand strong, and did not like what she saw. "What is this?" she asked as Cal Jacox of the local Black *Journal and Guide* and other reporters listened. The crowd was segregated. White spectators filled one side of the arena, while African Americans were seated on their own. A suit challenging the Virginia law that required segregation at public events was making its way through the courts, but until the matter was resolved, the separate seating remained. "I don't like it," Gibson announced as the writers transcribed her speech. "I don't want to skirt the law," she said. "But there must be something wrong with the law."[120]

Gibson went on with the match, beating Fageros 8–7, but her irritation lingered. Everywhere else the group had played with the Globetrotters, seating had been integrated, she said, or at least the law did not choose the spectators' seats for them. Ignoring her years in Wilmington, Lynchburg, and Tallahassee, Gibson claimed that she "didn't know this sort of thing existed here. Tennis is an international sport and yet you have some people sitting here and some people sitting there. Just what the hell is the matter?"[121] The sudden diatribe was her most emphatic public statement against segregation, and she intimated that she would say more. "I'm not attempting to be a pioneer or do anything that will discredit the group I'm with or Abe Saperstein, but, personally, I think I have the right to say the things I feel." She continued, "I'm not going to keep [racial discrimination] a secret. I think it's wrong."[122]

Teaching tennis was one way that Gibson demonstrated her opposition to segregation. She had enjoyed interacting with youngsters no matter their color or class during her State Department tours. When the Globetrotters came to San Francisco in January 1960, she and Fageros put on a tennis clinic for more than one hundred children and adults at Kezar Pavilion. All were welcome. Llewellyn and Paul Lippman, a reporter for the San Francisco *Examiner*, thought Gibson was an effective teacher, upbeat and clear in her instructions. She was so engaged that she lost track of time. Llewellyn had to tell her the session had ended. "She'd be out there six more hours if nobody interrupted her," he said. Lippman, taken by how good Gibson was with her pupils, asked why she did not pursue a career as a tennis teacher. Gibson did not confess her suspicion that racism led clubs to overlook her for positions. Instead, she repeated that she had "no desire to ever serve as a club pro" and explained her diverse interests. While she did "love to work with youngsters," she had "too many ambitions in other fields," including singing and acting. "I have so many irons in the fire I just don't know what I'm going to do. I guess I'll want to play it by ear until this tour is over."[123]

No longer under the watchful eye of either the ATA or the USLTA, Gibson exercised a newfound freedom to speak up against segregation, but she still contended with sexism during the tour. While "gentlemen" in other ways, she said, the Globetrotters could be chilly as they guarded the boundaries of gender in their show. Early in the tour, team members played along when she joined their pre-show warmup, giving her the ball for lay-ups and encouraging her attempts at shots from center court. Eventually, though, their mood soured. When Gibson "dunked the ball into the basket," the Globetrotters were displeased. "I didn't threaten to take their jobs away," she wrote, "but it was just a bit irritating to see a woman performing with almost as much skill as they, the greatest basketball players on earth." A handful of Black women had played in baseball's Negro Leagues earlier in the decade, to the chagrin of the men and the Black press, and there was no reason women could not compete with or against men in basketball, as Gibson had in her youth. The crowds loved her showboating, but the Globetrotters did not. Ever the competitor, she relished their reactions: "I enjoyed seeing them squirm."[124]

At other times, Gibson was left to figure out how to protect her own dignity where gender was concerned while doing what she could to sell tickets. With Fageros, she submitted to photographs of herself primping before mirrors and applying makeup before showtime and allowed photographers to snap pictures that showcased her legs, while Fageros's tennis panties were deliberately exposed. Gibson gave reporters food for thought when she called Maria Bueno and Christine Truman the most promising players in women's tennis. "They are aggressive," she said. "I prefer to call it that rather than masculine, but that's what it really is. A woman who plays a strong, hustling game has the advantage."[125] With the remark, she let out years of frustration over the ease with which women who played tennis boldly were cast as less than womanly. When local interviewers asked impertinent questions about marriage and her romantic life, Gibson responded with her blend of candor and vagueness. She would get married "in the future," she said in Tucson.[126] She would do so "very soon . . . very soon, now," she said in Cleveland.[127] Gibson, though, never named names, and in San Francisco in January, she said only that someone "male" had sent her the roses that had been delivered to her hotel room, where she met her interviewer while wearing a pink robe.[128] A reporter asked her whether she liked to cook. "Sometimes; it depends on how I feel," she responded. Gibson said that she cooked only for herself in New York and that she saw freedom from the expectation that women cook as a benefit of being on her own. "In a way, it's nice not being married. Then if I don't want to bother with cooking, I don't have to."[129] Reporters, though, bothered her with questions about domesticity that they would never consider posing to a man, and she parried each one.

The gulf between Gibson and domesticity contributed to the surprising announcement in early March that the Ward Baking Company had hired her as a community relations representative. She was following in the footsteps of Jackie Robinson, whom Chock Full O' Nuts, the coffee and restaurant company, had hired as personnel director after his retirement from the Dodgers in 1956. Ward distributed Tip-Top bread, which Gibson was to plug during public appearances nationwide. For decades, racial Whiteness was part and parcel of white bread's image of wholesomeness and purity, as most manufacturers relied on images and rhetoric of Whiteness to push the food-stuff into American homes. Bond Bread, in whose ads Gibson and Robinson along with his family had appeared in the 1940s, was an exception, and some African Americans assumed that Ward's retaining of Gibson would set off a competition among bread manufacturers to compete for Black dollars. Gibson was benefiting from corporate America's postwar recognition of the "Negro market," as companies realized, with the help of Black entrepreneurs, that African Americans had consumerist dreams and would be more likely to spend their cash with the encouragement of influential Black celebrities, including athletes who had crossed the color line.[130]

The community relation position allowed Gibson to give back while also getting paid. Ward paid her $25,000 ($250,233 in 2022) annually and introduced her as its spokesperson at two splashy luncheons at upscale hotels, the Waldorf-Astoria in New York and the Palmer House in Chicago, where Jesse Owens attended. She spoke at each affair with her blend of candor and charisma. Gibson was "thankful" that the community relations position would keep her in New York, "where I like to be," and would bring less travel than the professional tennis tour had demanded. No longer would she "live with a tennis racket in one hand and a suitcase in the other," she quipped. Her new job would "give me more time to be at home here. To meet and be with some of the people I have long neglected." It was a rare admission that her pursuits kept her from her parents and her siblings, all of whom were married, and their children, all daughters, and that she felt torn by her frequent absences. Over the years, Gibson wrote letters to Annie during her travels. It was a sign of love, letting her mother share in her life and career, but it was not the same as being with her.[131]

The service dimensions of the community relations job appealed to Gibson as much as and even more than the marketing aspect. The eponymous Althea Gibson Awards were to be given as "incentives to young people" selected by schools and local organizations for showing promise in sports and athletics. The awards were, said Gibson, "very close to a desire that I have had for a long time—to help others—as so many have helped me."[132] Soon she made her first trips for Ward, speaking and signing autographs at consumer expositions sponsored by Black newspapers. The events were staples of her deal with Ward. Every "Home-a-Rama" and "Home Service Show" showcased products, leisure, and convenience to housewives, and in their domesticity they were antithetical to the active life of gender defiance that she had lived.[133]

Gibson looked every bit the Black success story in the spring and summer of 1960. In March, she appeared on the cover of *Sport* magazine with Jackie

Robinson, Willie Mays, and Wilt Chamberlain for a special issue called "The Negro in American Sport."[134] After the tour with the Globetrotters ended in April, she beat Pauline Betz to win the World Pro Tennis Championship, sponsored by Pepsi-Cola, in Cleveland. Sportswriters raved at the intensity of the match, which required three sets and 140 minutes. "It is to be hoped that this will not be the last meeting between these two," *World Tennis* wrote of the well-matched meeting of Gibson and Betz, "two magnificent stars."[135] Gibson was thrilled by the victory—and undoubtedly by the opportunity to play against someone who could give her a true challenge. Only six women competed for the title, but she savored her victory all the same, believing that it confirmed that she was the best woman tennis player in the world.

Back in New York, Gibson went to the Vanderbilt Hotel in May to support junior tennis, a cause always close to her heart. She was one of several players, amateur and professional, who committed to lead a series of free tennis lessons in public parks in a program sponsored by the Eastern Tennis Patrons and the Department of Parks.[136]

Success for Gibson extended beyond the tennis court and America, too. In June, she returned to London to cover Wimbledon for the *Evening Standard* again. Her pieces were ghosted by Richard Evans, a new member of the newspaper's staff. Evans met Gibson for the first time at the Queen's Club and was instantly struck by her presence. She was "a tall, elegant young woman dressed in black" who "greeted me with a warm smile." Evans was in his early twenties and Gibson was among the few Black people he had ever met. He was awed by her expertise as they watched the men's and women's matches together at Wimbledon. Gibson gave Evans "a crash course in the intricacies of the game" that he would apply for the next sixty years as one of Britain's most revered tennis writers. Before attending the Wimbledon Ball together, they met at his mother's apartment for cocktails. Mrs. Evans had never entertained a Black guest in her home. At the ball, Gibson danced with Evans. He surmised that "all eyes were upon us."[137]

During the fortnight, Gibson stayed with Angela Buxton's family in their house in north London, where a housekeeper served her breakfast in bed. She made the trip into a working vacation. In addition to watching the tennis matches, she rented an Austin to drive around the city, attended a fashion show, spent time with Bill Davis, who hoped to qualify for Wimbledon, and visited acquaintances. She enjoyed delicious meals, made multiple trips to a hair salon, and shopped. Gibson shared with Black America the details of her trip in a series that the *Amsterdam News* and the *Chicago Defender* published as her "London Letter." She mentioned her new, larger apartment on Central

Park West, which Earle Zaidins had secured for her. Zaidins had overseen its decoration while Gibson was on the road with the Globetrotters. She dropped references to Tip-Top bread and her first business trips for Ward.[138]

Gibson's writing ambitions were further fulfilled in August 1960 when *Guideposts*, the magazine founded by the popular minister and motivational speaker Norman Vincent Peale, published her article "Persistence: A Form of Faith." The piece revealed the depth of her spirituality and how much Sydney Llewellyn had come to influence her decision-making on and off the tennis court. Gibson praised Llewellyn as "a coach-in-living" and credited him with helping her overcome the desire to quit tennis. He motivated her through parables, encouragement to read the Bible, philosophical advice, and tips supposedly based in psychology and science. Llewellyn taught Gibson, "If you are convinced of the merit of your goal, and if you want to reach it badly enough, paying the price of embarrassment is not so hard." Religious faith and the mental coaching from Llewellyn were driving her to keep pursuing a career in professional tennis against increasingly long odds.[139]

In September and October, Gibson was abroad yet again. Sponsored by tennis promoters in Latin America, she and Fageros played exhibition matches for two and a half weeks in Puerto Rico, the Virgin Islands, the West Indies, Haiti, Curaçao, Suriname, and Colombia. The *Amsterdam News* published her reports as a "Latin American Letter" series for its readers, adding more luster to her public image of glamour, wealth, and jet-setting.[140]

It looked as if all that Gibson touched after going professional had turned to gold, but inequity cast a shadow over her fortune and prospects, dimming her delight. Alex Olmedo, the Peruvian winner of the men's title at the World Pro, earned more than she did from the $10,000 purse ($102,518 in 2022), even though his match lasted only two sets and took fifty minutes. Gibson's check barely covered her travel expenses to Cleveland. The days and weeks that followed brought more disappointment. Gibson anticipated that her victory would lead to more opportunities. "In the past, title winners had been avalanched with offers to appear in some public exhibition or go on some tour or teach at some club," she wrote. "But the only avalanche that hit me was one of silence." Aside from Fageros, the other women in the competition were teaching pros at private clubs. All of them were White and, except for Betz, none of them had won majors.[141]

The lack of playing opportunities for women in professional tennis compounded Gibson's frustrations. The World Pro was the only opportunity for women to compete for a professional tennis title, and it was an inconsistent chance at that. The most recent inclusion of a women's division in the tournament had been in 1957, when Betz beat Doris Hart, and 1960 turned out to be the last time that women could enter the event for another eight years. Gibson and Betz faced off just one more time. The ATA invited them to come to Hampton Institute in Virginia to compete in an exhibition during the Nationals in August. Betz, forty-one and a mother of five, accepted and got revenge. Catching Gibson, days away from turning thirty-three, off guard, she won, 6–2, 6–3. The next day, Arthur Ashe, seventeen, won the ATA men's singles championship for the first time.[142]

By the fall, Gibson was shaken. She began to think that racism, like gender, was limiting her marketability and opportunities to capitalize on her success. She had long believed that she could live above the trap of racism. Respectability and showing that she was "worthy" would open doors for her that were closed to other African Americans who did not have her record of achievement, she thought. Reflecting on her life after amateur tennis, though, yielded darker thoughts as she realized that the White people who set the standards, trends, and tastes in tennis and other industries were overlooking her. "Suddenly it dawned on me that my triumphs had not destroyed the racial barriers once and for all as I had—perhaps naively—hoped. Or if I did destroy them, they had been erected behind me again."[143] Gibson was facing the openness of segregation in American business. Black and female, she did not fit Madison Avenue and corporate America's shared idea of the face and figure that would appeal to the interests and tastes of White consumers on Main Street, USA.

Even the achievements that Gibson did attain reflected segregation. In the weeks after *Sport* published its special issue on which she had been among the cover figures, the editors received crank letters. "You're supposed to be a sports magazine, not a striver for civil rights," a reader from Virginia wrote angrily. Another from Alabama regarded the issue as a regional attack. *Sport* was, he claimed, "trying to destroy the customs and necessary fundamentals of the greatest section of the United States—the South."[144] The reactions proved that hostility to serious coverage of African Americans' successes and struggles was alive and well and affirmed Gibson's hesitance to speak openly about her own tribulations. Her relationship with the racket manufacturer Harry C. Lee briefly took a promising turn that summer when the company featured her in print advertisements. Along with Fageros, she endorsed Lee's newest racket, "The Bat." Yet the promotion was not on par with what her White counterparts received. For years, leading American equipment manufacturers Wilson and Spalding had stamped the signatures and faces of star professionals on the necks of rackets. Marble, Hardwick, Hart, Palfrey,

Betz, Connolly, Riggs, Kramer, Pancho Gonzalez, and others all had auto-graph models. Harry C. Lee, however, put neither Gibson's brown face nor her curlicued signature on a racket. Instead, "The Bat" was adorned with a small picture of an actual black bat.[145]

Gibson's relationship with Ward was hardly better. Not only was she ef-fectively the "Negro liaison" for Tip-Top bread, but her work also reflected the exploitative practices of White businesses. Ward primarily assigned her to meet with Black audiences, and the advertisements in which she appeared were published in Black newspapers, not White ones. A Black businessman alleged that Ward stole from him the idea of Gibson's selection as a spokes-person. In August, Dolph Thompson, president of Associated Counselors Incorporated, a public relations firm based in Washington, D.C., sued Ward and Grey Advertising for appropriation. Thompson alleged that the businesses hired him to design a "comprehensive public relations plan" designed to make Tip-Top bread appeal to Black consumers, adopted his ideas, and then did not pay him.[146]

Gibson kept her self-described "disillusionment" to herself as she plotted the next steps of her career.[147] In October, she went to Los Angeles to sup-port a membership drive for the YMCA. When reporters asked her about the relationship between her tennis achievements and racial representation, she responded conservatively. "I won't be a soapbox orator for racial equality. Sure I think it's horrible that people can't get along because of the color of their skins," she commented. Long loath to admit it, Gibson said that she had known racism while growing up in Harlem. Yet talking about prejudice still did not interest her, and she echoed what she had told Fitzgerald for *I Always Wanted to Be Somebody*: "I feel I can do more good by serving as an example to others."[148] Silence would also keep her in the good graces of potential busi-ness partners.

Like generations of African Americans and women, Gibson hoped that entrepreneurship would mediate her problems with discrimination and give her more control over her career. She turned to Llewellyn and Zaidins for advice. Llewellyn was enmeshed in Gibson's affairs after two years as her manager, and she trusted him implicitly. She trusted Zaidins, too, though his reputation was dubious, whether she knew it or not. Billie Holiday's wid-ower, Louis McKay, was taking Zaidins to court. Zaidins claimed Holiday owed him $12,000 ($120,069 in 2022) when she died in July, and he sought 10 percent of her estate. Florynce Kennedy, the entertainment lawyer and ac-tivist, represented McKay in court. McKay accused Zaidins of giving money to Holiday even though he knew she would use it to buy drugs. Kennedy thought Zaidins "slimy" and "typical of the kind of sleazy people" Holiday selected for company.[149] He was also in Gibson's inner circle. She, meanwhile, seemed to have lacked a strong grasp on the operations of the corporation, Althea Gibson Enterprises, that she had formed with Zaidins and Llewellyn. In March, she told a reporter that the corporation was "doing a thriving business," but when asked, "What kind of business?" she said only, "You name it. We do it."[150]

Gibson declined Saperstein's offer to have the tennis troupe join the Globetrotters again, first in Latin America and then for a second American tour. She decided instead to compete with Saperstein and the Globetrotters. Hungry to pocket more in profits than Saperstein had given her from the tour's revenue, she chose to strike out on her own in the sports entertainment business. The Althea Gibson–Harlem Ambassadors Sports Show launched on October 31, 1960, in Decatur, Illinois. She and Fageros again faced off in tennis matches, and two teams, the Ambassadors and the New York Skyscrapers, played basketball games.[151]

The tour was a short-lived disaster. With the Globetrotters, Gibson and Fageros had consistently played before thousands of people and sellout crowds. Without the team's name recognition and brand and Saperstein's thirty-three years of experience, they floundered. For a month, more empty seats than fans saw Gibson, Fageros, the Ambassadors, and the Skyscrapers play, and the press noticed. A "disappointingly slim crowd of about 300" came out to see them at a high school gym in Port Huron, Michigan, while a "tiny crowd" showed up in Moline, Illinois.[152] Those were the good nights. Gibson's show traveled in the shadow of Saperstein's, following the Globetrotters' regional schedule to the point of sometimes playing just two weeks before or after the team arrived. Some thought the quality of her show was inferior. The advertisements suggested that the tour was not a top-tier operation. Gibson did not have a superstar on either basketball team, but advertisements billed "Oscar Robertson's Brother, 'Bailey Robertson'" as a leading attraction.[153] Splitting the profits this time, Gibson and Fageros played "faultless tennis"; second serves were not allowed, and to expedite play, there were no deuce games. Tennis fans among the sparse crowds were dissatisfied with the abbreviated matches, which they thought were too fast. Some contests lasted only thirty minutes.[154] Others thought the entire production lacked the zest of the Globetrotters' program. Gibson's show was, judged one critic, a "copy job" of a well-crafted product, just another float on the "parade of Globetrotters' imitators" that passed through the Midwest. Failure forced Gibson to see her bid to compete with Saperstein as a mistake, but it was too late.[155]

The troupe's problems soon grew bigger than a lack of originality. The press reported that Gibson "suffered a twisted back" in late November, forcing her to end the tour for two months.[156] She and Fageros traveled apart from the Skyscrapers and the Ambassadors. On the night of November 29, snow fell in Detroit, making it impossible to fly to New York, where the next engagement was in the city of Troy. Gibson chartered a limousine and relished the idea of reaching their destination faster and in comfort. At first, Fageros agreed. Then, at the last minute, she changed her mind. "I'm going to take the bus—it looks safer," she said. Gibson ducked inside the limo and Fageros boarded the bus with the Skyscrapers. Late in the night, a truck skidded on ice and crashed into the bus as it was traveling on the Ohio Turnpike. Fageros landed in a Youngstown hospital with broken ribs, a broken vertebra, and injuries to her neck and one of her legs. At twenty-six, her competitive tennis career was over.[157]

Gibson canceled the rest of the tour. The accident was cover for another reason to end the flagging show: she could not afford to keep it going. When strategizing with Llewellyn and Zaidins, Gibson "had failed to see clearly that if I stood to make the bulk of the profits on my own tour, I also stood to absorb the entire loss as well." Thirteen months removed from the announcement that she would make "near $100,000" as a professional tennis player, she estimated that her corporation was between $20,000 and $25,000 in debt ($200,186–$250,233 in 2022). By December 1960, Gibson was forced to face a cold reality. "I was, in effect, ruined."[158]

12

A Winner Who Hasn't Won Yet

Wanted: Young women for itinerant work, 3–4 days per week, 20-odd weeks per year. Must travel 300 to 1,000 miles between jobs, be in top physical condition, and emotionally tough enough to withstand a certain amount of male criticism. Pay varies, but $4,000–7,000 considered average.

—*EBONY*, 1971

AT THE END of 1960, Gibson was on the verge of losing her queer ways. The abrupt end of the tennis tour with Fageros took her away from sports. She spoke freely of her desire for open tennis and was among those who believed it was necessary for the game to remain popular, but the men who ran the sport disagreed.[1] The International Lawn Tennis Federation had met in July to vote on whether to allow professionals and amateurs to compete against each other at last. The resolution failed by a mere five votes. Gibson's entertainment career, whether as an unconventional crooner or as a hard-to-cast actress, was finished, too. Producers and booking agents were not inviting her to do anything. Will Darben did. Will was rising through the ranks at the Bendix Corporation, where he had been promoted to expeditor and production analyst. Away from the company, he cared for his mother after his father's death two years earlier. Will presented Gibson with a one-carat diamond engagement ring and asked her to marry him.[2] She accepted. She told her family and friends on Christmas Day at a party at her apartment and planned for a spring wedding in 1961.[3]

"This was no spur of the moment decision," Gibson said of their engagement. "I was quite surprised when he asked me and of course I accepted because I am so much in love with him." The press misidentified Will as her "childhood sweetie."[4] They had not known each other that long, but the almost ten years in which they had was a short yet eventful lifetime for the peripatetic Gibson. Will had wanted to marry her since he first proposed in 1953, but, less certain of marriage then, she declined.

Eight years later, little had changed. In late March 1961, Gibson announced that her engagement with Will was "definitely off."[5] The decision was not as mutual as she made it seem. Declaring himself "very reluctant to make any comment" to the press, the taciturn Will refused to say that the engagement was indeed over. As was her wont, Gibson did all the talking. "We came to an agreement that this was not the right time to be married because of extenuating circumstances," she said. She explained that "there are a lot of things I am obliged to do." She had already bought a house for her parents. With its ten rooms, 109-21 201st Street in Hollis, Queens, New York, was Gibson's "long cherished dream," as she called it, to give back to her parents, but, she told reporters, she also wanted to "build a nice home" for them, too. "This is a difficult job. I don't think it's right for me to involve myself in such a serious matter as marriage before completing this very necessary obligation. . . . I don't want to involve Mr. Darben in such a personal matter as this. It's my responsibility, not his."[6] She said nothing of her debt, a compelling reason of its own, though not one that dissuaded Will.

The major reason for the breakup emerged in April, when Gibson went to Pennsylvania for speaking engagements for the Ward Baking Company. In Philadelphia, she faced several reporters, but only one, syndicated entertainment columnist Art Peters, dared ask her about the broken engagement. Gibson confided to Peters that she was "too busy to make a success of marriage."[7] Then in Pittsburgh, she revealed to another reporter over lunch at the Penn-Sheraton Hotel that golf was her new focus. "It's a challenge, and I must have a challenge," she said, dramatically curling her fingers into a fist.[8] In fact, she had been on an extended golf trip to California in March just before she announced the end of the engagement.[9]

Gibson's decision was personal. Golf was rousing her spirit from the depths of disappointment and despair brought on by the failure of her pro tennis career and the pressure to pay down her massive debt. She comforted herself with "eccentric thoughts" that the $25,000 that she owed her creditors was a sign of her importance. Few people either owed that much money or earned it annually, she reasoned. Yet Gibson did not believe her self-talk and her actions showed how unhappy she had become. "I was weary with myself," she said later. Gibson was stuck in a "routine" of traveling alone for Ward, speaking to audiences of often inattentive children, and returning to her hotel room in cities where she knew no one. More sedentary than active for the first time in her life, she gained weight, adding to her sense that things were out of her control. "I got bored and angry with myself for my inactivity and with-drawal from life."[10]

At thirty-three, Gibson still craved competition, and golf was effectively her most logical and only outlet. Like tennis, it required that she swing an object at a ball. "I thought I could adapt easily to it," she reasoned. Gender factored into her change of sports, too. "Golf was the only sport I had noticed that a group of ladies could play."[11] Aside from the newly formed Professional Women's Bowling Association, the LPGA was the only professional sports organization for women, offering regular tournaments, prizes, and purses. By playing on the circuit, she could do what she had always wanted: play sports for money.

For the next ten years, Gibson opened herself to the glory and challenge of her new game. Golf became her obsession. No athlete "who wishes to develop to the perfect extent of her ability" could "neglect her intellectual faculties . . . To succeed, the athlete must think, she must read, and she must communicate," Gibson wrote later. "If [the athlete] fails to do these things, she cannot hope to compete successfully against opponents who have been thoughtful enough to avail themselves of the growing amount of knowledge relative to athletics."[12] Feeling that she had to make up for lost time—time when her opponents had been honing their game—Gibson read numerous golf books, practiced whenever she could, sought lessons, and studied the games of others. She allowed the game to blend with her search for a pur-pose in life as she felt increasingly lost. Satisfying her competitive appetite, extending her sports career, and putting her nonconformity of gender and race on full display, golf brought the challenges, if not the rewards, that she longed for.

———

Just three years earlier, Gibson had expressed skepticism that golf was worthy of her time and talents. "I don't see any sense in hitting a ball and then walking a couple hundred yards to hit it again," she said during a press conference in Minneapolis.[13] Others, however, thought she was selling the game, and her-self, short.

Gibson's introduction to golf at FAMC had been inauspicious. She hit golf balls on the college's practice football field during P.E. classes and made "big divots." Jake Gaither never complained. The dense packets of flying sod were proof that she was intent on making solid contact with every swing.[14] When women from FAMC and Tuskegee Institute met for a golf tournament in Alabama in May 1951, Gibson won. According to a news report about the tournament, she shot 124 for nine holes. Gibson later claimed that she scored 99 or only a few strokes higher (she changed the number over the years) on a course that had "oiled sand greens."[15] It was her first and only golf tournament, but it was enough to earn a varsity letter. Hansel Tookes, FAMC's golf coach, imagined that Gibson would have succeeded in the game if she had played more than the occasional round over the years. "She was a fearless competitor and had a burning desire to excel," Tookes said of her college days. "If she had devoted as much time to golf as she did to tennis, she would have been a golf champion."[16]

Gibson's friend Eoline Thornton agreed. Whenever she visited with Eoline and her husband, James "Spot" Thornton, during trips to Los Angeles in the 1950s, she faced the same good-natured proselytizing. "Why don't you try this golf, girl? It's fabulous," Eoline would say. She was biased. In 1951, Eoline won the women's national championship of the United Golfers Association (UGA). Founded in 1926, the UGA was the Black-run counterpart of the Professional Golfers' Association. It held tournaments at public golf courses outside the South and at country clubs owned and operated by African Americans. UGA tournaments were open to all people regardless of race. Gibson's response to Eoline's entreaties was always the same, "Nah. I'll stick to tennis," and she played golf at most six times a year.[17]

Once she left amateur tennis, Gibson changed her mind. Shortly after announcing her sabbatical from the game, she told the press that golf would be a "wonderful" complement to her singing career and estimated that with her self-belief and "six months training from a good pro," she would get "good" at the game."[18] More than a year later, Ed Fitzgerald asked Gibson during the roundtable with *Sport* magazine about the possibility that she would "take up golf," first as an amateur and then as a professional. She did not deny her interest and stated that she was "play[ing] golf at a lot of places now without any trouble."[19]

"Trouble" was a byword for African Americans' relationship with golf, the last American sport to admit Blacks on the elite level. The PGA, the governing body that oversaw professional tournaments for men and teaching jobs at clubs and courses, had barred African Americans from membership since its founding in 1916. The ban was formalized in 1934 when members added the "Caucasian clause" to the PGA's constitution. The clause stated that only "professional golfers of the Caucasian race . . . residing in North or South America" were eligible for membership. The ban placed a variety of monetary privileges—not just the ability to compete in tournaments, which offered purses and prizes, but also assistance in finding jobs and discounts on the purchase of equipment—out of the reach of African Americans.[20] By the early 1950s, the PGA utilized the invitational system that governed tennis: entries were by invitation only, and tournament committees and sponsors did not have to explain or justify their rationale for either inclusion or exclusion. A handful of Black men, notably Teddy Rhodes, Bill Spiller, Howard Wheeler, and Charlie Sifford, received invitations to play in a limited number of PGA-sanctioned tournaments, most often in California, the Midwest, and Canada, but they still faced barriers in the Golden State, the Southwest, and the center of the country. Sponsors in the South gave Black golfers only silence and cold shoulders. The United States Golf Association (USGA), which established rules and oversaw national championships, had no ban on African Americans as members, and indeed several Black golfers played in USGA events. Yet race remained a factor and barrier in that association's competitions, too. Black golfers could play in USGA-sanctioned national tournaments only if the host site approved of their entry.[21]

Gibson embarked on her golf career at a time of transition in the sport. Charlie Sifford had honed his game under the sponsorship of Billy Eckstine, working as the singer's valet and golf instructor. Winner of the UGA national championship six times between 1952 and 1960, Sifford was widely regarded as the best Black golfer in the country. In 1957, he won the Long Beach Open, an unofficial PGA event. In the fall of 1959, Sifford caught an unexpected break during a chance meeting while playing golf in Los Angeles with Eckstine at Hillcrest Country Club, founded by Jews decades earlier in response to anti-Semitic exclusion. Eckstine introduced Sifford to Stanley Mosk, the attorney general of California. Mosk, who preferred tennis, had opened a civil rights division in his office. He was appalled to learn, while chatting casually with Sifford, that African Americans could not enter PGA events, including some prestigious tournaments in California. Mosk contacted the PGA for clarification on race and its membership policies. Within months, the PGA awarded Sifford status as an "approved tournament player," enabling him to play in more tournaments, but still denied him full-fledged membership. In November 1960, the PGA voted 64–17 at its annual meeting to keep the Caucasian clause. For the next year, the PGA faced bad publicity, including editorials written by Jackie Robinson, an avid golfer, threats of lawsuits from Mosk and the NAACP, and the possibility of losing money between legal battles and moving tournaments out of states where attorneys general sided with Mosk by refusing to sympathize with segregation and white supremacy.[22]

Gibson's fate as an attempted integrator of the LPGA Tour was unclear in 1961; yet again she was entering uncharted territory of race and gender.

Founded in 1950 by thirteen White women, including Babe Didrikson Zaharias, the LPGA by all published accounts had yet to face the issue of whether, when, and how to admit a Black player. Black women had played golf across the country for decades, forming clubs of their own and competing in events organized by the UGA, which established a women's division in 1930. Despite this feature, Black women still faced sexism and barriers to being made to feel as if they fully belonged in the association. Women did not compete in the first four UGA national championships, even though some wanted to enter. What is more, while UGA tournaments typically offered both amateur and professional divisions for men, women could only compete as amateurs. In 1947, the UGA excluded women from competing in the Joe Louis Open because, according to historian Lane Demas, "some complained about the large discrepancy between male and female prize money."[23]

While Gibson had been rising through the ranks of tennis, three other women were making names for themselves on the Black golf circuit. Thelma Cowans, Ethel Funches, and Ann Moore Gregory were the best Black women golfers in the country after World War II. Between 1946 and 1963, the three dominated the UGA women's national championship. Cowans, whose husband, Russ, had excoriated Gibson as a "jackass" for her attitude toward the press after Wimbledon in 1957, and Funches, who represented Wake-Robin Golf Club, the Black women's group in Washington, D.C., each won the title five times. Gregory, a housewife living in Gary, Indiana, captured the UGA title three times. Cowans and Gregory also played against White women in a few tournaments. Both entered the Tam O'Shanter All-American Open, a tournament organized in the Chicago suburbs by White businessman George S. May, who urged the integration of golf. None of the three women, however, pursued professional golf and LPGA membership.[24]

Born in Aberdeen, Mississippi, in 1912, Gregory had been the most likely candidate to become the first Black female touring professional. Beginning in 1956, she played in several USGA Women's Amateurs and Women's Opens, firsts for a Black woman. With each entry, Gregory endured harassment, including death threats, from spectators and club and tournament workers. In 1959, at the Congressional Country Club in Bethesda, Maryland, a favorite course of President Eisenhower's, she was barred from attending a gala dinner launching the week's U.S. Open festivities. Tying her results at the previous year's open at Forest Lake Country Club in Bloomfield Hills, Michigan, Gregory won her first two matches, respectable finishes given that she practiced and played almost exclusively on municipal courses with conditions far below the standard of the facilities that hosted elite amateur and professional events for White golfers. Black men who played in limited PGA events faced the same reality. Players at tournaments treated Gregory politely enough, though at the 1963 U.S. Amateur in Williamstown, Massachusetts, a competitor mistook her for a maid at the tournament inn. Realizing her error when she noticed that Gregory was wearing golf togs, the player, Polly Riley, apologized.[25]

In 1958, Gregory received two sponsorship offers that would have enabled her to play professionally, but she turned them down. She was a wife and the mother of a teenage daughter. "I might have inspired more Negroes to play golf, but my family came first," Gregory explained in 1965. "I thought it was more important to build my daughter's character at that formative stage." Money was among Gregory's concerns, too. Once her daughter graduated from college, Gregory believed she could afford to enter professional golf, but, at fifty-two, she never tried. Gregory opined that financial backing was the biggest barrier for any Black woman who aspired to tour across the country as a member of the LPGA.[26]

Gibson resolved not to let lack of money or the prejudice and ignorance of others dampen her pursuit of a professional golf career. She immersed herself in improving her game, practicing and playing whenever and wherever she could. She played at public golf courses in New York and New Jersey, arriving at 8:00 A.M. and staying until dark. The only Black woman on the properties, she endured the "stares" and "funny looks" of the other golfers, most of whom were White men, as she "took my place on the practice tee or putting green." She was convinced that her good shots, especially her long drives, earned the "appreciation, respect and even envy" of the skeptics and gawkers who surrounded her.[27]

That Gibson could even set foot on the sites was a departure from recent history. Since the 1940s, and especially after the *Brown* decision in 1954, public golf courses had been legal battlefields as African Americans filed lawsuits against cities for access and White course operators and recreation officials resisted, often through nefarious privatization schemes or by shutting down the facilities entirely. The first major battle over integration in Greensboro, North Carolina, was over one of its golf courses, Gillespie Park, beginning in December 1955, not the Woolworth's lunch counter in February 1960. A private club would have been better for Gibson's preparations, giving her access to the kinds of course conditions that characterized sites that hosted elite amateur and professional events. Finances, race, and gender, though, stymied her access to a membership. Golf and country clubs were notoriously cool to giving women unlimited time on their courses, and African

Americans remained verboten as members. Pushback against Black golfers, whether at public or private courses, existed beyond the South. In the early 1960s, reports of African Americans being denied memberships at golf clubs, the ability to enter city tournaments, and the chance to play on public courses in Connecticut, New York, and Colorado cropped up in the Black press. Even celebrity did not guarantee entrée to membership in a private club. None other than Jackie Robinson was denied membership in 1956 at High Ridge Country Club, located between Stamford, Connecticut, and Pound Ridge, New York. The membership committee approved his application, but a group of White women complained.[28]

Gibson was confidently stitching together a way forward in golf in 1961. She was disenchanted with tennis and hardly played anymore. She joined Sarah Palfrey, Bill Talbert, and Mercer Beasley in New York as part of the second annual junior tennis program sponsored by the Department of Parks. In June, she went to the Bahamas for an exhibition with Donald Budge and Ellsworth Vines. They promoted "Paradise Tennis," a combination of regulation tennis and table tennis that Paradise Island used as a tourist attraction. It was typical of Gibson at the time: she only played tennis when she was to be paid. The *Evening Standard*'s decision to hire Jaroslav Drobny, the men's champion of 1954, to cover Wimbledon ended her visits to London. "There isn't much work now for a lady pro tennis player," she bemoaned.[29]

Golf was completely Gibson's game. When she was home in New York, she practiced her short game, chips and putts, in her apartment with a putter and wedge that she kept beside her front door as reminders to work at her new craft. Golf courses became her spiritual haven. Alone on courses, she found herself thinking about God. "I contemplated the presence of a spiritual Being very grand and very gentle who could provide for us, on a few privileged occasions in our lives, a setting as moving as this by which we could glimpse His scheme." Despite the calamities and disappointments of the preceding years, Gibson still felt "thankful for the blessings bestowed on me," she wrote later, and "any bitterness I felt over the misfortunes in my life fled."[30]

A self-described "student of the game," Gibson sought the help of expert teachers. Since the previous fall, she had taken four lessons each from three teaching professionals—Jimmie DeVoe of Los Angeles and New York's Walter Reabley and Charley Brown. Gibson visited an LPGA tournament in the spring and studied the techniques of players. Using a movie camera, she shot footage of their swings and had conversations with some of the top stars, including Louise Suggs, Marilynn Smith, and Marlene Bauer Hagge. Based upon her interactions with assorted women, Gibson judged that the atmosphere of the LPGA would not be inhospitable: "They seemed to be a fine group. If I get my game into good enough shape, I'm sure they would welcome me on the circuit."[31]

There were suggestions that some in the ATA had become unwelcoming toward Gibson, adding to her feeling that the time was right to leave tennis behind. For the first time since she had become serious about the sport, Gibson did not attend the ATA Nationals that summer. Containing harsh words about her visits to the Nationals since becoming a champion of Wimbledon and Forest Hills, the tournament program for the National Junior Championships, held during the week of August 8 to 13, held clues about her absence. During the 1959 Nationals week, Gibson had played a singles exhibition with Karol Fageros and teamed with Gunter Polte, a White player from Springfield, Ohio, in a mixed doubles exhibition against Clyde Freeman and Gwen McEvans, the association's reigning national doubles champions. A caption for a picture of the four players questioned why Polte was her partner rather than Dr. Eaton or Dr. Johnson: "These two doctors made Althea what she is today. What did Mr. P[o]lte do?" Another picture showed Gibson with Darlene Hard during their visit in 1957. Its caption noted that the picture was "conspicuous by the absence of the two men who made Althea" and pointed out that she "learned her tennis in North Carolina and Virginia and not on New York sidewalks," a crack at a line used often in the media to describe her background.[32] While Gibson's knowledge of the rancorous picture captions is unknown, perceptions of her within the ATA seemed to have soured, especially after the controversy over Ralph Bunche and the West Side Tennis Club. After 1958, Gibson made gifts of between $25 and $50 ($250 to $500 in 2022) through her corporation to the Junior Development Program led by Dr. Johnson, but she seems not to have sought either a leadership role in the organization or opportunities to play in any more exhibitions. She was thoroughly ready to move on.[33]

Feeling prepared to enter golf tournaments, Gibson turned to the UGA. That summer, she finished in third place in her first event, the Quaker City Open, in Philadelphia, and won her next three in Chicago, Cleveland, and Pittsburgh. Confident that she was moving in the right direction, she set her sights on winning the UGA women's national championship at the end of August at the Ponkapoag Golf Course in Canton, Massachusetts. For two weeks, she worked hard on her game, fitting in practice sessions between her Ward duties in New York, Detroit, and Chicago. When the tournament began on August 21, though, Gibson struggled. Seeing the rain clouds blanketing the Boston suburb, she expected her round to be postponed. It was not; unlike tennis players, golfers played in rain. Already unfamiliar with the course, she "wasn't prepared" for the weather.[34] Despite shooting a 52 on her first nine holes, including a nine on the par-5 first and a triple bogey on her last hole, she played well enough to qualify for the match-play portion of the tournament, when players faced off one-on-one against opponents until a winner was declared. In the quarterfinals, Gibson met Ethel Funches, the two-time defending champion. Their match ended on the sixteenth green, where Funches won convincingly, three holes up with two to play.[35]

Gibson kept the loss in perspective, and she kept up her devotion. In September, she led a charity drive for Chicago's Crusade for Mercy. Entrants struck tee shots that were measured for length, and dollars were raised accordingly. She won the contest with a drive of 270 yards. She had a chance meeting with President Eisenhower, who was speaking at the McCormick Place Convention Center on the same day. The press speculated that they discussed golf during their first, and only, tête-à-tête.[36] Weeks later, Gibson went to Allentown, Pennsylvania, where she played with a group of White women, including noted amateur Gloria Ehret, at a public course. The visit exemplified the rare space that Gibson occupied in comparison to other Black golfers, and she knew it. "I've had an advantage others lack," she told the *Boston Globe* during the UGA Championship. "I've been invited to courses because of my sports record and the contacts I made in tennis. I've had many more opportunities to play. The others haven't been so fortunate."[37]

The fortunes of Black golfers with professional ambitions changed in November 1961. At its annual meeting, the PGA voted to rescind the "Caucasian clause." Lou Strong, the association's president, implied that continued concerns over international perceptions of racial discrimination in the United States during the Cold War compelled the PGA to make the decision: "The action was a realization of changing conditions in the world situation. This was a constructive measure, coinciding with decisions set forth by the United States government."[38] There was no indication that the LPGA, which was run by its players, was opposed to having a Black member. The PGA's decision, and the harm to its image in the months before the erasure of the clause, made it unlikely that LPGA players would protest the integration of their ranks. The door to a career in professional golf was open for Gibson. She just needed to be ready to enter.

Gibson did not plan to turn professional right away. By 1962, reports of her switch to golf were appearing regularly in the press, Black and White. Writers speculated that she could dominate the LPGA. The 270-yard tee shot in Chicago was no fluke. Driving had become the best part of her game, though sometimes she pushed the ball far to the left because of the strong right hand that she had developed in tennis. Yet there was more to golf than long drives. Gibson's short game—chips, putts, pitches, and sand shots—needed attention, but she was unintimidated by the challenge of improving. "A little hard work will fix that up," she said in February after winning the women's title at Ray Mitchell's North-South Winter Golf Tournament, a star-studded Black golf tournament in Miami, by twenty-six strokes over her nearest competitor. Mindful of her amateur status, Gibson said only that she wanted to be "the best woman golfer ever." She cautiously predicted that she was two to three years away from "the real bigtime" in golf.[39] The timeline might have been shorter without her day job and her debt.

Gibson wished that she did not need the Ward job, but, unable to quit, she used the work and other public speaking engagements to achieve her brand of social good that focused on gender equality, education, and physical fitness. A visit to the University of Nebraska–Lincoln in mid-March exemplified her point of view. She came to the university to give the keynote address for the regional conference of the Athletic and Recreational Federation of College Women, where 125 to 150 students and faculty from the Midwest convened for a three-day event. Gibson expressed her wide-ranging opinions in press conferences and interviews during the trip. She joined the chorus of observers who charged that tennis was losing players to other sports because of money. Baseball, basketball, and football offered aspirants financially viable career paths. Tennis did not. "You can't live on $15 a day," Gibson scoffed. Wading into the concerns about the physical fitness of young people that occupied educators, the media, and even the White House, she insisted that American cities and towns bore a responsibility for the health of children. Speaking like a PAL beneficiary, she called for urban design and city planning to prioritize physical wellness: "There isn't enough public playground area for our youngsters. If the community isn't interested—the child won't be." She proposed building tennis courts on rooftops, an idea that she also expressed in 1961.[40]

Gibson's statements about women during the conference were among the boldest that she made about a social issue up to that point in her life. "The Role of Women in Sports" was the topic of her speech, and she did not hold back. Gibson was adamant that she had no reservations about girls' and women's engagement with sports. "Sports participation for girls is very important and proper," she said, adding that "women are just as strong as men, and it is very helpful for a woman to participate in physical activity." She also disagreed with the notion that sports made women unfeminine: "To this I can only say—in a ladylike way—Baloney!" Gibson named Jacqueline Kennedy, the First Lady and an avid equestrian, as an exemplar of femininity and athleticism. Drawing on her personal experience, Gibson decried the double standards faced by women in sports that were also played by men: "We must play by their rules and still maintain our own standards."[41]

In Nebraska, Gibson did not limit herself to addressing only the restrictions that women faced in athletics. She linked the gender barriers in sports to the pressures and problems of women in a male-dominated society. "Being a good woman is a tough job—a job not made easier by men," she said. "They put us on a pedestal and then put it in an enclosure. They look up to us and they look down on us at the same time." She cited housework and childrearing as examples. Men "expect us to be glamorous at night after a day of scrubbing floors, and wiping runny noses and other ends," she joked. Humorously pointing to domestic life again, she bristled at the stereotype that men were innately more skilled at tasks that required dexterity. "Have you ever seen a man try to put a diaper on a baby for the first time? He's like a man putting up a pup tent in a high wind."[42] Gibson further astonished her audience during a tennis demonstration at the university's famed Coliseum, where she towered over the two coeds invited to join her on the tennis court and smashed serves and traded cannon-like passing shots with Don Gibson, a man from Nebraska's tennis team, in a one-set match. They were tied 2–2 when he abruptly and suspiciously ended the match to attend a class, allowing him to say that he had not lost to a woman.[43]

Gibson would make hundreds of addresses and public appearances until Ward chose not to renew her contract for 1965. Most of the events required that she don her elegant dresses and smart skirted business suits, smile no matter her true feelings, shake hands with distinguished figures, and distribute checks from Ward to local charities. She attended gatherings of the National Urban League, the National Association of Negro Business and Professional Women's Clubs, and the National Negro Publishers Association, and came to groundbreakings, including for the Bethune House, public housing projects in Washington, D.C. Gibson especially enjoyed being among children. She regularly attended Chicago's Bud Billiken Parade, the annual festival founded for Black children by *Defender* publisher Robert S. Abbott to celebrate Black life, culture, and achievements. She sometimes gave clinics in tennis, paddle tennis, and golf to youngsters, too. The appearances raised money for Black causes and put her closer to "my people," as she called African Americans.[44] Whether young or old, Black men and women, boys and girls, could look to her as a source of inspiration. Gibson's work for Ward was a much-needed job, but it was something more. She had told Ed Fitzgerald during their book collaboration that anything she did to support the advancement of African Americans she would have to do "my way." Her work for Ward was her way in action.

Gibson took her position seriously and resolved to be more than a mere corporate mouthpiece, spouting a checklist of talking points of the supposed virtues of Tip-Top bread. By 1962, she had made education her platform for Ward. She set out, she explained in Nebraska, "to stimulate young people to realize that education is a very important factor and they should prepare themselves well for adult life."[45]

The topic was personal for Gibson, and she treated the talks the same way. She called them "family chats" and, speaking as much from her heart as from her prepared speech, she revealed an honesty and a vulnerability that few associated with her. She went to schools, libraries, and community centers and, before audiences of mostly Black children, teenagers, teachers, and parents, described her own journey from the streets of New York to her place in front of them. Education, she emphasized, was the vehicle that brought her to their town. "The years I spent away from classrooms were wasted years for I overlooked the most important part of my life, my education," she told an audience at an elementary school in Hackensack, New Jersey.[46] Her message in Bridgewater was blunt: "Without education, one has no hope in life."[47] Listeners who came to the Phyllis Wheatley Branch of the YWCA in St. Louis heard Gibson describe learning as holistic and as giving her opportunities that she otherwise would have missed: "Through education I've learned the value of being a human being. I've traveled around the world two times." "Going to school," she reminded her listeners, was not as "tough" as the responsibilities of adulthood. Schooldays were "the easiest time of your life" because "your only responsibility is to yourself, your parents," and studying.[48] She did not limit herself to groups who came to see her in person. She talked about her past as a self-described "dropout" on television, too.[49]

"I never planned it to happen," Gibson said of her lecturing role. She embraced the work nonetheless. "Knowing what I'd gone through as a youngster, I'm glad I have the chance to do it."[50] Sometimes she sang "So Much to Live For" at the end of her program, but the "chats" alone resonated with Gibson's spirituality. She considered it "a sin not to be able to use your talents."[51] She believed, too, that she was using her own talents to uplift and advance others, including her people.

————

After more than a year of accepting invitations from contacts to play at their home clubs, Gibson acquired a private membership of her own. Located in Bergen County, New Jersey, Englewood Golf Club was co-owned by Jerry Volpe, a teaching professional, and Guido Fusco Jr., co-owner of his family's restaurant, Fusco's, in Manhattan's financial district. "She's a dues paying member, classified as a single female golfer with all rights and privileges of any other member, no special dispensation needed," Fusco told reporters when Gibson's membership made news in May 1962.[52] However, in *So Much to Live For*, she remembered things differently. Volpe "invited me to use the facilities of his club" and "made me an honorary member," she wrote, suggesting that she paid little or nothing at all to belong at Englewood. She also thought the invitation was a sign that God "listened to my prayers."[53] No matter the terms, Volpe, Fusco, and Gibson each benefited from the arrangement. She was spared the greens fees, costs of range balls, and prying eyes at public golf courses, and her association with the club, which would be mentioned alongside her name in the press for years to come, brought it publicity. The club's only Black member, she knew that the invitation was a "break," financially and racially.[54]

Excited to have a new and promising pupil, Volpe worked with Gibson and acted as her cheerleader. He was used to helping famous people with their golf games. Volpe's first job, at sixteen, was for Bernarr Macfadden, the famed physical culturist. Volpe gave lessons to Ed Sullivan, Buddy Hackett, Joey Bishop, and members of the New York Yankees, and, with Gibson, played with Jackie Robinson, too. Her level of dedication struck Volpe as entirely different from anything he had previously seen. "She can practice endlessly for hours and hours," said the garrulous Volpe. "I've never seen anyone like her. She gets me tired just watching. This girl will take a wedge and work the same shot over and over again until you think she isn't human. With her will and desire alone she's got to be great. Althea has everything to be tops," including, Volpe pointed out, the ability to "hit [the ball] as long as any woman ever did."[55] Volpe sometimes said that she "hits just like a man."[56] He predicted publicly that she would win the U.S. Women's Open in four years.[57]

Fortified by her new club membership, Gibson launched herself into high-profile competitive opportunities. She worked her way down to a four handicap, typically shooting in the low eighties and high seventies, and accepted invitations to join other celebrities in pro-am competitions that preceded LPGA tournaments in New York and New Jersey. She played other events that raised money for charities. Teamed with Jackie Robinson, she won an exhibition match against Ann Gregory and Joe Louis in Chicago. The match benefited Provident Hospital, the NAACP, and the Urban League, and gave Gibson a chance to catch up with Louis. An avid golfer who hosted a UGA tournament and pushed the PGA to integrate, Louis had been among those who encouraged her to play golf. She played in more UGA events and began to enter elite White amateur tournaments, too.[58]

Played at the Country Club of Rochester in August, the U.S. Women's Amateur was the most prestigious event on Gibson's calendar in 1962. She beat fifteen-year-old Jeanie Butler of Harlingen, Texas, in the first round. In the second, she faced Alice Dye, the women's state golf champion of Indiana and wife of famed course architect Pete Dye. The tournament format was match play and, attracting the largest gallery of the day, Gibson got off to a hot start, three up after eight holes. By the sixteenth, Gibson's lead vanished as her short game let her down again and again. Dye won the match two up on the eighteenth green. Gibson bristled when, walking off the eighteenth green, a member of the gallery offered sympathy and encouragement to return the next year. "I don't feel bad at all," she responded. "And I expect I will be back."[59]

If nothing else, Gibson was a problem-solver, even if her solutions sometimes created more problems. Diagnosing a "lack of tournament experience" as the culprit in her loss to Dye, she decided to enter as many tournaments as her schedule allowed. Gibson ended 1962 with two victories, winning her division in the Women's New Jersey State Golf Association Championship in September and capturing Englewood's women's club championship the following month. The next year began auspiciously. Gibson's first event of 1963 was the LPGA's St. Petersburg Open. Weeks before its start, she wrote a letter to the tournament's organizers to express her interest in entering. There was a subtext to the missive: she was trying to gauge their openness to having a Black woman among the contestants. To her relief and possible surprise, they expressed no opposition; Billy Watts, who was both the pro at the tournament site, the Sunset Golf and Country Club, and the tournament director, approved. She was the first African American in the tournament's history.[60] The invitation was a good omen. It was also a reminder that such opportunities were still not guaranteed for Black golfers.

St. Petersburg held two professional golf tournaments, the LPGA event at the Sunset in February and the PGA tournament at the Lakewood Country Club in March. Charlie Sifford informed the local media that he wanted to play in the men's St. Petersburg Open. Watts went on record to say that he was in favor of Sifford's entry. Whether he knew it or not, Watts had gone out on a limb. Others in the city's golf glitterati refused to say whether they would support Sifford's entry, and an agreement between St. Petersburg and Lakewood complicated matters. Though the city leased the club for the week of the tournament, Lakewood's members and operators had final say over who could use the clubhouse and its locker rooms. The arrangement exemplified the long-standing machinations that private clubs deployed, and municipal leaders accepted, to keep African Americans out of golf tournaments. Officials allowed Sifford and Howard Brown, another Black professional, to enter the PGA's St. Petersburg Open. After the women's open ended, Watts resigned from the city's golf committee. According to the local press, Watts, never a yes-man, was disturbed to know that he had been among the few who felt that letting Gibson play in the women's open was the right thing to do.[61]

If Gibson was aware of the controversy, she said nothing about it. She knew Sifford. In early 1960, she had played a round with him and Eoline Thornton at the Western Avenue Golf Course during a swing through Southern California with the Globetrotters. In St. Petersburg, she shot 327, sixteen strokes behind Mickey Wright and Marilynn Smith, who tied for first place after four rounds and headed for a playoff the next day. Two weeks later, Gibson won the women's division of the North-South Winter Golf Tournament at the public Miami Springs Golf Course for the second straight year. She was surrounded by good company. The North-South was the premier pro-am in Black golf. Sidney Poitier, Martin Luther King Jr., Joe Louis, Ralph Metcalfe, and Maury Wills were among the celebrities who trod the fairways by day and relaxed by night to the hot jazz and good food at the Hampton House Motel, the accommodations of choice for well-heeled African Americans visiting Miami.[62]

Gibson entered more events as an amateur until July 6. Exactly six years after her first capture of Wimbledon, she turned professional as a golfer. Leonard Wirtz, the LPGA's tournament director, announced the news during a stop in Sutton, Massachusetts. Wirtz was effusive in his praise and outlook for her. Gibson was "a wonderful person and a great competitor," he said. As if anticipating curiosity about racial animus among the women of the LPGA, Wirtz insisted, "We're glad she's joining our organization" and "Every member of the troupe is happy she's joining us."[63] Gibson had the potential to be good for the LPGA's business. Yet it remained to be seen whether the business of golf would be good for—and good to—her.

—·—

Turning professional was inevitable for Gibson, but the timing was hardly opportune. She would have to balance her playing schedule with her work commitments for Ward. Her abilities posed a problem, too. Most of the top players in the LPGA had been playing golf since they were either children or adolescents, and they had the requisite tournament experience and skills to be consistently competitive. Joining the tour with her four handicap, Gibson faced on-the-job training that would prove costly.

One LPGA tournament did not a member make. LPGA rules required that women interested in joining the circuit finish in the top 80 percent in three out of four events. The association further required that all nonmembers pay one-tenth of 1 percent of the total prize money for each tournament entered plus an additional $50. Aspirants who passed the 80 percent test earned credit toward their LPGA player's card and were reimbursed the $50 fees up to $200. Cardholders were then obligated to play in 60 percent of all tournaments. After four years, a member earned Class A status and the freedom to play as often or as little as she wished if she continued to pay her membership dues.[64]

The process was intended to develop a tour for women who were committed to competing regularly for years to come in the face of dismal odds, doubts, and inequality. LPGA members played tournaments and did service, too, from the presidency to course setups to public relations and more. The LPGA was, wrote *Golf Digest*, "an infant—walking but still struggling to run—when compared to its male counterpart and the $100,000-plus tournaments" sponsored by the PGA.[65] That infancy and inequality showed most in tournament purses. In 1963, LPGA players played for a total of $300,000 in thirty-two tournaments. Even the most significant events offered little bounty. When Mary Mills won the U.S. Women's Open in July 1963, she earned $2,000; the entire purse was $9,000. Julius Boros alone received a check for $17,000 when he won the men's National Open in June.[66] Staging tournaments in small towns and midsized cities across the country, LPGA players were reductively referred to in the press as "proettes," "gal pros," and "gal golfers" and vied for titles against a backdrop of notions that they were lesser golfers than men—not just the stars who played with the PGA but mediocre men who hacked their way across courses, whether well-maintained country club greens or poor-quality "dog track" courses, from coast to coast.[67] Undermining the gendered discourse of golf, the women of the LPGA played from the so-called men's tees, though their scores were higher than if they had teed off from even just a few yards up. Lenny Wirtz insisted that the additional challenge and yardage were worth it so that players "play the course as it was designed" and "get the test the architect planned." Gender figured into the association's course setups, too. "If a girl's playing badly from the ladies' tees, some woman in the crowd is going to say she could do better herself," Wirtz explained. "If the same girl's playing well from the men's tees, then the men in the gallery are likely to be dazzled and admit she's getting figures they couldn't beat."[68]

Hopes abounded that Gibson might fill perceived voids in the LPGA. Her fame generated excitement that she could attract fans to tournaments. Players and sportswriters believed that the tour needed a star. No member of the LPGA had come close to matching the star power and influence of Babe Didrikson Zaharias since her death from colon cancer in 1956. A funny and flamboyant braggart, Zaharias was undeniably one of the greatest golfers of all time. Though her self-confidence and abrasiveness often irritated her fellow pros, Zaharias brought national attention to the LPGA. People bought tickets to see her wallop the ball and became interested in women's golf after seeing her in the media. Zaharias played her harmonica and sang on *The Ed Sullivan Show*, acted alongside Katharine Hepburn in the film *Pat and Mike* (1952), and had a regular presence in magazines and newspapers, including in advertisements for the many products she endorsed. Topping the list of earners and winners on the LPGA year after year, Mickey Wright effectively replaced the late Zaharias as the best player on the circuit. Wright, however, admitted that "I'm not the type who captures the 'public's imagination.'" As she told *Golf Digest* in 1963, "I never will be. Babe Zaharias was uninhibited, outgoing, a person who loved to be the center of attention. She wanted publicity and thrived on it. My needs are different."[69]

What Wright lacked in flamboyance, she made up for in long driving, the second feature that players, press, and public opined was vital for the success of the LPGA, and another asset that Gibson could contribute. "The customers want to see the bomb, the real long gone bomb," observed a writer for the *Boston Globe*.[70] Shirley Englehorn, the LPGA's public relations director and one of its longest drivers, agreed: "What we need are players who hit the ball the way men do." Englehorn spoke for many who believed that Gibson's prowess off the tee could help bring spectators to tournaments. *Golf Digest* estimated that only five to ten thousand people came to watch LPGA tournaments, which lasted three or four rounds. "It will take her a little time to perfect her golf game as she perfected her tennis. But while she is polishing up her game, she'll be wowing them with the long ball," Englehorn said of Gibson. "She can hit that ball as well as many men and better than most."[71] Published reports estimated that Gibson's tee shots averaged 250 yards, placing her in the company of some of the tour's biggest hitters and names—Wright, Englehorn, Kathy Whitworth, and Marilynn Smith. Wirtz, at the end of a three-year contract as tournament director and seeking a renewal, did not mince words about Gibson's value: "She'll be a tremendous asset to the LPGA both personally and as a gate attraction."[72]

Sportswriters and others had regarded Gibson as a much-needed star for the LPGA as soon as her interest in a golf career became public. Variations on "she could be another Babe Didriks[o]n Zaharias" were written in newspapers and uttered by observers.[73] Gibson encouraged them. The Associated Press reported that she said she wanted to be "the best woman golfer in the world and match" Zaharias's records, which included thirty-six LPGA tournament victories, ten of which were majors. "It's no secret the Babe always has been an inspiration to me," she said. "She was a great all-around athlete who took up golf late—in her thirties—and became the undisputed champion."[74] Gibson likened herself to the LPGA co-founder. "I feel somehow much like" her, she told a reporter. "I've competed in many sports and done fairly well at all of them. The Babe did many things well and I feel that I am much the same." She believed that God would guide her through Zaharias's path to the top. The bad breaks from the tremendous debt and the stalling of her professional tennis career had led Gibson to increasingly rely on faith. She applied her growing spirituality to her latest pursuit. "It's a sin if you don't use your God given talents. So, as long as I'm strong and healthy, with God's help I might reach the top again. Certainly, I intend to do my part."[75]

Gibson made her professional debut in July 1963 at the U.S. Women's Open in Cincinnati, Ohio, at Kenwood Country Club. Golfers often played practice rounds together before tournaments, studying the course, sharing insights, and lightly socializing all at once. She chose a different approach. The day before the championship began, she ventured around the golf course alone, taking only her caddy, who worked for the club. On each tee box, Gibson hit three balls. She seldom found the fairway. Her iron shots impressed observers, but the complexes at the end of each hole laid bare the weaknesses of her short game. "I never saw anything like those greens," she told Kenwood's pro.[76] She refused, however, to concede defeat before the tournament began, telling a reporter after her practice round, "I feel I'm good enough to play at this level. If I didn't think I was, I wouldn't be here. I like to think positively all the time." She did not expect to win. Instead, her goal was to make the cut—have among the lowest scores on the first two days, and then play the final two rounds on Saturday and Sunday for a chance to win a check, if not the title.[77]

Gibson came close. The leaders on the first day shot two-under-par 71s. She came to Kenwood's par-5 seventeenth just one shot over par, but two double bogeys—a seven there and a six on the par-4 eighteenth—gave her a 78 for the round. The next day, Gibson was again undone by the seventeenth hole, where she made another seven and shot 82. With her two-day score of 160, she missed the cut by one stroke. Gibson often compared tennis with golf, and immediately after the round she found a humorous and self-deprecating correlation between the two games: "In tennis, you try to stroke the ball to the worst possible spot to keep your opponent from hitting it back. I'm afraid I haven't quite gotten over the habit." She said that she "was not at all discouraged."[78] Days later, though, Gibson admitted that the outcome was still hard to accept. "If it had been five strokes it wouldn't have been so bad," she said ruefully in Detroit, "but just by one."[79] Misses, mostly far, filled the rest of her season, but she motivated herself with thoughts that her professional golf career served a social purpose, not simply a personal one.

Others agreed. The civil rights movement was in full swing in the South. Voter registration initiatives were under way in the Mississippi Delta, and Birmingham, Alabama, had become the cynosure of the movement. Martin Luther King Jr., who had brought his Southern Christian Leadership Conference to the city to challenge its segregationist policies, was arrested and detained in jail. Black residents, including children, were marching and voluntarily getting arrested to protest Jim Crow. Televisions, newspapers, and magazines across the country and around the world showed pictures of police officers and firefighters, acting on the orders of Bull Connor, the police commissioner, using dogs and high-power water hoses to attack demonstrators. The John F. Kennedy administration struggled to find ways to quell the violence, lessen the damage to the country's image, and bring calm to what many worried would be a difficult summer. A week after President Kennedy declared civil rights "a moral issue" in a televised address to the nation, officials reviewed a proposal from Time-Life to have "national leaders," Black and White, from a variety of arenas "make 1-minute appeals for reason in [the] upcoming period of racial tension." The media company wanted King, Roy Wilkins, James Baldwin, Langston Hughes, Lena Horne, Marian Anderson, Harry Belafonte, Louis Armstrong, and Leontyne Price to be among the African American speakers; Gibson's name appeared with Jackie Robinson, Joe Louis, and Willie Mays on the list of athletes.[80] The program seems never to have been produced and Gibson may never have known about the proposal, but her inclusion on the draft document was proof of her standing as a symbol of importance to the federal government.

That summer, the country, especially Black America, was abuzz with antic-ipation for the March on Washington. Organizers envisioned the gathering as a demonstration to compel the Kennedy administration to take decisive action on civil rights by supporting substantial legislation that would affirm fairness, equal access, and opportunity in public spaces and employment. Gibson identified with the objectives of the march, and not just because of her past. Thoughts of the lack of job opportunities in tennis lingered in her mind alongside the reality that the tentacles of discrimination—based on race and on gender—threaded through golf as well.

In the weeks leading up to the march, Gibson linked her golf aspirations to the battle for equal opportunity. "There is big money in professional golf and I want people of my race to get some of what the sport offers top players."[81] She said she was playing to make a point not just about money but also about women. "What I wanted to do when the chance came," she said of the desegregation of professional golf, "was to open the door to other Negro women golfers."[82] Breaking from her constant optimism and soon to turn thirty-six, she confessed that time and age might undermine her am-bition to be among the best golfers of all time. Still, she felt that something positive could come from her new career for all African Americans. "I cannot hope to go to the top in this game, as I did in tennis with such a late start," she told an audience. "However, I am hopeful that my success in entering the gates of professional golf for women will make it possible for others of my race to follow." There were, she added, "at least a few young golfers of my race who stand a good chance of winning their share of titles," in both amateur and professional golf.[83] Gibson was not among the estimated quarter of a million Americans, including Dr. Johnson, who came to the Lincoln Memorial for the March on Washington for Jobs and Freedom on August 28, but she did her part where she could. The day before, she gave golf, tennis, and table tennis demonstrations at the Century of Negro Progress exposition in Chicago.[84]

Gibson earned positive press in the African American media as she embarked on her golf career. While some reporters were skeptical about her chances for success, others predicted that she would excel. Cal Jacox thought she could "more than hold her own in competition with the cream of the [crop] of the nation's women golfers."[85] Gibson's decision to publicly posi-tion herself as a race leader in golf impressed Black news outlets, too. The *Chicago Defender* called her a "real pioneer," and Al Monroe, the syndicated columnist, praised her for entering golf not for herself but to "open a door that was shut via unwritten law." Monroe counted her among Black athletes who were working "quietly but with definite determination" to break down segregation.[86]

Like her comments, the compliment showed how much opinions of Gibson had changed since the height of her tennis career. Wilma Rudolph, thirteen years younger, had joined her as a world-famous Black sportswoman. Winner of three Olympic gold medals at the Rome Games in 1960, more than any other woman in a single Olympics at the time, Rudolph had replaced Gibson as a darling of the State Department. She met global audiences with her track and field teammates, was the subject of a USIA-produced propaganda film, and even met President Kennedy in the Oval Office. A. S. "Doc" Young observed that the White media preferred Rudolph's aesthetics over Gibson's. Rudolph "was . . . the first Negro woman athlete to draw worldwide praise for her beauty . . . and this is indisputable proof that 'things are getting better' for Negroes.' "[87]

Nevertheless, just a few years removed from accusing her of selfishness and racial disloyalty, the Black media was embracing Gibson again as a heroine. The intimations of lesbianism and the suggestions that she was odd for being over thirty and unmarried had faded. Back in August 1958, the *New York Amsterdam News* had responded to the description of her relationship with the army captain at Lincoln University in the *Saturday Evening Post* with a story, "Althea's Love Life—Almost Gave Up Tennis for a Man!" The title practically mocked, "Can you believe it?," and insinuated the ubiquity of the gay rumor.[88] The broken engagement to Will in 1961 had also drawn more attention to the supposed oddness of her decision not to marry. " 'Still No Wedding'—Althea," the *Pittsburgh Courier* headlined that spring.[89] Yet all of that was in the past. Her new image surely helped. Away from the golf course, Gibson was photographed in the custom-made business fashions and evening wear that she bought from couturiers in New York and New Jersey; her height necessitated the bespoke garments, she said. Gibson's appearance in Ward's advertisements stood out from the ways in which African Americans had long been portrayed in commercial art. She wore sweater sets, elegantly styled hair, and a diamond ring as she pitched Tip-Top bread in Black newspapers. This was "the new Althea," according to a feature article published in *Sepia*, another Black-targeted magazine.[90] Intended as a compliment, the notion fit the narrative that she had become a respectable, gender-conforming role model among African Americans. It also reminded the public that she had not always been that way. In July, Gibson was the celebrity guest for *Ebony's* monthly "Date with a Dish" series. Wearing pearls, a cap-sleeved top, and a skirt, she tossed a salad of Brussels Sprouts Italiano to accompany other favorite treats, porterhouse steaks and orange-flavored milk. Like the Ward advertisements, the *Ebony* feature stood out for domesticating Gibson. "Glowing with vitality and achievement" and fortified by "good nutrition," wrote *Ebony*, she was a picture of "business and sports success."[91]

As was often the case with Gibson, the image did not match her reality. Five months into her first season as a professional, her golf career was turning out to be a disaster. After the U.S. Open, she played in LPGA tournaments in Michigan, Wisconsin, Utah, California, Nevada, and Arizona. She made only a few cuts. She also made no money. She had started 1963 aware that it was less likely to be "a year of earning" than "one of learning."[92] Even so, earning nothing was a hard pill to swallow. During a tournament stop in Las Vegas, Gibson spoke with Maggie Hathaway, the nation's leading Black golf reporter. Gibson disclosed that she was "paying her own way" on the LPGA circuit.[93] She estimated that she needed $200 ($1,936 in 2022) every week to sustain herself and travel, which she did alone. Hathaway opined that the financial stress added pressure, and strokes, to Gibson's game: "It is a known fact that a professional can score better when someone else is paying the bill of about $15,000."[94]

To be sure, practically every woman in the LPGA had to be creative about finances at the start of her career and often for all of it. Top money-winners, like Mickey Wright and Kathy Whitworth, were exceptions, but even they had reputations for being moderate in their spending. *Golf Digest* estimated conservatively that players needed $150 per week to survive; $135 was possible but a stretch. Many cut costs by traveling in pairs or groups. During the brief off-season between November and March, players conducted clinics and worked at private clubs and public golf courses. Some had arrangements that took them abroad. Family and friends backed some players, too.[95]

Sponsorships helped. The magazine estimated that nearly 80 percent of LPGA players had sponsorship deals. The women represented equipment companies and "publicity-conscious" golf clubs.[96] Often the names of sponsors appeared on players' golf bags, and they were obligated to do some type of additional work for the entity that would further increase its name recognition. In exchange, players received money and equipment at no cost.

In December, Gibson landed a sponsor of her own when Dunlop Sports put her under contract. The only other Black professional golfers to have endorsement deals with sporting goods companies were Teddy Rhodes and Charlie Sifford, both with the Burke Golf Company. Gibson was glad for her deal with Dunlop but, speaking at the press conference in New York to announce the relationship, she was clear that whatever the company offered her—the terms were not made public—it was not enough: "I'll have to win something to keep going. Dunlop isn't paying all expenses."[97]

Gibson kept private her suspicions that race had hampered and delayed her ability to get a sponsor, but she was surrounded by evidence that she was right. By and large, major American companies were not hiring Black athletes, even undisputed stars like Willie Mays, Hank Aaron, Bill Russell, and Muhammad Ali, to pitch their products.[98] Some advertisers in 1963 were beginning to integrate African Americans into their appeals to consumers in mainstream media rather than exclusively in Black-targeted publications. The civil rights movement combined with the realization that African Americans accessed mainstream (White) publications launched the slow inclusion of Black faces and bodies in department store display windows, print media advertisements, and television commercials. Gibson was part of the slow trend. In June, the Equitable Life Assurance Society used a drawing of her playing tennis alongside a little White girl in an advertisement published in *Sports Illustrated*. "Will she be as great a player as Althea Gibson?" the copy asked.[99] Businesses tended to base decisions regarding race and the selection of models and spokespeople on the presumed comfort levels of their White consumers with having African Americans in their midst. As long as golf and country clubs continued to exclude African Americans as members and teaching professionals, the likelihood that Gibson would land other golf-related sponsorship deals would remain low.[100]

For the time being, Gibson was content to stay silent about the personal effect of the racial disparity and to insist that she could blend social advocacy and business. "My hope is, I can help bring more Negroes into the game of golf," she said at the Dunlop press conference. "Sports has a wonderful language—something everyone understands."[101] Money was like that, too, and Gibson understood that unless her fortunes changed, she would soon be out of it.

———

Race not only affected how much money Gibson made in professional golf but also impacted where she could play. The 1964 LPGA season started in March at the Women's Western Open in Pensacola, Florida, but she was not among the players gathered at Scenic Hills Country Club. The tournament was an invitational, and Gibson was not invited. The Western was not alone. The first several weeks of the LPGA schedule included tournaments in Georgia, Tennessee, South Carolina, and Louisiana, and their organizers did not invite her to play.[102]

In interviews, Gibson came across as blasé about the racial snubs, speaking about them cautiously. She brushed off questions about her inability to play in the other southern LPGA events: "I don't believe my game would be ready that early in the year."[103] When she made her season debut at the St. Petersburg Open, Gibson continued to be self-protective when a local reporter asked about her troubles with race, first in tennis and then in golf. Defying past statements and experiences, she insisted again that she had only recently learned what discrimination was: "I was in my late 20s before I even knew there was such a word." Taking a shot at those who objected to having her in their events, she referred to having received the Wimbledon trophy from Queen Elizabeth and sniffed, "I wonder how many of those people who'd bar me have ever done that."[104]

The civil rights movement was also about defiance, and Gibson again expressed her evolving belief that her golf career could be an instrument for fairness and change. "I want whatever I do to be a good reflection on myself and my race," she said. She was also taking to heart Martin Luther King's "I Have a Dream" speech from the March on Washington. "My goal right now is to become a good golfer, and to be judged by my ability, not by the color of my skin or hair or eyes," she said. "I detest violence. Martin Luther King is doing what he thinks is right, and I admire him for it. The people who go into the streets are doing what they think is right." Speaking of her golf career and her work for Ward, she added, "I'm doing what I think is right."[105]

Gibson found justification for her outlook during the St. Petersburg Open. She made the cut and earned $106.50—minus the required fees. Her 303 score for the four rounds included her "lifetime low on the tour," a 75 on the first day. "I only hope that this is a sign of better things to come for me," she told reporters.[106] Such things would have to wait five weeks, until she played her next event, the Muskogee Women's Golf Tournament, in Oklahoma. Until then, every LPGA tournament was in the Deep South, and she was shut out.

Gibson left St. Petersburg with a reminder that the region was not friendly territory. During tournament week, a man who identified himself as Al Watson sent her a threatening letter. Typed on plain white paper, Watson's message was simple and hostile: "Althea: Suggest in future you confine your playing to Northern cities. Colored not wanted in this locale."[107]

———

Gibson was glad to be invited to play at St. Petersburg for a second time. She had enjoyed being there in 1963. "Everyone was very hospitable and cordial. I was treated like one of the gang, which is all I want," she said.[108]

In many ways, Gibson was just one of the LPGA gang. Possibly linking dark skin with strength, co-founder Patty Berg called Gibson "the strongest looking woman I've ever seen," but the tour was filled with athletic women and several were tall and well muscled.[109] Stars Mary Mills, Kathy Whitworth, Mickey Wright, and Carol Mann were nearly or above six feet in height. More than anything, all the women pursued their careers passionately despite financial strain and the social stigmas that led the media to characterize them as queer because they were sportswomen and because they were not exclusively money-minded. The women of the LPGA were "good-looking but hardy," *Sport* magazine had written six years earlier, and they spent the ten-month golf season "looking for an elusive and somewhat limited pot of gold. But most of them don't do it for the money; they compete because they love the sport and they love the life." The magazine's conclusion—"And what's wrong with that?"—highlighted the general social judgment that women professional golfers were bucking social standards.[110] Underscoring the queerness of LPGA players, writer Frank Littler reminded readers of *Golf Digest* in 1964, "Hearth-and-home, it is believed, are more natural for nubile young women than a continuous trek around the country."[111] The very title of Littler's article, "The Unusual Life of a Woman Pro," underscored their status as outliers.

Together, LPGA players faced public scrutiny of their bodies as well as their gender expressions and choices, including what they wore to the golf course. The exclusively outdoor nature of golf combined with the duration of rounds and variations in temperature and terrain made pants and shorts practical and convenient choices, and like many of her new colleagues, Gibson reached for them often, even exclusively. The preference bothered some spectators. "I attended a recent Ladies PGA tournament and came to the conclusion that most of the touring lady professionals would do themselves a favor if they wore skirts instead of shorts or slacks," a reader wrote to *Golf Digest*.[112] The magazine published the letter in the same issue as "The Unusual Life of a Woman Pro," where Littler assuaged concerns among the public that the women of the LPGA were masculine and blithely unconcerned with meeting gender norms. "The modern proette is as feminine as a Dior model and as poised as a career diplomat," Littler promised. LPGA players, he concluded, were "as sharp-looking a group of women as you will find at any club in the country."[113]

That was not happenstance. Players were attuned to negative perceptions of sportswomen, and they were eager to combat them to sustain their tour. "The prototype image in the public's mind of a female athlete is not a pretty one, which holds true for any women's sport," one player reminded her peers during a meeting in 1961. "This element is being shattered by our dressing better and appearing as feminine as possible at all times."[114] The tour fined players for using profanity. Veterans reminded newcomers that everyone carried a responsibility for the image of the tour to dress femininely when attending public events away from the golf course. Players abided as a matter of "public relations," according to Littler, and received media training to further burnish the association's image. "Fashion-conscious regulars," including Marlene Bauer Hagge, a co-founder of the LPGA, gave others "a short course" in grooming.[115] Ambivalent about the program, Mickey Wright, the LPGA president, accepted it as necessary for the survival of women's sports. "Unfortunately, at that time it was not acceptable for a woman to be an athlete. We all felt that when we were in public, we had to be 'on' like being on a stage, and we had to watch our speech, our mannerisms, and everything we did. Not that anyone needed to, but when you are told that any woman who plays sports is nothing but an amazon; then you have to try to counter act it."[116]

The attentiveness to appearance went beyond concerns about masculinity. The LPGA had rules on players' makeup and the length of shorts. Wirtz kept a close eye on the women's weight, too. The association asked anyone deemed as having "baby fat trouble" or excess weight "between her knees and her waist" not to wear shorts. "The dress has to be pleasing," Wirtz told an interviewer.[117] "We want them to be the All-America type, the kind of girl you'd take home to your mother or son." Black and nearing forty, Gibson's claims to All-American girlhood were doubtful. However, well stocked by her mid-Atlantic couturiers, she had the golf wear, skirts, and dresses to be inconspicuous—sartorially, at least—among the other women on the tour.[118]

Yet Gibson was a conspicuous anomaly on the tour in other ways. Not since Zaharias had another woman on the circuit achieved world fame in one sport before taking up professional golf. Few rookies and relevant newcomers received as much major publicity as Gibson, either. Twice within her first eight months with the LPGA, she received substantive attention in *Golf Digest*, the sport's leading magazine. The first was a short profile in which she discussed her brief history in golf and reiterated her self-belief: "Right now I think I have a 50-50 chance to be the best player in women's golf."[119] Six months later, the magazine published a short first-person essay in which Gibson gave four tips to new golfers: take lessons, "hit the ball squarely," practice as much as possible, and learn to accept defeat.[120] They were universal suggestions, not specific to any particular race, gender, or class. Neither feature included her in cheesecake-style pictures or drew attention to her clothing or to her personal life.

Gibson's status as the only Black player in the LPGA made her among the most-discussed people on the tour. Reporters sought her out for interviews after her rounds and practice sessions, and their articles reminded readers that she was the first and only "Negro" on the circuit. They asked other players what they thought of her. Like Wirtz, the tournament director, most players were diplomatic and spoke of Gibson positively as a person, as a contributor to the development of the LPGA, and as a golfer with the "potential" to improve with more time. Indeed, "potential" was among the most oft-used words applied to Gibson and her game. Fellow players described her ability to hit long drives as the centerpiece of her competitive promise, but at least one colleague thought that driving was the beginning and the end of Gibson's game. Speaking anonymously at St. Petersburg, a player was candid: "That's all she's got, the long ball. She may make some money sometime. Maybe pick up a check for $50 now and then, but she started too late in life and can't compete with the rest of us."[121] Most LPGA players did not openly discuss race, but one suggested that players did not challenge Gibson's presence because she herself said little on the topic. Seemingly unaware of Gibson's statements ahead of the March on Washington, Shirley Englehorn told a reporter, "She would be a real asset to the tour, and I don't think she's trying to crusade for her race."[122] It was not the kind of standard and statement that either a tour leader or anyone else was likely to have applied to the other women of the LPGA.

Crusade or not, Gibson's golf in 1964 was marked by struggle. Her scoring average dropped from 84 to 77.5, an improvement but still too high to be consistently competitive every week. She tamped down her braggadocio, a sure sign that the failures were affecting her. "I'm not trying to be another Babe Zaharias," she said during a tournament stop in Rockton, Illinois. "I'm trying to be as great as I can. I hope to become as good a golfer as possible with the God-given talent I have."[123] Gibson did not conceal her annoyance when people scrutinized her game. When she noticed a reporter and a club pro watching her with more attention than she wanted during a round outside Baltimore, she told them, "I thought it was a very pleasant day until you came along. There's always got to be somebody around trying to spoil a man's fun."[124]

The summer brought the highlight of the year: Gibson earned her LPGA player's card. Getting it marked the end of paying the entry fees and percentages of tournament purses. According to one source, Gibson paid

$400 to the LPGA before getting the card. Starving for a competitive outlet, she ranked receiving her player's card alongside her Wimbledon and Forest Hills triumphs. It represented "a level of accomplishment I hadn't reached in about five years," she said, and made her feel "as if I'd been handed a second birth certificate."[125] Otherwise, the season was an imbrication of on-course failures. She played nearly twenty tournaments, never won, and earned between $560 and $649 in any given year—minus the entry fees and purse percentages. Gibson, in short, was paying to play and losing money. Mickey Wright won eleven of the twenty-seven events that she entered and a total of $32,000, less than a third of what Arnold Palmer won as the top earner on the PGA Tour in 1964, but enough for Wright to continue to invest in the stock market, one of her passions.[126]

In the fall, it looked as if Gibson might beat Wright, golf's "quiet queen."[127] She had a magical first round at the Thunderbird Women's Open in Phoenix. The round was the kind that epitomized why golfers kept playing. Her short-game woes appeared to be in remission. She made four birdies and chipped in from sixty feet for an eagle on the seventeenth hole at the Arizona Biltmore Golf Club. She shot a 69, her new career low. The score placed her one stroke ahead of Wright and gave her the outright lead for the tournament. Gibson was in awe when the round was over. "When you shoot a 69," she told the press after her round, "everything works."[128] In the second round, very little did, and she shot 78. It was not the low round that she had hoped for, but it would have meant that she would make the cut, play the weekend, and possibly earn a check of consequence. It was not to be. Gibson submitted an incorrect scorecard. Still dreaming about her eagle the day before, she wrote the wrong number in the square for the seventeenth hole. By the rules of golf, she was disqualified from the rest of the tournament. Wright finished second, three strokes behind the winner, Ruth Jessen, who pocketed $1,350.[129] The disqualification was an unforced error that she could scarcely afford.

———

Gibson spent the off-season in Southern California. Shirley Spork, one of the founders of the LPGA, invited Gibson to stay with her at Indian Wells Country Club, where Spork gave lessons. While working on her game in Palm Springs and Palm Desert, Gibson took advantage of her proximity to the best players in golf. The PGA's season began in January in the Golden State. She got advice from Arnold Palmer, the reigning Masters champion, in January, at Indian Wells. Julius Boros, who was nearly fifty and still winning on the men's circuit, gave her tips to improve her sand play, and she "eavesdropped" on a lesson that Jack Nicklaus, Masters champion of 1963 and Palmer's chief rival, gave to someone else.[130] She also pondered her future.

Every opportunity to play—and get paid—was precious. As 1965 got under way, golf was Gibson's only source of income. She and Ward ended their partnership that winter. She was more interested in her golf career than in touring the country for the firm. Ward, for its part, was disinterested in backing her foundering golf career and declined to renew her contract. The Dunlop sponsorship was all but finished, too. Gibson borrowed money and committed to penny-pinching, but those measures alone would not be enough to survive on tour. She would have to implement drastic changes in order to make it another year and beyond.[131]

Gibson began her new season inauspiciously for the third straight year at the St. Petersburg Open. She finished near the bottom of the leaderboard after shooting 75 and 80 in the first two rounds, then departed Florida for Wilmington. A reporter for the *Charlotte Observer* spotted her in the gallery watching the action at the PGA's Azalea Open at Cape Fear Country Club and was instantly struck by curiosity. The LPGA was in Mississippi for the Allstate Ladies' Invitational that week before sweeping through the South. Asked why she was not with her colleagues, Gibson answered honestly: "They won't let me play in the upcoming tournaments at Spartanburg (S.C.), Pensacola (Fla.), Jackson (Miss.) or Baton Rouge." She might have added Shreveport and Kentucky, too. The tournaments were invitationals, and none welcomed Gibson. She said years later that clubs that refused to have her on their grounds "would inform LPGA officials," who in turn "told me they didn't agree with the unfortunate decision." The LPGA did not have a "Caucasian clause" like the PGA, but the women's circuit held their events at the courses of Jim Crow clubs just the same.[132]

Gibson's candor in Wilmington was a personal turning point. Previously, she had kept both her concerns and experiences with discrimination in golf to herself, made light of her exclusion, or cast herself as superior to her antagonists; sometimes she did all three at once. She had embarked on her golf career with the "faith" that she would be admitted into all the tournaments that she wished. "If they like me as an individual, and are aware of my attributes, I'm sure they will welcome me," she had told Ed Fitzgerald in 1959.[133] Yet Gibson was not welcome everywhere. She had earned her player's card on a course where the members had not permitted her to use the clubhouse, including the locker room and showers. She never named the club, nor did she go public with the affront. "As long as I was allowed to play on the grounds, the use of the facilities was secondary," she reasoned.[134] Publicizing the situation would have created a headache for herself and for the tour, she thought. As an LPGA apprentice, and a winless one at that, Gibson had not previously felt positioned to speak up. She even accepted the exclusion. "I don't go where I'm not wanted," she told Robert Lipsyte of the *New York Times* in the summer of 1964. "I'm trying to be a good golfer. I have enough problems as it is."[135] Earning membership on the tour, though, emboldened Gibson. She anticipated that her player's card might guarantee her entry into every tournament, including the invitationals in the South. She saw the LPGA as "a kind of family" that would "assist me in getting a fair shake."[136] When she reached the status of LPGA member yet still found herself uninvited to tournaments, she began to complain.

Gibson's protests had the ring of a strategic campaign. Invitationals were one talking point. Back on tour for the Dallas Civitan Open, in late May, she told reporters that she could play everywhere "except when the girls play in Dixie where [tournament organizers] make it very simple": entries were "on an invitation-only basis."[137] Five weeks later, she came to the Atlantic City Country Club, in Northfield, New Jersey, for the U.S. Women's Open, a major and one of the most important tournaments of the year. She got in off the wait-list after an injured Mickey Wright withdrew. Speaking to the press, Gibson held nothing back. She said again that there were "seven tournaments in the South" where she could not play. She also leaned on her second talking point, her lack of a sponsor. "I have been on the golf tour for two years, and I still don't have a sponsor," she told the press. "I think I have done enough for sports and have made enough of a name for myself to deserve some sort of backing—most of the other girls have it. Sponsors help pay expenses when things are lean. They keep you in the fight. . . . It's hard on me when I have to pay my own way." Then, breaking from her habit of dissembling, Gibson openly blamed racism for killing her career: "This makes it very tough on me, because I started golf so late and need every chance I can get. But I don't get the breaks and it's all because of the color of my skin."[138] She missed the cut by five strokes at the open. Her short game and driving accuracy remained weak, but her insistence on talking about the role of race in her golf troubles was stronger than ever.

The next week, Gibson played the Lady Carling Open, in Columbus, Ohio, and spoke again about the problem: "I really can't understand it. I'm not bragging, but I think I've been good in athletics. I've always tried to set a good example for youngsters by living 'right,' but none of the sporting goods firms have offered to back me like they do the other athletes." She searched in vain for an alternative explanation, even as she was certain that she had the right one: "Way in the back of my mind I guess I think it's because of my race. But I hate to think that. And I hate to have the companies think that way. I'm not begging, but I just don't understand it."[139]

Gibson's candor about race and her plight in golf reflected the times. The passage of the Civil Rights Act of 1964, with its creation of the Equal Employment Opportunity Commission (EEOC), had drawn attention to employment discrimination. Gibson was attuned to the civil rights movement, though she was not marching in the streets. She became a shareholder in Freedom National Bank, Jackie Robinson's ambitious venture in Harlem aimed at building wealth among its majority-Black population. The investment showed her awareness that entrepreneurship and property ownership were essential to leveling all playing fields for African Americans. In Baltimore's *Afro-American*, Sam Lacy called her "a successful, if somewhat aloof, representative of colored progress."[140] Famous athlete though she was, Gibson was also a single Black woman shut out from opportunities to advance in her chosen profession, leading her to apply the discourse of inequality to her own situation. Not everyone was convinced that discrimination alone was to blame. The Associated Press, for one, circulated Gibson's quotes from the U.S. Women's Open in an article that ran for days under various headlines that described her as "tak[ing] a rap at," "angry," and "bitter" about discrimination. The AP also noted her undistinguished record as a golfer, "an uphill" battle that was unlikely to attract corporate backers.

Gibson agreed, but she also knew that she was caught in a cycle. The "best strategy" for fighting discrimination was "simply to be a winner," she thought, but discrimination undermined her chances of winning. Like the other women on tour, she expressed pride and pleasure in the circuit. "It's a tough life, but a good life," she told Lipsyte. "You go from country club to country club, stay in the best motels. You have to stay physically prepared, mentally prepared, swing in a groove."[141] Yet Gibson's life on tour was tougher than anything her White colleagues endured. Not being invited to invitationals reduced her earning potential. It also required her to play more tournaments back-to-back later in the season to meet the LPGA requirement that cardholders play 60 percent of all events. She seldom had weeks off to simply practice and rest. She had to play every round as if her career depended on it. Gibson boasted that "my golf game has no weaknesses" and "pressure doesn't worry me. I concentrate hard. I relax hard and let others get high blood pressure." But the racial restrictions in golf meant that her game was under constant stress.[142]

When she was not practicing or playing, Gibson was driving. Behind the wheel of her long and sleek 1963 Cadillac Coupe de Ville, she ferried herself from town to town. Her thoughts ("philosophical things," she said), the radio, and the ambient whir of the air conditioner were her only companions. She was "like a person with blinders on," she said decades later, just "looking straight ahead."[143]

Sometimes, though, Gibson's thoughts shifted to the past long enough to think of Will Darben. Connected by long-distance calls, they had never lost touch, despite the broken engagement in 1961. Will remained in New Jersey, working for Bendix. He held on to his hope that she would marry him and used sweet talk, reassurances about her career, and kindnesses as part of his constant campaign to convince her to do so. He proposed again in 1963, and again she refused. Gibson admired his steadiness and his devotion to his mother until her death in January 1965. On October 17 of that year, Gibson and Will married in Las Vegas. Annie and Daniel were among the small band of family and friends who gathered for the simple, private ceremony at the home of one of Gibson's friends, a local dentist. Four days later, she was back at work. With Will watching, she played in the Thunderbird Open in Phoenix. The next week, she ended her season in New Mexico at the Las Cruces Ladies' Open, where she finished twenty-nine strokes behind the winner, Clifford Ann Creed, and out of the money. She made $1,595 for the year.[144]

Gibson did not immediately tell the press about her marriage. The news simply "leaked out to reporters," said the *Philadelphia Tribune*. Black newspapers on the East Coast were the first to print that she had "at last taken the big plunge" nearly two months earlier, hardly concealing the perception that she was at least a decade behind the marriage trend.[145]

Dressed in their Sunday best, Gibson and Will allowed photographers into the Pleasant Way house to take their first public portraits as a married couple. Will gazed intently at Gibson, who smiled but looked straight ahead. He told reporters that he would support her golf career in hopes that she would have the same success in her second sport as she had achieved in tennis. The timing of the marriage was striking. Gibson could not land a sponsor, but she had found a husband.[146]

Their marriage was companionable in the off-season. Gibson and Will drove into Manhattan, where she introduced him as her husband at fashionable night spots such as the Chateau Madrid and the Living Room. Sometimes they went to the theater and visited friends. At home in Montclair, they played cards, entertained guests, and sat at the piano that she had given him as a wedding present, singing songs and writing them, too. They were like many other married couples approaching middle age in the mid-1960s, but when March began, the unusualness of their union was clear. Will stayed home in New Jersey, and Gibson packed the Cadillac with her gear and headed to Florida to resume her life alone on the golf circuit.[147]

Marriage added another layer to Gibson's status as an outlier within the LPGA. The consensus was that for women, a professional golf career and matrimony, or any committed relationship, did not mix. "I found out I couldn't have romance and golf at the same time," Mickey Wright confided in *Golf Digest*. "Romance is much more disconcerting to the active woman, golfer or not, than the ordinary man. Husbands are expected to be out earning a living—wives are expected to be raising a family."[148]

LPGA discouraged players from taking marriage vows. The appointed tournament director, Lenny Wirtz, was brazen in his, and the association's, preference for unmarried players. "We want quality players who are good-looking," he once told the *Los Angeles Times*. "And we definitely discourage the married ones. We don't even want the girls we have to get married, unless they want to quit golf." Wirtz connected marriage to the ever-present concern over the "image" and public relations of the LPGA. "No matter what they do it creates a bad image. It's bad for us [the LPGA] and it's bad for the girls," he continued. "If the husband travels with his wife, people say, 'What's he doing here? Is he a kept man or something? Why doesn't he get himself a job?' And if he gets a job, and the girl keeps playing golf, people say, 'What kind of marriage is that? Why doesn't she stay home with her husband?'" For the rest of Gibson's time on tour, she was one of a small group, typically only two players, who were married (or known to be), and Wirtz wanted to keep it that way. Of golfer-wives on the circuit, he said flatly, "We don't want any more."[149]

Playing as Althea Gibson Darben, she embraced her new status as a married woman and a full-time professional golfer. The press would butcher her new name for years, misidentifying her as Dobbin, Darbin, Darden, Darbien, Daren, and Darban. One report listed her as "Althea Gibson Darken." Whether that was an innocent mistake or an intentional and tasteless joke no one could say. Yet no matter how her name was misspelled, Gibson retained her feistiness when anyone suggested that she was too old to be successful in golf or pointed out that she was still winless. If she did "crack golf's elite," one writer scrawled, she would do it "at an age when other women are retiring." She paid them no mind, or just enough mind to show she intended to do as she wished whenever she wanted, and she referenced her marriage to justify her presence on tour. "This is my way of life," Gibson pointedly told reporters midway through the Louise Suggs Invitational in Delray Beach, Florida, in March 1966. "I just can't sit back and live off my laurels. Just as long as Mr. Darben lets me, what's gonna stop me?"[150]

Nothing and no one, it seemed. Gibson played in nearly twenty-five tournaments in 1966 and won a little more than $4,000, more than she had earned in her previous seasons combined. She still was not breaking even and never took home a trophy. Yet she had small wins. For one thing, her game showed signs of improvement. In the opening round of the Dallas Civitan Open in May, Gibson shot 31 on the front nine, reportedly the second-best score for nine holes at the host site, Glen Lakes Country Club. Two weeks later, she tied for sixth place at the Babe Zaharias Open. It was the best finish of her career to that point, and she proudly accepted her check for $475.[151]

The highlight of the season came in early August. Carling, the brewing company, was a devoted sponsor of the LPGA, supporting two tournaments for the season. The first Lady Carling Open of 1966 was held over three rounds in Sutton, a small town in central Massachusetts. Gibson found the course at Pleasant Valley Country Club to her liking on the first day. She had the type of round that would bring any golfer back for more. She overcame a three-putt from forty feet on the second hole by making birdies on two of her next three holes to shoot an even-par 37 on the front nine. Then Gibson caught fire on the back. With approach shots that landed as close as eighteen inches to three feet from the cup, she made five birdies to shoot a 31, the lowest score ever by a woman on Pleasant Valley's back nine. The 68, her lowest round on tour, gave her the overnight lead, four strokes ahead of Shirley Englehorn, and the women's course record at Pleasant Valley.[152]

It was too good to last. The next day, Gibson imploded with an 86. Golf is never the same game twice, even on the same course. The dreamy back nine of the day before turned into a nightmare. Gibson made a double bogey on Pleasant Valley's fifteenth hole, a quintuple bogey on the seventeenth, and a comparatively benign bogey on the eighteenth. Gibson was a methodical—some thought plodding—player anyway. The desire to succeed, and the pressure that she felt to play well, sometimes led her to move from shot to shot with indecision and deliberation. That took time, hers and that of the people who played either with or behind her. So did shooting 86. After the round, Wirtz gave Gibson a slow-play penalty of two strokes, making her official score 88. She shot 236 for the tournament, twenty-one strokes behind the winner, Kathy Whitworth, finished tied for twenty-fourth, and pocketed $120 for her trouble.[153]

On the upside, there were more golf courses where Gibson could find trouble. The specifics are hazy, but her comments about the racism behind the invitational system were yielding results. Sometime after she went public about discrimination on the circuit, the members of the LPGA held a meeting to discuss access to tournaments. Amid boycotts, protests, sit-ins, and desegregation efforts in public spaces and voting rights, prejudice and exclusion were not good for the image of the LPGA or any struggling business that craved all the attention, and ticket sales, that it could muster. Members voted that the association should hold events only at courses and clubs where everyone could play. Wirtz supported the outcome and went about the work of implementing it. He also had a private conversation with Gibson and asked her to stop talking about discrimination. She agreed. She noticed in the coming months that some cities and private clubs where she had previously encountered discrimination or had not been permitted to play were removed from the LPGA schedule.[154]

For the rest of her time with the association, Gibson would speak of racism on tour as a thing of the past. She did not deny that "unpleasant situations" had happened "in the South and West" and said that "some ugly scenes" had been part of her experience in golf, but she rarely went into the details.[155] She talked in general terms about not being allowed to eat, change shoes, or "fix my hair" in some clubhouses, but she did not say where or when the offenses occurred.[156] The LPGA "just never went back to those clubs," she insisted, and "won't stand for that."[157]

Midland, Texas, appears to have been one of the cities where the LPGA had to take a stand. In the 1980s, Gibson told Stan Hart, a tennis fan and writer, that she had not been permitted to use the clubhouse during a tournament there. She was in Midland four times during her golf career. She played its Tall City Open at the Hogan Park Golf Course in 1964, 1966, and 1968, and in 1967, when Midland Country Club hosted the event. If Gibson definitively named the site that refused to let her inside the clubhouse, Hart, in a book long on stories but short on fact-checking, either did not remember it or chose not to say. Hart did, however, write that tournament organizers eventually allowed Gibson to change her shoes inside the clubhouse.[158]

To Hart, Gibson also expressed gratitude for Marlene Bauer Hagge, whom she remembered as among the players who refused to play in any tournament that would not accept her. When a hotel in Columbus, Ohio, refused to honor Gibson's reservation, Hagge let her stay in her room. Hart wrote that Hagge was Gibson's "roommate" on tour. In *So Much to Live For*, she thanked Hagge's sister, Alice Bauer Hovey, too. Gibson's touching yet vague remembrance of Hovey as having gone "out of her way on one occasion to give me a lesson in humanity as well as golf" suggests that the younger sister had been an ally to Gibson in a different way. Lenny Wirtz recalled intervening when a different hotel claimed to have lost her reservation. When tournament sponsors said they did not want Gibson to attend social functions such as dinners, Wirtz would take her to restaurants, where he noticed that some waitstaff were deliberately slow in serving them, prompting the pair to leave and find another place to eat.[159]

The recognition also showed Gibson's entrenched reluctance to speak openly about the indignities she faced. In her 2017 memoir, Shirley Spork wrote, "When we played the U.S. Women's Open in Oklahoma, the tournament site had a 'White Only' policy in their clubhouse. If Althea couldn't go in, the rest of us wouldn't either. We all changed our shoes in the car."[160] Press coverage proves that Gibson played all four rounds, finished twelve strokes out of first place, and won $455 at the 1970 U.S. Women's Open, held at Muskogee Country Club in July, but an account of a protest by as many as 134 players, the number entered in the tournament, appears either not to have been recorded by or to have escaped the notice of the media. Spork told the story as evidence of the LPGA's unity: "We were a small group, but we were a family, and we stuck together." Yet the Open would have been run by the USGA, not the LPGA. One wishes for extant records to verify and give specifics to Spork's story, especially since Gibson seems never to have spoken of either clubhouse restrictions or a unified protest in Muskogee and because it is unclear that Spork was in Oklahoma for the tournament. A news account places her in Carefree, Arizona, for a teaching seminar that week.[161]

Of course, Gibson had long since renewed her habit of speaking minimally about racism. Prejudice was "something I can live with" and the preoccupation of "people who think irrationally," she said. She felt "sorry for" the bigots, not for herself.[162] She could even find humor in their ignorance, quipping to *Ebony* a few years later, "I don't know if they thought I was going to eat the grass. All I wanted to do was hit the ball off it."[163] By 1967, she had what she wanted: "I'm a member of the LPGA and wherever the tour goes I play."[164]

Gibson also had more money in the bank. She actively sought financial support. Speaking to a reporter in Worcester, Massachusetts, she made a clever appeal that further revealed her faith. "I'm just hoping . . . that some good Samaritan would come along with a kind heart and see the predicament that I might be in and say, 'Well, here, Althea, go out and play a few years longer.' "[165] The Beverly Hills chapter of the NAACP could not fulfill her request for support due to lack of money, but two black doctors did. William

Cassio of Montclair and William Hayling of Newark sponsored her for the year with $500 each, and Cassio committed to a second, too. Corporate America could be ambivalent toward Gibson, but she had a knack for securing aid from Black doctors.[166]

By 1967, Gibson was not the only Black woman playing the tour. Renee Powell, twenty-one, had just started her first season with the LPGA as a professional that summer after two years of entering tournaments as an amateur. Gibson and Powell had played in some of the same LPGA and UGA tournaments for years. In 1963, Powell, then seventeen, teamed with Ted Beattie, an accomplished White junior golfer from Cincinnati who held the UGA's national boys' title, to beat Gibson and Joe Louis in an amateur exhibition event at Chicago's Pipe-O-Peace Golf Course. It was the type of victory that validated *Ebony*'s description of Powell as the "Girl Golfing Marvel" and its prediction that she "may become the Althea Gibson of golf."[167] As a rookie professional, in July, Powell paired with Gibson in Grand Blanc, Michigan, for the Yankee Women's Open, a rare team event on the women's circuit. Sixty miles away, Detroit was literally on fire. Sparked by a police raid on a bar that operated without a license on the famed 12th Street, the Detroit Uprising of 1967 raged for nearly a week as thousands of Black Detroiters let out their fury over decades of marginalization and mistreatment by the state, including the police. The Motor City was not alone, as Los Angeles, Oakland, Plainfield, New Jersey, Washington, D.C., and other cities in the urban North and West became sites of rebellion in the mid- and late 1960s. When the uprising in Detroit ended, forty-three people were dead, hundreds of others were injured, and more than seven thousand people were arrested.[168]

The number on Gibson's and Powell's minds was eight—as in the number of strokes that they finished behind the winners, Gloria Ehret and Judy Kimball. Gibson and Powell were outside the top ten, but far from the smoke and flames in Detroit they achieved a first: never had two Black women teamed in an LPGA event. When a reporter asked Gibson that weekend about prejudice in golf, she returned to her old dissembling habit of seeing sports through rose-colored glasses: "We've got no problems. People in sports are very liberal minded. They don't judge you by the color of your skin or the color of your eyes. All they're interested in is your ability."[169] Apparently satisfied with Wirtz's efforts on her behalf, she saw golf as unlike the rest of America, especially Detroit.

Gibson and Powell shared a desire to play golf as a way of life, not as a political undertaking. Powell's parents, William and Marcella Powell, were the proprietors of their own nine-hole golf course in East Canton, Ohio, and she began playing at age three. Clearview Golf Course was the first golf course constructed, owned, and operated exclusively by individual African Americans. The Powells launched Clearview with money borrowed from William's brother Barry and two Black doctors and from a second mortgage on their house. Their project was a pursuit of democracy and an act of defiance. William had caddied as a boy, belonged to the golf team at Wilberforce University with Barry in the 1930s, and played golf with White soldiers while stationed in England during World War II. Yet when he returned to Canton after the war, none of the public golf courses would allow him to play. Renee Powell had encountered discrimination, too. As with Gibson, the invitational system had limited her ability to enter tournaments earlier in her career, and she, too, had faced other hostilities. At the start of the 1967 season, Powell received death threats when she played in the St. Petersburg Open. Nevertheless, she played on, reasoning, "You're going to do something, right? So this way I'm doing something I really enjoy."[170]

Powell surmised that personal satisfaction guided Gibson in golf, too. Gibson continued to believe that her career could be a source of inspiration for other Black people, especially women and girls. "If my being out here and playing golf can be some stimulation to other young ladies of my race to play golf," she said in Wisconsin, "then I feel I've made a contribution. In everything, there has got to be a beginning."[171] Powell appreciated what Gibson had endured in tennis and golf as a living Black first. Where racial strife was concerned, "Althea went through more of that than I did," Powell said years later.[172] She thought Gibson was a blend of stoicism and vulnerability, "hardened to" discrimination with the outward appearance that racist "things didn't bother her," and a "gentle person," too.[173] Still, Powell deduced, Gibson made decisions with her own best interest in mind. "I remember Althea told me she was on her own at the age of fourteen. It didn't matter to her, I don't think, what anybody thought or how they felt."[174] She "was focused on playing the game," Powell said fifty years after the Yankee Open. "She wasn't trying to open doors. She was just trying to play [golf] and make a living."[175]

Gibson earned some of the largest checks of her career that season and came as close to making a living in golf as she ever had, but the money still was not enough. She won $570 with a fifth-place finish at the Venice Open in March. She credited Teddy Rhodes with the result. Rhodes, who wintered in Florida, gave Gibson direct and indelicate advice after watching her shoot 79 in the third round: "Get that big butt around! Get your hips pointed toward where you want the ball to go."[176] She listened and the next day shot 68. Weeks later, her team won the pro-am at the Azalea Open in Raleigh, North

Carolina, and split $1,500. Excited by her turnaround, Gibson visited Rhodes at Cumberland Golf Course in Nashville, Tennessee, for more lessons. "No one has made golf as emphatic and clear to me as Teddy Rhodes," she said.[177]

Gibson felt empowered after their visit. In Milwaukee for the Jaycees Open, she faced down questions about her record of defeat and whether her career remained viable. She insisted that she was "beginning to feel" that she would win a tournament soon: "It's because I'm Althea Gibson. Maybe because I'm a champion I think like a champion."[178] She backed up her talk by tying for sixth place and winning $800. A few days later, Gibson was brimming with pride when she finished in second place at a charity pro-am in Chicago: "I'm beginning to come into my own. I have had three years of experience as a golf pro. It's starting to come."[179] In September, Gibson finished in a tie for third at the Pacific Ladies' Golf Classic in Junction City, Oregon, and won $940. Otherwise, she picked up checks for a couple of hundred dollars here, a hundred dollars there, and even as low as $33 at the Azalea. Players estimated that they needed between $6,000 and $8,000 to last on tour for a season. Only twenty-five players made that much money in 1967. With $5,567.50 in twenty-five tournaments, Gibson was not one of them. Another golf season ended, and she was still barely getting by.[180]

⸺

Daniel mellowed with age, putting to rest the rage and frustration that had led him to mistreat his family, especially Gibson, when he was younger. He quietly lived out his days in the house that she had bought for him and for Annie. Gibson's second cousin Don Felder had neither memory nor knowledge of Daniel's abusive behavior until he read *I Always Wanted to Be Somebody* as an adult. The Uncle Dush that the adolescent Felder knew played cards and sat innocuously enough when relatives visited on weekends. Daniel's death in May 1967 put Gibson in a reflective mood. He had been sick for a few years, but she still found a shocking suddenness in his death. She was glad that he had lived long enough to "see me make something out of myself and to receive a few of the humble benefits of my success."[181] Daniel's dream had been for Gibson to make reams of money as a professional athlete, if not in boxing, then in tennis. He never saw that. Dissatisfied with the way that her first stint in professional tennis had gone, she decided to give it another try.

The financial prospects in the sport were better than ever by 1968. In February, the USLTA voted in favor of open tennis, joining its British counterpart, the Lawn Tennis Association (LTA). The next month, the leaders of French tennis threw their support behind amateurs and professionals facing off in competition, too. The International Lawn Tennis Federation (ILTF) approved as well. "The time for a change is now, for a better world of tennis," said Bob Kelleher, the USLTA president.[182]

Plenty of players agreed. On April 1, Billie Jean King, Rosie Casals, Ann Jones, and Françoise Dürr joined the newly formed National Tennis League tour, the brainchild and investment of George MacCall, a player turned promoter. MacCall signed King, the Wimbledon women's singles champion of 1966 and 1967, to a two-year contract worth $80,000 ($681,100 in 2022) and guaranteed her more money based upon her finishes at events. Maxwell House, the coffee company, gave King her first endorsement deal. King was thrilled by the turn of events: "I was finally getting a living wage for doing what I loved."[183]

It was an experience that Gibson had yet to know in golf, and 1968 was no different. Her fifth full season with the LPGA was another bust. There were highlights, to be sure. She finished sixth at the Azalea Open in Raleigh in April, just six strokes behind Carol Mann, the tournament winner and the best player on tour, and won more than $700. Playing at Moselem Springs Golf Club in Reading, Pennsylvania, Gibson made the cut for the first time at the U.S. Women's Open. Still, the lows outnumbered the highs: scores in the 80s, penny-ante checks, and, most dramatic of all, a dressing down from Lenny Wirtz. After a round at the Pabst Classic Golf Tournament in Columbus, Ohio, in July, Wirtz reportedly "bawled out Althea" in the parking lot of the tournament motel for playing too slowly and holding up the players who followed behind her.[184] By August, she had had enough. Gibson took the $2,700 that she earned in nineteen tournaments and ended her season. She returned to New Jersey to see Will and to have surgery to remove a minor growth from her left arm.[185]

Gibson initially denied that she wanted to make a comeback in professional tennis. "Are you kidding? At my age?" she responded when asked. "I ran around the tennis courts for 20 some years. That's enough. I retired as undefeated champion, and that's the way it's going to stay."[186]

But it was not. Soon after her release from Newark's Presbyterian Hospital, Gibson began to plot a strategy to be a dual-sport athlete. She imagined playing golf in early 1969 and then spending several weeks preparing for the U.S. Open, which began in August. She ignored that she had not played a competitive match since 1961. "As long as I've got the big serve, I'm all right," she reasoned.[187]

It did not take long for Gibson to secure a tournament invitation. After meeting her at Forest Hills in September, King's husband, Larry, invited her to the International Invitational Pro Tennis Tournament in Oakland. Scheduled for February, the tournament had a $10,000 purse, with $2,500 guaranteed for the winner. King invited Gibson to join her in leading a tennis clinic sponsored by Planters Peanuts for children in Philadelphia a few weeks before the tournament. King had seen her play only once, at the Pacific Southwest in Los Angeles in 1957 when King was just thirteen years old, and she once described herself as "more impressed with" Maureen Connolly.[188] The overtures were, King said later, gestures of gratitude for a "long-ago inspiration."[189]

Gibson dove headfirst into preparing for the tournament. Her name helped. Businessman Leonard Bordonaro invited her to practice and play at the Eastern Indoor Tennis Courts, the tennis bubble that he co-owned in Hackensack. Her association with the Eastern brought publicity to the club. Through the fall and winter, Gibson worked out for as many as five hours a day, hitting balls against Steve Siegel, the sixteenth-ranked amateur in the country, and Jim Federici, the club's pro. Getting back in shape hurt. Her hands felt weak and her muscles ached, but she refused to quit. Gibson had "been through the hard knocks" and believed that she could summon the strength to be competitive again. Just before Christmas, she went public with her decision to play the tournament in Oakland, explaining, "Tennis is my first love and that's where the money is." She was also out to prove that her best days were not behind her. She was searching for an agent, and the visibility that came with playing tennis again might help, but no one was expressing interest in representing her: "It's almost as if they're saying I'm a has-been."[190]

So Much to Live For, Gibson's second memoir, was intended to fight the perception that she was a washed-up athlete, but the results were mixed. Curious about her decision to leave amateur tennis, Richard Curtis, a freelance writer from New York, approached her about writing a book that described her life since 1958. She gave a candid account of her myriad disappointments and pursuits—the album that "sank beneath a sea of indifference," the challenges of portraying Lukey with dignity in *The Horse Soldiers*, the financial failure and disillusionment that followed her tennis tour, the draining work for Ward, her difficult transition to golf, and reuniting with Will, whom she dispassionately likened to "a vital organ."[191] She also refrained from the kind of controversial comments about race that earned the scorn of critics who read her first book. Instead, *So Much to Live For* showed Gibson as willing to fight for her right to earn a living in professional golf. The book ended as a promotional appeal. Gibson described at length the "nonprofit academy" she hoped to lead for young athletes, her interest in a career as a singer, her search for a manager, and the need for sponsorship so that she could remain on the LPGA Tour.

G. P. Putnam's Sons published *So Much to Live For* in the fall of 1968. The company marketed the book in a series, Sports Shelf Biographies, intended for young adults, an odd choice given its mature story of loss, disenchantment, and a desperate comeback. Gibson was the only female athlete with a book in the series, and Putnam's, apparently unsure of the best marketing strategy, hedged. One cover showed an illustration of Gibson's face surrounded by her golf clubs, while another depicted a golfer, a race car driver, and basketball, football, and baseball players, none of whom were women. Filled with over-wrought prose and "word jumbles," according to *Kirkus Reviews*, *So Much to Live For* received generic reviews and was not given the splashy promotional campaign that Harper and Row had given *I Always Wanted to Be Somebody* ten years earlier.[192] The treatment from Putnam's and the bland reception were further evidence of how considerably her fame had diminished.

Times had changed in the modern sports scene, making it harder for Gibson to remain relevant. Sports integration was no longer controversial or novel. Black athletes played in all three of the major professional sports leagues and golf. The college conferences, even those in the South, were inte-grating. Winning and profits, as much as developing social consciences, had led even die-hard segregationists to change their minds.[193]

Ostensibly, the civil rights and Black Power movements had given younger generations of Black athletes greater latitude when talking about race than Gibson had ever been able to practice. Some, like Arthur Ashe and O. J. Simpson, were moderate or even conservative in their rhetoric. Others spoke candidly about their personal experiences with racial prejudice and shared their passionate observations about the endurance of racism in America. "The Black Athlete: A Shameful Story," a five-part series published in *Sports Illustrated* in the summer of 1968 and later expanded into a book, brought Americans face to face with the inequality that divided sports, especially the collegiate scene, and disabused readers of facile notions that African American athletes were content at predominantly White schools. The integration of college sports brought together young African American men on teams across the country while the winds of activism and social awareness swirled. Fed up with prejudice on their campuses and aware that their athletic skills gave them power, Black athletes staged protests and demonstrations, which sometimes included refusing to play scheduled games until their demands were met. The movement came to be known as the Revolt of the Black Athlete. The Summer Olympics drew further attention to the discontent of many Black athletes through the long public debate about whether the Mexico City games should be boycotted, and again after the event got began and Tommie Smith and John Carlos staged their famous protest on the medal podium, where they raised their black-gloved fists in a Black Power salute. Yet the swift and lingering backlash to Smith and Carlos's action showed that it was still risky for Black athletes to speak or act against racism. Branded as radicals, both men were excoriated in the press, were ostracized by the public, and endured years of job discrimination that set off financial problems. Their experience was a cautionary tale whose moral was that athletes who kept their thoughts about prejudice to themselves could also keep their careers and prosper financially.[194]

At the same time, a generational changing of the guard was happening. Younger African Americans did not automatically respect Black sports legends. While doing community outreach in New York, Jackie Robinson faced ridicule for being "an Uncle Tom," and in Mexico City Black members of the U.S. Olympic track and field team insulted Jesse Owens, who opposed both the proposed boycott and Smith and Carlos's demonstration. The chosen models for activist-minded young Black athletes were men like Muhammad Ali, for whom race and religion were at the center of his opposition to the Vietnam War, and Bill Russell, the center and coach for the Boston Celtics who was vocal in his opposition to racism, his support for social justice, and his quest for diversity and fairness in the NBA. When it came to Black athletes in the late sixties, the media, many members of the public, and budding sports stars were interested in militancy, masculinity, youth, and victories, leaving no room for Gibson.[195]

When Gibson arrived at the Oakland Coliseum Arena for the International Invitational Pro Tennis Tournament, she was noticeably different from her competitors. She had won five majors on her own, one fewer than Jones, King, Dürr, and Casals combined, but that had been a dozen years earlier. At forty-one, she was eleven, fifteen, sixteen, and twenty-one years older than the other women, respectively. She was also the only player who did not have a professional contract. King, who was recovering from knee surgery, was diplomatic when asked how Gibson looked in their warm-up sessions, saying that it was "hard to evaluate how tough she'll be here from watching her practice."[196] Gibson insisted that she was ready: "If I didn't think I could play, I wouldn't be trying this." Yet she also sounded a note of caution, adding that she would "still have to prove a few things."[197] Gibson would not prove them in Oakland. The synthetic court was too fast, her volleys missed their targets, and she had a tough time returning serves. Awarded a bye in the first round, she lost her subsequent matches to Jones,

Dürr, and Casals, and won $500. King, the tournament winner, thought Gibson "or anyone attempting a comeback like this needs at least a year to get back into form."[198] Others were not sure that Gibson should give her sports career another day. Bill Nunn Jr., who had written about her since her first and more successful foray in tennis, said, "I hope the time comes when . . . Althea Gibson would realize that her days as a super athlete are behind her."[199]

———

Gibson returned to the LPGA tour in the spring. Her decisions, travels, and statements all suggested that she was still confident in her golf game. Bragging to build herself up was a reflex for her, so she claimed again that she still hoped to "match" Babe Zaharias's accomplishments.[200] Gibson accepted financial backing from Abe Margolies, the president of Zales Jewelers, who gave her $150 a week to stay afloat through the fall. She played one tournament after another, including the Tournament of Champions in Winnipeg in August and the Molson Canadian Classic in September. When a reporter asked Gibson whether she had a favorite player in mind to win the Molson, she shot back with laughter, "Yeah, me!"[201] Yet money and marriage prevented her from keeping up the façade that she was happy. She was looking for a way out of professional golf.

Gibson had driven all the way to Canada from Missouri only to earn nothing in Winnipeg and somewhere between $33 and $36 in Vancouver. The Molson ended on Sunday, September 7, as the U.S. Open was being waged at Forest Hills. Margaret Court won the women's singles title and received a check for $6,000.[202] During the trip to Canada, Gibson spoke openly about her finances and her golf career. After years of being reluctant to use money as a measure of her success in golf, she made an abrupt about-face: "You cannot play professional tennis if there is no income, and I'm not making much income at this golf either."[203] She needed money for golf, but she did not play golf for the money, she said: "I don't really have to play golf for the money. But any money I do win sure helps pay the bills."[204] She was responsible for paying those bills on her own. Speaking to reporters in the clubhouse at Shaughnessy Golf and Country Club, Gibson spoke of Will and their modern marriage. They had, wrote Ann Barling of the *Vancouver Sun*, a "mutual agreement that Althea was to play golf as long as she was still interested and perhaps as long as she could make some sort of living on her own—to pay her own way."[205] Others suggested that Will supported her career and that friends gave her money, too.[206]

More and more, Will factored into Gibson's growing disenchantment with golf. She had been on the road for months and would not return to New Jersey until the end of October. Golf was a hard game as it was. Playing with guilt made it tougher. "I'm feeling my responsibility towards my husband right now," she confessed in Canada.[207] A week after their fourth wedding anniversary, Gibson was in Texas for the Dallas Civitan Open, and her mind was filled with doubts: "I'm just not sure I want to stay on the road for months at a time without accomplishing much." That she had decided long ago that God and spirituality were driving forces behind her golf career made the decision to leave the game and the circuit more difficult. It did not help that she had fallen into the trap of believing that she had to win to prove to others—and even to herself—that she was "worthy of being loved and respected."[208]

Gibson thought about giving her singing career another try. She claimed to be working with a contact who was making an act for her, though she was not keen on "night club work, although it would be lucrative." She found being "a recording artist" appealing.[209] Gibson wrote in *So Much to Live For* that Nat Sackin, the former owner of the Bon Soir in Greenwich Village, where Woody Allen and Barbra Streisand launched their careers, was "regularizing my business affairs and cultivating my talents," while pianist Sammy Benskin helped her select songs and seek "maximum effectiveness" when she sang. Sackin questioned whether she was directing her time and energy to a music career.[210] As long as she remained on the golf circuit, the answer was no.

Yet, fighter that she was, Gibson refused to give up her unorthodox way of looking at her golf career. "I'm a winner who hasn't won yet," she rationalized to a reporter in Dallas. She decided that not every victory came with a check or a trophy. "When you consider the time I've had to play the game of golf, and the fact that I've improved consistently," she meditated, "maybe I have won something."[211] She would spend the next nine months, her longest break from golf, thinking about it.

For the first time in years, March did not find Gibson in Florida, preparing to begin her golf season. Instead, she was still at home in New Jersey in the spring of 1970. The Essex County Park Commission announced that it had hired her to work as its "special sports consultant." She would develop and encourage athletic participation among the county's citizens, especially in the cities and schools and among girls in basketball and tennis. Gibson's appointment coincided with celebrations of the seventy-fifth anniversary of the Essex County parks system, among the oldest such institutions in the country. She expressed satisfaction in the appointment. While not the leadership role at the sports academy she dreamed of, the county job was something. "It gives me a chance to use the talents which God endowed me with to make a contribution to the lives of young people."[212] It also gave her a dignified exit out of golf.

Before doing so, Gibson made one last campaign for her own cause. She started her season in the late spring, and when she arrived at the Immke Buick Open in Columbus, Ohio, she was as fresh as she had been in years. Gibson shared the first-round lead of 71, one under par. She had caught a break in the scheduling: she started and finished her round before a thunderstorm delayed play for more than two hours. In the second round, she shot a 68 to take the overnight lead outright.[213]

If she had shot 76, four over par, in the third and final round, Gibson would have won. Instead, nervous and unfamiliar with the feeling of playing with the lead when the trophy was on the line, she shot 77 and found herself in a playoff with two experienced winners, Sandra Haynie and Mary Mills, the LPGA's rookies of the year for 1961 and 1962, respectively. Haynie lost when she made par on the first extra hole and Gibson and Mills made birdies.[214]

Standing on the tee box of the par-4, four-hundred-yard fourth hole at Raymond Memorial Golf Course, Gibson looked to be Mills's equal. She was as tall as Mills and as strong, and like Mills, she hit her drive straight down the middle of the fairway. Mills hit her second shot onto the green, her ball landing fifteen feet from the cup. Catching more sod than ball, Gibson hit her shot fat. She missed the green short. Minutes later, her pitch to the cup left her with a par putt that she missed. Mills, who had been eight strokes behind at the start of the round, two-putted for par and won the tournament. The playoff loss was as close as Gibson ever came to winning on the LPGA Tour.[215]

13

The Harvest

They called me a pioneer, but pioneers don't reap the harvest.

—ALTHEA GIBSON

THE DAY AFTER her forty-third birthday, Gibson teamed with Australian Judy Tegart Dalton to win a doubles match in the first round of the Marlboro Open in South Orange, New Jersey. Gibson's "comeback," as the press called it, was short-lived.[1] A Russian doubles team knocked her and Dalton out of the tournament in the second round. Gibson put her rackets and golf clubs away, while Dalton survived until the singles semifinals, then prepared to play in the First Houston Women's International Tennis Tournament, an event for eight players at the Houston Racquet Club. Gladys Heldman, the founder of *World Tennis* magazine, organized the event. Billie Jean King, the face of women's tennis, and Rosie Casals would be there, too. Less than two full days before the tournament began—but after years of sexist disrespect in amateur and professional tennis, including huge disparities in prize money—King, Dalton, Casals, and the other players defied the wishes of the USLTA and signed contracts with Heldman to form their own professional tennis tour. The name of the tournament changed to the Virginia Slims Invitational of Houston, reflecting the sponsorship of Philip Morris, the tobacco company that saw tennis as an attractive way to promote its newest line of cigarettes to women. Including Heldman, the group of founders came to be known as the Original 9. With Heldman as its promoter and Philip Morris as its lead sponsor, the Virginia Slims Circuit changed sports forever. At last women tennis players had a viable league for consistent competition and could make livelihoods through their sport.[2]

The Virginia Slims Circuit proved a lasting success. By 1971, its players traveled together, played wherever a tennis court could be found or made, and went out of their way to publicize their tournaments, including through their attire, designed by Teddy Tinling. Setting up the tour was hard work, but, as

King reminisced five decades later, it was also "glorious, side-splitting, outrageously good fun. It felt like we were spinning straw into gold." Across the country, the press covered the circuit and the public bought tickets. King felt gratified: "For the first time, a lot of women players were making real money, and we were determined to keep it going." The founding of the Virginia Slims Circuit was, in a word, "revolutionary."[3]

But the revolution came too late for Gibson. She had lived most of her life reaching milestones—graduating from high school and college, winning her major tennis titles, embarking on her golf career, and marrying—at advanced ages compared to her peers and most others. "You've come a long way, baby" was the famous slogan of Virginia Slims. It was clear that Gibson had come along too early to reap the rewards that were coming to King, Dalton, and the other women a dozen years after she and Karol Fageros had tried to make sustainable careers in professional tennis. "They called me a pioneer, but pioneers don't reap the harvest," Gibson noted poignantly yet matter-of-factly.[4]

Still, Gibson refused to give up the toil; after a lifetime of playing sports, she could not, for both personal and professional reasons. She would spend the rest of her life cobbling together a livelihood through gigs—sophisticated ones, but gigs all the same. In the 1970s, she took advantage of America's warmth to the idea that women and girls, including those who were Black, deserved more and better opportunities in sports than she had known, vocally supporting the changes and speaking up for women's rights, all while seeking opportunities to sustain her name recognition and achieve her career goals.

The transition was born of necessity. Gibson took a long, hard look at her finances in 1970 and faced a sobering reality long in the making. She recounted the realization years later: "You gotta eat. You gotta pay the rent. You gotta pay bills, car insurance, and things like that. I wasn't making enough money to do that."[5]

———

Gibson embarked on her new job as the sports consultant for the Essex County Park Commission at the end of the year. The work was hardly glamorous and required her to limit her travels to New Jersey, but she made the most of it. Emceeing an ice show that was a fundraiser for skating clinics in Newark looked like a fall for the mighty, but she rose to the occasion, raising her commanding voice and presence to do the job. Other activities, like running day camps in tennis and basketball for girls and visiting high school assemblies to talk with students, were more her speed.[6]

When the Girls Athletic Council at Montclair High School invited Gibson to speak, she accepted and led a "chat" that came straight from her days as the public relations rep for Ward. She boasted plenty, describing herself as "a fabulous basketball player, a good bowler and the greatest quarterback and passer my block ever saw on a touch football team." She also implored the students to stay in school.[7]

Gibson took seriously her interactions with the youths and saw herself as having a special mission, especially with female members of her audiences. "I try to offer something to the young ladies, and the women, something to stimulate them to take up a sport," she told an interviewer in March 1971. She was promoted to recreation supervisor for the county by the summer. The job was full-time and gave her a steady paycheck as well as a chance to serve the public good. She accepted the opportunity, saying, "I hope that maybe in some way I can make a contribution."[8]

Yet Gibson remained frustrated by the feeling that her past contributions, made without recompense during her amateur tennis days, were not being satisfactorily rewarded. When Linda Elliott, a reporter for the fledgling magazine *Black Sports*, interviewed her, Gibson did not hold back regarding what Elliott perceived as her "disappointment." "When I came out of tennis as the world champ and turned pro in golf in '63, I was a big name in sports. You'd think some sporting goods company would have signed me, but to this day I still haven't received an invitation to associate with any firm," she said, overlooking the eventual though short-lived association with Dunlop. Gibson argued that it would be "good business to put my name on a tennis racquet or a golf club or even to have used me for endorsements." She explained that racism, sexism, and ageism stymied her career. "It appalls me that as a Black female athlete I have not been approached to be sponsored by any major manufacturers or asked to affiliate with any sporting goods companies," she continued. "I'm convinced that the answer has nothing to do with 'too many players are now on staff' or 'I'm too old,'" as corporate representatives told her again and again. Speaking with Elliott, Gibson's frustrations boiled over. "I'm just as vibrant and talented at golf at 43 as I was when I first started playing and I'm still acceptable to offers of sponsorship." Gibson expected others to believe that she could provide a high return on investment for a corporate sponsor despite her age, her lack of success in golf, her loss of the ability to compete at the highest level in tennis, and her decline in fame. Her primary concern remained herself, and she readily admitted that she still faced the "same problem" in her golf career that she had in professional tennis: "being financed."[9] She played fewer than ten LPGA tournaments in 1971. When she did not miss cuts, she took home only a few hundred dollars. Despite her limited resources, Gibson still held on to her dream of staying on the tour if she could "get a sponsor." Her most ardent wish was for the disparity between men's and women's purses in golf to shrink. "I'd like to see the ladies make a good buck every week," she told *Ebony*. "I think they put as much time and effort into the sport as men do."[10]

Gibson came to New York that September with mixed emotions. The National Lawn Tennis Hall of Fame and Museum inducted her along with Vic Seixas and others during a ceremony at the West Side Tennis Club. The induction was an honor, and its timing was bittersweet, given Dr. Johnson's death in June. The distinction brought wistful feelings for another reason. She wanted money that would allow her to have a future competing in sports, not just a medal like the one she got at Forest Hills to commemorate her past.[11]

Gibson was facing her future without Will. Early in the year, a journalist asked about the state of her domestic life amid her travels. "I have an understanding fella," she replied. The "trace of a sigh" that the writer detected was a clue that something was amiss.[12] There was. Press clippings suggest she had separated from Will by this time. Gibson had sat for the interview with *Black Sports* at an apartment in East Orange where the couple had moved after 1968, but Elliott called the trophy- and memorabilia-lined space "Althea's apartment in East Orange." Gibson told Elliott that Will accompanied her to "most of the major tournaments. It makes me feel even more confident when I know my husband's in the stands cheering for me," but she was entering fewer significant tournaments in either golf or tennis. The claim sounded like an act intended to make her career and her marriage sound stronger than they were.[13] By 1974, Gibson and Will were indeed separated. To those who observed the marriage, the break was not a surprise, including for Will. "He saw it coming," Rosemary, his sister, told author Bruce Schoenfeld in the early 2000s. "She was traveling all over; she had made mistakes. He couldn't establish a home with her. She wouldn't stay still."[14]

The end of the marriage, first with a separation and then with the divorce, finalized by 1976, was a defeat, and Gibson did not like to lose. It also gave her something in common with many other Americans as the divorce rate surged to an all-time high in the 1970s. In June 1974, she acknowledged during an interview at an LPGA tournament in Canada that she was single again. Around the same time, Kay Gilman, a writer for the New York *Daily News*, found her reluctant to talk about the end of her "six-year marriage," a further suggestion that Gibson and Will were not living together after 1971. "The fact that it didn't work out had nothing to do with my career," she insisted. "With understanding and sincere concern, a couple can make it no matter what their careers are or where they have to go." She added that each party in a married couple "should help one another."[15] Her response, honest yet cryptic, suggests that Will was not agreeable to blindly sponsoring her sports exploits. But marriages are private affairs, and Gibson was likely holding back details.

Schoenfeld, not naming names of either lovers or sources, writes that "accusations of infidelity on both sides" surrounded Gibson and Will's split.[16] Infidelity was possible. If Fred Kovaleski and even her own boasts during her trip to Hollywood are to be believed, Gibson reserved the right to look beyond Will for affection. She was famous and charismatic, and she traveled all over the country and even the world. Whether single or married, Gibson was, as *Black Sports* titled its profile of her, "The Self-Liberated Sister." That said, her devotion to her sports career showed all the signs of an addictive affair. Golf enthusiasts joked about the golf widow, the cultural figure of the wife who stayed home alone while her husband spent hours on the golf course. There was no male equivalent, and yet Gibson, in her devotion to her career and competition, had made Will into a golf widower.

—•—

By the spring of 1972, Gibson had decided to resume her tennis career. She resigned from her Essex County post and took a new job as the teaching professional and program director at Valley View Racquet Club, a private tennis facility in Bergen County's Northvale, near the New York border. "You can't play very much tennis when you have committed yourself to the kind of schedule I used to have," she said in May, applying the same rationale that had led her to quit the jobs she had had in the 1940s to play basketball and tennis. "Now I'll have a lot more freedom and, of course, the courts will be right where I work." According to reports, the terms of her contract with Valley View were potentially generous: five years, "a five-figure contract," and a 5 percent ownership.[17]

The time seemed right for a change. Tennis was hot. The women's game was major news. The Virginia Slims Circuit was roaring and the USLTA refused to be left behind. The association beefed up its own schedule of tournaments and prize money for women and boasted its own constellation of stars. Australia's Evonne Goolagong, England's Virginia Wade, and Chris Evert, the teenage phenom from Fort Lauderdale, were the biggest names on the USLTA tour, attracting fans in droves. Arthur Ashe and Jimmy Connors revitalized interest in men's tennis in the United States, while Australians Rod Laver, John Newcombe, Ken Rosewall, and Tony Roche captured the public's imagination, too. The game was different from the one Gibson had played. Crisp white togs were out. Instead, players wore colorful and color-coordinated tops, bottoms, and even shoes. Players were also less phlegmatic, tending to show more personality, including displeasure with fans and officials. Gibson would have fit right in, and with the advent of increased prize money, she wanted to. "The big money in tennis has given women the chance to become full-time professionals," she said. "If I'm able to get back some semblance of my form, I hope to join the circuit when it swings this way in a few months."[18]

The Valley View job brought perks and challenges. The club advertised in newspapers across the New York metropolitan area, keeping her name in the public eye with the reminder that she was the "former world famous Tennis Champion." The weeks between sessions of tennis lessons at the club allowed her to play in select LPGA tournaments and travel to speaking engagements and tennis clinics elsewhere. Still, the job was a real job; it was not a ceremonial position for which she was paid effectively only for the use of her name, like the arrangement Billie Jean King had at the Hilton Head Racquet Club in South Carolina, or Arthur Ashe's position as director of tennis at the famous Doral Hotel and Country Club in Miami. From September through April, Gibson had to work for her money through teaching, the very career she had said she did not want, even though she was by many accounts good at it. The job came with bitter irony, too. It had taken more than a decade for such a position to come her way. She claimed that the slight "didn't bother me . . . I felt it was their loss."[19] Perhaps, but she did not hesitate to point out how long it had taken.

Gibson made the best of the situation because that was all that she could do. In June, she flew to Minneapolis to give a clinic to youths as part of the Inner City Tennis Program. In the spirit of "tennis for everyone," political affiliation aside, she played an exhibition tennis tournament at a fundraiser in Ossining for New York's Democratic Party. At Valley View's grand opening in October, Gibson hosted King and Casals for exhibition matches. It was good business; King's name was sure to move tickets, priced at $7.50 apiece. It was also a sign of respect. Gibson thought King was the best player in women's tennis.[20]

The networking and visibility were helping Gibson survive. In April 1973, she played in the Dinah Shore-Colgate Winners Circle Tournament in Palm Springs and won a new car, a Mercury sedan, when her tee shot landed thirty-seven inches from the cup, closer than anyone's, on the seventeenth hole in the third round. For years, she drove the car, a steel and rubber reminder of her life's creed: if you don't play, you can't win. In May, Pepsi announced that Gibson was the new national director and technical advisor of its Mobile Tennis Program. Riding in a van stocked with equipment, she would go to inner-city neighborhoods and introduce youngsters to tennis. For decades, Pepsi, like its rival, Coca-Cola, had sought to appeal to Black consumers. Pepsi hired Black employees and used Black models and images in advertisements placed in the Black press. With the Mobile Tennis Program, Pepsi was raising its presence in Black sporting communities just as more attention was being paid to the conditions of Black people's lives in urban America. Since 1962, Pepsi had operated its International Golf Tour (IGT), trips on which Black golfers, often hundreds of them, traveled around the world to play. Black celebrities, including Jim Brown and Jackie Robinson, often went, too. The Mobile Tennis Program resonated with Gibson's past: her youth with PAL, her vagabond tours in professional tennis, and her years with Ward. The Pepsi initiative was another example of corporate America seeking to make money by turning to a Black celebrity to appeal to Black consumers.[21]

Still, Gibson believed in the program. It was another way for her to evangelize for tennis—and get paid for it. The Mobile Tennis Program "provides constructive competition, better use of leisure time and a sense of achievement and enjoyment to youngsters who have never had an opportunity or even considered the possibilities of playing tennis or entering tournaments before," she said in Atlanta. Reluctant to give up tradition, Gibson donned her tennis whites—a collared knit shirt and shorts—and, joined by staffers, gave demonstrations and lessons to children. She was especially pleased that the program, which lasted for weeks in a community, was not a "token" arrangement. She traveled across the country, including Atlanta, Boston, and Chicago, but worked close to home, too, with stops in Essex County and Harlem. Gibson was especially proud that the program gave "steady participants" equipment, including rackets, to keep.[22] Pepsi's program was also a chance for Gibson to keep herself in the spotlight. At the announcement luncheon, she mentioned her plan to play competitive tennis again. She conjectured that she could beat "80 per cent" of the women in professional tennis and crowed that when she was at her best between 1957 and 1958 there would have been no contest: "I would definitely win. No doubt about it." She dismissed the idea that she was making a comeback. "I never really left the game," she said, conveniently forgetting the definitive statements that she had made in the 1960s. "Just call it a return," she punned.[23]

Armchairs and sidelines were as close as Gibson was getting to realizing her dream and profiting handsomely from open tennis. When the Massachusetts

Institute of Technology (MIT) hosted the ATA Nationals in August, she joined Bud Collins of the *Boston Globe*, who was becoming the leading journalistic voice in tennis, to cover the finals for PBS. Maureen Connolly, Sarah Palfrey, and even Angela Buxton had covered televised tennis matches in the fifties, but this was a first for Gibson. It was also another short-term gig. A year later, Billie Jean King signed a contract to broadcast with ABC Sports.

Gibson could not play on the courts of majors, either. Neither the USLTA nor the Women's Tennis Association would automatically allow her to play singles at Forest Hills based upon her past. Instead, they required Gibson to qualify, a requirement she found odious. She did not like the idea of a "world champion" losing to an "up-and-coming" player, she said. She claimed that she would not lose, but the possibility—more than slight—that she would was plainly on her mind. Whether it was endorsements, sponsorships, or Forest Hills, Gibson could never agree with the notion that sports were not about ceremony but rather were tests of what players had done lately. The inability to play in that year's open was a particular disappointment; it was the first that would see the men's and women's champions receive equal prize money. Offended by the perceived snub but also aware that she would likely lose in a qualifying match, she decided not to "pursue it any further."[24]

There was nothing to prevent Gibson from playing doubles if someone invited her, however. Arthur Ashe, the golden Black man in American tennis, did just that, teaming with her in mixed doubles. They had paired the year before in an indoor charity event that carried his name. Their teaming at the U.S. Open in 1973 was inspired: Ashe and Gibson were Dr. Johnson's most successful protégés, the first and only Black winners at Forest Hills. She felt that their pairing might spur on others. "I sincerely feel as the only Negro player, I have an image to maintain for young ladies," she told journalist Grace Lichtenstein. "I don't mean to be blowing any horns, but whom do they have to look up to?" Yet Gibson and Ashe did not gel as doubles partners. They lost in the first round, 6–2, 6–2.[25]

Ashe's success had placed a shadow over Gibson's. As early as 1957, he was said to be "following in . . . [her] footsteps."[26] In the sixties, sportswriters credited Gibson's "pioneering" with opening doors for Ashe and called him her "male counterpart," someone who would attract Black men and boys to tennis.[27] By the early seventies, though, Ashe's celebrity had surpassed Gibson's, and her victories, achieved years ahead of his, had been forgotten.

Ashe was loath to acknowledge Gibson's impact on his career. Asked once whether he had been "inspired" by her achievements, he replied incredulously, "Why, she's a woman!"[28] Individuals get to choose their heroes. Gibson certainly had, choosing Black male boxers and Alice Marble, a White woman, as her lodestars rather than the women of the ATA, such as Ora Washington. Ashe continued, "I guess a boy needs 'man heroes.'" Pancho Gonzales was his "idol," he proclaimed. "Skin-wise, [Gonzales] was the nearest thing to me, and he was also the greatest player in the world. That's a pretty good combination."[29] Ashe carried no qualms about benefiting from male privilege. In the sixties, he spoke openly and without irritation about gender and his opportunities to prosper. "Really, being the first works to my advantage," he said of his historic selection for the Davis Cup team in 1965. "As a man, I can do much more than Althea Gibson did if I reach the top."[30]

Once Ashe got there, he did not support equal prize money for women. He used the same rhetoric as his White male contemporaries and predecessors to justify the gender pay gap in tennis. "Men are playing for a living now. They don't want to give up money just for girls to play," he said in 1970. "Why should we have to split the money with them? . . . We're supporting families and we're the drawing cards."[31] Ashe was single and childless at the time. Six years later, when the WTA threatened to boycott Wimbledon unless the tournament offered equal prize money, Ashe did not step forward as an ally. "Equal prize money at Wimbledon is basically two questions for me," he explained. "The first is the quality and the depth of the field. The other is the number of drawing cards the women have. I think on both counts that they would do better not to compare themselves with the men but to look at the women's situation as it really is. They have been piggybacking on us for a long time." Later, Ashe named Chris Evert and Evonne Goolagong as the only women who should receive the same prizes as men.[32]

On the fringes of professional tennis, Gibson chose to be creative and used every opportunity to push her name and potential. When Bobby Riggs, the men's singles champion at Wimbledon and Forest Hills in 1939, began to agitate tennis and the rest of the world with his chauvinistic boasts about male supremacy, she spoke up. Gibson predicted that Australia's Margaret Smith Court, thirty years old and the winner of seven singles titles at Wimbledon and Forest Hills, would defeat Riggs, fifty-five, not because of the difference in their ages but because they would play on a hard court. Though Riggs won against the ill-prepared Court in the May match that came to be known as the "Mother's Day Massacre," Gibson refused to back down in her belief that a woman could beat a man in a tennis match. She had done it often enough. When Billie Jean King, feeling the need to defend the progress that women's tennis was making, accepted Riggs's challenge to play him, Gibson sided with King on the premise that her youth, mental tenacity, and careful study of

Riggs's style of play in beating Court gave King the edge. King was "going to run Bobby's little legs off," she told the Associated Press on the eve of the match, dubbed the "Battle of the Sexes."[33] Gibson's praise was generous, but she could not resist using the match, televised around the world from the Houston Astrodome, as a chance to promote herself. Interviewed at Forest Hills, she confessed "one reservation" about King's game: "Billie Jean doesn't have that big first service it takes to beat Bobby. I think, because of my service and net play, I'd have a better chance."[34] When Gibson did face Riggs two years later in the less publicized "Challenge of the Sexes" in Mission Viejo, California, she lost, 8–4, in a "pro set"—first to win at least eight games by two.[35]

Gibson's imagination and confidence were bigger than her ability. Just how much bigger, the tennis world soon learned. She remained active, working out at a YMCA near her apartment and shooting baskets, she said. She liked telling people that her fitness level was high. Gibson allowed that gaining more than fifteen pounds since her major-winning days had cost her some speed, but, she said, she made up for it with experience. In January 1974, Gibson, forty-seven, played in a charity basketball game to raise money for a teenager who had been paralyzed in an accident. Her team nearly won. The following month, she went to Fort Lauderdale to be honored alongside Nancy Chaffee, Sarah Palfrey, and Gussie Moran in the S&H Green Stamps $50,000 Women's Tennis Classic. Chris Evert and Kerry Melville reached the final round, but when Melville broke her toe in a freak accident the night before the title match, forcing her to default, Evert was declared the winner. With thousands of fans hungry to see a tennis match, tournament organizers recruited Gibson to play Evert in an exhibition match.[36]

Gibson required no cajoling. This was the chance she had dreamed of. During tournament week, she said that she could have beaten Evert and King "in my prime."[37] As the announcer called her name, she ran onto the tennis court, smiling and waving to the packed crowd, and then peeled off her red track jacket and pants to reveal her white shorts, shirt, and wristbands. Evert, nineteen and skeptical about what was to unfold, got to work, winning 6–1, 6–2. No one thought Evert would lose. Still, she was surprised by Gibson's ability: "I don't think there is anyone in women's tennis today that serves it with that much pure power."[38] A writer for the *Miami Herald* was impressed with Gibson's "blazing serves" and her "excellent condition."[39]

Gibson was not crestfallen by the defeat. Rosie Casals had dubbed Billie Jean King "the Old Lady." Gibson joked that at forty-six to Evert's nineteen, she was the "Big Mama."[40] The loss did not stop her from saying for years afterward that she could have beaten Evert, King, and their peers in her heyday.[41] The line, like the exhibition, drew exposure, the currency that she needed to survive.

Gibson came back to the LPGA in the spring with mixed results. Between tournaments in Raleigh and Baltimore, she won close to $850. In Canada for a tournament in Quebec's Candiac, she put up the same valiant defense with reporters that she had used in the past. Before the tournament began, Gibson pushed the line that she would not have entered if she did not think that she could win. Then she played badly, and her emotions deflated. Heading off the eighteenth hole after shooting a 75 in the first round, she was in no mood to talk and walked straight through a crowd of people without acknowledging them. Nonplussed, a young female reporter, Pat Boland of the *Montreal Star*, offered to buy her a drink. Caught off guard, Gibson turned defensive. "Who are you?" she asked. Boland caught "an icy stare and a chill" in the question but plowed through and identified herself. Gibson relaxed and committed to be interviewed after she practiced her sand game. Back from her practice session, she was candid, as if she was looking for a chance to unburden herself. "I play when the spirit strikes me, but I still get pretty mad at myself when I blow a shot. It hurts even though it's a hobby—I guess it's my competitive nature." Old habits die hard. Some pains never went away, too. Gibson smarted over her inability to support herself through tennis, and she allowed that her golf record was unimpressive. She gave the short highlight reel of her LPGA career and closed by telling Boland, "You don't get rich at the game when you can name your tournament successes too readily and with a couple of sentences." Where tennis was concerned, she refused to give up the idea that she could beat the best players of the seventies. "I was the queen of tennis" in the 1950s, "and I'd be the queen today against the likes of Billie Jean King and Margaret Court." The thing was, she would never know. Life didn't work that way. After a few minutes, the bad feelings passed, and Gibson returned to sounding optimistic: "Now I'm just trying to make the best of the times."[42]

———

More people were playing tennis than ever before. The shift to open tennis, the construction of public tennis courts, Billie Jean King's celebrity (especially after the Battle of the Sexes spectacle), and the founding of World TeamTennis were reasons that thirty-four million people played, up from just ten million in 1970. Many of the converts were women and girls who, with the passage of Title IX in 1972, were beginning to take a stronger interest in sports. The tennis boom and the growth in interest in sports among women were good for Gibson's business. Golf and tennis were major attractions for fundraisers, and her name still had enough cachet to get her invited to high-profile charity events across the color line and at integrated affairs. She attended functions with the likes of Charlton Heston, Bill Cosby, Ruby Dee and Ossie Davis, multiple Kennedys, and Bob Hope. Gibson was in heady company, to be sure, but she was also replaying a theme of her life: circulating among people with more wealth than she would ever know.[43]

Everywhere Gibson went amid the tennis boom, people asked how she felt about the money that was available to contemporary tennis players and the amateurism of her time. She often answered evenly. She was impressed that King's leadership in women's tennis had created the windfall in purses, and she could be gracious about the way things were changing in sports: "I'm glad to see women are able to make a decent living at a sport which they have spent most of their life playing and learning."[44] Yet, despite insisting that she was not bitter (reporters asked), Gibson's responses sometimes revealed that the situation had left a bad taste in her mouth. "I was sure born at the wrong time to cash in on today's game" was one of her more matter-of-fact assessments.[45] At other times, though, bite accompanied her admitted frustrations. "Do I think about the money today's stars get?" she once asked a writer rhetorically. "Of course. I'd be stupid if I didn't."[46]

Other people thought about Gibson and money and saw dollar signs. She had gotten involved in questionable investment programs. She floated in interviews that she co-owned Vanguard Sports, Ltd. with Wilma Rudolph and Dave Stallworth, a former member of the New York Knicks. Vanguard's exact mission was unclear. Sometimes its mission was described as seeking career opportunities for former athletes. At other times, Gibson said Vanguard was devoted not to looking out for past sports greats but to looking for future ones. Vanguard would nurture the talents of the budding stars in cities and support them as they fielded scholarship offers. The company would manufacture sports equipment and "help train and develop athletes in all sports."[47] The specifics were a moving target, a sure sign of a shady deal. Later, Gibson invested in a television studio that Gil Fuller was building. A former jazz composer turned businessman, Fuller was also her manager and occasional spokesperson. Will never trusted him. Fuller envisioned that his Videoplaza would woo production companies to Newark to shoot films and commercials. He imagined Gibson, Elston Howard (the first Black member of the Yankees), and Reggie Jackson (among the most popular players in Major League Baseball in the 1970s) shooting commercials there. "Athletes need a second career and commercials are right for them," Fuller told a New

Jersey newspaper.[48] Gibson agreed. She called the Videoplaza among the "few things pending" for her outside of sports and anticipated "shooting some things in it, maybe commercials. That's what I feel I have to look forward to."[49] It never happened.

———

By the fall of 1975, hobnobbing brought Gibson her most impressive paid gig to date. Weeks after she attended a reception at Morven, New Jersey's governor's residence, to show support for the Equal Rights Amendment, Brendan Byrne, New Jersey's Democratic governor, nominated Gibson to serve as the state athletic commissioner. She knew the governor socially. He had once hosted her for an afternoon of tennis; they tied 2–2 in their four-game singles match. Afterward, she told watchers that she had allowed Byrne to win a second game so that he would not lose outright. If Byrne, who seemed neither to have expected nor wanted the gift of the game, was put off by her remarks, he got over it. Byrne made her the honorary professional at the Morven tennis court and golfed with her in a charity tournament weeks later. By selecting Gibson for the commissioner's role, Byrne gave her a steady albeit part-time job that kept her in the public eye and brought her an annual salary of $7,000 to $7,500 ($41,302 in 2021), more than she had ever made in any of her seasons on the LPGA tour.[50]

As was so often the case in her life and career, Gibson's nomination set a precedent and broke a barrier, while revealing other people's discomfort as she veered from the status quo. There had never been an athletic commissioner like her. She was the first African American nominated to serve in the position and the first woman, too. The latter development raised the hackles of Bob Curley, a writer for *The News*, based in Paterson, New Jersey. Curley questioned the possibility that a tennis player and golfer could succeed as the athletic commissioner, a role that was primarily devoted to overseeing and regulating boxing and wrestling concerns in the state. Curley doubted that Gibson could do the job well precisely because she was a woman. "It's a woman's world, but boxing certainly isn't . . . as Helen Reddy sings it . . . 'No Way to Treat a Lady' . . . Promoters, performers and spectators would rather see male competence at the top, rather than an attractive female with a great reputation in other sports." Curley thought that Byrne should have nominated "some man with boxing savvy, leadership and integrity" and named retired boxers Jersey Joe Wolcott, who was Black, and Paul Cavaliere, a White man, as alternatives.[51] Gibson was a dilettante where politics was concerned, but her swearing-in ceremony in November showed that she was hardly a babe in the woods in sports. Promoter Don King, Elston Howard, and Don Bragg, the Olympic pole vaulter, were in the audience, and afterward she threw a football with one of Byrne's aides, all the better for showing the energy and strength she boasted she still possessed.[52]

Gibson addressed the matter of identity and her commissionership head-on as soon as she was in office. In interviews and meetings, she was decisive that she was no fan of assessments like those made by the Associated Press, which reported that Byrne had "scored a double kayo" with her appoint-ment, a sporting equivalent to later, lazy descriptions of women of color as "twofers" in workplaces.[53] Such phrases erased the skills, experience, intel-lect, and ambitions that the professionals, Gibson included, brought to their work. Gibson broached the subject within days of being sworn in and clearly articulated that she did not want perceptions of her race and gender to impact or influence how people worked with her or what they expected from her. "I know what is running through your minds," she told a gathering of the New Jersey Boxing Writers Association, a group composed entirely of men, a week after taking the oath of office. "Do not think of me as a woman. I'm a human being."[54] When a writer for the *New York Times* interviewed Gibson about her new role and pointed out the historic dimensions of her appointment, she reiterated her stance and added race: "I have often been referred to as the only black or the only woman in this or that. Don't look at me as a woman or a black. I'm human."[55] For the length of her tenure, Gibson did not discuss either race or gender when outlining her vision for improving New Jersey's sports profile. Instead, she spoke of changing sports and entertainment promoters' habit of looking first to New York and Philadelphia as venues for their events while New Jersey remained an afterthought. She proposed building new sports facilities across the state and hinted that she might be able to convince Don King to stage a fight in New Jersey for Muhammad Ali, on whose television special she had made a cameo during the summer. She wanted boxing to boom again so that the state could profit from the sport's taxes and fees.[56]

Gibson plainly drew on her personal experiences in her new post. State athletic commissioner was a dream job for her, or at least an ironic and appro-priate position for a woman whose father had wanted her to become a boxer. "Boxing had a special place in my heart," she explained early in her tenure. Still ignoring propriety and respectability, Gibson reminisced that Daniel "taught me how to put up my dukes when I was a mere tot" and recalled memories of New Jersey as a center of the boxing world when she was a child. "The sports pages always had plenty of boxing news. It looked to me at times as if a boxing arena was operating every night in New Jersey."[57] Borrowing from her years in PAL, she argued that sports were a panacea for crime: "Right now people have too much time to make all the wrong decisions. If the muggers and robbers were more concerned about playing a game and winning, they wouldn't be mugging and robbing." She resurrected one of her favorite lines about fighting juvenile delinquency, "Keep 'em on the courts, not in the courts"; supported the establishment of "recreational programs" for youths and adults; and advocated for gymnasiums to be open at night, just as she experienced in Harlem in the 1940s.[58]

Gibson's ambitions exceeded boxing and wrestling. She aspired for New Jersey to be a staging ground for, and to make money from, all professional sports, and wanted to relocate the commission's office from Trenton, the capital, to Newark, which was closer to New York.[59] She spoke in tones that conjured the ATA's collaborative approach to social change. "I'll consider all of you as assistant commissioners," she told boxing writers and wrestling and boxing promoters in November 1975. "We all have a part to play for the benefit of the whole. When we want things to grow, we have to assist and help each other."[60] Another time, the lessons she had drawn as an ATA protégé were crisp: "You've got to have cooperation. You can't do everything by yourself. You need people to help people."[61]

———

Gibson had minimal experience with political bureaucracy. In the sixties, she had been a member of the State Recreation Council for Governor Nelson Rockefeller in New York and was one of a dozen unpaid sports commissioners for New York City under Mayor John Lindsay. Those had been ceremonial posts that were good for public relations for herself and the politicians who had appointed her. Now she enjoyed the appearance of power that came with her state job in New Jersey. "What can I do for you, babe?" she would ask people who approached her.[62] Yet she still had to help herself. The title of state athletic commissioner was impressive. It was also inflated, the employment equivalent of being land-poor.

Gibson fit tennis clinics and exhibitions, public speaking engagements, and golf tournaments around her work schedule for the state. It was necessary work. Her job at Valley View was on hold during her commissionership. Title IX and the tennis boom had given her a niche and a new lifeline. At colleges and universities, churches, and community centers, Gibson gave speeches on "the role of the woman athlete" and tennis as a sport for people of all walks of life. One speech in her repertoire, "30 Years Old, Winner at Wimbledon,

Winner at Forest Hills—What Do You Do Next?," plainly belied her insistence that she was neither bitter nor interested in thinking about her past.[63]

Gibson got another chance to be a part of the changing action for women in sports at the start of 1976. She went to Rotonda, Florida, to join twenty-three other women for the second edition of the ABC television network's *Women Superstars*. Aired in 1975, the original event was the brainchild of Larry King, Billie Jean King's husband. *Women Superstars* was an offshoot of *Superstars*, which brought together male athletes from across sports and generations to compete for cash prizes and bragging rights. Larry King pitched the idea of a women's version to Sidney Schlenker, the vice president and manager of the Houston Astrodome. When ABC Sports and International Management Group partnered with the Kings and Schlenker as co-producers, the prize money was raised to equal the men's purse. Each woman was guaranteed $1,000, too.[64]

When Gibson competed, she joined a who's who of the best women in sports: swimmer Diana Nyad, golfers Jane Blalock and Amy Alcott, the USLTA's Martina Navratilova, boxer Jackie Tonawanda, and two Olympic gold medalists, speed skater Anne Henning and track star Wyomia Tyus. Like its male predecessor, *Women Superstars* was a contrived, "made-for-TV" event of short matches. It also gave the women rare chances to compete in a sports smorgasbord in front of a national television audience for a top prize of $50,000 ($260,350 in 2022), just as men did, and to come together for competition and camaraderie, experiences missing from Gibson's life with her limited appearances on the LPGA Tour. Billie Jean King and Keith Jackson, one of the network's leading analysts, did play-by-play. Critics dismissed *Superstars* and its ilk as "TrashSports," but *Women Superstars* gave sportswomen exposure and opportunities that had long been denied their sex. Gibson regarded women's inclusion in the wave of made-for-TV sports matchups, tennis and otherwise, as an idea whose time was overdue: "It's entertainment, of course, and it's nice for the men to be making that kind of money, but I'd like to see women playing in them, too."[65]

In *Women Superstars '76*, Gibson, the oldest entrant, held her own. She was firmly in the middle of the pack in the qualifying rounds in January, reached the finals in February, and finished alone in eighth place, ahead of softball player Irene Shea, Tyus, and Navratilova, to win $1,400. That was in addition to her guarantee.[66] Gibson's tenacity and personality left a lasting impression on Shea: "She's 48 and she's lost some of her speed, but she still has the natural grace of an athlete and she's a fine, warm human being."[67]

The *Women Superstars* appearance, combined with the media coverage that came with the athletic commissionership, brought Gibson national publicity. *WomenSports*, the monthly magazine launched by Billie Jean and Larry King in 1974, honored her in its February and March issues in its "Foremothers" section devoted to remembering the accomplishments of women in the history of sports. Drawing from her autobiographies and media profiles, the two-part feature introduced Gibson to a younger generation unfamiliar with her accomplishments and her struggles. *People* magazine published a one-page article about her in February, too. The new celebrity-focused magazine wrote about Gibson's ambitions to shake up New Jersey's sports scene and included pictures that showed the many facets of her life: tennis skirt at Wimbledon, short skirt and tall boots while working in her Newark office, sweatpants on the basketball court with two men, and a close-up portrait of her face as she grimaced while wearing a track jacket during a workout. "If Commissioner Gibson gets her way . . . she could be known as the 'Black Queen of All Sports.'"[68]

Yet Gibson was not getting her way in New Jersey politics. She was having trouble charming her political colleagues into supporting her agenda. Governor Byrne did not take up her proposals for the construction of a sports and entertainment arena in Newark and for a mentorship program that paired youths with successful athletes. Byrne's foes were against her, too. Frank J. Dodd, the state senator representing Essex County and one of Byrne's frequent adversaries, co-sponsored the Comprehensive Boxing and Wrestling Act, a bill that would have changed the way boxing and wrestling were regulated in New Jersey and increased the number of commissioners. Dodd, in crafting the bill, bypassed Gibson, never seeking her input. He and his co-sponsor, Senator Matthew Feldman of Bergen County, reportedly ignored her request to delay the hearing so that she could offer a thorough response to its content. Others took notice of Dodd and Feldman's unusual and questionable tactics. Asked whether she thought the senators were overriding her because she was a woman, Gibson sidestepped the question: "I don't know their reasons; they might have gotten the bill underway before I was appointed."[69]

Dodd's attempt ultimately failed because Gibson refused to play his game. Members of the media questioned Dodd's reasons for seeking to pass the bill so quickly, and boxing promoters sided with her that the bill was not in the best interest of either their industry or the state. Fighting back, Gibson came to the hearing on March 30 at the State House in Trenton and made her disapproval of the bill known. Reading from a prepared statement, she called Dodd's bill "regressive and short-sighted in concept, import and function" and decried it as "inefficient and ineffective." She described herself as "ready, willing, and able" to meet with Dodd, Feldman, and other legislators "in an atmosphere of functional reciprocity at any mutually convenient time" to share her thoughts and research. Gibson believed New Jersey needed "a truly comprehensive sports act dealing with all aspects of professional sports activities and not just boxing and wrestling." Pulling no punches, she emphasized that the Athletic Commission was underresourced, with only a part-time leader, "an understaffed office, and a debilitating organizational structure."[70] She was willing to be the full-time athletic commissioner, she said, if the salary were right.[71]

Outnumbered and overwhelmed, Dodd backpedaled. Facing opposition and looking foolish as other speakers took to the floor to disagree with his bill, Dodd confessed that he had acted in haste. He promised Gibson that by proposing multiple commissioners he was not trying to diminish her role and, sounding like her, insisted that he would seek input from others, including members of the boxing industry, as he drafted a new bill. Gibson left the State House chamber while the hearing was still in session.[72] It was a dramatic conclusion, like ending a tennis match with an ace and heading for the locker room while her overconfident and ill-prepared opponent stood flat-footed, dumbfounded, and alone on the court. Only later did she learn that her victory was pyrrhic.

Riding a wave of confidence, Gibson returned to Florida A&M in May for an emotional visit. She was the guest speaker for the Student Government Association, but the applause from the beyond-capacity crowd went on so long that she could not begin her speech on time. Gibson openly cried as she received the warm reaction. That a Black institution, and one of her own, was honoring her was especially touching. She felt there was a "need for blacks [to recognize] other blacks." Indeed, her livelihood depended in part on Black communities reaching out to her. Standing behind the rostrum, Gibson felt every one of the years that had passed. She had been on top of the world when she came back as an honored guest for the Orange Blossom Classic in the fall of 1957, with three Grand Slams behind her and two more ahead. So much had seemed possible then. Twenty years later, her life had not turned out as she had hoped. She did not sound maudlin, but it was clear that the many things that had not happened for her were on her mind. That season, Chris Evert, twenty-one, reached $1 million in career tournament winnings. "I like to see professional women athletes given the opportunity to earn a living from a sport that they have put so much time and hard work into," she said during a press conference in Tallahassee. "My only regret might be that it didn't happen when I was champ." For effect, she added colloquially, "I was the world champ, and I didn't have no money." She still didn't. Gibson promised the university $500 for a scholarship that would bear her name. She wanted the award to support a female tennis player. Her heart was in the right place. It was money, though, that she surely needed for herself.[73]

———

Ever the athlete, Gibson still spoke of the ways in which the lessons she had learned in sports helped her in the other dimensions of her life. "Training for tennis I learned to lock the outside out of what I'm doing," she said soon after joining the Byrne administration. "If I concentrated on the people watching me, I'd never see that ball."[74] Politics is like tennis and golf in at least one way: players tend to grow cautious after their strokes fly past their targets. By the summer, Gibson, keenly aware that New Jersey's political class and others were watching her closely, was acting with obvious reserve as she faced an issue that seemed tailor-made for her skills and passion.

The advances that women were making in society, under the law, and in sports combined with the rising popularity of prizefighting in the seventies to rekindle interest in women's boxing. California held its first fight between two women in April, and women were seeking licenses to fight in Nevada, Arizona, Oregon, Ohio, and elsewhere. New Jersey's turn in the sport's growing spotlight came in July. Supported by promoter Lou Duva, Cathy "Cat" Davis hoped the state would license her. Davis, a Louisiana native and college student, was an all-around athlete with a specialty in fencing. She had already won fights in Maine and Washington when the New York State Athletic Commission (NYSAC) rejected her bid to fight in the Empire State. In 1975, NYSAC had also denied Jackie Tonawanda, the best-known boxer among women. Tonawanda briefly turned to kickboxing and took her case to the New York Supreme Court, which eventually ruled in her favor.[75]

Albany's dismissal of Davis would seem to have created a golden opportunity for New Jersey to carve out a niche for itself, but Gibson was reluctant to consent. Speaking to the press, Davis, and Duva, she explained, "Far be it for me to deprive anyone from making a living, but I have to be sure this is the right thing for the people of New Jersey." She chose to assemble and convene a six-member Boxing Advisory Board to review Davis's case. As far as anyone knew, two women had never fought as boxers in the state, leaving Gibson to ask, "Is New Jersey ready for this?"[76] According to a member of California's Athletic Commission, not only was Gibson personally supportive of women's boxing, but she also influenced his decision to support licensing women to box after telling him about her upbringing in Harlem, about Daniel's demand that she learn to fight, and that girls could fight as well as boys could.[77]

Gibson took the middle ground in her own state. She approved Davis to fight an exhibition bout versus Jean Lang, on the condition that both women adhere to protective standards set by the advisory board. Wearing chest protectors, a rule in other states where women boxed, was among the prerequisites. Gibson argued that the exhibition was an important test. "I want to get a reaction from the public as well as see for myself what a women's bout is like."[78] The decision ensured that she would make history as the commissioner for New Jersey's first approved prizefight between two women.

The fight was historic though not memorable. Lang was not up to the task. Davis knocked her out after only thirty seconds in the second round as twenty-four hundred spectators watched at Hinchliffe Stadium in Paterson. Gibson sat at ringside with James Farley, the athletic commissioner for New York. Farley told the press he still disapproved of women's boxing. She again held back. "I'm reserving my statements until I talk with the advisory board," she reportedly said.[79] Another source noted that Gibson said women should "train in the state for a longer period before the next bout."[80] The press agreed that the Davis-Lang fight was not a convincing advertisement for women's boxing, but Gibson received criticism over her next exercise of hesitation. Don King announced an interest in staging a doubleheader in New Jersey, George Foreman versus Joe Bugner and Duane Bobick versus Ken Norton. Officials from Maryland and Pennsylvania expressed a desire to do business with King. Gibson told members of the New Jersey Boxing Writers Association that she would decide after she had consulted with the state attorney general. Asking permission had never been her way.[81]

———

Gibson felt herself turning into someone she was not. She had returned to FAMU in the fall to be inducted into its new Sports Hall of Fame. Jake Gaither, her mentor who could tell stories about her passion and ambitions, was inducted, too. The trip was a reminder of the firebrand she had once been. Her flame for the commissionership had died.[82]

Gibson resigned as state athletic commissioner in January 1977 after fourteen months. Speaking of her decision soon after submitting her resignation letter, she conveyed that state politics had given her yet another encounter with disillusionment in a life that had been filled with it. The gap between her aspirations for sports in New Jersey and what its politics allowed was so wide as to be insurmountable. "I don't wish to be a figurehead," she said. "I wanted to make the commissioner's job a viable post, but it seemed everything I wanted to do was knocked down." As recently as the fall, Gibson had suggested that all state agencies with any influence over sports—the Athletic Commission, the Racing Commission, and the Sports and Exposition Authority—should be combined. Nothing happened. "I found I didn't have a voice," she explained exasperatedly. "Fighting the bureaucracy is a tough task for someone not used to it."[83] Later, she described the job as a "bureaucratic maze of intrigue."[84]

Some in New Jersey's sports industry expressed agreement, support, and understanding for her decision. The structure that the state had established to oversee boxing specifically and athletics generally was a mess, they complained, and the state needed a full-time commissioner. Good for Gibson, they praised, for standing by her principles. Others, though, harped that she was inherently poorly suited for the role. The *Herald-News* of Passaic editorialized, "The world of wrestling and boxing is a man's preserve still, and Althea was not at ease in it."[85] On the contrary, the patriarchs of the Garden State's government were not ready for the pace with which Gibson wanted to move. Byrne, the governor, accepted her resignation "with regret" and pointed to dollars rather than disillusionment as the more likely reason for her exit. He had nominated her knowing that she was "making a financial sacrifice to accept the position."[86]

Gibson agreed to stay on until Byrne identified her successor, but the waiting frustrated her. She was still working for the state at the end of March, driving her to confess that money factored into her decision to step down: "I tried to do the job, but I was knocking my head against the wall. The job is interfering with my making a living. I could be doing other things. I don't want to be involved in anything that I can't make any headway in."[87] Byrne eventually nominated Jersey Joe Wolcott to replace her.[88]

Gibson needed to get away. The cold, snow, and winter drear of New Jersey were tough, especially after what she had gone through in state politics. She also needed money. The commissionership had not paid much, but quitting created a shortfall all the same. The University of California, Davis rescued her momentarily. In mid-February, Gibson came to the campus, just outside of Sacramento, as a guest of the Women's Center, the Minority Subcommittee on the Status of Women Committee, and the Affirmative Action Council. In this instance, her multiple identities were advantageous. She gave a tennis demonstration in the morning, meeting campus leaders for the kind of fun-and-games schtick mixed with chances to awe her audience with her skills that had become her stock in trade. In the afternoon, she gave half-hour tennis clinics.[89]

Anyone with five dollars and a willingness to learn could register for one of the clinics. For free, they could expose themselves to some of Gibson's other ideas. Her noontime speech, "Women in Sports," was part of the university's Minority Women Lecture Series. The topic was apt, as the media, including *Sports Illustrated*, *Newsweek*, and *Time*, regularly published reports on barriers that women encountered in athletics. It was also a subject that was close to her heart.[90]

Gibson delivered a speech about women in sports under different names over the years—"The Role of the Sportswoman," "The Role of the Female Athlete," "The Sportswoman's Role in Society," and "Women in Sports"— and each time her passion and honesty were irrepressible. She opened by asking her audience to "acknowledge the indigenous obligation which has always belonged to women. This is simply being women—perpetuating the idea of femininity." The introduction allowed Gibson to argue that the hurdles women faced in sports derived from and impacted society at large. She did not define femininity, calling it instead "the contrast to masculinity." Gibson noted, however, that maintaining strict delineations between masculinity and femininity was designed to be detrimental to women and beneficial to men. Sports was a stage where the examples were on full display. "The arguments most often used to justify discrimination against women in sports—that athletics are bad for their health and femininity, that women are not skilled enough or interested in playing games—have on the surface a nice paternalistic, even altruistic quality," she pointed out. "Recent studies show such assumptions are incorrect and self-serving nonsense." Those same studies, Gibson posited, proved that it was "in the best interest of the male athletic establishment to maintain the existing situation" of prioritizing men and boys. "Anything beyond token sexual equality in athletics represents a formidable threat to male pride and power" that was endemic in other aspects of American life.[91]

Personal experience informed other observations Gibson made in the speech. Fearlessly, she denounced commonplace assertations about women in sports. "Male defensiveness about female athletic prowess is not restricted to head-to-head confrontations," she noted. "Accomplished women athletes, even when they are competing against one another, seem to ruffle the psyches of many men." Alluding to the Battle of the Sexes, Gibson acknowledged that "a hundred or so male tennis players could defeat Billie Jean King." That said, "hundreds of thousands . . . would be fortunate to win a set from King." Gibson saw a direct correlation between a man's athletic ability and his vitriol toward women's participation in sports: "For obvious reasons it is often the unathletic, spectator oriented man who has the most derogatory things to say about outstanding sportswomen." Unflinchingly, she critiqued a line that had often been applied to her own athletics skills: "She plays like a man." Relying on colloquialisms, Gibson emphasized that the statement was not a "compliment" but rather "[a] frequent ploy used to maintain the illusion of total male athletic superiority . . . a barb . . . the insinuation that this babe's hormones are probably so weird that she is or nearly is a man." "Many men feel menaced by the athletic activities of women," she concluded.[92]

A proponent of Title IX, Gibson used her speech to raise awareness and pitch ideas. She updated her listeners on the legal battles and argument that had followed passage of the law. Armed with statistics and facts, she decried that women and girls were "getting the short end of the stick" where sports financing was concerned. The nation was still entangled in the Cold War, but Gibson made the radical proposal that American sports follow the lead of the Russians: "Have men's and women's teams, and you score them together." Sounding like the goodwill ambassador that she had once been, she implored, "We are living in an active age which requires preparedness and alertness of body and mind. Athletics can and does do much to keep us in step with the tempo of the times." Equal opportunities for women in sports was, for Gibson, a matter of being modern.[93]

The unequal distribution of money was not the only thing that irritated Gibson; without the implementation of Title IX, female athletes were "being denied a desirable educational process" and the society would suffer because of the outcomes. She had long believed that women and girls had everything to gain and nothing to lose by playing sports. She told audiences across the country, "The competitive spirit of sports breeds a desire for success and encourages discipline. If women are exposed to sports, they will become more confident and will develop a sense of identity."[94] Other times, she phrased the idea more bluntly: "Competition is good for women. Life is competition."[95] In her speech, Gibson maintained that "most women" were strengthened "physically and mentally" by "a continuing program of physical exercise," and the country was better off, too. Like their male counterparts, sportswomen, watched by a "sports loving" public, could improve the nation through demonstrations of honorable "conduct" and "certain aspects of citizenship" learned through athletics. When institutions denied women and girls equal access to and opportunities in sports, they hurt the country, as "there never has been a really successful society in which women were suppressed."[96]

Gibson was glad the women's rights movement had turned its attention to sports, and she identified herself as an advocate for its causes, but she thought its leaders' interests were overdue. "The most aggressive leaders of the movement have been more intellectual than physical types," she observed. "But now, the movement is becoming active in this area." Feminists' regard for sport was, she thought, linked to their broader goal for women to have the same types of power and opportunities that society granted men. "We've become conscious of the body," said. "It is a woman's right to control her body, be it wanting an abortion or wanting to strengthen it through sports."[97]

At Davis, Gibson did not hold back. She told her audience in the Memorial Union that "our male-dominated society prefers women [to be] physically and psychologically dependent." Sports were the solution, as "better athletic programs will develop more aggressive women with confidence and a strong sense of identity."[98] Still hovering over her resignation from the commissionership was the possibility that her own "confidence" and "strong sense of identity" had once again been unappreciated by men in positions of power.

Gibson refused to give up on state politics so easily. In April, she announced her candidacy for the New Jersey State Senate in the 26th District. It was a stunning about-face, given her displeasure with bureaucracy and her open aversion to politics in the past. Running as a Democrat, she was challenging the reelection of Frank Dodd. Eldridge Hawkins, a lawyer from Newark, was her other opponent. Gibson had been "persuaded" to run, she told the press, though by whom she did not say. The decision was also a matter of conscience. "You hear about politicians being crooked. I thought, why would I want to get into something like that? I believe I can be a politician but a fair one."[99]

Attempting to enter electoral politics, Gibson was again positioning herself to enter a sphere where White men were the majority. The previous dozen years had seen some changes. Cleveland, Detroit, Atlanta, Los Angeles, and Newark had elected Black mayors by 1977. All of them were men. There were four Black women in the U.S. Congress, including Shirley Chisholm from New York and Barbara Jordan from Texas. New Jersey state politics had seen progress of its own. The State Senate had gotten its first female member, Mildred Barry Hughes, in 1965, and a Black woman, Wynona Lipman, was elected in 1972.[100]

Nevertheless, Gibson—a divorced, childless Black woman with no substantial political experience—was an unconventional candidate. Her platform was thin. She reiterated her goal of making New Jersey a center of the sports world. As athletic commissioner, she had argued for the construction of stadiums across the state but said that she did not know how the projects would be funded. Taxes were the most obvious answer, but on the campaign trail, she was careful in how she spoke about the five-letter word. Reporters present when Gibson filed her campaign forms noted that she "thought the state income tax could be improved," while her campaign brochure mentioned only "equity in taxation."[101] Gibson's political novelty was underscored by an outfit she wore at a campaign event in East Orange. She chose a green dashiki and white bell-bottoms for a combination concert-rally held near her apartment. She was fond of touting her physical fitness as a qualification for public service. Reluctant to confess her age, even though it was a matter of public record since she had been in the public eye for decades, she invited the press to "come down and watch me hit [a] golf ball and see if you think I look like 50 . . . or watch me move on the tennis court."[102]

Neither Gibson's physical fitness nor her political platform was enough to win the State Senate race. She finished in third place behind Dodd, the winner, and Hawkins. Dodd won his reelection bid in November. Months later, he bragged about his ability to influence voters and select viable candidates: "When people are looking for athletic ability, they go to a stadium. When they're looking for candidates with proven ability in public office they knock on this man's door."[103] It was a shot at Gibson and a clear statement that, where politics was concerned, she had been out of her league.

———

Sports, like acting, was a business in which players aged out of roles, some faster than others. But, with a compulsion to compete since her earliest years, for Gibson the identity of athlete came first, before any other. "As long as I'm physically able to play, I will," she said in 1978. "I'm a competitor and an athlete."[104] Gibson was also like a gambler who could not rise from the slot machine or the card table of her own volition. That she was a woman did not matter. It was common for the best athletes to have trouble deciding when and how to retire. Billie Jean King, with whom she had much in common, was going through it in the late seventies. Ty Cobb, with whom Gibson had comparatively little in common except for a passion to win, had faced the conundrum, and the associated fear and anxiety, fifty years earlier. Babe Ruth eloquently summarized what life could be like for athletes after they left the sports arena for good: "It's hard to be on the outside of something you love. Just looking in doesn't help."[105] That was from a man who, unlike Gibson, had been rewarded with cheers and checks.

With her fifty-first birthday looming, Gibson gave the LPGA Tour one more try in 1978. She left her job at Valley View to devote herself full-time to golf. She was less style-focused than she had been during her first attempt at the tour. Her golf clothes were plain rather than custom-made, and her hair was noticeably thicker and curlier than the coiffed straightness that had been her habitual look for years. She put her furniture and trophies into storage and got back out on the road, chasing checks and an elusive win. She still had no sponsor and, surrounded by women twenty-five and even thirty years younger, she was the aged oddity on the circuit once again. Within two years, the PGA Tour would establish a circuit that gave male professional golfers over the age of fifty a viable place to play. Women, though, had nothing of the kind. When faced with skepticism about her ability to win, Gibson responded with her brand of magical thinking: "I am closer than most people think. It's just a matter of being consistent. That's all it would take for me."[106] Asked whether she was "crushed" by bad rounds, she retorted, "I ain't the crushing type. I ain't the give-up type."[107] Victory was "on the horizon," she predicted.[108] In truth, the sun had set on her golf career long before. The only consistencies were scores in the eighties (and some in the nineties), aches, pains, and a balky back exacerbated by driving for hours on end. There was also Nancy Lopez, the twenty-one-year-old golf sensation from New Mexico who won nine tournaments and was voted the AP Woman Athlete of the Year. Winless, Gibson left the LPGA for good, though she retained her amateur status and played in charity tournaments in the ensuing years. She loved golf, even though the game did not love her back.[109]

Tennis was different. The game was home, and Gibson returned. She would not play. Instead, grudgingly accepting that those days were over, she turned to coaching. She taught anyone who paid her. She gave a terse response to those who did not offer to pay her but asked about her methods: "That's my secret."[110] By 1979, she was sharing her secrets with young African Americans, including women and girls.

The tennis boom had not eluded African Americans. They were reaching for rackets in greater numbers, too, and as had been the case two decades earlier, they had a hero. Arthur Ashe's success after capturing Forest Hills in 1968—winning the Australian Open in 1970 and Wimbledon in 1975—had attracted more African Americans to the game and further inspired those who were already devotees. Ashe flourished on the court and off. Stoked by his presence in what was still often perceived as a White sport and by his conservative politics, he, like O.J. Simpson, landed lucrative, multiyear endorsement deals that had been previously unheard of for Black sportsmen. Ashe's achievements had also drawn more attention to the paucity of African Americans in tennis. Editorials and articles routinely asked why there were not more African Americans in professional tennis and mulled who the next Black tennis champion might be.

Gibson fielded the questions, too. "The same old reasons" that had held back Black athletes in the fifties were hindrances in the seventies as well: "Lack of opportunity, lack of facilities, lack of money. Tennis being what it is, you can't just go out on a street and backyard and start playing. You need a racquet, uniform, court, and instruction. In short, it's far more expensive than basketball, baseball or football pickup games." She did not think, though, that the situation was impossible. Discrimination existed, but, she allowed, "you can overcome even that if you try hard enough."[111] She thought that, compared to her prime years, the "door is wide open for black tennis players, both men and women."[112]

Still, Gibson questioned why more Black women had not reached the top in tennis. She speculated that money was one factor and thought the still-pervasive idea of the rigor required for success in sport was another, influencing them to choose other pursuits. "The black man is different, much different, I believe," she said in 1978. "Men are much more willing to take the abuses of sports and traveling." It was another way of admitting that she had been different. Where Black women in tennis were concerned, Gibson thought of herself as a "pioneer" without "too many followers."[113]

Bonnie Logan was among those few followers. Logan had been a championship-winning sensation in the ATA throughout the sixties. A native of Durham, North Carolina, she had grown up admiring Gibson and followed in her footsteps as one of Dr. Johnson's protégés. Logan, at the time a student at Morgan State University, was the first Black woman on the Virginia Slims Circuit in 1971. When Gibson had tried to make a comeback in tennis the following year, 1972, she said that African American women were on her mind. "There are a lot of Black women playing who have the ability," she had told a writer in East Orange. "I made it in tennis when things were a lot harder, and I want to show them that they can certainly make it now."[114]

Yet things were still hard. Two more Black women, Ann Koger, also of Morgan State, and Sylvia Hooks, a P.E. teacher from East Orange, joined the Slims Circuit by 1973, after the Women's International Tennis Federation (the short-lived incorporated name of the Slims Circuit) partnered with the ATA to give as many as six women the chance to qualify for the professional tour. The USLTA was disinterested in partnering with the ATA for a similar arrangement.[115] Slims players gave 10 percent of their prize money back to the circuit to pay the salaries of officials and to support a fund that helped defray costs for African American players who showed promise but lacked money. The fund ended in 1973. Gibson refused to join what journalist Grace Lichtenstein called a "movement by the tennis establishment in encouraging an 'affirmative action' program for minority players." "I've never been militant," she told Lichtenstein. "I don't believe in fights. Talent wins out." Lichtenstein found her "more interested" in talking about her past accomplishments than in thinking about the problems of others. Smoking a cigarette over dinner, Gibson recounted her dominance in 1956 and 1957 and mused, "These girls today wouldn't have had a chance against me."[116]

Sylvia Hooks was disappointed in Gibson's attitude. Hoping to keep her game sharp in the early seventies, Hooks had asked Gibson whether she could practice during slow hours at Valley View, Gibson's club in Northvale. Gibson hedged. In interviews, she boasted about her salary and ownership stake in Valley View, but she gave Hooks a different story. "Althea told me she was just 'a figurehead on the totem pole' and just about refused," Hooks said to a reporter in December 1972 as she prepared to join the Slims Circuit after Gladys Heldman, its commissioner, sent her a contract and made financial arrangements. Stunned by Gibson's response to her query, Hooks was at a loss to reconcile what she had heard with what she thought she knew about the great Black tennis legend: "I knew Althea before and knew of her reputation for wanting to help black players and the best she could do was promise to call me back." According to Hooks, "she never did."[117]

The response was all the more jarring because, once they joined the Slims Circuit, Logan (reeling from Dr. Johnson's death and the loss of his mentorship), Koger, and Hooks faced hardships like those Gibson had endured twenty years earlier. Florida was especially bad. Employees at a tennis club in Boca Raton tried to make the three players take the service entrance rather than the front door. The women arrived at Miami's famed Jockey Club for a tournament to find Confederate flags atop the flagpoles that adorned the grandstand. Logan, Koger, and Hooks stayed at a nearby Holiday Inn when the club would not give them rooms. Beleaguered by the stress of racism and a lack of money, the professional careers of the trio came to a close quickly and without victories.[118]

The story of Black women in professional tennis would not end with them. Gibson followed the careers of Renee Blount, Andrea Whitmore Buchanan, Kim Sands, and Leslie Allen, the next generation. In the spring of 1979, Jim Smith, the operator of Franklin Field Tennis Center, invited Gibson to Dorchester, one of Boston's most racially diverse neighborhoods, for a special short-term teaching opportunity. Franklin Field was part of Sportsmen's Tennis Club, the home of Black tennis in the area since the sixties. She spent four weekends coaching Buchanan, Allen, and Sands as well as Zina Garrison, a fifteen-year-old amateur from Houston. More than the paycheck motivated

Gibson as she watched, coached, and took notes on each player: "I want to give these kids self-confidence, develop the attitude that they can be winners," she told Lesley Visser of the *Boston Globe*. "They need polish, everything from overheads to court demeanor."[119]

Gibson was not a powder puff when it came to coaching. Like Dr. Eaton and Dr. Johnson, rules, attire, and deportment mattered to her, as did fitness, concentration, and strategy. She did not go easy on Garrison just because she was the youngest in the group. "Althea gave me a lot of one-on-one attention," Garrison wrote in her autobiography. "She pushed me as if I were a pro, not a junior." The lessons left an indelible impression on Garrison, who trained "from dawn to dusk" with her coach in Houston, but not at the "level of intensity" that Gibson demanded. "We did mental drills, physical drills, and every other kind of drill. It became clear to me that playing at the pro level required much more than physical talent and preparation. Total concentration for extended periods of time was essential." Garrison recognized Gibson's attention as a one-of-a-kind opportunity, but she also began to worry that she simply did not have what it took—or what Gibson said it took—to become a champion.[120]

Facing discrimination was part of being a Black tennis champion, and Gibson tried to prepare Garrison and the Black women for the differences that they would encounter. Twenty years later, Garrison remembered Gibson telling her "that nothing was going to be given to me, and that I would always have to work harder than the white girls on the tour. She said I had to be far better than everyone else, and even then I'd probably find myself in a situation where being the best wasn't good enough." It was as if Gibson was still smarting over the snubs from 1957, when few in the White media in America and England would acknowledge that she was the best player in women's tennis.[121]

Gibson thought Leslie Allen had what it took to be the best. Allen's mother, Sarah, had played in ATA tournaments, and the family even had an autographed picture of Gibson in their living room. But Allen was late in growing serious about tennis and had not grown up idolizing her. Yet when Gibson saw Allen, who was an inch shy of six feet tall, she saw a potential champion. "With your wingspan," she told her, "you need to think about winning WTA tournaments."[122] When Gibson spoke, Allen listened. "Not only can she tell me what it's like to be on the Centre Court at Wimbledon," Allen said, "she can say what it's like to be a black woman."[123] They were soon working together at Gibson's new club, the Rallye Racquet Club in East Orange, and Gibson came to believe that Allen was the world's best Black woman tennis player. "She's tall, lean, mean and hungry and she reminds me of me," she said at the U.S. Open at the end of the season. Allen was learning her lessons well, and not just the ones about shots. "You're an advertisement," Allen said about race. "But you have to play for yourself, and that's what I'm doing."[124] Gibson also imparted her self-confidence and passion for winning. She taught Allen that it was not enough "just [to be] happy to be in the game" or to think, "I hope I do well here." Instead, the attitude had to be, "Try and win the game!"[125] The attitude was neither ladylike nor polite. It never had been. But it was pure Gibson.

Gibson's work at Franklin Field Tennis Center and with Allen was reflective of the ways in which her attitude about race had evolved in some respects yet remained entrenched in others. She was still a hybrid. She sometimes still identified as a "Negro." She would never wear an Afro in the seventies, and she confessed that she preferred straightened hair over the natural style. She remained critical of social movements: "Some are good, some are bad. The trouble is that too often people get caught up in the movements themselves and lose sight of what the real goals are all about." Living as one chose without being encumbered by worries over racial representation and perceptions remained Gibson's preference: "You make your own life. And if you don't do anything yourself, nothing of value will happen for you."[126] She thought she was "on the right side" of racial matters because she did not identify with Black Power and did not want to be seen as "militant."[127] Yet Gibson identified strongly as a Black woman and was as adamant as ever that her sports careers had been socially valuable, if not materially so, at least not for herself: "I am not a militant person and I still feel that my life as a black woman and international golf and tennis player speaks loudly and clearly for my race. I feel I have set a good example which can be followed by any young people. I have proved that it is the person [who] counts in the long run, regardless of race, creed, or color."[128]

14

Two Deaths

*Unlike most, a ball player must confront two deaths. . . .
As his major league career is ending, all things will end.
However he sprang, he was always earthbound. Mortality
embraces him. The golden age has passed as in a moment.
So will all things. So will all moments. Memento mori.*

—ROGER KAHN, *The Boys of Summer*, 1971

SEPTEMBER 16, 1980, was a rare night when Gibson got the recognition that she deserved. At the "Salute to Women in Sports," held in New York City, she was one of nine women inducted into the new International Women's Sports Hall of Fame. The event was a gala fundraiser to benefit the Women's Sports Foundation, the organization founded six years earlier by Billie Jean and Larry King, swimmer Donna de Varona, and businessman James Jorgensen. Enshrined as a "pioneer," the category for women who had made their mark in sports before 1960, Gibson was celebrated along with Patty Berg, Amelia Earhart, Gertrude Ederle, Eleanor Holm, and Babe Didrikson Zaharias for paving the way for the careers of contemporary honorees King, Janet Guthrie, and Wilma Rudolph.[1]

The night, like so many of Gibson's days, was laced with reminders of the things that did not happen for her because she came along too soon. The foundation honored nineteen-year-old Tracy Austin, the winner of the U.S. Open in 1979, who had already earned more than a million dollars in career prize money. Guthrie, the first woman to race at the Indianapolis 500 and the Daytona 500, spoke of the perception of inadequacy that society had for so long foisted upon women of accomplishment, including those in sports: "Women tend to lose their history. The result is when . . . a woman capable of achieving something really remarkable comes along, she's made to feel like a freak."[2] Rudolph spoke of power and her hope that the Women's Sports Foundation, which aspired in part to help women and girls access money to support their careers, would "create great leverage for young women."[3] Guthrie's and Rudolph's words gave Gibson occasion to nod knowingly. She was doing then what she would do for the rest of her life: paying the heavy price in her senior years for having been an outsider in her prime. It was her last sport, a game of catch-up that she would never win.

———

Everything old was new again where movies were concerned. The major American studios had been churning out period pieces set in the 1940s and the 1950s, Gibson's heyday, throughout the seventies and into the eighties. Television got in on the act, too. With public interest in sportswomen and the seemingly never-ending fascination with Black men in sports flowing, the three major networks produced heavily romanticized and fictionalized made-for-TV biopics about Maureen Connolly, Zaharias, Rudolph, and Jesse Owens. Wanting a piece of the action, Gibson explored having her autobiography turned into a film. Tamara Dobson, the actress best known for playing the lead character in the Cleopatra Jones blaxploitation films, reportedly talked with Gibson about writing the screenplay. Gibson was said to have liked the idea. Standing 6'2", Dobson might also have played the lead. Yet Gibson's effort to bring her story to national television proved futile. Questions surrounded her possession of the copyright to her first book. In 1974, she had sold the rights to her story to a company called Geocine Films, which went on to produce a documentary about her. Vanguard, the business firm that she had invested in during the seventies, tried to interest the three major television networks in acquiring and broadcasting the documentary. By the early 1980s, none had accepted.[4]

The failure proved costly through the opportunities that Gibson did not receive. Rudolph's resurgence was a testament to the power of media and publicity. Like Gibson, Rudolph found that fame did not lead to fortune. She graduated from college and shifted from one job to another in teaching, coaching, and administration. Rudolph's life changed with the publication of her autobiography, *Wilma*, in 1977, and NBC's airing of a biopic based on the book later that year. By 1978, she was traveling regularly across the country, making paid appearances and giving speeches, mostly to youth groups. She was glad for the work, but she also knew that being a Black sportswoman lowered her bottom line. "Black women athletes in this country are on the lowest rung of the sports ladder," she told Associated Press reporter Will Grimsley.[5] Her male counterparts were on a different plane. "Black male athletes have carved out niches for themselves in our society. . . . They have become rich and famous. They are constantly sought out for personal appearances, movie roles and lucrative TV commentator jobs. They've got it made."[6]

Gibson had only to look to Arthur Ashe to agree. By 1980, Ashe, thirty-seven, had retired from professional tennis. He had also earned fame beyond compare as the leading Black man in the sport, the only one to win a major, and the admiration of people around the world for his budding, and gradualist, activism, typified by his stature as among the first Black American athletes to compete in South Africa amid apartheid. Ashe was also rich. Between tournament prizes, endorsements, and work as a color analyst for televised tennis coverage, he lived comfortably.[7]

Ashe knew that he benefited financially from male privilege and public interest in Black male athletes, and he observed that Yannick Noah would profit, too. He had discovered Noah, a Black native of France, in Cameroon in the 1970s and sponsored him. By the end of the decade, Noah was considered "the next Arthur Ashe" and bristled at the expectations that came with the mantle. Ashe opined that Noah would grow in time: "Yannick will come to know, like I came to know, that being black and very good will give him enormous financial advantages. With it goes a tremendous responsibility to the sport, to himself."[8] As Billie Jean King and the WTA continued to stand up for the cause of equal prize money, Ashe's outlook evolved, leading him to drop his public opposition to pay equity. He also became a mentor to several up-and-coming Black women in tennis. Leslie Allen and Zina Garrison consistently expressed their gratitude during and after their own careers for his encouraging words and lessons during programs, practice sessions, and clinics.[9]

Charity continued to bring Gibson and Ashe together over the years. Together, they played exhibitions to support the United Negro College Fund, HBCUs, the United Nations Children's Fund (UNICEF), and the Black Tennis and Sports Foundation (BTSF). Co-founded by Ashe in the 1970s, the BTSF was designed to benefit children in cities through after-school and weekend programs. Gibson was named a director of the BTSF, which was plagued by funding problems throughout its short existence. She expressed pride in Ashe's success. Gibson called herself "the happiest person in the world" when he won the U.S. Open. His interest in social matters gave her pleasure, too: "I'm proud of the way he has stood up for himself in such things as the South Africa affair." Still, she felt compelled to explain her comparative inaction where activism was concerned during her own playing days: "You know, I was never concerned with how people felt about me—about the color of my skin—I always knew I was a person as good as anyone else."[10]

Ashe's fame and reputation, buttressed by his charitable turn, were important for keeping Gibson in the public eye. By the 1980s, she was a relative afterthought whenever most people thought about African Americans in tennis. Ashe was top of mind. She had, in her own words, "helped open the opportunity for Arthur," but on everything, including the tennis fundraisers, his name came first.[11]

———

Gibson had become a relic. She still traveled, spoke, and gave tennis exhibitions. Organizations gave her awards and invited her to galas. She even picked up honorary degrees, first from Monmouth College and later from Drew University, but her activities and presence were based on her past. There were no entries in lucrative tournaments, broadcast jobs for cable television or the major networks, or books that she had been contracted to write. "The praise and accolades I received as I toured and lectured and sang were directed at someone who was once somebody. I was an ex—former amateur champion, former pro champion, former Woman Athlete of the Year, former movie actress, former recording artist."[12] Gibson wrote those lines in *So Much to Live For* to describe her life in the early sixties. Twenty years later, the description still applied. Her name throughout the press had become some variation on "Althea Gibson, former tennis champion." Sometimes Wimbledon or Forest Hills was named. Just as often, though, they were not. She was, in a sense, stripped of her titles.[13]

A new generation of Black women were making names for themselves in tennis in the eighties. Few had been born when Gibson won her Grand Slams. Most had enrolled at predominantly White colleges and universities, where they played on the tennis team. It was a landscape entirely different from the one she had known. Unlike in her day, these Black women would not be the only ones. "They're right there on the horizon," she said of the generation's chances of winning tournaments and succeeding in professional tennis. "If they keep working, they can make it."[14]

Gibson's protégés from her weekends at Boston's Franklin Field were leading the way. Renee Blount, a UCLA product like Ashe, was soldiering along in professional tennis, buoyed by a win in 1979 on the developmental tour sponsored by Avon, the cosmetics firm that briefly replaced Virginia Slims as the sponsor of the WTA. Gibson and Leslie Allen traveled abroad together around this time. When Allen played in tournaments in Europe and Africa, Gibson came with her, playing an exhibition doubles match in Benin City, Nigeria. Allen observed the dramatic difference between the way Gibson was treated there and how people responded to her when she attended tournaments in the United States. People in Benin City received her as "absolute royalty. They knew who she was and so she got her due respect." In the U.S. events where they worked together, "some of them big events," Allen noticed, "it was a sort of perfunctory or cursory acknowledgment of presence."[15]

In February 1981, Allen won the Avon Championship in Detroit. She was the first Black woman to win a major professional tennis title since Gibson. Gibson heard the news early the next morning as she made breakfast. "I was overwhelmed," she remembered when Will Grimsley called her for her reaction. "My heart started pounding away—with love and pride and concern." She still believed that Allen had what it took to win a major. Getting the first tournament win was "the biggest obstacle to overcome. Now Leslie may go on to be a champion." Grimsley recorded a message that she wanted to share: "I would like to tell Leslie, and the other black girls on the tour, that there are no obstacles out there, nothing to fear. Work hard and play tennis."[16]

Just watching Allen win the first set of her first-round match at the previous year's U.S. Open had been enough to make Gibson rise with emotion. Allen remembered looking up and seeing Gibson in the Past Champions' Box, where she "jump[ed] to her feet, cheer[ed], and rais[ed] her arms with clenched fists."[17] By the time of the Avon Championship, Bob Ryland, a standout former player in the ATA, was her coach, but in the days after the tournament, Allen sounded like Gibson when addressing questions about race: "I never think of being black. I look upon myself as a tennis player trying to win. It never occurs to me that I am an inspirational symbol for my race, a Jackie Robinson or an Althea Gibson." When Allen reminded Grimsley that she played on "the international circuit," she might as well have been reading the speech that Gibson had given at the Wimbledon Ball in 1957: "We all dress in the same locker room, we sit around tables and talk—some of us are Japanese, Indian, Swedish, black, yellow, and white. I can only regard myself as an American." Allen acknowledged that there had been much that Gibson "had to go through," but she insisted that the path that she and the other Black women in tennis trod was uncomplicated. "It's a different atmosphere now. None of us [Black players] learned the game on the sidewalks of Harlem. We haven't run into any barriers. Wherever we go, we are accepted."[18]

Yet things could still be difficult for Black women in tennis. After Allen won in Detroit, Zina Garrison won the Junior Wimbledon and U.S. Open titles. In Garrison's account, slights nearly circumvented her victories. Garrison was one of the highest-ranked juniors in U.S. tennis, but, she recalled, she was "the sixth person . . . to be chosen for the Wimbledon junior draw." Then, after she won at Junior Wimbledon, the USTA placed her on "an alternate list" for the U.S. Open Junior Championships in 1981. The treatment infuriated Garrison's coach, John Wilkerson. It led Garrison, seventeen at the time, to remember Gibson's message to her about what lay ahead in tennis: "Even when you unquestionably have proven yourself to be the best, you're not always going to be recognized as the best."[19]

Stories of Black women being received with hostility from White players were not unheard of. The following year, a report surfaced that Andrea Jaeger, a promising young White player, had attacked Renee Blount in the locker room after a doubles match in Los Angeles. Jaeger denied the accusation, but others saw what happened. Camille Benjamin, another Black woman on the circuit, recounted Jaeger's ominous words about her doubles teammate, Blount: "There's something about her I don't like."[20] The sneer and the mere suggestion of the attack hardly suggested acceptance.

Leslie Allen was loath to admit it, but she, too, was experiencing racially insensitive treatment on tour. Security guards at tournament venues repeatedly stopped her and asked "May I help you?" rather than allow her to move freely to the places where she needed to go. She watched as those same guards let her White peers walk through entrances without being questioned. Allen resorted to "calling out to one of [my white counterparts] to alert the guard that I belonged. To validate me."[21]

The 1983 French Open brought a particularly ugly scene. Allen and Charles Strode faced Eliot Teltscher and Barbara Jordan in the mixed doubles final. When Allen questioned a call, Teltscher "got very upset and started yelling like crazy," she told a reporter the next week.[22] Allen and Strode lost the point. She remembered that Teltscher approached her during the changeover and "called me the 'N' and the 'C' word." In a subsequent media interview, she said only that Teltscher had "made this very obscene remark" that was sexist.[23] In 2020, Allen, in an essay published online, accused him of using the racist slur, too. She still practiced restraint, calling him only "my white male opponent" and never stating Teltscher's name. She was clear, though, about which match had been the setting for the verbal attack. Allen recalled refraining from spitting in Teltscher's face as they shook hands at the net after the match and being "reluctant to talk much about the incident" afterward. Why? Because she feared being ostracized and met with retaliation by the tennis community even though she had done nothing wrong.[24]

Organizations invited Gibson to speak during events dedicated to women, women in sports, and African Americans. She accepted; her insights and stories about what it had meant to be first a Black girl and later a Black woman had become commodities of sorts in the post-civil-rights and women's rights eras. In February 1980, Black History Month, she spoke at Maryland's Catonsville Community College at a conference dedicated to women and sports. "Even the exceptional woman athlete used to have many barriers," she told her audience. "Many were only able to succeed because they had the support of wealthy patrons or families. Most black girls had nowhere to turn and therefore were seldom seen in individual sports because they couldn't afford the lessons." Gibson was describing herself, and she did not stop there. Hitting the lectern for emphasis, she told the audience of her career: "I was lean, mean, and hungry." She had succeeded in tennis, she said, because of her tenacity and her unwillingness to give any opponent a chance to overtake her: "It takes a lot to become a champion. You need to be a killer. If you can't look over that net and see Public Enemy Number One, then you aren't going to be a champ."[25] Gibson's career was over, but she never missed an opportunity to tell anyone who would listen how good she was. That her career was finished made the narrative even more imperative.

For all the braggadocio, her private pain sometimes showed in public. Gibson's voice broke at Catonsville, and she cried when she spoke the guiding principle of her life: "An athlete must learn to look out for number one." She fumbled to explain her sudden loss of composure. The pang and the tears came from the chasm between her words and her reality: "I don't do this a lot. There isn't a lecture a week."[26] Usually, the chances were not grand, either. She spoke with ironic regret. Some people talk about the chances that they did not take that might have led to major sports careers, or the intrusions, especially sudden injuries, that disrupted their sports dreams. Gibson implied that she regretted having been an athlete at all: "Sometimes, I wish I had gone into some other things. I wanted to be a doctor, I wanted to sing. But I was talked out of it and became a world champion instead."[27]

At Catonsville, she talked about money. Renting an apartment in East Orange at the Beechwood Gardens complex, Gibson was not living like a queen. When an audience member asked what she knew in her sports afterlife that she had not known in her prime, she answered candidly: "I would know how to protect myself. The athlete provides a livelihood for others. Others must protect them so there is some financial security later in life." Gibson plainly recognized that many people—those in tennis and golf associations around the world, and those in businesses, including Dot Records, Gil Fuller, and Saperstein and the Globetrotters—had profited from her name and her labor. In contrast, she was left with the wish but not the unfettered ability "to be able to do the small things when I want to do them whenever I want to do them."[28] Speaking off the cuff, Gibson fell into a pool of self-recrimination. "Like many athletes before me, I did not make the most of the lucrative years, because of mismanagement and the poor handling of supposed friends," she confessed. "Even when I was making money, I did not have the sense not to be fleeced." Gibson knew she was not alone. Her speech conjured the images of two men she had met and admired. Jesse Owens was dying in Tucson, and Joe Louis was not far behind him in Las Vegas. Debt and tax troubles had become as much a part of each man's legacy as his victories. "Most athletes don't have good business sense, so they have to trust other people who aren't always trustworthy," she acknowledged ruefully. "An athlete is so busy that underhand[ed] things occur that she's not aware of."[29] She recognized that time had not been on her side, either, a result of the years when she had played tennis and her age when she had taken up golf: "We all know the pro athlete's life is short-lived. If you don't make it after a certain span of years, you won't make it financially."[30]

Money was not the only thing on Gibson's mind. She thought about social interactions and her quality of life: "I want good friends and good relationships with people." Confessing the desire, Gibson all but admitted what she lacked.

Gibson married Sydney Llewellyn with little fanfare in April 1983.[31] Llewellyn had been married when they worked together in the 1950s. There was no definitive indication that he and Gibson were romantically involved then, but the formation of intimate bonds between male coaches and female athletes and between female stars and male agents is not un-heard of. Any fame that Llewellyn had was bound up with Gibson's name. He had been living in New York since their collaboration on the professional tours ended, teaching tennis at Fred Johnson Park, which had been named for Gibson's first instructor, and coaching leading ATA players. As a junior, Arthur Ashe took lessons with Llewellyn, whom he impressed with his "very subtle, low-key," and "persistent desire to win."[32] Yet as an adult, Ashe did not cite Llewellyn as a factor in his on-court success. "I contend it takes a chump to make a champ," Llewellyn liked to say.[33] Coaching the two most successful African American tennis champions had not been enough to make him rich.

Gibson's second marriage would be as unconventional as her first. Only she and Llewellyn knew the reason for their nuptials. They did not live together. She remained in her apartment filled with memorabilia in East Orange, while he kept his flat in New York. Few, if anyone at all, thought love had anything to do with the marriage. Speculation abounded among friends and family that Llewellyn's citizenship, the few rewards that still came with Gibson's celebrity, and money had brought the pair back together. He had at least two inventions to promote, an exercise machine called the Equiform and a tennis contraption—an elastic band with a ring attached to either end, one for the arm and another for the foot—that he promised would train users to move their bodies and their tennis rackets in unison during strokes. She envisioned that the Equiform would hit it big and allow her to make some of her own dreams come true. "We're spending quite a bit of time on it," she told the *St. Petersburg Times*. "I hope through this and other means we can set up a tennis academy. I've always wanted that—to teach kids how to play tennis effectively."[34]

The windfall and the academy never happened, leaving Gibson to work on someone else's grounds and terms. She was the director of recreation for East Orange and gave lessons at the city's Rallye Racquet Club. East Orange was "an urban ghost town," not a tennis mecca, as writer Stan Hart discovered when he met Gibson there in 1983. Hart was on a mission to interview and play with past tennis greats for the book that became *Once a Champion: Legendary Tennis Stars Revisited*. Hart called her to request an interview and playing session, but she refused to talk with him until Llewellyn, who was her business manager again, gave his "approval." Gibson gave Hart Llewellyn's telephone number and let the matter go. Reached by phone, Llewellyn explained that Gibson would only talk if she were paid. Hart agreed to pay her $100 for a tennis lesson and an hour-long interview. Gibson was indeed looking out for herself.[35]

Tall and proud, Gibson alighted from her long Mercury sedan on a Sunday morning to meet Hart. She wore a maroon jogging suit accented with a light stripe down the sides of her pants and the sleeves of her jacket. Her nails were painted, and her hair was styled. She looked the part of the athletically elegant teaching professional, but some of her first words to Hart underscored the comparative harshness of their surroundings: "Don't leave anything in the locker room."[36] Hart understood her to mean that neither his pants nor any cash from his pockets would be there when he returned. It was not the kind of thing that Gibson had had to worry about in the clubhouses and locker rooms at either Wimbledon or Forest Hills. It was another reminder that she was out of place.

Gibson carried out the lesson with Hart and the interview with the same intensity and thoroughness with which she had gone about most everything else in her sports careers. She pointed out his flaws and weaknesses, as her many coaches had done for her, but she also showed her independent streak, admitting that since Hart was only a casual player, sticking with his "old ways," primarily his grip, was fine. She beat him 8–6 in a pro set—though Hart questioned her eyesight, because of the glasses that she had worn for years to correct her nearsightedness, and thus her ability to see whether a ball was in or out.[37]

Llewellyn had been correct when he told Hart to be prepared for Gibson to be "negative at first" but to reveal herself as "a very warm and generous human being" as their time together progressed. When the lesson was over, she regaled Hart with the highlights of her tennis and golf careers and her thoughts about the present. She regretted not winning Australia's national title in 1957, which would have given her the career Grand Slam, though she took some solace in having beaten Shirley Fry in Perth. Gibson was not reluctant to discuss the best parts of her game: "I . . . had a great overhead, and I was fast. No one could hardly pass me, especially if I got the ball deep." By forgetting her early struggles, she exhibited the clichéd trait of most great athletes: a short memory. "I won on all surfaces: grass, hard court, and clay, as well as wood." Gibson remembered her last Grand Slam match, her defeat of Darlene Hard at Forest Hills in 1958, as her greatest victory. She was also unapologetic about her playing mentality: "People thought I was ruthless, which I was. I didn't give a darn who was on the other side of the net. I'd knock you down if you got in the way." When Hart asked whether Gibson could beat Martina Navratilova, the most dominant player in women's tennis in the early 1980s, she did not hedge. Twice she said, "I would win."[38]

Yet when Gibson spoke of her present and future, Hart felt that she was the one who had been knocked down. It was the matter of the disintegration of her career in pro tennis, the long, drawn-out end of her foray into golf, and her work in municipal sports in New Jersey. He listened in disbelief, and even challenged her, as she explained her difficulties in getting Black youths excited about tennis: "Black boys think [tennis] is not manly enough, and their girlfriends don't take it up because they are told that they will get muscles. So it is hard to get them going, although we have the facilities." The "sissy sport" stigma and the lesbian connotations of the game, raised with the outings of Billie Jean King and Navratilova two years earlier, were as rampant in 1983 as they had been during her own career. Gibson was less forthright when Hart asked her to share her thoughts about racism. She allowed that discrimination was "passed on down the line" through generational observations and habits and cited slavery as the origins, but she was hesitant to talk about the ways in which prejudice had impacted her own life. Moving to North Carolina and facing segregation on the public buses had made her think about "race problems" as she never had in Harlem, she said. Nearly forty years later, it was clear that she was still reluctant to think about them.[39]

Hart spent two hours with Gibson and came away with the impression that her life "was a mosaic, with the pieces slowly—sometimes almost simultaneously—beginning to fall into place," but he suspected, rightly, that there were fractures, too. She drove Hart to his hotel when the interview was over and pointed out public housing for the elderly along the way. "You know, I could live in any one of those apartments," she said. "They are all clean, roomy, and fit to live in." She had toured the property through her work for the city. Gibson, fifty-five, added in passing, "That is my dream. To afford my own house." Hart, a resident of Martha's Vineyard, sat silently in the passenger seat and reviewed the facts of Gibson's life to himself: "She has an apartment and is already contemplating the possibility that when she gets old, she will be living in the project we have just passed. She wants her own house but can't afford it. She went from Harlem to Wimbledon to Hollywood to the great golf courses of America and now works as a functionary for the city of East Orange. It doesn't seem fair," Hart concluded. "Something went wrong somewhere down the line."[40]

———

No single thing had gone wrong for Gibson. She was instead living with the consequences of having never fit neatly into society when she was younger and of being ahead of the times throughout her life. Once a gender-nonconforming child and teenager and then an adult woman who defied social norms and restrictions, she was moving into trying to survive as a senior citizen whose resources were deeply affected because she had not followed a traditional life path.

Gibson maintained her pride to the point of vanity. "Biographical Information: Althea Gibson, Tennis Champion/Sportswoman" was a four-page document that she attached to her resume. The package was convenient for teaching or reminding others about all that she had done. The first two sentences of the narrative were unsurprising. They gave the date and the location of her birth and stated that she lived in East Orange. The third sentence, however, stood out for its swagger: "Miss Gibson is 5'10½" and weighs 165 pounds and her physical condition is excellent."[41] Aesthetics mattered to her.

She dyed her hair without fail. "As long as I am in the public eye," Gibson told Hart, "I don't want to look my age. When I let it all hang out, I'll look all gray and distinguished, but now is not the time."[42] She knew well that keeping up a certain image was important for keeping herself relevant in the eyes of the public and for getting those much-needed speaking engagements. Nevertheless, people still remarked on her supposed strangeness. In early 1983, Gibson sat for a portrait session as part of a photography exhibition, "Women of Quality," that was to be presented at the Kennedy Center in Washington, D.C. She was uncomfortable with the sitting, which required that she wear a necklace of De Beers diamonds. The photographer, Paul Jasmin, dismissively diagnosed the reason for her fidgeting: "Gibson looks like an athlete and acts like an athlete—you could tell she probably never wore a diamond in her life."[43] Jasmin offered no such commentary on the other women, mostly actresses and ballerinas, who filled out the series. The only athlete featured in the exhibition, Gibson still carried the stigma of being a sportswoman.

Still, past fame yielded present rewards. When Wimbledon celebrated its one hundredth anniversary in the summer of 1984, Gibson was there with Llewellyn. The All England Club invited past champions to return with their spouses. It was the first time that Llewellyn made the trip to Wimbledon with his star pupil, three decades after her wins there, and her first trip back since 1960. Louise Brough was among the players who came back, too. Brough lived comfortably in California, where she taught tennis and split her time between two houses, one in Pasadena and another in San Diego, with her husband of nearly thirty years, a dentist. Brough and the others who returned took note of Gibson's behavior as she racked up bills for personal services, including hair salon visits and laundry. "She charged it all to the All England Club, but she didn't get away with it," Brough told author Bruce Schoenfeld. Flouting good taste and trying to get the best deal for herself, her behavior was, he concluded, "vintage Althea." During the trip, she and Llewellyn came unannounced to the tennis academy that Angela Buxton ran in Hampstead and gave impromptu lessons for hours to one group after another of astonished housewives. Weeks later, Gibson was in Los Angeles as a dignitary for the Olympic Games. Then it was back to New York to participate in Ashe's "Artists and Athletes Against Apartheid," an event at Columbia University to raise money to bring justice to South Africa.[44]

Gibson and Llewellyn put their teamwork to use for history at the end of October 1984. Filmmaker William Miles interviewed them for *Black Champions*, his oral history project devoted to capturing the stories of African American athletes, the famous and the forgotten. Wearing a green zippered jogging suit and pink lipstick that matched her socks, Gibson sat on a bench and reminisced, holding a Babolat tennis racket as a prop. The session was pleasant until the interviewer asked her to discuss "the modern game of tennis." Abruptly, Gibson refused to continue: "I don't want to talk about that." Setting the conditions of her interviews was nothing new. She had once decided not to talk to reporters over the telephone. Another time, she refused to talk on the grounds that she "wouldn't want to give out details" that she could include in a third memoir. Gibson told the crew to turn off their cameras and called for Llewellyn. Only after they conferred would she agree to continue. She lamented that contemporary players did not hit with the same "forward drive" that she and her peers used in the 1950s and that topspin had come to dominate the game. Then, as if on cue, Gibson broached the subject of money. She confessed that the money that players made "impressed" her. "In my day, it was for peanuts and for . . . cups, and for silverware, and not . . . [for] the bread. I wish I was able to play today to make the kind of money that they're making. I wouldn't have to worry about a thing."[45] The modern game, or modern money, clearly depressed her.

If Gibson had played in the modern era, her outlook on race would have been different, too. She consented to an interview for *Ladies of the Court*, a book collaboration between three-time Grand Slam singles winner Virginia Wade and journalist Jean Rafferty in anticipation of Wimbledon's centenary. Gibson was unchanged in all the expected ways. "Fiercely" she insisted that she, not Billie Jean King, had been the first woman to make $100,000 in professional tennis, even though she had long ago admitted that she earned far less. She did not seek to rewrite the historical record on her attitude about being either a racial symbol or an ambassador during her playing days, either. "At the time I felt I was just representing myself," she said. "My people weren't in that sport anyway." In *I Always Wanted to Be Somebody*, she had used "my people" to refer to African Americans. However, the phrase could just as easily have applied to not only race but class, specifically poor and working-class Black people like her family and the folks she had known in Harlem. "I never thought of myself as a spokesman. I was a competitor. I didn't much enjoy being a spokesman for anything," she continued.[46]

Yet with the passage of time, Gibson imagined that she would be a different kind of competitor in the eighties, a player who was more attuned to playing for something outside of herself: "What I feel right now is that if I played tennis, I would be playing for myself and for my people."[47] How she would have done it was anyone's guess. Beginning in 1969, the NCAA made changes directed at stamping out protests like the ones that characterized the Revolt of the Black Athlete. No longer would athletic scholarships be guaranteed no matter whether a player "played or protested" or even "quit the team." In 1973, the NCAA decreed that scholarships could be "one-year renewable agreements" rather than four-year guarantees, and gave coaches the power to decide. As one historian has written, this gave a coach the authority to "kick [a] player off the team and get [the] scholarship back for any arbitrary reason." Influenced by these restrictions as well as corporate America's continued queasiness about offending the sensibilities of White consumers, many Black athletes of the 1980s effectively operated with the same race politics that Gibson had adopted in the 1950s.[48]

Gibson lived somewhere between the past and the present. She took on speaking engagements, and she also had her job at the tennis club and her sporadic commitments for New Jersey's Athletic Control Board, but she looked for more ways to fill her time. Organizers for a minor tennis tournament in Kansas City were stunned when she accepted their invitation to attend and play in an exhibition mixed doubles match. "Oh, well, it's a possibility," she told Benita Givens, the tournament director, who called her. "I'm free that weekend. Send me a letter showing the things you want." Givens was dumbstruck that "a former Wimbledon champion" would be willing to listen. The reasons for Gibson's alacrity lay in the opportunity to travel and pass the time but also in the tournament's purpose: to raise money for the Niles Home, a center that treated abused children. She was still looking to give back and thinking about her own past.[49]

Time and time again, Gibson said some variation on "you can't go back," but interviews and speaking engagements inevitably led her there. Sometimes the time travel was fun. In April 1987, she was an honored guest at the dedication of the Alice Marble Stadium Court at the Palm Desert Resort and Country Club. Wearing a light tan skirt, a maize blazer, and a light green tie that matched her shirt, Gibson, on the cusp of her sixtieth birthday, was the picture of gender hybridity. She teared up as she remembered the impact of Marble's editorial in *American Lawn Tennis*. The essay led not only to her debut at Forest Hills in 1950 but also, she said, to her victory there in 1957. She claimed to have shed tears and said a prayer for Marble after beating Brough in the final.[50]

At other times, though, looking back was painful, as it forced Gibson to ponder what might have been and what never was. She did not hold back in sharing her thoughts. "I guess you could say my timing was off," she might say. "If I had played today, a lot of things would have been easier for me."[51] "The only regret I have is that the (tennis) money wasn't there when I was coming along," she allowed another time. "I'd no doubt be a millionaire if I were coming along now."[52]

It was impossible to reasonably compare players of one era to those of another, but Gibson was willing to try. She decided that Germany's Steffi Graf was her modern equivalent. "I was a phenomenon—and believe you me, I was a phenomenon," she told the *Detroit Free Press* in 1987 while in town to promote an exhibition match, the Ocean Spray Challenge of the Champions; Billie Jean King and Martina Navratilova were competing against Pam Shriver and Chris Evert Lloyd for $225,000. Ashe was to be one of the play-by-play announcers. "So I see someone with Graf's type of game—who knows how to attack a ball—and I'm impressed." Graf played the kind of forceful power game that Gibson preached was required of champions. "You have to learn to wheel and deal with that racket: You have to know how to use it deftly, how to use it ruthlessly and how to use it with finesse. The American girls," she added, when asked, "just aren't taught that, and in Europe," speaking of Graf, "evidently they are."[53]

Gibson judged that the African American women on the professional circuit were not measuring up. Her coaching relationship with Leslie Allen had long since ended, but Gibson still felt that she had skin in the game. "I notice a lot of players, especially some of our black young ladies . . . don't seem to have the intensity, the drive to want to win," she told William Miles's crew. She did not name a specific player, but she described her concerns: "I was looking at a match at the U.S. Open . . . recently, and I was noticing one of our black young ladies playing. To me, she had the match won, but then I noticed something there. There was no drive. [It] seemed like she just quit all of a sudden without continuing on to force that drive and intensity that is required, particularly for her to win that particular match." Gibson concluded ominously that "some of our black players . . . don't seem to have that willingness to want to win."[54] The statement was a broad generalization and one that showed how much she had forgotten, or had chosen not to remember, about her own career. For one thing, White players had always been allowed simply to play without categorization. For another, she had had to learn how to close matches, especially those played on the biggest stages, and learning took time.

Then again, Gibson had developed the habit of misremembering several points about her career. "On the court, I always conducted myself like a lady," she told a reporter for the *Miami News*. The remark plainly overlooked the time in 1956 when she had smashed a ball into the grandstand and nearly struck the Australian prime minister. "And I never thought about the disadvantages of being a woman in a man's world. I was just worried about accomplishing all that I could with the gifts I had." That might have been true of her amateur tennis days, but, by the sixties, she had openly questioned the impact of her race and gender on her trouble attaining corporate sponsorship. Gibson's revised version of her own story served a purpose. It was more appealing to the kinds of general audiences that she addressed, including for the Women's Sports Foundation. Stories of self-reliance told without implicating systems of oppression never go out of style. Nevertheless, she conceded that all the women tennis players of her era had been at a disadvantage.[55]

Speaking in support of women in sports became chief among Gibson's interests in her last years. "I have seen the need to make people aware of the state of women's athletics. It's a challenge. But even at my age, I still think I can look challenges right in the eye," she said. She openly marveled at the ways in which times had changed with Title IX. The law "has given modern female athletes a chance to compete in fields that might have been more restrictive in my time," she told an audience in Miami. Still, Gibson recognized that opportunities and recompense for women were not the same across all sports. She cited tennis and golf as leaders as each had "come the farthest toward equality for women." Her beloved basketball, which at that point still had no professional league for women, lagged far behind. Access to coaching concerned her, too. Ironically, she thought that women's sports were regressing where class was concerned. "I don't think individualized coaching that was available years ago to women is available to women today. Today coaches are highly-paid, highly-specialized people. . . . If you're a woman and you can afford the proper instruction, you can get it. If you are like I was—a child raised in Harlem—it becomes very difficult to afford that type of instruction."[56] For Gibson, and sports, everything came back to money.

For all the doubts that Gibson harbored, she still marveled over her achievements. She also knew that her life was a remarkable story. In April 1988, she came to Washington, D.C., to share part of that story with the nation. She donated one of her tennis outfits, a Harry C. Lee tennis racket, and her two most prized possessions, her Wimbledon trophies, to the National Museum of American History at the Smithsonian Institution. Dr. Eaton, seventy-one, attended the transfer presentation. They did not see each other often, though the past year had brought them together. In 1987, the University of North Carolina–Wilmington made her an honorary doctor of letters, two years after making Dr. Eaton an honorary doctor of laws. The bestowals were further signs that times had changed and that institutions were recognizing the parts Dr. Eaton and Gibson had played in creating those transformations. The two were still fond of each other, like family and warriors who had gone through battles together. Dr. Eaton kept a portrait of Gibson in his office in Wilmington. Autographed, the picture was in the center of a wall display that included a plaque from the NAACP, a family portrait, and his award for being North Carolina's Doctor of the Year.[57]

At the Smithsonian, Dr. Eaton recalled Dr. Johnson and their collective opinion about what Gibson needed to make it across the color line in tennis: "She was a fine player, but she had too many rough edges to go into those tennis clubs." Gibson recalled that she passed the gender comportment tests of the doctors and the country clubs with flying colors: "No one would say anything to me because of the way I carried myself. Tennis was a game for ladies and gentlemen, and I conducted myself in that manner." That she carried herself like a "lady" was increasingly important to the narrative that she was crafting to support her legacy. Exceptionalism was part of that narrative, too. In case no one knew, or remembered, her accomplishments, Gibson reminded her listeners grandly. "Who could have imagined? Who could have thought? Here stands before you a Negro woman, raised in Harlem, who went on to become a tennis player . . . and finally wind up being a world champion, in fact, the first black woman champion of this world. And believe it or not," she added, "I still am."[58]

"I still am" had become the theme of Gibson's life as she searched for opportunities to remain in the public eye. She was intent on finding ways to show that although she was thirty years removed from the height of her tennis career, she still had relevant things to say and contributions to make. "Coaches on the Court," an essay written by Gibson in 1988, was a case in point. Presenting herself as a strategist and commentator, Gibson cast a critical eye on what she saw as the deficiencies of modern tennis. Tennis had changed and not for the better, she thought. Tournament purses made the game "almost difficult to recognize as a sport," and while "players have changed in ability for the positive," their "behavior" had altered "in a negative way." "I find it upsetting to see and hear players shouting obscenities at umpires, linepersons, and fans and hitting the ball in anger over a bad call," she wrote, likely with John McEnroe in mind; McEnroe was one of the most talented and temperamental players in men's tennis at the time. She surmised that privilege and a shift in modern attitudes about decorum on the tennis court made such displays acceptable. Gibson recalled that race, "being the first black on my level," necessitated that she conceal her emotions. "I know that if I had made a gesture or argued one call they would have tried to boot me out of the game," she said, finally acknowledging the double standards that she faced during her tennis career. There were times when "maybe I would get a bad call followed by another bad call. I would think, 'What are they trying to do to me,'" but "I would SAY nothing. No argument, no emotion." Outbursts by players were "not healthy for the game." Instead, they were "hurting the dignity of the game."[59]

Yet the purpose of "Coaches on the Court" was as much about creating space for Gibson as it was about improving tennis. She argued that allowing coaches to interact with their students between breaks in matches would "reduce the players['] stress," leading to "more exciting tennis." Having coaches on the sidelines would also "bring more personalities to the sport" and lengthen careers. "Wouldn't the fans like to see players who are winding up their careers stay in the sport or former greats return to the sport?" If the answer were yes, she might have stayed in tennis a little longer. She might also have found her way back to tennis in the eighties and to a salary of $30,000 ($75,107 in 2022), which, she informed her audience, was the going rate for coaches. "I am still around this great game," she said at the end, "as a written consultant and, yes, coach." She had a persistent "daydream" of being back at Wimbledon "on the court as a coach" guiding a future winner.[60] The essay was an appeal. It was also an expression of what she had learned over the years: that she had to work to make her dreams come true.

Gibson would do that work without Sydney Llewellyn. They divorced in 1988. Many of Gibson's relatives had never liked him, accusing him of infidelity, abuse, greed, and giving her poor financial advice. If Gibson thought badly of Llewellyn, she did not say so in public. She merely called him "my former coach and husband" and fondly recalled how he had helped her become a champion. She remembered his characteristic reaction after a "bad set" when an opponent had gotten the best of her: "'You are having fun while she is working. Go out there now, Althea, and work and win.' And I did."[61]

———

Gibson spoke proudly of her accomplishments, but she remained ambivalent about the racial significance of her achievements. In January 1990, a reporter for the *Daily Utah Chronicle* interviewed her to promote her upcoming visit to Provo to appear on a panel convened to celebrate Martin Luther King Jr. Day at the University of Utah. Gibson was emphatic that personal strength had helped her tune out hecklers: "I couldn't afford to let anything bother me because I was out there to play tennis to win." Being a symbol, she confessed, was a responsibility that she had never wanted. "The obstacles I had to over-come were being the first," she explained. "I didn't like being a pioneer, because I believed my abilities and talents were why I was there." She acknowledged that she was not allowed to enter some tournaments. When her entry forms were accepted, she insisted, everything was fine as far as she was concerned: "Once I was entered and displayed my talents, I had no problems." She also showed the degree to which she operated at cross purposes to Dr. Eaton, Dr. Johnson, and the ATA. "I wasn't set up to represent any group," she told the writer. "I was a representative of myself, although," she added, "it was an honor because I was black and I'm sure my people were joyous." Gibson defended her decision not to be vocal about racial injustice during her tennis career: "In sports, you can't let other things interfere with the game you're playing on the court. I was out there to play and to win. I wasn't out there representing a cause." African Americans were not her focus, she explained, but they benefited indirectly from the matters that she cared about: "I was representing myself and my country. And blacks are part of the United States. I did it my way, by winning, and won just about anything I played."[62]

Others were vying to join Gibson in the winner's circle. Zina Garrison and Lori McNeil were the two African American women most likely to win Grand Slams. Two years after turning professional, Garrison won her first WTA title, the European Indoors, in 1984. She won at least one title every year for the next five years. McNeil, Garrison's childhood friend and doubles partner, won her first professional title, the Virginia Slims tournament in Oklahoma City, in September 1986 by defeating Garrison. It was a historic match, the first WTA final that featured two Black women. McNeil won six more titles during the decade and reached her career-best ranking of ninth in the world in 1988. The following year, Garrison was ranked fourth, her personal best. Despite their successes, both women had difficulties landing significant sponsorship deals. The year 1990 appeared to be a competitive turning point. Garrison beat powerhouses Monica Seles and Steffi Graf to reach the Wimbledon final. It was the first time a Black woman had reached a Grand Slam title match since Gibson at Wimbledon and Forest Hills in 1958. Hours after she defeated Graf, Reebok and Yonex signed Garrison to major contracts.[63]

The All England Club arranged for Gibson to attend the Wimbledon final as an honored guest. She watched Garrison practice hours before the final, unwittingly disconcerting her heir apparent. "You wouldn't believe how nervous I felt just knowing that that tough, charismatic lady would be watching," Garrison wrote in 2001. "I was fine until Althea walked on the court during one of my warm-up sessions. Just seeing her and thinking about what she had achieved on this same court caused me to sweat. Her presence made me realize that I had an opportunity to do something that would make history."[64] Gibson gave Garrison a tour of select parts of the clubhouse. With Garrison's present and future on the line, Gibson made her personal past the center of their interactions. "She pointed to the bathroom stall she used, and she showed me the little corner she rested in before playing her final match," Garrison remembered. Gibson shared little advice or wisdom: "The only thing she actually told me to do was to get out there and go for it."[65]

Garrison gave the match her all, but it was not enough to win. Resplendent in a white tracksuit, Gibson sat in the Royal Box with Angela Mortimer Barrett, who had won her Wimbledon title in 1961, Kathleen McKane Godfree, the champion of 1924 and 1926, and Sidney Wood, men's champion of 1931. Together, they watched as Navratilova beat Garrison, 6–4, 6–1, in seventy-five minutes. After the match, Garrison denied that Gibson's presence affected her performance. She also revealed a clear difference in their outlooks. "I can't even comprehend winning one Wimbledon; it's amazing that someone can do this," Garrison said, speaking of Navratilova's capture of her ninth Wimbledon singles title. "She really believes this is her court and that no one can take it away from her."[66] It had taken time, but Gibson had learned to play that way, too.

———

Even at sixty-four, Gibson could not give up competition. Tennis was out, given a bad left knee and the qualifying rules, but there was nothing to stop her from making another bid at glory in professional golf. She traveled to Rancho Mirage, California, in September 1990 for an LPGA qualifying tournament. She did not see age as a hindrance: "I thought about my age and said, 'That doesn't matter.' I can still play." Gibson's presence pointed to a gender gap in golf. There was still no tour for women over the age of fifty, a lacuna that she hoped to see filled. "My attempting this, being a senior, hopefully might prompt a women's senior tour. I think we need one badly. We can bring out the great ones if the money is right, if you can make a living at it." Like the others, this golf comeback was part of her way of satisfying her need to compete and her interest in improving society—on her own terms. "I hope I'm encouraging [Black women to play golf], senior golf, ladies golf. I feel I'm doing my part." Twenty-five years earlier, she had said the same. Still, more than competition and inspiring society were at stake; she was making a bid for financial survival, too. Seeing Beth Daniel, one of the LPGA's best players, win $100,000 ($226,684 in 2022) in a tournament inspired her latest comeback.[67]

Gibson made ends meet with her work for New Jersey's Governor's Council on Physical Fitness and Sports, the state version of the councils convened by American presidents for decades. The New Jersey council maintained a speaker's bureau, distributed awards, and convened conferences and seminars. Gibson was at the center of it all. Some of her talks discouraged students, including children in the third and fourth grades, from using drugs and dropping out of school.[68] She even appeared in a state-sponsored film for students called *Talk Drugs Out*. In other speeches, she encouraged senior citizens to remain physically active regardless of their athleticism. Thinking specifically about women's health, she said, "It's not necessary for a woman to excel [in sports] to enjoy sports." Still aware of the stigmas that female athletes faced, she told her audiences that exercise did not reduce a woman's femininity, a message that could potentially lengthen and improve the quality of the lives of the older women who came out to hear her. Gibson shared her high-mindedness about the power of women in sports to be positive examples for all who watched them. "The female athlete is a role model and is obligated to keep her life on the highest moral plane," she opined. Preaching had never been her way and she did not judge the way others lived their lives, so she did not define what it meant to be "moral."[69] Gibson knew well that many of her listeners faced financial challenges as they aged, and she proposed a solution: "As seniors, our thoughts are more on our pensions than our passions. We have to use our time to assist one another."[70] Old habits died hard, leading her to point out that she was "still the only Negro woman's tennis champion today," even though "Black" and "African American" had long since become the socially accepted terms.[71] While her racial identity was stuck in the past, she had come to identify as an older person for whom age and ageism had become hurdles. "Being young is a special blessing," she told children. "Unfortunately, you may not realize it until you're all grown up."[72] Senior citizens had to "push through doors marked pull," she liked to say.[73]

That was what Gibson was doing—or trying to do—in Palm Springs: defying expectations of what women over the age of sixty could do. She bragged to a local sportswriter about her out-of-state speaking invitations: "I get so many offers, so many requests to make appearances. I only respond to the ones that have the most money." The explanation was sensible and sounded grand, but she followed by giving a peek into her less-than-comfortable financial circumstances and the reason that she was entered in the tournament: "I've got to pay the rent, the gas bill, the electric bill. I'm all alone. I've got no one to support me."[74]

Gibson would not support herself through golf. After shooting 85 in her first round, she tried to convince the press and herself of her athletic bona fides. "I am a natural athlete. I don't like to brag about myself, but I can play any sport you mention. I carry a 200 average in bowling. I've played semi-professional basketball in Harlem. I've thrown a football 50 yards." As for the game at hand, Gibson maintained that she had a chance. "I can still play golf," she insisted. "I could be great at this game if I can hit the greens like I know I can." Instead, she took to the course at Mission Hills Resort on the second day and shot herself out of the tournament with an 86.[75]

Her dreams of returning to the professional golf circuit for anything other than celebrity pro-ams dashed, Gibson returned to the gig life she had been living all along. Within months, the NCAA flew her to Nashville to present her with its highest honor, the Theodore Roosevelt Award, at its annual convention. She was investing in and managing a deli and catering service, Around the Corner, but it did not last. Gibson went back to giving her speeches. She would speak for any organization that invited her. Often, she showed up in school gymnasiums, dressed in a jogging suit and polo shirt. Audiences, young and old, were often spellbound by the way she talked about her life and encouraged them to either take up a sport or not try drugs.[76] She embellished stories about her life. She claimed that when lightning struck the stadium at Forest Hills during her match against Louise Brough, one of the decorative stone eagles "fell right at my feet." This, she said, was a message from God: "It told me that Our Creator wasn't ready for me to win yet." Gibson described her skills as magical, too. Her serve was "like a bolt out of the blue" and she could "dance around the court."[77] Sometimes she ended her talks by singing "So Much to Live For." Just as often she closed by telling assemblies that she loved them. Gibson faced impertinent questions with aplomb. She had lived a life filled with accomplishments that most people could only dream of and turns of fate and fortune found in film scripts and novels. Nevertheless, during question-and-answer periods, she was sometimes asked whether she was married, as if the listener had noticed a gap in what she had chosen to reveal about herself. Gibson answered simply and directly: "Yes I was—twice; and divorced—twice." She treated the question as if it were like any other search for basic facts and added, "You probably want to know how old I am, too."[78] Listeners called her "a treasure," "an inspiration," and "sincere and honest."[79] In those moments, she seemed to be living without acrimony over missing out on the riches that had come to those tennis players who came after her.

Others, though, thought Gibson had become churlish with the years and their many disappointments. Fred Kovaleski, who had known Gibson in Egypt in 1956, remembered hearing that the warm-hearted woman he had known "in those early good years" had changed: "From everything I've heard, she turned a little disillusioned and colder as she got older."[80] Lenny Simpson, who had gone from playing on Dr. Eaton's and Dr. Johnson's respective tennis courts to playing World TeamTennis, encountered her in Hilton Head, where she was playing in a celebrity golf tournament. They talked long enough for Simpson to feel that Gibson, despite her protests over the years, had indeed grown "bitter."[81] She miffed reporters who tracked her down at her office in Trenton in hopes of discussing her career. She again refused to give telephone interviews on the grounds that she would not want to divulge anything that could appear in another book. After all, a third book, if she ever got around to writing it, could mean money. In the meantime, she limited herself to sharing her wisdom, stories, and charisma in the speaking engagements that carried her across the country and the state. It was all part of her life on the road.[82]

That life as Gibson knew it ended on the night of January 14, 1992. She was in West Orange to give a keynote address at an awards dinner for the Essex County Council of the Boy Scouts of America, where Dr. Stanley Bergen Jr., the president of New Jersey's University of Medicine and Dentistry, was the guest of honor. However, before rising to speak, Gibson fell over in her chair. Emergency medical technicians arrived and carried her to an ambulance. Checked into Newark's University Hospital, she remained for days and refused to allow staff to tell the press and the public what had happened. She had suffered a stroke.[83]

At first Gibson rallied. By the spring, she had resumed her work for the Governor's Council. In May, she was back on the road, promoting the annual New Jersey Senior Games for residents fifty-five and older for competition and to showcase the mental and physical value of exercise. Medalists were guaranteed spots in the national games the following year. Gibson dove back into her role, joking with audiences across the state about the effects of aging on her own athleticism. Tennis was out because of her knee, she said, and her body ached after golf. Still, regular exercise and a healthy diet were musts. The message was personal, given her own health scare. "Enjoy your life much longer and you can avoid the alternative," she said.[84]

Bad news reached Gibson and her six colleagues on the council in June. The Republican-controlled state legislature cut their funding in the state budget for 1993. Harry Carson, the council's executive director, had argued against the elimination, to no avail. The winner of a Super Bowl with the New York Giants, Carson knew that he would be fine. He could make up his annual salary, $68,000 ($143,547 in 2022), in a matter of days with paid speeches and public appearances. Carson led the council not for the money, he said, but because he believed the work improved the lives of New Jersey's residents. The council had been vulnerable to budget cuts because its work was marginalized as unsubstantial. "The problem is, we're sports," Carson said ruefully. "We're not on the part of the budget that's on the front page." Being an outsider had cost Gibson again. On July 1, she was jobless.[85]

In a bitter irony, *Ebony* placed Gibson on its cover for August, her first national magazine cover since the sixties. In the special issue, called "Winning," *Ebony* covered African Americans in sports from 1947 to 1992. The timing was right, as 1992 was an Olympic year and the country was at a fever pitch over the Barcelona Games. For the first time, American professional athletes were competing, leading to the gold-medal-winning dominance of USA Basketball, the "Dream Team," led by Michael Jordan. The year was also the forty-fifth anniversary of Jackie Robinson's entry into Major League Baseball. Gibson was on the cover as part of a collage with Robinson on one end and herself on the other. They looked like sentinels guarding their lieutenants— Muhammad Ali, Florence Griffith-Joyner, Carl Lewis, and Jordan—in the middle. Inside, Gibson held and shared the spotlight. The editors allowed her to stand alone as a trailblazer for Black women in sports, with a full-page portrait in its "Women's Hall of Fame," called her first Wimbledon singles title "perhaps the greatest breakthrough in individual sports," and credited her as having "opened the door for Arthur Ashe." Nevertheless, her Wimbledon win tied his 1975 title for fifth place on the list of the ten "most dramatic moments" in the history of sports. Ashe, who had written *A Hard Road to Glory*, on the history of Black athletes since 1619, contributed an essay in which he imagined a bright future of historic advances for Black athletes, coaches, and business leaders. Every reference to and image of Gibson was about her past.[86]

The council work had been more than a job for Gibson; it had been a lifeline. The position gave her benefits beyond much-needed health insurance. The work brought her chances to meet people and to connect with them, if only from afar and for the time that it took to give a speech, shake a hand, or trade stories one-on-one when the speech was over. "I showed off on the football field because throwing passes better than the varsity quarterback was a way for me to express myself, to show that there was something I was good at," she had written of her high school days.[87] Her public-facing work for the Governor's Council was much the same. She had never been a homebody, and the travel got her out of her apartment and on the road. That disappeared with her job. The invitations to lecture were drying up, but the state of her health made it harder for her to do basic things anyway.

The news that Ashe was living with AIDS only added to the bleakness. Ashe had been diagnosed in the late eighties. His doctors attributed his condition to a blood transfusion that he had received years earlier after bypass surgery. When the press learned of his diagnosis in the spring of 1992, Ashe was forced to go public. Asked for comment, Gibson said what many people thought: "I feel terrible hearing Arthur has this kind of disease. It's sad news, this happening to such a great man, too."[88] By February 1993, Ashe was dead. He was only forty-nine.

June brought a special invitation and an opportunity for ambivalent feelings. More than three decades after the Eisenhower administration passed on having her at the White House, President Bill Clinton invited Gibson to attend the National Sports Awards Reception in the East Room on June 20. The honorees were Kareem Abdul-Jabbar, Muhammad Ali, Arnold Palmer, Ted Williams, and Wilma Rudolph. Gibson was only to be a guest. She seems not to have attended. Relegation to the sidelines made the request hard but bearable; an aversion to the thought that people would see how much weight she had lost and the toll that her waning health was having on her appearance were bigger obstacles to overcome. Increasingly, she could not.[89]

Despair surrounded Gibson. The divorce long behind them, she and Will had made peace with each other. They met regularly for lunch at a diner near the senior citizens' center where he lived, keeping each other company but also seeing each other's decline. Gibson began to think more and more about death. She had never had complete possession of her own life. Forces and her own decision-making had conspired that way. Now the notion struck her that her death was something she could control.[90]

Late one afternoon in March 1995, Gibson called Angela Buxton. They had stayed in touch over the years. When Buxton came to New York for the U.S. Open, she would reach out to Gibson. They met for lunch in East Orange or visited at Gibson's apartment. Sometimes they watched the tennis matches together at Flushing Meadows. Buxton had experienced her own share of losses in the years after her divorce: the sicknesses and eventual deaths of her son Joseph, her partner, Jimmy, and her mother, Violet. She had sold her house and bought a condo in Florida to spend part of the year there and start anew. Gibson's call was supposed to be a final goodbye. She told Buxton about her health troubles and that she was running out of money to pay her rent, utilities, and medical bills. Bounced checks had become a way of life for Gibson. There was one solution left, she thought: "I'm going to commit suicide."[91]

It never happened. "I just took her as she was," Buxton said of the time she had spent with Gibson in the fifties. "What I saw was what I got and I liked it, and we got on very well."[92] After forty years, Buxton refused to let go of their friendship. She held Gibson on the telephone line. She committed to send money, too. Days later, Buxton enlisted the help of the *Boston Globe*'s Bud Collins, who also worked for NBC Sports. Collins, the ultimate tennis insider, spread the word about Gibson's condition. Members of the tennis community mailed checks to her. The money was welcome. A close friend later estimated that Gibson had just $3,000 ($5,830 in 2022) in savings and was living on her monthly social security check. She suffered a further emotional setback when Will died from complications of diabetes in September, pushing her further into a state of depression.[93]

Withdrawing from life, Gibson refused to see people. Alone in her apartment, she eased her pain with cigarettes and liquor. New York mayor David Dinkins, whom she had known for years through the Black tennis community and Ashe's fundraisers, and Zina Garrison were among the many whose calls she let go to voicemail. Sometimes she answered, saying just enough to make Dinkins or anyone else on the other end feel concerned. Living in Virginia, Annie worried about Gibson as much then as she had fifty years earlier. Annie asked her grandnephew, Don Felder, who lived in the metro area, to check on her. He called Gibson again and again, but she would neither pick up the telephone nor call back.[94]

———

By 1996, Gibson's situation had become national news. *Tennis Week* reported on her condition. Soon, newspapers and magazines across the country were telling the story. David Dinkins went public, too. Gibson had told him that she was dying, he said. Bill Hayling, who was Gibson's physician as well as her former golf sponsor in the late sixties, took the extraordinary measure of revealing her condition. Two strokes and an aneurysm were taking their toll on her. She weighed close to one hundred pounds. Even so, she wanted to remain independent. She was "trying to take care of things" on her own, Hayling said. "She doesn't want to be pitied," Dinkins added. "If she had been a half-step later [in her tennis career], she would have been a multimillionaire." The cruelness of time—not to mention Gibson's myriad non-conformities—was to blame.[95]

Gibson had come full circle. The kindness of strangers—Buddy Walker, Marsden Burnell, Rhoda Smith, Fred Johnson, Edna and Sugar Ray Robinson, Dr. and Mrs. Eaton, and Dr. Johnson—had gotten her off the streets of Harlem. Astonished by her potential, others, including Alice Marble, had given her chances to make it in tennis. It was the stuff that led Ted Poston, reflecting on Gibson's rise in the wake of her first Wimbledon singles title, to call her a "nationwide community project."[96] Back then, people noticed her talent. Four decades later, after being brushed aside because her novelty had worn off, Gibson, aged and vulnerable, was externally supported once again. People saw her suffering. Money came from all over, from individuals, groups, and tennis associations. Even schoolkids mailed dollars. Funds came from people who remembered Gibson's glorious tennis past. Others who had only learned who she was after news of her troubles circulated in newspapers and magazines across the country and around the world gave, too. Yet the sympathy was not enough to lead to a lasting tribute on a grand scale. In August 1997, days before her seventieth birthday, the stadium at the National Tennis Center in Flushing was named not for her but for Ashe, who, according to an advocate for the decision, was "universally acknowledged as a man of genuine historic importance."[97]

Gibson lived out the rest of her days in seclusion. Annie's death in Virginia in 2001, on Gibson's seventy-fourth birthday, dealt another blow. She had already lost her sisters Mildred and Ann. Frances Clayton Gray, whom Gibson had known for decades through her work for Newark and the surrounding area, and her partner, Carol Gaither, were among the few whom Gibson allowed inside her apartment. Rosemary Darben, her former sister-in-law, visited, too, cooking her favorite foods to cheer her up. Gaither and Gray became Gibson's major caregivers, with Gray taking the lead role in managing her bills and her medical care; she also became Gibson's spokesperson and set up the Althea Gibson Foundation in hopes of raising money for scholarships and mentorship programs and to cover her healthcare costs. Gibson seldom left the apartment. She was an active homebody at best, described as "alert." Yet the public did not hear from Gibson directly. Gray and Rosemary communicated for her, giving her peace while also making it difficult for others to surmise her true condition.[98] After 1998, Buxton would not see her again. When neighbors spotted Gibson around the complex, she waved but said little, mainly speaking only when someone spoke to her. The woman who had boasted about her tennis skills now shut down conversations about what she had once been able to do. Yeses and nods were as much as she would give anyone who asked.[99]

———

Gibson died on September 28, 2003, felled at last by a heart attack suffered months earlier and respiratory problems. Gray made the arrangements for Gibson's last rites, seeing to it that her body, dressed all in white, including her pants, lay in repose at the Newark Museum the day before her funeral at Trinity & St. Philip's Cathedral, where Zina Garrison and Leslie Allen spoke of what her coaching and life meant to them. Gibson was buried beside Will in Montclair at Rosedale Cemetery. They share a headstone, but her portion, complete with an etching of a tennis racket and a list of her Grand Slam victories, is larger than Will's, which describes him as "The Love of Her Life."[100]

Television had been Gibson's constant companion through her long end. Alone in her apartment, the rise of Venus Williams roused her. Venus had been among the most-watched players in junior tennis, and turning professional in October 1994 at the age of fourteen had made her a sensation. Like the rest of the tennis world, Buxton was fascinated by Venus's abilities, but her interest was personal, too. Venus's "formidable serve, cat-like court coverage and controlled aggression" reminded her of Gibson "in her prime."[101]

Through a contact, Buxton received an invitation to the home in Palm Beach Gardens where Venus lived with her parents, Oracene and Richard, and her sister Serena, a competitive player who was finding her game while living in Venus's shadow. On New Year's Day 1997, Buxton and a friend watched Venus practice. When Buxton offered to telephone Gibson, Venus was noticeably excited. Gibson answered and gave Venus advice that Buxton recorded: "Play aggressively and with spirit. You should revel in playing in such wonderful arenas. I know I did." Gibson knew all too well what it was like to be an outsider in tennis, and she encouraged Venus to look upon the status as an asset: "Since you'll be the underdog, you'll have nothing to lose. The crowds will love you. . . . But most of all, be who you are and let your racquet do the talking." Venus treasured the call.[102] Close by during the conversation, Serena gained from Gibson's message, too. Her capture of the U.S. Open in 1999 over Martina Hingis meant that Gibson was no longer the only living Black Grand Slam tennis champion in singles. Months earlier, Serena had reached out to her, faxing a letter and questions to the Althea Gibson Foundation as part of an interview for a school assignment.[103]

When Venus won Wimbledon in 2000, she remembered Gibson: "I know she's somewhere watching this." Venus, twenty, spoke about race with a candor and confidence that had eluded Gibson in her prime and decades after: "You realize not everyone wants you to win, not everyone is going to support you—and that's okay." Thinking of Serena, she continued, "We're Black. We have fought for everything we have. People are turning on their TV and suddenly they see this Black girl playing tennis. . . . We're doing something different that hasn't been done very often." But not never.[104]

Gibson was indeed watching. She had been thrilled by the telegrams that awaited her after her victory at Wimbledon in 1957. Forty-three years later, she passed her joy, and the torch, along to Venus with a telegrammed message of her own:

YOU HAVE NOW MOVED YOURSELF TO ANOTHER LEVEL IN YOUR ATHLETIC ADVENTURE. YOU ARE NOW IN THE HISTORY BOOKS FOREVER. I GLADLY PASS THE TORCH TO YOU AND SERENA. I KNOW THAT YOU TWO WILL CARRY IT WELL BECAUSE YOU AND YOUR SISTER HAVE BEEN PREPARED FOR THIS DAY BY YOUR PARENTS. CONGRATULATIONS ON YOUR MAGNIFICENT VICTORY.[105]

The harvest was complete.

Notes

INTRODUCTION

1. Althea Gibson, *I Always Wanted to Be Somebody*, ed. Ed Fitzgerald (New York: Harper and Row, 1958), 133–139; "London Letter: Champion's Songs," *Birmingham Post and Gazette*, July 8, 1957, 4.

2. Edith Evans Asbury, "City Pays Tribute to Althea Gibson," *New York Times*, July 12, 1957, 23.

3. Serrell Hillman, "That Gibson Girl," *Time*, August 26, 1957, 48; Russ J. Cowans, "Sports Writers Sour on Althea," *Chicago Defender*, July 27, 1957, 2; Wendell Smith, "Has Net Queen Althea Gibson Gone High Hat?," *Pittsburgh Courier*, July 27, 1957, 18.

4. Smith, "Has Net Queen Althea Gibson Gone High Hat?"

5. Cowans, "Sports Writers Sour on Althea."

6. Cowans, "Sports Writers Sour on Althea"; Leon Fischer, quoted in Smith, "Has Althea Gibson Gone High Hat?"; Russ J. Cowans, "Russ' Corner: She Should Be Told," *Chicago Defender*, July 27, 1957, 24.

7. Josh Greenfeld, "Althea Against the World," *Sport*, July 1958, 37.

8. Bill Nunn Jr., "Change of Pace: Althea Gibson Speaks Her Mind," *Pittsburgh Courier*, August 17, 1957, 20.

9. Hillman, "That Gibson Girl," 48.

10. Gibson, *I Always Wanted to Be Somebody*, 149.

11. William J. Baker, *Jesse Owens: An American Life* (New York: Free Press, 1986); Amy Bass, *Not the Triumph but the Struggle: The 1968 Olympics and the Making of the Black Athlete* (Minneapolis: University of Minnesota Press, 2004); Lane Demas, *Integrating the Gridiron: Black Civil Rights and American College Football* (New Brunswick, NJ: Rutgers University Press, 2011); Douglas Hartmann, *Race, Culture, and the Revolt of the Black Athlete: The 1968 Olympic Protests and Their Aftermath* (Chicago: University of Chicago Press, 2004); James S. Hirsh, *Willie*

Mays: The Life, the Legend (New York: Scribner, 2010); Gregory J. Kaliss, *Men's College Athletics and the Politics of Racial Equality: Five Pioneer Stories of Black Manliness, White Citizenship, and American Democracy* (Philadelphia: Temple University Press, 2012); Charles H. Martin, *Benching Jim Crow: The Rise and Fall of the Color Line in Southern College Sports, 1890–1980* (Urbana: University of Illinois Press, 2010); Arnold Rampersad, *Jackie Robinson, a Biography* (New York: Alfred A. Knopf, 1997); Charles K. Ross, *Outside the Lines: African Americans and the Integration of the National Football League* (New York: New York University Press, 2001); Theresa Runstedtler, *Jack Johnson, Rebel Sojourner: Boxing in the Shadow of the Global Color Line* (Berkeley: University of California Press, 2012); Randy Roberts, *Papa Jack: Jack Johnson and the Era of the White Hopes* (New York: Free Press, 1983); Thomas G. Smith, *Showdown: JFK and the Integration of the Washington Redskins* (Boston: Beacon Press, 2011); Douglas Stark, *Breaking Barriers: A History of Integration in Professional Basketball* (Lanham, MD: Rowman and Littlefield, 2018); Jules Tygiel, *Baseball's Great Experiment: Jackie Robinson and His Legacy* (New York: Oxford University Press, 1983); and Geoffrey C. Ward, *Unforgivable Blackness: The Rise and Fall of Jack Johnson* (New York: Alfred A. Knopf, 2004). See also Patrick B. Miller, "Muscular Assimilationism: Sport and the Paradoxes of Racial Reform," in *Race and Sport: The Struggle for Equality On and Off the Field*, ed. Charles K. Ross (Oxford: University of Mississippi Press, 2004), 147–149.

12. Darlene Clark Hine, "Rape and the Inner Lives of Black Women in the Middle West," *Signs* 14, no. 4 (1989): 915, 916.

13. Businesswoman Effa Manley is a notable exception. See James Overmyer, *Queen of the Negro Leagues: Effa Manley and the Newark Eagles* (Lanham, MD: Rowman and Littlefield, 2020).

14. Exemplary histories of women in sports include

15. Admirable exceptions are Theresa Rundstedtler, "In Sports the Best Man Wins: How Joe Louis Whupped Jim Crow," in *In the Game: Race, Identity, and Sports in the Twentieth Century*, ed. Amy Bass (New York: Palgrave Macmillan, 2005), 47–92, and Roberts, *Papa Jack*.

16. My intersectional analysis of Gibson's life is indebted to the work of theorist and legal scholar Kimberlé Crenshaw. See Kimberlé Crenshaw, "Demarginalizing the Intersection of Race and Sex: A Black Feminist Critique of Antidiscrimination Doctrine, Feminist Theory and Antiracist Politics," *University of Chicago Legal Forum* 1 (1989): 139–167. See also Kimberlé Crenshaw, "Mapping the Margins: Intersectionality, Identity Politics, and Violence Against Women of Color," *Stanford Law Review* 43, no. 6 (1991): 1241–1299. My considerations of Gibson and gender performativity are informed by Judith Butler, *Gender Trouble* (1990; repr., New York: Routledge, 2007), 185–193.

17. Gwen Knapp, "Repaying a Proud Pioneer," *San Francisco Examiner*, November 10, 1996, D-3; Neil Amdur, "Althea Gibson Congratulates the Sisters," *New York Times*, September 9, 2001, SP 4; Bruce Schoenfeld, *The Match: Althea Gibson and Angela*

Buxton: How Two Outsiders—One Black, the Other Jewish—Forged a Friendship and Made Sports History (New York: Amistad Press, 2004); Frances Clayton Gray and Yanick Rice Lamb, *Born to Win: The Authorized Biography of Althea Gibson* (Hoboken, NJ: John Wiley and Sons, 2004); Eunice Lee, "Statue of First Black Woman to Win Wimbledon Unveiled in Newark Park," March 29, 2012, *Newark Star-Ledger*, https://www.nj.com/news/2012/03/statue_of_first_black_woman_to.html; "Stamp Announcement 13-36: Althea Gibson Stamp," United States Postal Service, July 25, 2013, https://about.usps.com/postal-bulletin/2013/pb22 368/html/info_007.htm; *Althea*, dir. Rex Miller (2014), https://www.rexpix.com/althea; Cody Benjamin, "CBS Sports Network to Premiere Arthur Ashe and Althea Gibson Documentary in Celebration of Black History Month," CBS Sports, February 14, 2019, https://www.cbssports.com/tennis/news/cbs-sports-network-to-premiere-arthur-ashe-and-althea-gibson-documentary-in-celebration-of-black-history-month/; Amanda N'Duka, "Four Daughters Sets 'The Match' as First Feature with Francesca Gregorini Directing," *Deadline*, May 15, 2020, https://deadline.com/2020/05/four-daughters-the-match-feature-francesca-gregorini-directing-1202936067/; "Althea Gibson Movie," Indiegogo, https://www.indiegogo.com/projects/althea-gibson-movie#/ (accessed August 19, 2022); Joel Drucker, "*I Always Wanted to Be Somebody*: Althea Gibson's Reissued Autobiography Remains a Seminal and Significant Text," *Tennis*, February 17, 2022, https://www.tennis.com/news/articles/i-always-wanted-to-be-somebody-althea-gibson-s-reissued-autobiography-remains-a-; Witherspoon, "New York City Renaming West 143rd Street in Althea Gibson's Honor," 10sballs.com, July 25, 2011, https://www.10sballs.com/2022/07/25/new-york-city-renaming-west-143rd-street-in-althea-gibsons-honor/.

18. Richard Gonzales, "New Statue at U.S. Open Honors African American Tennis Pioneer Althea Gibson," National Public Radio, August 29, 2019, https://www.npr.org/2019/08/26/754562253/new-statue-at-u-s-open-honors-african-american-tennis-pioneer-althea-gibson; George Vecsey, "A Sport Salutes Its Jackie Robinson," *New York Times*, September 8, 2004, D1; Angela Buxton, "Advice from a Legend," *Tennis*, August 1997, 16; Neil Amdur, "Serena Williams Has Tie to a Legend," *New York Times*, September 16, 1999, D4; Kevin Skiver, "USTA to Honor Althea Gibson, the First Black Grand Slam Champion, with Statue," CBS Sports, March 1, 2018, https://www.cbssports.com/tennis/news/usta-to-honor-althea-gibson-the-first-black-grand-slam-champion-with-statue/; Katherine Acquavella, "Althea Gibson, Iconic Tennis Champion and Trailblazer, Honored with Sculpture at U.S. Open," CBS Sports, August 28, 2019, https://www.cbssports.com/tennis/news/althea-gibson-iconic-tennis-champion-and-trailblazer-honored-with-sculpture-at-us-open/; Katrina M. Adams, *Own the Arena: Getting Ahead, Making a Difference, and Succeeding as the Only One* (New York: Amistad, 2021), 57–63.

19. "Artist Eric Goulder on His Althea Gibson Sculpture at the U.S. Open," *Thirty Love: Conversations About Tennis* (podcast), interview by Carl Bialik, featuring

Eric Goulder, August 27, 2019, https://medium.com/@bialik/thirty-love-podc ast-artist-eric-goulder-on-his-althea-gibson-sculpture-at-the-us-open-d5c89528f a31; Peter Bodo, "A Stadium by Any Other Name," *Tennis*, April 1997, 24–25.

20. Nina Pantic, "Althea Gibson Sculpture Pays Tribute to a Legend," *Tennis Magazine*, August 26, 2019, https://www.tennis.com/baseline/articles/althea-gibson-sculpt ure-pays-tribute-to-a-legend.

21. Tweet by Serena Williams, embedded in Skiver, "USTA to Honor Althea Gibson, the First Black Grand Slam Champion, with Statue."

22. Debert Cook, "Four Black Women Now Permeate the LPGA Tour," *African American Golfer's Digest*, August 25, 2016, https://africanamericangolfersdigest. com/four-black-women-now-permeate-the-lpga-tour/.

23. Cahn, *Coming on Strong*, 14, 15; Greg Ruth, *Tennis: A History from American Amateurs to Global Professionals* (Urbana: University of Illinois Press, 2021); George B. Kirsch, *Golf in America* (Urbana: University of Illinois Press, 2009), 166; Susan Ware, *Title IX: A Brief History with Documents* (Boston: Bedford/St. Martin's, 2007).

24. Aram Goudsouzian, *King of the Court: Bill Russell and the Basketball Revolution* (Berkeley: University of California Press, 2010); Eric Allen Hall, *Arthur Ashe: Tennis and Justice in the Civil Rights Era* (Baltimore: Johns Hopkins University Press, 2014); Raymond Arsenault, *Arthur Ashe: A Life* (New York: Simon and Schuster, 2018); Brad Snyder, *A Well-Paid Slave: Curt Flood's Fight for Free Agency in Professional Sports* (New York: Viking, 2006); David Remnick, *King of the World: Muhammad Ali and the Rise of an American Hero* (New York: Vintage, 1998); Susan Ware, *Game Set Match: Billie Jean King and the Revolution in Women's Sports* (Chapel Hill: University of North Carolina Press, 2011).

25. Marion E. Jackson, "Sports of the World," *Atlanta Daily World*, August 29, 1962, 7.

26. Kennett Love, "Althea Is at Home Abroad on Tennis Court," *New York Times*, June 24, 1956, S3.

27. Gibson, *I Always Wanted to Be Somebody*, 158.

28. Sam Lacy, "Don't Count Words, Measure Inches," *Baltimore Afro-American*, February 20, 1965, 10.

29. Patricia Hill Collins, "Learning from the Outsider Within: The Sociological Significance of Black Feminist Thought," *Social Problems* 33, no. 6 (1986): S14–S15.

30. Representative texts include Tomiko Brown-Nagin, *Civil Rights Queen: Constance Baker Motley and the Struggle for Equality* (New York: Pantheon, 2022); Melinda Chateauvert, *Marching Together: Women of the Brotherhood of Sleeping Car Porters* (Urbana: University of Illinois Press, 1997); Paula J. Giddings, *When and Where I Enter: The Impact of Black Women on Race and Sex in America* (1984; repr., New York: Perennial, 2001); Paula J. Giddings, *Ida, a Sword Among Lions* (New York: Amistad Press, 2008); Evelyn Brooks Higginbotham, *Righteous Discontent: The Women's Movement in the Black Baptist Church, 1880–1920* (Cambridge, MA: Harvard University Press, 1994); Tera W. Hunter, *To 'Joy My*

Freedom: Southern Black Women's Lives and Labors After the Civil War (Cambridge, MA: Harvard University Press, 1997); Jacqueline Jones, *Labor of Love, Labor of Sorrow: Black Women, Work, and the Family from Slavery to the Present* (1985; repr., New York: Basic Books, 2010); Kate Clifford Larson, *Walk with Me: A Biography of Fannie Lou Hamer* (New York: Oxford University Press, 2021); Alison M. Parker, *Unceasing Militant: The Life of Mary Church Terrell* (Chapel Hill: University of North Carolina Press, 2020); Barbara Ransby, *Ella Baker and the Black Freedom Movement: A Radical Democratic Vision* (Chapel Hill: University of North Carolina Press, 2003); Rosalind Rosenberg, *Jane Crow: The Life of Pauli Murray* (New York: Oxford University Press, 2017); Jeanne Theoharis, *The Rebellious Life of Mrs. Rosa Parks* (Boston: Beacon Press, 2013); Victoria W. Wolcott, *Remaking Respectability: African American Women in Interwar Detroit* (Chapel Hill: University of North Carolina Press, 2001).

31. "Lady Pros Seek Golf Glory," *Ebony*, July 1971, 111.

32. Althea Gibson, "Coaches on the Court," unpublished essay, April 1988, Althea Gibson Collection, Felder Family Archives, South Orange, NJ (hereafter "Gibson Collection").

33. Maureen Connolly, *Forehand Drive* (London: Macgibbon and Kee, 1957), 88.

34. United Press, "Irate Miss Gibson Bows to Miss Fry," *New York Times*, December 16, 1956, S1.

35. Billie Jean King with Cynthia Star, *We Have Come a Long Way: The Story of Women's Tennis* (New York: McGraw-Hill, 1988), 62–96; Dr. Hubert A. Eaton Sr., quoted in Ted Poston, "The Story of Althea Gibson: Article III," *New York Post Daily Magazine*, August 28, 1958, M2.

36. Ashley Brown, "Swinging for the State Department: American Women Tennis Players in Diplomatic Goodwill Tours, 1941–59," *Journal of Sport History* 42, no. 3 (2015): 290, 298–303.

37. Althea Gibson, "The Role of the Sportswoman"/"The Role of the Female Athlete"/ "The Sportswoman's Role in Society" (lecture, n.d. but after 1973), Gibson Collection.

38. Grace Lichtenstein, *A Long Way, Baby: Behind the Scenes in Women's Pro Tennis* (New York: William Morrow, 1974), 201.

39. Hall, *Arthur Ashe*, 2; Goudsouzian, *King of the Court*, 133; Mary Jo Festle, "'Jackie Robinson Without the Charm': The Challenges of Being Althea Gibson," in *Out of the Shadows: A Biographical History of African American Athletes* (Fayetteville: University of Arkansas Press, 2006): 189.

40. William H. Borders, *Seven Minutes at the Mike in the Deep South*, 2nd ed. (Atlanta: B. F. Logan Press, 1943), foreword, 101; "Courier Presents Readers Famous Poem," *Pittsburgh Courier*, February 20, 1943, 14; "Race Contribution Cited by Borders," *Atlanta Daily World*, February 16. 1942, 6.

41. William H. Wiggins Jr., "Contemporaries Heroes and Heroines Day: Cultural Resources," The African American Lectionary, February 24, 2008, http://www.

theafricanamericanlectionary.org/PopupCulturalAid.asp?LRID=11; Taylor Branch, *Parting the Waters: America in the King Years, 1954–63* (New York: Simon and Schuster, 1988), 53–54, 101; William H. Wiggins Jr., "Good Friday: Cultural Resources," The African American Lectionary, April 22, 2011, http://www.theafrica namericanlectionary.org/PopupCulturalAid.asp?LRID=205; Martin Luther King Jr., *Why We Can't Wait* (1963; repr., New York: Signet Classics, 2000), 21, 33, 93.

42. Martin Luther King Jr., *Where Do We Go from Here, Chaos or Community?* (Boston: Beacon Press, 1968), 127. King was not the only prominent thinker to recognize her symbolism. Historian Richard Bardolph concluded his book *The Negro Vanguard* with a tribute to Gibson, whom he saw as one of several Black athletes who, while not "entering the polemics of the [race] struggle, have . . . been concerned about 'The Problem,' but have hoped that their individual achievements would speak for themselves as an advertisement for the race." See Richard Bardolph, *The Negro Vanguard* (New York: Rinehart, 1959), 340, 334.

43. Stan Hart, *Once upon a Champion: Legendary Tennis Stars Revisited* (New York: Dodd, Mead, 1985), 27.

44. Gibson, *I Always Wanted to Be Somebody*, 1.

45. Judith Halberstam, *In a Queer Time and Place: Transgender Bodies, Subcultural Lives* (Durham, NC: Duke University Press, 2005), 1–7.

46. Gibson, *I Always Wanted to Be Somebody*, 48, 44.

47. Gibson, quoted in Hart, *Once a Champion*, 28.

48. Schoenfeld, *The Match*, 266; *Althea*, dir. Miller; Evelyn C. White, "Before Serena Williams, There Was Champion Tennis Player Althea Gibson," Bitch Media, September 3, 2015, https://www.bitchmedia.org/article/serena-williams-there-was-champion-tennis-player-althea-gibson; Arthur Carrington, interview by author, June 7, 2017.

49. Elizabeth Lapovsky Kennedy and Madeline D. Davis, *Boots of Leather, Slippers of Gold: The History of a Lesbian Community*, 2nd ed. (New York: Routledge, 2014), 169, 188.

50. I have previously explored Gibson's queerness and its implications on her career and sports integration and the Black media's interest in it. See Ashley Brown, "'Uncomplimentary Things': Tennis Player Althea Gibson, Sexism, Homophobia, and Anti-Queerness in the Black Media," *Journal of African American History* 106, no. 2 (Spring 2021): 249–277, esp. 250. See also Lisa Duggan, "Making It Perfectly Queer," *Socialist Review* 22, no. 1 (March 1992): 11–31, esp. 20; Cathy Cohen, "Punks, Bulldaggers, and Welfare Queens: The Radical Potential of Queer Politics?," in *Black Queer Studies: A Critical Anthology*, ed. E. Patrick Johnson and Mae Henderson (Durham, NC: Duke University Press, 2005), 21–51.

51. Brown, "'Uncomplimentary Things,'" 258, 251, 274; Susan K. Cahn, "From the 'Muscle Moll' to the 'Butch' Ballplayer: Mannishness, Lesbianism, and Homophobia in U.S. Women's Sport," *Feminist Studies* 19, no. 2 (Summer 1993): 350, 351, 354; Higginbotham, *Righteous Discontent*; Kathy Peiss, *Hope in a Jar: The Making of*

America's Beauty Culture (1998; repr., Philadelphia: University of Pennsylvania Press, 2011), 203–37; Anastasia C. Curwood, *Stormy Weather: Middle-Class African American Marriages Between the Two World Wars* (Chapel Hill: University of North Carolina Press, 2010), 5–6, 83–108, 33; Jeffrey B. Ferguson, *The Harlem Renaissance: A Brief History with Documents* (Boston: Bedford/St. Martin's, 2008), 22.

52. Brown, "'Uncomplimentary Things,'" 251.

53. Brown, "'Uncomplimentary Things,'" 258.

54. Pat Griffin, "The Lesbian Athlete: Unlearning the Culture of the Closet," in *A Queer World: The Center for Lesbian and Gay Studies Reader*, ed. Martin Duberman (New York: New York University Press, 1997), 564–566.

55. Gibson, *I Always Wanted to Be Somebody*, 156–157.

56. Cahn, "From the 'Muscle Moll' to the 'Butch' Ballplayer"; Pat Griffin, "Changing the Game: Homophobia, Sexism, and Lesbians in Sport," in *Women and Sports in the United States: A Documentary Reader*, ed. Jean O'Reilly and Susan K. Cahn (Boston: Northeastern University Press, 2007), 218–219.

57. Gibson, *I Always Wanted to Be Somebody*, 159.

58. Gibson has also been the subject of individual chapters in monographs and anthologies. See Sundiata Djata, *Blacks at the Net: Black Achievement in the History of Tennis, Volume One* (Syracuse, NY: Syracuse University Press, 2006), 28–41; Cecil Harris and Larryette Kyle-DeBose, *Charging the Net: A History of Blacks in Tennis from Althea Gibson and Arthur Ashe to the Williams Sisters* (Chicago: Ivan R. Dee, 2007), 46–75; Festle, "'Jackie Robinson Without the Charm,'" 187–205; Jennifer H. Lansbury, *A Spectacular Leap: Black Women Athletes in Twentieth-Century America* (Fayetteville: University of Arkansas Press, 2014), 75–113; Cecil Harris, *Different Strokes: Serena, Venus, and the Unfinished Black Tennis Revolution* (Lincoln: University of Nebraska Press, 2020), 76–92.

59. David Bromwich, "The Uses of Biography," *Yale Review* 73, no. 2 (1984): 167.

60. Denice C. Morgan, "Jack Johnson: Reluctant Hero of the Black Community," *Akron Law Review* 32, no. 3 (1999): 529–556; Neil Lanctot, *Campy: The Two Lives of Roy Campanella* (New York: Simon and Schuster, 2011), 177–178, 293, 308–310; Bardolph, *The Negro Vanguard*, 334; Hirsh, *Willie Mays*, 6, 231, 234; Leola Johnson and David Roediger, "'Hertz, Don't It?': Becoming Colorless and Staying Black in the Crossover of O. J. Simpson," in *Reading Sport: Critical Essays on Power and Representation*, ed. Susan Birrell and Mary G. McDonald (Boston: Northeastern University Press, 2000), 40–73; David L. Andrews, "Excavating Michael Jordan's Blackness," in *Reading Sport: Critical Essays on Power and Representation*, ed. Susan Birrell and Mary G. McDonald (Boston: Northeastern University Press, 2000), 166–205; Orin Starn, *The Passion of Tiger Woods* (Durham, NC: Duke University Press, 2011), 68–71, 92–99. Michael Jordan stands out for his business investments and philanthropy since his retirement from professional basketball.

61. Lynda Whitley, "Althea Gibson Rose to the Top in Grand Style," *Daily Press* (Newport News, VA), April 4, 1987, B8.

CHAPTER 1

1. Edith Evans Asbury, "City Pays Tribute to Althea Gibson," *New York Times*, July 12, 1957.
2. "Reception for Althea Gibson at Waldorf Astoria Hotel After Ticker-Tape Parade," July 11, 1957, http://www.wnyc.org/people/renville-h-mcmann/. Richard C. Patterson was the commissioner of commerce and public events.
3. Althea Gibson, *I Always Wanted to Be Somebody*, ed. Ed Fitzgerald (New York: Harper and Row, 1958), 1.
4. Evelyn Brooks Higginbotham, *Righteous Discontent: The Women's Movement in the Black Baptist Church, 1880–1920* (Cambridge, MA: Harvard University Press, 1994), 185–229, 8; Randall Kennedy, "Lifting as We Climb: A Progressive Defense of Respectability Politics," *Harper's Magazine*, October 2015, 24–34, esp. 24–27, 29. For a discussion of the milquetoast ways in which women, mainly White women, were expected to tell and indeed generally told the stories of their lives, see Carolyn G. Heilbrun, *Writing a Woman's Life* (1988; repr., New York: W. W. Norton, 2008), esp. 11–15, 23–24, 27. On middle-class Black women and the long-standing cultural imperative of concealing dimensions of their intimate lives, see Lisa B. Thompson, *Beyond the Black Lady: Sexuality and the New African American Middle Class* (Urbana: University of Illinois Press, 2009), 2–8.
5. Gibson, *I Always Wanted to Be Somebody*, 2.
6. Robert Lipsyte, "Althea Gibson: Golf Is Just Another Challenge," *New York Times*, August 23, 1964, 12S; Gibson, *I Always Wanted to Be Somebody*, 9; Frances Clayton Gray and Yanick Rice Lamb, *Born to Win: The Authorized Biography of Althea Gibson* (Hoboken, NJ: John Wiley and Sons, 2004), 8; Astrology Chart Notes by Althea Gibson, n.d., Gibson Collection.
7. James A. Burchard, "Althea Gibson's Story—From Harlem to Wimbledon," *New York World-Telegram*, June 23, 1956. Some sources say "Charlie."
8. Ted Poston, "The Story of Althea Gibson: Article I," *New York Post Daily Magazine*, August 26, 1957, M2.
9. Gibson, *I Always Wanted to Be Somebody*, 9; Susan K. Cahn, *Coming on Strong: Gender and Sexuality in Women's Sport*, 2nd ed. (Urbana: University of Illinois Press, 2015), 53.
10. Obituary, Annie Bell Gibson, August 31, 2001, Gibson Collection; Gray and Lamb, *Born to Win*, 8–9; Clyde Reid, "Althea to Wimbledon: Won 14 Titles Abroad," *New York Amsterdam News*, June 9, 1946; Althea Gibson, Handwritten Astrology Chart, n.d., Gibson Collection; Gibson, *I Always Wanted to Be Somebody*, 3. For a picture of Annie and Daniel side by side, see Associated Press, "Mr. and Mrs.

Daniel Gibson Admiring Pictures at Their Home in New York," *New York Times*, July 7, 1957.

11. Gibson, *I Always Wanted to Be Somebody*, 3.

12. Gibson, *I Always Wanted to Be Somebody*, 3.

13. Althea Gibson, birth certificate, Gibson Collection; Poston, "The Story of Althea Gibson: Article I." Previous biographers quote sources that only raise further questions. Daniel's father was a landowner, write Lamb and Gray, while Annie's father was a "tenant farmer" who "ran a big farm." See Lamb and Gray, *Born to Win*, 8–9, 6–7.

14. Gibson, *I Always Wanted to Be Somebody*, 4; Poston, "The Story of Althea Gibson: Article I"; Edward Royce, *The Origins of Southern Sharecropping* (Philadelphia: Temple University Press, 1993).

15. Marguirite De Laine, F. S. Corbett, and Cecil J. Williams, *Clarendon County* (Charleston, SC: Arcadia, 2002).

16. Ossie Davis and Alice Bernstein, *The People of Clarendon County: A Play by Ossie Davis with Photographs and Historical Documents, and Essays on the Education That Can End Racism* (Chicago: Third World Press, 2007), xxiii–xxv. See also De Laine, Corbett, and Williams, *Clarendon County*, esp. 56, 119, 111, and 95.

17. Hansi Lo Wang, "S.C. Judge Rules 1944 Execution of 14-Year-Old Boy Was Wrong," NPR, December 18, 2014. See also "Racism Fueled Rush to Judgment Against Teen?," NPR, October 3, 2011.

18. Eric Arnesen, *Black Protest and the Great Migration: A Brief History with Documents* (Boston: Bedford/St. Martin's, 2003), 1–7; Isabel Wilkerson, *The Warmth of Other Suns: The Epic Story of America's Great Migration* (New York: Random House, 2010); James R. Grossman, *Land of Hope: Chicago, Black Southerners, and the Great Migration* (Chicago: University of Chicago Press, 1991).

19. One account says the family moved when Althea was a year old. See Serrell Hillman, "That Gibson Girl," *Time*, August 26, 1957, 44. Hillman interviewed Althea for the article. Others say that Althea was two years old. See Poston, "The Story of Althea Gibson: Article I." Also, James A. Burchard, "Althea Gibson's Story—From Harlem to Wimbledon: She Made It the Hard Way," *New York World-Telegram and Sun*, June 23, 1956. Burchard interviewed Annie, while Poston interviewed Althea and Daniel. Althea, through Ed Fitzgerald, noted that she was still living in Silver with her family when she was three years old. See Gibson, *I Always Wanted to be Somebody*, 9. Annie's obituary states that the family moved in 1931, the latest date this biographer has found. See Obituary, Annie Bell Gibson.

20. Gibson, *I Always Wanted to Be Somebody*, 4.

21. Gibson, *I Always Wanted to Be Somebody*, 4.

22. Gibson, *I Always Wanted to Be Somebody*, 4–5. On Pullman porters, see Larry Tye, *Rising from the Rails: Pullman Porters and the Making of the Black Middle Class* (New York: Henry Holt, 2004).

23. Jonathan Gill, *Harlem: The Four Hundred Year History from Dutch Village to Capital of Black America* (New York: Grove Press, 2011), 282–300, 329–332; Erik S. McDuffie, *Sojourning for Freedom: Black Women, American Communism, and the Making of Black Left Feminism* (Durham, NC: Duke University Press, 2011), 1–3, 58–90.

24. Gibson, *I Always Wanted to Be Somebody*, 5.

25. Gibson, *I Always Wanted to Be Somebody*, 5, 22–23, 56–57, 60, 86, and 176. Mary Jo Festle finds Gibson to be "not clear" in her explanation of what it means to "be somebody." See Mary Jo Festle, "'Jackie Robinson Without the Charm': The Challenge of Being Althea Gibson," in *Out of the Shadows: A Biographical History of African American Athletes*, ed. David K. Wiggins (Fayetteville: University of Arkansas Press, 2006), 204. In contrast, I interpret Gibson to consistently express an overwhelming desire to be independent, self-supporting, and free to live without regulations, which were long a feature of her life.

26. Gibson, *I Always Wanted to Be Somebody*, 5; Darlene Clark Hine, "Black Migration to the Urban Midwest: The Gender Dimension, 1915–1945," in *The Great Migration in Historical Perspective: New Dimensions of Race, Class, and Gender*, ed. Joe William Trotter Jr. (Bloomington: Indiana University Press, 1991), 127–146.

27. Gibson, *I Always Wanted to Be Somebody*, 6–7.

28. Lamb and Gray, *Born to Win*, 12.

29. Gibson, *I Always Wanted to Be Somebody*, 7–8.

30. Gibson, *I Always Wanted to Be Somebody*, 7.

31. Gibson, *I Always Wanted to Be Somebody*, 6–8; Robin Bernstein, *Racial Innocence: Performing Childhood from Slavery to Civil Rights* (New York: New York University Press, 2011); *Ethnic Notions: Black People in White Minds*, dir. Marlon Riggs, California Newsreel, 1987.

32. Gibson, *I Always Wanted to Be Somebody*, 8; Kennett Love, "Althea Is at Home Abroad on Tennis Court," *New York Times*, June 24, 1956, S3; Charles McGeehan, "Althea Gibson Gives Legacy to Young Women," *Baltimore Sun*, February 24, 1980, C9. Like the dates of Althea's and Daniel's arrivals in New York, it is unclear when the family began to live together in the apartment. Anecdotal evidence suggests that Gibson and the family lived at the 143rd Street address in 1940, but the family was not counted in the census. Historically, African Americans and other people of color have been undercounted in the census. See Cristian Salazar, Deepti Hajela, and Randy Herschaft, "1940 Census: Tennis Legend Didn't Exist," *Post and Courier* (Charleston, SC), November 2, 2016, https://www.postand courier.com/archives/1940-census-tennis-legend-didn-t-exist/article_83ad2008-7551-56b8-9885-1c37cda258f1.html. Buddy Walker told a reporter in 1957 that he encountered Althea playing paddle tennis on 143rd Street when she was "about 12, not yet 13," which would indeed place the family there in the summer of 1940. See Ted Poston, "The Althea Gibson Story: Article II," *New York Post Daily Magazine*, August 23, 1957, M2. See also Christy Munro, "Althea Gibson . . . Tragic Success

Story," *Look*, November 12, 1957, 136; Apartable, "135 W 143rd Street, New York, NY 10030, Harlem," http://apartable.com/buildings/135-west-143-street-manhat tan (accessed December 11, 2015; no longer available). Another article explicitly states that she was eleven years old before she had a permanent home with her family; see Josh Greenfeld, "Althea Against the World," *Sport*, July 1957, 67.

33. Gibson, *I Always Wanted to Be Somebody*, 8.

34. I am indebted to the research by Dr. Stephen Robertson of George Mason University for this material about Harlem's schools. Stephen Robertson, "Schools in 1920s Harlem," *Digital Harlem Blog*, July 16, 2018, https://drstephenrobertson. com/digitalharlemblog/maps/schools-in-1920s-harlem/; Hillman, "That Gibson Girl," 45; Sam Lacy, "Althea Gibson," *Baltimore Afro-American Magazine*, June 2, 1956, 5. On school name, see "Lincoln Nurses Play Thursday," *New York Amsterdam News*, January 22, 1944.

35. Hillman, "That Gibson Girl," 45.

36. Gibson, *I Always Wanted to Be Somebody*, 1.

37. Gibson, *I Always Wanted to Be Somebody*, 1.

38. Lamb and Gray, *Born to Win*, 19.

39. Gibson, *I Always Wanted to Be Somebody*, 9. Scholarship on the history of race and policing nationwide has surged in recent years, yielding many notable works, including Simon Balto, *Occupied Territory: Policing Black Chicago from Red Summer to Black Power* (Chapel Hill: University of North Carolina Press, 2020); Max Felker-Kantor, *Policing Los Angeles: Race, Resistance, and the Rise of the LAPD* (Chapel Hill: University of North Carolina Press, 2020); Jeffrey S. Adler, *Murder in New Orleans: The Creation of Jim Crow Policing* (Chicago: University of Chicago Press, 2019).

40. Gibson, *I Always Wanted to Be Somebody*, 18.

41. Gibson, *I Always Wanted to Be Somebody*, 17.

42. Gibson, *I Always Wanted to Be Somebody*, 18.

43. Gibson, *I Always Wanted to Be Somebody*, 11, 21.

44. Gibson, *I Always Wanted to Be Somebody*, 21.

45. Lamb and Gray, *Born to Win*, 18.

46. Lamb and Gray, *Born to Win*, 18.

47. Gibson, *I Always Wanted to Be Somebody*, 19, 21.

48. Brian Lanker, "Althea Gibson," in *I Dream a World: Portraits of Black Women Who Changed America* (New York: Stewart, Tabori and Chang, 1989), 47.

49. Stephanie Coontz, *The Way We Really Are: Coming to Terms with America's Changing Families* (New York: Basic Books, 1997), 43–44.

50. Michael Eric Dyson, "Punishment or Child Abuse," *New York Times*, September 18, 2014; Erin Killeen, "The Increased Criminalization of African American Girls," *Georgetown Journal on Poverty and Law Policy* blog, April 17, 2019, https://www.law. georgetown.edu/poverty-journal/blog/the-increased-criminalization-of-african-american-girls/; Phillip Atiba Goff, "Black Boys Viewed as Older, Less Innocent

Than Whites, Research Finds," American Psychological Association, March 2014, https://www.apa.org/news/press/releases/2014/03/black-boys-older.

51. Lamb and Gray, *Born to Win*, 19.

52. Gibson, *I Always Wanted to Be Somebody*, 10.

53. Poston, "The Althea Gibson Story: Article I," M2. Also, Hillman, "That Gibson Girl," 45.

54. Poston, "The Althea Gibson Story: Article I," M2.

55. Malissa Smith, *A History of Women's Boxing* (New York: Rowman and Littlefield, 2014), 11, 19–21.

56. Smith, *A History of Women's Boxing*, 66, 73–74, 69–71; Jeffrey T. Sammons, *Beyond the Ring: The Role of Boxing in American Society* (Urbana: University of Illinois Press, 1988), 53–59. By the 1970s, women were challenging restrictions on their participation in boxing. See Gerald Eskenazi, "2 Women Boxers Ask Licenses," *New York Times*, October 8, 1974.

57. "Girl Boxers Touring Again," *New York Amsterdam News*, January 3, 1934. See also Pete Richardson, "Clocking the Bronx," *New York Amsterdam News*, February 15, 1947; Elaine Weintraub, "Boxing Her Way to Equality and Justice," *Vineyard Gazette*, July 18, 2013, https://vineyardgazette.com/news/2013/07/18/boxing-her-way-equality-and-justice.

58. "Rufe and Rastus in the Late War," *New York Amsterdam News*, December 29, 1926.

59. "Colored Girl Boxers to Challenge Jeanne Le Mar if She Gets License," *New York Amsterdam News*, January 5, 1927. On La Mar, see Smith, *A History of Women's Boxing*, 73–76, 85. The newspaper misspelled La Mar's last name. It also misspelled Wheeldin's surname (and first name) several times across several articles.

60. "New Show Seen in Long Island," *New York Amsterdam News*, September 2, 1931; "Girl Boxers Touring Again," *New York Amsterdam News*.

61. Weintraub, "Boxing Her Way to Equality and Justice."

62. "Girl Boxers Touring Again," *New York Amsterdam News*.

63. Gibson, *I Always Wanted to Be Somebody*, 11.

64. Gibson, *I Always Wanted to Be Somebody*, 12.

65. Smith, *A History of Women's Boxing*, 71–72. For description of these gangs and their colors, see Roger Wilkins, *A Man's Life: An Autobiography* (New York: Simon and Schuster, 1982), 26, 28. On Harlem and gangs generally, see Gill, *Harlem*, 339, 355–356. On Althea's possible gang ties, see Poston, "The Althea Gibson Story: Article I," M2.

66. Wilkins, *A Man's Life*, 28.

67. Gibson, *I Always Wanted to Be Somebody*, 14.

68. For a thorough description of playing the dozens, see Wilkins, *A Man's Life*, 23, 24. Also, Robin D. G. Kelley, *Yo' Mama's Disfunktional: Fighting the Culture Wars in Urban America* (Boston: Beacon Press, 1998), 1–2; Poston, "The Althea Gibson Story: Article I," M2. Daniel Jr. told this story to reporters at least three times and in slightly different forms. To Poston, he said the bully verbally attacked the entire

family. To another reporter, he said he alone was the subject of the offenses. See Edith Evans Asbury, "Miss Gibson's Kin Proud of Punch," *New York Times*, July 9, 1957, 33. He told Yanick Rice Lamb that Annie was the target of the taunts. See Gray and Lamb, *Born to Win*, 19–20.

69. Gibson, *I Always Wanted to Be Somebody*, 14.

70. Gibson, *I Always Wanted to Be Somebody*, 12–13.

71. On Louis's body language, see Chris Mead, *Joe Louis: Black Champion in White America* (Mineola, NY: Dover, 1985), 52. Several authors have analyzed Louis's social and cultural standing as a hero. See Randy Roberts, *Joe Louis: Hard Times Man* (New Haven, CT: Yale University Press, 2010); William H. Wiggins Jr., "Joe Louis: American Folk Hero," in *Sport and the Color Line: Black Athletes and Race Relations in Twentieth-Century America*, ed. Patrick B. Miller and David K. Wiggins (New York: Routledge, 2004), 127–146; Theresa Runstedtler, "In Sports the Best Man Wins: How Joe Louis Whupped Jim Crow," in *In the Game: Race, Identity, and Sports in the Twentieth Century*, ed. Amy Bass (New York: Palgrave Macmillan, 2005), 47–92.

72. Gibson, *I Always Wanted to Be Somebody*, 11.

73. Gibson, *I Always Wanted to Be Somebody*, 10.

74. Hillman, "That Gibson Girl," 45.

75. Gibson, *I Always Wanted to Be Somebody*, 10.

76. Inger E. Burnett-Zeigler, "The Strong and Stressed Black Woman," *New York Times*, April 25, 2018.

77. Kathy Peiss, *Hope in a Jar: The Making of America's Beauty Culture* (New York: Henry Holt, 1998), 206; Judith Halberstam, *Female Masculinity* (Durham, NC: Duke University Press, 1998), 5–6; E. Patrick Johnson, *Black. Queer. Southern. Women: An Oral History* (Chapel Hill: University of North Carolina Press, 2018), 137–138; Deborah Gray White, *Too Heavy a Load: Black Women in Defense of Themselves: 1894–1994* (New York: W. W. Norton, 1999), 106.

78. Gibson, *I Always Wanted to Be Somebody*, 9.

79. Gibson, *I Always Wanted to Be Somebody*, plate 1. Althea is just as tall as the three men in the picture.

80. Gibson, *I Always Wanted to Be Somebody*, 42; Leisa D. Meyer, *Creating GI Jane: Sexuality and Power in the Women's Army Corps During World War II* (New York: Columbia University Press, 1996), 152–155.

81. Poston, "The Althea Gibson Story," Article I, M2.

82. Salazar, Hajela, and Herschaft, "1940 Census: Tennis Legend Didn't Exist."

83. Gibson, *I Always Wanted to Be Somebody*, 11.

84. Kortney Ziegler, "Black Sissy Masculinity and the Politics of Dis-respectability," in *No Tea, No Shade: New Writings in Black Queer Studies* (Durham, NC: Duke University Press, 2016), 197, 198; Thaddeus Russell, "The Color of Discipline: Civil Rights and Black Sexuality," *American Quarterly* 60, no. 1 (March 2008): 104, 105; Cookie Woolner, "'Woman Slain in Queer Love Brawl': African American

Women, Same-Sex Desire, and Violence in the Urban North, 1920–1929," *Journal of African American History* 100, no. 3 (Summer 2015): 407–427; Lillian Faderman, *Odd Girls and Twilight Lovers: A History of Lesbian Life in Twentieth-Century America* (New York: Columbia University Press, 1991), 79.

85. James Baldwin, "Freaks and the American Ideal of Manhood," in *Collected Essays*, ed. Toni Morrison (New York: Library of America, 1998), 819; Russell, "The Color of Discipline," 108. Baldwin details his struggles elsewhere. See James Baldwin, *The Fire Next Time* (1963; repr., New York: Vintage International, 1993), 15–47.

CHAPTER 2

1. Edith Evans Asbury, "Miss Gibson's Kin Proud of Punch," *New York Times*, July 9, 1957.
2. Transcript, "Interview with Althea Gibson," Washington University in St. Louis, October 21, 1984, http://repository.wustl.edu/concern/videos/8s45qd665.
3. "Althea Hopes to Add Golf Crown to Her Collection," *Philadelphia Tribune*, March 20, 1962, 11.
4. Ted Poston, "The Story of Althea Gibson: Article I," *New York Post Daily Magazine*, August 26, 1957, M2.
5. Asbury, "Miss Gibson's Kin Proud of Punch."
6. Serrell Hillman, "That Gibson Girl," *Time*, August 26, 1957, 45.
7. Althea Gibson, *I Always Wanted to Be Somebody*, ed. Ed Fitzgerald (New York: Harper and Row, 1958), 2; Josh Greenfield, "Althea Against the World," *Sport*, July 1958, 67.
8. Robert A. Caro, *The Power Broker: Robert Moses and the Fall of New York* (New York: Vintage, 1975); Elliott J. Gorn and Warren Goldstein, *A Brief History of American Sports* (New York: Hill and Wang, 1993), 169–182; Police Athletic League of New York City, "History," https://www.palnyc.org/history (accessed September 1, 2022); Gibson, *I Always Wanted to Be Somebody*, 27.
9. Stan Hart, *Once a Champion: Legendary Tennis Stars Revisited* (New York: Dodd, Mead, 1985), 32.
10. Susan K. Cahn, "From the 'Muscle Moll' to the 'Butch' Ballplayer: Mannishness, Lesbianism, and Homophobia in U.S. Women's Sport," *Feminist Studies* 19, no. 2 (Summer 1993): 344.
11. Pat Griffin, "The Lesbian Athlete: Unlearning the Culture of the Closet," in *A Queer World: The Center for Lesbian and Gay Studies Reader*, ed. Martin Duberman (New York: New York University Press, 1997), 564. On this same page, Griffin notes that "team sports, like football, basketball, ice hockey, and baseball," especially are training and proving grounds for masculinity.
12. Poston, "The Story of Althea Gibson: Article I"; Hillman, "That Gibson Girl," 44–45; Brian Lanker, "Althea Gibson," *I Dream a World: Portraits of Black Women Who Changed America* (New York: Stewart, Tabori and Chang, 1989), 47; "Sports About Harlemtowne," *New York Amsterdam News*, July 8, 1944.

13. Hillman, "That Gibson Girl," 45; Althea Gibson, "How I Feel About Being 'On Stage,'" n.d., Gibson Collection.

14. Fessenden S. Blanchard, *Paddle Tennis* (New York: A. S. Barnes, 1944), 1–17. See also Howard Cohn, "Paddle Game a Welcome Member of Tennis Family," *American Lawn Tennis*, January 1950, 10–12, 31.

15. Althea Gibson, oral history, International Tennis Hall of Fame and Museum, Newport, RI, July 14, 1979; Gibson, *I Always Wanted to Be Somebody*, 27; Poston, "The Story of Althea Gibson: Article I"; "Harlem Playground Now Fully Equipped," *New York Amsterdam News*, October 24, 1936; "Sports Clips: Everybody Wants a Bonus," *New York Amsterdam News*, May 19, 1956.

16. Poston, "The Althea Gibson Story: Article I."

17. Ted Poston, "The Althea Gibson Story: Article II," *New York Post Daily Magazine*, August 27, 1957, M2. All from *New York Amsterdam News*: "Musician Gets Young Spouse," July 6, 1935; "Dinner-Dance to Be March 3," February 23, 1935; "Compliments Auxiliary," June 22, 1935; "Club Chats," June 1, 1935; "Benefit Dance," February 8, 1936; Bill Chase, "All Ears," April 23, 1938; "Amsterdam News Boys Club," February 16, 1935; "Amsterdam News Boys Club," March 9, 1935; "4 Youngsters Receive Awards from Council," July 18, 1936; "Socially Speaking," February 21, 1942.

18. Gibson, *I Always Wanted to Be Somebody*, plate 1. The *New York Times,* the *New York Herald Tribune*, and the *New York Amsterdam News* appear not to have published articles to back Althea's statement about her victory. For another description of Beal, see "Around the World," *World Tennis*, September 1958, 54.

19. Poston, "The Althea Gibson Story: Article II," M2; Edith Evans Asbury, "City Pays Tribute to Althea Gibson," *New York Times*, July 12, 1957; "2 Harlem Play Areas to Open Tomorrow," *New York Times*, March 31, 1939. On Moses, Rockefeller, and the Harlem Lane Playground, see Hilary Ballon and Kenneth T. Jackson, *Robert Moses and the Modern City: The Transformation of New York* (New York: W. W. Norton, 2007), 182–183.

20. Gibson, *I Always Wanted to Be Somebody*, 27.

21. "Musician Gets Young Spouse"; Thelma Berlack-Boozer, "Millions Spent in Harlem for Dress," *New York Amsterdam News*, July 5, 1941; "Fern Walker Is Christened," *New York Amsterdam News*, April 2, 1938.

22. David W. Dunlap, "At 50, Harlem River Houses Still Special," *New York Times*, April 23, 1987; Meghan White, "The Experimental History Behind Harlem River Houses," National Trust for Historic Preservation, August 28, 2017, https://savin gplaces.org/stories/the-experimental-history-behind-the-harlem-river-houses#. X2z23D-SmUk.

23. Gibson, *I Always Wanted to Be Somebody*, 27.

24. Althea Gibson, interview by Bud Lessor, July 14, 1979, Bud Lessor Oral History Archive, International Tennis Hall of Fame and Museum, Newport, RI.

25. Allen Guttmann, *Sports: The First Five Millennia* (Amherst: University of Massachusetts Press, 2004), 62, 63, 101; Joanna Davenport, "The History and Interpretation of Amateurism in the United States Lawn Tennis Association," Ph.D. diss., Ohio State University, 1966, 14–15; Helen Irene Driver, *Tennis for Teachers* (Madison, WI: H. I. Driver and Associates, 1956), 22.

26. Greg Ruth, *Tennis: A History from American Amateurs to Global Professionals* (Urbana: University of Illinois Press, 2021), 7, 11–12; Guttmann, *Sports*, 101; E. Digby Baltzell, *Sporting Gentlemen: Men's Tennis from the Age of Honor to the Cult of the Superstar* (New York: Free Press, 1995), 40, 19–27; Driver, *Tennis for Teachers*, 23; Allison Danzig, "Sphairistike, History of the United States Lawn Tennis Association," in *The Fireside Book of Tennis*, ed. Allison Danzig and Peter Schwed (New York: Simon and Schuster, 1972), 14–15; Davenport, "History and Interpretation of Amateurism," 20.

27. Edwin Bancroft Henderson, *The Negro in Sports* (Washington, DC: Associated, 1939), 170–175; Sundiata Djata, *Blacks at the Net: Black Achievement in the History of Tennis* (Syracuse, NY: Syracuse University Press, 2006), 1–5; Sundiata Djata, "Game Set, and Separatism: The American Tennis Association, a Tennis Vanguard," in *Separate Games: African American Sport Behind the Wall of Segregation*, ed. David K. Wiggins and Ryan A. Swanson (Fayetteville: University of Arkansas Press, 2016), 165–178; At a meeting in February 1922, the USLTA rejected Howard University's request for membership. The association's official position was that African American clubs that sought to become part of the USLTA would be denied. It set out to convey that position to "each of [its] regional sections." See Cecil Harris, *Different Strokes: Serena, Venus, and the Unfinished Black Tennis Revolution* (Lincoln: University of Nebraska Press, 2020), 50, 51.

28. Hubert A. Eaton, "*Every Man Should Try*" (Wilmington, NC: Bonaparte Press, 1984), 27; Henderson, *The Negro in Sports*, 178, 180; Hazel Garland, "Things to Talk About," *Pittsburgh Courier*, September 16, 1950.

29. D. Ivison Hoage, "Greetings from the President of the A.T.A.," *Official Bulletin of the American Tennis Association Twenty-Fifth Annual National Championship*, August 18–23, 1941, 4, 31, papers of Dr. Hubert A. Eaton Sr., Special Collections, Randall Library, University of North Carolina–Wilmington (hereafter "Eaton Papers"); "The Death Roll: Dr. David Ivison Hoage Dies," *American Lawn Tennis*, March 1945, 26; "Jim Crow Tennis," *Time*, August 28, 1939, 41.

30. Club names taken from "Roster of ATA Associations and Clubs," *ATA Executive Bulletin* no. 14, July 1948, n.p.; Jeane Hoffman, "Althea's Rise Credited to U.S. Assist," *Los Angeles Times*, September 18, 1956, 6.

31. "Club Chats," *New York Amsterdam News*, July 24, 1929; "Cosmopolitan Net Club in Gala Start," *New York Amsterdam News*, May 3, 1933.

32. "Ideal Set-Up for Tennis," *New York Amsterdam News*, June 1, 1935; Roi Ottley, "Hectic Harlem," *New York Amsterdam News*, June 20, 1936. Three years prior, the Cosmopolitan Tennis Club leased two courts and a clubhouse at a site on 124th

Street. See "Cosmopolitan Net Club in Gala Start," *New York Amsterdam News*, May 3, 1933. By 1935, the club was on 149th Street. See "Ideal Set-Up for Tennis."

33. Ottley, "Hectic Harlem."

34. Al Laney, "2,000 Negroes Acclaim Budge as He Defeats Their Champion," *New York Herald Tribune*, July 30, 1940; "State Tennis Championships August 3," *New York Amsterdam News*, July 25, 1936.

35. Gibson, *I Always Wanted to Be Somebody*, 26–28; Poston, "The Althea Gibson Story: Article II"; Gibson interview by Bud Lessor. Gibson and Poston gave two different spellings for the surname of the teacher: Poston called him Juan Surreals, and Gibson called him Juan Serrell. I located a "Sarreals" who was active in Black tennis circles in New York. Sadly, none of the six articles gave his first name. There was also EsCobedo Sarreals, a young socialite and Fisk University leader who married a tennis player. See "Ora Washington Only Net Champ Winner," *New York Amsterdam News*, August 15, 1936. For EsCobedo Sarreals, see "Miss Sarreals to be Married on August 6," *New York Amsterdam News*, August 1, 1936.

36. Roger Wilkins, *A Man's Life: An Autobiography* (New York: Simon and Schuster, 1982), 21.

37. "Has Sugar Hill Gone to the Dogs?," *Jet*, March 26, 1953, 12, 15; Carla Kaplan, *Miss Anne in Harlem* (New York: HarperCollins, 2013), 143–144.

38. Gibson, *I Always Wanted to Be Somebody*, 28; Gibson interview by Bud Lessor.

39. Eric Allen Hall, "'I Guess I'm Becoming More and More Militant': Arthur Ashe and the Black Freedom Movement," *Journal of African American History* 96, no. 4 (Fall 2011): 479.

40. Poston, "The Althea Gibson Story: Article II," M2.

41. Gibson interview by Bud Lessor.

42. Poston, "The Althea Gibson Story: Article I," M2.

43. Poston, "The Althea Gibson Story: Article II," M2; Dorothy Davies Randle and Marjorie Hillas, *Tennis Organized for Group Instruction* (New York: A. S. Barnes, 1932), 161.

44. Poston, "The Althea Gibson Story: Article I," M2.

45. Marion E. Jackson, "Sports of the World," *Atlanta Daily World*, May 26, 1963; Lou Eastwood Anderson, *Tennis for Women* (New York: A. S. Barnes, 1926), 2–5; Arthur E. Francis, "New Yorkers Again Extract Sting of the Famous New Jersey Mosquitoes," *New York Amsterdam News*, July 22, 1925; "B'klyn Vanquishes Cosmopolitan Club," *New York Amsterdam News*, July 24, 1937.

46. Eaton, *"Every Man Should Try,"* 29.

47. Jackson, "Sports of the World," May 26, 1963.

48. Poston, "The Althea Gibson Story: Article II," M2; Gertye West, "Tennis Still Keeps Up Racial Barriers, Which Have Been Breached Only Slightly," *New York Amsterdam News*, December 10, 1949.

49. Poston, "The Althea Gibson Story: Article II," M2; Gibson, *I Always Wanted to Be Somebody*, 28; "Burrell Releases N.J. Tennis Ratings," *New York Amsterdam News*, May 4, 1932.

50. Gibson, *I Always Wanted to Be Somebody*, 28–29.

51. T.E.B., "Chatter and Chimes: La Fonle Surprises Rhoda Smith," *New York Amsterdam News*, December 10, 1938, 10. "Married Here 25 Years Ago," *New York Amsterdam News*, August 3, 1940; "B.W.I. Tennis Star Is Feted," *New York Amsterdam News*, March 29, 1947; Les Matthews, "The Sports Whirl," *New York Amsterdam News*, July 8, 1978; Bertram L. Baker, "Rhoda Smith: Woman in Tennis," *New York Amsterdam News*, July 8, 1978.

52. Poston, "The Althea Gibson Story: Article II," M2.

53. Betty Granger, "The Truth About Althea Gibson," *New York Amsterdam News*, July 21, 1956, 14.

54. Evelyn Brooks Higginbotham, *Righteous Discontent: The Women's Movement in the Black Baptist Church, 1880–1920* (Cambridge, MA: Harvard University Press, 1994), 185–229, 8; Randall Kennedy, "Lifting as We Climb: A Progressive Defense of Respectability Politics," *Harper's Magazine*, October 2015, 24–34, esp. 24–27, 29; James R. Grossman, *Land of Hope: Chicago, Black Southerners, and the Great Migration* (Chicago: University of Chicago Press, 1989), 123–160.

55. Higginbotham, *Righteous Discontent*; Kevin K. Gaines, *Uplifting the Race: Black Leadership, Politics, and Culture in the Twentieth Century* (Chapel Hill: University of North Carolina Press, 1996); Anastasia C. Curwood, *Stormy Weather: Middle-Class African American Marriages Between the Two World Wars* (Chapel Hill: University of North Carolina Press, 2010), 4, 6; Michele Mitchell, *Righteous Propagation: African Americans and the Politics of Racial Destiny After Reconstruction* (Chapel Hill: University of North Carolina Press, 2004).

56. Gibson, *I Always Wanted to Be Somebody*, 30.

57. Hoage, "Greetings," 4.

58. Hoage, "Greetings," 4.

59. Henderson, *The Negro in Sports*, 175, 174; David Wiggins, "Edwin Bancroft Henderson, African-American Athletes, and the Writing of Sport History," in *Sport and the Color Line*, ed. David Wiggins and Patrick Miller (New York: Routledge, 2006), 271–288.

60. Anderson, *Tennis for Women*, 2–5.

61. Lester Granger, "Manhattan and Beyond," *New York Amsterdam News*, September 23, 1961.

62. "La Foule Surprise Bon Voyage Fete," *New York Amsterdam News*, December 19, 1938; "These Frolickers Had a Ball at the Lincoln University Tennis Meet," *New York Amsterdam News*, August 27, 1938; Roi Ottley, "This Hectic Harlem," *New York Amsterdam News*, July 26, 1933.

63. Arthur E. Francis, "Tennis," *New York Amsterdam News*, April 10, 1929. For more on Conick, see A-J Aronstein, "Elsie Conick: A Biography in Fragments," *Guernica*, September 8, 2020, https://www.guernicamag.com/elsie-conick-a-biography-in-fragments/.

64. Henderson, *The Negro in Sports*, 237.

65. Chester L. Washington, "'Sez Ches': Uncle Sam Has Called Many of the Netmen to the Colors," *Pittsburgh Courier*, September 12, 1942.

66. "Still the Best at Tennis," *New York Amsterdam News*, August 30, 1941; "Action! Camera! Beauty, Sports, Theatre on Parade," *New York Amsterdam News*, August 12, 1939; "Saitch, Weir, McDaniel's Prey," *New York Amsterdam News*, August 12, 1939; "News Reel to Feature Aces," *New York Amsterdam News*, August 19, 1939; "McDaniel Nips Cohen to Win," *New York Amsterdam News*, August 31, 1940; St. Claire Bourne, "Confidentially Yours: At the New York State Tennis Tourney," *New York Amsterdam News*, August 17, 1940.

67. "Harlem Playground Renamed for Tennis Coach and Player," *Jet*, November 11, 1971, 54.

68. Poston, "The Althea Gibson Story: Article II."

69. Brian Lanker, *I Dream a World: Portraits of Black Women Who Changed America* (New York: Stewart, Tabori, and Chang, 1989), 47.

70. Gibson, *I Always Wanted to Be Somebody*, 31–32.

71. "M'Daniel Retains Title," *New York Times*, August 11, 1940; "Weir Beats Grasing in U.S. Negro Tennis," *New York Times*, August 19, 1944; "Cohen Gains Tennis Final; Beats Russell, 6–3, 6–1, 6–1, in Negro State Title Tourney," *New York Times*, August 22, 1943.

72. "Doyle Wins Net Crown; Beats Paul in Parks Tourney Final—Mrs. Irwin Victor," *New York Times*, August 24, 1942; "Miss Irwin Takes Net Final," *New York Times*, July 25, 1942; "Annual New York State Open Tournament Due Aug. 10 to 15," *New York Amsterdam News*, August 8, 1942; "Parks Net Title to Rubel," *New York Times*, August 16, 1943.

73. Gibson, *I Always Wanted to Be Somebody*, 32.

74. Gibson, *I Always Wanted to Be Somebody*, 33; Hillman, "That Gibson Girl," 45.

75. "Pictorial Story of Folk Around Elizabeth," *New York Amsterdam News*, August 19, 1939; "Jimmie McDaniel Beats Cohen for Tennis Title," *New York Amsterdam News*, August 16, 1941; "East, West Set for Tilt," *New York Amsterdam News*, August 17, 1940; "Title Won by Jim M'Daniel," *New York Amsterdam News*, July 20, 1940; Hillman, "That Gibson Girl," 45.

76. Hillman, "That Gibson Girl," 45; Gibson, *I Always Wanted to Be Somebody*, 33. Davis recounted this story in *Time* in 1957, and Gibson and Fitzgerald reprinted it in the autobiography. The *Time* version does not state that Althea refused to shake Davis's hand.

77. Greenfield, "Althea Against the World," 67.

78. Gibson, *I Always Wanted to Be Somebody*, 16; Denzil Batchelor, "The Different Gibson Girl," *Picture Post*, June 30, 1951, 30; liner notes, *Althea Gibson Sings*, Dot Records, DLP 3105, 1958.

79. Gibson, *I Always Wanted to Be Somebody*, 18.

80. Harlem Education History Project, "Wadleigh High School and Junior High School," https://harlemeducationhistory.library.columbia.edu/collection/wad

(accessed October 19, 2020). Also, Harlem Education History Project, "Wadleigh Yearbooks,"   https://harlemeducationhistory.library.columbia.edu/collection/wad_yb (accessed October 19, 2020); Kimberly Johnson, "Wadleigh High School: The Price of Segregation," in *Educating Harlem: A Century of Schooling and Resistance in a Black Community*, ed. Ansley T. Erickson and Ernest Morrell (New York: Columbia University Press, 2019), 77–95.

81. Gibson, *I Always Wanted to Be Somebody*, 19, 22.

82. Gibson, *I Always Wanted to Be Somebody*, 19.

83. Sam Lacy, "Althea Gibson," *Baltimore Afro-American Magazine*, June 2, 1956, 5; Gibson, *I Always Wanted to Be Somebody*, 19, 22.

84. Hillman, "That Gibson Girl," 45.

85. Gibson, *I Always Wanted to Be Somebody*, 19.

86. Gibson, *I Always Wanted to Be Somebody*, 10.

87. Gibson, *I Always Wanted to Be Somebody*, 20.

88. Anne Reiniger, Joseph T. Gleason, et al., *The New York Society for the Prevention of Cruelty to Children, 1874–2000* (New York: RPM, 2000), n.p.; Gibson, *I Always Wanted to Be Somebody*, 20–21.

89. Gibson, *I Always Wanted to Be Somebody*, 21.

90. Lanker, "I Dream a World," 47; Gibson, *I Always Wanted to Be Somebody*, 21–25.

91. Gibson, *I Always Wanted to Be Somebody*, 21.

92. Gibson, *I Always Wanted to Be Somebody*, 24; Nina Bernstein, "Ward of the State; The Gap in Ella Fitzgerald's Life," *New York Times*, June 23, 1996. See also Nina Bernstein, *The Lost Children of Wilder: The Epic Struggle to Change Foster Care* (New York: Vintage Books, 2001), 3–35, and Prison Public Memory Project, "New York State Training School for Girls," September 22, 2014, http://www.prisonpublicmemory.org/blog/2014/new-york-state-training-school-for-girls; "Equality Is Won by Negro Girls in State School," *New York Herald Tribune*, November 20, 1936; Geoff K. Ward, *The Black Child Savers: Racial Democracy and Juvenile Justice* (Chicago: University of Chicago Press, 2012); Marcia Chatelain, *South Side Girls: Growing Up in the Great Migration* (Durham, NC: Duke University Press, 2015).

93. Hillman, "That Gibson Girl"; Althea Gibson, "Ward Baking Company Welcome Speech," March 9, 1960, Chicago, IL, Gibson Collection; Gibson, *I Always Wanted to Be Somebody*, 22–24.

94. Lacy, "Althea Gibson."

95. J. Thomas Jable, "The Philadelphia Tribune Newsgirls: African American Women's Basketball at Its Best," in *Separate Games: African American Sport Behind the Walls of Segregation*, ed. David K. Wiggins and Ryan Swanson (Fayetteville: University of Arkansas Press, 2016), 37–60; "Metropolitan Stars Defeat Y Senior 5," *New York Amsterdam News*, January 5, 1946; "Harlem Mysterious Five Seeking Cage Contests," *New York Amsterdam News*, December 9, 1939; "Stabs Young Boxer as Gang Wars Go On," *New York Amsterdam News*,

October 27, 1945; Dan Burley, "Confidentially Yours," *New York Amsterdam News*, November 6, 1943.

96. "Mysterious Girls Beat Metropolitan Life and Templars," *New York Amsterdam News*, January 15, 1944; Dan Burley, "Confidentially Yours," *New York Amsterdam News*, November 6, 1943; Dan Burley, "Confidentially Yours," *New York Amsterdam News*, April 3, 1943; "Sports About Harlemtown," *New York Amsterdam News*, February 12, 1944; Marsden Burnell, "Harlem Yankees, Rens Play 2nd Game in Jasper Oval," *New York Amsterdam News*, July 29, 1944; "Mysterious Girls Victors, 37 to 17," *New York Amsterdam News*, January 20, 1945.

97. "Mysterious Girls AC Feature Teamwork Above Anything Else," *New York Amsterdam News*, January 22, 1944, 17; Burnell was the likely author. The scoring estimate is affirmed by other articles. See "Ft. Wayne Nips Washington Bears, 60–58," *New York Amsterdam News*, April 17, 1943; "Mysterious Girls Win," *New York Amsterdam News*, December 18, 1943.

98. "It's Tender . . . Delicious . . . The Finest Bread Baked!," advertisement, *New York Amsterdam News*, October 23, 1944; "Mysterious Girls AC Feature Teamwork Above Anything Else"; Gibson, *I Always Wanted to Be Somebody*, 30, 16.

99. Joe Bostic, "The Scorecard: Althea Gibson a Solid Athlete from Way Back," *New York Amsterdam News*, March 26, 1949.

100. Susan K. Cahn, *Coming on Strong: Gender and Sexuality in Women's Sport* (1993; repr., Urbana: University of Illinois Press, 2015), 85, 87; Rita Liberti, "'We Were Ladies, We Just Played Like Boys': African-American Womanhood and Competitive Basketball at Bennett College, 1928–1942," *Journal of Sport History* 26, no. 3 (Fall 1999): 567–584; Marc Katz, "Althea Gibson at 50: Golf Gold Comes Hard," *Dayton Daily News*, June 11, 1978, 9-D.

101. For pictures of Jenkins, Nightingale, and Irving, see "Harlem Mysterious Girls' A.C.," *New York Amsterdam News*, February 7, 1942; Gibson, *I Always Wanted to Be Somebody*, 13; Gibson interview by Bud Lessor. See also James Wells Champney, "Boon Companions," oil on canvas, 1879, Smith College Museum of Art.

102. "Sports About Harlemtowne: Reports on Sports," *New York Amsterdam News*, June 17, 1944; Poston, "The Althea Gibson Story: Article I," M2; "Sports About Harlemtowne," *New York Amsterdam News*, April 15, 1944; "Bowling Notes," *New York Amsterdam News*, December 15, 1945.

103. Gibson, *I Always Wanted to Be Somebody*, 16.

104. "Bowling Notes." Inexplicably, in the article Gibson appears to have been referred to by a nickname, perhaps "Toni" or "Ton" (the text of the original is difficult to make out).

105. Gibson, *I Always Wanted to Be Somebody*, 35.

106. Corey Kilgannon, "Once the King of Harlem Hairdressers, Now Nearly Forgotten," *New York Times*, March 24, 2013, http://cityroom.blogs.nytimes.com/2013/03/24/sugar-rays-barber/; Kenneth L. Shropshire and Scott Brooks, "Sugar Ray Robinson—The Businessman," in *Race and Sport: The Struggle*

for Equality On and Off the Field, ed. Charles K. Ross (Oxford: University of Mississippi Press, 2004), 26–39; "Sugar Ray Is 'Santa' for 100 Youngsters," *Philadelphia Tribune*, August 31, 1946; Herb Boyd and Ray Robinson, *Pound for Pound: A Biography of Sugar Ray Robinson* (New York: Amistad Press, 2006), 80.

107. Gibson, *I Always Wanted to Be Somebody*, 34–36; liner notes, *Althea Gibson Sings*; Boyd and Robinson, *Pound for Pound*, 80.

108. "Edna Mae Robinson, 86, Dancer and Boxer's Wife," *New York Times*, May 7, 2002; "Edna Mae Robinson, 86; Ex-Wife of Boxing Great, Performer and Activist," *Los Angeles Times*, May 5, 2002; Hillman, "That Gibson Girl," 45.

109. "Cohen Gains Tennis, Final," *New York Times*, August 22, 1943, 2S; "Little Jean Branche," *Call and Post* (Cleveland, OH), September 11, 1943; "Cohen Captures Net Title," *Baltimore Afro-American*, August 28, 1943; SNS, "Southern Tennis Stars Defeat Monopolize National Tourney," *Atlanta Daily World*, August 22, 1944; "Pvt. Scott Is Net Champion: 1944 Ratings of ATA Are Announced," *Chicago Defender*, June 16, 1945; Marsden Burnell, "Rens Trounce Harlem Yankees by 5–4 Count," *New York Amsterdam News*, September 2, 1944.

110. Arthur Daley, "Sports of the Times: The Half-Century Look," *New York Times*, January 6, 1950; United Press, "Flam Loses Final in Straight Sets," *New York Times*, June 2, 1957.

111. Sam Lacy, "Prairie View Player Scores Upset; Roumania Peters Women's Winner," *Baltimore Afro-American*, August 26, 1944.

112. Gibson, *I Always Wanted to Be Somebody*, 29.

113. J.D.H., "Styles of the Great IV: Alice Marble," *World Tennis*, March 1960, 27.

114. Ashley Brown, "Swinging for the State Department: American Women Tennis Players in Diplomatic Goodwill Tours, 1941–59," *Journal of Sport History* 43, no. 5 (Fall 2015): 292–295; "Dr. Weir Upset in Negro Title Tennis by Scott," *New York Herald Tribune*, August 20, 1944; "American T A Championships," *American Lawn Tennis*, November 1944, 28–29.

115. Gibson, *I Always Wanted to Be Somebody*, 31. Gibson recounted this story to Ted Poston. See Poston, "The Althea Gibson Story: Article I."

116. Gibson, *I Always Wanted to Be Somebody*, 33; Sam Lacy, "Scott Retains Nat'l Singles Tennis Crown," *Baltimore Afro-American*, August 25, 1945; Poston, "The Althea Gibson Story: Article I."

CHAPTER 3

1. Althea Gibson, *I Always Wanted to Be Somebody*, ed. Ed Fitzgerald (New York: Harper and Row, 1958), 33.

2. Judith Halberstam, *In a Queer Time and Place: Transgender Bodies, Subcultural Lives* (New York: New York University Press, 2005), 1, 7; Serrell Hillman, "That Gibson Girl," *Time*, August 26, 1957, 45.

3. Gibson, *I Always Wanted to Be Somebody*, 34.

4. Dr. Hubert A. Eaton Sr., quoted in Ted Poston, "The Althea Gibson Story: Article III," *New York Post Daily Magazine*, August 28, 1957, M2.

5. Cleveland Jackson, "Peters Sisters Annex Two Titles, Freeman Bros. Capture 3 Victories," *Call and Post* (Cleveland, OH), August 31, 1946, 8-B; Lulu Jones Garrett, "McDaniel Takes Men's Net Crown," *Baltimore Afro-American*, August 31, 1946, 16.

6. "Dick Cohen, Althea Gibson Cop Eastern Net Titles in N.J.," *Baltimore Afro-American*, August 3, 1946, 17.

7. "Lloyd Scott, Kathryn Irvis Top '45 ATA Net Ratings," *Baltimore Afro-American*, April 13, 1946, 18; "Cohen Cops Eastern Net Crown. Lillian Van Buren Upset," *Call and Post*, August 10, 1946, n.p.

8. "Athea [*sic*] Gibson Gains Women's Singles Title," *New York Amsterdam News*, August 17, 1946, 10.

9. Edwin Bancroft Henderson, *The Negro in Sports* (Washington, DC: Associated, 1949), 422, 426.

10. Garrett, "McDaniel Takes Men's Net Crown."

11. Gibson, *I Always Wanted to Be Somebody*, 36–37.

12. Fay Young, "McDaniel, Roumania Peters Win National Net Titles," *Chicago Defender*, August 31, 1946.

13. Fay Young, "Through the Years," *Chicago Defender*, August 31, 1946, 11.

14. Gibson, *I Always Wanted to Be Somebody*, 36.

15. Althea Gibson, "Dear Miss Marble," *American Lawn Tennis*, February 1951, 15.

16. Gibson, *I Always Wanted to Be Somebody*, 37.

17. Gibson, *I Always Wanted to Be Somebody*, 37.

18. Gibson, *I Always Wanted to Be Somebody*, 37.

19. Gibson, *I Always Wanted to Be Somebody*, 32.

20. Gibson, "Dear Miss Marble," 15.

21. Dr. Robert Walter Johnson, quoted in Poston, "The Althea Gibson Story: Article III."

22. Hubert A. Eaton, *"Every Man Should Try"* (Wilmington, NC: Bonaparte Press, 1984), 27; Dr. Johnson, quoted in Poston, "The Althea Gibson Story: Article III."

23. Dr. Johnson, quoted in Poston, "The Althea Gibson Story: Article III."

24. Eaton, *"Every Man Should Try,"* 27.

25. Ol' Harrington, "Over the Top for Jim Crow," *New York Amsterdam News*, August 31, 1940, 14.

26. Brenda L. Moore, "African Americans in the Military," in *The Columbia Guide to African American History Since 1939*, ed. Robert L. Harris Jr. and Rosalyn Terborg-Penn (New York: Columbia University Press, 2006), 122–123, 265.

27. Charles Ross, *Outside the Lines: African Americans and the Integration of the National Football League* (New York: New York University Press, 1999), 82, 83; Thomas Zeiler, *Jackie Robinson and Race in America: A Brief History with Documents* (Boston: Bedford/St. Martin's, 2014), 20, 19.

28. Eaton, *"Every Man Should Try,"* 27.

29. Eaton, *"Every Man Should Try,"* 27.

30. Gibson, "Dear Miss Marble," 15.

31. Poston, "The Althea Gibson Story: Article III."

32. Gibson, *I Always Wanted to Be Somebody*, 37, 38, 53.

33. Dr. Eaton, quoted in Poston, "The Althea Gibson Story: Article III."

34. Gibson, *I Always Wanted to Be Somebody*, 37.

35. Eaton, *"Every Man Should Try,"* 27; Gibson, *I Always Wanted to Be Somebody*, 37, 38.

36. Gibson, *I Always Wanted to Be Somebody*, 39.

37. Eaton, *"Every Man Should Try,"* 28.

38. Edwin Bancroft Henderson, *The Negro in Sports* (Washington, DC: Associated, 1939), 178; "Gerald F. Norman, Taught at Long Island City High," *New York Times*, April 4, 1973, 46; Al Laney, "2,000 Negroes Acclaim Budge as He Defeats Their Champion," *New York Herald Tribune*, July 30, 1940, 24A; Sam Lacy, "Prairie View Player Scores Upset; Roumania Peters Women's Winner," *Baltimore Afro-American*, August 26, 1944, 18; "USLTA Stars Win Mixed Matches," *Baltimore Afro-American*, August 25, 1945, 18.

39. Lacy, "Prairie View Player Scores Upset; Roumania Peters Women's Winner"; Jackson, "Peters Sisters Annex Two Titles."

40. "Al Laney of the *New York Herald Tribune* Writes," *Official Bulletin of the Twenty-Fifth Annual National Championships*, August 18–23, 1941, 35, Eaton Papers.

41. Al Laney, "Views of Sport: Pros Not So Squeamish," *New York Herald Tribune*, August 12, 1944, 13A.

42. Randy Roberts, *Papa Jack: Jack Johnson and the Era of White Hopes* (New York: Free Press, 1983).

43. Laney, "Views of Sport."

44. Larry Engelmann, *The Goddess and the American Girl* (New York: Oxford University Press, 1988), 328.

45. Gibson, *I Always Wanted to Be Somebody*, 42.

46. Gibson, *I Always Wanted to Be Somebody*, 38.

47. "Lynching: Notorious Lynchings—Moore's Ford," *New Georgia Encyclopedia*, last edited August 12, 2020, https://www.georgiaencyclopedia.org/articles/history-archaeology/lynching; "Graphic Photos of Georgia Lynchings," *New York Amsterdam News*, August 3, 1946, 1; "Harlem Rallies Protest Lynching of Four," *New York Amsterdam News*, August 3, 1946, 2; "Death to Lynchers Mass Meeting Packs Mother Zion," *New York Amsterdam News*, August 10, 1946, 4.

48. Gibson, *I Always Wanted to Be Somebody*, 41.

49. Gibson, *I Always Wanted to Be Somebody*, 42.

50. For a picture of the Eaton house, see City of Wilmington Historic Preservation Planner, "Hubert Eaton House," in *A Guide to Wilmington's African American Heritage* (Wilmington, NC: City of Wilmington, 2013), 25, https://www.wilmingtonnc.gov/home/showdocument?id=16; Gibson, *I Always Wanted to Be Somebody*, 42; Carolyn Eaton, email message to author, October 30, 2020.

51. Gibson, *I Always Wanted to Be Somebody*, 42.

52. Gibson, *I Always Wanted to Be Somebody*, 42; Gibson, "Dear Miss Marble," 28.

53. Gibson, *I Always Wanted to Be Somebody*, 42.

54. "Wife—Celeste Marie Burnett Eaton (1938)," in Eaton, *"Every Man Should Try,"* plate 13; "People Are Talking About," *Jet*, November 8, 1951, 42.

55. Eaton, *"Every Man Should Try,"* 17.

56. Eaton, *"Every Man Should Try,"* 17–18; Charles W. Wadelington, "Palmer Memorial Institute," in *North Carolina Encyclopedia* (Chapel Hill: University of North Carolina Press, 2006), https://www. ncpedia.org/palmer-memorial-institute; Deborah Elizabeth Whaley, *Disciplining Women: Alpha Kappa Alpha, Black Counterpublics, and the Cultural Politics of Black Sororities* (Albany: State University of New York Press, 2010); "Mrs. Marie Eaton Succumbed Last Thursday," *Carolina Times*, July 22, 1972, 4A.

57. Eaton, *"Every Man Should Try,"* v, 182.

58. Eaton, *"Every Man Should Try,"* 28.

59. Eaton, *"Every Man Should Try,"* 28, 182.

60. Caleb Crain, "City Limits," *New Yorker*, April 27, 2020, 67–71, esp. 68, 69, 67; Eaton, *"Every Man Should Try,"* 43; David Zucchino, *Wilmington's Lie: The Murderous Coup of 1898 and the Rise of White Supremacy* (New York: Grove Press, 2021).

61. On Community Hospital, see City of Wilmington Historic Preservation Planner, *A Guide to Wilmington's African American Heritage*, 26; Eaton, *"Every Man Should Try,"* 17, 10, 53, 21.

62. Eaton, *"Every Man Should Try,"* 4, 25.

63. Eaton, *"Every Man Should Try,"* 14; Lawrence C. Ross Jr., *The Divine Nine: The History of African American Fraternities and Sororities* (New York: Davina Books, 2000), 73–100.

64. Eaton, *"Every Man Should Try,"* 18, 25.

65. Eaton, *"Every Man Should Try,"* 26, 25. Perry was a champion tennis player and, in at least one instance, a champion for justice. In 1933, he and fellow tennis player Henry "Bunny" Austin wrote a letter of protest to the *London Times* when the German Davis Cup team, in acquiescence to Adolf Hitler's opposition to Jews, refused to allow its best player, Daniel Prenn, to compete in the matches. See Larry Engelmann, *The Goddess and the American Girl: The Story of Suzanne Lenglen and Helen Wills* (New York: Oxford University Press, 1988), 329–330.

66. Eaton, *"Every Man Should Try,"* 29, 27.

67. Eaton, *"Every Man Should Try,"* 29; Gibson, *I Always Wanted to Be Somebody*, 45, 46.

68. Eaton, *"Every Man Should Try,"* 29.

69. Eaton, *"Every Man Should Try,"* 33.

70. "Socially Speaking," *New York Amsterdam News*, August 25, 1945; Dr. Eaton, quoted in Poston, "The Althea Gibson Story: Article III," M2.

71. "Tennis Tourney Patter," *Jet*, September 8, 1955, 44; Dr. Eaton, quoted in Poston, "The Althea Gibson Story: Article III"; Gibson, *I Always Wanted to Be Somebody*, 42.

72. Gibson, *I Always Wanted to Be Somebody*, 48.

73. Eaton, *"Every Man Should Try,"* 4; Dr. Eaton to A.A. Morisey, September 18, 1951, Eaton Papers.

74. Kate Masur, "Color Was a Bar to the Entrance: African American Activism and the Question of Social Equality in Lincoln's White House," *American Quarterly* 69, no. 1 (March 2017): 2.

75. "These Nets for White Fish Only," editorial, *Call and Post*, July 29, 1939, 10.

76. Gibson, *I Always Wanted to Be Somebody*, 44.

77. Gibson, *I Always Wanted to Be Somebody*, 44.

78. Dr. Eaton, quoted in Poston, "The Althea Gibson Story: Article III"; Dr. Eaton, quoted in Hillman, "That Gibson Girl," 46.

79. Hillman, "That Gibson Girl."

80. Eaton, *"Every Man Should Try,"* 30.

81. Gibson, *I Always Wanted to Be Somebody*, 44–45.

82. Daniel L. McGuire, *At the Dark End of the Street: Black Women, Rape and Resistance—A New History of the Civil Rights Movement from Rosa Parks to the Rise of Black Power* (New York: Vintage Books, 2010).

83. Eaton, *"Every Man Should Try,"* 31; Chuck Caree, "The Natural," *Wilmington Star News Online*, May 6, 2007, https://www.starnewsonline.com/story/sports/2007/05/06/the-natural/30305045007/. Dr. Hubert A. Eaton Jr. told Caree that his father omitted from his autobiography that the children were locked in the bathroom and that Gibson may not have been home when his parents arrived.

84. Eaton, *"Every Man Should Try,"* 31, 32.

85. Gibson, *I Always Wanted to Be Somebody*, 44.

86. Eaton, *"Every Man Should Try,"* 33, 31.

87. Eaton, *"Every Man Should Try,"* 30, 33, 32.

88. Eaton, *"Every Man Should Try,"* 32, 33.

89. Gibson, *I Always Wanted to Be Somebody*, 38.

90. Gibson, *I Always Wanted to Be Somebody*, 47.

91. Gibson, *I Always Wanted to Be Somebody*, 46–47; Eaton, *"Every Man Should Try,"* 30; Victoria W. Wolcott, *Race, Riots, and Roller Coasters: The Struggle over Segregated Recreation in America* (Philadelphia: University of Pennsylvania Press, 2012).

92. Gibson, *I Always Wanted to Be Somebody*, 47.

93. Gibson, *I Always Wanted to Be Somebody*, 43; Eaton, *"Every Man Should Try,"* 30.

94. "Bowling Notes," *New York Amsterdam News*, December 15, 1945, 14; "Bowling Notes," *New York Amsterdam News*, December 15, 1945, 14; Althea Gibson with Richard Curtis, *So Much to Live For* (New York: G. P. Putnam's Sons, 1968), 22.

95. Gibson, *I Always Wanted to Be Somebody*, 49.

96. Gibson, *I Always Wanted to Be Somebody*, 48.

97. Susan K. Cahn, "From the 'Muscle Moll' to the 'Butch' Ballplayer: Mannishness, Lesbianism, and Homophobia in U.S. Women's Sport," *Feminist Studies* 19, no. 2 (Summer 1993): 350–351.

98. Gibson, *I Always Wanted to Be Somebody*, 48–49.

99. "Photos: Williston Through the Years: 8/15," *Wilmington Star News*, January 14, 2019, https://www.starnewsonline.com/photogallery/NC/20190114/NEWS/114009990/PH/1 (no longer available; accessed November 22, 2020).

100. Eaton, *"Every Man Should Try,"* 31.

101. Gibson, *I Always Wanted to Be Somebody*, 49, plate 3; Eaton, *"Every Man Should Try,"* 31.

102. John McPhee, *Levels of the Game* (New York: Farrar, Straus and Giroux, 1969), 38, 43, 39, 26, 38.

103. Doug Smith, *Whirlwind, the Godfather of Black Tennis: The Life and Times of Dr. Robert Walter Johnson* (Washington, DC: Blue Eagle, 2004), 9, 19, 25, 21, 34, 39; McPhee, *Levels of the Game*, 24–25.

104. McPhee, *Levels of the Game*, 261; "Top Net Stars to Be in Lynchburg Doubles Tourney," *Chicago Defender*, August 26, 1944, 7; Edwin Bancroft Henderson, "Henderson's Comment: Interest in Youth Development Brings Plaudits to 'Whirlwind,'" *Baltimore Afro-American*, November 4, 1950, 17; Selena Roberts, *A Necessary Spectacle: Billie Jean King, Bobby Riggs, and the Tennis Match That Leveled the Game* (New York: Crown Books, 2005); Bobby Johnson, interview by author, Silver Spring, MD, September 26, 2015. The photograph of the segregated seating at the exhibition match is part of Bobby Johnson's personal collection.

105. Gibson, "Dear Miss Marble," 28.

106. Gibson, "Dear Miss Marble," 28; Gibson, quoted in Ted Poston, "The Althea Gibson Story: Article I," *New York Post Daily Magazine*, August 26, 1957, M2.

107. Bobby Johnson, interview by author; Dr. Johnson, quoted in Poston, "The Althea Gibson Story: Article III."

108. McPhee, *Levels of the Game*, 26, 28, 29, 28, 29.

109. Dr. Johnson, quoted in Poston, "The Althea Gibson Story: Article III."

110. Robert W. Johnson III, interview by author, September 26, 2015, College Park, MD.

111. Gibson, *I Always Wanted to Be Somebody*, 47.

112. Gibson, *I Always Wanted to Be Somebody*, 50.

113. Susan Sessions Rugh, *Are We There Yet? The Golden Age of American Family Vacations* (Lawrence: University Press of Kansas, 2008), 68–91; Mia Bay, *Traveling Black: A Story of Race and Resistance* (Cambridge, MA: Belknap Press of Harvard University Press, 2021); Gibson, *I Always Wanted to Be Somebody*, 50–51; Langston Hughes, "The Miracle of the Gotham," *Ebony*, August 1947, 30.

114. Picture, "Miss Gibson Eyes National Title," *Norfolk Journal and Guide*, August 16, 1947, 21. For a list of the tournaments that Althea won, see "Sensational Young

Tennis Player Seeks Added Titles," *Norfolk Journal and Guide*, August 9, 1947, 12; "Miss Stanfield Is First Place Winner of Indianapolis Title," *Norfolk Journal and Guide*, August 16, 1947, 21.

115. Gibson, "Dear Miss Marble," 28.

116. Betty Granger, "Conversation Piece," *New York Amsterdam News*, July 6, 1957, 10.

117. Robert W. Johnson III (grandson of Dr. Johnson), interview by author, September 26, 2015.

118. Capt. R. Darnaby, "Bitter Battle Among Women: Gibson vs. Peters Predicted," *Chicago Defender*, August 16, 1947, 11.

119. Fay Young, "George Stewart, Panama, and Althea Gibson Win Nat'l Net Titles," *Chicago Defender*, August 30, 1947, 11; R. S. Darnaby, "Panama Star Defeats Scott for Tennis Title," *Norfolk Journal and Guide*, August 30, 1947, 10.

120. The team changed its name to the Guardians in July 2021.

121. Fay Young, "Through the Years: Miss Althea Gibson," *Chicago Defender*, August 30, 1947, 11; Picture, "Ranking Tennis Stars Rest After Exhibition," *Norfolk Journal and Guide*, September 6, 1947, 1.

122. Young, "Through the Years: Miss Althea Gibson."

123. Young, "Through the Years: Miss Althea Gibson."

124. Fay Young, "Through the Years," *Chicago Defender*, August 31, 1946, 11.

125. "George Stewart, Althea Gibson Star in Sectional Net Meets, Eye National Titles," *Call and Post*, July 26, 1947, 3-A.

126. Orlando G. Rodman, "Va. and Tex. Players Win Midwest Tennis Tourney," *Indianapolis Recorder*, August 23, 1947, 11.

127. "Vivacious Althea Gibson to Defend Her National Women's Title This Week," *Pittsburgh Courier*, August 21. 1948, 11; A. A. Morisey, "George Stewart, Miss A. Gibson Annex Southeastern Net Titles," *Norfolk Journal and Guide*, August 21, 1948, 21; Joe Bostic, "The Scorecard: Pounding the Sports Beat," *New York Amsterdam News*, August 28, 1948, 26; Gertye West Brown, "Tennis Keeps Up Racial Barriers Which Have Been Breached Only Slightly," *New York Amsterdam News*, December 10, 1949, 42.

128. Rodman, "Va. and Tex. Players Win Midwest Tennis Tourney."

129. "Stewart Defeats Chandler to Take Pa. Net Crown," *Baltimore Afro-American*, August 9, 1947, 13; "Top Sepia Racquet Wielders to Meet at Tuskegee on August 18–23," *Call and Post*, August 9, 1947, 8-B. On the perpetuation of similar rhetoric to describe women who play tennis, see Susan K. Cahn, *Coming on Strong: Gender and Sexuality in Twentieth-Century Women's Sport* (Cambridge, MA: Harvard University Press, 1994), 2.

130. Sam Lacy, "Scott Retains Nat'l Singles Tennis Crown," *Baltimore Afro-American*, August 25, 1945, 18.

131. Associated Negro Press, "Craig, Miss Gibson Tennis Champs," *New York Amsterdam News*, August 14, 1948, 26.

132. Mary Etta Fine, quoted, Dennis Dodd, "Althea Gibson Doesn't Miss Spotlight," *Kansas City Times*, June 13, 1985, C-5.

133. "Vivacious Althea Gibson to Defend Her National Women's Title This Week."

134. Ric Roberts, "Three-Star Performer," *Pittsburgh Courier*, August 21, 1948, 11.

135. "Negress Stars in Eastern," *American Lawn Tennis*, April 1949, 29.

136. Jimmy Booker, "First Woman to Enter Tennis Tourney: Weir and Eight Other Negro Stars in Met's Indoor Championships," *New York Amsterdam News*, March 5, 1949; "Gibson, Weir in Nationals," *New York Amsterdam News*, March 19, 1949, 26.

137. Clyde Reid, "Demands of Negro Tennis 'Too Much' Says Weir," *New York Amsterdam News*, March 31, 1956, 27.

138. Harrold Rosenthal, "National Tennis Accepts Entry of First Negro in Its History," *New York Herald Tribune*, March 9, 1948, 27.

139. Rosenthal, "National Tennis Accepts."

140. Alrick H. Man, quoted in Allison Danzig, "Negro to Compete for First Time in a National Tennis Tournament," *New York Times*, March 9, 1948, 30.

141. "Bill Talbert," International Tennis Hall of Fame and Museum, Newport, RI, https://www.tennisfame.com/hall-of-famers/inductees/bill-talbert (accessed June 20, 2022); Allison Danzig, "Talbert Puts Out Weir in U.S. Tennis," *New York Times*, March 14, 1948, S1.

142. Booker, "First Woman to Enter Tennis Tourney."

143. Fred Hawthorne, "Kovaleski Beats Borotra in Duel," *New York Herald Tribune*, March 23, 1949, 34; John M. Ross, "Make Way for Fancy Nancy," *Sport*, September 1950, 88.

144. Gibson, *I Always Wanted to Be Somebody*, 55, 56.

145. This quote appears in a newspaper clipping found in the archives of the West Side Tennis Club in Forest Hills, New York. In addition to the article's text, only the name of the author, Alex Schults, has survived. The title of the article, the name and location of the newspaper, and the page number are missing. I thank Bea Hunter for sharing this material with me.

146. Jules Tygiel, *Baseball's Great Experiment: Jackie Robinson and His Legacy* (New York: Oxford University Press, 1983), 8, 9.

147. Eric Avila, *Popular Culture in the Age of White Flight: Fear and Fantasy in Suburban Los Angeles* (Berkeley: University of California Press, 2004), 150–151.

148. Dick Edwards, "Sports Scenes," *Philadelphia Tribune*, April 2, 1949, 10.

149. Cal Jacox, "From the Press Box," *Norfolk Journal and Guide*, April 2, 1949, 13.

150. Jacox, "From the Press Box."

151. Jacox, "From the Press Box."

152. National Negro Press Association, "Tennis Stars Make Good Showing in Net Tourney," *Norfolk Journal and Guide*, April 2, 1949, 13; Allison Danzig, "Borotra Eliminated by Kovaleski in Title Indoor Tennis, 7–5, 16–14," *New York Times*, March 23, 1949, 39.

153. Edwards, "Sports Scenes."

154. "Negress Stars in Eastern," 29. On offensiveness of "negress," see Marie Brenner, *Great Dames: What I Learned from Older Women* (New York: Random House, 2000), 44; Jack Greenberg, *Crusaders in the Courts: How a Dedicated Band of Lawyers Fought for the Civil Rights Revolution* (New York: Basic Books, 1994), 33.

155. Mary V. Ransom, "Women in Year's National Spotlight," *Norfolk Journal and Guide*, December 31, 1949, 6.

156. Gibson, *I Always Wanted to Be Somebody*, 56; Eaton, *"Every Man Should Try,"* 31; "Talk by Althea Gibson," March 14, 1959, National Archives and Records Administration, RG 306, 306-ENTT-2367; "Tennis Champ Wields Saxophone," *Norfolk Journal and Guide*, May 28, 1949, 17.

157. Gibson, *I Always Wanted to Be Somebody*, 57; "Wiggins Cops Florida Schoolboy Tennis Title," *Baltimore Afro-American*, May 7, 1949, 8.

158. Walter M. Austin to Dr. Hubert A. Eaton, May 9, 1949, Box 27, Folder 4, Eaton Papers; William H. Wiggins to Dr. Eaton, May 9, 1949, Box 27, Folder 4, Eaton Papers.

159. Susan Ware, *Title IX: A Brief History with Documents* (Boston: Bedford/St. Martin's Press, 2007); Billie Jean King with Frank Deford, *Billie Jean* (New York: Viking Press, 1982), 58; A. S. Gaither to Mary Jackson White, July 2, 1952, Box 11, Folder 14, and Sarah L. Powell to Jake Gaither, November 14, 1955, Box 11, Folder 14, both Gaither Collection, Meek-Eaton Southeastern Regional Black Archives Research Center and Museum, Florida A&M University, Tallahassee.

160. "Reception for Althea Gibson at Waldorf Astoria Hotel After Ticker-Tape Parade," July 11, 1957, WNYC, http://www.wnyc.org/people/renville-h-mcmann/.

161. Sarah Palfrey, "Althea," *Sports Illustrated*, September 2, 1957, 28.

162. Eaton, *"Every Man Should Try,"* 33, 30.

163. Eaton, *"Every Man Should Try,"* 31, 29.

164. Gibson, *I Always Wanted to Be Somebody*, 48.

165. Eaton, *"Every Man Should Try,"* 33.

CHAPTER 4

1. Althea Gibson, *I Always Wanted to Be Somebody*, ed. Ed Fitzgerald (New York: Harper and Row, 1958), 57, 60; "Five Negro Net Champs to Play in Famcee Meet," *Tallahassee Democrat*, June 26, 1949, 7; "Famcee Net Squad to Leave for Meet at Wilberforce," *Tallahassee Democrat*, August 19, 1949, 8; Austin to Dr. Eaton, May 9, 1949, Box 27, Folder 4, Eaton Papers; D. C. Collington, "Campus Chatter," *New York Age*, August 3, 1957, 6; "Famcee Netters in National Tournament," *Philadelphia Tribune*, August 23, 1949; "Althea Gibson Retains Women's Tennis Championship," *Atlanta Daily World*, August 31, 1949, 5.

2. Gibson, *I Always Wanted to Be Somebody*, 53–54.

3. Gibson, *I Always Wanted to Be Somebody*, 57.

4. Gibson, *I Always Wanted to Be Somebody*, 47.

5. Alice Rabby, *The Pain and the Promise: The Struggle for Civil Rights in Tallahassee, Florida* (Athens: University of Georgia Press, 1999), 1–9, 12; Gibson, *I Always Wanted to Be Somebody*, 59; Erik Robinson, *Images of America: Tallahassee* (Charleston, SC: Arcadia, 2003); Althemese Barnes and Ann Roberts, *Black America Series: Tallahassee, Florida* (Charleston, SC: Arcadia, 2000).

6. Gibson, *I Always Wanted to Be Somebody*, 56–57; Ted Poston, "The Story of Althea Gibson: Article III," *New York Post Daily Magazine*, August 28, 1958, M2; Peter Wallenstein, "Black Southerners and Nonblack Universities: The Process of Desegregating Southern Higher Education, 1935–1965," in *Higher Education and the Civil Rights Movement: White Supremacy, Black Southerners, and College Campuses* (Gainesville: University Press of Florida, 2008), 43–44, 51.

7. Gibson, *I Always Wanted to Be Somebody*, 153.

8. "History of Florida Agricultural and Mechanical University (FAMU)," https://www.famu.edu/index.cfm?AboutFAMU&History (accessed November 30, 2020).

9. "Remember," *The Rattler 1950*, n.p. *The Rattler* was FAMC's yearbook.

10. Gibson, *I Always Wanted to Be Somebody*, 59.

11. Gibson, *I Always Wanted to Be Somebody*, 59.

12. Florida Agricultural and Mechanical College, *Bulletin* 1, no. 4 (December 1948): 32, 30; Gibson, *I Always Wanted to Be Somebody*, 60.

13. Florida Agricultural and Mechanical College, *Bulletin* 1, no. 4 (December 1948): 32.

14. Florida Agricultural and Mechanical College, *Bulletin* 1, no. 4 (December 1948): 31.

15. Gibson, *I Always Wanted to Be Somebody*, 60; Rabby, *The Pain and the Promise*, 38.

16. Gibson to Dr. Eaton, October 4, 1949, Eaton Papers; Gibson to Dr. Eaton, November 24, 1949, Eaton Papers.

17. Derrick E. White, *Blood, Sweat, and Tears: Jake Gaither, Florida A&M, and the History of Black College Football* (Chapel Hill: University of North Carolina Press, 2019); Gibson to Dr. Eaton, October 4, 1949, Eaton Papers.

18. Gibson to Dr. Eaton, October 4, 1949, Eaton Papers.

19. "Women's Senate" and "Freshman Women Council," *The Rattler 1950*, n.p.; Gibson to Dr. Eaton, February 10, 1950.

20. Gibson to Dr. Eaton, February 10, 1950, Eaton Papers.

21. Gibson to Dr. Eaton, February 10, 1950, Eaton Papers.

22. Gibson to Dr. Eaton, February 10, 1950, Eaton Papers; "More Black Youngsters Playing Tennis Today," *New York Amsterdam News*, September 28, 1974, C14; Betty Granger, "Conversation Piece," *New York Amsterdam News*, April 16, 1977, A9; Julius J. Adams, "Sports Figures Gain Ground in Many Fields During Year 1949," *New York Amsterdam News*, December 31, 1949, 22.

23. Nick Carr, "A Fireplace Between Two Columns" and "Paratus et Fidelis," www.scoutingny.com/a-peek-inside-the-worlds-largest-armory/ (accessed December 7, 2020).

24. "Miss Gibson Takes Final," *New York Times*, March 5, 1950, S7.

25. Bill Lauder Jr., "Patty's Rally Defeats Masterson, in Indoor Tennis," *New York Herald Tribune*, 30; Michael Strauss, "M'Neill Is Victor over Budge Patty," *New York Times*, March 24, 1950; Allison Danzig, "M'Neill Conquers Kovaleski in Final," *New York Times*, March 25, 1950, S1; John M. Ross, "Make Way for Fancy Nancy," *Sport*, September 1950, 47, 87–88; "Wins Tennis Title," *New York Times*, March 26, 1950, S1.

26. "Myrick, Kingman Honored," *New York Times*, March 29, 1950, 42; Francis, quoted in "The New Gibson Girl," *Sports Illustrated*, July 2, 1956, 20. For a biography of Baker, see Ron Howell, *Boss of Black Brooklyn: The Life and Times of Bertram L. Baker* (New York: Empire State Editions, 2019).

27. Francis, quoted in Ted Poston, "The Althea Gibson Story: Article IV," *New York Post Daily Magazine*, August 29, 1957, M2.

28. Howard Cohn, "The Gibson Girl," *American Lawn Tennis*, July 1, 1950, 6; Francis, quoted in "The New Gibson Girl," 20.

29. "Althea Gibson Earns Chance to Play in National Tennis Tourney," *Pittsburgh Courier*, April 1, 1950, 23.

30. James L. Hicks, "Althea Gibson Earns Bid to U.S. Tennis Nationals," *Baltimore Afro-American*, April 1, 1950, 17.

31. Al Laney, "Don McNeill, Miss Chaffee Win Net Titles," *New York Herald Tribune*, March 26, 1950, B1.

32. "Oldtime Champ at the Charleston," *Life*, April 3, 1950, 32–33.

33. Gordon Parks, "New Tennis Threat," *Life*, April 3, 1950, 32.

34. James L. Hicks, "Big Time," *Baltimore Afro-American*, July 23, 1949.

35. Hicks, "Althea Gibson Earns Bid."

36. "Wins Eastern Indoor Title," *Baltimore Afro-American*, March 18, 1950, 17; Gibson, *I Always Wanted to Be Somebody*, 61.

37. Serrell Hillman, "That Gibson Girl," *Time*, August 26, 1957, 46.

38. J. D. Advent and A.L. Burwell, "The College Song," *The Rattler 1950*, front inside cover; Gibson, *I Always Wanted to Be Somebody*, 61.

39. Gibson, *I Always Wanted to Be Somebody*, 53.

40. Dr. Eaton to Gibson, April 6, 1950, Eaton Papers.

41. "Students Hear Dr. Gore at Fla. A. and M.," *Atlanta Daily World*, April 11, 1950.

42. Rabby, *The Pain and the Promise*, 38.

43. Chestine Everett, "Althea Gibson Looks Forward to Bid to Compete in National This Summer," *Chicago Defender*, June 17, 1950, 19.

44. Dr. Eaton to Gibson, April 6, 1950, Eaton Papers; Gibson to Dr. Eaton, May 10, 1950, Eaton Papers.

45. Gibson to Dr. Eaton, May 10, 1950, Eaton Papers; "The New Gibson Girl," 60.

46. "The New Gibson Girl," 20; Sylvester B. Smith, "Message from the President," ATA National Junior Championships, Tournament Program, August 8–13, 1960, 5, 36, Eaton Papers; Sylvester B. Smith, "Report of the Office of the President," August

16–22, 1959, 7, American Tennis Association, Eaton Papers; Neil Lanctot, *Negro League Baseball: The Rise and Ruin of a Black Institution* (Philadelphia: University of Pennsylvania Press, 2004), 437; Jeff Wiltse, *Contested Waters: A Social History of Swimming Pools in America* (Chapel Hill: University of North Carolina Press, 2007), 121–180.

47. "Tennis Assn. Gives Tray to Francis," *New York Amsterdam News*, January 26, 1963, 37; "The New Gibson Girl," 20, 60.

48. Dr. Eaton to Gibson, May 22, 1950, Eaton Papers.

49. Arthur E. Francis to Maplewood Country Club, June 14, 1950, Eaton Papers; Francis to Robert Clark, June 14, 1950, Eaton Papers.

50. Francis typed in a letter to Dr. Eaton that the official was "Mr. Harold Annerman." I have found no one of that name in news of the New Jersey tennis community published in the *New York Times* between 1945 and 1965. I did, however, locate Harold E. Ammerman of Orange, New Jersey, who was the treasurer of the Eastern Lawn Tennis Association in 1951 and for several years after that. "Savitt Nominated as Tennis Leader," *New York Times*, January 13, 1951, 18. In 1959, the USLTA bestowed an award on Ammerman for his service as an umpire. "Ammerman Is Honored," *New York Times*, September 11, 1959, 35; "The New Gibson Girl," 60.

51. Gibson, *I Always Wanted to Be Somebody*, 67.

52. Dr. Eaton to Francis, June 17, 1950, Eaton Papers.

53. Gibson to Dr. Eaton, July 4, 1950, Eaton Papers.

54. Francis to Dr. Eaton, July 12, 1950, Eaton Papers; Gibson to Dr. Eaton, July 4, 1950, Eaton Papers.

55. Married three times, Sarah Palfrey Cooke was known by various surnames during her careers as a tennis player and as an author. In the early 1980s, she told writer Stan Hart that she preferred to be known professionally as Sarah Palfrey, her family name. See Stan Hart, *Once a Champion: Legendary Tennis Stars Revisited* (New York: Dodd, Mead, 1985), 36.

56. Tom Carter, *First Lady of Tennis: Hazel Hotchkiss Wightman* (Berkeley, CA: Creative Arts, 2001), 101–105; Gibson to Dr. Eaton, July 4, 1950; "Sarah Palfrey," International Tennis Hall of Fame and Museum, Newport, RI, http://www.tennisfame.com/hall-of-famers/inductees/sarah-palfrey (accessed December 28, 2020); "Alice Marble," International Tennis Hall of Fame and Museum, Newport, RI, http://www.tennisfame.com/hall-of-famers/inductees/alice-marble (accessed December 28, 2020).

57. Sarah Palfrey Cooke, *Winning Tennis and How to Play It* (Garden City, NY: Doubleday, 1946), 1.

58. Associated Press, "Pro Charges Hang Over U.S. Champion," *New York Times*, April 8, 1947, 39; Allison Danzig, "Miss Betz to Play Miss Cooke Sunday," *New York Times*, May 2, 1947, 32; Pauline Betz, *Wings on My Tennis Shoes* (London: Sampson Low, Marston, 1949), 150–154; Allison Danzig, "Plan for Pro Tour Bars Tennis Stars," *New York Times*, April 9, 1947, 32; Mary Hardwick, "Pauline's Exodus Leaves

Gap in Women's Racket Ranks," *American Lawn Tennis*, June 1947, 9; Jack Miller, "Net Queens Abdicate," *American Lawn Tennis*, 7.

59. Althea Gibson, foreword, *Tennis for Anyone* (1966; repr., New York: Cornerstone Library Publications, 1971), 7.

60. Francis to Dr. Eaton, July 12, 1950, Eaton Papers.

61. Francis to Dr. Eaton, July 12, 1950, Eaton Papers; Hillman, "That Gibson Girl," 60.

62. Alice Marble, "A Vital Issue," *American Lawn Tennis*, July 1, 1950, 14.

63. Cohn, "The Gibson Girl," 31.

64. Cohn, "The Gibson Girl," 6.

65. Baker to Dr. Eaton, July 7, 1950, Eaton Papers.

66. "Justice at Forest Hills," editorial, *New York Herald Tribune*, July 5, 1950, 22.

67. "Justice and the Courts (Tennis)," editorial, *Life*, July 17, 1950, 40.

68. Edwin Bancroft Henderson, *The Negro in Sports* (Washington, DC: Associated, 1939), 178; Francis to Dr. Eaton, July 12, 1950, Eaton Papers.

69. Victoria W. Wolcott connects the maintenance of the color line in recreational settings with the fluidity of gender contact. See Victoria W. Wolcott, *Race, Riots, and Roller Coasters: The Struggle over Segregated Recreation in America* (Philadelphia: University of Pennsylvania Press, 2012), 8, 16. Dr. Johnson, quoted in Frances Clayton Gray and Yanick Rice Lamb, *Born to Win: The Authorized Biography of Althea Gibson* (Hoboken, NJ: John Wiley and Sons, 2004), 55.

70. Althea Gibson, "Dear Miss Marble," *American Lawn Tennis*, November 1950, 15.

71. Robert Cromie, "River Forest Meet Attracts Top Net Stars," *Chicago Daily Tribune*, July 16, 1950, A6.

72. Jules Tygiel, *Baseball's Great Experiment: Jackie Robinson and His Legacy* (New York: Oxford University Press, 1983).

73. Wendell Smith, "Wendell Smith's Sports Beat: Thar's Gold in Them Thar Forest Hills," *Pittsburgh Courier*, July 29, 1950, 22.

74. Bruce Schoenfeld, *The Match: Althea Gibson and Angela Buxton: How Two Outsiders—One Black, the Other Jewish—Forged a Friendship and Made Sports History* (New York: Amistad, 2004), 51; Smith, "Thar's Gold in Them Thar Forest Hills." The ellipsis is Smith's.

75. Susan K. Cahn, "From the 'Muscle Moll' to the 'Butch' Ballplayer: Mannishness, Lesbianism, and Homophobia in U.S. Women's Sport," *Feminist Studies* 19, no. 2 (Summer 1993): 350–353.

76. Arch Ward, "In the Wake of the News," *Chicago Daily Tribune*, July 22, 1950, B1.

77. Robert Cromie, "Tony Mottram Last Foreigner in Clay Courts," *Chicago Daily Tribune*, July 22, 1950, B2.

78. Robert Cromie, "6 Clay Courts Stars Upset in 1st Round," *Chicago Daily Tribune*, July 19, 1950, B1.

79. "Drawing Seeded Players for U.S. Tennis Championships," *New York Times*, August 24, 1950, 44; Gibson, *I Always Wanted to Be Somebody*, 67.

80. Hillman, "That Gibson Girl," 60; "Expert Advice," *New York Herald Tribune*, July 31, 1950, 18.

81. "Grassy Battlefield," *Sports Illustrated*, August 29, 1955, 12–14; Allison Danzig, "The West Side Story," in *The Fireside Book of Tennis*, ed. Allison Danzig and Peter Schwed (New York: Simon and Schuster, 1972), 89–93.

82. Philip Benjamin, "City Investigates Tennis Club Bias," *New York Times*, July 10, 1959, 1.

83. Gibson, *I Always Wanted to Be Somebody*, 69.

84. Gibson, *I Always Wanted to Be Somebody*, 69.

85. Hillman, "That Gibson Girl," 60.

86. Gibson, *I Always Wanted to Be Somebody*, 67.

87. Associated Press, "Althea Gibson Wins in Grass Court Net Play," *New York Herald Tribune*, August 1, 1950, 26.

88. Allison Danzig, "Miss Gibson Conquers Mrs. Johnson as Eastern Grass Court Tennis Starts," *New York Times*, August 1, 1950, 29.

89. Allison Danzig, "Flam's Stirring Rally Halts Brown in Eastern Grass Court Tennis," *New York Times*, August 2, 1950, 34.

90. Associated Press, "Mrs. duPont Gains in Eastern Grass Court Tennis," *New York Herald Tribune*, August 2, 1950, 25.

91. Ted Poston, "The Althea Gibson Story: Article IV," *New York Post Daily Magazine*, August 29, 1957, M2.

92. Danzig, "Flam's Stirring Rally Halts Brown."

93. M. J. Sleet, "Cal. Tennis Ace Retains Crown," *New York Amsterdam News*, August 19, 1950, 24

94. James Edmund Boyack, "Althea Gibson Wins Fight to Play at Forest Hills," *Pittsburgh Courier*, August 12, 1950, 20; "Will Act on Miss Gibson," *New York Times*, August 16, 1950, 36.

95. "Althea Gibson, Oscar Johnson Dominate 33rd Annual ATA Matches," *Pittsburgh Courier*, September 2, 1950, 16; "Althea Gibson Awaits Forest Hills Bid," *Baltimore Afro-American*, August 26, 1950, 16.

96. "Althea Gibson Awaits Forest Hills Bid."

97. "Title Tennis Admits First Negro, a Girl," *New York Times*, August 22, 1950, 1.

98. Gibson, *I Always Wanted to Be Somebody*, 68.

99. "A. Gibson Gets Nat'l Tennis Bid," *Pittsburgh Courier*, August 26, 1950, 16.

100. "A. Gibson Gets Nat'l Tennis Bid."

101. "Title Tennis Admits First Negro, a Girl."

102. "New York Girl Will Enter National Tennis Championship," *New York Herald Tribune*, August 22, 1950, 1.

103. Sam Lacy, "Althea Gibson: A Profile of Our Top Woman Tennis Champion," *Baltimore Afro-American Magazine*, August 26, 1950, 1.

104. M. J. Sleet, "Fans Await Althea's Appearance at Forest Hills; 1st Negro to Play in Nationals," *New York Amsterdam News*, August 26, 1950, 23.

105. "Tennis Joins the Parade of Democracy in Sports," editorial, *Norfolk Journal and Guide*, August 26, 1950.

106. D'Weston Haywood, *Let Us Make Men: The Twentieth-Century Black Press and a Manly Vision for Racial Advancement* (Chapel Hill: University of North Carolina Press, 2018).

107. "A. Gibson Gets Nat'l Tennis Bid."

108. Lacy, "Althea Gibson: A Profile," 1.

109. "Tennis Comes of Age," editorial, *Philadelphia Tribune*, August 26, 1950, 4.

110. Gibson, *I Always Wanted to Be Somebody*, 69.

111. Ted Poston, "The Althea Gibson Story: Article V," *New York Post Daily Magazine*, August 30, 1957, M2; Gibson, *I Always Wanted to Be Somebody*, 69.

112. Gibson, *I Always Wanted to Be Somebody*, 69.

113. Gibson, *I Always Wanted to Be Somebody*, 69.

114. Sam Lacy, "From A to Z," *Baltimore Afro American*, September 2, 1950, 17, B1; Al Laney, "McNeill Upsets McGregor in National Tennis; Louise Brough, Althea Gibson Gain," *New York Herald Tribune*, August 29, 1950, 24.

115. Laney, "McNeill Upsets McGregor"; Arnold de Mille, "Althea Loses, but Shatters Many Traditions," *Chicago Defender*, September 9, 1950, 17; Buddy Walker quoted in Poston, "The Althea Gibson Story: Article V"; Gibson, *I Always Wanted to Be Somebody*, 72.

116. Laney, "McNeill Upsets McGregor."

117. Laney, "McNeill Upsets McGregor."

118. Arnold de Mille, "Althea Gibson Uses Racket to Smash Color Bar: Althea Gibson and Her Benefactors," *Chicago Defender Magazine Section*, September 9, 1950, 13; Cecil Layne, "Eaton, Francis, Althea, Smith, Baker, Walker, and Johnson," August 28, 1950, Althea Gibson Portrait Collection, Schomburg Center for Research in Black Culture, New York.

119. Gibson, *I Always Wanted to Be Somebody*, 70; "Championed by a Champion," *Pittsburgh Courier*, September 2, 1950, 16; de Mille, "Althea Gibson Uses Racket to Smash Color Bar"; "Althea Did a Splendid Job," *New York Amsterdam News*, September 2, 1950, 1; *This Is Your Life*, tribute to Alice Marble, episode 75, February 3, 1954, revised television script, Container 11, Folder 4, Ralph Edwards Productions Radio and Television Scripts, Manuscript Division, Library of Congress, Washington, DC.

120. Gibson, *I Always Wanted to Be Somebody*, 71.

121. Hicks, "Althea Gibson Earns Bid to U.S. Tennis Nationals."

122. Sam Lacy, "From A to Z," *Baltimore Afro-American*, September 2, 1950.

123. Betram Baker quoted in Poston, "The Althea Gibson Story: Article IV."

124. M. J. Sleet, "Alethea [*sic*] Beats Rhoda Smith, but Was Sorry," *New York Amsterdam News*, August 12, 1950, 23. Elsewhere, Smith was said to have been "like a mother to her for many years." See de Mille, "Althea Gibson Uses Racket to Smash Color Bar," 13.

125. Al Laney, "Patty Top Seed in Nationals at Forest Hills," *New York Herald Tribune*, August 24, 1950, 25; Sam Lacy, "From A to Z," *Baltimore Afro-American*, September 9, 1950.

126. Al Laney, "McNeill Upsets McGregor in National Tennis; Louise Brough, Althea Gibson Gain," *New York Herald Tribune*, August 29, 1950, 24; Associated Press, "Rain Halts U.S. Net Play as Gibson Leads Brough," *Chicago Tribune*, August 30, 1950, B2.

127. Associated Press, "Rain Halts U.S. Net Play."

128. Gibson, *I Always Wanted to Be Somebody*, 72; Eaton, *"Every Man Should Try,"* 35; Sam Lacy, "From A to Z," *Baltimore Afro-American*, September 9, 1950.

129. Laney, "McNeill Upsets McGregor in National Tennis."

130. Al Laney, "Althea Gibson Leads Louise Brough in 3d Set of Tennis Match Delayed by Rain," *New York Herald Tribune*, August 30, 1950, 27.

131. Eaton, *"Every Man Should Try,"* 35; Gibson, *I Always Wanted to Be Somebody*, 72.

132. Gibson, *I Always Wanted to Be Somebody*, 172; James Edmund Boyack, "Handles Self Well in Women's Nat'l," *Pittsburgh Courier*, September 9, 1950, 18.

133. Gibson, *I Always Wanted to Be Somebody*, 73.

134. Gibson, *I Always Wanted to Be Somebody*, 73.

135. Allison Danzig, "Miss Gibson Bows to Louise Brough," *New York Times*, August 31, 1950, 29.

CHAPTER 5

1. Associated Press, "Althea Gibson Loses Poise and U.S. Net Match," *Chicago Daily Tribune*, August 31, 1950, B2; Allison Danzig, "Sedgman Checks Clark's Rally to Advance in U.S. Tennis: Miss Gibson Bows to Louise Brough," *New York Times*, August 31, 1950, 29; James Edmund Boyack, "Tennis Star Althea Gibson Vows 'I'll Be Back,'" *Pittsburgh Courier*, September 9, 1950, 18.

2. Sam Lacy, "Gibson Loses After Rocking Tennis World," *Baltimore Afro-American*, September 9, 1950, 17.

3. Boyack, "Tennis Star Althea Gibson Vows."

4. Arnold de Mille, "Althea Loses, but Shatters Many Traditions; Newsreel, Radio Photographers Have Field Day," *Chicago Defender*, September 9, 1950, 17; Boyack, "Tennis Star Althea Gibson Vows."

5. Al Laney, "Mulloy Beats Cochell, Flam Downs Talbert in National Tennis: The Summaries," *New York Herald Tribune*, September 3, 1950; B3; Boyack, "Tennis Star Althea Gibson Vows."

6. "Althea Gibson to Be Welcomed," *Tallahassee Democrat*, September 26, 1950, 8; "A&M Greets Tennis Star," *Tallahassee Democrat*, September 27, 1950, 9; Gibson to Dr. Eaton, October 5, 1950, Eaton Papers.

7. Alvin Moses, Associated Negro Press, "American Sports Show Interracial Trend During 1950: New Athletes Gain Stardom in Sports," *Atlanta Daily World*, December 27, 1950, 5; Buddy Walker, "Buddy Walker Thinks Storm Played a Dirty Trick on Althea Gibson," *Chicago Defender*, September 9, 1950, 17.

8. Boyack, "Tennis Star Althea Gibson Vows"; Sam Lacy, "From A to Z," *Baltimore Afro-American*, September 9, 1950, 17.

9. "All Honors Althea," editorial, *Chicago Defender*, September 16, 1950, 6.

10. "Alonzo 'Jake' Gaither, Florida A&M Coaching Boss Is the Winningest in Negro College Football," *Ebony*, November 1960, 162; Gibson to Dr. Eaton, November 9, 1950, Eaton Papers.

11. Adam Green, *Selling the Race: Culture, Community, and Black Chicago, 1940–1955* (Chicago: University of Chicago Press, 2009), 129–178; Maren Stange, "'Photographs Taken in Everyday Life': *Ebony's* Photojournalistic Discourse," in *The Black Press: New Literary and Historical Essays*, ed. Todd Vogel (New Brunswick, NJ: Rutgers University Press, 2001), 207–227; John H. Johnson with Lerone Bennett Jr., *Succeeding Against the Odds: The Inspiring Autobiography of One of America's Wealthiest Entrepreneurs* (New York: Warner Books, 1989), 153, 155.

12. "Althea Gibson: Tomboyish Coed Startles Tennis World with Natural Ability on Court," *Ebony*, November 1950, 100, 96, 97, 99.

13. Arnold de Mille, "Along Celebrity Row," *Chicago Defender*, November 25, 1950, 8.

14. De Mille, "Along Celebrity Row"; Sam Lacy, "From A to Z: Special Note," *Baltimore Afro-American*, April 7, 1951, 16; Gibson to Dr. Eaton, October 5, 1951, Eaton Papers.

15. Layne's Studio, "Robinson, Gibson, Reynolds, Sampson, Battle, and Marble," November 29, 1950, Althea Gibson Collection, Schomburg Center for Research in Black Culture, New York.

16. Gibson to Dr. Eaton, January 6, 1951, Eaton Papers.

17. Lua Stewart Bartley, *A Brief History of the Division of Health, Physical Education and Recreation at Florida Agricultural and Mechanical University from 1918 Through 1978 (60 Years)* (Tallahassee: FAMU, 1978), 11, 17, 19, http://famu.digital.flvc.org/islandora/object/famu%3A7026#page/Page+i/mode/1up; Marion E. Anderson, "Sports of the World," *Atlanta Daily World*, December 13, 1949, 5.

18. Gibson to Dr. Eaton, January 6, 1951, Eaton Papers; Joe Bostic, "The Scoreboard," *New York Amsterdam News*, October 7, 1950, 27.

19. Tony Layng, "Black Students at Rollins," *Rollins College Alumni Record*, 1970-02, 6–8, http://archives.rollins.edu/cdm/compoundobject/collection/students/id/381/rec/9; Pauline Betz, *Wings on My Tennis Shoes* (London: Sampson Low, Marston, 1949), 102–116; Doris Hart, *Tennis with Hart* (Philadelphia: J. B. Lippincott, 1955), 74; Peter Wallenstein, ed., *Higher Education and the Civil Rights Movement: White Supremacy, Black Southerners, and College Campuses* (Gainesville: University Press of Florida, 2008), 17–59.

20. Gibson to Dr. Eaton, January 12, 1951, Eaton Papers.

21. "How the Stars See God," *Ebony*, April 1959, 101. She also spoke of God often in *So Much to Live For*. See Althea Gibson with Richard J. Curtis, *So Much to Live For* (New York: G. P. Putnam's Sons, 1968), 42, 64, and 111.

22. Gibson to Dr. Eaton, January 22, 1951, Eaton Papers.

23. Gibson to Dr. Eaton, January 22, 1951, Eaton Papers; Fred Hawthorne, "Gibson Scores in Jamaica," *American Lawn Tennis*, April 1951, 10; Associated Press, "Miss Rosenquest Victory," *New York Times*, February 12, 1945, 16; United Press, "Clark Wins in Jamaica: Beats Grigry in Singles Final—Althea Gibson Also Scores," *New York Times*, February 11, 1951, S5.

24. Gibson to Dr. Eaton, January 6, 1951, Eaton Papers; "Sports and Video Figures Help at ANTA Benefit," *New York Herald Tribune*, February 17, 1951, 6; "Jackie Robinson Star of Tennis Show Here," *New York Times*, February 17, 1951, 11.

25. Billie Jean King, *All In: An Autobiography* (New York: Alfred A. Knopf, 2021), 186; Teddy Tinling with Robert Oxby, *White Ladies* (London: Stanley Paul, 1963), 141–142.

26. Al Laney, "Seixas Is Upset by Shields in Indoor Tennis," *New York Herald Tribune*, February 18, 1951, B1; Bill Lauder Jr., "Althea Gibson, Balbiers Gain in Title Tennis," *New York Herald Tribune*, February 21, 1951, 24; Allison Danzig, "Althea Gibson Defeats Mrs. Buck in U.S. Indoor Tennis," *New York Times*, February 21, 1951, 37.

27. Danzig, "Althea Gibson Defeats Mrs. Buck in U.S. Indoor Tennis"; Al Laney, "Nancy Chaffee Wins, 6–1, 6–3, over Althea Gibson in Tennis," *New York Herald Tribune*, February 23, 1951, 26.

28. Ned Kellogg, "Talbert and Chaffee Take Indoor Titles," *American Lawn Tennis*, April 1951, 5.

29. Laney, "Nancy Chaffee Wins."

30. Associated Press, "Cochell Defeats Larned in Tennis," *New York Times*, April 18, 1949, 20; Eddie Herr, "Patty and Gibson Win Caracas," *World Tennis*, May 1958, 14–17; Arthur L. Himbert, "Miami Beach Story: Success of a Resort City Built on Climate Will be Celebrated on 35th Anniversary," *New York Times*, March 12, 1950, X15.

31. "Rattler Net Ace to Be Featured in New Reel," *Tallahassee Democrat*, March 18, 1951, 11; Amanda Jenkins, "All-American News: The First African American Newsreel," *Now See Hear! The National Audio-Visual Conservation Center Blog*, Library of Congress, February 15, 2019, https://blogs.loc.gov/now-see-hear/2019/02/all-american-news-the-first-african-american-newsreel/.

32. Marion E. Jackson, "Sports of the World," *Atlanta Daily World*, January 18, 1951, 5; "Gibson in Mixed Play," *Pittsburgh Courier*, March 24, 1951, 1.

33. "Admiral Hotel," postcard, c. 1940, author's personal collection.

34. Furman Bisher, "What About the Negro Athlete in the South?," *Sport*, May 1956, 86.

35. Chanelle Nyree Rose, *The Struggle for Black Freedom in Miami: Civil Rights and America's Tourist Paradise, 1896–1968* (Baton Rouge: Louisiana State University Press, 2015).

36. Althea Gibson, *I Always Wanted to Be Somebody*, ed. Ed Fitzgerald (New York: Harper and Row, 1958), 76.

37. "Gibson in Mixed Play"; Lacy, "From A to Z: Special Note," April 7, 1951.

38. Gibson, *I Always Wanted to Be Somebody*, 76.

39. "Good Neighbor Honors Go to Flam," *International Tennis News*, April 1951, 9.

40. Karla Schuster, "Herr, Tennis Legend, Dies," *South Florida Sun Sentinel*, June 18, 2000, www.sun-sentinel.com/news/fl-xpm-2000-06-18-0006180119-story.html; Bill Wallace, "Cold Snap Cuts Play," *Miami Daily News*, December 20, 1954, 21-A; Edwin Pope, "Althea Gibson: Pent-Up Power, Poise, Skill and Conversation," *Miami News*, April 6, 1958, 3D; Charles C. North, "Negro Community News: Miss Althea Gibson," March 21, 1951, *Miami Daily News*, 6-C; Charles C. North, "News About Miami Negro Community," *Miami Herald*, March 25, 1951, 13–A; Gibson to Dr. Eaton, April 8, 1951, Eaton Papers (Gibson's handwriting is difficult to read in this instance. The friend might also have been named Leonard. Gibson used female pronouns to refer to the individual); Jimmy Burns, "Spotlighting Sports: They'll Always Remember Knute Rockne," *Miami Herald*, March 31, 1951, 14-A; Charles C. North, "News About Miami Negro Community: Althea Gibson Honored," April 1, 1951, *Miami News*, 6-B.

41. "Gibson in Mixed Play"; Lacy, "From A to Z: Special Note," April 7, 1951.

42. Sam Lacy, "From A to Z," *Baltimore Afro-American*, April 7, 1951, 16; North, "Negro Community News: Miss Althea Gibson," 6-C.

43. "Good Neighbor Honors Go to Flam," 8; Sam Lacy, "Vanquished Rival Lauds Althea Gibson," *Baltimore Afro-American*, April 7, 1951, 16.

44. "Good Neighbor Honors Go to Flam," 9; Lacy, "From A to Z: Special Note," April 7, 1951; Associated Press, "Flam Overcomes Mulloy in 5 Sets," *New York Times*, April 2, 1951, 32.

45. Charlie Nobles, "For Slim Harbett, Tennis Is Still a Love Affair," *Miami News*, May 21, 1983; Gibson to Dr. Eaton, April 8, 1951, Eaton Papers.

46. Dr. Eaton to Gibson, April 11, 1951, Eaton Papers; Tyler Stovall, *Paris Noir: African Americans in the City of Light* (New York: Houghton Mifflin, 1996).

47. Omega Psi Phi and Fitness Through Athletics, *The Rattler 1951*, n.p.; 1951 Intercollegiate Athletics Varsity "F" Recipients, 1, 2, Alonzo "Jake" Gaither Collection, Box 5, Folder 10, Meak-Eaton Black Archives Research Center and Museum, Tallahassee (hereafter "Gaither Collection").

48. Joanna Davenport, "The History and Interpretation of Amateurism in the United States Lawn Tennis Association," Ph.D. diss., Ohio State University, 1966, 76–83, 178; William T. Tilden II, *My Story* (New York: Hellman, Williams, 1948), 204; Ed Linn, "Is Amateur Sport Dead?," *Sport*, July 1956, 87.

49. Obituary, "S. E. Davenport, Tennis Official, 69," *New York Times*, May 27, 1958, 31; Jack Kramer, *The Game: My 40 Years in Tennis* (New York: G. P. Putnam's Sons, 1979), 69, 70, 71. Kramer won Forest Hills in 1946, too.

50. "Alonzo 'Jake' Gaither, Florida A&M Coaching Boss," 168–169.

51. Wendell Smith, "Wendell Smith's Sports Beat: Thar's Gold in Them Thar Forest Hills," *Pittsburgh Courier*, July 29, 1950, 22.

52. Greg Ruth, *Tennis: A History from American Amateurs to Global Professionals* (Urbana: University of Illinois Press, 2021), 67, 98–109; Tilden, *My Story*, 116.

53. Davenport, "History and Interpretation of Amateurism," 2, 176, 38, 68–70; Angela Lumpkin, *Women's Tennis: A Historical Documentary of the Players and Their Game* (Troy, NY: Whitson, 1981), 68–69; Al Stump, "The Terrible-Tempered Mrs. Todd," *Sport*, April 1951, 91; Tilden, *My Story*, 204.

54. Dr. Eaton to Gibson, April 11, 1951, Eaton Papers; Hubert A. Eaton, "*Every Man Should Try*" (Williston, NC: Bonaparte Press, 1984), 29; Robert Walter Johnson to Bertram L. Baker, April 15, 1951, Eaton Papers; Dr. Eaton to Gibson, April 11, 1951, Eaton Papers.

55. Dr. Johnson to Baker, April 15, 1951, Eaton Papers.

56. Dr. Johnson to Baker, April 15, 1951, Eaton Papers.

57. Dr. Johnson to Baker, April 15, 1951, Eaton Papers.

58. Associated Negro Press, "Althea Gibson Ready to Quit Florida A&M?," *Philadelphia Tribune*, April 24, 1951, 10; Associated Negro Press, "Althea Gibson May Quit School," *Los Angeles Sentinel*, April 26, 1951, B6; "To Compete in Wimbledon; Althea Reported to Be Leaving Fla. A&M," *New York Amsterdam News*, April 28, 1951, 15; Associated Negro Press, "Althea Refutes Previous Report of Leaving College," *New York Amsterdam News*, May 5, 1951, 13.

59. Dr. Eaton to Gibson, April 11, 1951, Eaton Papers.

60. Gibson, *I Always Wanted to Be Somebody*, 77. "Poor Althea, Support for Coaching Fades," *Call and Post* (Cleveland, OH), April 21, 1951; Dr. Eaton to Gibson, April 19, 1951, Eaton Papers.

61. "Jim Crow Tennis," *Time*, August 28, 1939, 41; Sean Jacobs, "Not So Quiet Resistance," *Africa Is a Country* (blog), March 10, 2022, https://africasacountry.com/2022/03/not-so-quiet-resilience.

62. Sam Lacy, "From A to Z," *Baltimore Afro-American*, June 16, 1951, 17.

63. Sam Lacy, "Althea Gibson on Way to Wimbledon," *Baltimore Afro-American*, June 9, 1951, 16.

64. "Pace-Setting Women," editorial, *Pittsburgh Courier*, June 16, 1951, 20.

65. Marion E. Jackson, "Sports of the World: Tipoff," *Atlanta Daily World*, April 8, 1951, 7.

66. Marion E. Jackson, "Sports of the World," *Atlanta Daily World*, June 29, 1951, 7.

67. Bertram Baker to Jake Gaither, March 29, 1951, Eaton Papers; Gibson, *I Always Wanted to Be Somebody*, 76.

68. Bertram Baker to Slazenger Limited, May 24, 1951, Eaton Papers.

69. Bertram Baker to Jake Gaither, March 29, 1951, Eaton Papers.

70. Gibson, *I Always Wanted to Be Somebody*, 75–76; Jake Gaither to Bertram Baker, April 7, 1951, Eaton Papers.

71. "Althea Gibson Set to Play in Wimbledon Matches; Net Star Permitted to Take Early Exams," *New York Amsterdam News*, May 26, 1951, 19.

72. Gibson, *I Always Wanted to Be Somebody*, 76; "William C. Matney, Jr., 76, Pioneering Broadcaster Joined NBC News in Chicago in 1963," *Chicago Tribune*, June 19, 2001; "Hotel Gotham: Detroit's 200-Room Hostelry Is Finest in Negro America," *Ebony*, August 1947, 28; Dr. Gibson to Eaton, May 24, 1951, Eaton Papers.

73. Jean Pitrone, *Jean Hoxie: The Robin Hood of Tennis* (Hamtramck, MI: Avenue, 1985), 18–21, 92–93; "Jean Hoxie—Globe-Trotter," *American Lawn Tennis*, June 1949, 34–35. Years later, Hoxie gave tennis lessons to Jacqueline Kennedy and served on President Dwight Eisenhower's National Youth Fitness Committee.

74. Pitrone, *Jean Hoxie*, v; Fred Kovaleski, "Hamtramck," in *The Fireside Book of Tennis*, ed. Allison Danzig and Peter Schwed (New York: Simon and Schuster, 1971), 461. Kovaleski won the National Public Parks singles and doubles titles in 1947 and the National Intercollegiate Doubles, with Tut Bartzen, in 1948.

75. Pitrone, *Jean Hoxie*, 71.

76. Gibson, *I Always Wanted to Be Somebody*, 77. Hoxie's dubious qualities went beyond pedagogy. According to her biographer, Hoxie was a publicity- and fortune-seeking fabulist given to lying about everything, including her family background, her education and age, and even her husband's education and business dealings. As a teaching professional at Orchard Lake Country Club, Hoxie was routinely accused of improper billing. See Pitrone, *Jean Hoxie*, 71, 36, 31, and 80.

77. Meeting Minutes, American Tennis Association, August 21, 1951, 15, Eaton Papers.

78. Meeting Minutes, American Tennis Association, August 21, 1951, 15, Eaton Papers; Emerson W. Craig to Baker, April 8, 1951, Eaton Papers.

79. Meeting Minutes, American Tennis Association, August 21, 1951, 15, Eaton Papers; Associated Negro Press, "Althea Gibson to Play at Wimbledon," *Atlanta Daily World*, June 6, 1951, 7; Allison Danzig, "Miss Gibson Gets Wimbledon Offer," *New York Times*, May 31, 1951, 33.

80. "Sports Group Backs Althea Gibson's Trip," *Call and Post*, April 28, 1951, 1-D; Gibson, *I Always Wanted to Be Somebody*, 77; Gibson to Dr. Eaton, May 24, 1951, Eaton Papers.

81. "Poor Althea, Support for Coaching Fades."

82. Joe Bostic, "The Scorecard," *New York Amsterdam News*, June 9, 1951.

83. "Althea to Get Wimbledon Trip," *Call and Post*, June 9, 1951, 2D. Another source says Louis "spearheaded the drive which raised two thousand dollars" for Althea, but it offers no explanatory details; see "Billy Rowe's Notebook," *Pittsburgh Courier*, June 5, 1951, 18.

84. Gibson, *I Always Wanted to Be Somebody*, 77.

85. Gibson, *I Always Wanted to Be Somebody*, 77; Randy Roberts, *Joe Louis* (New Haven, CT: Yale University Press, 2010), 233–239, 241–242, 249–250; Associated Negro Press, "Government Files $507,610 Tax Lien Against Ex-Bomber Louis," *Philadelphia Tribune*, December 19, 1955, 6.

86. Gibson to Dr. Eaton, May 24, 1951, Eaton Papers; Gibson, *I Always Wanted to Be Somebody*, 77; "Althea Gibson Off for Wimbledon," *New York Herald Tribune*, June 3, 1951, B3.

87. "Colour Bar in Tennis," *Hull Daily Mail*, August 16, 1950, 5; Fred Perry, "Concentration Can Make Frank Sedgman a Champion," *Liverpool Echo*, May 12, 1951, 3.

88. "Wimbledon Newcomers," *Leicester Evening Mail*, May 31, 1951, 12; "Coloured Girl in Tennis Semi," *Dundee Courier and Advertiser*, June 8, 1951, 2; *The Sphere* (London), June 23, 1951, 501; "Wimbledon 'Ladies' Day Hold-Up," *Leicester Evening Mail*, June 26, 1951, 12; "Althea's Ace Too Much for Susan," *Daily Mirror* (London), June 15, 1951, 10.

89. Bruce Harril, "Notes from My Diary: Hard Feelings," *Londonderry Sentinel*, June 9, 1951, 8.

90. Perry, "Concentration Can Make Frank Sedgman a Champion"; Maureen Connolly, *Forehand Drive* (London: Macgibbon and Kee, 1957), 55–56; Bruce Harril, "Notes from My Diary: Hard Feelings," *Londonderry Sentinel*, June 9, 1951, 8.

91. "Wimbledon Newcomers," *Leicester Evening Mail*, May 31, 1951, 12.

92. "A&M Photo Feature," *Tallahassee Democrat*, May 15, 1951, 2; Denzil Batchelor, "The Different Gibson Girl," *Picture Post*, June 30, 1951, 29.

93. Mary L. Dudziak, *Cold War Civil Rights: Race and the Image of American Democracy* (Princeton, NJ: Princeton University Press, 2000). See also "Robeson's Attorneys Say Passport Ban Restrictive," *Atlanta Daily World*, August 22, 1951, 1.

94. Batchelor, "The Different Gibson Girl," 30.

95. "Expert Praise for Althea," *Daily Mirror*, June 5, 1951, 10.

96. "A Victory Full of Promise for the Winner—and Loser," *Daily Mirror*, June 6, 1951, 11.

97. "Althea Beaten in Semi-Final," *Daily Mirror*, June 9, 1951, 10; "Like 'Sugar Ray,'" *Belfast Telegraph*, June 5, 1951, 8.

98. "Quick Work by the Gibson Girl," *Daily Mirror*, June 13, 1951, 10; United Press, "Mulloy Advances in English Tennis," *New York Times*, June 13, 1951, 41.

99. "Susan Shines, Outplays French Girl," *Birmingham Gazette*, June 13, 1951, 5; "Kay Reaches Semi-Final; Jean Is Out," *Daily Mirror*, June 22, 1951, 10.

100. Gibson to Dr. Eaton, June 9, 1951, Eaton Papers.

101. Batchelor, "The Different Gibson Girl," 30–31.

102. Gibson to Dr. Eaton, August 2, 1951, Eaton Papers.

103. Batchelor, "The Different Gibson Girl," 29, 30; Ollie Stewart, "Althea Bows at Queen's Box at Match," *Baltimore Afro-American*, July 7, 1951; Stan Hart, *Once a Champion: Legendary Tennis Stars Revisited* (New York: Dodd, Mead, 1985), 27.

104. "Wimbledon Newcomers," *Leicester Evening Mail*, May 31, 1951, 12; Helen Wills, "A Review of Wimbledon," Paul E. Deutschman, "The One and Only," C. M. Jones, "Nine Decades of Splendor," and Lance Tingay, "More than a Tennis Tournament," all in *The Fireside Book of Tennis*, ed. Allison Danzig and Peter Schwed (New York: Simon and Schuster, 1971), 108–127.

105. Connolly, *Forehand Drive*, 57–58.

106. Deutschman, "The Only and Only," 112.

107. Lynda Whitley, "Althea Gibson Rose to the Top in Grand Style," *Daily Press* (Newport News, VA), April 7, 1987, 9.

108. Virginia Wade, *Ladies of the Court: A Century of Women at Wimbledon* (New York: Atheneum, 1984), 103.

109. Whitley, "Althea Gibson Rose to the Top in Grand Style."

110. Mary Hawton, "What Makes Wimbledon Different?," *Tennis in Australasia*, September 1956, 6; Deutschman, "The One and Only," 111; "English Girls Are Improving," *Birmingham Gazette*, June 27, 1951, 6; Tinling, *White Ladies*, 142; "15,000 Shiver in Wimbledon Rain," *Birmingham Gazette*, June 27, 1951, 1.

111. "The Backhand According to Beverley," *Daily Mirror*, June 30, 1951, 10.

112. "Althea Made Her Exit Quietly—Beaten by Nerves," *Daily Mirror*, June 30, 1951, 10; United States Tennis Association, "USTA Junior Nationals Girls' Champions," https://www.usta.com/en/home/about-usta/usta-history/natio nal/usta-national--junior-championships---girls-.html (accessed February 7, 2021); Ed Fitzgerald, "It's Now or Never for Beverly," *Sport*, July 1959, 21; Norman Harnett, "Sedgman in Form at Wimbledon: Unusual Style," *Yorkshire Post and Leeds Mercury*, June 30, 1951, 7.

113. United Press, "Viera 4-Set Victor over Young U.S. Ace," *New York Times*, July 1, 1951.

114. Connolly, *Forehand Drive*, 58.

115. National Negro Press Association, "Althea Finds Odds Against Her at Wimbledon," *Journal and Guide* (Norfolk, VA), June 30, 1951, 1–2.

116. Dick Knight, "'Sugar' Ray Rides into Town in a Limousine," *Birmingham Gazette*, July 5, 1951, 1, 3.

117. Knight, "'Sugar' Ray Rides into Town"; Associated Press, "New York Girl Captures German Tennis Tourney," *New York Times*, July 9, 1951; Associated Press, "Miss Gibson Net Victor," *New York Times*, July 22, 1951.

118. "Back from Wimbledon 'First,'" *Baltimore Afro-American*, August 4, 1951, 2.

119. Malcolm Poindexter, "Three Events Halted by Sudden Rainfall at Germant'wn Meet," *Philadelphia Tribune*, July 31, 1951, 10; Mary Ransom Hunter, "National Social Whirl," *Journal and Guide*, August 4, 1951; Betty Granger to Dr. Eaton,

July 24, 1951, Eaton Papers; Dr. Eaton to Granger, July 26, 1951, Eaton Papers; Dr. Eaton to Gibson, n.d., 1951, Eaton Papers; Baker to Dr. Eaton, July 12, 1950, Eaton Papers; Meeting Minutes, American Tennis Association, August 21, 1951, 14, Eaton Papers; "Queen of the Courts," *Our World*, September 1951, 46–49; "ATA Welcomes Althea Home," *Pittsburgh Courier*, August 18, 1951, 16; "Althea's Day," *Pittsburgh Courier*, August 18, 1951, 16; Al Moses, Associated Negro Press, "Beating the Gun," *Atlanta Daily World*, August 15, 1951, 5.

120. "Ted Tinling," International Tennis Hall of Fame and Museum, Newport, RI, January 18, 2022, https://www.tennisfame.com/hall-of-famers/inductees/ted-tinling; Tinling, *White Ladies*, 142.

121. Allison Danzig, "Richardson Upsets McGregor in Eastern Tennis," *New York Times*, August 2, 1951, 26; Connolly, *Forehand Drive*, 18; Al Laney, "Sedgman, Talbert, Savitt, McGregor and Flam Gain 4th Round in National Tennis," *New York Herald Tribune*, August 29, 1951, 25; Gibson to Dr. Eaton, August 2, 1951, Eaton Papers.

122. "ATA Sidelights," *Baltimore Afro-American*, September 1, 1951, 16; "ATA Welcomes Althea Home"; Gibson to Dr. Eaton, August 2, 1951, Eaton Papers; Dr. Eaton to Gibson, handwritten note, n.d. [1951], Eaton Papers.

123. Biddy Wood, "Stewart, Gibson Win ATA Nationals; Interracial Finals Over in 33 Minutes," *Baltimore Afro-American*, September 1, 1951, 16.

124. "ATA Sidelights."

125. Meeting Minutes, "Special Meeting for Gibson Conference," American Tennis Association, August 21, 1951, 4, Box 34, Folder 1, Eaton Papers.

126. Meeting Minutes, "Special Meeting for Gibson Conference," American Tennis Association, August 21, 1951, 4, Box 34, Folder 1, Eaton Papers.

127. Allison Danzig, "Sedgman and Mulloy Gain Tennis Quarter-Finals," *New York Times*, August 30, 1951.

128. Connolly, *Forehand Drive*, 16, 12, 72, 15, 73, 33–34, 26.

129. Connolly, *Forehand Drive*, 35; "Young Queen," *Time*, September 17, 1951, 54; Al Moses, Associated Negro Press, "Beating the Gun," *Atlanta Daily World*, August 15, 1951; "Althea Gibson, George Stewart Retain Singles Titles at Annual Tennis Tourney at Wilberforce," *New York Amsterdam News*, August 30, 1952, 28; Bill Nunn Jr., "Althea, George Stewart Cop ATA Championships," *Pittsburgh Courier*, August 29, 1953, 26.

130. Gibson to Dr. Eaton, September 25, 1951, Eaton Papers.

131. Flavio G. Martinez and Francisco C. Lona to George W. Gore, September 2, 1951, Eaton Papers.

132. "Jake Gaither," *Ebony*, November 1960, 168; Mary Hardwick, "Althea Gibson as I Know Her," *British Lawn Tennis and Squash*, July 1951, 4.

133. Lona to Gibson, September 14, 1951, Eaton Papers. The letter consists of a reprint of the committee's telegram to Gore and Gore's short refusal.

134. Gibson to Dr. Eaton, December 7, 1951, Eaton Papers.

135. Bruce Schoenfeld, *The Match: Althea Gibson and Angela Buxton: How Two Outsiders—One Black, the Other Jewish—Forged a Friendship and Made Sports History* (New York: Amistad, 2004), 52.

136. "The Rattler Plays: Tennis," *The Rattler 1951*, n.p.

137. Schoenfeld, *The Match*, 52; transcript, "Interview with Althea Gibson," Washington University in St. Louis, October 21, 1984, http://repository.wustl.edu/concern/videos/8s45qd665.

138. Gibson to Dr. Eaton, January 12, 1952, Eaton Papers.

139. Gibson, quoted in Sam Lacy, "From A to Z," *Baltimore Afro-American*, September 1, 1951, 15.

140. Lacy, "From A to Z," September 1, 1951.

141. "Althea Gibson's Experimentation Hurts Game," *Los Angeles Sentinel*, September 13, 1951, B4.

142. Pamela Grundy, *Learning to Win: Sports, Education, and Social Change in Twentieth-Century North Carolina* (Chapel Hill: University of North Carolina Press, 2001), 158–189; A. S. "Jake" Gaither, speech, "The Responsibility of the Team," n.d., Box 4, Folder 18, "1950–1954," Gaither Collection.

143. Martha H. Verbrugge, *Active Bodies: A History of Women's Physical Education in Twentieth-Century America* (New York: Oxford University Press, 2012); Bartley, *A Brief History*, 11, 17, 19; *1950–1951 Bulletin and Course Catalog*, Florida Agricultural and Mechanical University, 135.

144. Gibson to Dr. Eaton, January 12, 1952, Eaton Papers.

145. A. P. Stewart to Gaither, August 7, 1953, Box 5, File 5, "Health and P.E. Meetings and Etc. Minutes, 1953–1959," Gaither Collection.

146. Pamela Grundy and Susan Shackleford, *Shattering the Glass: The Remarkable History of Women's Basketball* (New York: New Press, 2005), 109–123; A. S. Gaither and M. W. Smith, Minutes of the Physical Education Department, January 25, 1952, Box 5, File 5, "Health and P.E. Meetings and Etc. Minutes, 1953–1959," Gaither Collection.

147. Gibson to Dr. Eaton, February 4, 1952, Eaton Papers.

148. "Althea Gibson Sharpening Game," *Tallahassee Democrat*, February 11, 1952, 6.

149. Allison Danzig, "Savitt and Talbert Advance to U.S. Indoor Tennis Final," *New York Times*, February 24, 1952, S1; Associated Press, "Mrs. Todd in Net Final," *New York Times*, March 7, 1952, L27; Associated Press, "Seixas Defeats Vincent," *New York Times*, April 12, 1952, 17; Marion Jackson, "Sports of the World," *Atlanta Daily World*, December 20, 1952, 5.

150. Associated Press, "Savitt Tennis Victor," *New York Times*, March 5, 1952, 35. After marrying, Rosenquest played as Betty Rosenquest Pratt.

151. "Althea Gibson Scores in Bermuda Net Tournament," *Journal and Guide*, August 9, 1952, 24; Gibson to Dr. Eaton, July 8, 1952, Eaton Papers.

152. "Althea Gibson Thrills Fans at Bermuda Tourney," *Call and Post*, August 9, 1952, 2D; "Miss Versatility," *New York Amsterdam News*, August 9, 1952, 26.

153. Tania Grossinger, *Growing Up at Grossinger's* (New York: Skyhorse, 2008); Grossinger's, "Sportsnatches at Grossinger's," advertisement, *New York Times*, August 16, 1952, 18; Grossinger's, "Marciano Training at Grossinger's," advertisement, *New York Times*, August 17, 1952, X15; Arnold Rampersad, *Jackie Robinson* (New York: Alfred A. Knopf, 1997), 221.

154. Gibson to Dr. Eaton, September 22, 1952, Gibson to Dr. Eaton, April 15, 1953, Eaton Papers.

155. "Althea Gibson on Campus, Considers P.Ed. Staff Position," *Lincoln Clarion*, May 23, 1953, 1.

156. Eaton, *"Every Man Should Try,"* 33.

157. Associated Negro Press, "Althea Gibson Praises Others for Her Success," *Philadelphia Tribune*, January 18, 1955, 10.

158. Associated Press, "Maureen Connolly and Vic Seixas Take National Clay Court Crowns," *New York Times*, July 20, 1953, L23.

159. "Althea Gibson Drops Exhibition Match to Miss Connolly, 6–1, 4–6, 6–1," *Chicago Defender*, May 24, 1952, 16; Associated Press, "Maureen Connolly and Vic Seixas Take National Clay Court Crowns."

160. Associated Press, "Net Skein May Be Ended by Miss Brough's Injury," *New York Times*, August 9, 1951, 29; Allison Danzig, "Seixas and Trabert Reach Final of Pennsylvania Tennis Tourney," *New York Times*, July 26, 1953, S3.

161. Gibson to Dr. Eaton, July 26, 1953, Eaton Papers.

162. "National Tennis Title Tourney May Produce New Crop of Stars," *New York Amsterdam News*, July 4, 1953, 28; "Rosemary Darben Gains Fourth Round," *Montclair Times*, July 26, 1951, 4; "Y-Teen Clubs Plan Mid-Winter Activities," *Montclair Times*, February 15, 1951; Gibson, *I Always Wanted to Be Somebody*, 78–79; Gibson, *So Much to Live For*, 113.

163. Obituary, Robert E. Darben, *Montclair Times*, June 5, 1958, 19; Obituary, "Mrs. Robert Darben Succumbs at 76," *Montclair Times*, January 14, 1965, 6.

164. Astrology Chart Notes by Althea Gibson, c. 1995, Gibson Collection; Gibson, *So Much to Live For*, 114, 113; Gloria Pritchard, "Payola Made Record Falter, Althea Says," *Pittsburgh Courier*, January 23, 1960, 12.

165. Gibson, *I Always Wanted to Be Somebody*, 152, 156.

166. Gibson, *So Much to Live For*, 113.

167. John M. Ross, "They're Murdering Tennis!," *Sport*, August 1954, 88; Gibson to Dr. Eaton, July 16, 1953, Eaton Papers.

168. Astrology Chart Notes by Althea Gibson, c. 1995, Gibson Collection; transcript, "Interview with Sydney Llewellyn," Washington University in St. Louis, October 21, 1984, http://repository.wustl.edu/concern/videos/rb68xg9ow; Stacey Baker, "Tennis in Harlem," *6th Floor* (blog), *New York Times*, August 30, 2013 https://archive.nytimes.com/6thfloor.blogs.nytimes.com/2013/08/30/tennis-in-harlem/; Gussie Moran, "Can Althea Gibson Make It?," *Sport*, October 1956, 50, 51, 70.

169. Transcript, "Interview with Sydney Llewellyn"; "California Tennis Ace Beats Stewart; Gibson Wins Easily," *New York Amsterdam News*, August 12, 1950, 24; Moran, "Can Althea Gibson Make It?"

170. Transcript, "Interview with Sydney Llewellyn."

171. Ted Poston, "The Story of Althea Gibson: Article II," *New York Post Daily Magazine*, August 27, 1957, M2; Serrell Hillman, "That Gibson Girl," *Time*, August 26, 1957, 46–48; transcript, "Interview with Sydney Llewellyn."

172. Moran, "Can Althea Gibson Make It?," 50; Lillian S. Calhoun, "Tennis Great Succeeds in Business World," *Chicago Defender*, April 8–14, 1961, 22.

173. Transcript, "Interview with Althea Gibson."

174. Gibson, *I Always Wanted to Be Somebody*, 80, 81, 82; Gibson to Dr. Eaton, July 6, 1953, Eaton Papers; "Among the Top," *Call and Post*, July 25, 1953; "Wheeler, Johnson Bow in Net Meet; Tourney's Listed," *Journal and Guide*, August 1, 1953, 19.

175. Gibson, *I Always Wanted to Be Somebody*, 80. The germane passage in the autobiography reads as if the *Jet* piece that led to his insistence that they work together was published in 1950.

176. Johnson, *Succeeding Against the Odds*, 207, 237.

177. A. S. "Doc" Young, "Inside Sports," *Jet*, January 1, 1953, 55.

178. Young, "Inside Sports."

179. Marion E. Jackson, "Sports of the World," *Atlanta Daily World*, August 29, 1952, 7; "Althea Wins 1st Round with Ease," *Pittsburgh Courier*, September 6, 1952, 24; John McPhee, *Levels of the Game* (New York: Farrar, Straus, and Giroux), 26–28.

180. Althea Gibson, "Dear Miss Marble," *American Lawn Tennis*, February 1951, 15.

181. Cal Jacox, "From the Press Box: Thoughts While Thinking," *Journal and Guide*, June 6, 1953, 23.

182. Jacox, "From the Press Box: Thoughts While Thinking."

183. Cal Jacox, "From the Press Box: In '53 We'd Like to See," *Journal and Guide*, January 10, 1953, 20.

184. Malcolm Poindexter Jr., "Sports-I-View: Miss Gibson Ready for Forest Hills; Improved Play Favors Star's Chances," *Philadelphia Tribune*, August 25, 1953, 11.

185. Marion E. Jackson, "Sports of the World," *Atlanta Daily World*, July 9, 1953, 5; Alvin Moses, "Beating the Gun: Q) I Attended the Recent ATA Tennis Meet," *Atlanta Daily World*, September 12, 1951, 4; Poindexter, "Sports-I-View: Miss Gibson Ready for Forest Hills."

186. Cal Jacox, "From the Press Box: Here . . . and There," *Journal and Guide*, August 1, 1953, 19.

187. Gibson, *I Always Wanted to Be Somebody*, 77.

188. Will Grimsley, Associated Press, "Florida Vet Double Faults 16 Times," *Washington Post*, September 6, 1953, M6.

189. Connolly, *Forehand Drive*, 88.

190. Allison Danzig, "Nielsen Is Ousted," *New York Times*, September 6, 1953, S1, S3; Connolly, *Forehand Drive*, 88.

191. Connolly, *Forehand Drive*, 88.

192. Sam Lacy, "Foul Calls Help Defeat Althea at Forest Hill [*sic*]," *Baltimore Afro-American*, September 12, 1953, 15.

193. Lacy, "Foul Calls."

194. Lacy, "Foul Calls"; Danzig, "Nielson Is Ousted"; Associated Press, "Seixas and Hoad Drub Tennis Foes," *Los Angeles Times*, September 6, 1953, A7.

195. Connolly, *Forehand Drive*, 67, 71–74, 88–89.

CHAPTER 6

1. Lawrence Larsen, *A History of Missouri*, vol. 4, *1953–2003* (Columbia: University of Missouri Press, 2004), 5–6, 58, 2.

2. Missouri Census Data Center, University of Missouri, "Missouri Population, 1900–1990," http://mcdc.missouri.edu/trends/tables/cities1900-1990.pdf (no longer active; accessed February 10, 2016).

3. Althea Gibson, *I Always Wanted to Be Somebody*, ed. Ed Fitzgerald (New York: Harper and Row, 1958), 81, 85.

4. Larsen, *A History of Missouri*, 171; Arnold G. Parks, *Lincoln University, 1920–1970* (Charleston, SC: Arcadia, 2007), 7–9, 19.

5. Rawn James Jr., *Root and Branch: Charles Hamilton Houston, Thurgood Marshall, and the Struggle to End Segregation* (New York: Bloomsbury Press, 2010), 120–121, 150–151; Parks, *Lincoln University*, 27, 28, 102–103, 45, 83.

6. "The Leo Lewis Story," *The Lincoln Archives 1955*, 149–150; "Leo Lewis," Lincoln University, https://lubluetigers.com/honors/hall-of-fame/leo-lewis/11 (accessed February 19, 2021). *The Lincoln Archives* was Lincoln University's yearbook.

7. Parks, *Lincoln University*, 117.

8. Parks, *Lincoln University*, 25, 29; "Gov. Donnelly Slashes Pres. Scruggs' Budget Recommendations; President's Request Includes Many Campus Improvements," *Lincoln Clarion*, February 27, 1953; Zora Neale Hurston, *Their Eyes Were Watching God* (1937; repr., New York: Harper Collins, 1991), 22.

9. Gibson to Dr. Eaton, July 22, 1953, Eaton Papers.

10. "Phy. Ed. Dept. Adds 3 to Staff," *Lincoln Clarion*, September 25, 1953, 3; Martha H. Verbrugge, *Active Bodies: A History of Women's Physical Education in Twentieth-Century America* (New York: Oxford University Press, 2012), 185–186; Gibson, *I Always Wanted to Be Somebody*, 82; Gibson to Dr. Eaton, May 30, 1955, Eaton Papers.

11. Harriet A. Washington, *Medical Apartheid: The Dark History of Medical Experimentation on African Americans from Colonial Times to the Present* (New York: Doubleday, 2006); Verbrugge, *Active Bodies*, 20, 176, 182–183.

12. Luix Virgil Overbea, Associated Negro Press, "Beating the Gun: Althea Gibson as a Teacher," *Philadelphia Tribune*, May 15, 1954, 10.

13. Verbrugge, *Active Bodies*, 177, 181, 178; "Majorettes and 'Cheerleaders,'" *The Lincoln Archives 1955*, 155; Gibson to Dr. Eaton, September 12, 1953, Eaton Papers.

14. "Tennis Team Cops Title," *Lincoln Clarion*, May 21, 1954, 5; Edwin Bancroft Henderson, *The Negro in Sports*, rev. ed. (Washington, DC: Associated, 1949), 296; "Blames Evils on College Heads: Coaches Are Followers of Policies," *Chicago Defender*, June 5, 1954, 22; "Tigers Will Defend Long Win Streak," *Lincoln Clarion*, May 28, 1954, 7.

15. "Netmen Lose to Concordia," *Lincoln Clarion*, May 7, 1954, 1; "52 Athletes Get Letters at All-Sports Banquet," *Lincoln Clarion*, May 28, 1954, 7.

16. Susan K. Cahn, "From the 'Muscle Moll' to the 'Butch' Ballplayer: Mannishness, Lesbianism, and Homophobia in U.S. Women's Sport," *Feminist Studies* 19, no. 2 (Summer 1993): 347–351; Lillian Faderman, *The Gay Revolution: The Story of the Struggle* (New York: Simon and Schuster, 2015), xi–49; Verbrugge, *Active Bodies*, 178, 7, 23–25, 45, 23.

17. Gibson, *I Always Wanted to Be Somebody*, 85.

18. "Blames Evils on College Heads"; Gibson, *I Always Wanted to Be Somebody*, 85; Ted Poston, "The Story of Althea Gibson: Article V," *New York Post Daily Magazine*, August 30, 1957.

19. Verbrugge, *Active Bodies*, 187.

20. "Althea Gibson," *The Lincoln Archives 1954*, n.p.

21. Joseph Summers and Dorothy S. Dallmeyer, *Jefferson City, Missouri* (Chicago: Arcadia, 2000), 101; Gibson, *I Always Wanted to Be Somebody*, 84, 83; James W. Loewen, *Sundown Towns: A Hidden Dimension of American Racism* (New York: Touchstone, 2006), 4; Parks, *Lincoln University*, 78.

22. Gibson, *I Always Wanted to Be Somebody*, 84.

23. "Donald W. McMoore," *Lincoln Archives 1955*, 21; "William McMoore," *Lincoln Archives 1955*, n.p.; "Phy. Ed. Dept. Adds 3 to Staff"; Gibson, *I Always Wanted to Be Somebody*, 84.

24. Gibson, *I Always Wanted to Be Somebody*, 84; Robert Lipsyte, "Althea Gibson: Golf Is Just Another Challenge," *New York Times*, August 23, 1964, 12S.

25. Gibson, *I Always Wanted to Be Somebody*, 85.

26. "TV and Tennis," *Journal and Guide* (Norfolk, VA), February 13, 1954, 1; *This Is Your Life*, tribute to Alice Marble, episode 75, February 3, 1954, revised television script, Container 11, Folder 4, Ralph Edwards Productions Radio and Television Scripts, Manuscript Division, Library of Congress, Washington, DC.

27. Donald Bogle, *Primetime Blues: African Americans on Network Television* (New York: Farrar, Straus, and Giroux, 2001).

28. Bogle, *Primetime Blues*, 81.

29. "Under the Command of Capt. Dova L. Jones," *Lincoln Archives 1954*, n.p.; "From L to R, Flanking Capt. Dova Jones," *Lincoln Clarion*, May 14, 1954; Capt. Dova

L. Jones, *Lincoln Archives 1955*, 112; "Capt. Dova L. Jones Is New PMS and T," *Lincoln Clarion*, December 11, 1953, 1.

30. Gibson, *I Always Wanted to Be Somebody*, 81, 82.

31. "Capt. Jones Talks on Army Career," *Lincoln Clarion*, February 26, 1954, 2; Gibson, *I Always Wanted to Be Somebody*, 82.

32. Gibson to Dr. Eaton, April 13, 1954, Eaton Papers.

33. Gibson, *I Always Wanted to Be Somebody*, 83.

34. Brenda L. Moore, *To Serve My Country, to Serve My Race: The Story of the Only African American WACs Stationed Overseas During World War II* (New York: New York University Press, 1996); Leisa D. Meyer, *Creating GI Jane: Sexuality and Power in the Women's Army Corps During World War II* (New York: Columbia University Press, 1996), 74–75; Gibson, *I Always Wanted to Be Somebody*, 82; Dr. Eaton to Gibson, February 16, 1955, Eaton Papers; Gibson to Dr. Eaton, April 13, 1954, Eaton Papers; Gussie Moran, "Can Althea Gibson Make It?," *Sport*, October 1956, 50.

35. Cal Jacox, "From the Press Box: Thoughts While Thinking," *Journal and Guide*, June 6, 1953, 23.

36. Bill Nunn Jr., "Change of Pace: Archie, Ez Called Turn on Jackson," *Pittsburgh Courier*, July 24, 1954, 23; Cliff W. Mackay, "News in Tabloid," *Baltimore Afro-American*, May 8, 1954, 4.

37. Gibson, *I Always Wanted to Be Somebody*, 160, 170–171; Gibson, "Coaches on the Court," unpublished essay, April 1988, Gibson Collection; Moran, "Can Althea Gibson Make It?," 69.

38. Bill Nunn Jr., "Change of Pace: New York Upbeat," *Pittsburgh Courier*, June 26, 1954, 25; "Title to Althea Gibson: She Defeats Isabel Troccole by 10–8, 6–3 in State Tennis," *New York Times*, July 12, 1954, 25.

39. National Negro Press Association, "Althea Upset in Opening Rounds of Clay Court Nets," *Baltimore Afro-American*, July 24, 1954, 16.

40. Cal Jacox, "From the Press Box: Rambling at Will," *Journal and Guide*, September 4, 1954, 18. Ramsey trained with Dr. Johnson, albeit briefly, in the summer of 1953. Robert W. Johnson III, email to author, October 17, 2015.

41. C. Gerald Fraser, "Althea Gibson Loses Tourney to Perez," *New York Amsterdam News*, September 4, 1954, 7, 24.

42. Maureen Connolly, *Forehand Drive* (London: Macgibbon and Kee, 1957), 99–100, 65, 93, 107–109.

43. Allison Danzig, "Seixas and Doris Hart Rally to Win National Tennis Crowns at Forest Hills," *New York Times*, September 7, 1954, 31.

44. "The Truth About Women Athletes," *Jet*, August 5, 1954, 56–58.

45. "The Truth About Women Athletes," 58; Ann Aldrich, *We Walk Alone Through Lesbos' Lonely Groves* (New York: Gold Medal Books, 1955), 18, 30, 38, 22, 10 (Aldrich was a pen name of Marijane Meaker); Lauren Jae Gutterman, "Another Enemy Within: Lesbian Wives, or the Hidden Threat to the Nuclear Family in Post-War America," *Gender and History* 24, no. 2 (2012): 476.

46. "The Truth About Women Athletes," 58.

47. John H. Johnson with Lerone Bennett Jr., *Succeeding Against the Odds* (New York: Warner Books, 1989), 205–209, 237; Beth Bailey, *Sex in the Heartland* (Cambridge, MA: Harvard University Press, 2002), 40; Yvonne Keller, "'Was It Right to Love Her Brother's Wife So Passionately': Lesbian Pulp Novels and U.S. Lesbian Identity, 1950–1965," *American Quarterly* 57, no. 2 (2005): 385–410.

48. Thaddeus Russell, "The Color of Discipline: Civil Rights and Black Sexuality," *American Quarterly* 60, no. 1 (2008): 112, 113.

49. Sam Lacy, "From A to Z," *Baltimore Afro-American*, September 12, 1953, 16; "Girl Tennis Star," *Ebony*, June 1952, 41–44.

50. "Sports Salute," *New York Amsterdam News*, August 22, 1953, 24.

51. Overbea, "Beating the Gun."

52. "In Milwaukee Net Meet," *Journal and Guide*, August 1, 1954, 19; Arthur Carrington, "The American Tennis Association: Roll of Champions: 1917–Present," International Tennis Hall of Fame and Museum, Newport, RI, n.d., 8, author's personal collection.

53. Fraser, "Althea Gibson Loses to Perez."

54. Joe Bostic, "The Scorecard: These Are the Things I Hope for in '54," *New York Amsterdam News*, January 9, 1954, 20.

55. "Conservatism May Have Caused Winn Victory," *Philadelphia Tribune*, July 25, 1953, 11; John McPhee, *Levels of the Game* (New York: Farrar, Straus, and Giroux, 1969), 26, 29.

56. "Althea Gibson on Campus, Consider P. Ed. Staff Position," *Lincoln Clarion*, May 23, 1953, 1.

57. "Althea Gibson," *Lincoln Archives 1954*, 22; Gibson to Dr. Eaton, February 9, 1955, Eaton Papers; Gibson to Dr. Eaton, May 20, 1954, Eaton Papers .

58. Associated Press, "Prison Riot Ended with Deaths at 4," *New York Times*, September 24, 1954, 50.

59. "Owens Head Polio Drive," *Lincoln Clarion*, February 19, 1954, 1; "Extravaganza Audience Takes 'Jet Around the World,'" *Lincoln Clarion*, February 26, 1954, 2; "6th Extravaganza Depicts Life 'On the Sunny Side of the Street,'" *Lincoln Clarion*, February 25, 1955, 1; Peter Wilson, "The Girl Globe-Trotter from Harlem," *Daily Mirror* (London), May 26, 1956, 19; "AKA's Give Party at Club Contessa," *Lincoln Clarion*, February 25, 1955, 6; Gibson, *I Always Wanted to Be Somebody*, 85; "Pla-Mors Elect Two to Office," *Lincoln Clarion*, December 11, 1953, 5; "Pla-Mor Honors Won by Talbots," February 19, 1954, 4; Ted Poston, "The Story of Althea Gibson: Article V," *New York Post Daily Magazine*, August 30, 1957, M2.

60. Gibson, *I Always Wanted to Be Somebody*, 83; Gibson to Dr. Eaton, March 27, 1955.

61. Lew Larkin, "'K.C. Star' Prints Article of Concern to Lincoln U," *Lincoln Clarion*, January 20, 1956, 2; "The School That Was Too Good to Die: Lincoln University in Jefferson, City, Mo., Proves Boon to Negroes, Whites in Area," *Ebony*, March 1958, 17–24.

62. Gibson, *I Always Wanted to Be Somebody*, 85.

63. Gibson, *I Always Wanted to Be Somebody*, 78–79; Gibson to Dr. Eaton, June 9, 1955, Eaton Papers.

64. Gibson to Dr. Eaton, June 9, 1955, Eaton Papers.

65. Carrington, "The American Tennis Association: Roll of Champions," 5, 8, 11; Gibson to Dr. Eaton, June 9, 1955, Eaton Papers.

66. Gibson, *I Always Wanted to Be Somebody*, 85–87; "Althea Gibson Victory," *New York Times*, July 17, 1955, 8S; Allison Danzig, "Tennis Title Goes to Miss Brough," *New York Times*, July 24, 1955, S1, S12.

67. "The New Gibson Girl," *Sports Illustrated*, July 2, 1956, 20.

68. United Press, "Miss Gibson Keeps Laurels in Tennis," *New York Times*, August 21, 1955, 4S. Wilberforce was renamed Central State College in 1951. For the sake of continuity, I will continue to refer to the institution as Wilberforce.

69. "Fear Chicago Boy Kidnaped: Armed Trio Seizes Visitor in Mississippi," *Chicago Tribune*, August 29, 1955, 1; "Kidnaped Boy Whistled at Woman: Friend," *Chicago Tribune*, August 30, 1955, 2; "Find Kidnaped Chicago Boy's Body in River," *Chicago Tribune*, September 1, 1955, 1; "Southern Jury Indicts Two in Till Slaying," *Chicago Tribune*, September 7, 1955, 5; Elliott J. Gorn, *Let the People See: The Story of Emmett Till* (New York: Oxford University Press, 2018).

70. "Treatment of Minorities in the United States: Impact on Our Foreign Relations," report, National Archives (hereafter "NA"), Record Group (hereafter "RG") 59, 811.411/12-458, 2; see also Mary L. Dudziak, *Cold War Civil Rights: Race and the Image of American Democracy* (Princeton, NJ: Princeton University Press, 2000).

71. Harold E. Howland to Edwin S. Baker, letter, January 17, 1955, NA, RG 59, 511.913/1-1755, Box 2230.

72. Howland to Tony Trabert, letter, January 10, 1955, NA, RG 59, 511.903/1-1055, Box 2224.

73. Howland to Hamilton Richardson, letter, January 7, 1955, NA, RG 59, 511.903/1-755, Box 2224.

74. Howland to Hamilton Richardson, letter, January 7, 1955, NA, RG 59, 511.903/1-755, Box 2224; Howland to Talbert, letter, January 10, 1955, NA, RG 59, 511.903/1-1055, Box 2224; Howland to Embassies of Colombo, Karachi, Kuala Lumpur, New Delhi, Rangoon, and Saigon, instructions, March 1, 1955, NA, RG 59, 511.903/3-155, Box 2224; Howland to Edwin Baker, letter, March 11, 1955, NA, RG 59, 511.913-3-1155, Box 2230; Amrit Kaur to Donald Kennedy, letter, January 13, 1955, NA, RG 59, 891.453/2-2855, Box 5060; Howland to Baker, January 17, 1955, NA, RG 59, 511.913/1-1755, Box 2230.

75. Allison Danzig, "Trabert, Bartzen and Hoad Victors," *New York Times*, September 8, 1955, 38; Gibson, *I Always Wanted to Be Somebody*, 89.

76. Kenneth Osgood, *Total Cold War: Eisenhower's Secret Propaganda Battle at Home and Abroad* (Lawrence: University Press of Kansas, 2006); Laura A. Belmonte, *Selling the American Way: U.S. Propaganda and the Cold War* (Philadelphia: University

of Pennsylvania Press, 2008); Damion L. Thomas, *Globetrotting: African American Athletes and Cold War Politics* (Urbana: University of Illinois Press, 2012), 9, 10.

77. Harold E. Howland, "The Case for the State Department Athlete," *Sports Illustrated*, July 16, 1956, 67.

78. "Capsule Court News: Gussy Moran Takes North India Title from Pat Todd" and "Americans Star in Down Under Exhibitions," *American Lawn Tennis*, February 1950, 21; Ashley Brown, "Swinging for the State Department: American Women Tennis Players in Diplomatic Goodwill Tours," *Journal of Sport History* 42, no. 3 (2015): 289–309.

79. ABC, "Contrast in Manners," letter to editors, *New York Herald Tribune*, September 13, 1950, 22.

80. "Tennis Joins the Parade of Democracy in Sports," editorial, *Journal and Guide*, August 26, 1950, n.p.; Arnold de Mille, "Along Celebrity Row," *Chicago Defender*, December 9, 1950, 9; Alvin Moses, Associated Negro Press, "Beating the Gun: Althea Gibson," *Atlanta Daily World*, May 30, 1951, 5; Alvin Moses, Associated Negro Press, "Beating the Gun," *Atlanta Daily World*, August 15, 1951, 5.

81. Argus J. Tresidder to State Department, Washington, dispatch, August 7, 1951, NA, RG 890.4533/8-751.

82. Gibson, *I Always Wanted to Be Somebody*, 101.

83. Gibson to Dr. Eaton, October 31, 1955, Eaton Papers.

84. Gibson to Dr. Eaton, October 31, 1955, Eaton Papers; Dr. Eaton to Gibson, November 10, 1955, Eaton Papers; Brenna Wynn Greer, *Represented: The Black Imagemakers Who Reimagined African American Citizenship* (Philadelphia: University of Pennsylvania Press, 2019), 197–247; Johnson, *Succeeding Against the Odds*, 229–233.

85. Osgood, *Total Cold War*, 229; Penny M. Von Eschen, *Satchmo Blows Up the World: Jazz Ambassadors Play the Cold War* (Cambridge, MA: Harvard University Press, 2004), 29.

86. Gibson, *I Always Wanted to Be Somebody*, 90; Angela Buxton, interview by author, October 24, 2014; Dorothy Kilgallen, "Coco Captivates Night Club Set," *Washington Post and Times Herald*, September 14, 1955, 22.

87. Gibson, *I Always Wanted to Be Somebody*, 79; Evelyn Boyden, "Day In and Day Out," *Baltimore Afro-American*, October 15, 1955, 13.

88. Althea Gibson with Richard J. Curtis, *So Much to Live For* (New York: G. P. Putnam's Sons, 1968), 113.

89. Gibson to Dr. Eaton, June 22, 1955, Eaton Papers.

90. Osgood, *Total Cold War*, 228; "Former World Tennis Champion Alice Marble, Recognized a Rising Star," *Daily News* (Colombo), October 22, 1955; "Asian Tennis Tourney: Ranked Americans to Play; Richardson and Miss Gibson as Draw-Cards," *Hindusthan Standard*, September 30, 1955; "Althea Gibson, the Prevailing Young Negro Tennis Player . . . ," *Daily News*, October 12, 1955.

91. "Former World Tennis Champ Aids Negro Girl's Career," *Daily News*, September 14, 1955.

92. Howland to Embassies of Calcutta, Colombo, Dacca, Lahore, Karachi, New Delhi, and Rangoon, instructions, October 21, 1955, NA, RG 59, 511.903/10-2155.

93. Gibson, *I Always Wanted to Be Somebody*, 89–90; Howland to Embassies of Calcutta, Colombo, Dacca, Lahore, Karachi, New Delhi, and Rangoon, instructions, October 21, 1955, NA, RG 59, 511.903/10-2155; Jack Kofoed, "Karol Is Tennis' New Glamour Girl," *Sport*, May 1957, 40–41, 86; "'Absence Makes the Heart Grow Fonder': Star Turn," *Daily News*, January 11, 1956.

94. Fred Russell, "Davis Cup Student," *Sport*, September 1955, 36, 92, 90, 91; Howland to Embassies of Calcutta, Colombo, Dacca, Lahore, Karachi, New Delhi, and Rangoon, instructions, October 21, 1955, NA, RG 59, 511.903/10-2155.

95. "U.S. Tennis Stars Arriving December 3," *Nation* (Bangkok), November 30, 1955; "U.S. Tennis Stars to Play at Hyderabad," *Dawn* (Karachi), January 13, 1956.

96. Osgood, *Total Cold War*, 244–251.

97. Gibson, *I Always Wanted to Be Somebody*, 101–102.

98. Osgood, *Total Cold War*, 246–247; Dudziak, *Cold War Civil Rights*, 76–77; Gibson, *I Always Wanted to Be Somebody*, 102.

99. "U.S. Tennis Group Off to Tour Asia," *New York Times*, November 30, 1955, 43; Howland to Embassies in Calcutta, Dacca, Karachi, Lahore, New Delhi, and Rangoon, instructions, November 15, 1955, NA, RG 59, 511.903/11-1555, Box 2224.

100. Wilson, "The Girl Globe-Trotter from Harlem."

101. "Sven Davidson Tops Seeding List; National Championship Starts Today," *Hindusthan Standard*, December 10, 1955; "Asian Tennis Championships," advertisement, *Hindusthan Standard*, December 23, 1955; "Double Crown Annexed by Miss Gibson," *Hindusthan Standard*, December 19, 1955; "Two Titles for Miss Gibson: Asian Tennis Championships," *Pakistan Times*, January 2, 1956.

102. Gray and Lamb, *Born to Win*, 86.

103. Gray and Lamb, *Born to Win*, 86.

104. "Miss Kamo Triumphs," *New York Times*, July 15, 1957, 27; "Sport in Brief: Asian Lawn Tennis Championships," *Dawn*, January 1, 1956, 10; "Davidson Wins Title for 3rd Time, Exciting 4-Set Duel, Althea Gibson Overwhelms Miss Kamo," *Statesman* (New Delhi), December 19, 1955, 8; "Gallant Display by Miss Kamo," *Statesman*, January 2, 1956, 8; "'Asian Tennis Has Greatly Improved'; Foreign Stars Speak Well of Indian Players," *Hindusthan Standard*, January 3, 1956, 8.

105. "Althea Gibson Wins Championship," *Nation*, January 2, 1956; "British Pair Win Final; Kumar and Krishnan Defeated; Two Titles for Miss Gibson," *Hindu* (Madras), January 2, 1956; "Indians' Bid for Doubles Title; to Meet British Pair in Final; Fine Tennis in Ladies' Singles," *Hindusthan Standard*, December 31, 1955.

106. "Ranked Americans to Play," *Hindusthan Standard*, September 30, 1955; "Asian Tennis Tourney Must be Improved," *Daily News*, January 11, 1956; "Davidson Top Seed in Asian Tennis; Pride of Place for Miss A. Gibson," *Hindustan Times*,

December 23, 1955; "Althea Gibson Will Start Off a Firm Favourite for National Tennis Title," *Times of India*, December 1, 1955.

107. Gibson, *I Always Wanted to Be Somebody*, 102.

108. "Segregation in Sports: Georgia Governor's Action Resented," *Hindu*, December 5, 1955; "Georgia Bans Games with Mixed Teams," *Times of India*, December 4, 1955; Marion E. Jackson, "Sports of the World," *Atlanta Daily World*, December 27, 1955. On the Georgia athletic ban, see Charles H. Martin, *Benching Jim Crow: The Rise and Fall of the Color Line in Southern College Sports, 1890–1980* (Urbana: University of Illinois Press, 2010), 80–83; Reuters, "Georgia State Parks to Be Sold If Segregation Be Disallowed," *Burman* (Rangoon), December 14, 1955, 4; Jeanne Theoharis, *The Rebellious Life of Mrs. Rosa Parks* (Boston: Beacon Press, 2013), 46–115; "Segregation in Buses," *Pakistan Times*, January 6, 1956.

109. Gibson, *I Always Wanted to Be Somebody*, 90, 102.

110. Gibson, quoted in Serrell Hillman, "That Gibson Girl," *Time*, August 26, 1957, 46.

111. Gibson, *I Always Wanted to Be Somebody*, 102.

112. Frances Clayton Gray and Yanick Rice Lamb, *Born to Win: The Authorized Biography of Althea Gibson* (Hoboken, NJ: John Wiley and Sons, 2004), 85.

113. Gibson to Dr. Eaton, January 14, 1956, Eaton Papers; "Exhibition Matches at Bangkok," *Nation*, January 12, 1956, 8; Howland to American Embassy, Bangkok, instructions, December 23, 1955, NA, RG 59, 511.903/12-2355.

114. "Exhibition Tennis Matches in Dacca," *Pakistan Times*, January 4, 1956; "U.S. Tennis Stars to Play at Hyderabad"; "U.S. Tennis Stars Applauded in Final Display," *Dawn*, January 18, 1956, 7; "U.S. Stars Play Exhilarating Game: Exhibition Tennis Matches in Karachi," *Dawn*, January 16, 1956.

115. "Tennis Demonstrations," *Dawn*, January 17, 1956; "American Stars Arrive Today," *Dawn*, January 14, 1956; "Treatment of Minorities in the United States," 1, 14, 17–19.

116. "Tennis Team from America," *Hindusthan Standard*, December 13, 1955; "Asian Lawn Tennis Starts Today: Array of Stars Promise Thrilling Encounters," *Statesman*, December 23, 1955; Karol Fageros and Steve Gelman, "Play Tennis and See the World," *Sport*, December 1959, 86–87; Gibson, *I Always Wanted to Be Somebody*, 94; "U.S. Tennis Stars Give Last Display," *Nation*, December 10, 1955, 8.

117. "Asian Lawn Tennis Starts Today." On "off-stage public relations work" and "performance," see Osgood, *Total Cold War*, 228.

118. Transcript, "Interview with Althea Gibson," Washington University in St. Louis, October 21, 1984, http://repository.wustl.edu/concern/videos/8s45qd665.

119. Gibson, *I Always Wanted to Be Somebody*, 101.

120. "Ambition Breeds Success," *Montclair Times*, November 12, 1970, 6.

121. Gibson, *I Always Wanted to Be Somebody*, 88–108; Fageros and Gelman, "Play Tennis and See the World," 86–87.

122. Bill McIntyre, "Change of Pace Provided by Richardson at TD Club," *Shreveport Times*, October 25, 1966, 2-C.

123. Bruce Schoenfeld, *The Match: Angela Buxton and Althea Gibson: How Two Outsiders—One Black, the Other Jewish—Forged a Friendship and Made Sports History* (New York: Amistad Press, 2004), 27–30; "Althea and Angela Pair Up," *Daily Mirror*, February 3, 1956, 19.

124. Gibson, *I Always Wanted to Be Somebody*, 89.

125. Gibson, *I Always Wanted to Be Somebody*, 99, 91; Jeff Wiltse, *Contested Waters: A Social History of Swimming Pools in America* (Chapel Hill: University of North Carolina Press, 2010).

126. Gibson, *I Always Wanted to Be Somebody*, 91.

127. Dr. Eaton to Gibson, November 10, 1955, Eaton Papers.

128. Photograph of tennis team with dignitaries and USIS people, *Statesman*, December 16, 1955; "Althea Gibson, One of the Top Women Players of America, Who Has a Good Record Both at Forest Hills and Wimbledon," *Dawn*, December 23, 1955; "Exhibition Tennis Match in Dacca," *Pakistan Times*, January 4, 1956; "American Woman Beats Man," *Dawn*, January 3, 1956; "Talk by Althea Gibson," 1959, State Department, Sound Recording, National Archives and Records Administration, 306-ENTT-2367.

129. Gibson, *I Always Wanted to Be Somebody*, 91.

130. Gibson, *I Always Wanted to Be Somebody*, 91–92.

131. Biff Benntt, "SPORTalk: Pretty Karol Fageros," *Sport*, July 1954, 9; Tony Galli, "Althea Gibson Eases by Karol Fageros, 6–3, 6–2," *Atlanta Daily World*, September 6, 1956, 5; "Golden Goddess of Tennis," *New York Herald Tribune*, July 28, 1957, B5; Kofoed, "Karol Is Tennis' New Glamour Girl," 40.

132. Gibson, *I Always Wanted to Be Somebody*, 92, 94.

133. Fageros and Gelman, "Play Tennis and See the World," 87; Allison Danzig, "Louise Brough Upset in Tennis; Coast Girl Extends Miss Gibson," *New York Times*, July 26, 1956, L29.

134. Becky Machemahl, quoted in Gibson, *I Always Wanted to Be Somebody*, 108.

135. Bill Lipper, quoted in Gibson, *I Always Wanted to Be Somebody*, 108.

136. Gibson, *I Always Wanted to Be Somebody*, 102.

137. "Miss Kamo Triumphs."

138. Associated Press, "Krishnan Thanks State Department," *Washington Post and Times Herald*, August 1, 1957, C2.

139. Schoenfeld, *The Match*, 11, 141–143, 157–160; Doris Hart, *Tennis with Hart* (Philadelphia: J. B. Lippincott, 1955), 187; Gibson, *I Always Wanted to Be Somebody*, 167; Angela Buxton, interview by author, October 24, 2014.

140. Sydney Llewellyn, quoted in Moran, "Can Althea Gibson Make It?"

141. Gibson to Dr. Eaton, February 8, 1956, Eaton Papers; Associated Press, "Mary Ann Mitchell Gains Tennis Final," *Los Angeles Times*, October 15, 1955, 7; United Press, "Patty Defeats Davidson," *New York Times*, January 30, 1956, 31; "British Pair Win," *Birmingham Daily Post*, January 28, 1956, 14.

142. Angela Mortimer, *My Waiting Game* (London: Frederick Muller, 1962), 13, 14, 43.

143. Mortimer, *My Waiting Game*, 84, 81.

144. "Two Titles for Angela Buxton," *Coventry Evening Telegraph*, February 13, 1956, 8; "Miss Gibson Triumphs in West German Tennis," *New York Times*, February 6, 1956, 20; "Summary: Lawn Tennis," *Daily Mirror*, February 27, 1956, 18.

145. "Quick Consolation for Shirley," *Birmingham Gazette*, April 4, 1956, 6; Associated Press, "Althea Gibson Wins Two Titles in Italy," *Washington Post and Times Herald*, April 9, 1956, 16; United Press, "Merlo Turns Back Stewart in 4 Sets," *New York Times*, April 10, 1956, 38; Associated Press, "Miss Gibson Wins on Naples Court," *New York Times*, April 16, 1956, 32; Associated Press, "Miss Gibson Wins on Naples Court: She Beats Mrs. Brewer in Tennis Final . . . ," *New York Times*, April 16, 1956, 32; United Press, "Miss Gibson Wins Sixth Final in a Row," *New York Times*, May 9, 1956, 42; "Angela Keeps Title," *Leicester Evening Mail*, March 10, 1956, 20; Associated Press, "Hoad Is Extended to Five Sets in Defeating Davidson at Cairo," *New York Times*, March 12, 1956, 30; "Sport in Brief," *Belfast Telegraph*, March 26, 1956, 10; Gibson, *I Always Wanted to Be Somebody*, 111.

146. "Angela Will Defend Her Title," *Birmingham Gazette*, May 25, 1956, 8.

147. "Angela Will Defend Her Title"; Clifford Webb, "Exit Angela—and 'History' Final," *Daily Herald* (London), May 25, 1956, 10.

148. Clifford Webb, "Angela Is Favourite for Title," *Daily Herald*, May 26, 1956, 9.

149. Webb, "Exit Angela—and 'History' Final"; Webb, "Angela Is Favourite for Title."

150. Gibson, quoted in "Althea the New Champ," *Sunday Mirror* (London), May 27, 1956, 22.

151. Stanley Doust, "Angela Mortimer Loses Her Record," *Sunday Dispatch* (London), May 27, 1956, 14.

152. "Angela Is Beaten," *Sports Argus*, May 26, 1956, 1.

153. Doust, "Angela Mortimer Loses Her Record."

154. Peter Wilson, "Triumph for the Black Windmill," *Daily Mirror*, May 28, 1956, 19.

155. C. M. Jones, "Hoad 'Terrific' in One-Man Doubles Victory," *Daily Mirror*, May 26, 1956, 19.

156. Clifford Webb, "Once She Quit: Now Angela Buxton Is Among Champions," *Daily Herald*, May 28, 1956, 10.

157. Gibson, quoted in Webb, "Once She Quit."

158. C. M. Jones, "A Smile Helps Angela to Win," *Daily Mirror*, May 28, 1956, 19; Gibson, *I Always Wanted to Be Somebody*, 112.

159. Jones, "A Smile Helps Angela to Win."

160. Doust, "Angela Mortimer Loses Her Record"; Ray Canton, "Persistent Belief in Own Ability Made Althea Gibson Champion," *Minneapolis Morning Tribune*, January 25, 1958, 18.

161. Wilson, "The Girl Globe-Trotter from Harlem."

162. Wilson, "Triumph for the Black Windmill."

163. Wilson, "The Girl Globe-Trotter from Harlem."

164. Billie Jean King and Cynthia Starr, *We Have Come a Long Way: The Story of Women's Tennis* (New York: McGraw-Hill, 1988), 53–96; Virginia Wade and Jean Rafferty, *Ladies of the Court: A Century of Women at Wimbledon* (New York: Atheneum, 1984), 77–104; also, Tony Mottram, "It's Such an Open Wimbledon: Brough Defends," *Birmingham Gazette*, June 25, 1956, 8.

165. "Althea Has Right Look," *Birmingham Gazette*, May 30, 1956, 7; "Althea Wins Again," *Weekly Dispatch* (London), June 3, 1956, 14.

166. United Press, "Miss Gibson Takes English Net Final," *New York Times*, June 10, 1956, 1, 12.

167. United Press, "Miss Gibson Takes English Net Final"; Associated Press, "Miss Gibson Wins Bristol Net Final," *New York Times*, June 16, 1956, 17; "Lew Hoad and Ken Rosewall Top Seeds," *Coventry Evening Telegraph*, June 19, 1956, 16; Laurence Tingay, quoted in Associated Press, "Miss Gibson Is Hailed: British Writers Rate U.S. Star World Top Tennis Player," *New York Times*, June 12, 1956, 43.

168. Gibson, *I Always Wanted to Be Somebody*, 145.

169. United Press, "British Select Team," *New York Times*, May 30, 1956, L16; Fred Tupper, "U.S. Beats British Wightman Team for 20th Time in Row," *New York Times*, June 19, 1956, L21; Gibson, *I Always Wanted to Be Somebody*, 145.

170. Tony Mottram, "Mrs. Fleitz Shows Good Promise of Proving a Winner," *Yorkshire Observer*, June 27, 1956, 6; Clifford Webb, "The Gibson Girl Flattens Edda," *Daily Herald*, June 27, 1956. 10.

171. Mottram, "Mrs. Fleitz Shows Good Promise of Proving a Winner"; Tony Mottram, "Learn How to Play the Forcing Game," *Belfast Telegraph*, June 27, 1956, 10.

172. Tony Mottram, "Four 'Seeds' Only Remain in Men's Wimbledon Singles," *Bradford Observer*, June 29, 1956, 4; "Ken Rosewall Is Too Good for Larsen," *Sports Argus*, June 30, 1956, 1; "Althea Center of British Rhubarb," *Baltimore Afro-American*, July 21, 1956, 14. Gibson specifically referenced this article in her first book; see Gibson, *I Always Wanted to Be Somebody*, 116–117. Maurice Smith, "This Gibson Girl May Shock Wimbledon," *The People* (London), July 1, 1956, 14.

173. Alan Dick, "Mr. Dick Meets the Slamming Sourpusses," *Daily Herald*, June 28, 1956, 4; Peter Wilson, "1) Lackadaisical Lew; 2) Bev, the Girl with the Look of a Cheeky Peke," *Daily Mirror*, July 2, 1956, 19.

174. Wilson, "1) Lackadaisical Lew."

175. Angela Buxton, interview by author, October 24, 2014.

176. Gibson, *I Always Wanted to Be Somebody*, 153, 154.

177. Connolly, *Forehand Drive*, 117.

178. Kennett Love, "Althea Is at Home Abroad on the Tennis Court," *New York Times*, June 24, 1956, S3.

179. Peter Wilson, "The Bargain Basement," *Daily Mirror*, July 4, 1956, 19.

180. Wilson, "The Bargain Basement."

181. Scottie Hall of the *Sunday Graphic*, quoted in Gibson, *I Always Wanted to Be Somebody*, 115.

182. Associated Press, "Winning Streak Ends," *New York Times*, July 4, 1956, 23; Wilson, "The Bargain Basement."

183. "Angela Was Fry-ed!," *The People*, July 8, 1956, 12.

184. "Althea's Odyssey," *Life*, July 2, 1956, 88, 91.

185. Angela Buxton, interview by author, October 24, 2012; "Light-Foot Favorite," *Time*, June 4, 1956, 66.

186. On dime and dollar, see "Debra Martin Chase: Biography," https://www.thehi storymakers.org/biography/debra-martin-chase-40, n.d. (accessed April 2, 2021); Wilson, "The Bargain Basement."

187. "Angela Was Fry-ed!"

CHAPTER 7

1. "Mayor Wagner Learning a Few Things About Tennis," *New York Times*, July 12, 1956, L17.

2. "We Make a Motion," editorial, *New York Amsterdam News*, June 9, 1956, 10.

3. "How About a Royal Welcome?," illustration, *New York Amsterdam News*, June 9, 1956, 10; "Althea Wins Doubles Match at Wimbledon; Plan NYC Welcome," *Philadelphia Tribune*, July 10, 1956, 10; "Mayor to Greet Net Champion," *Baltimore Afro-American*, July 14, 1956, 1.

4. Simon Anekwe, "Earl Brown Dies in Hospital at 77-Years of Age," *New York Amsterdam News*, April 19, 1980, 2; "Squabbling Council Hails Tennis Stars," *New York Times*, July 11, 1956, L19.

5. Bertram L. Baker to President Dwight D. Eisenhower, June 26, 1956, in Kevin McCann to Bertram L. Baker, July 9, 1956 (Case File), GF 117 G 1956, Box 666, General File, Eisenhower, Dwight D.: Records as President (White House Central Files), Dwight D. Eisenhower Presidential Library, Abilene, KS (henceforth "McCann to Baker Case File").

6. "Althea Wins Doubles Match at Wimbledon; Plan NYC Welcome."

7. Ruth Feldstein, *Motherhood in Black and White: Race and Sex in American Liberalism, 1930–1965* (Ithaca, NY: Cornell University Press, 2000), 102–108; Jeanne Theoharis, *The Rebellious Life of Mrs. Rosa Parks* (Boston: Beacon Press, 2013), 118, 122, 126–130; Glenda Alice Rabby, *The Pain and the Promise: The Struggle for Civil Rights in Tallahassee, Florida* (Athens: University of Georgia Press, 1999), 1.

8. Marcia G. Synnott, "African American Women Pioneers in Desegregating Higher Education," in *Higher Education and the Civil Rights Movement: White Supremacy, Black Southerners, and College Campuses*, edited by Peter Wallenstein (Gainesville: University Press of Florida, 2008), 204.

9. Marion E. Jackson, "Sports of the World," *Atlanta Daily World*, December 27, 1956, 5.

10. Marion E. Jackson, "Sports of the World," *Atlanta Daily World*, March 9, 1956, 7.

11. Howland, quoted in Marion E. Jackson, "Sports of the World," *Atlanta Daily World*, December 27, 1956, 5.

12. Associated Press, "Shirley Fry Ousts Althea Gibson at Wimbledon," *Washington Post and Times Herald*, July 4, 1956, 18.

13. Kenneth Osgood, *Total Cold War: Eisenhower's Secret Propaganda Battle at Home and Abroad* (Lawrence: University Press of Kansas, 2006), 5, 215, 218–220, 220; "Mayor to Greet Net Champion"; Marion E. Jackson, "Sports of the World," *Atlanta Daily World*, March 9, 1956.

14. E. B. Henderson, letter to editor, "Spingarn Medalist," *Baltimore Afro-American*, July 28, 1956, 4.

15. "We Make a Motion"; "Mayor to Greet Net Champion"; William F. Talbert, "Tennis—with Emotions," *Sports Illustrated*, July 16, 1956, 27.

16. Jeane Hoffman, "Althea's Rise Credited to U.S. Assist," *Los Angeles Times*, September 18, 1956, Part II, 6.

17. Associated Press, "Althea Gibson Given Official Welcome Home by New York," *Washington Post and Times Herald*, July 12, 1956, 50.

18. "Squabbling Council Hails Tennis Stars."

19. Clyde Reid, "Althea Back Home; Ticker Parade Off," *New York Amsterdam News*, July 14, 1956, 1; Kevin McCann to Bertram L. Baker, July 9, 1956, McCann to Baker Case File.

20. "We Make a Motion"; Jacob Seidenberg to Maxwell M. Rabb, July 19, 1956, McCann to Baker Case File.

21. Ann Whitman to Max Rabb, undated, McCann to Baker Case File.

22. "The New Gibson Girl," *Sports Illustrated*, July 2, 1956, 61.

23. "A Good Envoy," editorial, *New York Times*, May 13, 1956, 10E.

24. "Britain's Tennis Cup Chances Slim—Captain," *Bradford Observer*, June 11, 1956, 7; "Shock Defeat for Louise Brough; Wightman Cup Fillip for US," *Birmingham Daily Gazette*, June 11, 1956, 7; "Harlem to Wimbledon," advertisement, *Daily Mail* (London), June 15, 1956, 1.

25. Kennett Love, "Althea Is at Home Abroad on Tennis Court," *New York Times*, June 24, 1956, S3.

26. Angela Buxton, interview by author, October 24, 2014.

27. Mary Hawton, "Hawton-Long Win Title," *Tennis in Australasia*, September-October 1956, 11.

28. Fred Kovaleski, interview by author, October 23, 2014.

29. Buxton, interview by author, October 24, 2014.

30. Transcript, "Interview with Althea Gibson," Washington University in St. Louis, October 21, 1984, http://repository.wustl.edu/concern/videos/8s45qd665.

31. Louise Brough, quoted in Billie Jean King and Cynthia Star, *We Have Come a Long Way: The Story of Women's Tennis* (New York: McGraw-Hill, 1988), 95.

32. Althea Gibson, quoted in King and Star, *We Have Come a Long Way*, 95.

33. "Gibson's Impact Is Still Felt," *Miami Herald*, August 26, 2007, 12D.

34. Buxton, interview by author, October 24, 2014.

35. Gussie Moran, "Can Althea Gibson Make It?" *Sport*, October 1956, 50.

36. Darlene Clark Hine, "Rape and the Inner Lives of Black Women in the Middle West," *Signs* 14, no. 4 (Summer 1989): 915.

37. Love, "Althea Is at Home Abroad on Tennis Court."

38. Ralph Hewins, "Why She Aims to Reach the Top," *Daily Mail*, June 19, 1956, 4.

39. Associated Press, "Miss Gibson Rival to Louise Brough," *New York Times*, June 24, 1956, S3.

40. Fay Young, "Fay Says," *Chicago Defender*, July 7, 1956, 17.

41. Love, "Althea Is at Home Abroad on Tennis Court."

42. Buxton, interview by author, October 24, 2014; Angela Buxton, "My Friend, Althea," *British Lawn Tennis and Squash*, July 1956, 11.

43. Ralph Hewins, "Harlem to Wimbledon," *Daily Mail*, June 18, 1956, 4.

44. "Althea Gibson Seeded Fourth at Wimbledon," *Call and Post* (Cleveland, OH), June 30, 1956, 3C; "Althea Gagged, Seeded Fourth," *Baltimore Afro-American*, June 30, 1956, 15.

45. E. Hampson, "Tennis Topics: Super Form Needed in Davis Cup," *Star Green 'Un* (Sheffield, UK), June 9, 1956, 3.

46. Hewins, "Why She Aims to Reach the Top."

47. Hewins, "Why She Aims to Reach the Top."

48. Charles H. Martin, *Benching Jim Crow: The Rise and Fall of the Color Line in Southern College Sports, 1890–1980* (Urbana: University of Illinois Press, 2010), 83–85; Barent S. Meier, "Letter from America: Coloured People Are Barred from Sport," *Belfast Telegraph*, August 2, 1956, 4. See also Meier, "American Letter: Deep South's Colour Ban Bill Shock," *Halifax Daily Courier and Guardian*, August 1, 1956, 3.

49. "Althea Center of British Rhubarb," *Baltimore Afro-American*, July 21, 1956, 14. Althea specifically referenced this article in her first book. See Althea Gibson, *I Always Wanted to Be Somebody*, ed. Ed Fitzgerald (New York: Harper and Row, 1958), 116–117.

50. Gibson, *I Always Wanted to Be Somebody*, 118.

51. Gibson, *I Always Wanted to Be Somebody*, 118.

52. Gibson, *I Always Wanted to Be Somebody*, 118.

53. "Jackie Robinson Cited," *New York Times*, June 15, 1956, 27.

54. Arnold Rampersad, *Jackie Robinson: A Biography* (New York: Alfred A. Knopf, 1997), 165–167; James Hirsch, *Willie Mays: The Life, the Legend* (New York: Scribner, 2010), 234.

55. "Orchids to Althea," editorial, *Pittsburgh Courier*, July 7, 1956.

56. "Althea Has Finally Arrived," *Ebony*, August 1956, 35, 38.

57. "Althea Has Finally Arrived."

58. "A Bubble Bursts," *Call and Post*, July 21, 1956, 3C; "Althea at Wimbledon," editorial, *Baltimore Afro-American*, July 21, 1956, 4.

59. Malcolm Poindexter, "Sports-I-View," *Philadelphia Tribune*, July 24, 1956, 11.

60. "No Apex," *Baltimore Afro-American*, June 30, 1956, 1. On Apex, see "Apex Inaugurates Expansion Project," *Baltimore Afro-American*, December 1, 1956, 9. Thanks to Michael Gnat.

61. "Althea's Odyssey," *Life*, July 2, 1956, 81; "Althea, Queen of Pops," *Baltimore Afro-American*, July 21, 1956, 14. The caption identifies the second woman in the picture as Rosemary, though she bears a striking resemblance to Gibson and might very well be one of her sisters, particularly Lillian, the youngest.

62. L. Masco Young, Associated Negro Press, "The Low Down," *Atlanta Daily World*, August 12, 1956, 7.

63. Peter Wilson, "The Girl Globe-Trotter from Harlem," *Daily Mirror* (London), May 26, 1956, 19.

64. Gibson, *I Always Wanted to Be Somebody*, 103–104.

65. Bruce Schoenfeld, *The Match: Althea Gibson and Angela Buxton*: How Two Outsiders—One Black, the Other Jewish—Forged a Friendship and Made Sports History (New York: Amistad Press, 2004), 159; Angela Buxton, interview by author, October 24, 2014.

66. Fred Kovaleski, interview by author, October 23, 2014.

67. Marion E. Jackson, "Sports of the World," *Atlanta Daily World*, August 5, 1956.

68. Gibson, *I Always Wanted to Be Somebody*, 105.

CHAPTER 8

1. "Althea Returns from Tennis Tour," *New York Times*, July 12, 1956, L17.

2. "Althea Returns from Tennis Tour."

3. "Flam, Shirley Fry Win in U.S. Tennis," *New York Times*, July 24, 1956, L31.

4. Allison Danzig, "Miss Gibson Gains Merion Laurels," *New York Times*, July 29, 1956, S1.

5. Associated Press, "Miss Gibson 6–1, 6–3 Victor over Brough," *Washington Post and Times Herald*, August 13, 1956.

6. "Grossinger News-Notes," advertisement, *New York Times*, August 12, 1956, 18X; "A Tennis Pro Writes Again," advertisement, *New York Times*, August 14, 1956, L23.

7. "Althea Returns from Tennis Tour."

8. Associated Press, "Althea Gibson Tops Miss Brown in Final," *New York Times*, August 26, 1956, 12S.

9. "Althea Gibson Honored: Her Goodwill Tour Cited by Paddle Tennis Association," *New York Times*, August 29, 1956, L33.

10. "National Tennis Off Until Today," *New York Times*, September 1, 1956, 12; Allison Danzig, "Miss Gibson's Match Will Open National Title Tennis Tomorrow," *New York Times*, August 30, 1956, L29; Allison Danzig, "Richardson Wins; Miss

Gibson, Schmidt Also Move Ahead in U.S. Singles," *New York Times*, September 2, 1956, S1.

11. Allison Danzig, "Hoad Drops First Set Before Advancing in U.S. Tennis," *New York Times*, September 4, 1956, L39.

12. Associated Press, "Hoad and Rosewall Lead Aussies into Quarters," *Los Angeles Times*, September 6, 1956, Part II, 2; "Seixas, Three Aussies in Semifinals," *Los Angeles Times*, September 8, 1956; Will Grimsley, Associated Press, "Rosewall, Hoad Gain U.S. Finals," *Washington Post and Times Herald*, September 9, 1956, C1.

13. Allison Danzig, "Rosewall Defeats Hoad, Miss Fry Defeats Miss Gibson for U.S. Tennis Titles," *New York Times*, September 10, 1956, L34; PWW, "On the Courts; Jubilee," *New Yorker*, September 15, 1956, 144; United Press, "Rosewall Upsets Hoad," *Los Angeles Times*, September 10, 1956.

14. Serrell Hillman, "That Gibson Girl," *Time*, August 26, 1957, 48.

15. Ted Poston, "The Story of Althea Gibson: Article VI," *New York Post Daily Magazine*, August 31, 1957; Hillman, "That Gibson Girl," 48.

16. "Triumph of Tenacity," *New York Times*, September 10, 1956, L34.

17. "There Were Cold Wins and Disappointments . . . ," *Sports Illustrated*, September 17, 1956.

18. Gussie Moran, "Can Althea Gibson Make It?," *Sport*, October 1956, 70.

19. Moran, "Can Althea Gibson Make It?," 69.

20. International News Service, "Shirley Fry Beats Althea Gibson: Fry Jinx Top Althea for 3rd Time," *Chicago Defender*, September 10, 1956, 24; Moran, "Can Althea Gibson Make It?," 69; Maureen Connolly, *Forehand Drive* (London: Macgibbon and Kee, 1957), 131–132.

21. Althea Gibson, *I Always Wanted to Be Somebody*, ed. Ed Fitzgerald (New York: Harper and Row, 1958), 119.

22. Canadian Press, "Miss Gibson Wins 2 Finals in Tennis," *New York Times*, September 13, 1956, L45; Hugh Stewart and Jennifer Hoad, "Hoad and Gibson Win O'Keefe Invitation Titles at Toronto," *World Tennis*, November 1956, 36, 38.

23. Ham Richard and Jackie Tegland, "The Pacific Southwest: Flam Beats Rosewall, Althea Wins over Kiner," *World Tennis*, November 1956, 25–27, 23; "Pacific Southwest Champions," Tournament Program, Pacific Southwest Tennis Championships, September 15–23, 1956, 56; "1956 Center Court," Tournament Program, Pacific Southwest Tennis Championships, September 12–22, 1957, 28–29.

24. Tournament Program, Pacific Southwest Tennis Championships, 1956, 12, 8.

25. On clubs, see "Gay 'Pot Luck' Follows Turnabout Installation," *Los Angeles Sentinel*, January 27, 1949, C2; Harry Adams, "Pacific Town Club, Los Angeles, 1954," photograph, 1954, California State University–Northridge Libraries, Digital Collections, https://digital-collections.csun.edu/digital/collection/Bradley/id/157/; Jessie Mae Brown, "Your Social Chronicler," *Los Angeles Sentinel*, September 27, 1956, B2; "They're the Tops," *Chicago Defender*, October 1, 1956, 19; Will Friedwald, *Straighten Up and Fly Right: The Life and Music of Nat King Cole*

(New York: Oxford University Press, 2020), 222–224; Gibson, *I Always Wanted to Be Somebody*, 120.

26. Gardnar Mulloy, "Larsen and Gibson Take Colorado State Titles," *World Tennis*, November 1956, 42, 45.

27. International News Service, "Althea Eyes '57 Win at Forest Hills Meet," *Journal and Guide* (Norfolk, VA), September 22, 1956, 18.

28. International News Service, "Althea Eyes '57 Win."

29. Mulloy, "Larsen and Gibson Take Colorado State Titles," 42.

30. Jeane Hoffmann, "Althea's Rise Credited to U.S. Assist," *Los Angeles Times*, September 18, 1956, 6.

31. Richardson and Tegland, "The Pacific Southwest," 27.

32. Gardnar P. Mulloy, *As It Was* (New York: Flexigroup, 2009), 204.

33. Mulloy, *As It Was*, 204.

34. Mulloy, *As It Was*, 204.

35. Ann Ledesma, "Ex-Tennis Ace Serves Formula—Play Sports and Cut Crime," *Central New Jersey Home News*, November 25, 1975, 17.

36. Maureen Connolly, "Tennis Girls of Tomorrow," *Sport*, August 1956, 50.

37. Angela Buxton, "My Friend, Althea," *British Lawn Tennis and Squash*, July 1956, 11.

38. Mulloy, quoted in "Singles Worries Hurt Althea as Team Player," *Baltimore Afro-American*, September 29, 1956, 16.

39. Associated Press, "Davidson, Miss Gibson Win," *New York Times*, October 15, 1956, L32; United Press, "Miss Gibson Team Wins," *New York Times*, October 14, 1956, S9.

40. Darlene Hard, quoted in Billie Jean King and Cynthia Star, *We Have Come a Long Way: The Story of Women's Tennis* (New York: McGraw-Hill, 1988), 95.

41. Gibson, *I Always Wanted to Be Somebody*, 120; Claude E. Harrison Jr., "People in Sports," *Philadelphia Tribune*, September 18, 1956, 10.

42. On the racial and gender politics of magazine covers, see Brenna Wynn Greer, *Represented: The Black Imagemakers Who Reimagined African American Citizenship* (Philadelphia: University of Pennsylvania Press, 2019), 1–2, 142–196; Chester Himes, *If He Hollers, Let Him Go* (1945; repr., New York: Thunder's Mouth Press, 2002), 78.

43. Moran, "Can Althea Gibson Make It?," 50, 69.

44. Moran, "Can Althea Gibson Make It?," 51, 69, 70.

45. Moran, "Can Althea Gibson Make It?," 69.

46. Hoffmann, "Althea's Rise Credited to U.S. Assist."

47. Associated Press, "Miss Fry Beaten by Miss Gibson," *New York Times*, November 17, 1956, L 25; United Press, "Miss Gibson Captures Aussie Tennis Laurels," *New York Times*, December 2, 1956, S5.

48. Associated Press, "Shirley Fry Wins Aussie Net Tourney," *Los Angeles Times*, December 16, 1956, Part III, 2; United Press, "Miss Fry Victor in Tennis Final,"

New York Times, January 29, 1957, L36; "Billy Knight in Final," *Weekly Dispatch* (London), January 27, 1957, 11.

49. "Althea Smiles at 5 'Faults,'" *Argus*, December 15, 1956, 14.

50. United Press, "Miss Gibson Captures Aussie Tennis Laurels."

51. "Althea Will Make Long Tour Again," *Pittsburgh Courier*, September 15, 1956, 19.

52. "Hoad Wins," *Liverpool Echo*, January 5, 1957, 15; Associated Press, "Rosewall Beats Hoad in 5 Sets," *Los Angeles Times*, December 18, 1956, Part IV, 4.

53. "Althea Smiles at 5 'Faults.'"

54. United Press, "Irate Miss Gibson Bows to Miss Fry," *New York Times*, December 16, 1956, S1.

55. "Gibson Gets 21 'Calls' in Singles Final," *Sydney Morning Herald*, December 16, 1956; "Miss Gibson Shows Temper Down Under," *Pittsburgh Courier*, December 22, 1956, 27; Alan Stewart, "Althea to Keep Her Stance," *Herald* (Melbourne), December 17, 1956, 26; United Press, "Irate Miss Gibson Bows to Miss Fry."

56. Associated Press, "Shirley Fry Wins Aussie Net Tourney"; United Press, "Irate Miss Gibson Bows to Miss Fry"; Marilyn Lake and Henry Reynolds, *Drawing the Global Colour Line: White Men's Countries and the International Challenge of Racial Equality* (Cambridge: Cambridge University Press, 2008), 137–165.

57. "Althea Loses Set and Temper," *Baltimore Afro-American*, December 22, 1956, 14.

58. United Press, "Irate Miss Gibson Bows to Miss Fry"; "Althea Loses Set and Temper."

59. On gender hierarchy in amateur tennis, see Al Stump, "The Terrible-Tempered Mrs. Todd," *Sport*, April 1951, 92. See also Alan Stewart, "Tennis Official Did Fine Job," *Herald*, December 17, 1956, 25.

60. Doris Hart, *Tennis with Hart* (Philadelphia: J. B. Lippincott, 1955), 97, 105–106, 52.

61. Adrian Quist, "Delayed Start Ruins Men's Singles Final," *Herald*, December 16, 1956.

62. "Talking to the Stars: Take Heart, Says Althea," *British Lawn Tennis and Squash*, April 1957, 12.

63. Gibson, *I Always Wanted to Be Somebody*, 121, 122. Gibson writes that in Melbourne she and Fry stayed with an affable married couple, whom she names as "Dr. Robert Mitchell and Dr. Gwonne Villiars" (possibly Gwynne Villiers).

64. Gibson, *I Always Wanted to Be Somebody*, 124.

65. Gibson, *I Always Wanted to Be Somebody*, 124; Angela Mortimer, *My Waiting Game* (London: Frederick Muller, 1962), 48.

66. Gibson, *I Always Wanted to Be Somebody*, 120–121; "Triumph of Tenacity," L34; Mortimer, *My Waiting Game*, 110–111.

67. Gibson, *I Always Wanted to Be Somebody*, 123–125.

68. Atlas, "Althea Gibson of New York City, U.S.A. a Leading World Tennis Player," *Daily News* (Colombo), January 16, 1957.

69. "Hi! There, Greeting from Althea," *Daily News*, February 8, 1957.

70. "Star-Studded Tennis Tourney," *Daily News*, February 6, 1957; "Championships Start Today: Good Job of Work by the C.L.T.A.," *Daily News*, February 11, 1957.

71. "Hi! There, Greeting from Althea."

72. "Indians Upset in Doubles; Women Added a Dash of Colour," *Daily News*, February 14, 1957; "Glamour of Tennis," *Daily News*, February 15, 1957.

73. "Althea Gibson Misses the Coveted Prize," *Daily News*, February 25, 1957.

74. Gibson, *I Always Wanted to Be Somebody*, 126.

CHAPTER 9

1. Christy Munro, "Althea Gibson . . . Tragic Success Story," *Look*, November 12, 1957, 134; Samuel A. Haynes, "Althea to Be a Bride? She's Mum," *Baltimore Afro-American*, March 16, 1957, 2.

2. Haynes, "Althea to Be a Bride?"; "Althea to Marry," *New York Amsterdam News*, March 9, 1956. Also, "Flash News in Brief: The Happiest News of the Week," *Baltimore Afro-American*, March 16, 1957.

3. Elaine Tyler May, *Homeward Bound: American Families in the Cold War Era*, 4th ed. (New York: Basic Books, 2017), 1, 3.

4. May, *Homeward Bound*, 1, 3; Thaddeus Russell, "The Color of Discipline: Civil Rights and Black Sexuality," *American Quarterly* 60, no. 1 (March 2008): 113–124.

5. Associated Press, "'Little Mo' Gives Up Tennis," *New York Times*, June 9, 1955, L38.

6. Maureen Connolly, *Forehand Drive* (London: Macgibbon and Kee, 1957), 185; Associated Press, "Shirley Fry Wed in Australia," *New York Times*, February 17, L12; Haynes, "Althea to Be a Bride?"

7. Quoted in Gussie Moran, "Can Althea Gibson Make It?," *Sport*, October 1956, 70.

8. "Althea Eyes '57 Win at Forest Hills," *Journal and Guide* (Norfolk, VA), September 22, 1956, 18.

9. "Talking with the Stars: Take Heart, Says Althea," *British Lawn Tennis and Squash*, April 1957, 12.

10. Haynes, "Althea to Be a Bride?"

11. "Althea's Aim," *Lancashire Evening Post*, March 16, 1957, 3.

12. "Talking with the Stars: Take Heart, Says Althea."

13. Associated Negro Press, "Althea Gibson Making Plans for 1957 Wimbledon Matches," *Philadelphia Tribune*, March 19, 1957, 10.

14. "Birdland Bon Voyage to Althea," *Baltimore Afro-American*, May 4, 1957, 15; "Althea's Singing Is Bon Voyage Party Hit," *New York Amsterdam News*, May 25, 1957, 20; Associated Negro Press, "Althea Gibson Star of Own Bon Voyage," *Los Angeles Sentinel*, May 16, 1957, B2.

15. *Hep*, June 1957, cover; Yvonne Keller, "'Was It Right to Love Her Brother's Wife So Passionately': Lesbian Pulp Novels and U.S. Lesbian Identity, 1950–1965," *American Quarterly* 57, no. 2 (June 2005): 385–410.

16. St. Clair Johns, "The Strange Case of Althea Gibson," *Hep*, June 1957, 19, 20.

17. Susan K. Cahn, *Coming on Strong: Gender and Sexuality in Women's Sport*, 2nd ed. (Urbana: University of Illinois Press, 2015), 77–79. *Hep* even named McCormack

and Marlene Bauer as having "full-flowered charms." See Johns, "The Strange Case of Althea Gibson," 51; Pamela Grundy, *Learning to Win: Sports, Education, and Social Change in Twentieth-Century North Carolina* (Chapel Hill: University of North Carolina Press, 2001), 226–257. On Temple, see Cahn, *Coming on Strong*, 133. For emblematic spreads, see John G. Zimmerman, "Tennis Preview," *Sports Illustrated*, September 2, 1957, 30; Biff Bennett, "SPORTalk: Pretty Karol Fageros," *Sport*, July 1954, 9; Maureen Connolly, "Tennis Girls of Tomorrow," *Sport*, August 1956, 48–51; Jack Kofoed, "Karol Is Tennis' New Glamour Girl," *Sport*, May 1957, 40–41, 86.

18. Johns, "The Strange Case of Althea Gibson," 20.

19. Johns, "The Strange Case of Althea Gibson," 51, 50; table of contents, *Hep*, June 1957, 4.

20. Johns, "The Strange Case of Althea Gibson," 20.

21. Table of contents, *Hep*, June 1957, 4.

22. Althea Gibson, *I Always Wanted to Be Somebody*, ed. Ed Fitzgerald (New York: Harper and Row, 1958), 128.

23. Gibson, *I Always Wanted to Be Somebody*; "Richardson Is Named; He and Flam Will Represent U.S. in Wimbledon Tennis," *New York Times*, April 24, 1957, L40; Althea Gibson to Dr. Eaton, March 28, 1957, Eaton Papers.

24. "Strong Challenge to American Star," *Leicester Evening Standard*, May 24, 1957, 20.

25. Associated Press, "Miss Gibson Reaches London," *New York Times*, May 25, 1957, L17; Gibson, *I Always Wanted to Be Somebody*, 128.

26. Gibson, *I Always Wanted to Be Somebody*, 131.

27. Gibson, *I Always Wanted to Be Somebody*, 128.

28. Gibson, *I Always Wanted to Be Somebody*, 131–132, 129.

29. C. M. Jones, "The Gibson Girl Hurt by Politeness," *Daily Mirror* (London), June 18, 1957, 20; Roy McKelvie, "Worried Althea Ought to Win," *Daily Mail* (London), June 24, 1957, 8.

30. C. M. Jones, "Althea in Storm over Rain," *Daily Mirror*, June 8, 1957, 13.

31. Jones, "Althea in Storm over Rain"; "Northern Tennis: L. Hoad Defeats Krishnan," *Northern Daily Mail*, June 8, 1957, 7.

32. Ted Stevens, "Pre-Wimbledon Scare for Althea Gibson," *Daily Herald*, June 15, 1957, 8; "It Made No Difference . . . Christine Still Lost," *Daily Herald*, June 15, 1957, 3.

33. "Althea and Becker Win Surrey Titles," *The People*, June 2, 1957, 16; "Althea Had a Hard Final," *The People*, June 9, 1957, 12; Stanley Doust, "Hard Fight for Althea," *Weekly Dispatch* (London), June 16, 1957, 14; Ted Stevens, "Whirlwind Win by Gibson," *Daily Herald* (London), May 28, 1957, 8.

34. Stanley Doust, "Althea Was Not Impressive," *Weekly Dispatch*, June 2, 1957, 14; "Althea and Becker Win Surrey Titles."

35. Stanley Doust, "Hoad Looks Good for Wimbledon," *Weekly Dispatch*, June 9, 1957, 11.

36. Stevens, "Pre-Wimbledon Scare for Althea Gibson."

37. Stevens, "Pre-Wimbledon Scare for Althea Gibson."

38. "Althea Gibson: Is This Her Year?," *World Tennis*, June 1957, cover.

39. Susan Noel, "The Gibson Girl: Best of the 'Old-Stages,'" *World Sports*, June 1957, 7.

40. Charles Radclyffe, "Around the Centre Court," *The Sketch*, June 19, 1957, 608; Tony Mottram, "Hoad's Power 'Pack' a Wimbledon Ace," *Coventry Evening Telegraph*, June 19, 1957, 12; Jack Peart, "42,000-Pound Racket," *Daily Mirror and Sunday Pictorial*, June 23, 1957, 19; Peter Wilson, "Party Piece—Then the Kill," *Daily Mirror*, June 26, 1957, 17.

41. Peart, "42,000-Pound Racket."

42. Mottram, "Hoad's Power 'Pack' a Wimbledon Ace"; "Wimbledon Hope Is Shirley," *Leicester Evening Mail*, June 20, 1957, 16; "Miss Bloomer Made to Fight," *Birmingham Daily Post*, June 13, 1957, 12; Noel, "The Gibson Girl"; Angela Mortimer, *My Waiting Game* (London: Frederick Muller, 1962), 65; Frank Shaw, "The Line-up for a Royal Wimbledon," *Tatler and Bystander*, June 19, 1957, 14; John Ballantine, "Our Wimbledon Hopes Recede," *Western Mail*, June 20, 1957, 10.

43. "Christine on Test: Power-Practice," *Daily Herald*, June 14, 1957, 10.

44. Peter Wilson, "Shirley's the Girlie for My Bet," *Daily Mirror*, May 4, 1957, 13.

45. Cahn, Coming on Strong, 57.

46. Jack Wood, "Althea Was Not Fooled," *Daily Mail*, June 13, 1957, 13.

47. Jack Wood, "Doubt Nags at Althea, Tigress of the Court," *Daily Mail*, June 14, 1957, 12.

48. Peart, "42,000-Pound Racket."

49. Wood, "Althea Was Not Fooled"; "Christine on Test."

50. Peter Wilson, "Party Piece—Then the Kill," *Daily Mirror*, June 26, 1957, 17.

51. Wood, "Doubt Nags at Althea," 12.

52. Clifford Webb, "Althea Beats Her Bogy—and Fans," *Daily Herald*, June 26, 1957, 8; Gibson, *I Always Wanted to Be Somebody*, 129.

53. Webb, "Althea Beats Her Bogy"; Norman Cook, "These Give Me Telly-Ache!," *Liverpool Echo*, June 29, 1957, 6.

54. David Talbot, "Wimbledon Players and Prospects," *Birmingham Post and Gazette*, June 24, 1957, 4.

55. John Ballantine, "Winning Ace for Worried: Tough First Game with Hungary's No. 1," *Western Mail*, June 26, 1957, 10.

56. Webb, "Althea Beats Her Bogy."

57. Webb, "Althea Beats Her Bogy"; "A Listless Hoad Puts Lesch Out: Nervous," *Torbay Express and South Devon Echo*, June 27, 1957, 1; Associated Press, "The Summaries," *New York Times*, June 29, 1957, L15.

58. "Triumph of Althea," *Newsweek*, July 15, 1957, 64; Webb, "Althea Beats Her Bogy"; "Christine Toast of Wimbledon: Britain's 'Little Mo' Meets Favourite Gibson Next," *Western Mail*, July 3, 1957, 10.

59. C. M. Jones, "Christine Is Best We've Seen Since Little Mo," *Daily Mirror*, July 1, 1957, 19; "Christine Toast of Wimbledon"; Steve Roberts, "Wimbledon's Wonder Girl," *Liverpool Echo*, July 4, 1957, 6.

60. Jack Wood, "Victory—Then Miss Truman Calls for an Iced Lolly," *Daily Mail*, July 3, 1957, 1.

61. Shaw, "The Line-up for a Royal Wimbledon."

62. "The Kid . . . and the Crow," *Daily Mail*, July 4, 1957, 10.

63. Gibson, *I Always Wanted to Be Somebody*, 129–130, 29.

64. Roberts, "Wimbledon's Wonder Girl"; Official Programme, "Thursday 4th July Tenth Day: The Lawn Tennis Championships 1957," Robert Kelleher Collection, International Tennis Hall of Fame and Museum, Newport, RI.

65. Clifford Webb, "Christine Crumples to Defeat in 41 Minutes," *Daily Herald*, July 5, 1957, 10.

66. Webb, "Christine Crumples"; Gibson, *I Always Wanted to Be Somebody*, 130.

67. Jack Wood, "It Was Murder on the Centre Court," *Daily Mail*, July 5, 1957, 1.

68. C. M. Jones, "Beaten by Her Team Boss," *Daily Mirror*, July 3, 1957, 19; Webb, "Christine Crumples to Defeat in 41 Minutes."

69. Webb, "Christine Crumples to Defeat in 41 Minutes."

70. "Christine Gets Tennis Lesson," *Western Mail*, July 5, 1957, 12.

71. "Christine Gets Tennis Lesson."

72. Peter Wilson, "Poor Chris Didn't Get a Look In," *Daily Mirror*, July 5,1957, 19.

73. Roy Ullyett, "It's Althea vs. the Rest," *Pittsburgh Courier*, July 13, 1957, 4.

74. Gibson, *I Always Wanted to Be Somebody*, 131.

75. Gibson, *I Always Wanted to Be Somebody*, 132.

76. "Constance Noville's London Letter: Cool, Classic Look for Wimbledon," *Torbay Express and South Devon Echo*, June 19, 1957, 4.

77. Gibson, *I Always Wanted to Be Somebody*, 132–133.

78. Angela Buxton, "My Friend, Althea," *British Lawn Tennis and Squash*, July 1956, 11; "How the Stars See God," *Ebony*, April 1959, 104.

79. Clifford Webb, "Darlene Hard Laughs Off 'White Hope" Label," *Daily Herald*, April 24, 1957, 8.

80. Jack Peart, "Althea—But So Dull!," *Sunday Mirror*, July 7, 1957, 23.

81. "Althea Gibson Makes History at Wimbledon," *Liverpool Echo*, July 6, 1957, 9; Maurice Smith, "Althea Is Queen of Wimbledon: Darlene Loses 'Duel in the Sun' in 49 Mins," *The People* (London), July 7, 1957, 12.

82. Fred Tupper, "Miss Gibson Wimbledon Victory," *New York Times*, July 7, 1957; Jennifer, "Social Journal," *Tatler and Bystander*, July 17, 1957, 99; Gibson, *I Always Wanted to Be Somebody*, 134; "Triumph of Althea"; William "Sheep" Jackson, "Althea Gibson Changed Crowd," *Cleveland Call and Post*, July 27, 1957, 3C.

83. Jackson, "Althea Gibson Changed Crowd."

84. Associated Press, "Good Loser," *New York Times*, July 7, 1957, S1.

85. David Talbot, "Miss Gibson's Easy Task," *Birmingham Gazette*, July 8, 1957, 4.

86. Gibson, *I Always Wanted to Be Somebody*, 136.

87. John Rolls, "Life in the Mirror: Some Girl," *Daily Mirror*, July 8, 1957, 2; Gibson, *I Always Wanted to Be Somebody*, 138.

88. John Ballantine, "A Lack-Lustre Wimbledon," *Western Mail*, July 8, 1957, 8; "London Letter: Champion's Songs," *Birmingham Post and Gazette*, July 8, 1957, 4.

89. Gibson, *I Always Wanted to Be Somebody*, 139.

90. Peggy Pascoe, *What Comes Naturally: Miscegenation Law and the Making of Race in America* (New York: Oxford University Press, 2010); Rolls, "Life in the Mirror"; "London Letter: Champion's Songs."

91. "London Letter: Champion's Songs"; Gibson, *I Always Wanted to Be Somebody*, 138–139.

92. Edward Murrain, "Althea Returns Triumphant: Wimbledon Crown Tops Harlemite's Net Career," *New York Age*, July 13, 1957, 3.

93. *Althea*, dir. Rex Miller (2014), https://www.rexpix.com/althea.

94. Edith Asbury Evans, "'Queen' Althea Hailed by Harlem Neighbors: Wimbledon Victor Is Acclaimed on Street Where She Played," *New York Times*, July 10, 1957, A1, A22

95. Murrain, "Althea Returns Triumphant"; George Barner, "Things Normal Again at Home of Gibsons," *New York Amsterdam News*, July 20, 1957, 32.

96. Stanley Doust, "Harlem Girl Gains Tennis Crown and Her Life Ambition," *Weekly Dispatch*, July 7, 1957, 14; Peart, "Althea—But So Dull!"; "Singles and . . . ," *Daily Mail*, July 9, 1957, 5.

97. Murrain, "Althea Returns Triumphant"; Michelle Curry, interview by author, September 3, 2021.

98. Gibson, *I Always Wanted to Be Somebody*, 142.

99. Gibson, *I Always Wanted to Be Somebody*, 142; Edith Evans Asbury, "Miss Gibson's Kin Proud of Punch," *New York Times*, July 9, 1957, L33; Peter Wilson, "The Heroine Came Home Quietly," *Daily Mirror*, July 11, 1957, 19.

100. Gibson, *I Always Wanted to Be Somebody*, 140; Milton Gross, "Speaking Out," *New York Post*, July 8, 1957, 48.

101. Evans, "'Queen' Althea Hailed by Harlem Neighbors."

102. Evans, "'Queen' Althea Hailed"; on reference to football, see Marion E. Jackson, "Sports of the World: Quote: Althea Gibson," *Atlanta Daily World*, July 14, 1957, 8.

103. Edith Evans Asbury, "City Pays Tribute to Althea Gibson," *New York Times*, July 12, 1957, L23; George Barner, "Althea's Homecoming Was as Tough as Wimbledon," *New York Amsterdam News*, July 20, 1957, 1; Rita Liberti and Maureen M. Smith, *(Re)Presenting Wilma Rudolph* (Syracuse, NY: Syracuse University Press, 2015), 20–22.

104. "Reception for Althea Gibson," sound recording, July 11, 1957, WNYC, http://www.wnyc.org/people/renville-h-mcmann/.

105. "Reception for Althea Gibson."

106. "Reception for Althea Gibson."

107. "Reception for Althea Gibson"; Melinda Schwenk, "'Negro Stars' and the USIA's Portrait of Democracy," *Race, Gender and Class* 8, no. 4 (October 31, 2001): 116–139.

108.. "Reception for Althea Gibson."

109. "Reception for Althea Gibson"; "City Will Pay Tribute to Miss Gibson Today," *New York Times*, July 11, 1957; Barner, "Things Normal Again at Home of Gibsons"; "Johnson, Eaton Played Major Roles in Net Success of Althea Gibson," *Journal and Guide*, August 3, 1957, 20; Gibson, *I Always Wanted to Be Somebody*, 143.

110. Ted Poston, "Althea Would Love All the Acclaim—If She Could Only Get Some Sleep," *New York Post*, July 10, 1957, 2; Barner, "Things Normal Again at Home of Gibsons."

111. Murrain, "Althea Returns Triumphant."

112. Serrell Hillman, "That Gibson Girl," *Time*, August 26, 1957, 48; Quentin Reynolds, "Personal History: Long Road to the Center Court," *Saturday Review*, November 29, 1958, 16. See also Jack Olsen, *The Black Athlete: A Shameful Story— The Myth of Integration in American Sport* (New York: Time-Life Books, 1968). The *Baltimore Afro American* credited the Chicago White Sox with being the first integrated baseball team in the American League to place their white and black players in the same hotel, the Lord Baltimore. See "Tan Stars at Hotel," *Baltimore Afro American*, August 3, 1957.

113. Reynolds, "Personal History."

114. Russ J. Cowans, "Sports Writers Sour on Althea," *Chicago Defender*, July 27, 1957, 2.

115. Wendell Smith, "Has Net Queen Althea Gibson Gone High Hat?," *Pittsburgh Courier*, July 27, 1957, 18.

116. Cowans, "Sports Writers Sour on Althea."

117. United Press, "Althea Gibson and Seixas Gain U.S. Clay Court Tennis Crowns," *New York Times*, Monday, July 22, 1957, L24; Herb Lyon, "Tower Ticker," *Chicago Tribune*, July 23, 1957, Part 2, 2.

118. Cowans, "Sports Writers Sour on Althea."

119. Russ J. Cowans, "Russ' Corner: She Should Be Told," *Chicago Defender*, July 27, 1957, 24.

120. Smith, "Has Net Queen Althea Gibson Gone High Hat?"

121. Gordon B. Hancock, Associated Negro Press, "Between the Lines," *Atlanta Daily World*, July 24, 1957, 6.

122. "NCNW Urges Woman to Post of Juvenile Court Judge," *Atlanta Daily World*, July 17, 1957, 6.

123. Bill Nunn Jr., "Change of Pace: A Whirl Around the World of Sports," *Pittsburgh Courier*, August 3, 1957, 18.

124. Evelyn Cunningham, "The Women: Things I'll Remember About Famous People," *Pittsburgh Courier*, August 16, 1952, 29.

125. Evelyn Cunningham, "Althea Learning That It's Tough Wearing a Crown," *Pittsburgh Courier*, July 20, 1957, 18.

126. Cunningham, "Althea Learning That It's Tough."

127. "Althea Gibson: What Makes Her a Champion?," *Los Angeles Sentinel*, August 8, 1957, B1.

128. Hazel Garland, "'Queen' Althea Holds Court at Country Club Reception," *Pittsburgh Courier*, August 17, 1957, 16.

129. Garnet R. Ford, letter to editor, *Baltimore Afro-American*, August 31, 1957, 4.

130. Sarah Palfrey, "Althea," *Sports Illustrated*, September 2, 1957, 28.

131. Palfrey, "Althea," 28; "First of the Americans," *Pittsburgh Press*, August 6, 1957, 27; Gibson, *I Always Wanted to Be Somebody*, 145–146; "Talking with the Stars: Take Heart, Althea Says."

132. Gibson, *I Always Wanted to Be Somebody*, 145–146.

133. Bill Nunn Jr., "Change of Pace: Althea Gibson Speaks Her Mind," *Pittsburgh Courier*, August 17, 1957, 20.

134. Nunn, "Change of Pace: Althea Gibson Speaks Her Mind."

135. "Althea Hits Back; Says She's Same," *New York Amsterdam News*, August 17, 1957, 4.

136. "Althea Has No Time to Spare," *Pittsburgh Press*, August 7, 1957, 34.

137. "Althea Says Press Is Wrong in Calling Her 'Bigheaded'; Paces U.S. to Wightman Cup," *Philadelphia Tribune*, August 13, 1957, 10.

138. "Althea Hits Back."

139. "Althea Hits Back"; Nunn, "Change of Pace: Althea Gibson Speaks Her Mind."

140. "Althea Hits Back."

141. Berger, "The Wightman," *Pittsburgh Press*, August 7, 1957, 34.

142. Gibson, *I Always Wanted to Be Somebody*, 145; "Capacity Crowds for Wightman Cup," *Leicester Evening Mail*, August 10, 1957, 9; Associated Press, "Althea Gibson Paces U.S. to 3–0 Wightman Cup Lead," *New York Times*, August 11, 1957, S1.

143. I. Ball, "Wightman Cup Net Patter," *Pittsburgh Courier*, August 17, 1957, 23.

144. "Meet Hazel Wightman, the Game's 'First Lady,'" *American Lawn Tennis*, December 1947, 16; Ball, "Wightman Cup Net Patter."

145. "Wightman Cup Matches at Sewickley Thrill Socialites," *Pittsburgh Press*, August 11, 1957, 2, Section 1; "Althea Gibson Paces U.S. to 3–0 Wightman Cup Lead"; Associated Press, "U.S. Women Keep Wightman Cup, 6–1," *New York Times*, August 12, 1957, L25; Maureen Connolly, "Your Tennis Girls Will Beat Us Next Year," *Daily Mail*, August 13, 1957, 7; Mary Hardwick, "The Wightman Cup Story," *World Tennis*, October 1957, 57.

146. Associated Press, "Miss Gibson Takes Semi-final Match," *New York Times*, August 18, 1957, S1, S12; Associated Press, "Miss Gibson Wins Essex Club Final," *New York Times*, August 19, 1957, L15; Associated Press, "Cooper-Fraser Take U.S Title in Tennis Doubles at Brookline," *New York Times*, August 28, 1957, L33; "Louise Brough," International Tennis Hall of Fame and Museum, Newport, RI, https://

www.tennisfame.com/hall-of-famers/inductees/louise-brough (accessed May 26, 2021).

147. Herb Ralby, "Big Improvement Seen in Althea's Court Work," *Boston Globe*, August 30, 1957, 20.

148. "20 Days in One or What You Missed in Sports," *Boston Globe*, August 30, 1957, 20.

149. Associated Press, "Miss Gibson Wins Essex Club Final"; "Gibson's Impact Is Still Felt," *Miami Herald*, August 26, 2007, 12D.

150. John G. Zimmerman, "Althea Gibson Meets Her Biggest Test at Forest Hills," photo, *Sports Illustrated*, September 2, 1957, cover.

151. Marion E. Jackson, "Sports of the World," *Atlanta Daily World*, August 22, 1957, 5.

152. Boris Chaliapin, "Althea Gibson," *Time*, August 26, 1957, cover.

153. Hillman, "That Gibson Girl," 57, 44.

154. Hillman, "That Gibson Girl," 45, 46.

155. Hillman, "That Gibson Girl," 45, 44.

156. Sarah Palfrey, "Preview: Althea," *Sports Illustrated*, September 2, 1957, 28. Gibson is misquoted as saying Dr. Eaton "took such good care of me down in South Carolina when I was a kid." The line should say North Carolina.

157. John G. Zimmerman, "Althea," photo, *Sports Illustrated*, September 2, 1957, 29.

158. John G. Zimmerman, "Preview: More Stars in Color," photo, *Sports Illustrated*, September 2, 1957, 30.

159. William F. Talbert, "A Year for the Newcomers," *Sports Illustrated*, September 2, 1957, 31.

160. Hillman, "That Gibson Girl," 44.

161. Hillman, "That Gibson Girl," 48.

162. George Barner, "Will Another Tennis Champ Come from the ATA?," *New York Amsterdam News*, June 29, 1957, 30.

163. Cal Jacox, "From the Press Box: Dissension in the Ranks," *Journal and Guide*, July 20, 1957, 16.

164. P. L. Prattis, "Althea Gibson," *Pittsburgh Courier*, July 20, 1957, 4.

165. Joan Cook, "Anna Hedgeman Is Dead at 90; Aide to Mayor Wagner in 1950's," *New York Times*, January 26, 1990, D18; Jennifer Scanlon, *Until There Is Justice: The Life of Anna Arnold Hedgeman* (New York: Oxford University Press, 2016); Anna Arnold Hedgeman, "Althea Impresses City Official," *New York Amsterdam News*, August 31, 1957, 24.

166. Gibson, *I Always Wanted to Be Somebody*, 146, 148; Brochure, Manger Vanderbilt Hotel, 1958, 2, author's personal collection.

167. Fred Tupper, "Althea Gibson Gains in Tennis After Difficult Match with Karol Fageros," *New York Times*, September 1, 1957, S4.

168. "More Stars," *Sports Illustrated*, 30; Palfrey, "Althea," 28.

169. Gibson, *I Always Wanted to Be Somebody*, 146.

170. Allison Danzig, "Flam Put to Rout: Cooper Tops American in Tennis Semi-final—Davidson Beaten," *New York Times*, September 8, 1957, S1; Mary

Hardwick, "Althea Gibson Defeats Brough," *World Tennis*, October 1957, 18–19; Will Grimsley, "Gibson, Brough Gain Final," *Washington Post and Times Herald*, September 8, 1957, C4.

171. Gibson, *I Always Wanted to Be Somebody*, 148; Vanderbilt Hotel Service Directory, 1–4, author's personal collection; Brochure, Manger Vanderbilt Hotel, 1.

172. Gibson, *I Always Wanted to Be Somebody*, 148–149.

173. Allison Danzig, "Anderson and Miss Gibson Capture National Tennis Titles at Forest Hills: Women Tense, Cautious," *New York Times*, September 9, 1957, L33; Mary Hardwick, "Althea Gibson Defeats Louise Brough," *World Tennis*, October 1957, 19.

174. Danzig, "Anderson and Miss Gibson Capture National Tennis Titles at Forest Hills"; Evan Thomas, *Being Nixon: A Man Divided* (New York: Random House, 2015); Michael Beschloss, "Jackie Robinson and Nixon: Life and Death of a Political Friendship," *New York Times*, June 6, 2014, D3; Murray Illson, "Champion's Game Is Country-Bred," *New York Times*, September 9, 1957, 33; "The United States Champions," photo, *World Tennis*, October 1957, cover.

175. Althea Gibson quoted from *The Thrill of Sports: Actual Sounds and Voices*, Columbia Masterworks, ML 5294, 1958.

176. "A Cowpuncher and a Negro Make Tennis History," *Life*, September 23, 1957, 56; Danzig, "Anderson and Miss Gibson Capture National Tennis Titles at Forest Hills"; Gibson, *I Always Wanted to Be Somebody*, 150.

177. Emma Harrison, "From Streets of Harlem to Victory at Forest Hills: Miss Gibson Reaches Her Goal After 7-Year Quest," *New York Times*, September 9, 1957, L33.

178. Vincent Harding, Robin D. G. Kelley, et al., "We Changed the World, 1945–1970," in *To Make Our World Anew, Volume II: A History of African Americans from 1880* (New York: Oxford University Press, 2005), 196–198.

179. "President's Statements," *New York Times*, September 24, 1957, 1.

180. "Eisenhower Address on Little Rock," *New York Times*, September 25, 1957, 14.

181. Kenneth T. Walsh, *Celebrity in Chief: A History of Presidents and the Culture of Stardom* (New York: Routledge, 2016), 159–178; Maurice Isserman and Michael Kazin, *America Divided: The Civil War of the 1960s* (New York: Oxford University Press, 2000), 32; Gibson, *I Always Wanted to Be Somebody*, 139–140; Louis Lautier, "In the Nation's Capital: Althea to the White House," *Atlanta Daily World*, July 14, 1957, 4; Sam Lacy, "Sports: A to Z," *Baltimore Afro-American*, November 30, 1957, 13; Robert F. Burk, *The Eisenhower Administration and Black Civil Rights* (Knoxville: University of Tennessee Press, 1984), 260.

182. *Althea Gibson, Tennis Champion* (dir. Walter de Hoog, 1957), United States Information Service, NA II, RG 306.3105; Schwenk, " 'Negro Stars' and the USIA's Portrait of Democracy."

183. Hazel Garland, "Things to Talk About: A Study in Contrasts," *Pittsburgh Courier*, September 14, 1957, 13. Hollywood gossip columnist Hedda Hopper felt similarly, writing weeks later, after Gibson competed in the Pacific Southwest

Tennis Championships, "There never was a greater contrast than watching Althea Gibson perform magnificently on Los Angeles tennis courts and seeing pictures of the National Guard keeping one little Negro girl from entering a school-house." Hopper called seeing Gibson receive the Wimbledon trophy from Queen Elizabeth II "one of the most moving things I've ever witnessed." See Hedda Hopper, "Warner Gives Fuller Triple Duty on Film: Couldn't Resist," *Los Angeles Times*, September 23, 1957, C10.

184. Hazel Garland, "Things to Talk About: A Study in Contrasts," *Pittsburgh Courier*, September 14, 1957, 13.

185. *New York Age*, September 14, 1957, 3; *New York Age*, September 28, 1957, 1.

186. Penny M. Von Eschen, *Satchmo Blows Up the World: Jazz Ambassadors Play the Cold War* (Cambridge, MA: Harvard University Press, 2004), 63–64; Stanley Robertson, "L.A. Confidential: 'The Horn Don't Know No Race,'" *Los Angeles Sentinel*, September 26, 1957, 4.

187. Stanley Robertson, "L.A. Confidential: Have Eartha and Louis Awakened?" *Los Angeles Sentinel*, September 26, 1957, 4.

188. Jeane Hoffman, "Confidence Big Help to Althea," *Los Angeles Times*, September 19, 1957, C6; Gibson, *I Always Wanted to Be Somebody*, 61–62.

189. Associated Press, "Althea Gibson Criticized," *Washington Post and Times Herald*, September 7, 1957, A9.

190. Perry T. Jones to Holcombe Ward, August 2, 1943, Lawrence A. Baker Collection, Box 8, Folder 4.14.1, "Racial Issues," International Tennis Hall of Fame and Museum, Newport, RI; "Althea Gibson Arrives for Net Tourney," *California Eagle*, September 19, 1957, 3; "Committees of the Tennis Patrons," Program Booklet, Thirty-First Anniversary Pacific Southwest Tennis Championships, September 12–22, 1957, 3, author's personal collection.

191. Arnold Beisser, "The Pacific Southwest Championships: The Women's Singles," *World Tennis*, November 1957, 14, 15.

192. Hoffman, "Confidence Big Help to Althea."

193. Beisser, "The Pacific Southwest Championships: The Women's Singles," 14, 15.

194. L. I. Brockenbury, "Gibson Gal Darling of 100% Wrong Club," *Los Angeles Sentinel*, September 26, 1957, B2.

195. Associated Press, "Althea Gibson Wins Colorado Tennis," *Washington Post and Times Herald*, September 16, 1957, A18; Gardnar Mulloy, "Olmedo and Gibson Win Colorado State," *World Tennis*, November 1957, 36; "Althea Gibson Arrives for Net Tourney," *California Eagle*, September 19, 1957, 3; "100% Wrong Club Honors Miss Gibson," *California Eagle*, September 26, 1956, 9.

196. L. I. Brockenbury, "Tying the Score: Althea Gibson Is Quite a Girl," *Los Angeles Sentinel*, September 26, 1957, B4; Brockenbury, "Gibson Gal Darling of 100% Wrong Club."

197. Brockenbury, "Tying the Score: Althea Gibson Is Quite a Girl."

198. Bion Abbott, "Seixas Easily Beats Gil Shea," *Los Angeles Times*, September 23, 1957, C1; "Althea Nabs 2 Wins in One Week Stay," *Los Angeles Sentinel*, September 26, 1957, B3; "And Still Champion," *New York Times*, September 23, 1957, 32; United Press, "Davidson Beats Seixas," *New York Times*, October 1, 1957; "Althea Gibson to Present Net Winners' Awards," *California Eagle*, October 3, 1957, 8; "Althea Presents Awards," *California Eagle*, October 10, 1957, 7; "Althea Star in AKA Program," *Los Angeles Sentinel*, October 10. 1957, C2.

199. Gibson, *I Always Wanted to Be Somebody*, 61.

200. John E. Meeks, letter to the editor, *Time*, September 9, 1957, 10.

201. R. M. Shaw, letter to the editor, *Time*, September 9, 1957, 10.

202. Brockenbury, "Althea Gibson Is Quite a Girl."

CHAPTER 10

1. Jeane Hoffman, "Confidence Big Help to Althea," *Los Angeles Times*, September 19, 1957, C6; Emma Harrison, "Althea, Pride of West Side, Becomes Queen of Another," *New York Times*, September 9, 1957, L33;.

2. Jun L'Rhue, "Manhattan Council, NCNW Hold World Fellowship Luncheon," *New York Age*, November 9, 1957, 14; Myrtle Cook, "Althea Gibson to Appear at Opening of Net Club," *Montreal Star*, November 12, 1957, 37; Myrtle Cook, "Net Ace Arrives for Exhibition," *Montreal Star*, November 21, 1957, 56; Myrtle Cook, "Althea Gibson Shows Class," *Montreal Star*, November 25, 1957, 32.

3. Associated Press, "Accidents Claim Lives of 4 in State," *Courier-News* (Bridgewater, NJ), November 29, 1957, 30; "A Great Year for FAMU," *Tallahassee Democrat*, December 16, 1957, 4; Althea Gibson to George W. Gore, November 7, 1957, Gaither Collection.

4. A. S. "Doc" Young, "How Althea Conquered Herself," *Jet*, August 1, 1957, 54.

5. "Tennis Queen from Harlem," *Ebony*, October 1957, 56.

6. Hoffman, "Confidence Big Help to Althea."

7. Christy Munro, "Althea Gibson . . . Tragic Success Story," *Look*, November 12, 1957, 132–133, 134.

8. "Miss Gibson Gains Best-of-'57 Prize," *New York Times*, January 12, 1958, 4S; Associated Negro Press, "Laud Althea as Top Girl Star of Year," *Chicago Daily Defender*, February 18, 1924, 24.

9. Althea Gibson with Richard J. Curtis, *So Much to Live For* (New York: G. P. Putnam's Sons, 1968), 17, 20.

10. Ted Poston, "The Althea Gibson Story: Article VI," *New York Post Daily Magazine*, September 1, 1957, M5.

11. Hoffman, "Confidence Big Help to Althea"; Harrison, "Althea, Pride of West Side Becomes Queen of Another."

12. Sarah Palfrey, "Althea," *Sports Illustrated*, September 2, 1957, 28; John M. Ross, "There's No Tennis Like Pro Tennis," *Sport*, March 1956, 47.

13. Dick Phelan, "The Small Green Empire of Jack Kramer," *Sports Illustrated*, February 24, 1958. See also John M. Ross, "They're Murdering Tennis," *Sport*, August 1954, 89; Ross, "There's No Tennis Like Pro Tennis," *Sport*, March 1956, 47, 88, 89; Greg Ruth, *Tennis: A History from American Amateurs to Global Professionals* (Urbana: University of Illinois Press, 2021), 115–137.

14. Phelan, "The Small Green Empire of Jack Kramer."

15. Jack Kramer with Frank Deford, *The Game: My 40 Years in Tennis* (New York: G. P. Putnam's Sons, 1979), 96.

16. "Althea to Be Busy in Retirement," *British Lawn Tennis and Squash*, October 1958, 14.

17. Kramer, *The Game*, 79, 80.

18. Kramer, *The Game*, 93–95.

19. "Will Little Mo Come Back Against Althea?," *Sport*, March 1958, 31; "Maureen Connolly Rejects Kramer Bid," *Washington Post and Times Herald*, February 8, 1958, A10. When the horseback riding accident happened, Kramer was negotiating a contract worth $100,000 for Connolly to oppose Betz. See Kramer, *The Game*, 95–96. "Kramer Hopes to Sign Christine," *Daily Herald* (London), June 21, 1958, 8; "Christine to Continue as Amateur," *Belfast Telegraph*, June 21, 1958, 10; Ted Stevens, "So Three Gals Clean Up in Record Time," *Daily Herald*, June 25, 1958, 10.

20. Palfrey, "Althea"; George Barner, "Althea Wants: 1. Apt., 2. Pro Singing Career," *New York Amsterdam News*, September 14, 1957, 1.

21. Barner, "Althea Wants"; Gibson, *So Much to Live For*, 17; Kramer, *The Game*, 71.

22. Palfrey, "Althea," 28; Peter Wilson, "The Heroine Came Home Quietly . . . ," *Daily Mirror* (London), July 11, 1957, 19; Ted Poston, "The Story of Althea Gibson: Article VI."

23. Ted Poston, "The Story of Althea Gibson: Article VI"; Munro, "Althea Gibson . . . Tragic Success Story," 136; Gibson, *So Much to Live For*, 66; Palfrey, "Althea," 28.

24. Christopher Lehmann-Haupt, "Overcoming a Lifetime's Motivations to Drink," *New York Times*, July 5, 1990, C15; David K. Kirkpatrick, "Edward Fitzgerald, 81, Book-of-Month Executive," *New York Times*, February 19, 2001, B8; Ed Fitzgerald, *A Nickel an Inch: A Memoir* (New York: Atheneum, 1985), 84–95.

25. Fitzgerald, *A Nickel an Inch*, 95.

26. Fitzgerald, *A Nickel an Inch*, 95.

27. Fitzgerald, *A Nickel an Inch*, 96.

28. "Althea to Be Busy in Retirement," *British Lawn Tennis and Squash*, October 1958, 14; Fitzgerald, *A Nickel an Inch*, 96, 95.

29. Hoffman, "Confidence Big Help to Althea"; Barner, "Althea Wants."

30. Gibson, *I Always Wanted to Be Somebody*, 154–155; Gibson, *So Much to Live For*, 22–23.

31. Althea Gibson, *I Always Wanted to Be Somebody*, ed. Ed Fitzgerald (New York: Harper and Row, 1958), 154, 155; "Handy Feted as 'Father of Blues,'"

Baltimore Afro-American, November 30, 1957, 5; Ruth Ellington, "This Is New York: Flowers While He Lives," *Pittsburgh Courier*, November 30, 1957, 10.

32. Gibson, *So Much to Live For*, 23, 29. Dot had a reputation for making recording deals with people with well-known names but questionable talent. See *Tab Hunter Confidential*, dir. Jeffrey Schwarz, 2015, Amazon Prime Video.

33. Gibson, *So Much to Live For*, 30, 31.

34. Gibson, *So Much to Live For*, 31.

35. Stephanie Brown, "Calm Althea in City: Tennis Star Asks Only Time to Eat," *Minneapolis Star*, January 24, 1958, 11A; Ray Canton, "Althea Draws Record Crowd," *Minneapolis Sunday Tribune*, January 26, 1958, S3; Sid Hartman, "Hartman's Roundup: Great Athlete," *Minneapolis Morning Tribune*, February 1, 1958, 18.

36. Canton, "Althea Draws Record Crowd"; "500 Student Tickets Set for Gibson-Arth Match," *Minneapolis Sunday Tribune*, January 5, 1958, 6.

37. Brown, "Calm Althea in City"; Jack Goodwin, "Althea Gibson Goal: 'To Prove I Rank with Women Tennis Greats,'" *Minneapolis Star*, January 24, 1958, 9B.

38. Ray Canton, "Persistent Belief in Own Ability Made Althea Gibson Champion," *Minneapolis Morning Tribune*, January 25, 1958, 18.

39. Claude E. Harrison Jr., "People in Sports," *Philadelphia Tribune*, February 1, 1958, 13.

40. Althea Gibson, "How I Feel About Being 'On Stage,'" n.d., Gibson Collection; Gibson, *I Always Wanted to Be Somebody*, 153.

41. Peter Wilson, "Songbird Althea Flops on Tennis 'Hit' Parade," *Daily Mirror*, April 23, 1958; Gibson, *I Always Wanted to Be Somebody*, 173.

42. Associated Press, "Miss Gibson Defeated," *New York Times*, March 8, 1958, L11; Sam Lacy, "Sports A to Z," *Baltimore Afro-American*, March 29, 1958, 13; Eddie Herr, "Patty and Gibson Win Caracas," *World Tennis*, May 1958, 14, 15.

43. "The Caribe Hilton Championships: Patty and Fleitz Take Titles," *World Tennis*, May 1958, 51; Gibson, *I Always Wanted to Be Somebody*, 166.

44. "The Caribe Hilton Championships."

45. Gibson, *I Always Wanted to Be Somebody*, 161.

46. Gibson, *I Always Wanted to Be Somebody*, 161, 162, 164, 167.

47. Gibson, *I Always Wanted to Be Somebody*, 105.

48. Gibson, *I Always Wanted to Be Somebody*, 165.

49. Fred Kovaleski, interview by author, October 23, 2014; "What Winning at Tennis Cost Althea Gibson," *Jet*, August 7, 1958, 58.

50. Brown, "Calm Althea in City."

51. Gibson, *I Always Wanted to Be Somebody*, 165, 164, 156.

52. Associated Press, "Miss Gibson Takes Final," *New York Times*, March 31, 1958, L32; Sidney Phillips, "The Caribbean Championships," *World Tennis*, June 1958, 71; Associated Press, "Janet Hopps Scores over Althea Gibson," *New York Times*, April 6, 1958, S1.

53. Tommy Fitzgerald, "Althea Gibson Is Beaten by Janet Hopps in Upset," *Miami News*, April 6, 1958, 1C, 4C; United Press, "A Champion Can Have Off Day, Says Tennis Star Althea Gibson," *Washington Post and Times Herald*, April 7, 1958, A15.

54. Fitzgerald, "Althea Gibson Is Beaten by Janet Hopps."

55. Fitzgerald, "Althea Gibson Is Beaten by Janet Hopps."

56. "Miss Gibson Intends to Win Again," *Birmingham Daily Post*, April 23, 1958, 23; Gibson, *I Always Wanted to Be Somebody*, 173; United Press, "A Champion Can Have Off Day."

57. Edwin Pope, "Althea Gibson: Pent-Up Power, Poise, Skill and Conversation," *Miami News*, April 6, 1958, 3D.

58. Pope, "Althea Gibson."

59. Tommy Fitzgerald, "Althea's Road Tough to Hoe," *Miami News*, April 7, 1958, 1-C.

60. Peter Wilson, "Poor Chris Didn't Get a Look In," *Daily Mirror*, July 5, 1957, 19.

61. Hoffman, "Confidence Big Help to Althea."

62. United Press, "A Champion Can Have Off Day."

63. Craig Werner, *A Change Is Gonna Come: Music, Race, and the Soul of America* (Ann Arbor: University of Michigan Press, 2006).

64. Cover, *Althea Gibson Sings*, Dot Records, DLP 3105, 1958; Mary Hawton, "An Overseas Tennis Tour," *Tennis in Australasia*, September 1956, 12; Gussie Moran, "Can Althea Gibson Make It?," *Sport*, October 1956, 70. On Eckstine, see Cary Ginell, *Mr. B: The Music and Life of Billy Eckstine* (Milwaukee, MI: Hal Leonard, 2013). Althea Gibson, "How I Feel About Being 'On Stage,'" n.d., Gibson Collection.

65. Allison McCracken, *Real Men Don't Croon: Crooning in American Culture* (Raleigh, NC: Duke University Press, 2015), 2–4; Ann Simer, "Althea's After a New Kind of Record," *Corpus Christi Caller-Times*, October 26, 1969, 1.

66. "Album Reviews: 'Althea Gibson Sings,'" *Variety*, June 11, 1958, 44, 50.

67. Lew Matthews, "Althea's Voice Not as Good as Tennis Playing," *Chicago Defender*, April 30, 1958, 23.

68. Masco Young, "The Grapevine: Althea Gibson," *Pittsburgh Courier*, May 3, 1958, 18.

69. Ed Sullivan, "Can TV Crack America's Color Line?," *Ebony*, May 1951, 60, 61; "Television: Negro Performers Win Better Roles in TV Than in Any Other Entertainment Medium," *Ebony*, June 1950, 20; Suzanne E. Smith, *Dancing in the Street: Motown and the Cultural Politics of Detroit* (Cambridge, MA: Harvard University Press, 1999), 133–134.

70. Sam Lacy, "NBC Answers Query: Mahalia to Break Tan Drought on Shore Show," *Baltimore Afro-American*, May 31, 1958, 7; Donald Bogle, *Prime Time Blues: African Americans on Network Television* (New York: Farrar, Straus, and Giroux, 2001), 74–77; James Maguire, *Impresario: The Life and Times of Ed Sullivan* (New York: Billboard Books, 2006), 4, 15.

71. *The Ed Sullivan Show*, August 23, 1959.

72. I have copied these lyrics verbatim from Gibson's May 25, 1958, performance on *The Ed Sullivan Show*.

73. Gibson, *I Always Wanted to Be Somebody*, 156.

74. Earl Wilson, "'Dodgers, Go,' in LA Signs: The Midnight Earl," *Miami News*, May 30, 1958, 7B; Gibson, *So Much to Live For*, 32.

75. Gibson, *So Much to Live For*, 32.

76. "Around the World," *World Tennis*, July 1958, 53.

77. "Tele Follow-Up Comment: Ed Sullivan," *Variety*, May 28, 1958, 39.

78. John P. Shanley, "Althea Gibson Sings," *New York Times*, May 26, 1958, L51.

79. Marion E. Jackson, "Sports of the World," *Atlanta Daily World*, May 27, 1958.

80. "Miss Gibson Has Quick Win in Surbiton," *Birmingham Daily Post*, May 28, 1958, 30.

81. "May Have a 7-Match Day," *Liverpool Echo*, May 31, 1958, 35; Roy McKelvie, "Maria Bueno Is Only Threat to Champion Althea," *Daily Mail* (London), June 30, 1958, 8; "So Easy for Althea," *Manchester Evening News*, June 7, 1958, 8.

82. "Althea Keeps the Trophy," *British Lawn Tennis and Squash*, July 1958, 19.

83. Bruce Schoenfeld, *The Match: Althea Gibson and Angela Buxton: How Two Outsiders—One Black, the Other Jewish—Forged a Friendship and Made Sports History* (New York: Amistad Press, 2004), 251–252; Angela Buxton, interview by author, October 24, 2014.

84. Wilson, "Songbird Althea Flops"; "So Easy for Althea."

85. Peter Wilson, "Pal Mal to Stride to Royal Road—And Althea to Keep Her Crown," June 23, 1958, 19; Tony Mottram, "It Looks Like Being a Lean Wimbledon," *Belfast Telegraph*, May 10, 1958, 10.

86. "Sports in Brief," *Los Angeles Times*, February 21, 1958, C2; Jack Peart, "Althea—But So Dull!," *Sunday Mirrorl*, July 7, 1957, 23; Roy McKelvie, "Weak U.S. Tennis Cup Team," *Daily Mail*, May 14, 1958, 15; "Althea Wins Easily; Wightman Cup Tennis," *Liverpool Echo*, June 13, 1958, 20; Peter Wilson, "England Regains Wightman Cup," *World Tennis*, August 1958, 11.

87. "Britain's Wonder Girls of Tennis," *Liverpool Echo*, June 19, 1958, 6; "Can Christine Lift Title?," *Star Green 'Un* (Sheffield, UK) June 21, 1958, 10.

88. Roy McKelvie, "But Fans Rate It a Women's Wimbledon," *Daily Mail*, June 23, 1958, 9; Wilson, "England Regains Wightman Cup," 12–13; Ralph Hadley, "We've Done It After 28 Years," *The People* (London), June 15, 1958, 16.

89. Denzil Batchelor, "Little Miss Greatheart's Mightiest Triumph," *Sunday Dispatch* (London), June 15, 1958, 12.

90. "Miss Bloomer Loses Petticoat Gracefully," *Washington Post and Times Herald*, June 14, 1958, A15; Associated Press, "U.S. Loses First Time in 20 Years," *Washington Post and Times Herald*, June 15, 1958, C3.

91. George Casey, "So the Toast Is Christine," *Sunday Mirror*, June 22, 1958, 23; J. L. Manning, "Christine, 17, Beats That Gibson Girl," *Sunday Dispatch*, June 15, 1958, 1.

92. Manning, "Christine, 17, Beats That Gibson Girl," 1.

93. Gibson, *I Always Wanted to Be Somebody*, 173; Paul Tanfield, "And the Girls That All Wimbledon Will Watch," *Daily Mail*, June 16, 1958, 12.

94. Associated Press, "Althea Sights Victory over English Star," *Miami News*, June 23, 1958, 3C.

95. Gibson, *I Always Wanted to Be Somebody*, 173, 174.

96. Robert Musel, "California Girl Star of Tourney," *Washington Post and Times Herald*, June 29, 1958, C1; "Christine and Althea Winners," *Liverpool Echo*, June 24, 1958, 10; John Ballantine, "Bobby Wilson Left to Carry British Hopes," *Western Mail*, June 27, 1958, 12; Roy McKelvie, "Ann and Angela Crash to the Semi-Final: Very Competent," *Daily Mail*, July 2, 1958, 9; Gibson, *I Always Wanted to Be Somebody*, 174.

97. McKelvie, "Ann and Angela Crash to the Semi-Final"; "Christine Has a Quick Triumph," *Western Mail*, June 25, 1958, 10; Gibson, *I Always Wanted to Be Somebody*, 174; "Ann Haydon Loses to Miss Gibson," *Birmingham Daily Post*, July 4, 1958, 23.

98. Peter Wilson, "The Write-Off Is in the Final," *Daily Mirror*, July 4, 1958, 23.

99. Monty Court, "Now Pickard Puts Tennis Before Love: Engagement," *Daily Mail*, July 5, 1958, 1; "Foot-Faults but Title Althea's," *Belfast Telegraph*, July 5, 1958, 10; Sam Leitch, "Meet Miss Sport—and Miss Sense," *Daily Herald*, July 4, 1958, 10.

100. Angela Mortimer, *My Waiting Game* (London: Frederick Muller, 1962), 129; "Gibson Wins Singles, Doubles at Wimbledon," *Washington Post and Times Herald*, July 6, 1958, C1.

101. Mortimer, *My Waiting Game*, 129.

102. Associated Press, "Althea Wins 2 Net Titles," *Miami Herald*, July 7, 1958, D1; "Gibson Wins Singles, Doubles at Wimbledon"; Jack Peart, "Althea Smashes Plucky Angela," *Sunday Mirror*, July 6, 1958, 23.

103. "Gibson Wins Singles, Doubles at Wimbledon."

104. Wilson, "Pal Mal to Stride to Royal Road."

105. Gibson, *I Always Wanted to Be Somebody*, 174.

106. Gibson, *I Always Wanted to Be Somebody*, 168–169.

107. "Jockey, 52, Wins Big One After 9 Years," *Miami Herald*, July 7, 1958, D1.

108. Gibson, *So Much to Live For*, 44; Obituary, "Zaidins—Earle Warren," *New York Times*, January 20, 2003, B7; "Kefauver Accused of Quashing Report," *New York Times*, May 6, 1957, 19; "Three Girls Whose Engagements Are Announced," *New York Times*, January 22, 1952, 34; Julia Blackburn, *With Billie: A New Look at the Unforgettable Lady Day* (New York: Pantheon, 2006), 299–308.

109. United Press International, "MacKay Gets Top Seeding," *Washington Post and Times Herald*, July 13, 1958, C4; "Mrs. Knode, Christine Truman Top Seeded at Essex," *Boston Globe*, August 12, 1958, 44.

110. William J. Clothier II, "The Pennsylvania Grass Courts," *World Tennis*, September 1958, 46; Betty Pratt, "Gibson Wins Women's Title at Orange," *World Tennis*, October 1958, 57.

111. "Video Encore," *Baltimore Afro-American*, August 23, 1958, 7; William Ewald, "Althea Goes on TV Sock What Line?," *Chicago Daily Defender*, August 13, 1958, 17; *What's My Line?*, August 10, 1958. *What's My Line?* featured many athletes during its run, including Arnold Palmer and Willie Mays. Lew Hoad appeared after winning Wimbledon in 1957.

112. Frances Gray and Yanick Rice Lamb, *Born to Win: The Authorized Biography of Althea Gibson* (Hoboken, NJ: John Wiley and Sons, 2005), 119; Jack Walker, "Izzy Rowe's Notebook," *Pittsburgh Courier*, August 2, 1958, A14.

113. "Longwood Bows to Althea: Ed Sullivan Show Date Forces Net Final Shift," *Boston Globe*, August 23, 1958, 1, 12; "Althea Set for TV Debut," *Pittsburgh Courier*, May 24, 1958, 22.

114. Allys Swanson and Sharon L. Van Oteghen, "Oral History of Jeanne Arth Interview with Jeanne Arth," 2002, 39, Nutrition and Exercise Sciences Faculty Scholarship, St. Catherine University, https://sophia.stkate.edu/exsci_fac/9. On Wightman's home as lodging for tennis players, see Tom Carter, *First Lady of Tennis: Hazel Hotchkiss Wightman* (Berkeley, CA: Creative Arts, 2001), 106–113.

115. "Aces-Deuces," *Boston Globe*, August 24, 1958, 72; Allison Danzig, "Richardson-Olmedo Upset Australians in Four Sets," *New York Times*, August 24, 1958, S1.

116. Jose, "Tele Follow-Up Comment: Ed Sullivan Show," *Variety*, August 27, 1958, 29.

117. Elizabeth W. Driscoll, "TV Notebook: Althea Scores Hit with TV Net Work," *Boston Daily Globe*, August 25, 1958, 5.

118. Mary Hardwick, "The National Championships: The Women's Singles," *World Tennis*, October 1958, 21, 22, 24, 27; Hoffman, "Confidence Big Help to Althea"; George Minot, "Across the Net," *Washington Post and Times Herald*, July 27, 1958, C5.

119. Hardwick, "The Women's Singles," 24; Transcript, "Interview with Althea Gibson," Washington University in St. Louis, October 21, 1984, http://repository.wustl.edu/concern/videos/8s45qd665.

120. "Rule Book Doesn't Offer, but Althea Finds a Seat," *New York Times*, September 10, 1958, 32.

121. Transcript, "Interview with Althea Gibson."

122. Steve Snider, United Press International, "Anderson Loses in Five Sets," *Washington Post and Times Herald*, September 8, 1958, A16; Allison Danzig, "Cooper and Althea Gibson Win National Tennis Titles," *New York Times*, September 8, 1958, 1, 32.

123. Hardwick, "The Women's Singles," 25; Associated Press, "Gibson Tired, to Sing for a Year at Least," *Miami News*, September 8, 1958, 2-C.

124. Will Grimsley, Associated Press, "Althea May Never Play Tourney Tennis Again," *Washington Post and Times Herald*, September 8, 1958, A15; United Press International, "Dulles Gives Out Tennis Trophies," *Washington Post and Times Herald*, September 8, 1958, A16; Associated Press, "Gibson Wins U.S. Title, Quits Tennis," *Miami Herald*, September 8, 1958, C1; Gibson, *So Much to Live For*, 15.

CHAPTER 11

1. Althea Gibson with Richard J. Curtis, *So Much to Live For* (New York: G. P. Putnam's Sons, 1968), 26.

2. "Is Althea Gibson Really Broke?," *Pittsburgh Courier*, November 23, 1957, 8.

3. Christy Munroe, "Althea Gibson . . . Tragic Success Story," *Look*, November 12, 1957, 136.

4. "What Winning at Tennis Cost Althea Gibson," *Jet*, August 7, 1958, 56, 58.

5. Wills's autobiography was serialized in June and July 1933. Letters to the editor from Rev. Cordell A. Dickey, Rev. George E. Blanchard, Margaret Makin, and Mrs. Wayne B. Vinson, *Saturday Evening Post*, September 28, 1958, 4.

6. "War Film Slated by New Company," *New York Times*, March 27, 1958, 41; Harnett T. Kane, "Yankee Raiders Deep in Dixie," *New York Times*, February 19, 1956, BR3; Orville Prescott, "Books of the Times," *New York Times*, February 24, 1956, 23; Neil Longley York, *Fiction as Fact: The Horse Soldiers and Popular Memory* (Kent, OH: Kent State University Press, 2001), 1–24; Oscar Godbout, "Paramount Seeks to Enjoin Holden," *New York Times*, September 11, 1958, 42.

7. Althea Gibson, "How I Feel About Being 'On Stage,'" n.d., Gibson Collection; Greg Harris, "The Greg Harris Notebook," *Chicago Daily Defender*, September 23, 1958, 8; Morton Cooper, "Althea Gibson, Bundle of Energy, Talent and Drive," *Chicago Defender*, August 3–9, 1963.

8. Hazel Washington, "This Is Hollywood," *Chicago Daily Defender*, October 1, 1958, 17; Greg Harris, "The Greg Harris Notebook," *Chicago Defender*, September 23, 1958, 8; "Hear Althea Gibson Passed Test; Gains Berth for Top Film," *Chicago Defender*, October 11, 1958, 19.

9. Thomas Cripps, *Making Movies Black: The Hollywood Message Movie from World War II to the Civil Rights Era* (New York: Oxford University Press, 1993); Donald Bogle, *Bright Boulevards, Bold Dreams: The Story of Black Hollywood* (New York: Ballantine Books, 2005), 287–360; Charles C. Alexander, *Ty Cobb* (New York: Oxford University Press, 1984), 129; Seàn Crosson, *Sport and Film* (New York: Routledge, 2013), 34-35; Donald Bogle, *Toms, Coons, Mulattoes, Mammies, and Bucks: An Interpretive History of Blacks in American Films*, 5th ed. (New York: Bloomsbury Academic, 2016), 166, 167.

10. Pat Ford to John Ford, September 1958, Box 3, Correspondence, John Ford Collection, Lilly Library, Indiana University, Bloomington; Scott Eyman, *Print the Legend: The Life and Times of John Ford* (New York: Simon and Schuster, 1999), 145. According to another account, Althea refused to go to Louisiana. See "New York Beat," *Jet*, November 13, 1958, 63. Althea did not discuss her exclusion, chosen or otherwise, in *So Much to Live For*.

11. Walter Winchell, "Stars Furious at Louisiana Racial Ban," *Miami Herald*, November 14, 1958, 7-B.

12. Pearlie Cox Harrison, "Washington Report: Dems and Pigskins Took the Spotlight on Washington Scene," *Baltimore Afro-American*, November 15, 1958, 16; Lawrence

A. Oxley to Dr. Hubert A. Eaton Sr., July 12, 1958; Eaton to Oxley, July 25, 1958; Oxley to Eaton, August 21, 1958; Oxley to Sidney [*sic*] A. Llewellyn, August 21, 1958, all Eaton Papers; Associated Negro Press, "Pigskin Club Honors Althea," *Los Angeles Sentinel*, November 6, 1958, 4.

13. Edward White, *The Tastemaker: Carl Van Vechten and the Birth of Modern America* (New York: Farrar, Straus, and Giroux, 2014); Nancy Cuhl, *Extravagant Crowd: Carl Van Vechten's Portraits of Women* (New Haven, CT: Yale University Press, 2007); Carl Van Vechten to Langston Hughes, New York, September 20, 1958, in *Remember Me to Harlem: The Letters of Langston Hughes and Carl Van Vechten, 1925–1964*, ed. Emilie Bernard (New York: Alfred A. Knopf, 2001), 302.

14. Earle Warren Zaidins to Carl Van Vechten, December 10, 1958, James Weldon Johnson MSS 1050, Box 49, Folder 944, Carl Van Vechten Papers Relating to African American Arts and Letters, Series I Correspondence, Beinecke Library, Yale University. My interpretation of the photographs is based on a visit that I made to the main reading room of the Beinecke Library at Yale University July 17–18, 2014. The series is held in the Carl Van Vechten Papers, Yale Collection of American Literature, Beinecke Rare Book and Manuscript Library, Yale University. It is also available online: http://brbl-dl.library.yale.edu/vufind/Search/Results?look for=Althea+Gibson&type=AllFields&submit=Find&filter%5B%5D=genre_fa cet%3A%22Studio+portraits%22&limit=16&sort=relevance (accessed October 24, 2016).

15. "Althea Off for Role in Hollywood," *New York Amsterdam News*, December 6, 1958, 16.

16. Vernon Scott, United Press International, "Tennis Queen to Stick to Movies if Debut Clicks," *Chicago Defender*, December 20, 1958, 18; Gibson, "How I Feel About Being 'On Stage.'"

17. Army Archerd, "Just for Variety: Good Morning," *Variety*, December 9, 1958, 2.

18. Hazel Washington, "This Is Hollywood," *Chicago Defender*, January 8, 1958, 17.

19. Althea Gibson, "I Wanted to Be Somebody," *Reader's Digest*, December 1958, 68–80; "Althea Tells of Rise from Slums," *Atlanta Daily World*, November 6, 1958, 1; Althea Gibson, *I Always Wanted to Be Somebody*, ed. Ed Fitzgerald (New York: Harper and Row, 1958), 62.

20. Gibson, *I Always Wanted to Be Somebody*, 157–158.

21. Arnold Rampersad, *Jackie Robinson, a Biography* (New York: Alfred A. Knopf, 1997), 272–278; Gibson, *I Always Wanted to Be Somebody*, 158.

22. Gibson, *I Always Wanted to Be Somebody*, 158, 159. On homophobia, heteronormativity, and Althea's evolving image in the Black media, see Ashley Brown, "'Uncomplimentary Things': Tennis Player Althea Gibson, Sexism, Homophobia, and Anti-Queerness in the Black Media," *Journal of African American History* 106, no. 2 (Spring 2021): 249–277.

23. Gibson, *I Always Wanted to Be Somebody*, 159, 160.

24. Allison Danzig, "Off the Court There Were Victories Too," *New York Times*, December 7, 1958, BR3.

25. Robert E. Lee Baker, "Race Relations' Brighter Side," *Washington Post and Times Herald*, December 21, 1958, E6.

26. Review of *I Always Wanted to Be Somebody*, *Kirkus Reviews*, November 26, 1958.

27. "Althea Commits a 'Foot Fault,'" editorial, *Call and Post* (Cleveland, OH), November 15, 1958, 2D.

28. Sam Lacy, "Sam Lacy's A to Z," *Baltimore Afro-American*, November 22, 1958, 13.

29. Screenplay, *The Horse Soldiers*, 35, 36, 54, 114, 70, Box 6, Folder 34: Scripts and Production Materials, John Ford Collection, Lilly Library, Indiana University, Bloomington (hereafter "Screenplay, *The Horse Soldiers*").

30. Screenplay, *The Horse Soldiers*, 62.

31. Screenplay, *The Horse Soldiers*, 73, 72; Micki McElya, *Clinging to Mammy: The Faithful Slave in Twentieth-Century America* (Cambridge, MA: Harvard University Press, 2007).

32. Gibson, "How I Feel About Being 'On Stage.'"

33. Gibson, *So Much to Live For*, 36; Marion E. Jackson, "Sports of the World," *Atlanta Daily World*, November 6, 1958, 5.

34. Gibson, "How I Feel About Being 'On Stage'"; Gibson, *So Much to Live For*, 35, 36.

35. Gibson, "How I Feel About Being 'On Stage.'"

36. Robert Gooding-Williams, *Look, A Negro! Philosophical Essays on Race, Culture, and Politics* (New York: Routledge, 2004), 17–34.

37. Gibson, *So Much to Live For*, 36–37; "Althea's Film Debut," *Ebony*, July 1958, 73, 74.

38. On the mammy archetype, see Bogle, *Toms, Coons, Mulattoes, Mammies, and Bucks*, 6–7.

39. "Althea's Film Debut"; "Credit Where Credit's Due," *California Eagle*, June 18, 1959, 10; "Movie of the Week," *Jet*, July 2, 1959, 65; Hedda Hopper, "Doris Day Stars in 'Who Is Sylvia?,'" *Los Angeles Times*, December 10, 1958, C10.

40. Gibson, "How I Feel About Being 'On Stage.'"

41. "Playboy Interview: John Wayne," *Playboy*, May 1971, 80–82, 84.

42. Gibson, *So Much to Live For*, 39.

43. Neil Lanctot, *Campy: The Two Lives of Roy Campanella* (New York: 2011), 106; Jesse H. Walker, "About People and Things," *New York Amsterdam News*, January 24, 1959, 9; "Tennis Champ," *New York Age*, January 24, 1959, 9; Associated Press, "Althea No Surprise as Woman of the Year," *Miami News*, December 26, 1958, 11; "Versatile Althea," *Jet*, February 12, 1959, 37; Gibson, *So Much to Live For*, 61.

44. Stanley Nelson to Dr. Eaton, February 2, 1959, Eaton Papers.

45. R. Burke to James A. Donovan Jr., Outgoing Airgram, December 29, 1958, NA, RG 511.203/12-2958; Hare to Secretary of State, Cairo, Incoming Telegram, January 30, 1958, NA, RG 032 Gibson, Althea/1-3058.

46. Phifer P. Rothman to American Embassy, Caracas, Venezuela, Foreign Service Despatch, September 15, 1958, NA, RG 511.313/9-1558; "The Day Venezuela Attacked Nixon," Association for Diplomatic Studies and Training, May 6, 2013, https://adst.org/2013/05/the-day-venezuelans-attacked-nixon; Hewson A. Ryan

to State Department, Washington, DC, Foreign Service Despatch, March 13, 1959, NA, RG 032 Gibson, Althea/3-1359.

47. "Talk by Althea Gibson," March 1959, Sound Recording, NA, 306-ENTT-2367. The recording is undated. The *Washington Post* article about Gibson's talk to State Department staff says only that she visited "the other day." See George Minot, "Althea May Defend Her Wimbledon Title," *Washington Post and Times Herald*, March 15, 1959, C6.

48. Ryan to State Department, Despatch, March 13, 1959.

49. "Talk by Althea Gibson."

50. Bob Addie, "Bob Addie's Column," *Washington Post and Times Herald*, September 10, 1958, D2.

51. Addie, "Bob Addie's Column"; "Doris Hart Returns as Tennis Pro Here," *Miami News*, November 6, 1956, 12A; Steve Snider, United Press International, "Anderson Loses in Five Sets," *Washington Post and Times Herald*, September 8, 1958, A16.

52. George Minot, "Olmedo Charms His Fans at Peruvian Embassy," *Washington Post and Times Herald*, April 12, 1959, C2; "Talk by Althea Gibson."

53. Gloria Pritchard, "Payola Made Record Falter, Althea Says," *Pittsburgh Courier*, January 23, 1960, 12.

54. *Person to Person*, featuring Edward R. Murrow, aired April 3, 1959, on CBS.

55. John A. Malone to Henry Lee Moon, August 13, 20, and 22, 1958, Papers of the NAACP, Part 24, Special Subjects 1956–1965, General Office File, and Mrs. I. J. K. Wells to Roy Wilkins, February 8, 1959, Papers of the NAACP, Part 24, Special Subjects 1956–1965, General Office File, Microfilm, Reel 29, both in Lauinger Library, Georgetown University.

56. Art Peters, "NAACP Lauds Althea Gibson as Credit to Race and Nation," *Philadelphia Tribune*, May 5, 1959, 1, 3.

57. "Film Review: *The Horse Soldiers*," *Variety*, June 12, 1959, 3.

58. Harry Levette, Associated Negro Press, "Althea Gibson in Hollywood Debut," *Atlanta Daily World*, June 25, 1959, 5; Levette, "Althea Gibson as Natural on Screen as Tennis Court," *Chicago Defender*, June 20, 1959, 18.

59. Levette, "Althea Gibson as Natural on Screen as Tennis Court"; Levette, "Althea Gibson in Hollywood Debut."

60. Jimmie Meyers, "Meyers' Mill," *California Eagle*, June 18, 1959, 9; *The Horse Soldiers*, Pressbook No. 10, Page 12, Walter Mirisch Papers, Box 17, Volume 10, Wisconsin Historical Society Archives, Wisconsin Center for Film and Theater Research, University of Wisconsin, Madison.

61. "Dixie Accepts, Hails First Althea Gibson Pix 'Horse Soldiers,'" *Chicago Defender*, June 25, 1958, 22.

62. George Minot, "1,400 See Richardson, Gibson Win Exhibition Matches Here," *Washington Post and Times Herald*, June 15, 1959, A16.

63. "Althea Denies Offer," *Leicester Evening Mail*, June 17, 1959, 16; Bruce Schoenfeld, *The Match: Althea Gibson and Angela Buxton: How Two Outsiders—One Black, the*

Other Jewish—Forged a Friendship and Made Sports History (New York: Amistad Press, 2004), 260, 261; "From Harlem to Wimbledon," *Leicester Evening Mail*, June 13, 1959, 14; "Brazilian Girl Wins—and Cries," *Leicester Evening Mail*, July 4, 1959, 1; Harold Harris, "Althea Content to Let Honour Go," *Evening Express* (Aberdeen), June 20, 1959, 4.

64. Philip Benjamin, "Color Line Bars Bunche and Son from Forest Hills Tennis Club," *New York Times*, July 9, 1959, 1, 15; Philip Benjamin, "Protestants Hit Tennis Club Bias," *New York Times*, July 12, 1959, 62. On race and the founding of country clubs, see Richard J. Moss, *Golf and the American Country Club* (Urbana: University of Illinois Press, 2001), 5–19.

65. Benjamin, "Color Line Bars Bunche and Son from Forest Hills Tennis Club."

66. Schoenfeld, *The Match*, 259–260; United Press International, "Club Under Fire, Bars Bunche Jr.," *Chicago Defender*, July 18, 1959, 1; Associated Press, "Althea Gibson Annoyed," *New York Times*, July 10, 1959, 13.

67. Philip Benjamin, "Stark Acts to Force Forest Hills to Drop Bias of Cup Matches," *New York Times*, July 11, 1959, 8; United Press International, "Ex-Tennis Club Leader Denies Racial Barrier," *Chicago Daily Defender*, July 13, 1959, 24; United Press International, "Althea Gibson," *Chicago Daily Defender*, July 13, 1959, 24.

68. Bertram L. Baker to Althea Gibson, August 8, 1959, printed in Executive Meeting Minutes for 1959, 15, Eaton Papers.

69. Sam Lacy, "Can Althea Play at Forest Hills? Many Answer 'No,'" *Baltimore Afro-American*, July 18, 1959, 13.

70. Ed Fitzgerald, "Round Table Discussion: The Negro in American Sport," *Sport*, March 1960, 30.

71. "Statements on the West Side 'Incident,'" *Pittsburgh Courier*, July 18, 1959, 8.

72. Fitzgerald, "Round Table Discussion," 30.

73. "Althea Pops Off," *Call and Post*, July 25, 1959, 1C; Alice A. Dunnigan, "Althea in Focus Due to Controversial Statement," *New York Amsterdam News*, July 25, 1959; James L. Hicks, "Another Angle: Althea Gibson," *New York Amsterdam News*, July 18, 1959, 10.

74. Chippey quoted in Lacy, "Can Althea Play at Forest Hills?"

75. Jimmy Booker, "Uptown Lowdown: Top Draw Stuff," *Amsterdam News*, July 18, 1959, 11.

76. Darcy DeMille, Associated Negro Press, "Columnist Hails Althea Gibson's Acting in 'Horse Soldiers,'" *Philadelphia Tribune*, July 21, 1959, 8.

77. P. L. Prattis, "Horizon: Althea Gibson," *Pittsburgh Courier*, August 8, 1959.

78. Sam Lacy, "Diahann Toasts Parents at Champagne Party," *Baltimore Afro-American*, July 25, 1959, 15; Lacy, "A to Z: Sports by the Afro," *Baltimore Afro-American*, July 25, 1959, 13.

79. Robert J. H. Johnston, "N.A.A.C.P. Scores Carolina Leader," *New York Times*, July 18, 1959, 5.

80. United Press International, "New Yorker Wins ATA Title," *Chicago Daily Defender*, August 24, 1959, 24; A. S. "Doc" Young, "The Big Beat: Dashing Along the Dotted Line," *Los Angeles Sentinel*, September 10, 1959, C1; Althea Gibson to Robert (Bob) Solomon, September 22, 1959, author's personal collection.

81. *The Ed Sullivan Show*, CBS, air date August 23, 1959.

82. Gibson, "How I Feel About Being 'On Stage.' "

83. Gibson, *So Much to Live For*, 41; Ed Sullivan, "Little Old New York," *New York Daily News*, August 2, 1959, 14; "Althea Defended by U.S. Official in Tennis Dispute," *Jet*, September 24, 1959, 57; "Miss Gibson Returning to Tennis Competition," New York Times, August 6, 1959, 24.

84. Joseph M. Sheehan, Associated Press, "Althea Gibson Wins Pan-American Games Tennis Final," *New York Times*, September 4, 1959, 18.

85. Associated Press, "Althea to Turn Pro, Start New All-Female Tour," *Los Angeles Times*, September 9, 1959, C2; "Pro Tennis Tour by Women Looms," *New York Times*, September 10, 1959, 45; Bob Addie, "Bob Addie's Column," *Washington Post and Times Herald*, September 13, 1959, C13; Ted Smits, Associated Press, "O'Brien Sets Games Shot Put Mark," *Washington Post and Times Herald*, September 2, 1959, C5.

86. "Althea Would Turn Pro If She Got Good Offer," *Philadelphia Tribune*, September 1, 1959, 11.

87. Jeane Hoffman, "Althea Gambling on New Career to Provide 'Potatoes on Table,' " *Los Angeles Times*, January 9, 1959, C3.

88. Gibson, *So Much to Live For*, 15.

89. "What Winning at Tennis Cost Althea Gibson," *Jet*, August 7, 1958, 56–57; Allen M. Hornblum, *American Colossus: Big Bill Tilden and the Creation of Modern Tennis* (Lincoln: University of Nebraska Press, 2018), 215.

90. Associated Press, "Miss Gibson Faces Rebuke on Pro Talk," *New York Times*, September 6, 1959, 10S; "Althea Defended by U.S. Official in Tennis Dispute," *Jet*, September 24, 1959, 57.

91. "No Sympathy for Althea," *Chicago Daily Defender*, September 2, 1959, 22.

92. Allison Danzig, "Olmedo, Laver and Buchholz Capture First-Round Matches in U.S. Tennis," *New York Times*, September 5, 1959, 9; Sam Lacy, "A to Z," *Baltimore Afro-American*, November 21, 1959, 13; Associated Press, "Miss Gibson Faces Rebuke on Pro Talk."

93. "Golden Girls," *Journal and Guide* (Norfolk, VA), October 24, 1959, 1; "Miss Gibson to Go on Tour as a Pro," *New York Times*, October 17, 1959, 20; "Althea Gibson Signs Pro Contract for Nearly $100,000," *New York Times*, October 20, 1959, 52; United Press International, "$100 G's Pot for Althea!," *Chicago Daily Defender*, October 20, 1959, 24.

94. Buck Francis, "Buckin' the Line: Karol Not in Althea's Class," *Corpus Christi Times*, November 21, 1959, B1.

95. Gibson, *So Much to Live For*, 52–53; John Meyer, "Gyms Not Ideal, but Net Stars Are Happy," *Gazette* (Cedar Rapids, IA), November 30, 1959, 22; Max Stultz, "Vaudeville Not Dead, Just Seriously Ill," *Indianapolis Star*, December 7, 1959, 33; Frank Dolson, "Time Out: Girls' Tennis on the Goober Circuit," *Philadelphia Inquirer*, March 24, 1960, 41.

96. William "Sheep" Jackson, "Althea Gibson Finds Pro Tennis 'Grand,'" *Call and Post*, December 12, 1959, 6A.

97. Francis, "Buckin' the Line"; "Tennis Champ Althea Gibson, Karol Fageros Carded Here," *Standard-Sentinel* (Hazelton, PA), November 20, 1959, 45.

98. Jackson, "Althea Gibson Finds Pro Tennis 'Grand.'"

99. "Good Luck, Al!," editorial, *Amsterdam News*, October 24, 1959, 10.

100. Rube Samuelson, "Rube-Barbs: The Offices," *Los Angeles Evening Citizen News*, November 9, 1959, 15.

101. Sam Lacy, "A to Z," *Baltimore Afro-American*, October 31, 1959, 13.

102. Gibson, *So Much to Live For*, 51, 69; Will Grimsley, Associated Press, "Top Tennis Women Set World Tour," *Washington Post and Times Herald*, October 17, 1959, A13; John Crittenden, "Salary Less for Karol, So's Misery" *Miami News*, June 25, 1961, 3C.

103. Gibson, *So Much to Live For*, 58; "Althea Sees Tennis Salvation in Open Tennis," *Minneapolis Morning Tribune*, February 22, 1960, 27.

104. Dan Burley, "Did Patterson Turn Down Louis as Pilot?," *Chicago Defender*, September 22, 1959, 26.

105. "Abe Saperstein's Fabulous Harlem Globetrotters," advertisement, *Cincinnati Inquirer*, November 26, 1959, 3-G; Wilbur Adams, "Yes, Karol Will Wear Her Gold Panties Tomorrow," *Sacramento Bee,* January 18, 1960, D2; Pat Harris, "Pace on Court Leads to Fatigue for Star," *Arizona Daily Star*, February 14, 1960, 2C; Associated Negro Press, "Althea Gibson Beats Man in Tennis Battle," *Los Angeles Sentinel*, February 25, 1960, B-9.

106. Jack Man, "One Man's Opinion: 'Sesquipedalian' Is the Word for Karol," *Newsday*, May 13, 1960, 21C.

107. Jeane Hoffman, "Althea Gibson Envisions Lucrative Pro Career if Amateurs Hold Out," *Los Angeles Times*, February 3, 1960, C5; Mary Frazer, "Victory Duo . . . On and Off Court," *Examiner*, January 28, 1960, Sec. II, 4; Gibson, *So Much to Live For*, 60.

108. Jane Hines, "Pro Tennis Gals Prefer Business, First, Last and Always—Social Life Is Just Out," *Lincoln Journal Star*, November 26, 1959, 25.

109. George Beahon, "In This Corner: Tennis Anyone?," *Rochester Democrat and Chronicle*, March 28, 1960, 22; "Gibson-Fageros Net Duels Make Big Hit with Fans," *Salisbury Times*, November 26, 1959, 42.

110. David Condon, "In the Wake of the News," *Chicago Tribune*, November 16, 1959, Part IV, 1.

111. Gibson, *So Much to Live For*, 58; "Court Queens Fresh Despite Tour Rigor," *Morning Call* (Allentown, PA), March 22, 1960; Dolson, "Time Out."

112. Gibson, *So Much to Live For*, 58; "Court Queens Fresh Despite Tour Rigor."

113. "Althea Gibson Tours State," *Cushing Citizen*, November 19, 1959, 5; "Tennis, Cage Comedy Entertains Slim Crowd," *Times Herald* (Port Huron, MI), November 27, 1960, Sec. 3, 1.

114. Francis, "Buckin' the Line."

115. "In Person: Harlem Globetrotters . . . and Professional Tennis," advertisement, *Miami Herald*, February 3, 1960, 8-C. While tracking newspaper coverage of the tour, I uncovered no evidence to corroborate Gibson's assertion on page 58 of *So Much to Live For* that the troupe "hit the Deep South" between jaunts in the Southwest and the East. What is more, one writer expressly remarked that she and Fageros did not join the Globetrotters on the team's southern swing. See Raymond Johnson, "One Man's Opinion: Globetrotters Returning to Nashville Next Week," *Tennessean*, March 2, 1960, 18.

116. Gibson, *So Much to Live For*, 58; Cal Jacox, "Althea Balks at Va. Seating Bias," *Journal and Guide*, December 26, 1959, 2–1.

117. Prescott Sullivan, "The Lowdown: Some Things You Should Know About Gold Panties," *Examiner*, January 27, 1960, Sec. IV, 5.

118. Myrna Odell, "Is There a Difference: Status Seeker or Social Climber," *Miami News*, June 4, 1961, 6D; Adams, "Yes, Karol Will Wear Her Gold Panties Tomorrow"; Sullivan, "The Lowdown."

119. Donna Gehrke, "Cancer Society's Shining Star: Afflicted Former Tennis Champ 'Doesn't Have Time to Die,'" *Miami News*, January 14, 1988, 10A; Frazer, "Victory Duo . . . On and Off Court."

120. Jacox, "Althea Balks at Va. Seating Bias."

121. Jacox, "Althea Balks at Va. Seating Bias."

122. Associated Press, "Althea Gibson Is Ruffled at Segregation of Fans," *Courier-Journal* (Louisville, KY), December 21, 1959, 15.

123. "Tennis Clinic Shifted Today," *Examiner*, January 23, 1960, Sec. 2, 3; Paul Lippman, "Althea Is a Real Champ with Kids," *Examiner*, January 24, 1960, Sec. 3, Page 7.

124. Amira Rose Davis, "No League of Their Own: Baseball, Black Women, and the Politics of Representation," *Radical History Review* 125 (May 2016): 74–96; Gibson, *So Much to Live For*, 61.

125. "The Week's Best Photos: Time Out," *Jet*, January 28, 1960, 31; Tony Cordaro, "4,900 Fans See Trotters, Althea Win," *Des Moines Register*, November 27, 1959, 13; Ike Skynook, "Karol Fageros Yearns for Rest, Heaps Praise on Althea Gibson," *Rochester Democrat and Chronicle*, March 30, 1960, 25; Sec Taylor, "Sittin' in with the Athletes: Aggressiveness Pays," *Des Moines Register*, December 7, 1959, 21.

126. Harris, "Pace on Court Leads to Fatigue for Star."

127. Jackson, "Althea Gibson Finds Pro Tennis 'Grand.'"

128. Frazer, "Victory Duo . . . On and Off Court."

129. Harris, "Pace on Court Leads to Fatigue for Star."

130. "Althea Gibson Signs Up with Tip Top Bread," *New York Amsterdam News*, March 12, 1960, 2; Aaron Bobrow-Strain, *White Bread: A Social History of the Store-Bought Loaf* (Boston: Beacon Press, 2012), 64–66, 93–97; "It's Tender . . . Delicious . . . the Finest Bread Baked!," advertisement, *New York Amsterdam News*, October 23, 1943, 8; "At Home with Jackie Robinson," advertisement, *Journal and Guide*, August 14, 1948, 10; Masco Young, "The Grapevine: The Rumors," *Pittsburgh Courier*, March 26, 1960, 22; Rampersad, *Jackie Robinson*, 304–305; Gibson, *So Much to Live For*, 86; Brenna Wynn Greer, *Represented: The Black Imagemakers Who Reimagined African American Citizenship* (Philadelphia: University of Pennsylvania Press, 2019).

131. Althea Gibson, "Ward Baking Company Welcome Speech," March 9, 1960, Chicago,, Gibson Collection; Don Felder, interview by author, August 30, 2021.

132. "Tennis Ace Althea Gibson Enters Community Relations Field," *Chicago Defender*, March 19, 1960, 13; "Althea Signs Up with Tip-Top Bread," *New York Amsterdam News*, March 12, 1960, 2; Gibson, "Ward Baking Company Welcome Speech."

133. "Courier-WAMO Home-A-Rama Promises to Be the 'Greatest,'" *Pittsburgh Courier*, April 30, 1960, 9; "*Chicago Defender* 1960 Home Show," advertisement, *Chicago Defender*, September 26, 1960, 8.

134. "Special Issue—The Negro in American Sport," *Sport*, March 1960, cover.

135. "Olmedo and Gibson Win World Pro Titles at Cleveland," *World Tennis*, July 1960, 27.

136. Byron Roberts, "Tennis Pros Begin Tournament Tonight," *Washington Post*, May 27, 1960, D1; Gibson, *So Much to Live For*, 74; Allison Danzig, "Stars to Coach Tennis Clinics," *New York Times*, May 5, 1960, L46.

137. Schoenfeld, *The Match*, 261–262; Richard Evans, "Hooked at Hello: How Shadowing Althea Gibson Changed One Writer's Life," *Tennis*, September 11, 2019.

138. For "London Letter," see "Net Star Reports on Wimbledon Tourney," *Chicago Daily Defender*, June 20, 1960, 22; "Althea Gibson Reports," *New York Amsterdam News*, July 2, 1960, 27; "Althea Reports Arrival at Wimbledon Tourney," *Chicago Daily Defender*, July 9, 1960, 24; "Althea Gibson Reports," *New York Amsterdam News*, July 16, 1960, 26. Also, Frazer, "Victory Duo . . . On and Off Court."

139. Althea Gibson, "Persistence: A Form of Faith," *Guideposts*, August 1960, 14.

140. For "Latin American Letter," see *New York Amsterdam News*, October 15, 1960, 29; October 22, 1960, 26; and November 5, 1960, 28.

141. Gibson, *So Much to Live For*, 74–76.

142. Gibson, *So Much to Live For*, 76; Roberts, "Tennis Pros Begin Tournament Tonight"; Byron Roberts, "Althea Gibson Gets into the Act of 'Perils of Pauline,'"

Washington Post, May 22, 1960, C8; Ernest C. Downing Jr., "Ashe, Karanek Win Men's Women's ATA Singles Net Titles," *Journal and Guide*, August 27, 1960, 17.

143. Gibson, *So Much to Live For*, 77, 76.

144. Letters to the editor from J.H. and Billy Melton, *Sport*, June 1960, 14.

145. Dan G. White, *A Collector's Guide to Signature and Photo Decal Wood Tennis Rackets* (Palm City, FL: Dan G. White, 2020); "The Bat," advertisement, *World Tennis*, July 1960, 35.

146. ACNS, "Begin Hearings on Half Million Tip Top Lawsuit: Bread Company Being Sued by Publicity Firm," *Philadelphia Tribune*, August 9, 1960, 3.

147. Gibson, *So Much to Live For*, 93.

148. "Althea Say It Isn't So!," *Los Angeles Sentinel*, October 20, 1960, B9.

149. Gibson, *So Much to Live For*, 44; Julia Blackburn, *With Billie: A New Look at the Unforgettable Lady Day* (New York: Pantheon, 2006), 286, 283. On Kennedy's relationship with Holiday and McKay, see Sherie M. Randolph, *Florynce "Flo" Kennedy: The Life of a Black Feminist Radical* (Chapel Hill: University of North Carolina Press, 2015), 64–66, 72, 73.

150. William "Sheep" Jackson, "Althea Finds Dough Promoting Baking Co.," *Call and Post*, March 19, 1960, 6C.

151. "Gibson-Fageros Net Duels Make Big Hit with Fans," *Salisbury Times*, November 26, 1959, 42; Gibson, *So Much to Live For*, 71; "Gibson, Fageros to Be Here Oct. 31, Along with Cage Game," *Decatur Herald*, October 16, 1960, 16.

152. Gibson, *So Much to Live For*, 78; "Tennis, Cage Comedy Entertains Slim Crowd," *Port Huron Times Herald*, November 27, 1960, Sec. 3, Page 1; "Tiny Crowd Sees Gibson Triumph," *Moline Dispatch*, November 14, 1960, 20.

153. "Basketball, Net Combo Here Again," *Dayton Daily News*, November 25, 1960, 20; "The Althea Gibson–Harlem Ambassadors Super Colossal Show for 1960–1961," advertisement, *Messenger-Inquirer* (Owensboro, KY), October 20, 1960, 10.

154. Lou Younkin, "Althea Gibson Wins Exhibition," *Decatur* (IL) *Review*, November 1, 1960, 14; Tony Chamblin, "Karol's Glamour Can't Match Althea's Skill," *Decatur* (IL) *Herald*, November 1, 1960, 13.

155. Paul Carlson, "Sports Seen," *Moline Dispatch*, November 15, 1960, 18; Gibson, *So Much to Live For*, 78.

156. "Gibson Tour Off in Four Maine Cities," *Bangor Daily News*, December 1, 1960, 30.

157. Jamie Jobb, "Fageros' Golden Tennis Bought Only Loneliness," *Miami Herald*, April 18, 1966, 4-D; Gwen Harrison, "Retired Racquet," *Miami Herald*, December 20, 1960, 4-D; Crittenden, "Salary Less for Karol, So's Misery"; "Teaching Racquet Karol's Ambition," *Miami Herald*, June 25, 1961, 3-D.

158. Bob Fallstrom, "Once Over Lightly: Some Decatur Views on the State of U.S. Amateur Tennis," *Decatur Herald*, January 6, 1961, 15; Gibson, *So Much to Live For*, 79.

CHAPTER 12

1. "Althea Sees Tennis Salvation in Open Tennis," *Minneapolis Morning Tribune*, February 22, 1960, 27.

2. Charles Johnson, "Charles Johnson's Lowdown on Sports: One Fling Enough," *Minneapolis Star*, February 19, 1961, 10B; Greg Ruth, *Tennis: A History from American Amateurs to Global Professionals* (Urbana: University of Illinois Press, 2021), 169; obituary, Robert E. Darben, *Montclair Times*, June 5, 1958, 19.

3. Associated Negro Press, "Althea Gibson to Marry Childhood Sweetie," *New York Amsterdam News*, December 31, 1960, 1, 27.

4. Associated Negro Press, "Althea Gibson to Marry Childhood Sweetie."

5. "Althea's Marriage Is Off!," *New York Amsterdam News*, April 1, 1961, 1.

6. Althea Gibson with Richard J. Curtis, *So Much to Live For* (New York: G. P. Putnam's Sons, 1968), 69–70; "'Still No Wedding'—Althea," *Pittsburgh Courier*, April 15, 1961.

7. Art Peters, "Off the Main Stem," *Philadelphia Tribune*, April 15, 1961, 5.

8. "Althea Gibson Aims Sights for Golf . . . Ward's Bread," *Pittsburgh Courier*, April 22, 1961, 14.

9. "Miss Gibson Turns Golfer," *Valley Times*, March 6, 1961, 10; Pete Kokon, "Pete Kokon's Column: Guth Stars for Brubabes," *Valley Times*, March 9, 1961, 11; "Netter Turns Golfer," *Valley Times*, March 18, 1961, 29.

10. Gibson, *So Much to Live For* 97, 98; Ann Simer, "Althea's After a New Kind of Record," *Corpus Christi Caller-Times*, October 26, 1969, 1.

11. Ann Barling, "Former Tennis Champ Is Still a Swinger," *Vancouver Sun*, September 8, 1969, 28.

12. Althea Gibson, "The Role of the Sportswoman"/"The Role of the Female Athlete"/"The Sportswoman's Role in Society," 3 (lecture, n.d. but after 1973), Gibson Collection.

13. "Althea: 'Golf? No Sense Just Hitting That Ball,'" *Minneapolis Star*, January 24, 1958, 9B.

14. Ken Small, "Marilynn Smith Leads as Althea Closes Golf Gap," *Miami Herald*, March 28, 1964, 4-E.

15. Chuck Smith, "Rattlers Get Three Firsts at Carnival," *Tallahassee Democrat*, May 6, 1951, 10; Dave Condon, "In the Wake of the News," *Chicago Tribune*, July 24, 1964, 3.1; Small, "Marilynn Smith Leads as Althea Closes Golf Gap"; Associated Negro Press, "Althea Might Try Golf Next," *Philadelphia Tribune*, September 23, 1958, 10.

16. Wilbert E. Hemming, "Fla. A&M University Faculty, Classmates Salute Miss Gibson," *Philadelphia Tribune*, July 16, 1957.

17. M. Mikell Johnson, *The African American Woman Golfer* (Westport, CT: Praeger, CT, 2008), 120–121; Lane Demas, *Game of Privilege: An African American History of Golf* (Chapel Hill: University of North Carolina Press, 2017), 85–87, 135; Associated Press, "Reluctant Althea Gibson Signs Pro Golf Contract," *Charlotte*

Observer, December 13, 1963, 7-C; United Press International, "Gibson Girl Pushes Search for Golf Title," *Miami Herald*, April 16, 1966, 5-C.

18. Associated Negro Press, "Althea Might Try Golf Next."

19. Sam Lacy, "A to Z," *Baltimore Afro-American*, November 14, 1959, 13; Ed Fitzgerald, ed., "Round Table Discussion: The Negro in American Sport," *Sport*, March 1960, 30.

20. Demas, *Game of Privilege*, 116, 210.

21. Demas, *Game of Privilege*, 85–87, 135; George B. Kirsch, *Golf in America* (Urbana: University of Illinois Press, 2009), 160.

22. Kirsch, *Golf in America*, 161–162; Charlie Sifford, *Just Let Me Play: The Story of Charlie Sifford, the First Black PGA Golfer* (Latham, NY: British American, 1992), 97–101, 106; Demas, *Game of Privilege*, 90, 212, 213.

23. Rhonda Glenn, *The Illustrated History of Women's Golf* (Dallas, TX: Taylor, 1991), 149, 159; Kirsch, *Golf in America*, 170–171; Demas, *Game of Privilege*, 97, 98, 114, 99.

24. Demas, *Game of Privilege*, 90–91, 104–105; Pete McDaniel, *Uneven Lies: The Heroic Story of African-Americans in Golf* (Greenwich, CT: American Golfer, 2000), 73. Gregory won the UGA national title a total of five times. Her last two victories came in 1965 and 1966. Funches won the title seven times, taking her last in 1973.

25. Peter F. Stevens, *Links Lore: Dramatic Moments and Neglected Milestones from Golf's History* (Dulles, VA: Brassey's, 2000), 72–81; Glenn, *The Illustrated History of Women's Golf*, 213–214.

26. On course conditions as barriers for Gregory and other Black golfers, see McDaniel, *Uneven Lies*, 71; Tommy Fitzgerald, "Family's First for Ann Gregory," *Miami News*, February 18, 1965, 3B.

27. Gibson, *So Much to Live For*, 108.

28. Demas, *Game of Privilege*, 141–187; Kirsch, *Golf in America*, 151–156; "New York Link Clip Biased Tourneys," *Pittsburgh Courier*, July 9, 1960; Associated Negro Press, "Connecticut Club Bars Negro Golfers," *Philadelphia Tribune*, July 4, 1961; Associated Negro Press, "Golf Meet Bars Denver Judge," *Baltimore Afro-American*, August 19, 1961; Jack Cavanaugh, "Remember Jackie Robinson, the Golfer," *New York Times*, April 27, 1997; Robinson quoted in Fitzgerald, ed., "Round Table Discussion: The Negro in American Sport," 30.

29. William J. Briordy, "Tennis Sessions Start Monday," *New York Times*, May 3, 1961, 47; "Arriving at Nassau," *Desert Sun*, June 26, 1961, 5; "And Still Champ," *Jet*, August 31, 1961, 59; Richard Evans, "Hooked at Hello: How Shadowing Althea Gibson Changed One Writer's Life," *Tennis*, September 11, 2019; AP, "Althea Gibson Would Put Tennis Courts on Roofs in Cities," *Fort Meyers News Press* (Florida), May 4, 1961, B1.

30. Gibson, *So Much to Live For*, 111.

31. Bob Maisel, "Morning After," *Baltimore Sun*, May 10, 1963, 17, 10; Associated Press, "Althea Gibson Points at Following Babe Zaharias' Example on Links," *Tucson Daily Citizen*, March 7, 1962, 37; Jerry Waggoner, "Former Tennis Champ

Now Seeks Golf Laurels," *Amarillo Globe Times*, November 3, 1966, 13, 14; Coult Aubrey, "Tennis Queen Althea Gibson Soon May Be Golf Princess," *Morning Call* (Allentown, PA), October 9, 1961, 14; "Netter Turns Golfer"; Associated Press, "Althea Gibson May Try Golf," *Tallahassee Democrat*, June 23, 1961, 15.

32. "The American Tennis Association: Roll of Champions," 2019, Museum of the International Tennis Hall of Fame and Museum, Newport, RI, 9, author's personal collection; Orlanda G. Rodman Sr., "Althea Gibson Thrills 'Em at ATA Tennis Tournament," *Indianapolis Recorder*, August 29, 1959, 11; Tournament Program, A.T.A. Junior Championships, August 8–13, 1960, 19, 26, Eaton Papers.

33. Tournament Program, A.T.A. Junior Championships, August 8–13, 1960, 47; "Contributors," Tournament Program, ATA National Championships Intercollegiate for 1961, n.p., Eaton Papers.

34. "Althea Switches Over to Golf, Wins," *Chicago Daily Defender*, August 7, 1961, 22; Neil Singelais, "Her Golf Fizzles in Drizzle, Althea Learns Key Lesson," *Boston Globe*, August 22, 1961, 41.

35. Singelais, "Her Golf Fizzles in Drizzle, Althea Learns Key Lesson"; Associated Press, "New England Sports Briefs," *Barre Times Argus*, August 22, 1961, 7; Associated Press, "Althea Gibson Faces Ethel Funches Today," *Bennington Evening Banner*, August 23, 1961, 12; "Althea Beaten in UGA Golf," *Baltimore Afro-American*, September 2, 1961, 14; Associated Press, "New England Sports in Brief," *North Adams Transcript*, August 26, 1961, 9.

36. "Golf Drives for Charity," *Chicago Daily Defender*, September 30, 1961; "Golf Talk," *Pittsburgh Courier*, September 30, 1961, sec. 2, 1.

37. Aubrey, "Tennis Queen Althea Gibson Soon May Be Golf Princess"; Arthur Siegel, "Chevalier, Sox Near Contract—'For Right Bonus,'" *Boston Globe*, August 22, 1961, 41.

38. Kirsch, *Golf in America*, 162.

39. United Press International, "Gibson Girl Pushes Search for Golf Title," *Miami Herald*, April 16, 1966, 5-C; "They Did It Up Real Brown in North-South Golf Meet," *Miami News*, February 24, 1962, 1B; Associated Press, "Althea Gibson Points at Following Babe Zaharias' Example on Links"; Don Bryant, "Althea Wants to Be History's Best Gal Golfer," *Lincoln Star*, March 16, 1962, 23.

40. "Tennis Champ Gibson to Speak at Center," *Lincoln Journal Star*, March 9, 1962, 11; Marilou Topa, "Tennis Challenges All Removed; Althea Gibson to Take Up Golf," *Lincoln Journal Star*, March 16, 1962, 18; Bryant, "Althea Wants to Be History's Best Gal Golfer"; United Press International, "Tennis Great Althea Gibson Claims Cities Lack Courts," *Hastings Daily Tribune*, March 16, 1962, 9; Associated Press, "Althea Gibson Would Put Tennis Courts on Roofs in Cities," *News-Press* (Fort Myers, FL), May 4, 1961, B1.

41. Bryant, "Althea Wants to Be History's Best Gal Golfer."

42. Bryant, "Althea Wants to Be History's Best Gal Golfer."

43. "Like This, Gals," *Lincoln Star*, March 17, 1962, 16; Don Bryant, "Althea Is Big Hit at Coliseum," *Lincoln Star*, March 17, 1962, 15.

44. "Tennis Queen Attends," *Pittsburgh Courier*, March 14, 1964, 6; Stanley S. Scott, "Publishers Honor Noted Americans with Top Awards," *Alabama Tribune*, June 30, 1961, 1, 8; "Ground Breaking in D.C. for Bethune House Project," *Pittsburgh Courier*, June 22, 1963, 7; United Press International, "Tennessee Negroes Join Chicago Parade," *Knoxville News-Sentinel*, August 13, 1961, A-7; Edward Barry, "Vienna Comes Alive Again at Park Concert," *Chicago Tribune*, August 12, 1962, 35; "Tennis Help from Althea," *New York Daily News*, August 12, 1962, 5M; Mary Pakenham, "Sports and Fashions to Mark Negro Fair," *Chicago Tribune*, August 26, 1963, sec. 3, 11.

45. Topa, "Tennis Challenges All Removed."

46. "Net Star Says School Beats Any Glory Gained in Sports," *Hackensack Record*, October 11, 1962, 2.7.

47. Joe Calabrese, "Westfielders Hear Gibson," *Courier-News* (Bridgewater, NJ), March 14, 1963, 33.

48. Ron Powers, "Althea Turns from Drop Shots to Dropouts," *St. Louis Post-Dispatch*, July 1, 1964, 4C.

49. Television listings, "Special: *Speak for Yourself*," *Burlington Free Press*, November 30, 1963, 22.

50. Powers, "Althea Turns from Drop Shots to Dropouts."

51. "Net Star Says School Beats Any Glory Gained in Sports."

52. "Guido Fusco, Restaurateur in Financial District, 77," *New York Times*, September 28, 1964, 29; "Althea Gains Another First," Cleveland Call and Post, May 19, 1962, 6-C.

53. Gibson, *So Much to Live For*, 112, 111.

54. Gibson, *So Much to Live For*, 112.

55. Oscar Fraley, United Press International, "Today's Sport Parade," *Bristol Courier and Levittown Times*, January 11, 1963, 15; Ed Sullivan, "Little Old New York," New York *Daily News*, April 27, 1962, C14; Associated Press, "Althea Gibson Plans to Conquer Women Golfers; Amateur Her Goal," August 3, 1962, 18.

56. Gibson, *So Much to Live For*, 99.

57. Fraley, "Today's Sport Parade."

58. Tod Oliver, "Tennis Star Visits City, Judges Show," *South Bend Tribune*, June 2, 1962, 16; Randall Cassell, "Most Anything: Court to Links," *Baltimore Evening Sun*, June 22, 1962, B12; Hennie M. Cisco, "Links Cotillion, Golf Tourney in Chicago Spotlight," *Pittsburgh Courier*, July 14, 1962, 10; McDaniel, *Uneven Lies*, 85–89; F. M. Williams, "Former Tennis Great Althea Gibson Now Finds Golf Her Game," *Tennessean*, April 26, 1967, 28.

59. Associated Press, "Girl Opposes Her Mother in National," *Newsday*, August 28, 1962, 24C; Jim Karl, "'I Will Be Back,' Althea Promises," *Rochester Democrat*

and Chronicle, August 29, 1962, 32; Associated Press, "Mrs. Mason Tops Orcutt Record," *Record* (Hackensack, NJ), September 22, 1962, 10.

60. Bob Lenoir, "Welcome Back, Althea Gibson," *St. Petersburg Times*, February 15, 1978, 3C; Karl, "'I Will Be Back,' Althea Promises"; Associated Press, "Mrs. Mason Tops Orcutt Record"; Sam Adams, "Sam's Song: Althea to Tee It Up Here," *Tampa Bay Times*, January 20, 1963, 6-D.

61. Harris Williams, "Negro Golf Ace Sifford Wants to Play in Open," *Tampa Bay Times*, February 2, 1963, 1-C, 3-C; "Two Qualify for Golfing Tournament," *St. Petersburg Times*, March 14, 1963, 13-B; Harris Williams, "Tee Talk: What's with Watts?," *St. Petersburg Times*, February 22, 1963, 2-C.

62. Clayton Moore, "Golforama," *Los Angeles Sentinel*, February 11, 1960, B-9; Rick Pezdirtz, "The Golfing Beat: When Baseball Men Talk . . . It's Golf," *Miami News*, February 17, 1963, 4C; Jack Kofoed, "We're Really Turning Other Cheek to Reds," *Miami Herald*, February 19, 1963, 7-B; Eve Lynn Reynolds, "Eve Lynn and 'The Grand' Take in Golf Tournament," *Pittsburgh Courier*, March 9, 1963, 6; "The Historic Hampton House Hotel," Greater Miami Convention and Visitors Bureau, https://www.miamiandbeaches.com/things-to-do/history-and-heritage/the-historic-hampton-house-motel (accessed January 10, 2022).

63. Bob Monahan, "Tennis Champion Althea Gibson Turns Golf Champion," *Boston Globe*, July 7, 1963, 60.

64. Tom McEwan, "The Morning After: Candy's Doing Just Fine," *Tampa Tribune*, April 28, 1966, D-1; Burke Evans, "Golfers, Who's Althea Gibson?," *Waterloo Courier*, July 12, 1963, 11, 12.

65. Frank Littler, "The Unusual Life of a Woman Pro," *Golf Digest*, December 1964, 32; Dick Forbes, "Kenwood Is Praised," *Cincinnati Enquirer*, July 17, 1963, 19.

66. Jack Berry, "LPGA Growing Up," *Detroit Free Press*, July 26, 1963, 2-D.

67. Bob Monahan, "Golf's Best Gals in Carling's," *Boston Globe*, June 17, 1964, 46; "40 Gal Pros Set for Venice Open," *Tampa Tribune*, March 27, 1966, 6-D; Bill Beck, "Gal Golfers Find Travel Biggest Woe," *St. Louis Post-Dispatch*, August 18, 1968, 3E.

68. Littler, "The Unusual Life of a Woman Pro."

69. Susan E. Cayleff, *Babe: The Life and Legend of Babe Didrikson Zaharias* (Urbana: University of Illinois Press, 1995); Gene Gregston, "The Quiet Queen of Golf," *Golf Digest*, September 1963, 22.

70. John Ahern, "Althea the Answer? LPGA Needs Long Ball to Draw Big Galleries," *Boston Globe*, July 8, 1963, 27.

71. Englehorn, quoted in Ahern, "Althea the Answer?"

72. Jack Berry, "The 'New' Althea in Town," *Detroit Free Press*, July 25, 1963, 5-D.

73. Dave Lewis, "Once Over Lightly," *Long Beach Independent*, January 10, 1961, C2.

74. "Babe Zaharias," LPGA, https://www.lpga.com/players/babe-zaharias/82800/bio (accessed July 16, 2022); Associated Press, "Althea Gibson Points at Following Babe Zaharias' Example on Links," 37.

75. Oscar Fraley, United Press International, "Althea Gibson Has Goal: Top Woman Golfer in 4 Years," *Sacramento Bee*, December 15, 1962, B4.

76. Forbes, "Kenwood Is Praised."

77. Jim Schottelkotte, "New Game but Same Althea," *Cincinnati Enquirer*, July 19, 1963, 21.

78. Dick Forbes, "Southern Gals Lead Way in First Round of Open," *Cincinnati Enquirer*, July 19, 1963, 21; Earl Ruby, "Ruby's Report," *Courier Journal* (Louisville, KY), July 20, 1963, 2.5.

79. Berry, "The 'New' Althea in Town."

80. Vincent Harding, Robin D. G. Kelley, et al., "We Changed the World, 1945–1970," in *To Make Our World Anew, Volume II: A History of African Americans from 1880*, ed. Robin D. G. Kelley and Earl Lewis (New York: Oxford University Press, 2005), 225–232; "From: Time-Life Broadcast," John F. Kennedy Presidential Papers, White House Central Subject Files, Box 360, Folder 9, page 52, John F. Kennedy Presidential Library.

81. Al Monroe, "So They Say: Althea Gibson Hopes," *Chicago Defender*, May 22, 1963, 24.

82. "Real Pioneer," *Chicago Daily Defender*, August 15, 1963, 30.

83. Monroe, "So They Say: Althea Gibson in Victory."

84. Harding, Kelley, et al., "We Changed the World, 1945–1970," 233–234; Robert Walter Johnson III, interview by author, September 26, 2015; Pakenham, "Sports and Fashions to Mark Negro Fair."

85. Cal Jacox, "From the Press Box: From the Sidelines," *Journal and Guide* (Norfolk, VA), December 28, 1963, 12.

86. "Real Pioneer"; Monroe, "So They Say: Althea Gibson in Victory."

87. On Rudolph's career, fame, looks, and State Department travels, see Rita Liberti and Maureen M. Smith, *(Re)Presenting Wilma Rudolph* (Syracuse, NY: Syracuse University Press, 2015), 42–70. See also Cat M. Ariail, *Passing the Baton: Black Women Track Stars and American Identity* (Urbana: University of Illinois Press, 2020), 139–164; A. S. "Doc" Young, *Negro Firsts in Sports* (Chicago: Johnson, 1963), 197.

88. "Althea's Love Life: Almost Gave Up Tennis for a Man!," *New York Amsterdam News*, August 30, 1958, 26; Ashley Brown, "'Uncomplimentary Things': Tennis Player Althea Gibson, Sexism, Homophobia, and Anti-Queerness in the Black Media," *Journal of African American History* 106, no. 2 (Spring 2021): 273.

89. "'Still No Wedding'—Althea."

90. "'Now That's What I Call Fresh Bread,'" advertisement, *New York Amsterdam News*, March 30, 1963, 9; "The New Althea," *Sepia*, July 1962, 29, 27.

91. "Brussels Sprouts Italiano," *Ebony*, July 1963, 120.

92. Gibson, *So Much to Live For*, 127.

93. Maggie Hathaway, "Althea Gibson Hurdles Color Barrier in Golf," *California Eagle*, October 17, 1963, 3.

94. Hathaway, "Althea Gibson Hurdles Color Barrier in Golf."

95. "On Tour with the Lady Golfers," *Sport*, July 1957, 46–47; Littler, "The Unusual Life of a Woman Pro," 35.

96. Littler, "The Unusual Life of a Woman Pro," 35.

97. Demas, *Game of Privilege*, 108, 110; United Press International, "Althea Gibson Signs as Golf Pro with Sporting Goods Company," *Sacramento Bee*, December 13, 1963, D3.

98. Leola Johnson and David Roediger, "'Hertz, Don't It?': Becoming Colorless and Staying Black in the Crossover of O. J. Simpson," in *Reading Sport: Critical Essays on Power and Representation*, ed. Susan Birrell and Mary G. McDonald (Boston: Northeastern University Press, 2000), 43.

99. Jesse W. Lewis Jr., "Negroes Gaining in Ad Field," *Miami Herald*, October 11, 1964, 13-B.

100. Lewis, "Negroes Gaining in Ad Field."

101. United Press International, "Althea Gibson Signs."

102. "Swinging on the Green," *Miami News*, March 15, 1964, 29; Tom Kelly, "Career No. 5," *St. Petersburg Times*, April 5, 1964, 1-C, 5-C.

103. United Press International, "Althea Gibson Signs."

104. Kelly, "Career No. 5," 5-C.

105. Kelly, "Career No. 5," 5-C.

106. Associated Press, "Faulk Says Things Are Going Up," *St. Petersburg Times*, April 6, 1964, 12; "Whitworth Leads by One," *St. Petersburg Times*, April 3, 1964, 3-C.

107. Al Watson to Althea Gibson, April 6, 1964, Gibson Collection.

108. Associated Press, "Reluctant Althea Signs Pro Golf Contract."

109. Dwayne Netland, "Patty Berg: Hazeltine Tougher Site for Open," *Minneapolis Tribune*, April 19, 1966, 21.

110. "On Tour with the Lady Golfers."

111. Frank Littler, "The Unusual Life of a Woman Pro," 35.

112. Keith Bein, letter to the editor, "Back to Skirts," *Golf Digest*, December 1964, 6.

113. Littler, "The Unusual Life of a Woman Pro," 87.

114. Anonymous pro quoted in Kirsch, *Golf in America*, 207.

115. Shav Glick, "Ladies' Pro Tour Seeks Lookers, Preferably Single," *Los Angeles Times*, September 27, 1967, 3.2; Littler, "The Unusual Life of a Woman Pro," 87.

116. Wright quoted in Kirsch, *Golf in America*, 207.

117. George Kolb, "Girl Watching in Style Here," *News and Observer* (Raleigh, NC), April 21, 1967, 36.

118. "Sponsors Banquet at Sunnyside," *Waterloo Daily Courier*, July 29, 1965, 8; also, Burke Evans, "Proettes Tune for Tourney," *Waterloo Courier*, July 28, 1965, 21.

119. "Althea Joins LPGA," *Golf Digest*, September 1963, 10.

120. Althea Gibson, "On Taking Up Golf," *Golf Digest*, March 1964, 33.

121. Milton Gross, "Can Althea Make It in Rugged Pro Golf?," *Boston Globe*, April 2, 1964, 44.

122. Ray Giffin, "Englehorn Talks Golf; Likes Tourney Ranking," *Idaho Statesman*, September 1, 1963, 11.

123. Gibson, *So Much to Live For*, 134; Condon, "In the Wake of the News."

124. Bob Maisel, "The Morning After," *Baltimore Sun*, June 13, 1964, 15.

125. McEwan, "The Morning After: Candy's Doing Just Fine"; Gibson, *So Much to Live For*, 134.

126. Gibson, *So Much to Live For*, 134.; United Press International, Steve Snider, "The Sports Patrol," *Shreveport Times*, December 25, 1964, C1; "Bio: Mickey Wright," LPGA Tour, accessed January 19, 2022, https://www.lpga.com/players/mickey-wright/82316/bio; Dick Hyland, "Hope Desert Classic to Pay $1000 Per Hole," *Palm Desert Post*, January 14, 1965, 12; Gregston, "Quiet Queen of Golf," 56.

127. Gregston, "The Quiet Queen of Golf," 22.

128. Associated Press, "Althea Gibson Leads Arizona Tourney on 69," *Chicago Tribune*, October 23, 1964, 3.1; Carl Soto, "Gibson Leads LPGA Open with 3-Under 69," *Arizona Republic*, October 23, 1964, 65.

129. Carl Soto, "Disqualification Hits Althea Gibson 1st Round Leader," *Arizona Republic*, October 24, 1964, 53; John Gates, "Gibson Out to Conquer Golf," *Charlotte Observer*, March 31, 1965, 12A; Associated Press, "Ruth Jessen 1st in Thunderbird Open," *Philadelphia Inquirer*, October 26, 1964, 33.

130. Steve Eubanks, "Pioneer Althea Gibson an Almost-Forgotten Figure in Two Sports," LPGA, February 19, 2020, https://www.lpga.com/news/2020/2020-pioneer-althea-gibson-an-almost-forgotten-figure-in-two-sports; "Pro Starlets Take Stage," *St. Petersburg Times*, March 17, 1965, 1C, 3C.

131. Gibson, *So Much to Live For*, 141, 142.

132. Gates, "Gibson Out to Conquer Golf"; "Gals' 1965 Tourney Trail," *Waterloo Courier*, July 28, 1965, 22; Fred Brown, "Darben Feels Sorry for Irrationals," *Pensacola News Journal*, June 26, 1969, 1B. That the LPGA held tournaments at clubs with racial restrictions runs counter to the memories of LPGA co-founder Shirley Spork that "the LPGA never excluded any woman from the day it was formed." See Shirley Spork, *From Green to Tee* (Scotts Valley, CA: CreateSpace, 2017), 193.

133. Gibson, quoted in Fitzgerald, ed., "Round Table Discussion: The Negro in American Sport," 30.

134. Gibson, *So Much to Live For*, 134.

135. Robert Lipsyte, "Althea Gibson: Golf Is Just Another Challenge," *New York Times*, August 23, 1964, 12S.

136. Gibson, *So Much to Live For*, 105.

137. Ed Fite, United Press International, "Golf Tougher for Althea Gibson," *Town Talk* (Alexandria, LA), May 27, 1965, 15.

138. Will Grimsley, Associated Press, "Althea Gibson Bitter: Lacks Sponsor in Golf," *Decatur Daily Review*, July 1, 1965, 13.

139. D. L. Stewart, "Althea Gibson's Confident," *Mansfield News-Journal*, July 9, 1965, 19.

140. Harding, Kelley, et al., "We Changed the World," 236–237; Smithsonian Institution, "Attached List of Objects," Althea Gibson Collection, 2014, author's personal collection; Arnold Rampersad, *Jackie Robinson* (New York: Alfred A. Knopf, 1997), 392–395; Sam Lacy, "Don't Count Words, Measure Inches," *Baltimore Afro-American*, February 20, 1965, 10.

141. Lipsyte, "Althea Gibson: Golf Is Just Another Challenge."

142. Condon, "In the Wake of the News."

143. Stan Hart, *Once a Champion: Legendary Tennis Stars Revisited* (New York: Dodd, Mead, 1985), 33.

144. Gibson, *So Much to Live For*, 153, 154, 139; obituary, "Mrs. Robert Darben Succumbs at 76," *Montclair Times*, January 14, 1965, 6; "Miss Althea Gibson Weds N.J. Man," *Pittsburgh Courier*, December 18, 1965, 5; Carl Soto, "Top Golf Events Coming for Fans," *Arizona Republic*, October 10, 1965, 8-C; Associated Press, "Las Cruces Golf Honors Go to Miss Creed," *Sacramento Bee*, November 1, 1965, B6.

145. "Tennis Champ Althea Gibson Weds N.J. Love in Las Vegas," *Philadelphia Tribune*, December 4, 1965, 1.

146. "Tennis Champ Althea Gibson Weds."

147. Charles McHarry, "On the Town," *New York Daily News*, December 29, 1965, 3; Earl Wilson, "It Happened Last Night: Gallant Betty Bacall," *Times Recorder* (Zanesville, OH), December 14, 1965, 5-A; Simer, "Althea's After a New Kind of Record"; Gibson, *So Much to Live For*, 154.

148. Gregston, "The Quiet Queen of Golf," 56. At the time of Wright's death in 2020, she was survived by Peggy Wilson, who had played on the LPGA Tour. See Michael Bamberger, "Why Mickey Wright Belongs on the Mount Rushmore of American Golf," *Golf*, February 18, 2020.

149. Glick, "Ladies' Pro Tour Seeks Lookers, Preferably Single."

150. Small, "Marilynn Smith Leads as Althea Closes Gap."

151. "Official 1966 LPGA Winnings," *Pensacola News Journal*, December 2, 1966, 4-C; Associated Press, "Wright Rally Ties for Lead," *Amarillo Globe-Times*, May 13, 1966, 11; United Press International, "Englehorn Captures Babe Zaharias Open," *Morning Telegraph* (Tyler, TX), May 23, 1966, 2.1.

152. Tom Fitzgerald, "Althea Gibson's 68 Leads Lady Carling," *Boston Globe*, August 6, 1966, 15, 17; Associated Press, "Althea Gibson's Record 68 Leads Women's Open," *Fresno Bee*, August 6, 1966, 9-A.

153. Bob Maisel, "The Morning After," *Baltimore Sun*, June 13, 1964, 13, 15; United Press International, "Mary Mills Has Lead in Sutton Golf," *Chicago Tribune*, August 7, 1966, 2.7; Associated Press, "Whitworth Wins Golf Tournament," *Palm Beach Post*, August 8, 1966, 16.

154. Anya Alvarez, "The Lesser-Known History of Althea Gibson the Golfer," ESPN, February 20, 2017, https://www.espn.com/espnw/culture/story/_/id/18724 493/the-lesser-known-history-althea-gibson-golfer; Gibson, *So Much to Live For*, 135–137.

155. Brown, "Darben Feels Sorry for Irrationals"; Gibson, *So Much to Live For*, 136.

156. Simer, "Althea's After a New Kind of Record"; Roland Wild, "Hurdle Barriers—Never Look Back," *The Province,* September 4, 1969, 19.

157. Wild, "Hurdle Barriers—Never Look Back."

158. Hart, *Once a Champion*, 30.

159. Frances Gray and Yanick Rice Lamb, *Born to Win: The Authorized Biography of Althea Gibson* (Hoboken, NJ: John Wiley and Sons, 2005), 154–155; Hart, *Once a Champion*, 30; Gibson, *So Much to Live For*, 128; Alvarez, "The Lesser-Known History of Althea Gibson the Golfer."

160. Spork, *From Green to Tee*, 193.

161. "Leaders," Los Angeles Times, July 6, 1970, Part III, 4; "Keeping up with Sports, " *Stilwell Democrat-Journal*, July 2, 1970, 10; Spork, *From Green to Tee*, 193. See Carl Soto, "Carefree Hosts Teach-In," *Arizona Republic*, July 2, 1970, 77.

162. United Press International, "Whitworth Leads Fems," *Waco Tribune-Herald*, November 7, 1964, 4-B; Naaman Nickell, "Whitworth Wins Tall City Open," *Odessa American*, May 9, 1966, 3-B; Associated Press, "Ailing Mann 2-Shot Winner," *St. Petersburg Times*, May 8, 1967, 2-C; United Press International, "Miss Wright Wins Easily," *Times Recorder*, May 13, 1968, 3-B; Brown, "Darben Feels Sorry for Irrationals."

163. "Lady Pros Seek Golf Glory," Ebony, July 1971, 111.

164. Brown, "Darben Feels Sorry for Irrationals."

165. United States Armed Forces Radio and Television Service, interview with Althea Gibson, March 1967, Library of Congress, Recorded Sound Research Center.

166. Gray and Lamb, *Born to Win*, 147; Linda Elliott, "The Self-Liberated Sister," *Black Sports*, August 1971, 21.

167. Tom Fitzgerald, "Renee Powell, 15, Amazing Golfer: Ohio Girl Crowds Althea for Spotlight at Ponkapoag," *Boston Globe*, August 23, 1961, 45; Associated Press, "Whitworth Triumphs in Golf," *Pentagraph* (Bloomington, IL), July 19, 1965, 15; "Ex-Champs Fall to Youth," *Baltimore Afro-American*, July 13, 1963, 9; "Trophy Winners," *Jet*, September 13, 1962, 55; "Girl Golfing Marvel," *Ebony*, August 1961, 101.

168. "Uprising of 1967," Detroit Historical Society, https://detroithistorical.org/learn/ encyclopedia-of-detroit/uprising-1967 (accessed January 19, 2022); United Press International, "Ladies Tied for Lead in Best-Ball Tourney," *Morning Telegraph*, July 29, 1967, 2.1.

169. John Falls, "It's Really Something Watching Gals Golf," *Detroit Free Press*, July 30, 1967, 2-D.

170. Demas, *Game of Privilege*, 145–147; "Spirit of the Game: Althea Gibson, a Multi-Talented Star," Northern California Golf Association, June 1, 2021, https://blog.ncga.org/spirit-of-the-game-althea-gibson-a-multi-talented-star; "Lady Pros Seek Golf Glory," *Ebony*, July 1971, 108.

171. Associated Press, "Althea Gibson Thinks Like 'True Champion,'" *Commonwealth Reporter* (Fond du Lac, WI), June 15, 1967, 33.

172. "Lady Pros Seek Golf Glory," 108.

173. Alvarez, "The Lesser-Known History of Althea Gibson the Golfer"; "Spirit of the Game."

174. Gray and Lamb, *Born to Win*, 197.

175. Alvarez, "The Lesser-Known History of Althea Gibson the Golfer."

176. Associated Press, "Whitworth First in Venice Golf," *Tampa Tribune*, March 27, 1967, 3-C; Dick Young, "Young Ideas," New York *Daily News*, April 2, 1967, 135.

177. "Gibson's Team Wins Pro-Am," *News and Observer*, April 21, 1967, 35; F. M. Williams, "Former Tennis Great Althea Gibson Now Finds Golf Her Game," *Tennessean*, April 26, 1967, 28.

178. Ken Hartnett, Associated Press, "Althea Gibson Hopes to Win First Golf Tourney," *Post-Crescent* (Appleton, WI), June 15, 1967, B14.

179. Associated Press, "Winnings and Scores in the 54-Hole Milwaukee Jaycee Open Golf Tournament," *Daily Telegram* (Eau Claire, WI), June 19, 1967, 3-B; Will Norton, "Beth Stone Tops Pro-Am Meet with 69," *Chicago Tribune*, June 20, 1967, 3.3.

180. Associated Press, "Miss Creed Is Pacific Classic Winner by Six," *Sacramento Bee*, September 11, 1967, B6; Associated Press, "Creed Takes Links Action," *Statesman Journal* (Salem, OR), September 11, 1967, 11; Associated Press, "Whitworth Is Winner," *Citizen Times* (Asheville, NC), April 24, 1967, 19; "Entry List Reaches 24 for Women's U.S. Open," *Pensacola News Journal*, May 11, 1969, B1.

181. Gibson, *So Much to Live For*, 144; obituary, Annie Bell Gibson, Gibson Collection; Don Felder, interview by author, August 30, 2021.

182. Ruth, Tennis, 176; Keller, quoted in Bud Collins, "USLTA Backs British Stand, Votes for Open Tennis, 15–1," *Boston Globe*, February 4, 1968, 50.

183. Billie Jean King, *All In* (New York: Alfred A. Knopf, 2021), 140–141.

184. Jimmy Mann, "Ex-Tennis Champ Althea Gets Last Links Laugh," *St. Petersburg Times*, March 12, 1968, 1-C, 2-C; "Higher Scores Expected in Kiwanis Golf Tourney," *Shreveport Journal*, May 2, 1968, D1; Dave Kindred, "Carol Mann Fires a 69, Wins Bluegrass by Four," *Courier-Journal*, June 10, 1968, B7; George Kolb, "Carol Mann Gets 3 Stroke Win," *News and Observer*, April 29, 1968, 17; "Mrs. Berning Captures Women's Open Crown," *Boston Globe*, July 8, 1968, 24; Barry McDermott, "A Case of Cool," *Cincinnati Enquirer*, July 23, 1968, 21.

185. Ed Nichols, "Shore Sports: It's Understandable," *Daily Times* (Salisbury, MD), January 7, 1969, 10; "Garden State Roundup: Tennis Star Ends Hospital Stay," *Herald-News* (Passaic, NJ), September 11, 1968, 3.

186. Tom Armistead Jr., "Over the Net: Althea Gibson Loves Her Golf," *Dayton Daily News*, July 28, 1968, 8-D.

187. John W. Cresbaugh Jr., "Looking Them Over: Althea Gibson Darben Considering a Tennis Comeback," *Montclair Times*, October 3, 1968, 42.

188. Murray Olderman, "Between You 'n' Me," *Petaluma Argus-Courier*, August 31, 1968, 6.

189. Hildy Weltman, "Can Ten Years Make a Difference," *Ridgewood* (NJ) *Herald-News*, January 16, 1969, 2, 3; Pat Frizzell, "Pro Tour Needs More Girls," *Oakland Tribune*, February 21, 1969, 59; "Net Clinic Scheduled by Billie Jean King," *Call-Chronicle* (Allentown, PA), February 2, 1969, C-7; King, *All In*, 152.

190. Weltman, "Can Ten Years Make a Difference," 3; Associated Press, "Sheila Moran," *Citizen-Times* (Asheville, NC), December 24, 1968, 14.

191. Gibson, *So Much to Live For*, 11, 34, 113.

192. Review of *So Much to Live For*, *Kirkus Reviews*, October 1, 1968.

193. Charles H. Martin, *Benching Jim Crow: The Rise and Fall of the Color Line in Southern College Sports, 1890–1980* (Urbana: University of Illinois Press, 2010).

194. Louis Moore, *We Will Win the Day: The Civil Rights Movement, the Black Athlete, and the Quest for Equality* (Santa Barbara, CA: Praeger, 2017), 159–188; Jack Olsen, *The Black Athlete: A Shameful Story: The Myth of Integration in American Sport* (New York: Time-Life Books, 1968); Amy Bass, *Not the Triumph but the Struggle: The 1968 Olympics and the Making of the Black Athlete* (Minneapolis: University of Minnesota Press, 2004); *1968—A Mexico City Documentary*, narrated by Serena Williams (2018), YouTube, posted by NBC Sports, October 17, 2018, https://www.youtube.com/watch?v=7Ss6qavj29c, approx. 42:30–1:04:00.

195. Eric Allen Hall, "'I Guess I'm Becoming More and More Militant': Arthur Ashe and the Black Freedom Movement, 1961–1968," *Journal of African American History* 96, no. 4 (2011): 474–502; 'Rampersad, *Jackie Robinson*, 418; William J. Baker, *Jesse Owens: An American Life* (New York: Free Press, 1986), 211–212; Mike Marqusee, *Redemption Song: Muhammad Ali and the Spirit of the Sixties* (New York: Verso, 1999); Aram Goudsouzian, *King of the Court: Bill Russell and the Basketball Revolution* (Berkeley: University of California Press, 2010).

196. Frizzell, "Pro Tour Needs More Girls."

197. United Press International, "At 41, Althea Returns to Net," *Independent Press-Telegram* (Long Beach, CA), February 23, 1969, S-5.

198. Associated Press, "Roche Defeats Laver," *Independent Journal* (San Rafael, CA), February 27, 1969, 24; Associated Press, "Billie Jean King, Laver Triumph in Net Tourney," *Independent Journal*, February 28, 1969, 40; Associated Press, "Althea's Comeback Knocked for Loss," *Newsday*, February 26, 1969, 41.

199. Bill Nunn Jr., "Change of Pace: Nobody Asked Me But," *Pittsburgh Courier*, April 5, 1969, 14.

200. Moran, "Althea Gibson Attempting Comeback on Tennis Court."

201. Robert Sylvester, "Dream Street: The Busy Sports," New York *Daily News*, October 30, 1969, 77; Jeff Cross, "Sandra Post Writes for Province," *The Province*, September 2, 1969, 15.

202. Eric Whitehead, "Frankly Speaking," *The Province*, September 8, 1969, 14.

203. Barling, "Former Tennis Champ Is Still a Swinger."

204. Whitehead, "Frankly Speaking."

205. Barling, "Former Tennis Champ Is Still a Swinger."

206. Rice and Gray, *Born to Win*, 146.

207. Barling, "Former Tennis Champ Is Still a Swinger."

208. Simer, "Althea's After a New Kind of Record"; Gibson, *So Much to Live For*, 153.

209. Simer, "Althea's After a New Kind of Record."

210. Gibson, *So Much to Live For*, 151, 152.

211. Simer, "Althea's After a New Kind of Record."

212. "Park Consultant," *The Record* (Hackensack, NJ), March 8, 1970, 10-C; Hildy Weltman, "Can Ten Years Make a Difference," *Herald-News* (Ridgewood, NJ), January 16, 1969, 2, 3; "Althea Signs to Spread Sports Word," *Daily News*, March 15, 1970, NK2.

213. Associated Press, "Althea Gibson Rips Par, Leads Tourney," *Sacramento Bee*, June 28, 1970, F8; United Press International, "Mary Mills Wins Playoff on Second Hole," *Cincinnati Enquirer*, June 29, 1970.

214. United Press International, "Mary Mills Wins Playoff on Second Hole"

215. United Press International, "Mary Mills Wins Playoff on Second Hole."

CHAPTER 13

1. Associated Press, "Althea Gibson Makes Comeback at Orange; Laver Edges Russell," *Philadelphia Inquirer*, August 27, 1970, 40; United Press International, "Althea, 43, to Play in Tennis Open," *Boston Globe*, August 25, 1970, 28.

2. Associated Press, "Russians Doing Well in Jersey," *Record* (Hackensack, NJ), August 28, 1970, B-8; "Maggie Court Upset in NJ by Patti Hogan," New York *Daily News*, August 30, 1970, 141; United Press International, "Women Net Rebels Planning Own Tour," New York Times, September 25, 1970, 52; Billie Jean King, *All In* (New York: Alfred A. Knopf, 2021), 171–174.

3. King, *All In*, 184–185, 182, 174.

4. "Sports in Brief: Althea: One Regret," *Florida Today*, May 14, 1976, 2C.

5. Willie Schatz, "At Age 51, Althea Gibson Is Giving Golf One More Try," *Miami News*, February 9, 1978, 2C.

6. "Althea Gibson Will Emcee South Mountain Ice Show," *Herald-News* (Passaic, NJ), November 6, 1970, 25; "Essex Parks Birthday to Have Lasting Effects," *Belleville* (NJ) *Times*, June 17, 1971, 7.

7. "Ambition Breeds Success," *Montclair Times*, November 12, 1970, 6.

8. Associated Press, "Darben—Once the Best at Tennis, Now Golf Trail," *Colorado Springs Gazette Telegraph*, March 26, 1971, 5-C.

9. Linda Elliott, "The Self-Liberated Sister," *Black Sports*, August 1971, 20.

10. "Lady Pros Seek Golf Glory," *Ebony*, 1971, 108.

11. "Morning Brief: Names in the News," *Los Angeles Times*, September 6, 1971, 3.2; Doug Smith, *Whirlwind, the Godfather of Black Tennis: The Life and Times of Dr. Robert Walter Johnson* (Washington, DC: Blue Eagle, 2004), 148.

12. Associated Press, "Darben—Once the Best at Tennis, Now Golf Trail."

13. Frances Clayton Gray and Yanick Rice Lamb, *Born to Win: The Authorized Biography of Althea Gibson* (Hoboken, NJ: John Wiley and Sons, 2004), 147; Elliott, "The Self-Liberated Sister," 18.

14. "Ambition Breeds Success"; Associated Press, "Althea Gibson Thinking of Comeback," *Asbury Park Press*, May 10, 1972, 34; Bruce Schoenfeld, The Match: Althea Gibson and Angela Buxton: How Two Outsiders—One Black, the Other Jewish—Forged a Friendship and Made Sports History (New York: Amistad Press, 2004), 267.

15. Phyllis Raybin Emert, "Althea! Part II," *WomenSports*, March 1976, 25; Elaine Tyler May, *Homeward Bound: American Families in the Cold War*, rev. ed. (1988; repr., New York: Basic Books, 2017), 7; Marv Gross, "Joanne and Her Golf Game: Nothing 'Fat' About Either," *Montreal Gazette*, June 26, 1974, 30; Kay Gilman, "Althea Gibson . . . Still Every Inch a Queen," New York *Daily News*, June 30, 1974, 103.

16. Schoenfeld, *The Match*, 267.

17. "Valley View Racquet Club," advertisement, *Record*, January 15, 1973, B-4; Associated Press, "Althea Gibson Thinking of Comeback"; Parton Keese, "Althea Gibson Is Back: Her New Life and Her New Career in Tennis," *Tennis*, March 1974, 37.

18. Associated Press, "Althea Gibson Thinking of Comeback."

19. "Althea Gibson's Tennis Day Camp," advertisement, *Record*, May 28, 1972, C-5; King, *All In*, 237; Raymond Arsenault, *Arthur Ashe: A Life* (New York: Simon and Schuster, 2018), 262; Paul Schwartz, "Gibson Missed Big Money," *Record*, July 28, 1974, C-8; Richard Zitrin, "Althea Gibson Has Conquered Modesty, Too," *Akron Beacon Journal*, March 3, 1973, B2, B7.

20. Jim Byrne, "Althea Also Star in Track," *Minneapolis Star*, June 24, 1972, 13A; Milton Hoffman, "Both Parties Seek Increased Vote Registration," *Daily Item* (Port Chester, NY), September 29, 1972, 11; "Valley View Racquet Club," advertisement, *Record*, October 8, 1972, C-9; Associated Press, "Althea Gibson Thinking of Comeback."

21. Braven Dyer, "Mickey Wright Grabs Colgate-Dinah," *Desert Sun* (Palm Springs, CA), April 16, 1973, C1; "Althea Gibson Still Has It," *Standard-Speaker* (Hazleton, PA), May 9, 1973, 42; Stephanie Capparell, *The Real Pepsi Challenge: The Inspirational Story of Breaking the Color Barrier in American Business* (New York: Wall Street

Journal Books, 2007); Lane Demas, *Game of Privilege: An African American History of Golf* (Chapel Hill: University of North Carolina Press, 2017), 207.

22. Stan Washington, "Althea Gibson Launches Mobile Tennis Program," *Atlanta Voice*, June 23, 1973, 9.

23. "Althea Gibson Still Has It."

24. "WMHT-TV Notes," *Bennington Banner TV Week*, August 11, 1973, 2; King, *All In*, 281, 207–208; United Press International, "Veteran Althea Gibson May Return to Courts," *Palm Beach Post*, May 6, 1973, E6; Stan Hart, *Once a Champion: Legendary Tennis Stars Revisited* (New York: Dodd, Mead, 1985), 30.

25. "Arthur Ashe Celebrity Tennis Exhibition," advertisement, *Montclair Times*, January 13, 1972, S-6; United Press International, "Althea Eyes Pairs," *Chicago Defender*, July 25, 1973, 29; Jimmy Mann, "Mann on the Move," *St. Petersburg Times*, September 12, 1968, 3-C; Arsenault, *Arthur Ashe*, 316; Grace Lichtenstein, *A Long Way, Baby: Behind the Scenes in Women's Pro Tennis* (New York: William Morrow, 1974), 201.

26. "Richmond's Arthur Ashe Shows Promise as Netter," *Journal and Guide* (Norfolk, VA), August 3, 1957, 20.

27. Claude E. Harrison Jr., "Sports Roundup: Thanks to Pioneering of Althea, Ashe Won't Travel Rocky Road," *Philadelphia Tribune*, February 22, 1964, 15; L. I. "Brock" Brockenbury, "Tying the Score: Sports Shorts," *Los Angeles Sentinel*, June 6, 1963, A20.

28. Bob Martin, "Ashe Just Plays as Individual," *Long Beach Independent*, June 16, 1965, C-3.

29. Bill Bryson, "Ashe's Idol," *Des Moines Tribune*, June 1, 1967, 27.

30. Associated Press, "Ashe Says Davis Cup Pressure's on Osuna," *Miami Herald*, July 26, 1965, 3-D.

31. Quoted in King, *All In*, 170 For a discussion of Ashe's sexism, see Eric Allen Hall, *Arthur Ashe: Tennis and Justice in the Civil Rights Era* (Baltimore: Johns Hopkins University Press, 2014), 189–192.

32. Ashe quoted in Arsenault, *Arthur Ashe*, 405–406, 407.

33. "Althea Picks Marge to Beat Bobby Riggs," New York *Daily News*, May 10, 1973, 139; "How Gardnar Mulloy, Althea Gibson See It," *Miami News*, September 18, 1973, 4B.

34. Associated Press, "Riggs a Sure Thing? So They Say at Open," *Meriden Journal*, September 6, 1973, 8.

35. United Press International, "Men Dominate 'Battle of Sexes,'" *Sacramento Bee*, October 2, 1976, B2; Hart, *Once a Champion*, 25.

36. "Althea Picks Marge to Beat Bobby Riggs," New York *Daily News*, May 10, 1973, 139; "Channel 7 Team Helps Build Bengaff Fund," *Record*, January 8, 1974, B-5; Rich Rein, "To the Top," *People*, February 2, 1976, 56; Hillary Male, "From 'Ladies on Lawn' to Women Tennis Pros," *Fort Lauderdale News*, February 3, 1974, 1K, 14K.

37. Male, "From 'Ladies on Lawn' to Women Tennis Pros," 14K.

38. Ray Recchi, "Chris Wins, Kerry Weeps, Althea Wishes," *Fort Lauderdale News*, February 11, 1974, 16A, 20A.

39. Jim Martz, "Melville's Stubbed Toe Gives Evert Tennis Crown by Default," *Miami Herald*, February 11, 1974, D1.

40. King, *All In*, 144; Recchi, "Chris Wins, Kerry Weeps, Althea Wishes."

41. "Tennis Stars Richer Now," *Herald-Palladium* (Saint Joseph, MI), April 15, 1975, 4; "People Are Talking About," *Jet*, July 15, 1976, 40.

42. "Raleigh Golf Tournament," *Herald-Sun* (Durham, NC), May 13, 1974, 3B; United Press International, "Judy Rankin Wins with Rain's Help," *News and Observer* (Raleigh, NC), June 3, 1974, 17; "Results: Peter Jackson Ladies' Classic," *News and Observer*, July 1, 1974, 19; Pat Boland, "Riches Eluded Althea Gibson during Reign as Tennis Queen," *Montreal Star*, July 8, 1974, C-7.

43. King, *All In*, 267, 268, 271; Susan Ware, *Title IX: A Brief History with Documents* (Boston: Bedford/St. Martin's Press, 2007); "1974 Courier Awards Dinner Highlights," *Pittsburgh Courier*, July 6, 1974, 6D; "Arthur Ashe Is Playing," advertisement, New York *Daily News*, October 9, 1975, 127; "Rainbow Room Becomes Racquet Club," New York *Daily News*, August 24, 1974, 19; Althea Gibson with Bob Hope, AP photo, *Asbury Park Press*, August 13, 1975, C2.

44. Gilman, "Althea Gibson . . . Still Every Inch a Queen"; Gerry Raker, "Above All—the Game," *Poughkeepsie Journal*, June 6, 1975, 9.

45. "Tennis Stars Richer Now."

46. "Computer Will Decide Who's Best," *Herald and Review* (Decatur, IL), October 23, 1974, 20.

47. Male, "From 'Ladies on Lawn' to Women Tennis Pros"; Gilman, "Althea Gibson . . . Still Every Inch a Queen"; "Athletic Unit Gets Althea Gibson," *The News* (Paterson, NJ), September 19, 1975, 4; Boland, "Riches Eluded Althea Gibson During Reign as Tennis Queen."

48. Gray and Lamb, *Born to Win*, 177–178; Joan Ryan, "Women Boxers' Bout Lacks Punch," *Austin American-Statesman*, August 20, 1976, D5; Bruce Chadwick, "Lights, Camera, Newark," New York *Daily News*, June 4, 1978, J2; Richard Hubbard, "Gibson: Master of Tennis, but Golf Evades Her," *Bradenton Herald*, February 26, 1978, D-3.

49. Chadwick, "Lights, Camera, Newark."

50. "Athletic Unit Gets Althea Gibson"; "Gov. Byrne, Wife Urge Passage of ERA," *Daily Register* (Red Bank, NJ), August 27, 1975, 17; United Press International, "Amateur Byrne Ties Tennis Pro," *Courier-Post* (Camden, NJ), August 1, 1974;, Althea Gibson with Bob Hope, AP photo, *Asbury Park Press*; "Althea Gibson Sworn to State Athletic Post," *Asbury Park Press*, November 18, 1975, A20.

51. Bob Curley, "Althea Laces Up Gloves," *The News*, October 20, 1975, 10.

52. Rein, "To the Top," 56.

53. Associated Press, "Althea Gibson Lifts Dukes to Support Boxing," *Daily Register* (Shrewsbury, NJ), December 16, 1975, 28.

54. Augie Lio, "Gibson Gives Boxing Writers Ol' 1-2," *Herald-News*, November 25, 1975, 24.

55. Lena Williams, "Miss Gibson Aims at Top in Sports," *New York Times*, November 30, 1975, Sec. Sports, 17.

56. Williams, "Miss Gibson Aims at Top in Sports"; "Muhammad Ali and Friends to KO Audiences on Special," *Jet*, September 18, 1975, 66.

57. Associated Press, "Althea Gibson Lifts Dukes to Support Boxing."

58. Mary Amoroso, "Althea Gibson, Champion for N.J.," *Record*, December 11, 1975, 1; Ann Ledesma, "Ex-Tennis Ace Serves Formula—Play Sports and Cut Crime," *Central New Jersey Home News*, November 25, 1975, 17.

59. "Foes KO Bill to 'Improve' N.J. Boxing," *The News*, April 1, 1976, 28; Williams, "Miss Gibson Aims at Top in Sports."

60. Lio, "Gibson Gives Boxing Writers Ol' 1-2."

61. Richard T. Pienciak, Associated Press, "Althea Gibson's Goal: Make N.J. A Key Sports Center," *Philadelphia Inquirer*, December 11, 1975, 15-B.

62. United Press International, "Althea Gibson on Rec Council," *Rockland County Journal News*, August 28, 1964, 25; United Press International, "Mayor Lindsay Names Sports Commissioners," *Bridgeport Telegram*, February 18, 1966, 21; Amoroso, "Althea Gibson, Champion for N.J."

63. Amoroso, "Althea Gibson Champion for N.J.," A-1, A-16; "Althea Will Speak on Women Athletes," *Fresno Bee*, March 6, 1976, B3; "Tennis Everyone?," advertisement, *Item of Millburn and Short Hills*, March 18, 1976, 9; "Althea Gibson Gives Lecture at Dartmouth," *Rutland Daily Herald*, July 16, 1974, 8.

64. "See Them Free!," advertisement, *News-Press* (Fort Myers, FL), January 16, 1976, 7A; Travis Vogan, *ABC Sports: The Rise and Fall of Network Sports Television* (Oakland: University of California Press, 2018), 161, 192; King, *All In*, 283–284.

65. Tim Morris, "Karen Logan Begins Quest," *El Paso Times*, January 18, 1976, 3-C; "The TV Week: Sunday, February 29: 2:00," New York *Daily News*, February 29, 1976, 3; Linda Peterson, "Althea Gibson—A Hard Road to the Top," *Journal-News*, March 15, 1976, 5A.

66. "Ching, Henning Pace Women's Superstars," *News-Press* (Fort Myers, FL), January 20, 1976, 1C; Associated Press, "Henning Superstar Winner," *Pensacola News Journal*, February 25, 1976, 5C.

67. Rudy Martzke, "A Superstar, Not a Libber," *Rochester Democrat and Chronicle*, February 1, 1976, 6D.

68. King, *All In*, 271–274; Susan Ware, *Game, Set Match: Billie Jean King and the Revolution in Women's Sports* (Chapel Hill: University of North Carolina Press, 2011), 78–90; Phyllis Raybin Emert, "Foremothers: Althea!," *WomenSports*, February 1976, 12–16; Emert, "Althea! Part II," 22–25; Rein, "To the Top," 56.

69. Amoroso, "Althea Gibson, Champion for N.J.," A-16; Joseph Santangelo, "Sports Agency Urged for N.J.," *Record*, April 1, 1976, A-3; Associated Press, "Sports Law

Proposals Criticized," *Central New Jersey Home News*, March 25, 1976, 21; Augie Lio, "Why Do Senators Ignore Althea?," *Home News* (Passaic, NJ), March 30, 1976, 22.

70. Lio, "Boxing Bill Finds Opposition"; Santangelo, "Sports Agency Urged for N.J."

71. Lio, "Boxing Bill Finds Opposition."

72. Lio, "Boxing Bill Finds Opposition"; "Foes KO Bill to 'Improve' N.J. Boxing."

73. Susan Lykes, "Althea Gibson Tells Crowd of Benefits of 'Hard Work,'" *Tallahassee Democrat*, May 14, 1976, 17; King, *All In*, 263; Jim Durham, "Tennis: Good Medicine for A&M, Tennis Is Althea Gibson," *Tallahassee Democrat*, May 14, 1976, 22.

74. Amoroso, "Althea Gibson, Champion for N.J.," A-16.

75. Malissa Smith, *A History of Women's Boxing* (Lanham, MD: Rowman and Littlefield, 2014), 111–136; Vinny DeTrani, "For the Record: A Real Cat Fight Brewing," *Record*, July 20, 1976, B-7.

76. Augie Lio, "Lou Pushing Althea for Women's Bout," *Herald-News*, July 22, 1976, D-1.

77. DeTrani, "For the Record"; Cheryl Bentsen, "California Has Its First Ms.-Match," *Los Angeles Times*, April 27, 1976, 3.1, 3.4.

78. Kathy Martone, "This Gal Really Does Fight for Her Rights," New York *Daily News*, August 11, 1976, 74JL.

79. Phil Laciura, "'Cat' Kayoes Gal Foe," *The News*, August 13, 1976, 14.

80. John Rowe, "Cat Shows She's a Tiger," *Record*, August 13, 1976, B-7.

81. Augie Lio, "Sports Smorgasbord: Get It for Jersey," *Herald-News*, November 12, 1976, C-2.

82. "A&M Greats," *Tallahassee Democrat*, October 24, 1976, 6D.

83. Associated Press, "Althea Quits State Sports Post," *Central New Jersey Home News*, January 19, 1977, 8.

84. Theresa A. Glab, "Ex-Tennis Star Scores in Camden High Talk," *Courier-Post* (Cherry Hill, NJ), February 19, 1977, 16.

85. "Cheers for Miss Gibson," *Asbury Park Press*, January 26, 1977, A14; Augie Lio, "Althea Gibson Justifies Resignation," *Herald-News*, February 10, 1977, D-4; "One Resigned," editorial, *Herald-News*, January 22, 1977, A-7.

86. "State Athletic Commissioner Resigns Post," *The News*, January 19, 1977, 3.

87. Augie Lio, "Gibson Hanging on as Governor Fails to Act," *Herald-News*, March 31, 1977, D-2.

88. "Jersey Joe Appointed Athletic Chief," *Asbury Park Press*, June 18, 1977, C12.

89. "Tennis Player Gibson to Speak Here" and "Tennis Anyone?," *California Aggie*, February 4, 1977, 7; "So Does Althea Gibson," *California Aggie*, February 16, 1977, 1.

90. "Tennis Player Gibson to Speak Here." *Sports Illustrated* published its cover story on May 28, 1973, while *Newsweek* published its story on June 3, 1974. *Time* followed with its issue for June 26, 1978.

91. Althea Gibson, "The Role of the Sportswoman"/"The Role of the Female Athlete"/"The Sportswoman's Role in Society" (lecture, n.d. but after 1973), Gibson Collection.

92. Gibson, "The Role of the Sportswoman," 5,

93. Kathy Schofield Zoed, "Tennis 'Pro' Turned Golfer," *Times Record* (Troy, NY), May 3, 1974, 11; Gibson, "The Role of the Sportswoman," 10, 12.

94. Zoed, "Tennis 'Pro' Turned Golfer."

95. Jessica Gammon, "Two Different Women," *Morning Herald* (Durham, NC), May 10, 1974, 1D.

96. Gibson, "The Role of the Sportswoman," 2, 4.

97. Gibson, "The Role of the Sportswoman," 9.

98. "Gibson Entertains," *California Aggie*, February 17, 1977, 1. The lines came from a long passage written by David Auxter, a scholar and coach. Gibson's marked-up copy of the speech suggests that she read the passage but did not name Auxter, at least not every time she delivered it. His name and brief biography are crossed out.

99. "Senate-Assembly Races Low-Key," *Asbury Park Press*, June 5, 1977, G18; Associated Press, "Althea Gibson Tries a New Game: Politics," *Daily Record* (Morristown, NJ), April 26, 1977, 3.

100. Ravi K. Perry, *Black Mayors, White Majorities: The Balancing Act of Racial Politics* (Lincoln: University of Nebraska Press, 2014); LaVerne McCain Gill, *African American Women in Congress: Forming and Transforming History* (New Brunswick, NJ: Rutgers University Press, 1997); "Milestones for Women in New Jersey Politics," Center for American Women and Politics, Eagleton Institute of Politics, Rutgers University, https://cawp.rutgers.edu/milestones-women-new-jersey-politics (accessed January 17, 2022).

101. "Ex-Tennis Star Files for Senate Race," *Asbury Park Press*, April 26, 1977, B7; Gray and Lamb, Born to Win, 181.

102. Gray and Lamb, *Born to Win*, 181; "Ex-Tennis Star Files for Senate Race."

103. John T. McGowan, "Menza to Field His Own Slates for Senate Bid," *Courier News* (Bridgewater, NJ), March 18, 1978, B-8.

104. Michael Janofsky, "Back to Square One," *Miami Herald*, June 15, 1978, 8-F.

105. King, *All In*, 298. For Cobb's difficulty and Ruth's observation, see Charles C. Alexander, *Ty Cobb* (New York: Oxford University Press, 1984), 211.

106. John T. McGowan, "Menza to Field His Own Slates for Senate Bid," *Courier News*, March 18, 1978, B-8; Barry Cooper, "LPGA a Heartache for Gibson," *Tallahassee Democrat*, June 26, 1978, 3B; Marc Katz, "Althea Gibson at 50: Golf Gold Comes Hard," *Dayton Daily News*, June 11, 1978, 9-D.

107. Tom Tucker, "The Best—and Worst—of Times," *Atlanta Constitution*, April 30, 1978, 8-D.

108. Cindy Morris, "Althea, 50, Still After One Victory," *Cincinnati Enquirer*, June 8, 1978, C-4.

109. Tucker, "The Best—and Worst—of Times"; Katherine M. Jamieson, "Reading Nancy Lopez: Decoding Representations of Race, Class, and Sexuality," *Sociology of Sport Journal* 15 (Winter 1998): 343–358; Hart, *Once a Champion*, 30.

110. Keese, "Althea Gibson Is Back," 39.

111. Keese, "Althea Gibson Is Back," 39.

112. Associated Press, "Althea Gibson Thinking of Comeback."

113. Associated Press, "Gibson: No Harvest from Golf," *Tallahassee Democrat*, June 9, 1978, 7B.

114. "Blacks to Play in Gals' Net Tour," New York *Daily News*, November 2, 1972, 123; Associated Press, "Althea Gibson Thinking of Comeback."

115. King, *All In*, 359; "Then and Now: Bonnie Logan," YouTube, posted by USTA North Carolina, March 19, 2021, https://www.youtube.com/watch?v=tklYfWt_L5EAP.

116. Lichtenstein, *A Long Way, Baby*, 200, 201.

117. "A Court Minority," *New York Times*, January 2, 1973, 76; Peter Bodo, "Sylvia Hooks on the Hook," *Herald-News*, December 21, 1972, 35, 38.

118. King, *All In*, 360–361.

119. Lesley Visser, "Gibson Comes to Coach in Roxbury," *Boston Globe*, May 20, 1979, 60. Sadly, Buchanan was murdered three years later. See Associated Press, "Woman Tennis Player Shot," *Desert Sun*, January 29, 1982, E1.

120. On Althea as coach, see Robert Lipsyte, "Tennis in the 70s: Frenzy Grips Net Buffs," *Palm Beach Post*, April 22, 1976, D1, D7; Zina Garrison with Doug Smith, *Zina: My Life in Women's Tennis* (Berkeley, CA: North Atlantic Books, 2001), 79, 80.

121. Garrison, *Zina*, 82, 83.

122. "Leslie Allen Reflects on Landmark Detroit Win," Women's Tennis Association, February 25, 2021, https://www.wtatennis.com/news/2043774/leslie-allen-reflects-on-landmark-detroit-win.

123. Visser, "Gibson Comes to Coach in Roxbury."

124. "Ex-Champ Althea Never Played Here," *Indianapolis News*, August 4, 1979, 4; Greg Logan, "She's Excelling in Tennis Studies," *Record*, August 23, 1979, D-2.

125. Allen quoted in Gray and Lamb, Born to Win, 194.

126. Amoroso, "Althea Gibson Champion for NJ," A-16; Ledesma, "Ex-Tennis Ace Serves Formula—Play Sports and Cut Crime."

127. Ann Simer, "Althea's After a New Kind of Record," *Corpus Christi Caller-Times*, October 26, 1969, 1.

128. Emert, "Althea! Part II," 25.

CHAPTER 14

1. Bill Eichenberger, "Suggs Turns Back the Clock," *Columbia* (SC) *Record*, April 30, 1983, 12-B; Susan Ware, *Game, Set, Match: Billie Jean King and the Evolution*

of Women's Sports (Chapel Hill: University of North Carolina Press, 2011), 95–96, 91, 97.

2. Billie Jean King, All In (New York: Alfred A. Knopf, 2021), 284; Associated Press, "9 Inducted into Women's Hall," *Star-Gazette* (Elmira, NY), September 17, 1980, 1C.

3. Associated Press, "9 Inducted into Women's Hall."

4. Marv Gross, "Joanne and Her Golf Game: Nothing 'Fat' About Either," *Montreal Gazette*, June 26, 1974, 30; "Law Students Work on Unraveling the Estate of Tennis Great Althea Gibson," *Clinic News*, Rutgers Law School, Fall 2019, http://www.evergreeneditions.com/publication/?i=625259&article_id=3500192&view=articleBrowser&ver=html5; Lane Crockett, "Tamara: Tall and Talented," *Shreveport Journal*, August 1, 1975, 2-B; Phyllis Raybin Emert, "Foremother: Althea! Part II," *WomenSports*, March 1976, 25.

5. James Goodrich, "The Plight of Olympic Star," *Jet*, July 17, 1969, 50–52.

6. Will Grimsley, Associated Press, "Rudolph Preaches Hope to Ghetto Kids," *Central New Jersey Home News*, June 8, 1978, 18.

7. On Ashe, see Eric Allen Hall, *Arthur Ashe: Tennis and Justice in the Civil Rights Era* (Baltimore: Johns Hopkins University Press, 2014); and Raymond Arsenault, *Arthur Ashe: A Life* (New York: Simon and Schuster, 2018). Golfer Lee Elder and tennis player Bonnie Logan competed in South Africa, too. See Lane Demas, *Game of Privilege* (Chapel Hill: University of North Carolina Press, 2017), 224–231, and King, *All In*, 359.

8. Jane Gross, "Noah: Leader in the Rise of Black Tennis Players," *New York Times*, September 3, 1979, C3.

9. Hall, *Arthur Ashe*, 189–192; Arsenault, *Arthur Ashe*, 406, 507; Zina Garrison with Doug Smith, *Zina: My Life in Women's Tennis* (Berkeley, CA: North Atlantic Books, 2001), 85–86, 151.

10. "Arthur Ashe Is Playing," advertisement, New York *Daily News*, October 9, 1975, 127; "Arthur Ashe Celebrity Tennis Exhibition," advertisement, *Montclair Times*, January 13, 1972, S-6; "Black Colleges Raising Dough," New York *Daily News*, October 4, 1976, ML7; Peter Bodo, "A Day in the Life of the National Tennis Center," advertisement, *New York Times*, August 30, 1987, T31; "Tennis at the National Tennis Center," advertisement, *New York Times*, July 26, 1987, S9; Arsenault, *Arthur Ashe*, 505, 617; "Black Tennis and Sports Foundation," photograph, n.d. (mid-1970s), Black Tennis History, https://blacktennishistory.com/black-tennis-sports-foundation/; calendar, *New York Times*, July 11, 1988, C11; "Tennis Tournament," *New York Times*, July 19, 1988, A28; Ira Berkow, Newspaper Enterprise Association, "Althea Gibson Returns Home," *Lead Daily Call*, August 23, 1973, 2.

11. "Monmouth College to Give 4 Honorary Doctor Degrees," *Asbury Park Press*, May 18, 1980, A22; "Drew Graduates Hear Halberstam," *Record* (Hackensack, NJ), May 17, 1992, A-3; Berkow, "Althea Gibson Returns Home."

12. Althea Gibson with Richard Curtis, *So Much to Live For* (New York: G. P. Putnam's Sons, New York, 1968), 92.

13. "Williams, Piniella Among 'Dimes' Banquet Honorees," *Ridgewood* (NJ) *Sunday News*, April 24, 1983, 87; Charles Clines, "Stonebridge a Killer for Weekend," *Fort Worth Star-Telegram*, September 20, 1989, sec. 3, 8.

14. Dave Anderson, New York Times Service, "Althea Gibson Was Somebody Special," *Victoria Times Colonist*, September 9, 1980, 10.

15. "Black Woman Wins Avon Futures Tennis Tourney," *Jet*, March 8, 1979, 51; Frances Clayton Gray and Yanick Rice Lamb, *Born to Win: The Authorized Biography of Althea Gibson* (Hoboken, NJ: John Wiley and Sons, 2004), 206–207.

16. Will Grimsley, Associated Press, "Grimsley's Sports World: Althea Gibson Turns Back the Clock," *Vidette-Messenger of Porter County*, February 10, 1981, 11.

17. Leslie Allen-Selmore, "Althea, Arthur, Then Me," *New York Times*, August 24, 1997, UO74.

18. "Quiet Leslie Allen Takes Net Victory in Stride," *Jet*, February 26, 1981, 46; Will Grimsley, Associated Press, "Decision to Continue Came Easy for Allen," *Record*, February 20, 1981, C-3.

19. Garrison, *Zina*, 82, 83.

20. "Female Tennis Players Clash in L.A. Lockerroom Probed," *Jet*, August 29, 1983, 52.

21. Leslie Allen as told to Jerry Bembry, "Tennis Champ Leslie Allen Takes USTA to Task over 'Tone-Deaf' Statement," *Andscape*, June 18, 2020, https://andscape.com/features/tennis-champ-leslie-allen-takes-usta-to-task-over-tone-deaf-statement/.

22. "Miss Allen Cites Insults," *New York Times*, June 7, 1983, B10.

23. Allen and Bembry, "Tennis Champ Leslie Allen Takes USTA to Task over 'Tone-Deaf' Statement"; "Miss Allen Cites Insults."

24. Allen and Bembry, "Tennis Champ Leslie Allen Takes USTA to Task over 'Tone-Deaf' Statement."

25. Linell Smith, "Althea Gibson: A Champ When It Wasn't Easy," *Evening Sun* (Baltimore), February 29, 1980, B1.

26. Charles McGeehan, "Althea Gives Legacy to Young Women," *Baltimore Sun*, February 24, 1980, C9.

27. Smith, "Althea Gibson: A Champ When It Wasn't Easy."

28. Mike Kelly, "Barrier-Breaker Gibson Set Up a Wall of Her Own; Tennis Champ Died in Reclusive Poverty," *Record*, September 30, 2003, A03; McGeehan, "Althea Gives Legacy to Young Women"; Smith, "Althea Gibson: A Champ When It Wasn't Easy."

29. Smith, "Althea Gibson: A Champ When It Wasn't Easy."

30. McGeehan, "Althea Gibson Gives Legacy to Young Women."

31. Sources vary on when Gibson and Llewellyn married. For April 11, 1983, see Jay Horning, "For Althea Gibson, Tennis Is Still First Love," *St. Petersburg Times*, January 6, 1985, 6A. Journalist Bruce Schoenfeld states 1984 without attribution.

See Bruce Schoenfeld, *The Match: Althea Gibson and Angela Buxton: How Two Outsiders—One Black, the Other Jewish—Forged a Friendship and Made Sports History* (New York: Amistad Press, 2004), 278. Still another source says 1983. See Gray and Lamb, Born to Win, 169.

32. Althea Gibson, *I Always Wanted to Be Somebody*, ed. Ed Fitzgerald (New York: Harper and Row, 1958), 80; obituary, Sydney Llewellyn, *Record*, October 21, 1999, L-6; transcript, "Interview with Sydney Llewellyn," Washington University in St. Louis, October 21, 1984, http://repository.wustl.edu/concern/videos/rb68xg90w.

33. Transcript, "Interview with Sydney Llewellyn"; Stacey Baker, "Tennis in Harlem," *New York Times*, August 30, 2013, https://archive.nytimes.com/6thfloor.blogs.nyti mes.com/2013/08/30/tennis-in-harlem/. Neither Eric Allen Hall nor Raymond Arseneault, authors of substantial biographies of Ashe that rely heavily on his three published memoirs, discuss Llewellyn's engagement with him.

34. Transcript, "Interview with Sydney Llewellyn." On speculation, see Schoenfeld, *The Match*, 278; Gray and Lamb, *Born to Win*, 169–170; Horning, "For Althea Gibson, Tennis Is Still First Love."

35. Stan Hart, *Once a Champion: Legendary Tennis Stars Revisited* (New York: Dodd, Mead, 1985), vii, 20–21.

36. Hart, *Once a Champion*, 25.

37. Hart, *Once a Champion*, 25–26, 32.

38. Hart, *Once a Champion*, 20, 32, 31, 28, 33. On outings, see King, *All In*, 343–344.

39. Hart, *Once a Champion*, 28–30, 31.

40. Hart, *Once a Champion*, 33, 34.

41. "Biographical Information: Althea Gibson, Tennis Champion/Sportswoman," Gibson Collection.

42. Hart, *Once a Champion*, 32.

43. Ruth La Ferla, "Jasmin's 'Women of Quality,'" *Palm Beach Daily News*, May 1983, 2.

44. Schoenfeld, *The Match*, 278, 279; Don Felder, interview by author, March 10, 2021; Hart, *Once a Champion*, 325; "Newswire: Former Tennis Star," *Los Angeles Times*, October 2, 1984, sec. 3, 5.

45. Transcript, "Interview with Althea Gibson," Washington University in St. Louis, October 21, 1984, http://repository.wustl.edu/concern/videos/8s45qd665; Jim Martz, "Tennis Boom Finding Way to Inner City," *Miami Herald*, March 24, 1974, 6-F; Dennis Dodd, "Althea Gibson Doesn't Miss Spotlight," *Kansas City Times*, June 13, 1985, C-1.

46. Virginia Wade with Jean Rafferty, *Ladies of the Court: A Century of Women at Wimbledon* (New York: Atheneum, 1984), 104.

47. Wade and Rafferty, *Ladies of the Court*.

48. Louis Moore, *We Will Win the Day: The Civil Rights Movement, the Black Athlete, and the Quest for Equality* (Santa Barbara, CA: Praeger, 2017), 188.

49. Dodd, "Althea Gibson Doesn't Miss Spotlight," C-5.

50. "Palm Desert Resort and Country Club: Alice Marble Stadium Court," advertisement, *Palm Desert Post*, April 9–15, 1987, 3; "Alice Marble: Tennis Champion," YouTube, posted by Karl Gluesing, August 8, 2010, https://www.youtube.com/watch?v=ufVT3_GaBXA.

51. Armando Salguero, "For Gibson, Better Is Not Good Enough," *Miami News*, June 26, 1987, 5B.

52. Lynda Whitley, "Althea Gibson Rose to the Top in Grand Style," *Daily Press* (Newport News, VA), April 4, 1987, B8.

53. Steve Crowe, "'Ruthless' Graf Impresses a Tennis Giant," *Detroit Free Press*, March 19, 1987, 2D; Whitley, "Althea Gibson Rose to the Top in Grand Style."

54. Transcript, "Interview with Althea Gibson."

55. Salguero, "For Gibson, Better Is Not Good Enough."

56. Salguero, "For Gibson, Better Is Not Good Enough."

57. Crispin Y. Campbell, Associated Press, "Althea Gibson Legend Lives On," *Sun Herald* (Biloxi, MS), May 1, 1988, D3; Frank Barrows, "A Big Victory in Life of Struggles," *Charlotte Observer*, August 19, 1980, 4B; "Honorary Degrees Conferred 1971," University of North Carolina–Wilmington, https://uncw.edu/facsen/documents/hon_deg/hondegre.pdf (accessed July 28, 2022).

58. Barrows, "A Big Victory in Life of Struggles"; Campbell, "Althea Gibson Legend Lives On."

59. Althea Gibson, "Coaches on the Court," unpublished essay, April 1988, Gibson Collection.

60. Gibson, "Coaches on the Court."

61. Gray and Lamb, *Born to Win*, 169–170; Gibson, "Coaches on the Court."

62. Cathy W. Kelly, "'57 Wimbledon Champ to Discuss Sports Changes," *Daily Utah Chronicle*, January 10, 1990, 9.

63. Garrison, *Zina*, 121, 203; Women's Tennis Association Tour, "Lori McNeil," https://www.wtatennis.com/players/130049/lori-mcneil#bio (accessed January 16, 2022); Peter Alfano, "Footnote to Forefront," *New York Times*, November 18, 1986, B9.

64. Garrison, *Zina*, 150.

65. Garrison, *Zina*, 150–151.

66. "Parade of Champs," *Modesto Bee*, July 8, 1990, C-8; Robin Finn, "Navratilova Captures Ninth Singles Title," *New York Times*, July 8, 1990, S1, S5.

67. Rick Kaplan, "Althea Gibson Gets Back in the Swing," *Desert Sun* (Palm Springs, CA), September 19, 1990, A12.

68. Shelly McKenzie, *Getting Physical: The Rise of Fitness Culture in America* (Lawrence: University Press of Kansas, 2013), 15, 52, 56; Matt Romanoski, "Will Council on Fitness Take Its Last Breath Tomorrow," *Courier News* (Bridgewater, NJ), June 24, 1992, D1; Nancy Shields, "Anti-Drug Rally Held by Pupils: Athlete Says Goals Vital to Clean Life," *Asbury Park Press*, May 24, 1989, B1, B2.

69. Gretchen Schmidhausler, "Tennis Great Serves Up Advice to Seniors," *Asbury Park Press*, October 24, 1988, A10.

70. Donna Mancuso, "Ex-Tennis Champ Gibson: Persistence Still Pays Off," *Central New Jersey Home News*, February 15, 1989, B8. See also Tina A. Brown, "Fitness Still Her Racket: Althea Gibson Big Hit as Speaker," *Asbury Park Press*, September 14, 1991, A3.

71. Schmidhausler, "Tennis Great Serves Up Advice to Seniors."

72. Elliott Denman, "Dare to Be Great: Former Tennis Great Althea Gibson Has Clear Message for Youngsters," *Asbury Park Press*, February 20, 1991, D1.

73. Mancuso, "Ex-Tennis Champ Gibson: Persistence Still Pays Off."

74. Rick Kaplan, "Althea Gibson Says She Can Still Do It All," *Desert Sun*, September 20, 1990, F3.

75. Kaplan, "Althea Gibson Gets Back in the Swing"; Kaplan, "Althea Gibson Says She Can Still Do It All."

76. Jeannie Roberts, "Being Somebody," *Tallahassee Democrat*, February 24, 1991, 1D, 9D; Brown, "Fitness Still Her Racket."

77. Denman, "Dare to be Great," D8.

78. Denman, "Dare to be Great," D8.

79. Roberts, "Being Somebody," 1D, 9D; Brown, "Fitness Still Her Racket."

80. Fred Kovaleski, interview by author, October 23, 2014.

81. Lenny Simpson, interview by author, August 26, 2014.

82. Roberts, "Being Somebody."

83. "Gibson in Newark Hospital," *Courier-News* (Bridgewater, NJ), January 17, 1992, B-6.

84. Tina A. Brown, "Retirees Get Pep Talk from 2 Star Athletes," *Asbury Park Press*, May 5, 1992, D3; Kathleen A. Rowley, "A Champ at State Senior Games," *Courier-Post* (Camden, NJ), May 12, 1992, D1.

85. Pat Politano, "The State Budget Debate: Winners and Losers," *Courier-News*, June 28, 1992, A-6; John Rowe, "N.J. Fumbles on Fitness," *Record*, June 24, 1992, C1; Romanoski, "Will Council on Fitness Take Its Last Breath Tomorrow"; Beau Phillips, "Out-of-Work Giants Veteran Calls Council Cut a Bad Move," *Asbury Park Press*, July 2, 1992, A3.

86. *Ebony*, August 1992, cover, 82, 78, 92, 132–133.

87. Gibson and Fitzgerald, *I Always Wanted to Be Somebody*, 48–49.

88. Arsenault, *Arthur Ashe*, 502–504, 545, 567, 571–573; Gene Policinski and Doug Smith, Gannett News Service, "Ashe: Got AIDS via Surgery," *Courier-News*, April 9, 1992, B-1.

89. President and Mrs. Clinton, White House Invitation, June 1993, Gibson Collection; "William J. Clinton: Remarks at the National Sports Awards Reception," June 20, 1993, American Presidency Project, University of California, Santa Barbara, https://www.presidency.ucsb.edu/documents/remarks-the-national-sports-awards-reception. Don Felder, Gibson's second cousin, found the invitation in Gibson's mail circa 2020–2021.

90. Gray and Lamb, *Born to Win*, 170; Schoenfeld, *The Match*, 282.

91. Don Felder, interview by author, August 30, 2021; Schoenfeld, *The Match*, 3, 280–281.

92. Angela Buxton, interview by author, October 24, 2014.

93. Schoenfeld, *The Match*, 5–6; Gray and Lamb, *Born to Win*, 171.

94. Don Felder, interview by author, March 10, 2021; obituary, Annie Bell Gibson, Gibson Collection; Gray and Lamb, *Born to Win*, 210, 171, 204.

95. Associated Press, "Althea Gibson Seriously Ill," *Sunday Record* (Hackensack, NJ), November 24, 1996, A-2.

96. Ted Poston, "The Story of Althea Gibson: Article IV," *New York Post Daily Magazine*, September 1, 1957, M5.

97. Jane H. Lii, "From New Ashe Stadium, Appeals for Mayor to Speak," *New York Times*, August 24, 1997, 29; Peter Bodo, "A Stadium by Any Other Name," *Tennis*, April 1997, 24–25.

98. Obituary, Annie Bell Gibson, Gibson Collection; Michelle Curry, interview by author, September 3, 2021; Amanda Gerut, "Lady of the Court," *Herald-News* (Passaic, NJ), October 2, 2003, A6; Neil Amdur, "Serena Williams Has Tie to a Legend," *New York Times*, September 16, 1999, D4.

99. Schoenfeld, *The Match*, 288; Kelly, "Barrier-Breaker Gibson Set Up a Wall of Her Own."

100. Gray and Lamb, *Born to Win*, 210; Kelly, "Barrier-Breaker Gibson Set Up a Wall of Her Own"; Elise Young, "Tennis, N.J. Mourn Pioneering Champion," *Record*, September 29, 2003, A-9; Steve Strunsky, "3 Days of Rites for Althea Gibson," *Record*, September 30, 2003, A-3.

101. Angela Buxton, "Advice from a Legend," *Tennis*, August 1997, 16.

102. Schoenfeld, *The Match*, 284; Buxton, "Advice from a Legend," 16.

103. Amdur, "Serena Williams Has Tie to a Legend."

104. "Venus Williams Wins Wimbledon 2000 Tennis Championship," *Jet*, July 24, 2000, 16, 18.

105. Telegram, Althea Gibson to Venus Williams, July 9, 2000, Gibson Collection.

Bibliography

ARCHIVES AND PRIMARY SOURCES

Alonzo A. "Jake" Gaither Collection ("Gaither Collection"), Meek-Eaton Black Archives Research Center and Museum, Florida A&M University, Tallahassee

Althea Gibson Collection ("Gibson Collection"), Felder Family Archives, South Orange, New Jersey

Althea Gibson Collection, Smithsonian Museum of African American History and Culture, Washington, D.C.

British Newspaper Archive (online)

Bud Lessor Oral History Archive, International Tennis Hall of Fame and Museum, Newport, Rhode Island

Columbia Broadcasting System (CBS) Database, Paley Center for Media, New York

Dwight D. Eisenhower Presidential Library and Museum, Abilene, Kansas

Foreign Newspaper Collection (microfilm), Serial and Government Publications Division, Library of Congress, Washington, D.C.

History, Humanities, and Social Sciences Division, Library of Congress, Washington, D.C.

Hubert A. Eaton Sr. Papers ("Eaton Papers"), University of North Carolina–Wilmington

James Weldon Johnson Collection, Beinecke Library, Yale University, New Haven, Connecticut

John F. Kennedy Presidential Library and Museum, Boston

John Ford Collection, Lilly Library, Indiana University, Bloomington: *The Horse Soldiers*, Scripts and Production Materials, Correspondence

Lawrence A. Baker Collection, International Tennis Hall of Fame and Museum, Newport, Rhode Island

National Archives and Records Administration ("NA"), College Park, MD: State Department Files, United States Information Agency Records

Motion Picture, Broadcasting, and Recorded Sound Division, Library of Congress, Washington, D.C.

Moving Image Research Center, Library of Congress, Washington, D.C.

National Association for the Advancement of Colored People (NAACP) Papers (microfilm), Georgetown University, Washington, D.C.

Newspapers.com (online)

ProQuest Historical Newspapers (online): Black Historical Newspapers, Historical Newspapers

Ralph Edwards Productions Radio and Television Scripts, Manuscript Division, Library of Congress, Washington, D.C.

Richard M. Nixon Presidential Library, Yorba Linda, California

Samuel L. Coleman Library, Special Collections, Florida A&M University, Tallahassee

Schomburg Center for Research in Black Culture, New York: Althea Gibson Photograph Collection, Althea Gibson Portrait Collection

Walter Mirsch Papers, Wisconsin Historical Society, Madison

NEWSPAPERS AND PERIODICALS

Accessed through microfilm, hard copy, and online databases, hundreds of articles from approximately 240 newspapers and magazines from around the world are fully cited in the endnotes.

INTERVIEWS

Angela Buxton, interview by author, October 24, 2014

Arthur Carrington, interview by author, June 7, 2017

Michelle Curry, interview by author, March 10, 2021, and September 3, 2021

Don Felder, interview by author, March 10, 2021, and August 30, 2021

Robert W. Johnson III, interview by author, September 26, 2015

Fred Kovaleski, interview by author, October 23, 2014

Lenny Simpson, interview by author, August 26, 2014

PUBLISHED SOURCES, DISSERTATIONS, AND THESES

Adams, Katrina M. *Own the Arena: Getting Ahead, Making a Difference, and Succeeding as the Only One.* New York: Amistad Press, 2021.

Adler, Jeffrey S. *Murder in New Orleans: The Creation of Jim Crow Policing.* Chicago: University of Chicago Press, 2019.

Aldrich, Ann. *We Walk Alone Through Lesbos' Lonely Groves.* New York: Gold Medal Books, 1955.

Alexander, Charles C. *Ty Cobb.* New York: Oxford University Press, 1984.

Althea Gibson. West Haven, CT: Academic Industries, 1984.

Anderson, Lou Eastwood. *Tennis for Women.* New York: A. S. Barnes, 1926.

Andrews, David L. "Excavating Michael Jordan's Blackness." In *Reading Sport: Critical Essays on Power and Representation*, edited by Susan Birrell and Mary G. McDonald, 166–205. Boston: Northeastern University Press, 2000.

Ariail, Cat M. *Passing the Baton: Black Women Track Stars and American Identity*. Urbana: University of Illinois Press, 2020.

Arnesen, Eric. *Black Protest and the Great Migration: A Brief History with Documents*. Boston: Bedford/St. Martin's, 2003.

Aronstein, A-J. "Elsie Conick: A Biography in Fragments." *Guernica*, September 8, 2020. https://www.guernicamag.com/elsie-conick-a-biography-in-fragments/.

Arsenault, Raymond. *Arthur Ashe: A Life*. New York: Simon and Schuster, 2018.

Avila, Eric. *Popular Culture in the Age of White Flight: Fear and Fantasy in Suburban Los Angeles*. Berkeley: University of California Press, 2004.

Bailey, Beth. *Sex in the Heartland*. Cambridge, MA: Harvard University Press, 2002.

Baker, William J. *Jesse Owens: An American Life*. New York: Free Press, 1986.

Baldwin, James. *The Fire Next Time*. New York: Vintage International, 1993.

Baldwin, James. "Freaks and the American Ideal of Manhood." In *Collected Essays*, edited by Toni Morrison, 814–829. New York: Library of America, 1998.

Ballon, Hilary, and Kenneth T. Jackson. *Robert Moses and the Modern City: The Transformation of New York*. New York: W. W. Norton, 2007.

Balto, Simon. *Occupied Territory: Policing Black Chicago from Red Summer to Black Power*. Chapel Hill: University of North Carolina Press, 2020.

Baltzell, E. Digby. *Sporting Gentlemen: Men's Tennis from the Age of Honor to the Cult of the Superstar*. New York: The Free Press, 1995.

Bardolph, Richard. *The Negro Vanguard*. New York: Rinehart, 1959.

Barnes, Althemese, and Ann Roberts. *Black America Series: Tallahassee Florida*. Charleston, SC: Arcadia, 2000.

Bass, Amy. *Not the Triumph but the Struggle: The 1968 Olympics and the Making of the Black Athlete*. Minneapolis: University of Minnesota Press, 2004.

Bay, Mia. *Traveling Black: A Story of Race and Resistance*. Cambridge, MA: Belknap Press of Harvard University Press, 2021.

Belmonte, Laura A. *Selling the American Way: U.S. Propaganda and the Cold War*. Philadelphia: University of Pennsylvania Press, 2008.

Bernard, Emilie, ed. *Remember Me to Harlem: The Letters of Langston Hughes and Carl Van Vechten, 1925–1964*. New York: Alfred A. Knopf, 2001.

Bernstein, Nina. *The Lost Children of Wilder: The Epic Struggle to Change Foster Care*. New York: Vintage Books, 2001.

Bernstein, Robin. *Racial Innocence: Performing Childhood from Slavery to Civil Rights*. New York: New York University Press, 2011.

Betz, Pauline. *Wings on My Tennis Shoes*. London: Sampson Low, Marston, 1949.

Biracree, Tom. *Althea Gibson: Tennis Champion*. New York: Chelsea House, 1989.

Blackburn, Julia. *With Billie: A New Look at the Unforgettable Lady Day*. New York: Pantheon, 2006.

Blanchard, Fessenden S. *Paddle Tennis*. New York: A. S. Barnes, 1944.

Bobrow-Strain, Aaron. *White Bread: A Social History of the Store-Bought Loaf*. Boston: Beacon Press, 2012.

Bogle, Donald. *Bright Boulevards, Bold Dreams: The Story of Black Hollywood*. New York: Ballantine Books, 2005.

Bogle, Donald. *Primetime Blues: African Americans on Network Television*. New York: Farrar, Straus, and Giroux, 2001.

Bogle, Donald. *Toms, Coons, Mulattoes, Mammies, and Bucks: An Interpretive History of Blacks in American Films*. 5th ed. New York: Bloomsbury Academic, 2016.

Bontemps, Arna. *Famous Negro Athletes*. New York: Dodd, Mead, 1964.

Borders, William H. *Seven Minutes at the Mike in the Deep South*. 2nd ed. Atlanta: B. F. Logan Press, 1943.

Boyd, Herb, and Ray Robinson II. *Pound for Pound: A Biography of Sugar Ray Robinson*. New York: Amistad Press, 2006.

Branch, Taylor. *Parting the Waters: America in the King Years, 1954–63*. New York: Simon and Schuster, 1988.

Brenner, Marie. *Great Dames: What I Learned from Older Women*. New York: Random House, 2000.

Bromwich, David. "The Uses of Biography." *Yale Review* 73, no. 2 (1984): 161-176.

Brooks, Evelyn Higginbotham. *Righteous Discontent: The Women's Movement in the Black Baptist Church, 1880–1920*. Cambridge: Harvard University Press, 1994.

Brown, Ashley. "'Uncomplimentary Things': Tennis Player Althea Gibson, Sexism, Homophobia, and Anti-Queerness in the Black Media." *Journal of African American History* 106, no. 2 (Spring 2021): 249–277.

Brown, Ashley. "Swinging for the State Department: American Women Tennis Players in Diplomatic Goodwill Tours, 1941–59." *Journal of Sport History* 43, no. 5 (2015): 289–309.

Brown, Ashley. "The Match of Her Life: Althea Gibson, Icon and Instrument of Integration." Ph.D. diss., George Washington University, 2017.

Brown-Nagin, Tomiko. *Civil Rights Queen: Constance Baker Motley and the Struggle for Equality*. New York: Pantheon, 2022.

Burk, Robert F. *The Eisenhower Administration and Black Civil Rights*. Knoxville: University of Tennessee Press, 1984.

Butler, Judith. *Gender Trouble*. 1990; repr., New York: Routledge, 2007.

Cahn, Susan K. *Coming on Strong: Gender and Sexuality in Women's Sport*, 2nd ed. 1994; repr., Urbana: University of Illinois Press, 2015.

Cahn, Susan K. "From the 'Muscle Moll' to the 'Butch' Ballplayer: Mannishness, Lesbianism, and Homophobia in U.S. Women's Sport." *Feminist Studies* 19, no. 2 (Summer 1993): 343–368.

Capparell, Stephanie. *The Real Pepsi Challenge: The Inspirational Story of Breaking the Color Barrier in American Business*. New York: Wall Street Journal Books, 2007.

Caro, Robert A. *The Power Broker: Robert Moses and the Fall of New York*. New York: Vintage, 1975.

Carter, Tom. *First Lady of Tennis: Hazel Hotchkiss Wightman*. Berkeley, CA: Creative Arts, 2001.

Cayleff, Susan E. *Babe: The Life and Legend of Babe Didrikson Zaharias*. Urbana: University of Illinois Press, 1995.

Chateauvert, Melinda. *Marching Together: Women of the Brotherhood of Sleeping Car Porters*. Urbana: University of Illinois Press, 1997.

Chatelain, Marcia. *South Side Girls: Growing Up in the Great Migration*. Durham, NC: Duke University Press, 2015.

Cohen, Cathy. "Punks, Bulldaggers, and Welfare Queens: The Radical Potential of Queer Politics?" In *Black Queer Studies: A Critical Anthology*, edited by E. Patrick Johnson and Mae Henderson, 21–51. Durham, NC: Duke University Press, 2005.

Collins, Patricia Hill. "Learning from the Outsider Within: The Sociological Significance of Black Feminist Thought." *Social Problems* 33, no. 6 (1986): S14–S32.

Connolly, Maureen. *Forehand Drive*. London: Macgibbon and Kee, 1957.

Cooke, Sarah Palfrey. *Winning Tennis and How to Play It*. Garden City, NY: Doubleday, 1946.

Coontz, Stephanie. *The Way We Really Are: Coming to Terms with America's Changing Families*. New York: Basic Books, 1997.

Crenshaw, Kimberlé. "Demarginalizing the Intersection of Race and Sex: A Black Feminist Critique of Antidiscrimination Doctrine, Feminist Theory and Antiracist Politics," *University of Chicago Legal Forum* 1 (1989): 139–167.

Crenshaw, Kimberlé. "Mapping the Margins: Intersectionality, Identity Politics, and Violence Against Women of Color." *Stanford Law Review* 43, no. 6 (1991): 1241–1299.

Cripps, Thomas. *Making Movies Black: The Hollywood Message Movie from World War II to the Civil Rights Era*. New York: Oxford University Press, 1993.

Crosson, Seàn. *Sport and Film*. New York: Routledge, 2013.

Cuhl, Nancy. *Extravagant Crowd: Carl Van Vechten's Portraits of Women*. New Haven, CT: Yale University Press, 2007.

Curtis, Cathy. *A Generous Vision: The Creative Life of Elaine de Kooning*. New York: Oxford University Press, 2017.

Curwood, Anastasia C. *Stormy Weather: Middle-Class African American Marriages Between the Two World Wars*. Chapel Hill: University of North Carolina Press, 2010.

Danzig, Allison. "Sphairistike, History of the United States Lawn Tennis Association." In *The Fireside Book of Tennis*, edited by Allison Danzig and Peter Schwed, 14–15. New York: Simon and Schuster, 1972.

Das, Joanna Dee. *Katherine Dunham: Dance and the African Diaspora*. New York: Oxford University Press, 2017.

Davenport, Joanna. "The History and Interpretation Amateurism in the United States Lawn Tennis Association." Ph.D. diss., Ohio State University, 1966.

Davidson, Sue. *Changing the Game: The Stories of Tennis Champions Alice Marble and Althea Gibson*. Seattle: Seal Press, 1997.

Davis, Amira Rose. "No League of Their Own: Baseball, Black Women, and the Politics of Representation," *Radical History Review* 125 (May 2016): 74–96.

Davis, Ossie, and Alice Bernstein, *The People of Clarendon County: A Play by Ossie Davis with Photographs and Historical Documents, and Essays on the Education that Can End Racism*. Chicago: Third World Press, 2007.

De Laine, Marguirite, F. S. Corbett, and Cecil J. Williams, *Clarendon County*. Charleston, SC: Arcadia, 2002.

Deans, Karen. *Playing to Win: The Story of Althea Gibson*. New York: Scholastic, 2007.

Demas, Lane. *Game of Privilege: An African American History of Golf*. Chapel Hill: University of North Carolina Press, 2017.

Demas, Lane. *Integrating the Gridiron: Black Civil Rights and American College Football*. New Brunswick, NJ: Rutgers University Press, 2011.

Djata, Sundiata. *Blacks at the Net: Black Achievement in the History of Tennis*. Syracuse, NY: Syracuse University Press, 2006.

Djata, Sundiata. "Game Set, and Separatism: The American Tennis Association, a Tennis Vanguard." In *Separate Games: African American Sport behind the Wall of Segregation*, edited by David K. Wiggins and Ryan A. Swanson, 165–178. Fayetteville: University of Arkansas Press, 2016.

Driver, Helen Irene. *Tennis for Teachers*. Madison, WI: H. I. Driver and Associates, 1956.

Dudziak, Mary L. *Cold War Civil Rights: Race and the Image of American Democracy*. Princeton, NJ: Princeton University Press, 2000.

Duggan, Lisa. "Making It Perfectly Queer." *Socialist Review* 22, no. 1 (March 1992): 11–31.

Eaton, Hubert A. *"Every Man Should Try."* Wilmington, NC: Bonaparte Press, 1984.

Engelmann, Larry. *The Goddess and the American Girl*. New York: Oxford University Press, 1988.

Eyman, Scott. *Print the Legend: The Life and Times of John Ford*. New York: Simon and Schuster, 1999.

Faderman, Lillian. *The Gay Revolution: The Story of the Struggle*. New York: Simon and Schuster, 2015.

Faderman, Lillian. *Odd Girls and Twilight Lovers: A History of Lesbian Life in Twentieth-Century America*. New York: Columbia University Press, 1991.

Fago, John Norwood, Frank Redondo, and Fred Carrillo. *Jim Thorpe/Althea Gibson*. West Haven, CT: Pendulum Press, 1979.

Feldstein, Ruth. *How It Feels to Be Free: Black Women Entertainers and the Civil Rights Movement*. New York: Oxford University Press, 2013.

Feldstein, Ruth. *Motherhood in Black and White: Race and Sex in American Liberalism, 1930–1965*. Ithaca, NY: Cornell University Press, 2000.

Felker-Kantor, Max. *Policing Los Angeles: Race, Resistance, and the Rise of the LAPD.* Chapel Hill: University of North Carolina Press, 2020.

Ferguson, Jeffrey B. *The Harlem Renaissance: A Brief History with Documents.* Boston: Bedford/St. Martin's, 2008.

Festle, Mary Jo. "'Jackie Robinson Without the Charm': The Challenge of Being Althea Gibson." In *Out of the Shadows: A Biographical History of African American Athletes*, edited by David K. Wiggins, 187–206. Fayetteville: University of Arkansas Press, 2006.

Fitzgerald, Ed. *A Nick an Inch.* New York: Atheneum, 1985.

Friedwald, Will. *Straighten Up and Fly Right: The Life and Music of Nat King Cole.* New York: Oxford University Press, 2020.

Gaines, Ann Graham. *Female Firsts in Their Fields: Sports and Athletics.* Philadelphia: Chelsea House, 1999.

Gaines, Kevin K. *Uplifting the Race: Black Leadership, Politics, and Culture in the Twentieth Century.* Chapel Hill: University of North Carolina Press, 1996.

Gallon, Kim. *Pleasure in the News: African American Readership and Sexuality in the Black Press.* Urbana: University of Illinois Press, 2020.

Garrison, Zina, with Doug Smith. *Zina: My Life in Women's Tennis.* Berkeley, CA: North Atlantic Books, 2001.

Gibson, Althea. *I Always Wanted to Be Somebody.* Edited by Ed Fitzgerald. New York: Harper and Row, 1958.

Gibson, Althea, with Richard Curtis. *So Much to Live For.* New York: G. P. Putnam's Sons, 1968.

Giddings, Paula J. *Ida, a Sword Among Lions.* New York: Amistad Press, 2008.

Giddings, Paula J. *When and Where I Enter: The Impact of Black Women on Race and Sex in America.* 1984; repr., New York: Perennial, 2001.

Gill, Jonathan. *Harlem: The Four Hundred Year History from Dutch Village to Capital of Black America.* New York: Grove Press, 2011.

Gill, LaVerne McCain. *African American Women in Congress: Forming and Transforming History.* New Brunswick, NJ: Rutgers University Press, 1997.

Ginell, Cary. *Mr. B: The Music and Life of Billy Eckstine.* Milwaukee, MI: Hal Leonard, 2013.

Glenn, Rhonda. *The Illustrated History of Women's Golf.* Dallas, TX: Taylor, 1991.

Gooding-Williams, Robert. *Look, A Negro! Philosophical Essays on Race, Culture, and Politics.* New York: Routledge, 2004.

Gormley, Beatrice. *Althea Gibson, Young Tennis Player.* New York: Aladdin, 2005.

Gorn, Elliott J., and Warren Goldstein. *A Brief History of American Sports.* New York: Hill and Wang, 1993.

Gorn, Elliott J. *Let the People See: The Story of Emmett Till.* New York: Oxford University Press, 2018.

Goudsouzian, Aram. *King of the Court: Bill Russell and the Basketball Revolution.* Berkeley: University of California Press, 2010.

Gray, Frances Clayton, and Yanick Rice Lamb. *Born to Win: The Authorized Biography of Althea Gibson*. Hoboken, NJ: John Wiley and Sons, 2004.

Green, Adam. *Selling the Race: Culture, Community, and Black Chicago, 1940–1955*. Chicago: University of Chicago Press, 2009.

Greenberg, Jack. *Crusaders in the Courts: How a Dedicated Band of Lawyers Fought for the Civil Rights Revolution*. New York: Basic Books, 1994.

Greer, Brenna Wynn. *Represented: The Black Imagemakers Who Reimagined African American Citizenship*. Philadelphia: University of Pennsylvania Press, 2019.

Griffin, Pat. "Changing the Game: Homophobia, Sexism, and Lesbians in Sport." In *Women and Sports in the United States: A Documentary Reader*, edited by Jean O'Reilly and Susan K. Cahn, 217–234. Boston: Northeastern University Press, 2007.

Griffin, Pat. "The Lesbian Athlete: Unlearning the Culture of the Closet." In *A Queer World: The Center for Lesbian and Gay Studies Reader*, edited by Martin Duberman, 564–566. New York: New York University Press, 1997.

Grossinger, Tania. *Growing Up at Grossinger's*. New York: Skyhorse, 2008.

Grossman, James R. *Land of Hope: Chicago, Black Southerners, and the Great Migration*. Chicago: University of Chicago Press, 1991.

Grundy, Pamela, and Susan Shackleford. *Shattering the Glass: The Remarkable History of Women's Basketball*. New York: New Press, 2005.

Grundy, Pamela. *Learning to Win: Sports, Education, and Social Change in Twentieth-Century North Carolina*. Chapel Hill: University of North Carolina Press, 2001.

Gutterman, Lauren Jae. "Another Enemy Within: Lesbian Wives, or the Hidden Threat to the Nuclear Family in Post-War America." *Gender and History* 24, no. 2 (2012): 475–501.

Gutterman, Lauren Jae. *Her Neighbor's Wife: A History of Lesbian Desire Within Marriage*. Philadelphia: University of Pennsylvania Press, 2019.

Guttmann, Allen. *Sports: The First Five Millennia*. Amherst: University of Massachusetts Press, 2004.

Halberstam, Judith. *Female Masculinity*. Durham: Duke University Press, 1998.

Halberstam, Judith. *In a Queer Time and Place: Transgender Bodies, Subcultural Lives*. New York: New York University Press, 2005.

Hall, Eric Allen. *Arthur Ashe: Tennis and Justice in the Civil Rights Era*. Baltimore: Johns Hopkins University Press, 2014,

Hall, Eric Allen. "'I Guess I'm Becoming More and More Militant': Arthur Ashe and the Black Freedom Movement." *Journal of African American History* 96, no. 4 (2011): 474–502.

Harding, Vincent, Robin D. G. Kelley, et al. "We Changed the World, 1945–1970." In *To Make Our World Anew, Volume II: A History of African Americans from 1880*, edited by Robin D. G. Kelley and Earl Lewis, 236–251. New York: Oxford University Press, 2005.

Harris, Cecil. *Different Strokes: Serena, Venus, and the Unfinished Black Tennis Revolution*. Lincoln: University of Nebraska Press, 2020.

Harris, Cecil, and Larryette Kyle-Debose. *Charging the Net: A History of Blacks in Tennis from Althea Gibson and Arthur Ashe to the Williams Sisters*. Chicago: Ivan R. Dee, 2007.

Hart, Doris. *Tennis with Hart*. Philadelphia: J. B. Lippincott, 1955.

Hart, Stan. *Once a Champion: Legendary Tennis Stars Revisited*. New York: Dodd, Mead, 1985.

Hartmann, Douglas. *Race, Culture, and the Revolt of the Black Athlete: The 1968 Olympic Protests and Their Aftermath*. Chicago: University of Chicago Press, 2004.

Haywood, D'Weston. *Let Us Make Men: The Twentieth-Century Black Press and a Manly Vision for Racial Advancement*. Chapel Hill: University of North Carolina Press, 2018.

Heilbrun, Carolyn G. *Writing a Woman's Life*. New York: W. W. Norton, 1988.

Henderson, Edwin Bancroft. *The Negro in Sports*. Washington, DC: Associated, 1939.

Higginbotham, Evelyn Brooks. *Righteous Discontent: The Women's Movement in the Black Baptist Church, 1880–1920*. Cambridge, MA: Harvard University Press, 1994.

Himes,Chester. *If He Hollers, Let Him Go*. 2002; repr., New York: Thunder's Mouth Press, 1945.

Hine, Darlene Clark. "Black Migration to the Urban Midwest: The Gender Dimension, 1915–1945." In *The Great Migration in Historical Perspective: New Dimensions of Race, Class, and Gender*, edited by Joe William Trotter Jr., 127–146. Bloomington: Indiana University Press, 1991.

Hine, Darlene Clark. "Rape and the Inner Lives of Black Women in the Middle West." *Signs* 14, no. 4 (1989): 912–920.

Hirsch, James. *Willie Mays: The Life, The Legend*. New York: Scribner, 2010.

Howell, Ron. *Boss of Black Brooklyn: The Life and Times of Bertram L. Baker*. New York: Empire State Editions, 2019.

Hunter, Tera W. *To 'Joy My Freedom: Southern Black Women's Lives and Labors After the Civil War*. Cambridge, MA: Harvard University Press, 1997.

Hurston, Zora Neale. *Their Eyes Were Watching God*. 1937; repr., New York: Harper Collins, 1991.

Isserman, Maurice, and Michael Kazin. *America Divided: The Civil War of the 1960s*. New York: Oxford University Press, 2000.

James, Rawn, Jr. *Root and Branch: Charles Hamilton Houston, Thurgood Marshall, and the Struggle to End Segregation*. New York: Bloomsbury Press, 2010.

Jamieson, Katherine M. "Reading Nancy Lopez: Decoding Representations of Race, Class, and Sexuality." *Sociology of Sport Journal* 15 (Winter 1998): 343–358.

Johnson, E. Patrick. *Black. Queer. Southern. Women: An Oral History*. Chapel Hill: University of North Carolina Press, 2018.

Johnson, John H., with Lerone Bennett Jr., *Succeeding Against the Odds: The Inspiring Autobiography of One of America's Wealthiest Entrepreneurs*. New York: Warner Books, 1989.

Johnson, Kimberly. "Wadleigh High School: The Price of Segregation." In *Educating Harlem: A Century of Schooling and Resistance in a Black Community*, edited by Ansley T. Erickson and Ernest Morrell, 77–100. New York: Columbia University Press, 2019.

Johnson, Leola, and David Roediger. "'Hertz, Don't It?': Becoming Colorless and Staying Black in the Crossover of O. J. Simpson." In *Reading Sport: Critical Essays on Power and Representation*, edited by Susan Birrell and Mary G. McDonald, 40–73. Boston: Northeastern University Press, 2000.

Johnson, M. Mikell. *The African American Woman Golfer*. Westport, CT: Praeger, 2008.

Jones, Jacqueline. *Labor of Love, Labor of Sorrow: Black Women, Work, and the Family from Slavery to the Present*. 1985; repr., New York: Basic Books, 2010.

Kaliss, Gregory J. *Men's College Athletics and the Politics of Racial Equality: Five Pioneer Stories of Black Manliness, White Citizenship, and American Democracy*. Philadelphia: Temple University Press, 2012.

Kaplan, Carla. *Miss Anne in Harlem: The White Women of the Black Renaissance*. New York: HarperCollins, 2013.

Keller, Yvonne. "'Was It Right to Love Her Brother's Wife So Passionately': Lesbian Pulp Novels and U.S. Lesbian Identity, 1950–1965." *American Quarterly* 57, no. 2 (2005): 385–410.

Kelley, Robin D. G. *Yo' Mama's Disfunktional: Fighting the Culture Wars in Urban America*. Boston: Beacon Press, 1998.

Kennedy, Elizabeth Lapovsky, and Madeline D. Davis. *Boots of Leather, Slippers of Gold: The History of a Lesbian Community*. 2nd ed. New York: Routledge, 2014.

King, Billie Jean. *All In: An Autobiography*. New York: Alfred A. Knopf, 2021.

King, Billie Jean, with Frank Deford. *Billie Jean*. New York: Viking Press, 1982.

King, Billie Jean, with Cynthia Starr. *We Have Come a Long Way: The Story of Women's Tennis*. New York: McGraw-Hill, 1988.

King, Martin Luther, Jr. *Where Do We Go from Here, Chaos or Community?* Boston: Beacon Press, 1968.

King, Martin Luther, Jr. *Why We Can't Wait*. 1963; repr., New York: Signet Classics, 2000.

Kirsch, George B. *Golf in America*. Urbana: University of Illinois Press, 2009.

Kovaleski, Fred. "Hamtramck." In *The Fireside Book of Tennis*, edited by Allison Danzig and Peter Schwed, 461–463. New York: Simon and Schuster, 1971.

Kramer, Jack. *The Game: My 40 Years in Tennis*. New York: G. P. Putnam's Sons, 1979.

Lake, Marilyn, and Henry Reynolds. *Drawing the Global Colour Line: White Men's Countries and the International Challenge of Racial Equality*. Cambridge: Cambridge University Press, 2008.

Lanctot, Neil. *Campy: The Two Lives of Roy Campanella*. New York: Simon & Schuster, 2011.

Lanker, Brian. *I Dream a World: Portraits of Black Women Who Changed America*. New York: Stewart, Tabori and Chang, 1989.

Lansbury, Jennifer H. *A Spectacular Leap: Black Women Athletes in Twentieth-Century America*. Fayetteville: University of Arkansas Press, 2014.

Larsen, Lawrence. *A History of Missouri, Vol. 4, 1953–2003*. Columbia: University of Missouri Press, 2004.

Larson, Kate Clifford. *Walk with Me: A Biography of Fannie Lou Hamer*. New York: Oxford University Press, 2021.

Liberti, Rita. "'We Were Ladies, We Just Played Like Boys': African-American Womanhood and Competitive Basketball at Bennett College, 1928–1942." *Journal of Sport History* 26, no. 3 (1999): 567–584.

Liberti, Rita, and Maureen M. Smith. *(Re)Presenting Wilma Rudolph*. Syracuse, NY: Syracuse University Press, 2015.

Lichtenstein, Grace. *A Long Way, Baby: Behind the Scenes in Women's Pro Tennis*. New York: William Morrow, 1974.

Loewen, James W. *Sundown Towns: A Hidden Dimension of American Racism*. New York: Touchstone, 2006.

Lumpkin, Angela. *Women's Tennis: A Historical Documentary of the Players and Their Game*. Troy, NY: Whitson, 1981.

Maguire, James. *Impresario: The Life and Times of Ed Sullivan*. New York: Billboard Books, 2006.

Martin, Charles H. *Benching Jim Crow: The Rise and Fall of the Color Line in Southern College Sports, 1890–1980*. Urbana: University of Illinois Press, 2010.

Masur, Kate. "Color Was a Bar to the Entrance: African American Activism and the Question of Social Equality in Lincoln's White House." *American Quarterly* 69, no. 1 (2017): 1–22.

May, Elaine Tyler. *Homeward Bound: American Families in the Cold War Era*. 4th ed. New York: Basic Books, 2017.

McCracken, Allison. *Real Men Don't Croon: Crooning in American Culture*. Raleigh, NC: Duke University Press, 2015.

McDaniel, Pete. *Uneven Lies: The Heroic Story of African-Americans in Golf*. Greenwich, CT, 2000.

McDuffie, Erik S. *Sojourning for Freedom: Black Women, American Communism, and the Making of Black Left Feminism*. Durham, NC: Duke University Press, 2011.

McElya, Micki. *Clinging to Mammy: The Faithful Slave in Twentieth-Century America*. Cambridge, MA: Harvard University Press, 2007.

McGuire, Daniel L. *At the Dark End of the Street: Black Women, Rape and Resistance—A New History of the Civil Rights Movement from Rosa Parks to the Rise of Black Power*. New York: Vintage Books, 2010.

McKenzie, Shelly. *Getting Physical: The Rise of Fitness Culture in America*. Lawrence: University Press of Kansas, 2013.

McPhee, John. *Levels of the Game*. New York: Farrar, Straus and Giroux, 1969.

Mead, Chris. *Joe Louis: Black Champion in White America*. Mineola, NY: Dover, 1985.

Meyer, Leisa D. *Creating GI Jane: Sexuality and Power in the Women's Army Corps During World War II*. New York: Columbia University Press, 1996.

Miller, Patrick B. "Muscular Assimilationism: Sport and the Paradoxes of Racial Reform." In *Race and Sport: The Struggle for Equality On and Off the Field*, edited by Charles K. Ross, 146–182. Oxford: University of Mississippi Press, 2004.

Mitchell, Michele. *Righteous Propagation: African Americans and the Politics of Racial Destiny After Reconstruction*. Chapel Hill: University of North Carolina Press, 2004.

Moore, Brenda L. "African Americans in the Military." In *The Columbia Guide to African American History Since 1939*, edited by Robert L. Harris Jr. and Rosalyn Terborg-Penn, 120–135. New York: Columbia University Press, 2006.

Moore, Brenda L. *To Serve My Country, to Serve My Race: The Story of the Only African American WACs Stationed Overseas During World War II*. New York: New York University Press, 1996.

Moore, Louis. *We Will Win the Day: The Civil Rights Movement, the Black Athlete, and the Quest for Equality*. Santa Barbara, CA: Praeger, 2017.

Morgan, Denice C. "Jack Johnson: Reluctant Hero of the Black Community." *Akron Law Review* 32, no. 3 (1999): 529–556.

Mortimer, Angela. *My Waiting Game*. London: Frederick Muller, 1962.

Moss, Richard J. *Golf and the American Country Club*. Urbana: University of Illinois Press, 2001.

Olsen, Jack. *The Black Athlete: A Shameful Story: The Myth of Integration in American Sport*. New York: Time-Life Books, 1968.

Osgood, Kenneth. *Total Cold War: Eisenhower's Secret Propaganda Battle at Home and Abroad*. Lawrence: University Press of Kansas, 2006.

Overmyer, James. *Queen of the Negro Leagues: Effa Manley and the Newark Eagles*. Lanham, MD: Rowman and Littlefield, 2020.

Palfrey, Sarah. *Tennis for Anyone*. 1966; repr., New York: Cornerstone, 1971.

Parker, Alison M. *Unceasing Militant: The Life of Mary Church Terrell*. Chapel Hill: University of North Carolina Press, 2020.

Parks, Arnold G. *Lincoln University, 1920–1970*. Charleston, SC: Arcadia, 2007.

Pascoe, Peggy. *What Comes Naturally: Miscegenation Law and the Making of Race in America*. New York: Oxford University Press, 2010.

Peiss, Kathy. *Hope in a Jar: The Making of America's Beauty Culture*. 1998; repr., Philadelphia: University of Pennsylvania Press, 2011.

Perry, Imani. *Looking for Lorraine: The Radiant and Radical Life of Lorraine Hansberry*. Boston: Beacon Press, 2018.

Perry, Ravi K. *Black Mayors, White Majorities: The Balancing Act of Racial Politics*. Lincoln: University of Nebraska Press, 2014.

Pitrone, Jean. *Jean Hoxie: The Robin Hood of Tennis*. Hamtramck, MI: Avenue, 1985.

Rabby, Alice. *The Pain and the Promise: The Struggle for Civil Rights in Tallahassee, Florida*. Athens: University of Georgia Press, 1999.

Rampersad, Arnold. *Jackie Robinson, a Biography*. New York: Alfred A. Knopf, 1997.

Randle, Dorothy Davies, and Marjorie Hillas. *Tennis Organized for Group Instruction.* New York: A. S. Barnes, 1932.

Randolph, Sherie M. *Florynce "Flo" Kennedy: The Life of a Black Feminist Radical.* Chapel Hill: University of North Carolina Press, 2015.

Ransby, Barbara. *Ella Baker and the Black Freedom Movement: A Radical Democratic Vision.* Chapel Hill: University of North Carolina Press, 2003.

Reid, Megan. *Althea Gibson: The Story of Tennis' Fleet-of-Foot Girl.* New York: Balzer + Gray, 2020.

Reiniger, Anne, Joseph T. Gleason, et al. *The New York Society for the Prevention of Cruelty to Children, 1874–2000.* New York: RPM, 2000.

Remnick, David. *King of the World: Muhammad Ali and the Rise of an American Hero.* New York: Vintage, 1998.

Roberts, Randy. *Joe Louis: Hard Times Man.* New Haven, CT: Yale University Press, 2010.

Roberts, Randy. *Papa Jack: Jack Johnson and the Era of White Hopes.* New York: Free Press, 1983.

Roberts, Selena. *A Necessary Spectacle: Billie Jean King, Bobby Riggs, and the Tennis Match That Leveled the Game.* New York: Crown Books, 2005.

Robinson, Erik. *Images of America: Tallahassee.* Charleston, SC: Arcadia, 2003.

Rose, Chanelle Nyree. *The Struggle for Black Freedom in Miami: Civil Rights and America's Tourist Paradise, 1896–1968.* Baton Rouge: Louisiana State University Press, 2015.

Rosenberg, Rosalind. *Jane Crow: The Life of Pauli Murray.* New York: Oxford University Press, 2017.

Ross, Charles. *Outside the Lines: African Americans and the Integration of the National Football League.* New York: New York University Press, 1999.

Ross, Lawrence C., Jr. *The Divine Nine: The History of African American Fraternities and Sororities.* New York: Davina Books, 2000.

Royce, Edward. *The Origins of Southern Sharecropping.* Philadelphia: Temple University Press, 1993.

Rugh, Susan Sessions. *Are We There Yet? The Golden Age of American Family Vacations.* Lawrence: University Press of Kansas, 2008.

Rundstedtler, Theresa. "In Sports the Best Man Wins: How Joe Louis Whupped Jim Crow." In *In the Game: Race, Identity, and Sports in the Twentieth Century*, edited by Amy Bass, 47–92. New York: Palgrave Macmillan, 2005.

Runstedtler, Theresa. *Jack Johnson, Rebel Sojourner: Boxing in the Shadow of the Global Color Line.* Berkeley: University of California Press, 2012.

Russell, Thaddeus. "The Color of Discipline: Civil Rights and Black Sexuality." *American Quarterly* 60, no. 1 (2008): 101–128.

Ruth, Greg. *Tennis: A History from American Amateurs to Global Professionals.* Urbana: University of Illinois Press, 2021.

Sammons, Jeffrey T. *Beyond the Ring: The Role of Boxing in American Society.* Urbana: University of Illinois Press, 1988.

Scanlon, Jennifer. *Bad Girls Go Everywhere: The Life of Helen Gurley Brown*. New York: Oxford University Press, 2009.

Scanlon, Jennifer. *Until There is Justice: The Life of Anna Arnold Hedgeman*. New York: Oxford University Press, 2016.

Schoenfeld, Bruce. *The Match: Angela Buxton and Althea Gibson: How Two Outsiders— One Black, the Other Jewish—Forged a Friendship and Made Sports History*. New York: Amistad Press, 2004.

Schultz, Jaime. *Qualifying Times: Points of Change in U.S. Women's Sport*. Urbana: University of Illinois Press, 2014.

Schwartz, Peggy and Murray. *The Dance Claimed Me: A Biography of Pearl Primus*. New Haven, CT: Yale University Press, 2011.

Schwenk, Melinda. "'Negro Stars' and the USIA's Portrait of Democracy." *Race, Gender and Class* 8, no. 4 (2001): 116–139.

Shropshire, Kenneth L., and Scott Brooks. "Sugar Ray Robinson—The Businessman." In *Race and Sport: The Struggle for Equality On and Off the Field*, edited by Charles K. Ross, 26–39. Oxford: University of Mississippi Press, 2004.

Sifford, Charlie. *Just Let Me Play: The Story of Charlie Sifford, the First Black PGA Golfer*. Latham, NY: British American, 1992.

Sklaroff, Lauren Rebecca. *Red Hot Mama: The Life of Sophie Tucker*. Austin: University of Texas Press, 2018.

Smith, Doug. *Whirlwind, the Godfather of Black Tennis: The Life and Times of Dr. Robert Walter Johnson*. Washington, DC: Blue Eagle, 2004.

Smith, Malissa. *A History of Women's Boxing*. New York: Rowman and Littlefield, 2014.

Smith, Suzanne E. *Dancing in the Street: Motown and the Cultural Politics of Detroit*. Cambridge, MA: Harvard University Press, 1999.

Smith, Thomas G. *Showdown: JFK and the Integration of the Washington Redskins*. Boston: Beacon Press, 2011.

Snyder, Brad. *A Well-Paid Slave: Curt Flood's Fight for Free Agency in Professional Sports*. New York: Viking, 2006.

Spork, Shirley. *From Green to Tee*. Scotts Valley, CA: CreateSpace, 2017.

Stange, Maren. "'Photographs Taken in Everyday Life': *Ebony's* Photojournalistic Discourse." In *The Black Press: New Literary and Historical Essays*, edited by Todd Vogel, 207–227. New Brunswick, NJ: Rutgers University Press, 2001.

Stanmyre, Jackie F. *Althea Gibson and Arthur Ashe: Breaking Down Tennis's Color Barrier*. New York: Cavendish Square, 2016.

Stark, Douglas. *Breaking Barriers: A History of Integration in Professional Basketball*. Lanham, MD: Rowman and Littlefield, 2018.

Starn, Orin. *The Passion of Tiger Woods*. Durham, NC: Duke University Press, 2011.

Stauffacher, Sue. *Nothing but Trouble: The Story of Althea Gibson*. New York: Dragonfly Books, 2011.

Stevens, Peter F. *Links Lore: Dramatic Moments and Neglected Milestones from Golf's History*. Dulles, VA: Brassey's, 2000.

Stovall, Tyler. *Paris Noir: African Americans in the City of Light*. New York: Houghton Mifflin, 1996.

Summers, Joseph, and Dorothy S. Dallmeyer. *Jefferson City, Missouri*. Chicago: Arcadia, 2000.

Synnott, Marcia G. "African American Women Pioneers in Desegregating Higher Education." In *Higher Education and the Civil Rights Movement: White Supremacy, Black Southerners, and College Campuses,* edited by Peter Wallenstein, 199–228. Gainesville: University Press of Florida, 2008.

Teresa, Carrie. *Looking at the Stars: Black Celebrity Journalism in Jim Crow America*. Lincoln: University of Nebraska Press, 2019.

Theoharis, Jeanne. *The Rebellious Life of Mrs. Rosa Parks*. Boston: Beacon Press, 2013.

Thomas, Damion L. *Globetrotting: African American Athletes and Cold War Politics*. Urbana: University of Illinois Press, 2012.

Thomas, Evan. *Being Nixon: A Man Divided*. New York: Random House, 2015.

Thompson, Lisa B. *Beyond the Black Lady: Sexuality and the New African American Middle Class*. Urbana: University of Illinois Press, 2009.

Tilden, Bill. *My Story*. New York: Hellman, Williams, 1948.

Tinling, Teddy, with Robert Oxby. *White Ladies*. London: Stanley Paul, 1963.

Tye, Larry. *Rising from the Rails: Pullman Porters and the Making of the Black Middle Class*. New York: Henry Holt, 2004.

Tygiel, Jules. *Baseball's Great Experiment: Jackie Robinson and His Legacy*. New York: Oxford University Press, 1983.

Verbrugge, Martha H. *Active Bodies: A History of Women's Physical Education in Twentieth-Century America*. New York: Oxford University Press, 2012.

Vogan, Travis. *ABC Sports: The Rise and Fall of Network Sports Television*. Oakland: University of California Press, 2018.

Von Eschen, Penny M. *Satchmo Blows Up the World: Jazz Ambassadors Play the Cold War*. Cambridge, MA: Harvard University Press, 2004.

Wade, Virginia, and Jean Rafferty. *Ladies of the Court: A Century of Women at Wimbledon*. New York: Atheneum, 1984.

Wallenstein, Peter. "Black Southerners and Nonblack Universities: The Process of Desegregating Southern Higher Education, 1935–1965." In *Higher Education and the Civil Rights Movement: White Supremacy, Black Southerners, and College Campuses,* edited by Peter Wallenstein, 17–59. Gainesville: University Press of Florida, 2008.

Walsh, Kenneth T. *Celebrity in Chief: A History of Presidents and the Culture of Stardom*. New York: Routledge, 2016.

Ward, Geoff K. *The Black Child-Savers: Racial Democracy and Juvenile Justice*. Chicago: University of Chicago Press, 2012.

Ward, Geoffrey C. *Unforgivable Blackness: The Rise and Fall of Jack Johnson*. New York: Alfred A. Knopf, 2004.

Ware, Susan. *Game Set Match: Billie Jean King and the Revolution in Women's Sports*. Chapel Hill: University of North Carolina Press, 2011.

Ware, Susan. *Title IX: A Brief History with Documents*. Boston: Bedford/St. Martin's, 2007.

Washington, Harriet A. *Medical Apartheid: The Dark History of Medical Experimentation on African Americans from Colonial Times to the Present*. New York: Doubleday, 2006.

Whaley, Deborah Elizabeth. *Disciplining Women: Alpha Kappa Alpha, Black Counterpublics, and the Cultural Politics of Black Sororities*. Albany: State University of New York Press, 2010.

White, Dan G. *A Collector's Guide to Signature and Photo Decal Wood Tennis Rackets*. Palm City, FL: Dan G. White, 2020.

White, Deborah Gray. *Too Heavy a Load: Black Women in Defense of Themselves: 1894–1994*. New York: W. W. Norton, 1999.

White, Derrick E. *Blood, Sweat, and Tears: Jake Gaither, Florida A&M, and the History of Black College Football*. Chapel Hill: University of North Carolina Press, 2019.

White, Edward. *The Tastemaker: Carl Van Vechten and the Birth of Modern America*. New York: Farrar, Straus, and Giroux, 2014.

Wiggins, David K. "Edwin Bancroft Henderson, African-American Athletes, and the Writing of Sport History." In *Sport and the Color Line*, edited by David Wiggins and Patrick Miller, 271–288. New York: Routledge, 2006.

Wiggins, William H., Jr. "Joe Louis: American Folk Hero." In *Sport and the Color Line: Black Athletes and Race Relations in Twentieth-Century America*, edited by Patrick B. Miller and David K. Wiggins, 127–146. New York: Routledge, 2004.

Wilkerson, Isabel. *The Warmth of Other Suns: The Epic Story of America's Great Migration*. New York: Random House, 2010.

Wilkins, Roger. *A Man's Life: An Autobiography*. New York: Simon and Schuster, 1982.

Wiltse, Jeff. *Contested Waters: A Social History of Swimming Pools in America*. Chapel Hill: University of North Carolina Press, 2007.

Wolcott, Victoria W. *Race, Riots, and Roller Coasters: The Struggle over Segregated Recreation in America*. Philadelphia: University of Pennsylvania Press, 2012.

Wolcott, Victoria W. *Remaking Respectability: African American Women in Interwar Detroit*. Chapel Hill: University of North Carolina Press, 2001.

Woolner, Cookie. "'Woman Slain in Queer Love Brawl': African American Women, Same-Sex Desire, and Violence in the Urban North, 1920–1929." *Journal of African American History* 100, no. 3 (2015): 407–427.

York, Neil Longley. *Fiction as Fact: The Horse Soldiers and Popular Memory*. Kent, OH: Kent State University Press, 2001.

Young, A. S. "Doc." *Negro Firsts in Sports*. Chicago: Johnson Publishing Company, 1963.

Zeiler, Thomas. *Jackie Robinson and Race in America: A Brief History with Documents*. Boston: Bedford/St. Martin's, 2014.

Ziegler, Kortney. "Black Sissy Masculinity and the Politics of Dis-respectability." In *No Tea, No Shade: New Writings in Black Queer Studies*, edited by E. Patrick Johnson, 196–215. Durham, NC: Duke University Press, 2016.

Zucchino, David. *Wilmington's Lie: The Murderous Coup of 1898 and the Rise of White Supremacy*. New York: Grove Press, 2021.

Index

For the benefit of digital users, indexed terms that span two pages (e.g., 52–53) may, on occasion, appear on only one of those pages.